Steamboat Connections:
Montreal to Upper Canada, 1816–1843

In *Steamboat Connections* Frank Mackey gives us a narrative account of the first twenty-five years of steam navigation along the St Lawrence and Ottawa Rivers. Relying on a wealth of primary archival sources, Mackey focuses on the development of steamer traffic from 1816 – when the foundations were laid for the first stage and steamboat line between Montreal and Upper Canada – to the early 1840s – when locks, canals, innovations, and human daring conquered the rapids on those rivers and allowed for navigation between Montreal and the Great Lakes. He shows how, starting in 1841, small steamers ran "the circuit" – down the rapids of the St Lawrence to Montreal and then back up to Kingston and other Great Lakes ports via the Ottawa River and the Rideau Canal.

Mackey introduces the entrepreneurs who forged this important link between Montreal and the nation's interior and chronicles the course of their industry, correcting previous misinterpretations. He sheds light not only on steamboats but also on the social, commercial, and geographical development they made possible. He shows that the history of this country, a land with vast expanses and a harsh climate, cannot be fully appreciated without looking at the different modes of transportation that made it possible.

FRANK MACKEY is a copy editor for the *Montreal Gazette*.

Steamboat Connections: Montreal to Upper Canada, 1816–1843

Frank Mackey

McGill-Queen's University Press

Montreal & Kingston · London · Ithaca

© McGill-Queen's University Press 2000
ISBN 0-7735-2055-4

Legal deposit fourth quarter 2000
Bibliothèque nationale du Québec

Printed in Canada on acid-free paper

This book has been published with the help of a grant
from the Humanities and Social Sciences Federation of
Canada, using funds provided by the Social Sciences and
Humanities Research Council of Canada.

McGill-Queen's University Press acknowledges the
financial support of the Government of Canada through
the Book Publishing Industry Development Program
(BPIDP) for its activities. We also acknowledge the support
of the Canada Council for the Arts for our publishing
program.

Canadian Cataloguing in Publication Data

Mackey, Frank
 Steamboat connections : Montreal to Upper Canada,
 1816–1843
 Includes bibliographical references and index.
 ISBN 0-7735-2055-4
 1. Steam-navigation – Saint Lawrence River – History.
 2. Steam-navigation – Ottawa River (Quebec and Ont.) –
 History. 3. Saint Lawrence River – History. 4. Ottawa
 River (Quebec and Ont.) – History. I. Title.
 VM626.M33 2000   386'.3'09714   C99-901497-8

Typeset in Aldus 10/12
by Caractéra inc., Quebec City

Contents

Illustrations

Preface

To the odd colonial, stirred by the sight of sail, the first puffing, shuddering paddlewheelers might have seemed "the ugliest species of craft that ever diversified a marine landscape."[1] So they might seem today to all but steamboat buffs. Ugly or not, to most Canadians of the early nineteenth century, they were welcome allies in the struggle with the elements and with the hardships, economic and social, of isolation. Besides their appeal simply as something ingenious and new, they promised ever-greater reliability and speed in transport and communications at a time when transport and communications were nearly synonymous: before the telegraph, telephone, or radio, any message addressed to a distant recipient had to be taken by land or water to its destination.

This is one sort of connection covered by the title of this work. The word "connections" was deliberately chosen for its ambiguity: it refers, of course, to the connections between different boats along a watercourse, but also to the connections between a succession of boats over time, between steamers and stages, between villages and cities served by the boats, between the owners and the makers of boats, between these people and the communities and times they lived in and the businesses and institutions they helped to establish, between the Canadas and the north-eastern United States, and so on. In fact, the title is an open invitation to readers so inclined to make their own connections and associations.

The aim of this book is a simple one: to trace the beginnings of steam navigation on the upper St Lawrence and lower Ottawa rivers. It is not an analysis of that traffic; nor is it a thesis or treatise on transport economics, shipbuilding, steam technology, early canals, or colonial trade. It is a narrative account, arranged chronologically and spanning slightly more than a quarter-century – from 1816, three years before the first steamer appeared on Lake St Louis, where the two rivers meet west of Montreal, to 1843, two years after steam vessels began to run in a triangular "circuit" from Montreal, up the Ottawa River and Rideau Canal to Lake Ontario, and down again by the St Lawrence.

Anyone acquainted with the origins of inland steam navigation in Canada may wonder about that reference to 1816 in connection with Lake St Louis – why not speak of it as the year of the building of the first Canadian steamboat on Lake Ontario, or as two years before regular steamer service began at the head of the St Lawrence between Prescott and Kingston, or as five years before the appearance, however fleeting, of the first steamboat on the Ottawa? That, of course, is a question of perspective, focus, and emphasis – bias, some hard-nosed reader might say, to which one might reply that there is no history without a vantage point.

This account is written from a Montreal perspective, which means, among other things, that the first steamers to run above Prescott are viewed more as extensions of Lake Ontario navigation and touched on only briefly. But the view is definitely to the west, not eastward along the St Lawrence toward Quebec, where the very first Canadian steamboats plied. That is another story, as is steam on the Great Lakes. Our concern is with the area between Montreal, a hub of transportation, and the lakes.

But why this area in particular, and why steamboats? To be blunt, this book had its origins in baffled curiosity, not in any fascination with marine history, love of old boats, or interest in colonial entrepreneurship. It began as a search for information about one steamer, the *Henry Brougham*, captured and sunk by rebels at Beauharnois on Lake St Louis in the Lower Canadian rebellion of November 1838. Most accounts of the rising mention this episode but provide few, if any, details about the *Brougham*, its crew and passengers, who were held captive, its owners, its purpose, or its ultimate fate. Neither do published works offer much help in situating this boat in the chronology of steam above Montreal. In my search for answers to these questions, it became clear that the *Brougham* was part of a chapter in the history of Canadian transportation that was perhaps known in its broad outlines but was nowhere set out in clear and accurate detail. Willy-nilly, what had started out as an investigation of an episode of local history, worth perhaps an article in a historical journal, broadened in scope to become this book.

But where should it begin? No one disputes the fact that the first Canadian steamer was launched at Montreal in 1809 (though within living memory of the event, two Montreal newspapers stated the year to have been 1811).[2] That boat, the *Accommodation*, ran between Montreal and Quebec. As concerns the first steamer to ply immediately above Montreal and the Lachine Rapids, however, historians and other writers, generally focusing on the Ottawa, have proffered a variety of names and dates. It is as though the answer were not ascertainable in fact, but to be treated as a matter of opinion. A sampling of the published sources will show how frustratingly elusive the facts can be.

Writing in 1831, Joseph Bouchette, surveyor general of Lower Canada, said: "The 'Union of the Ottawa,' the first steam-boat that plied upon this part of the river [between Grenville and Hull], was built in 1819, and formed an era in the history of the Ottawa settlements from its contributing materially to their acceleration."[3] In his well-known *Steam Navigation*, published in 1898, James Croil, ventured that steam navigation on the Ottawa *seemed* to have begun in 1820 with the appearance of a boat called the *Union*, built the year before.[4] In the mid-1920s H.R. Morgan asserted in a paper on the history of Ottawa River steamers that it began with the *Union*, but in 1822. At about the same time, A.H.D. Ross took Bouchette's word for it that the *Union of the Ottawa* had been the first and that it had exerted a significant influence on the development of the area from 1819.[5] Then in 1938, in his classic history of Canadian transportation, George Glazebrook rejected those earlier accounts and claimed that the first steamer to ply on the Ottawa was the *Ottawa* in 1819.[6] Historian Lucien Brault sought to set the record straight in 1946. "The first steamer to ply on the Ottawa was the *Union* built at Hawkesbury by Thomas Mears in 1821 (some authors claim that it was constructed in 1819)," he wrote.[7] By 1965, however, Brault had rallied to the view that the *Union* was built in 1819.[8]

In 1982 André Lamirande and Gilles Séguin seemed to settle the question as far as the Ottawa River was concerned. In their pictorial history *A Foregone Fleet*, they cited period documents proving that the *Union* had been built at Hawkesbury in 1822–23 and had operated between Grenville and Hull. As such, she was the first steamer on the Ottawa, they said.[9] In 1983, doubts about the name of the boat also seemed to be dispelled with the appearance of the second supplement to John Mills's catalogue of Canadian steam vessels. After listing her as *Union of the Ottawa* in his first compilation in 1979, Mills pointedly corrected the name to *Union*, plain and simple.[10] But a 1984 Parks Canada study of the Ottawa River canals stated that the *Union of the Ottawa* was the first steamer on the river and that she appeared in 1820.[11] Robert Legget, in his 1988 book on the Ottawa canals, presented both names as valid: *Union of the Ottawa* was the name given to the boat when she was built in 1822, but it was shortened to *Union* in 1830.[12] As recently as 1996, geographer Pierre Camu, in his historical survey of navigation on the St Lawrence and the Great Lakes up to the mid-nineteenth century, asserted that the steamboat era on the Ottawa began with the *Union of Ottawa* in 1822.[13]

As we shall see, the *Union*, built at Hawkesbury between December 1822 and May 1823, was the first steamer in regular service on the

Ottawa, but not the first to run on the river. That honour belongs to the *Perseverance*, built in 1821 at Lachine on Lake St Louis and generally ignored in accounts of Ottawa navigation. The origins of steam on that river, however, go back even farther, to 1819. Here it must be said that the start of steam navigation on the Ottawa cannot be separated from its beginnings on the St Lawrence above Montreal, specifically on Lake St Louis. Both had a common origin in the steamer *Ottawa*.

This boat was built at Hawkesbury, above the Long Sault rapids of the Ottawa, in 1819 with the idea that she should ply on both the St Lawrence and the Ottawa between Lachine, then the outport of Montreal on Lake St Louis, and Point Fortune at the foot of the Carillon Rapids. Run down to Lachine to receive her engine, she never made it back to the Ottawa: the rapids at the mouth of that river proved an insurmountable obstacle and she was confined to Lake St Louis. The *Perseverance* would also find the rapids a bar to regular service on the Ottawa and would wind up sailing around Lake St Louis, though she would return to the Ottawa, under altered circumstances, several years later.

The *Ottawa* and the *Perseverance* illustrate a hard fact of early inland steam navigation: that is, everything that goes down must come up – but it cannot. Until canals allowed them to bypass the rapids in their path, steamboats were generally confined to the lake or stretch of river on which they were built. If for some reason they were run down the rapids, they could not get back up, at least not so easily as to make the ascent a matter of routine. (The *Union* never ran any rapids, but she too was locked in – between the Long Sault and the Chaudière Falls at Hull – until the Rideau Canal opened.) In a nutshell, that is the central theme of this book: a disjointed transportation route, featuring a few isolated boats paddling up and down their own ponds, evolves into a through route between Montreal and the lakes, a kind of forerunner of the St Lawrence Seaway.

It is plain that some of the authors cited above conflated the *Ottawa* and the *Union*, both built at Hawkesbury. One can easily see how, in Bouchette's day, the blurred recollection of two facts – that a steamboat had been built at Hawkesbury in 1819, and that the *Union* was the first such boat to operate there – produced the fiction that the *Union* was built in 1819. There is a "connection" between the two boats that makes it impossible for both to have operated at the same time: the *Union* inherited the *Ottawa's* engine. As for Glazebrook's contention that the *Ottawa* had begun plying on the Ottawa River in 1819, he based it solely on the fact that the boat was built at Hawkesbury.[14]

The confusion grows as one moves beyond the basic point of determining which boat came first. After stating that steam navigation began on the Ottawa in 1819 or later, for example, some authors go on to speak of a St Andrews Steam Forwarding Company as active in the area in 1816.

The mystified reader is left to wonder how a steamboat company could have operated for at least three years before the first steamboat appeared, and that boat not even its own.[15] The truth is that there was no such company at that time. One writer places a steamer called *Queen Victoria* on the Ottawa in 1836 – a year before Victoria ascended the throne, two years before she was crowned. There was no Queen Victoria in 1836 and, needless to say, no *Queen Victoria*.[16] Chroniclers who might be presumed to speak with some authority can be the most misleading. Captain Robert Ward Shepherd, for example, after a lifetime spent in Ottawa River navigation, left a summary account of the development of steam there that is a hopeless tangle of omissions and errors insofar as the years before 1838 are concerned.[17]

In defence of the authors of an earlier day, it must be said that they did not have ready access to the documentation and facilities available to the modern researcher. They had to rely on their memories or the recollections of others. The accounts they left us are valuable, but for want of trustworthy information, they distorted the record they sought to preserve. *Scripta manent* – and their accumulated errors keep popping up in the accounts of writers and scholars to this day, forming a thicket of false leads.

To clear away the brush, some of the principal tools at hand are contemporary newspapers and notarial records. Combined with other archival materials, these sources enable us to identify the pieces of the puzzle and fit them together so that a picture takes shape of steam traffic and some of the forces that drove it. To a great extent, those forces – economic, technological, political, social – walked on two legs. It is impossible to dissociate what was what from who was who. For this reason, the lives of some of the figures associated with the boats require some attention.

These people are generally little known today, if at all. One reason is that few left any private papers behind for historians to pore over. Yet a knowledge gleaned here and there of who they were and the connections that existed between them can help us to glimpse, beyond the bare sequence of events, some of the *how* and *why* of things. Zeroing in on them also helps to eliminate some errors and confusion. Because Philemon Wright, a towering figure in the development of the area around Hull, which he founded, was one of the owners of the *Union*, some have hastened to credit him with introducing steam navigation on the Ottawa River, virtually ignoring Thomas Mears of Hawkesbury, whose claims are at least as valid. Likewise, the later involvement of the Molsons in steam navigation on the Ottawa-Rideau route has led some to presume that their role there must have been as important as on the St Lawrence between Montreal and Quebec: it was not. Without a closer look, one might never know that contemporary references to Captain Whipple at times concerned Asahel Whipple and at others, his younger brother, Daniel; or that the Mr Walker behind some of the earliest propeller boats in Canada was not Montreal machinist James Nelson Walker but Montreal jeweller Nelson Walker. Variations in spelling being commonplace at the time, one might assume that boat-building contemporaries William Parkin and William Parkyn were one and the same. And who would think that the stage-and-steamboat-line partner identified by the contemporary press as J.S. Bigelow was not Jacob Bigelow but his younger brother, Increase?

The first chapter of this chronicle focuses on the *Ottawa*, built by the same man who had overseen the construction of the *Accommodation* and fitted with an engine made by an individual who was associated with the building of the first steamer on Lake Champlain. The foundry that the latter established in Montreal became, under successive owners in the next two decades, one of the two major engine foundries there.

Chapter 2 looks at the *Perseverance* and her owners. For a time, she formed part of the first mail and passenger line of stages and steamboats between Montreal and Upper Canada, along the St Lawrence. Three other steamers, the *Dalhousie*, the *Union*, and the *St Andrews*, are also considered as they enter the picture during the *Perseverance's* era. The *Dalhousie*, which served first as a mail and passenger boat between Prescott and Kingston, ended her days on Lake St Francis. The other three formed part of the first line of stages and steamboats on the Ottawa River in the mid-1820s. A lock built by the owners of the *St Andrews* at Vaudreuil, at the mouth of the Ottawa, would serve for more than fifteen years as a gate controlling steamer access to that river, giving rise to a running controversy over "monopoly" and a grievance of no little significance in the minds of many Upper Canadians.

Chapters 3 to 6 examine the career of Horace Dickinson, a self-effacing American who moved to Canada after the War of 1812 to establish the first mail-stage line between Montreal and Kingston and developed it into a line of stages and steamboats, the only one on the upper St Lawrence in his day. A resident of Montreal, he was part of a close-knit American community whose members made significant contributions to the social and economic life of the city and to the development of transportation. Among his circle were the Ward brothers from New Jersey, who established what was perhaps the principal engine foundry in Canada in the first half of the nineteenth century. Here was only one important cross-border transfer of knowledge and technology. Anglo-Scottish merchants then dominated the Montreal business world, and a native Montrealer, soured by private experience, might have privately advised his connections to "have as little to do with the American houses in Montreal as possible ... because the best of them are but rotten Concerns – they do business on a fictitious Capital which does not belong to them."[18] That may have been true of some traders but not of Dickinson and his circle. They were more the sort of American which a clergyman of Scottish descent eulogized toward the close of the century as having generally exercised a civilizing influence on the city, not least on its Scottish fur barons:

Naturally shrewd, they were also frugal and industrious and presented a striking contrast to their neighbours, the fur traders, whose gains accumulated rapidly, and who, in consequence, lived luxuriously and spent freely ... They thus proved a "salt" to the city – they saved it from the effects of an unhealthy, overstimulated social life. The Puritan leaven which those prudent, thoughtful, sagacious New Englanders brought over with them to Montreal has not ceased to be felt even yet in our religious and social life ... and they were most useful citizens: wide awake in all respects, they introduced the best methods of doing business into the community.[19]

The last three chapters, 7 to 9, trace the commotion that followed the opening in the 1830s of an alternative water route to the St Lawrence between Montreal and the Great Lakes, via the Ottawa River and the Rideau Canal. A period of suicidal rivalry ensued between St Lawrence and Ottawa-Rideau interests, which saw Upper Canada embark on a ruinous program of canal building on the St Lawrence. In the interest of self-preservation, the forwarders on the two routes eventually combined in successive cartels, uniting the competing routes in one continuous circuit, with barges and, by 1841, "miniature" steamers, including the first propeller boats in Canada. Scarcely had steamboats begun to exploit this circuit when the Cornwall Canal opened. It was the first of several "improvements" on the St Lawrence that would soon allow steamers to run up that river to the Great Lakes and render the Ottawa-Rideau obsolete as a through route.

No thorough description of most of the boats dealt with here has come down to us. It is possible to gain an idea of the appearance of some of them from the odd contemporary sketch. But in some cases the depiction is dubious. The accuracy of Henri Julien's sketch of the rebel capture of the *Brougham* in 1838, for example, is highly suspect: it was drawn fifty years after the fact to illustrate a series of newspaper articles.[20]

As a rule, the steamers were flat-bottomed sidewheelers, of necessity smaller and with a shallower draught than those on the St Lawrence below Montreal and on the Great Lakes. They burned wood, causing them to spew sparks and ashes, and until the 1840s almost all were powered by low-pressure, single-cylinder beam engines. Some also had masts and sails. In the records uncovered, the power of their engines was generally noted, but little else of a technical nature.

Accommodations for passengers were limited for the most part to a bar and men's and women's cabins, sometimes a single cabin with the men's and women's quarters separated by sliding doors or some other divider. These cabins were dormitory-style rooms with double tiers of shelf-like beds along the walls. At first, these facilities were located below deck, but within a few years, cabins – usually the women's, smaller than the men's – were built on deck on some boats. Since the men's cabin often doubled as a dining room at meal times, sleeping in was impossible. "By the regulation of these conveyances in Canada, every one rises before eight, so that the beds may be curtained and breakfast decently prepared in the cabin."[21]

Decency also dictated that a stewardess be attached to the women's cabin. So little has come to light on these female attendants that it is impossible to identify them or say much more than that they did exist.[22] Women may also have worked as cooks on some of these boats, as they did elsewhere. The possibility is suggested, in a backhanded way, by an 1829 advertisement in which the owners of Ottawa River boats, seeking cooks for their steamers, felt obliged to specify that they wanted males.[23]

Information on male crew members is not plentiful, but the names of quite a few can be found in scattered records. By one account, the waiters on the Great Lakes steamers by 1841 were "usually coloured men."[24] This does not appear to have been the case aboard the early steamers on the upper St Lawrence and the Ottawa. No black men or women have been identified as working on these boats. More surprising, however, is the relative absence of French Canadians among the crews and owners of the boats above Montreal, notwithstanding the claim of the Montreal newspaper *La Minerve* in 1836 that, "on our steamboats here, and on those in the United States, the crews consist almost exclusively of French Canadians."[25]

Many French Canadians worked as captains, pilots, firemen, and deckhands on the steamers below Montreal and on the ferries serving the city. No doubt, these were the boats that the *Minerve* writer had in mind. Above Montreal, there certainly were plenty of French Canadians engaged in other river trades, from the celebrated voyageurs and raftsmen to the unsung barge and batteaux men, but few worked on the steamers. As we shall see, of the six crew members of the *Ottawa* in 1820, for example, only one, the fireman, was a French Canadian. There is nothing to indicate that there were ever more than one or two on any of the boats that concern us.[26] A Scottish immigrant travelling up the St Lawrence from Montreal in the mid-1840s was struck by this absence: "None of the crew of the boat [on Lake St Francis] were french canadians and only two or three on the Cheftain [*Chieftain*, on Lake St Louis] were French," he saw fit to note in a letter home.[27]

The situation cannot be attributed to a lack of training or experience: of the crew members identified, many had neither. One might be tempted to think that a malign prejudice was at work, but no such complaint was ever raised. The explanation seems to lie in the cultural, economic, geographic, and social realities of the day. The area discussed here was, in a sense, the gateway to Upper Canada. French Canada showed little inclination to pass through it. As Gerald Tulchinsky has observed, French-Canadian merchants "were almost entirely absent from the upriver forwarding business, in part because very few of their firms traded with Upper Canada."[28] Men of British and American origin, sometimes with the help of French-Canadian tradesmen, built the steamers and their engines for British and American entrepreneurs – forwarders, commission merchants, stage-line operators, mail contractors, and others – with interests in the Upper Canadian connection. Sometimes the boat builder went on to command the vessel; in other cases, the owners found a captain, as well as other members of the crew, among the people who, in the broadest sense – and the narrowest – spoke their language: family members, relatives, friends and acquaintances, compatriots, and so on. John Ward, an American engine builder at Montreal, considered that his ability to secure engine-maintenance contracts hinged on the placing of American engineers on the boats. French Canadians were out of the loop, so to speak. They did work on the steamers owned by English and Scottish merchants, as well as those owned by French-Canadian entrepreneurs, that ran between Montreal and Quebec.[29] But if these experienced hands did not seek jobs on the boats above Montreal, it was probably from a reluctance to leave home, to exchange heartland for hinterland, old associations for new, and big boats for smaller ones with fewer hands, all but the odd one English-speaking. Montreal seems to have marked a kind of psychological boundary as much as a break in navigation.

In the writing of this book, some arbitrary decisions on nomenclature had to be made for the sake of consistency. As much as possible, names of people are spelt as they themselves wrote them; in a quotation, however, if a writer used a variant, for example, Dickenson instead of Dickinson, it is left uncorrected. In cases where the way in which the bearer wrote his or her name is not known, or where he or she did not use a consistent spelling, one spelling has been adopted and used throughout. With regard to forwarding companies that operated under different names in Lower and Upper Canada, as much as possible only one name is used in the text. Thus Hooker and Henderson, the Upper Canadian name of one such company, prevails even if certain actions were undertaken by the company under its Montreal name, Henderson and Hooker. The names of boats do not generally pose a problem in the text, except for the two steamers called *Phoenix* that plied within a short time of each other on Lake Champlain. To distinguish them, the second has been identified as *Phoenix II*. For the index, where two or three boats might

be listed under the same name, each such entry is followed by a paren-
thetical word or two to distinguish it from the others.

In the case of place names, where the name itself has changed, the place
is identified by its old name, with an indication of its current one, for
example, New Edinburgh, now part of Ottawa, or St Catherine, now the
Montreal suburb of Outremont. The steamboat terminal at the eastern
end of Lake St Francis is identified in the text as Côteau. It was called at
the time Côteau du Lac (and later, until quite recently, Côteau Landing),
but the present municipality of Côteau-du-Lac does not encompass this
site, now in the adjoining municipality of Les Côteaux. Certain French
place names had English equivalents: the translated form is used here, as
it was by the subjects of this book and in the bulk of the documentary
sources (for example, St John's rather than Saint-Jean). To distinguish
between what was the Sainte-Anne suburb on the west side of the city
of Montreal and the village of Sainte-Anne at the western tip of the Island
of Montreal, both identified in English at the time as St Anne, St Anne's,
St Ann, or St Ann's, the suburb is here called St Ann, while St Anne is
used for the village (and nearby rapids).

In keeping with the language of the time, boats are designated by the
feminine pronoun "she." Boat dimensions and speeds are given as they
were recorded, in feet and inches and miles per hour, rather than in the
metric equivalents in use today. For consistency's sake, the imperial
system is used for all weights and measures. Unless otherwise specified,
costs and prices are given as stated in the documentary sources, in
pounds, shillings, and pence "currency," worth slightly less than sterling.
A dollar figure occasionally crops up because, while the pound was the
money of account, payments were actually made in dollars, the circulating medium. In the period that concerns us, one pound currency (twenty
shillings) was generally reckoned to be worth four dollars; one dollar
was therefore the equivalent of five shillings.

This work attempts to present a picture of steam navigation above
Montreal. It is meant as a general introduction, in the hope that the
information it contains, the references it identifies, and the questions it
raises might spur others – whether the reader with an active interest in
the field or the scholar with a specialist's skill – to embark on further
explorations and analyses.

Over the course of this project, the debts of gratitude have steadily
mounted. In the case of the late Peter Blaney of McGill-Queen's University Press, who accepted an early version of the manuscript over the
transom, all thanks come too late. For others, there is still time: particular
thanks then to marine historian Walter Lewis for his early research
pointers in a long-ago telephone conversation; to Jack I. Schecter, then
librarian-archivist at Upper Canada Village, and Arthur B. Cohn, director

of the Lake Champlain Maritime Museum, for their interest and support when the work was half-done; to Leslie M. Simon, associate archivist and archaeologist at the Cigna Archives in Philadelphia, for her help and the gift of a useful book on the history of the Aetna (fire) Insurance Company; to Susan M. Stanley of the United Church of Canada Archives in Montreal for her help and the gift of an account of the American Presbyterian Church in Montreal; to Miss J.M. Wraight of the National Maritime Museum in Greenwich, England, for assistance in tracking down William Annesley; and to Estelle Brisson of the Archives Nationales du Québec in Montreal for her interest and suggestions through the years. The book would not have been written without the great forbearance of Ann Carroll, Roselaine Mackey, Lia Haberman, and Daniel Mackey, who put up with a husband and father who, forgetful of the present and the future, acted as though nothing mattered but the past. It would not have been published in its present form without a grant from the Aid to Scholarly Publications Programme of the Humanities and Social Sciences Research Federation of Canada, and without the help of McGill-Queen's editors Aurèle Parisien and Joan McGilvray.

Steamboat Connections

CHAPTER ONE

Dead in the Water

When Robert Fulton successfully tried his *Steamboat* (later called the *Clermont*) on the Hudson River of New York in August 1807, he launched the steamboat era in North America. Early the next year the *Steamboat's* pilot, James Winans, and his older brother, ship carpenter John Winans, who had helped build Fulton's boat, moved from Poughkeepsie, New York, to Vermont, where they established a shipyard in association with British expatriate Joseph Lough,[1] a founder by trade. At Burlington they set to building the first steamer on Lake Champlain. Their 125-foot *Vermont*, powered by a second-hand engine of 20 horsepower – and a sail hoisted on her single mast when the wind was right – turned out to be the first steamer in international service. In June 1809, under John Winans's command, she began running on the 120-mile route between Whitehall, New York, at the southern tip of the lake, and St John's on the Richelieu River in Lower Canada, linking the Montreal–St John's stage with the stage line between Whitehall and Troy. The War of 1812 interrupted her cross-border service, but she returned to the route in 1815. Her career ended abruptly on 15 October that year when she sank in the Richelieu near Île aux Noix.[2]

The *Vermont's* incursions notwithstanding, steam navigation in Canada is usually reckoned to have begun with the launching of John Molson's *Accommodation* at Montreal on 19 August 1809, or at the beginning of November that year when she first ran the 180 miles between Montreal and Quebec on the St Lawrence. It was only after the war that steamers made their appearance on the Great Lakes: within weeks of each other, the 170-foot Canadian boat *Frontenac* and the 110-foot American *Ontario* began plying on Lake Ontario in the spring of 1817.[3] Between Montreal and the Great Lakes, a succession of rapids on the St Lawrence meant that steam navigation was out of the question except on two segments where the river broadened into lakes – Lake St Francis, extending 40 miles from

Cornwall, Upper Canada, to Côteau du Lac in Lower Canada, and Lake St Louis, which offered about 25 miles of relatively clear sailing just above Montreal at the confluence of the St Lawrence and Ottawa rivers. Lake St Louis was the first of these two expanses to see a steamer, the *Ottawa*, in 1819.

Her origins might be traced to the foundry company that Joseph Lough set up at Montreal three months after the sinking of the *Vermont*. Joseph Lough and Company was formed on 26 January 1816 to build and operate a "cast iron air furnace."[4] Joining Lough in this venture were Lake Champlain steamboat pioneer Jahaziel Sherman, Montreal merchant James Wildgoose, and Massachusetts-born Thomas Mears, a pioneer Ottawa valley entrepreneur and former member of the Upper Canada legislature for Prescott County, then temporarily residing in Montreal.[5] Their five-year agreement called for each of the partners to chip in £500 by 1 June, Wildgoose and Mears promising to advance an extra £500 apiece if needed.

Lough, the only founder in the group – and a "very clever man in that line," according to his friend and sometime lodger Jedediah Dorwin[6] – would move to Montreal from Whitehall and run the shop. He would be the first of what might be called the Lake Champlain steamboat contingent to move there. Three other notable figures connected with early steam navigation of the lake would follow within the next three years – captain George Brush, engineer John Dod Ward, and shipbuilder Alexander Young.[7] Each would leave his mark on the early steam navigation in Canada.

Under the terms of the foundry partnership, Lough was to receive an annual salary of £125 and a rent-free house on the premises, besides his quarter share of the foundry profits. Wildgoose was to import from England, free of commission, the iron and coal required for the foundry. Sherman supplied capital for the business but remained in Vermont, where he commanded the *Phoenix,* the second steamer on Lake Champlain.[8] The partnership deed spelled out precisely where the foundry was to be located – a riverside lot just east of John Molson's brewery in the east-side St Mary (or Quebec) suburb. The main building on the site was a large, two-storey stone gristmill, powered by horses. The property was not yet theirs, but a deal had clearly been struck: the lot was knocked down at a sheriff's sale on 10 February to two intermediaries, who then resold it on 8 March to Wildgoose, Lough, and Mears (Sherman appears not to have been a party to this transaction) for £1,600. One condition of the sale to Lough and his associates was that "the poor man who occupies the small House erected on the said premises is to remain there until May next without paying rent." The middlemen had until June to remove the mill equipment.[9]

Lough and Mears being away from Montreal, Wildgoose signed the purchase papers for them. Lough had probably returned to Vermont, where he was involved that spring in the building of the *Champlain*, the third steamer on Lake Champlain. His American wife, Maria Terboss, was expecting their second child, and he may have waited until some time after the boy was born on 3 April to move his young family to Montreal.[10] There was no rush: quite possibly, their new home on the foundry property was to be the house occupied by the "poor man" guaranteed possession until May. Besides, the mill machinery had to be removed before Lough could set to work. Mears, on the other hand, had left Montreal for good after a residence there of about one year. He returned to Hawkesbury, which had been his home for at least a decade and where he would spend the rest of his life. On 12 July he bowed out of the foundry partnership, selling his share in the business and in the property to Wildgoose.[11]

Toward the end of the year, Lough opened the Montreal Air Furnace in the old mill on St Mary Street, the eastern extension of Notre Dame Street beyond the limits of the old walled city. By January 1817 he was offering for sale stoves and stovepipes, and soliciting orders for castings and blacksmith's work.[12] Whatever his technical skills, he was not a success as a businessman. His start-up costs had left him nearly £3,000 in debt, more than £750 of that owed to Sherman. On 7 July 1817 Joseph Lough and Company was dissolved. Lough took the company's debts upon himself. He bought out Wildgoose's interest for a token £5 and mortgaged the foundry property to Sherman.[13]

Without partners, Lough soldiered on. It may be supposed that his Methodist conscience,[14] not to mention the fear of being cast into prison for debt, would not allow him to default on his obligations without a struggle. Part of his financial woes may have stemmed from his air furnace, a natural-convection furnace that produced superior-quality cast iron but consumed more fuel than a forced-air cupola furnace. For the production of everyday items such as stoves, a cupola furnace, easier to control and cheaper to operate, might have served him better.[15] Six weeks after the dissolution of the partnership, he advertised that "considerable improvements in these works by experienced workmen" enabled him to offer castings of up to 30 hundredweight (3,360 pounds) and wrought-iron work too.[16] In early 1818, stressing more "great improvements," he offered to produce not just castings and wrought iron but machinery of all sorts, including steam engines: "Steam Engines being a public utility in this province, he is ready to contract for the making of the same in all their parts, either in relation to Boats or Mills; and as the public may doubt his ability, he is ready to give bonds for the due performance of the same; the power not to exceed 30 horse."[17]

There were two other foundries in Montreal, both established by recent English immigrants. In early 1817 John Fellow, a twenty-six-year-old blacksmith and brass founder, had set up shop in the St Lawrence suburb, on the northern edge of the old city, competing with Lough for scrap copper and brass. By that fall Yorkshiremen Guy and Joseph Warwick, operating as Guy Warwick and Company, had opened the Phoenix Foundry on the west side of town. Neither foundry produced steam engines as a rule, though the Warwicks built one in 1820 for a small boat, the *Dalhousie,* named for the new governor general, Lord Dalhousie, and meant to run between Montreal and Terrebonne. Throughout the 1820s their foundry produced castings for several steamboat engines.[18]

Lough's "improvements" and venture into the making of steam engines did not save his business, but he struggled on for another year. By the summer of 1818 he still had not paid a penny of his debt to Sherman. That August a worried Sherman asked engineer John Dod Ward, a resident of Elizabethtown (now Elizabeth), New Jersey, then in Vergennes, Vermont, to help out with the Montreal foundry. Ward was only twenty-three years old but well versed in the building and fitting of marine engines, skills he had learned from his father, Silas Ward, and his uncle, Daniel Dod. He had first visited Vergennes in the spring of 1816, having gone to work at $2 a day for John Winans, who was then installing the salvaged engine of the *Vermont* in the Lake Champlain Steamboat Company's new steamer *Champlain.* George Brush superintended the building of this steamer, which he was also to command. In the fall, Ward had moved on to Sackets Harbor, on the New York shore of Lake Ontario, where he installed an engine made by his uncle in the *Ontario.* He had returned to Vergennes in April 1817 to overhaul the 45-horsepower engine of the *Phoenix* and place it in the *Champlain,* the old engine of the *Vermont* having proved inadequate. Sherman had then prevailed upon him to remain "some time in the character of Superintendant of the boats."[19]

Ward did not tarry long in Vermont. He was off working in Virginia by the time the *Champlain* burned at the dock at Whitehall on 6 September. That boat's destruction marked the end of George Brush's career as a Lake Champlain steamboat captain; he moved to Montreal, where, from 1818, he would command a succession of steamers on the Montreal-Quebec run, beginning with the *Car of Commerce.* It does not appear that he incurred any blame for the destruction of the *Champlain.* If anything, the fire, attributed by some to "the imperfect construction and arrangement of her boilers," seems to have had more to do with Ward's department. But Ward's reputation suffered no more than Brush's.[20]

Proud of his undoubted knowledge and skills, Ward never would allow, as Lough did, that "the public may doubt his ability."[21] Back in Vergennes in 1818, he wrote to his father on 16 August: "I have already since my arrival been strongly solicited to take a small part of Capt. Sherman's Montreal furnace establishment and take the entire management of it and I intend in a few weeks to take a trip to Montreal to view it."[22] But first, he had an engagement in neighbouring Ferrisburgh: there on 2 September he married Laura Maria Roburds, whose father and grandfather had been among the pioneers of Vergennes.[23] Perhaps his bride accompanied him when he travelled to Montreal. For reasons that are not recorded, Ward did not take over the management of Lough's foundry, but he moved there the following year, drawn by the opportunities that Montreal offered to a skilled engine builder.

The possibilities in Canada were almost limitless compared with those in the United States, where boat and engine builders were cramped by the patent claims and legislated monopoly of Robert Fulton and his partner, Robert R. Livingston. Ward knew something of this problem first-hand. The monopoly had frustrated the plans of his uncle and a partner, former New Jersey governor Aaron Ogden, to operate a steam ferry, the *Sea Horse*, between Elizabethtown and New York City. Years later, Ward wrote an account of that episode which he read before the New Jersey Historical Society. The Fulton-Livingston monopoly was finally broken by a ruling of the U.S. Supreme Court in 1824.[24] In Canada, John Molson had tried in 1810 to secure a law giving him the exclusive right to steam navigation between Montreal and Quebec. The assembly of Lower Canada had approved the bill in early 1811, but the Legislative Council had thrown it out. Molson renewed his attempts to get a bill passed in the next couple of years, but to no avail.[25] The field of steam navigation remained wide open, save for the requirement under Britain's navigation laws that the boats had to be owned by British subjects.

Ward moved to Montreal with his wife and eighteen-year-old brother, Samuel Shipman Ward. On his arrival in the late spring of 1819, he performed some work or service for Lough, for which the latter gave him a promissory note on 19 June for $385.80, or £96 9s. in the currency of Lower Canada, payable in ninety days. Ward wrote to his father that he was counting on that money, as well as on funds due him from his uncle and others, to pay for a share in a steamboat to be launched at Montreal on 19 August, ten years to the day after the launch of the *Accommodation*.[26] The money from these various sources did not come through, and he never bought his share, but that steamboat, the *Montreal*, launched Ward's career in Canada.

The boat's owners, including Guy and Joseph Warwick,[27] had retained him to supervise the installation of an English-made engine in their boat. The Warwicks' foundry had produced a model of the 20-horsepower engine, which they had shipped in the spring to the English manufacturer, the Eagle Foundry of Francis, Smith and Company in Birmingham.

Realizing that waiting for this engine meant that their boat, already launched, could not go into operation until late the following summer at the earliest, the owners chose to speed things up by hiring Ward to make one on the spot. In October he began setting up shop on land that he had bought on Queen Street in the St Ann suburb, just west of where the city walls had stood. That winter he built the 32-horsepower engine for the *Montreal,* for which the iron castings were probably made at the nearby Phoenix Foundry.[28] In the meantime, the 20-horsepower engine on order from England was sold to forwarders Levi Sexton and Company for use in a steamer built that winter at Prescott, Upper Canada, which was to be called *Dalhousie* (see chap. 2).

The *Montreal,* 116 tons burden, $75\frac{1}{2}$ feet long and 19 feet wide, with a 6-foot depth of hold and drawing no more than 32 inches,[29] was built to run as a ferry between Montreal and La Prairie, on the south shore of the St Lawrence, the starting point for the stages to St John's and the United States. Skeptics held that no boat could run up the strong current and shallow water at the foot of the Lachine Rapids to La Prairie.[30] As Jacob De Witt, one of the co-owners of the *Car of Commerce,* was later to recall, Canada's first two steamboats, the *Accommodation* and the *Swiftsure,* launched in 1809 and 1812 respectively, had steamed no farther upriver than John Molson's brewery "because the received opinion was, that we could not build a steamer that could overcome the current St Mary just below the city, much less one which could navigate the St Lawrence to La Prairie." The *Car of Commerce,* launched in October 1815, beat the St Mary's Current to become the first steamer to ply regularly between the actual port of Montreal and Quebec. And in May 1820 the *Montreal* proved that a steamer could make the crossing to La Prairie.[31] Her owners willingly gave Ward credit. In a letter to the *Canadian Courant,* they wrote:

The Proprietors of the Steam Boat Montreal, having observed remarks respecting the probability of the Boat's performing her destined trips through the season from Montreal to Laprairie, wherein is expressed doubts as to the depth of water, strength of current, &c. &c. they have deferred making any reply to such conjectures until they should have ascertained the fact, which (they can now say with confidence) is established, that the Boat will perform her regular trips without any impediment whatever through the season.

The Engine of this Boat was entirely built at this place, by Mr John D. Ward, upon a new and most simple plan, and does not weigh more than one half of an imported engine of the same power.

The proprietors feel a pleasure in thus publicly acknowledging, that to the superior abilities of the ingenious maker of this engine, much of the success of their enterprise is to be attributed – and they trust that he will meet with that encouragement in his profession which he so justly deserves.[32]

For Ward, it was a merry month of May. Not only had his engine-building skills confounded the skeptics and commanded public praise, but two weeks earlier, he had become a father.[33]

Operating at first on his own and then from 1825 in partnership with his twin younger brothers, Lebbeus Baldwin Ward and Samuel Shipman Ward,[34] John Ward went on to build engines for many boats on the St Lawrence, the Great Lakes, and Lake Champlain. The foundry that the Wards established, which they called the Eagle Foundry, survived into the twentieth century.[35] How bleak and short-lived was Lough's Montreal experience by comparison. In the end, it was not John Ward but a well-connected, middle-aged Scottish merchant, Thomas Andrew Turner, who took over the Montreal Air Furnace in 1819–20. With that change, plans for building the *Ottawa* moved briskly forward.

This boat at times seems an embodiment of Turner's frustrated ambitions – a kind of floating "picture of Dorian Gray," with sidewheels. His actions and the twists and turns of his career at this time, when he had reached his mid-forties, suggest a man whose accomplishments never quite measured up to his self-importance. A partner with Alexander Allison in the trading firm of Allison, Turner and Company, he had been the founding vice-president of the Bank of Montreal in 1817. But he had left that first Canadian bank after less than a year to preside over the founding of the rival Bank of Canada. He remained its president until 1822. When that bank ran into difficulties in 1823, he was among a group of major shareholders who urged its dissolution. By then he had also left the merchandise trade, his bread and butter from his earliest days in Canada, to become a newspaper publisher as owner of the *Montreal Gazette*. He collected a string of public appointments; in the 1820s he would serve as a captain of militia, a justice of the peace, treasurer of the board of trustees of Montreal's public market, a member of the board of examiners for flour inspectors, king's printer, a commissioner for the improvement of navigation on the St Lawrence, and warden (then master, from 1832) of Trinity House, the port and pilotage authority.[36]

Playing on Turner's name and multiple occupations, the *Scribbler*, a bawdy, satirical journal, mocked him under the moniker of Tommy Changeling. For the *Scribbler*, Turner, who "has always some new project on the *anvil* and is so fond of *turning*," was an officious toady; "whatever scruples Tommy might have once had, his conscience has been pretty well seared when he was a blacksmith, for that has been one of the many pursuits of this Jack of all trades."[37]

The pointed talk of anvils, metal turning, and blacksmith's work referred to Turner's association with the Montreal Air Furnace. That association began on 7 January 1819 when he bought all the foundry's equipment, tools, and supplies from Lough for £1,000. Lough retained the foundry itself, but it was heavily mortgaged. Sometime during the year it came under the control of Allison, Turner and Company, and on 5 July 1820 Turner acquired the property for £945 at a sheriff's sale. Lough's original debt to Sherman – £757 19s. 10½d., plus yearly interest of 6 per cent from 7 July 1817 – stood at close to £1,000 when it was assigned to Turner in February 1822. He paid £500 for it, probably to get rid of encumbrances on the foundry property more than in hope of collecting from Lough.[38]

Turner obviously had plans for the foundry. In the fall of 1818 he had expressed an interest in joining Lough's old associate, Thomas Mears, and other Ottawa River traders who had decided to build a steamboat. On 16 January 1819, only nine days after buying Lough's stock in trade, he formally joined a partnership to build the *Ottawa*. Nameless as yet, the boat was "to be navigated between Lachine and the Cascades and also as far up the Grand or Ottawa River as the Circumstances & practicability of the case may require."[39]

The initial capital of the steamboat partnership was £2,000. Along with Mears and Turner, the stockholders were Donald Duff, Alexander Grant, Robert Grant, John Macdonell, and Hezekiah Wing. Duff and Robert Grant were forwarders based at Lachine, partners in Grant and Duff since January 1818.[40] Merchant Alexander Grant, a former North West Company fur trader and a future legislative councillor of Upper Canada, had settled on the Ottawa at New Longueuil (now L'Orignal, Ontario) in 1805. Macdonell, who had succeeded Mears as member of the legislature for Prescott County in April 1815, also a former North West Company fur trader, had settled at Point Fortune on the Ottawa River, where he operated a forwarding business and served as judge of the Ottawa District court. Wing, a Connecticut Yankee who kept an inn at Lachine and operated a forwarding business on the Ottawa, signed up for a share in the boat, but was to give it up on 7 April "from the want of capacity to pay and discharge the instalments as they might fall due."[41]

The written partnership agreement seems skewed. It split the capital into sixteen shares of £125 each, but accounted for only thirteen: "Grant & Duff, four Shares, the said Thomas Andrew Turner, Two Shares, the said Alexander Grant, two Shares, the said John McDonell, two shares, the said Thomas Mears, two shares, the said Hezekiah Wing, one Share." There is no record of any change in this distribution, except for a marginal entry noting Wing's withdrawal. Still, the partners, all seasoned businessmen, endorsed the agreement, Turner, the banker, signing for himself as well as for Macdonell and Alexander Grant. The agreement makes no mention of Turner's business partner, Alexander Allison, yet he held a stake in the boat – probably from the first, certainly by the time it was ready for service.[42]

On 23 January, Lough was hired to build, "after a neat, good, perfect and substantial workmanlike manner, subject to Inspection by Competent Engineers, a Steam Engine of Eighteen horses power for a certain Boat to be Built for the said Thomas Mears and Thomas Andrew Turner and others concerned, of Seventy feet Keel, twenty feet Beam and four and a half feet hold." The engine, which he would build at the Montreal Air Furnace, was to be ready by 1 May for transport to Lachine, where Lough was to install it. He was to be paid in all £1,700.[43]

Two days after hiring Lough, the partners secured the services of John Bruce, a forty-year-old Scot, to build the boat.[44] Bruce had already been associated with two milestones in Canadian steam navigation. He had built the *Accommodation* in partnership with John Molson and engineer John Jackson, and while his bid to build the *Frontenac* had been turned down, he had acted as inspector of the timber used in her construction.[45] The *Accommodation* had turned out to be no great credit to Bruce's skill. This first Canadian steamer, 85 feet long and 16 broad and driven by a 6-horsepower engine, had left on her maiden run from Montreal to Quebec on 1 November 1809. With stops, the trip downriver took her three days; the return against the current, a week. Bruce and Jackson had soon pulled out of their partnership with Molson, unable to sustain the expense. Bruce stayed on as a Molson employee, sailing aboard the *Accommodation* as engineer and then captain, and superintending the construction of Molson's second steamer, the *Swiftsure*, in 1811–12. The *Accommodation* had sailed throughout 1810 and, after failing to repay her owner, had been scrapped early in the following year. In the words of one passenger who travelled in her to Quebec in September 1810, she was a "clumsy ill-constructed thing and the power of the works, which were out of order, was by no means adequate to its magnitude."[46]

For the building of the *Ottawa*, Bruce showed Turner and his partners his plans, which they approved with one modification: that the boat "shall be even Built flatter Bottom'd than in the said plan represented," to reduce her draught. The dimensions were as specified in Lough's contract, and the price was set at £800.[47] Together then, Bruce and Lough were to be paid £2,500 – £500 more than the capital investment foreseen in the partnership deed signed only nine days earlier. Bruce was to build the hull at Hawkesbury, above the Long Sault rapids on the Ottawa, "as near the house of the said Thomas Mears as circumstances will admit." She was to be run down to Lachine by 15 May to receive Lough's engine and machinery. Bruce proved punctual: the boat reached Lachine on Monday, 17 May.[48]

The *Frontenac*, from a sketch attributed to John Elliott Woolford; launched in 1816 and in operation from June 1817, she was the first Canadian streamer on the Great Lakes (NA/C-99574).

This was around the time when John Ward moved to Montreal. Ward and Lough had known each other since at least 1816, when they had both worked on the *Champlain* at Vergennes. Perhaps Ward had helped Lough build or install the engine of the *Ottawa,* a connection that might explain Lough's promissory note to him of 19 June. True to form, the debt-ridden Lough failed to pay the note on time, and Ward had him arrested by the sheriff on 29 September, claiming that he was about to abscond. Lough was freed on bail posted by Allison and Turner. By coincidence, debtor and creditor were thrown together a week later when they were named to arbitrate a dispute over founder John Fellow's bill for repairs to the engine of the *Caledonia,* a Montreal-Quebec steamer of which Turner was part owner. Fellow chose Lough to represent him, while Ward acted for the boat's owners. Perhaps in the course of their joint duties, Lough was able to convince Ward that he had no plans to skip town without paying his debt.[49]

Work proceeded on the steamboat during the summer. It was five long months after Bruce had delivered the hull before the *Ottawa*, as she was now called, underwent her trial on Tuesday, 19 October, sailing a total of about 14 miles from Lachine to the mouth of the Châteauguay River, on the south side of Lake St Louis, and back. Accounts of her speed varied – 50 minutes going up and $37\frac{1}{2}$ coming back down, said one; 72 minutes total, said another, which also noted that she was towing two boats at the time.[50] On average, then, if those reports are to be believed, she sailed at a good clip – roughly 9 to $11\frac{1}{4}$ miles an hour. "Her model is said to be very handsome, and her engine (the first made in Canada) to reflect great credit upon its fabricator Mr Lough," the *Courant* reported. "It is the opinion of those who were aboard her during the excursion, that she surpasses in speed any other steamboat navigating the waters of these Provinces. Mr Bruce has the merit of her construction."[51]

The *Courant* and at least one other Montreal newspaper spoke of Lough's engine as the first made in Canada.[52] Yet only ten years earlier, a Canadian-made engine had powered the *Accommodation;* that first engine had been assembled under John Jackson's supervision from parts supplied by the St Maurice Iron Works near Three Rivers and by blacksmith and

The *Vermont*, an American steamer that ran on Lake Champlain from 1809, sank in the Richelieu River in 1815 (courtesy of Martha Chodat).

hardware merchant George Platt and whitesmith Ezekiel Cutter. Bruce knew that, as did John Molson and others involved, but no one ventured to publish a correction. Perhaps no one cared to be reminded of that first experiment: every Montreal steamer since had run on imported English engines. Besides, John Jackson was no longer around, and George Platt was dead.[53] Though not the first engine made in Canada, Lough's did mark a fresh start. His work, it was said, "demonstrates the important fact, that we can now obtain Steam Engines, without expending our money to pay the labourers of the Old Country; and liberates us from the heavy charges, which always result, from one Country being totally dependant on another, for their most necessary articles."[54]

As far as the public was concerned, then, the *Ottawa* was off to a flying start. But an ominous note had been sounded behind the scenes. On 5 October, two weeks before her trial trip to Châteauguay, John Macdonell's older brother, Miles, had warned him: "I much fear that the Steam boat at Lachine is not going to do well – it is now said that she cannot even go to the Cascades for want of a sufficiency of water to float her. You & the other proprietors sustain a great loss should she not answer the intended purpose."[55] The *Ottawa* drew about $3\frac{1}{2}$ feet of water – rather deep for a boat meant to negotiate the rapids of Vaudreuil or St Anne's at the mouth of the Ottawa.[56] At Lachine and at the Cascades, too, the water at wharfside was only about four feet deep, except in the spring. Somewhat belatedly, a quick survey was made to determine whether the waters between Lachine and the foot of the Vaudreuil Rapids were indeed navigable by steamboats. They were found to be suitable, "with very little exception," the *Herald* reported in early November. Still, the *Ottawa* did not begin regular commercial service that year. Winter arrived and she was tied up at Île Perrot, at the mouth of the Ottawa River. The true test of her performance would wait until spring.[57]

It is possible that by the end of 1819 the owners had already secured the services of William McMaster of Lachine as captain. A full crew, however, was not hired before the spring of 1820. In the meantime, the owners got into a spat with Bruce. Once her paddlewheels had been installed, he had been required to cover them. For this and other finishing work, he charged extra, claiming that it was not part of his contract. The owners insisted that it was, and besides, they protested, his charges were outlandish. The dispute was resolved on 20 February 1820 when, reconsidering a decision to submit to arbitration, the parties came to terms without further ado.[58]

Two days later Adam Hall was hired as the engineer of the *Ottawa* for one full year, to begin on 1 April. He was to be paid in all £150 plus room and board. Once the navigation season ended and he was no longer needed on the boat, he was to serve out the year – at Allison, Turner's foundry, it seems – doing whatever engineering work was required of him.[59] For two months Hall had been a familiar figure around the Montreal Air Furnace, now renamed the St Mary Foundry. In December a client had commissioned the firm to cast engine parts for the *Catherine*, launched the previous October and meant to run from Montreal to the south shore or any downriver village that might promise a profit. The client had stipulated that Hall was to supervise the building of the engine. Allison, Turner was so proud of its handiwork that it put the *Catherine's* 32-horsepower engine on public display at its foundry in April. The partners boasted that it was "the second which has been completed at the *St Mary Foundry*" and that now that they had found "a person of science to superintend the work" – presumably a reference to Hall – they were ready to take on more contracts and to "finish the whole, or any part of the work of a Steam Engine."[60]

Without a hint of doubt in their boat, the owners drew up a schedule for the *Ottawa*. From Saturday to Wednesday she would leave Lachine at 6 a.m. for the Cascades, calling at Châteauguay and Île Perrot on the way up, and return to Lachine by about 1 p.m. For the rest of the day, until dusk, she would run as a ferry between Lachine and Châteauguay. Every Thursday at 9 a.m. she was to leave Lachine for Point Fortune, on the border of Lower and Upper Canada, and return to Lachine by 1 p.m. the next day, when she would again spend the afternoon and evening running as a ferry to Châteauguay. At some point in late summer, when low water would undoubtedly make the Vaudreuil Rapids impassable, she would remain on Lake St Louis, leaving batteaux and Durham boats to ply the twenty-six miles above the rapids to Point Fortune. That, at least, was the plan in mid-March, a month before the opening of navigation.[61]

No sketch or description of the *Ottawa* seems to exist. Nowhere is it even stated whether she carried mast and sails, as most early steamers did. Surviving documents give her bare dimensions – keel 70 feet, beam 20 feet, depth of hold $4\frac{1}{2}$ feet – and show that she was a flat-bottomed sidewheeler with covered paddlewheels. When she was later put up for sale, she was also said to be equipped with a cast-iron crane. She had at least one dormitory-style cabin for passengers: according to her fare schedules, cabin passengers from Lachine to the Cascades, for example, paid 7s. 6d., while deck passengers paid 5s.[62] The cabin was undoubtedly below deck, as was the case with sailing ships and other early steamers. But was there only one? If so, a divider would have separated the men's berths from the women's, as segregation of the sexes was *de rigueur*.

A Jamaican planter who travelled through the Canadas in 1816 left a description of the rather cramped accommodation that steamboats offered. Although he wrote after boarding one of the southbound Lake Champlain

THE PROPRIETORS OF THE STEAM BOAT OTTAWA, notify, that the Boat will commence running, from LACHINE, on the opening of the Navigation.

It is intended that she shall start from LACHINE for THE CASCADES, each morning, (*Thursdays and Fridays excepted*) punctually, at SIX o'Clock. She will land Passengers at CHATEAUGUY RIVER, and on ISLE PERRAULT, on her way up, and return to LACHINE about One o'clock P. M.

On THURSDAY, she will leave LACHINE at Nine o'Clock in the morning, and proceed to POINT FORTUNE on the Grand River; from whence she will return to Lachine about One o'Clock on Friday.

On her return from the CASCADES, she will ply between LACHINE and the mouth of the CHATEAUGUY RIVER, till Sundown, so that a regular daily traverse to *Chateauguy*, will be kept up after One o'Clock, during the Season, *Thursdays excepted*.

Every arrangement has been made for the safety and comfort of Passengers, and a Bar will be kept on board to furnish refreshments when required.

The proprietors will Transport GOODS AND PASSENGERS to and from the different places on the communication at the following rates, and, when low water, (as the season advances,) shall prevent the Boat from passing the Vaudreuil Rapids, the communication with Point Fortune will be regularly kept up by PACKET BOATS.

Nothing but accident will prevent the greatest punctuality in the departure of the Boat, so that the public may rely on meeting with no unnecessary detention.

RATES OF FREIGHT AND PASSAGE

Per Cwt. from Lachine to the Cascades	0	7½
per do do do to Vaudreuil	0	9
per do do do to Point Fortune	1	6
Cabin Passengers to the Cascades	7	6
Deck do do do	5	0
Cabin do to Vaudreuil	8	9
Deck do do do	6	3
Cabin do to Point Fortune	15	0
Deck do do do		
All passengers landed any where between Vaudreuil and Point Fortune	12	6
Pot or Pearl Ashes from Point Fortune per barl.	2	6
Packs of Fur do	1	3
Ashes from Vaudreuil per barl.	1	8
Grain do do in Bags per bush.		2½

Ashes or other produce at intermediate distances from Point Fortune to Vaudreuil, same rates as from Point Fortune.

	s.	D.
Ashes from the Cascades per barl.	1	6
Flour do do per do		10

(*Passengers as upwards.*)

Passengers to and from Chateauguy River each	1	3

Raftsmen returning from Montreal will be taken at the rate of 5s. for a Crew not exceeding 8, or 7½d. each man

N. B. Emigrants with their families and Luggage, will be conveyed at a very moderate rate.

For Freight or Passage, apply to the undermentioned Agents.

ALEXr. ALLISON, at Montreal
DONALD DUFF, LaChine
OR
JOHN McDONELL, Point Fortune.

TO BE LEASED, for the ensuing Season, THE BAR OF THE STEAM BOAT OTTAWA— Apply to the Subscribers here, or to Mr. Donald Duff, at La Chine.

ALLISON, TURNER & Co.

Montreal, 17th March 1820. tf.

The first advertisement for the *Ottawa* stated that she would run from Lachine up the Ottawa River to Point Fortune once a week (from the *Montreal Herald, 8 April 1820*).

steamers at St John's, he obviously meant his description to be more or less generic:

Those who have never been in a steam boat will hardly be able to conceive how 60 people or more can be lodged in one apartment, leaving room for all the tables chairs &c. in the middle necessary for the accommodation of double that number at other meals – There are two tiers of bed places divided by partitions of wood looking somewhat like the shelves of an open press – Each passenger has one to himself of about 5 ft 10 in length & two ft in bredth. These are provided with a mattress, bed blankets & quite all clean – ... The ladies have always a separate cabin to themselves often fitted up with elegance, as all the cabins are with neatness & cleanliness.[63]

While the small *Ottawa* would not have offered sleeping room for sixty men and an untold number of women, the arrangements would have been similar.

Like other steamers, the *Ottawa* also had a "bar." Charles Michael Connolly, a grocer and tavern-keeper originally from County Monaghan, Ireland, leased this food-and-drink concession on 10 April, promising to keep a stock of food, wines, and spirits "of unobjectionable qualities" on board. He was to pay £65 for the privilege. By this lease, the owners secured the services of a steward without having to pay him a wage. By the same token, they denied themselves a source of revenue which, to Connolly, was clearly worth more than £65. In a burst of enthusiasm, the fifty-year-old Connolly formed a company to operate a summer stage service, the Union Stage Coach, between the Molsons' Mansion House Hotel on St Paul Street in Montreal and the Free Mason's Arms in Lachine, to connect with the steamboat.[64]

The rest of the crew were hired on 19 April. Allan Cameron and Robert Bell of Montreal signed on as "mariners" at £3 a month. Labourer Baptiste Portugais, the only French Canadian among them, was hired as fireman, or stoker, at the same rate of pay. All told, then, the operation of the boat was placed in the hands of six men. On Sunday, 30 April, with all hands at their posts and the lake free of ice, the *Ottawa* went into service.[65]

On the first two days she left Lachine for the Cascades at 9 a.m. She switched to her advertised schedule of 6 a.m. starts on the Tuesday. On the Thursday, 4 May, she was supposed to make her first run up to Point Fortune. That trip, however, never came off. Sometime before, McMaster must have tried his luck at the mouth of the Ottawa, only to find that the steamer could not pass the shallow Vaudreuil Rapids where, over a distance of a few hundred feet, the Ottawa drops a mere three feet or so as it spills from the Lake of Two Mountains into Lake St Louis. That very Thursday the boat's owners announced that, for the time being, they had given up the idea of taking her up to Point Fortune: the *Ottawa* would work Lake St Louis, while Durham boats and batteaux would take care of business above the rapids.[66]

The idea now was that every day but Sunday the *Ottawa* would make two round trips daily to the Cascades, leaving Lachine at 6 a.m. and 1 p.m., and then run as a ferry to Châteauguay. (On Sundays she was to make a single trip to the Cascades, carrying passengers only.) Within two weeks, even those plans proved too ambitious. A round trip to the Cascades – about fifty miles – took her at least six hours. If she was to provide weekday ferry service to Châteauguay as well, one trip a day to the Cascades was all that she could manage. By 20 May one trip it was.[67]

While these developments represented setback after setback for the owners and no doubt a disappointment for settlers, traders, and forwarders on the Ottawa, not everyone was dispirited. Drawn by the novelty of a boat that could take them out for a spin and bring them back within a specified time, wind or no wind, pleasure-seekers with time and money to spare took to cruising in her on Lake St Louis. "It has now become a fashionable recreation for those whose business will afford a leisure day, to spend it by enjoying a jaunt as far as the Cascades in this boat," a newspaper reported.[68] Beginning in 1821, the *Montreal*, sailing from the port of Montreal, offered similar Sunday excursions on the waters below the city.[69]

These were short recreational trips, but they were symptomatic of a new phenomenon that would soon grow in importance. Improvements in the speed, safety, and reliability of transportation gave rise to a new class of traveller along the St Lawrence – the tourist. Where others travelled from necessity, tourists travelled for pleasure. Adventurers, businessmen, immigrants, soldiers, or other hardy souls, with no other purpose than to reach their destination, might be resigned to hardship on their journey, but tourists – not just men but whole families – were out to enjoy themselves in relative comfort. As a result, coaches had to meet steamboats, and tolerable lodgings, food, and drink were needed at the stopping points. With varying degrees of application and success, the owners of stages, steamboats, inns, and hotels sought to meet these demands. In the *Ottawa's* case, Michael Connolly launched his Montreal-Lachine stagecoach service to meet the boat. Before the *Ottawa* even got going, when Lough was fitting her engine at Lachine, William Jones moved there from St John's and, in a building that had formerly housed a tavern run by Bruce's brother-in-law, Daniel McArthur, opened the Steam Boat Hotel. The name itself testified to the hopes which the steamer inspired.[70]

The *Ottawa* brought other developments. The most practical and immediately beneficial was the towing of the forwarders' boats against the current to the Cascades. She could not help them up the rapids, of course, but any improvement to the supply line to Upper Canada was significant at a time when all the imports of the upper province – "every hat and every coat that is worn" – had to be shipped up the river.[71] The boat may also have added to the value of lakeside real estate: a property offered for sale at the Cascades in the fall of 1819 was touted as providing "an easy and expeditious communication to Montreal, by means of the Steam Boat now built at Lachine, which will land within a few acres of the Farm."[72]

Lord Dalhousie, who took up his duties as governor general at Quebec in June 1820, noted the impact of steam navigation on the river and on the shore as he travelled up to Montreal for the first time that August:

The steam boats have destroyed the posting altogether, & consequently the roads are not taken care of. The people of the villages naturally complain of these effects, the proprietors of lands feel them, and more than these, a large population that till now lived by the trade & employment arising from the small craft on the river that absolutely swarmed in large & small boats; that class of the people is deprived of their usual means or subsistance, & unwillingly, at first, to turn to a new pursuit in life. However the steamboats are admirably calculated to promote the public welfare, as well as public convenience, & those classes complaining, are not to be pitied, while they live on land of the richest nature.[73]

The *Ottawa* signalled the same kind of mixed blessing for people above Montreal. In short, she marked the coming of steam power and the Industrial Revolution, with all its benefits – as well as its disruptions, noise, and sooty smoke – to an area that had known only wind, water, and muscle.

She represented a substantial investment – at least £2,500 for the hull and engine. It is doubtful that she ever began to repay her owners. Perhaps a hint of their problems can be seen in their decision to halve the fare for day trippers to the Cascades as of mid-July: "parties going up on pleasure will be brought down gratis." In other words, a round trip would cost no more than a one-way fare.[74] Less than two weeks later came a sure sign of trouble. Whether because his bar was proving less profitable than he had hoped or because of some dispute with the owners – it seems that they may have withheld some of his revenues as security for the payment of his rent – Michael Connolly shut down the bar on 9 August and left the boat, breaking his lease.[75]

The *Ottawa* sailed to the close of navigation without serious accident, a feat in itself considering the mishaps that befell many early steamers. The *Frontenac*, for example, in operation only two months, ran up on rocks below Kingston in August 1817 and had to be hauled off. Only one day after she made it back to Kingston, two of her passengers fell overboard

and drowned. In September that year the *Champlain* burned to the waterline at Whitehall. In September 1819, at the same time as Lough was
working on the *Ottawa's* engine, six people lost their lives when the *Phoenix*
burned and sank north of Burlington.[76]

No crippling or fatal accident befell the *Ottawa*, yet her owners
resolved not to run her another year. Precisely when and why they
decided to get rid of her is a matter for conjecture. The public had no
reason to suspect that she would not sail again. In the early spring of
1821 it was even thought that she would take another run at the Ottawa
River, which suggests that any engine troubles or problems with her
design and manœuvrability were not generally considered so grave as to
make her a lost cause.[77] Her $3\frac{1}{2}$-foot draft of water posed a problem, as
John Macdonell's brother had suggested. "The Steam Boat was yet
aground when I left town," Mears wrote laconically after returning to
Hawkesbury from a visit to Montreal in August 1820.[78]

Even if she lost money in her first year, the *Ottawa's* owners might
have kept her, hoping for better days, had she proven herself on the river
from which she drew her name. That, after all, was the chief interest of
Mears, Macdonell, and Alexander Grant and possibly also of Robert
Grant. But she sat too low in the water to drag herself up the rapids. If
navigating the Ottawa was out of the question and she was to be confined
to Lake St Louis, what other motive but profit could have induced them
to hold on to her? Their decision to sell suggests that she offered no such
prospect. Quite apart from any defects in her design or in her engine, it
is possible that there was simply not enough business to repay her owners
for their large capital outlay.[79]

Some falling out among the owners might also have contributed to her
demise. On 22 January 1821 Grant and Duff broke up, the partners going
their separate ways in the forwarding line.[80] Captain McMaster, too, went
his own way. When he married Ellen McNabb of Lachine on 22 February
1821, a notice of the event identified him as "master of the Steam-Boat
Ottawa."[81] The fact is that he was already hard at work on the *Perseverance*, a new steamer of which he was co-owner and which he was to
command. He had begun work on her that winter, and it was no secret:
he was building her at Robert Grant's slip at Lachine. Aptly named, she
was meant to take a run at the Ottawa River. If the costly *Ottawa* had
failed to conquer the rapids and pay back her owners when she had Lake
St Louis to herself, she hardly stood a chance of competing with a rival
built and commanded by someone intimately acquainted with her weak-
nesses and bound to make every effort to correct them.

On 2 May, only a week before the launch of the *Perseverance*, the
Montreal brokers Macnider, Aird and Company announced that the
Ottawa would be sold at auction on the 19th. Her engine, billed as a

20-horsepower, was said to be "nearly new and in good order." In a tacit acknowledgment that she was unsuited to Lake St Louis, no mention was made of the lake, but it was suggested that the steamer was "particularly well adapted for the navigation of the River Chambly [the lower Richelieu], or to ply between Montreal and Longueuil and Boucherville, & might be brought down from LaChine with little or no risk."[82]

Three days after the auction date, Alexander Allison was offering the *Ottawa* for private sale, promising to deliver her at the port of Montreal if necessary.[83] Either at the auction or through some other transaction, he wound up as the sole owner of the unwanted steamer. It is possible that, even before the auction, some of the stockholders had forfeited their shares by failing to meet a call for funds from the management committee. Or perhaps the boat came into his hands in a division of assets on the dissolution of his partnership with Turner on 21 August. The breakup came only six days after a fire – their second within a year – destroyed Allison, Turner's trading house on St Paul Street.[84] Allison kept the St Mary Foundry going; he seems to have shown some zest for the job, even designing a new model of stove. But on 1 December he died of a liver complaint while on a trip to Quebec.[85] Turner, for his part, went on to buy the *Montreal Gazette* the following spring from publisher James Brown.

John Gray, founding president of the Bank of Montreal, was named curator of Allison's estate. He took over the foundry operation, leasing it from the estate for three years and then transferring its tools and equipment to a shop near his home at St Catherine (now Outremont).[86] But Gray had no plans to pump new life into the *Ottawa*. On 8 March 1822 he offered her for sale "for less than the cost of the Engine alone," suggesting that she could "easily be taken to Montreal or up the river to Lake St Francis, where she might be employed to great advantage, but would answer well on any part of the River, as she can be navigated at small expence."[87] Taking the boat down the Lachine Rapids would have been a challenge – no steamer had yet attempted that. How Gray expected anyone to haul her up the rapids from Lake St Louis to Lake St Francis when she had proved incapable of scaling the much tamer rapids of Vaudreuil he did not say, nor was he ever called on to prove that it could be done.

Gray had no more luck than Allison in disposing of the *Ottawa* by private sale. Tied up at Robert Grant's wharf, where she had been held in the grip of winter ice and buffeted by the winds and waves, she settled on the bottom in about four feet of water. She must have been a sorry sight when, on 20 July, shortly before noon, she went under the auctioneer's hammer, this time in four separate lots – hull, engine, fittings, and cast-iron crane – without any reserve price.[88]

Thomas Mears acquired Lough's engine for an unknown sum. In January 1823 he and the Quebec City timber-exporting partners William

Sheppard and John Saxton Campbell hired engineer Scott Burt to "take, erect & put up the Steam Engine & apparatus (which was originally on board the Ottawa) with all additional machinery that may be necessary on board of another boat now building at Hawkesbury."[89] This was the *Union*, like the *Ottawa*, built at Mears's place. She was to be the first steamer to provide regular service on the Ottawa, plying between Grenville, on the Lower Canadian side of the river opposite Hawkesbury, and Hull.

While fate gave Lough's engine a new life on the Ottawa River, it was not kind to Bruce's boat, no more than it had been to his *Accommodation* a decade earlier. The *Ottawa* went unsold. Gray was still trying to dispose of the hull and crane late in 1825.[90] By then, Captain McMaster, after four years commanding the *Perseverance*, had left that boat to see to the building of yet another steamer at Lachine, the *St Lawrence*, this one in association with Horace Dickinson, an American expatriate who operated the stage and steamboat line along the St Lawrence between Montreal and Upper Canada.

No more was heard of Joseph Lough. He had left Montreal, perhaps to return to the United States, if not by the end of 1819, then certainly by early 1822.[91] As for John Bruce, he died all but forgotten in the Montreal General Hospital on 29 December 1825 at the age of forty-seven. At the sale of his effects the following February, among his rulers and maps and saws, his planes and bevels and books on navigation, there was one boat model. Daniel McArthur, his brother-in-law, snapped it up for nine pence.[92]

The navigation season of 1827 had just begun when the Durham boat *Louisa* sailed from Kingston on 17 April, bound for Montreal.[93] She was carrying 538 bushels of peas, 143 barrels of flour, and 10 barrels of pork for forwarder James McCutchon.[94] George Horne, her master, ran her down the spring-swollen St Lawrence and through the Long Sault rapids above Cornwall without incident. At the eastern end of Lake St Francis, at present-day Les Côteaux, he stopped to take on a licensed pilot to guide the *Louisa* down the rapids of Côteau, Cedars, and Cascades.

That stretch of troubled water between Lakes St Francis and St Louis, where the river drops about eighty-two feet over eight miles, was the doom of many river boats. The worst part was the Cedars, and not just in the spring when the water ran high. "This Rapid is much more frightful than the Long Sault," the wife of Upper Canada's first lieutenant-governor, Elizabeth Simcoe, had noted in mid-summer 1796. "I cannot describe how terrifying the Extent of furious dashing white waves appeared, & how the Boat plunged & rose among them, the waves sometimes washing into the boat ... There is a place called the Run near the Locks which is like going down the stream of an overshot Mill & I really thought we should never have risen out of it."[95] There were men who scoffed that the rapids had more bark than bite and frightened only "the fair sex," but one who had sailed down the river in a Durham boat in the early 1820s was just as impressed as Mrs Simcoe with the Cedars run, where "the water curls up, roars, foams, and splashes over one, and where the only safe part of the channel is so narrow, that if the boats are not kept in an accurately straight line, they are inevitably lost."[96]

But luck was with the *Louisa*, and again she came through unscathed. She crossed Lake St Louis and on Sunday morning, 22 April, with the worst of the journey behind her, she made for the entrance of the Lachine Canal under a press of sail. Horne and his crew could look forward to a smooth ride through its six locks, which would ease them down the forty-two-foot drop to the port of Montreal, sparing them the ordeal of a run down the Lachine Rapids.

They were nearing the mouth of the canal when, out of the blue, an old ghost struck with a vengeance. The *Louisa* ran against the hulk of the steamer *Ottawa*, lying just below the surface. Her hull torn open, the *Louisa* sank. A passenger, a boy of fifteen, was reported to have drowned. His name went unrecorded. Horne and his crew were lucky; they suffered no more than a dunking. Peas, pork, and flour were ruined. Horne blamed his accident on the "sunken wreck or Hull of an old Steam Boat or Vessel called the 'Ottawa' said to be owned by one Horace Dickinson."[97] If Dickinson had indeed acquired the old hull, it seems that it was for use as a makeshift wharf at low water.[98]

The sinking of the *Louisa* and the drowning of her young passenger marked the last recorded episode in the career of the *Ottawa*. After this reminder of her brief, inglorious existence, she vanished from the record.

CHAPTER TWO

Years of Perseverance

For any disillusioned shareholder in the *Ottawa* who might have read it, Robert Gourlay's *Statistical Account of Upper Canada*, published in London in 1822, contained a cruelly ironic statement. "There is, at the extremity of that part of Ottawa river, called the lake of Two Mountains, a considerable current, but not such as to impede navigation," Gourlay wrote, "and when I left Canada, it was said that a small steam boat was established, to ply regularly from La Chine, near Montreal, to the lower part of Hawkesbury township."[1] Gourlay had left Canada in August 1819. By the time his book appeared, the "small steam boat" of which he wrote had been stymied by the very current that he pictured as surmountable. Even had news of the *Ottawa's* failure reached him, Gourlay might have deemed it inconclusive as regards the navigability of the rapids. William McMaster certainly did. In 1821 the persevering captain and his new associates hoped that, with skill and the right boat, they could succeed where the *Ottawa* had failed. For them, the right boat was the *Perseverance*.

Lachine had never seen a whoop-up like the launch of the *Perseverance*, though spring flings of a sort had become something of a tradition, thanks to the fur trade. For years, the canoe brigades of the Montreal-based North West Company had gathered there in early May to set off up the Ottawa River and beyond to the fur countries of the west. But the union of the North West and Hudson's Bay companies, negotiated in London the previous winter, meant that Lachine had seen the last of that bustling rite of spring. Most of the fur-trade traffic would now run between London and Hudson Bay or the Pacific coast.

The big fur brigades were gone, but there was no danger of Lachine becoming a ghost town. The fur trade, on the decline for several years, had given way to trade in timber, potash, and produce from the upper country. What Joseph Bouchette, surveyor general of Lower Canada, had observed in 1815 still held largely true: "La Chine is a place of greater importance than any other village on the island [of Montreal], being the centre of all the commerce between the upper and lower provinces, and the north-west country also: whatever merchandise is sent upwards is brought hither by land carriage from Montreal, and all the imports [from Upper Canada and the American shores of the Great Lakes] are here landed."[2] Durham boats and batteaux came and went, handling the growing trade with Upper Canada and with the developing country up the Ottawa.

At the time when Bouchette wrote, Lachine consisted of "only about 20 dwelling-houses, but a great number of store houses belonging to the merchants, besides the warehouses of the Indian department."[3] By the spring of 1821, it had not grown much in size; nor had it shrunk in importance. The *Ottawa* had proved deficient – though no one yet knew that she would never sail again – but she had brought steam power to the lake: towing power, new notions of speed, freedom from the whims of the wind, and other changes. There was no turning back. The *Perseverance* confirmed that fact. As the first steamer built at Lachine, she deserved a celebration when she was launched. There was more good news in the air: after years of talk, work was scheduled to start on the Lachine Canal that summer. It would not be built with steamboats in mind; its locks, 108 feet long by 20 wide, with a 5-foot depth over the sill, would be too narrow and its fixed bridges too low for boats with funnels or cabins on deck, but it would be a boon to Durham boats, batteaux, and barges running to Montreal.[4]

So people from miles around gathered on the afternoon of 9 May to see the new boat off, their spirits buoyed by good news, spring fever, and free beer. Scots, French, English, and Irish were joined by about a hundred Mohawks from Caughnawaga (Kahnawake), across the St Lawrence. When the *Perseverance* slid into the water, the Natives on her deck hooted with delight, and the crowd on shore shouted and applauded. Grasshoppers – a kind of brass artillery shell – were fired in quick succession, making a roar, and Captain McMaster was in his glory.[5] A spectator wrote up the event in doggerel, painting a Hogarthian scene:

> *The Launch of the Steam-Boat at Lachine*
> I sing not of Kings
> Nor of any such things,
> Tho' to mine I confess I am quite staunch;
> About Honour and Glory
> I weave no fine story:
> No, I sing of a wonderful boat launch.

True, as I am a sinner,
I bolted my dinner,
Nor e'en play'd on my bottle a solo;
But when I'd done stuffing,
Away, neck or nothing,
I scamper'd to see the raree show.

The good folks of La Chine,
To their best might be seen;
And better's not under the Sun, Sir;
Cochnowaga's fair Squaws,
With clean muzzles and paws,
Also had their share of the fun, Sir.

There were Sawneys and Paddies,
Old Wives and young Ladies,
Dress'd in white, red, black, green, blue & yellow;
All complexions were there,
Pale, tawny, and fair,
Negro black, ginger red, Sir, and sallow.

There were thick, short and tall,
Great, middling and small;
And, I say it with humble submission,
A more orderly set
Of good folks never met,
Tho' of high, low, and ev'ry condition.

There were lots of good cheer,
Bread, cheese, and strong beer,
Which knock'd many a stout fellow under;
While the Grasshoppers loud,
Astonish'd the crowd
With their noise, for they sounded like thunder!

Then to work they went steady,
And when all things were ready,
They clear'd ship for action at once, Sir;
But a delicate dandy,
At leaping not handy,
Got a pitch mop across his fine sconce, Sir.

Old John by command,
At the bow took his stand,
To baptise with a huge brandy bottle;

And he swore at the time,
That he thought it a crime,
Not to pour it all down his own throttle.

Well, the boat went at last,
Not too slow, nor too fast,
To the water she went like a goose, Sir,
Amid such ranting and tearing,
Huzzaing and swearing,
That it seem'd as if hell were let loose, Sir.

To give the Captain his due,
(Tho' my countryman too,)
He's a chap that's both active and clever;
While success I will sing
To my country and King,
The same to McMaster, for ever.[6]

The *Ottawa* might be termed the forwarders' boat, given the interests of several of her main backers. She represented a venture into steam navigation by those freight handlers specialized in inland water transport who in the next two decades would come to dominate steamer traffic between Montreal and Upper Canada. But the *Perseverance* was not part of this trend. There was not one forwarder among her owners. She was more of a tradesmen's boat.

As her builder and master, McMaster, then thirty-two, was the person most closely identified with the new steamer, but he was not her sole owner. At a meeting in Montreal on 14 December 1820, seven men had committed themselves to build her. Besides McMaster, there were his fellow Scot, plumber James Greenfield, merchant James Russell of the Cascades, a certain H. Halpin, and engineers William Brackenridge, John Bennet, and Scott Burt.[7] The plan seems to have been to split the ownership into nine shares. In early January 1821 Alexander Forbes, a cooper, did promise "to come a partner in the new Steam Boat now a Building by Captn McMaster, & promise to pay one ninth part of Said Boat which is said to cost nine hundred & Ten pounds for Engine & Building of Boat, also for Cables, anchors & Sales [*sic*] &c. all complete Providing the Builder & engineers will give Satisfactory Security that Said Boat & engines will give Satisfaction & answer the purpose Intended for."[8] When the time came to sign a formal contract on 31 January, however, the wary Forbes was out of the picture, as was Halpin, and the ownership was split into just five shares.[9] McMaster owned one, as did James Russell, though he sold it the following year to John McKenzie, partner in the dry goods importing firm of Hector Russell and Company.[10] Founder John Fellow also owned a full share, while Greenfield and Brackenridge split one. The fifth share went to Bennet, Briggs and Burt, blacksmiths, brass founders, millwrights, and makers of steam engines, of Panet Street in the St Mary suburb of Montreal. Greenfield and Fellow acted as managers of the concern.

John Bennet, a Scot and the mainstay of Bennet, Briggs and Burt, was Greenfield's engine builder of choice. He would construct the engines for all four steamers in which Greenfield was to have an interest.[11] Not that there was much choice: for more than a decade after the dissolution of Allison, Turner and Company in the summer of 1821 and the Phoenix Foundry's one stab at engine building for the Montreal-Terrebonne steamer *Dalhousie* in 1820, the only makers of marine engines left in Montreal were Bennet's successive partnerships and the Ward brothers. It would be 1833 before another engine maker appeared on the scene.[12]

Bennet had been sent out from Britain by Boulton and Watt in 1812 to install and maintain the engine of John Molson's second steamer, the *Swiftsure*, and he had stayed on to work for Molson.[13] Then in January 1820 he had formed a partnership with Burt and blacksmith Lot Briggs. They had opened for business that March.[14] The 10-horsepower engine of the *Perseverance* was the first steamboat engine they produced, with help from Brackenridge and castings from the Phoenix Foundry.[15] Evidently, the affairs of the partnership did not require their full attention: in January 1821 Bennet and Burt signed up for the year as engineers with John Molson and Sons, Bennet to work chiefly aboard the Montreal-Quebec steamer *Malsham*, and Burt aboard the *New Swiftsure* on the same route.[16] In June 1822 Burt, a drunkard who seems never to have held a job for very long, would withdraw from the partnership and give up his interest in the *Perseverance*. The business would continue under the name of Bennet and Briggs for another four years.[17]

The *Perseverance* was 80 feet long and 14 feet 10 inches broad, and drew less than 18 inches light. It was noted that she was "rather narrower than Steam-Boats are in general in proportion to her length." Certainly, she was sleeker than the *Ottawa* – about 5 feet narrower – although the two boats were roughly the same length, and her draft was less than half that of her predecessor. Her facilities included a bar and a cabin, the latter extending almost two feet above the deck. She had a mast and sails; in fact, the agreement with McMaster required him to supply three sails. She was built for £910 – £310 for the boat and fittings, £600 for the engine – the price agreed upon at the meeting of 14 December 1820.[18]

From the start, her owners showed a concern for economy. The *Ottawa*, built for £2,500 or more, seems a monument to extravagance by comparison. While the power of an engine determined its cost,[19] the owners of the *Perseverance* went for a weak engine, supplementing it with sails.

They had the reliability of steam power, but when the wind was favourable, they could hoist the sails and save fuel. The fact that the builders of boat and engine were among the partners also helped to keep costs down and gave them an added incentive to ensure that she would operate smoothly and at a profit. It was understood, as their agreement stated, "that the share or shares of the said William McMaster, John Bennet and Co. and William Breckenridge, are included in the said sum of nine hundred and ten pounds and their shares deducted, the remaining Balance to be paid by the rest of the said co-partners."[20] The schedule of payments also betrayed a cautious approach. Neither McMaster nor Bennet's firm and Brackenridge were to be fully paid until the boat had run for fifteen days and been pronounced sound. By contrast, the contracts for the *Ottawa* had specified that John Bruce was to receive his final payment when he delivered the boat, and Joseph Lough was to get the last of his money once his engine had been installed "and found sufficient, but prior to the said Boat performing a trip."[21]

Unlike the *Ottawa*, the *Perseverance* was launched with her engine on board. A month passed, however, before the finishing work was done and she was ready to make her first run to the Cascades. On Sunday, 10 June, she made the round trip, calling at Châteauguay on the way, in something less than four hours. McMaster showed his passengers every courtesy, and they in turn had nothing but praise for him and his boat. The *Perseverance*, like the *Ottawa* before her, was off to a fine start.[22]

Her owners ran her for almost two weeks before deciding on the frequency of her sailings. They waited another two weeks, until her machinery was well broken in, before pitting her against the rapids at the mouth of the Ottawa River on Friday, 6 July. Instead of tackling the Vaudreuil Rapids to the west of Île Perrot, as the *Ottawa* had tried to do, she went for the more direct route – twelve miles shorter – up the St Anne Rapids on the northeast side. Once her crew had found a channel and marked it with buoys, she accomplished the job in fifteen to twenty minutes, not by steam power alone but by warping: an anchor was thrown into the stream ahead of the boat, and her crew hauled her up by reeling in the hawser.[23]

Some fifty passengers sailed on this triumphant journey. "Being the only vessel of that description that ever ascended the Ottawa so far," she was cheered from shore by the inhabitants along the route as she proceeded past the rapids and on through the Lake of Two Mountains. At Point Fortune, at the foot of the Carillon Rapids, the jubilation reached its peak as the people crowded her deck, dancing and partying into the night. If McMaster and his crew were any the worse for wear the morning after, they still managed to sail back to Lachine without incident in about five hours.[24]

The *Montreal Herald* hailed the feat as "a subject of no small congrat-
ulation to the province in general and that part of it in particular, as until
then it was much doubted whether a steam-boat could penetrate so far."
The same paper noted the strategic value of the demonstration. The War
of 1812 had shown how easily an American force might stop up the
military supply lines along the narrow bottleneck of the St Lawrence
between the Great Lakes and Montreal. British military experts, pushed
for the development of a navigable route away from the border, using the
Ottawa River up to Hull and then the Rideau River and the chain of lakes
down to Kingston. "Now," said the *Herald,* the introduction of steam
navigation on the Ottawa "secures a comparatively easy communication
with a rapidly improving section of the country, and greatly facilitates
the route to which recourse must be had in the event of a future war."[25]

But that glorious progress up the Ottawa had not proven as easy as the
newspaper made it out to be. Significantly, none of the published schedules for the *Perseverance* in 1821 made any mention of the Ottawa River
and Point Fortune. They simply listed the hours of her departures for the
Cascades and Châteauguay and the fares and freight rates on Lake St
Louis.[26] Still, there are strange gaps in her timetables for that year. The
schedules show her as operating seven days a week, with her sailing times,
destinations, and layovers all clearly stated – except for a mid-week
mystery trip. The summer schedule has her leaving Lachine on Wednesdays at 4 p.m. for an unnamed destination, then sailing from Lachine again
the next day at 1 p.m. for the Cascades, with no mention of an intervening
return trip. Similarly, the fall schedule, in effect from 5 September, has
her leaving Lachine on Wednesday mornings at 8, destination unspecified,
and then Lachine again on Thursdays at noon for the Cascades. How did
she get from Lachine ... to Lachine? In the unlikely event that she ever
did try sailing up the Ottawa again, these gaps in her schedule, particularly that twenty-eight-hour one in the fall, are the only possible times
when she could have done so.

If the Ottawa River remained out of bounds, the *Perseverance* was a
sure bet on Lake St Louis, barring accidents. One mishap in her first
summer nearly ended her career. It was around 9 o'clock on 7 August,
one of those Tuesday nights when her schedule called for her to lie over
at the Cascades. Her fireman stacked logs to dry around the furnace and
left them unattended. The logs caught fire, and in a flash, the area below
deck was aflame. The alarm was raised too late to allow the fire to be
doused with buckets of water. The only hope of saving the boat lay in
scuttling her. Her hull was opened with an axe and the *Perseverance* sank
in about five feet of water.[27]

Upon examination, her stern was found to be intact, but the walls and
flooring in her centre and bow had been scorched to a depth of an inch

or more. Since her timbers were untouched, however, it was thought that she might be refitted quickly enough and at no great cost. Within a week, she was raised and taken down to Lachine. As her owners had hoped, the damage was repaired without difficulty, and she was back in business by the end of August.[28]

At the end of the year, after all the celebrations and that one brush with disaster, her owners must have felt reasonably satisfied with her performance. Captain McMaster had reason to feel doubly contented. His creation had proved an improvement on the *Ottawa:* at least she would not be discarded after one year. And three days after Christmas, his wife gave birth to their first child.[29] By then, plans were already in train for the *Perseverance's* second year: her owners had already put out a call for 600 cords of firewood – tamarack and hemlock – for the 1822 season.[30] In this, as in all subsequent wood contracts, they stipulated that part of the wood was to be delivered at Lachine and part at the Cascades or Châteauguay; no more than in her schedules did the name of Point Fortune or any other Ottawa River location crop up. After that first year, in fact, it seems that they gave up on the Ottawa to concentrate on serving Lake St Louis and fitting into an ever more integrated system of land and water transport on the St Lawrence route between Montreal and Upper Canada.

The rough state of the roads meant that, where practicable, steamers were preferable to stagecoaches, both for comfort and for speed. In the *Perseverance's* first year, it had been suggested that the travelling to and from Upper Canada would be improved if the boat were to run in conjunction with Horace Dickinson's stage line to Upper Canada. That connection was made, beginning in 1822.[31] Incorporating the *Perseverance* into the line made good business sense for her owners and for Dickinson, and smoothed the way for travellers. The logic of integration seems inescapable. One wonders why Dickinson and the owners of the *Ottawa* had not worked out such a mutually beneficial agreement, and indeed, whether the *Ottawa* might not have survived had she formed part of the line to Upper Canada instead of sailing in isolation on Lake St Louis.[32]

The *Canadian Courant* published a sketch of the stage and steamer connections on the Upper Canada Line for the benefit of its readers considering an excursion up the river in the summer of 1822:

The present travelling establishment on the route to Upper Canada, is highly worthy of notice; and the enterprise and laudable spirit of the proprietor [Horace Dickinson] cannot but be considered entitled to the patronage of the public. We are informed that the accommodations on that route are nearly equal to any in the U. States; upwards of sixty horses are employed; and the carriages are of the most substantial kind; besides the journey between Kingston and Montreal has that variety of land and water carriage so pleasing to travellers, affording that

LAKE ONTARIO.

THE
STEAM-BOAT

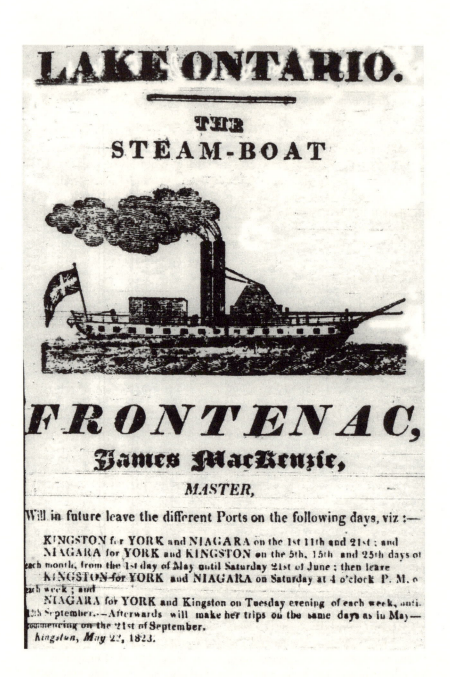

FRONTENAC,
James MacKenzie,
MASTER,

Will in future leave the different Ports on the following days, viz :—

KINGSTON for YORK and NIAGARA on the 1st 11th and 21st ; and NIAGARA for YORK and KINGSTON on the 5th, 15th and 25th days of each month, from the 1st day of May until Saturday 21st of June ; then leave KINGSTON for YORK and NIAGARA on Saturday at 4 o'clock P. M. o each week ; and NIAGARA for YORK and Kingston on Tuesday evening of each week, until 13th September.—Afterwards will make her trips on the same days as in May— commencing on the 21st of September.

Kingston, May 22, 1823.

THE BAY AND RIVER STEAMER "CHARLOTTE," BUILT AT ERNESTTOWN, U. C., 1818.

The *Charlotte*, as depicted in this engraving published in *Eighty Years' Progress*, is the same boat shown in an 1823 advertisement for the *Frontenac* in the *Kingston Chronicle*; in fact, this was a generic illustration used by the *Chronicle* and is a true picture of neither boat.

delightful change of scene so much to be desired in a pleasure jaunt. From Montreal to Lachine passengers take the stage; from the latter place to the Cascades the Steam Boat *Perseverance* runs regularly, and is comfortably arranged for the accommodation of travellers. The voyage is a delightful one, and is performed very expeditiously. The stage is again taken at the Cascades to Coteau du Lac; from which place a passage is made in a commodious *Team Boat* across the Lake St François to Cornwall at the rate of four miles an hour. From Cornwall to Prescott in the Stage. Whence the rest of the journey to Kingston is performed by the Steam Boat *Charlotte*.[33]

Nothing is known of the Lake St Francis team boat, or horse boat, or whether its owners were Canadian or from the New York side of the river. If they were New Yorkers, perhaps the same might have been said of their boat as of team boats on the Hudson River: "They are not employed as being cheaper to navigate with horses than with steam but because the family of Fulton have a monopoly of the Steam Engine as used on the United States waters & all interlopers must pay the patentee a considerable duty."[34] The steamer *Charlotte*, for her part, 130 feet long by 18 feet beam, had been built by Henry Gildersleeve at the same yard as the *Frontenac* at Ernestown (now Bath), Upper Canada, in 1817–18. From the spring of 1818, she ran twice a week between Prescott and the Bay of Quinte.[35]

The *Courant* article went on to state that the "beautiful new Steam-Boat *Dalhousie*," partly owned by Dickinson, was about to join the line, to carry passengers and mail between Prescott and Kingston. This side-wheeler was 76 feet long, with a breadth of 31 feet 4 inches outside the paddle boxes, and had a 4-foot draft of water. She had a "handsome and commodious Cabin, containing sixteen berths, with a swing division to separate the Ladies' from the Gentlemen's apartment."[36]

The *Dalhousie* presents a puzzle. A subscription to build her was launched in 1818, and by all accounts, she was built the following year, yet she did not make her first trip from Prescott to Kingston until the end of August 1822.[37] The explanation for the long delay between the times of her building and her first sailing appears to lie in the imbroglio surrounding the 20-horsepower engine ordered from the Eagle Foundry of Francis, Smith and Company in Birmingham by Guy Warwick and Company in June 1819 for the Montreal–La Prairie ferry *Montreal*.

In the autumn of 1819 the owners of the *Montreal* had changed their minds, as we have seen, and rather than wait for the arrival of the English engine, they had hired John Ward to build one on the spot. Then in December, Guy Warwick and Company had sold the now-redundant English engine, complete with boiler, paddlewheels, and shafts, to St Lawrence River forwarders Levi Sexton and Company for £1,292, promising to have the machinery shipped from Liverpool and delivered at Montreal by the following 1 June. Included in the sale price were the services of an engineer, to be sent to Prescott by Guy Warwick and Company, to fit the engine into "the Steam Boat now [December 1819] Lying on the Stocks at Prescott," that is, the *Dalhousie*.[38]

Because of an accident and other circumstances, the machinery – in more than one thousand pieces – was slightly late in arriving. On 2 June, with the cargo landed at Quebec and awaiting shipment to Montreal, Levi Sexton and Company gave notice that because the due date was passed, it would refuse to take delivery. Guy Warwick and Company was caught in a vise: it needed to collect from Levi Sexton and Company to pay the English manufacturer. Under the circumstances, the Warwicks in turn refused to accept the machinery when it reached Montreal on 7 June, alleging that the shipment was not only late but damaged: many parts had rusted in transit. Left with no other choice, Francis, Smith and Company sued Guy Warwick and Company in October, claiming £1,331 for the costs of making, shipping, and storing the engine. The Court of King's Bench found against the Warwicks on 18 June 1821 and awarded Francis, Smith and Company all that it asked, including interest and court costs. The evidence – from John Molson and John Ward, among others – had shown that the slight delay in the arrival of the engine was not of major importance and that all imported English engines suffered from rusting on the transatlantic passage. To collect the award, Francis, Smith and Company seized the assets of Guy Warwick and Company, which led to further court action in the fall. This last matter appears to have been settled in early 1822.[39] By then, however, Levi Sexton and Company was no more. The company had been dissolved on 16 July 1821.[40]

It is not clear whether, in the end, the contentious 20-horsepower engine from the Eagle Foundry ever made it into the *Dalhousie*. It would seem so: only after the dust from the legal tussles in Montreal had settled was the steamer fitted with her engine, a 20-horsepower. But a contemporary newspaper reported her engine as being Canadian-made, and a modern source identifies it as one produced by John Ward. It is possible that Ward, rather than making a whole new engine, refurbished the English one. After all, he had estimated that it could be put in working order at a cost of at most £25. It is also conceivable that the engine stayed in Montreal: early in 1823 Froste and Porter, as agents of Francis, Smith and Company, offered for sale a steam engine "made to order for a vessel of 18 feet beam by 75 feet keel, by one of the first Houses in Birmingham."[41] These boat dimensions were very close to those of the *Montreal* and the *Dalhousie*.

Dickinson's stake in the *Dalhousie* in 1822 foreshadowed the direction he was soon to take: he would carry integration of land and water transport further by launching his own steamers. But for the moment, the straitlaced Yankee worked hand in hand with the owners of the *Perseverance*, led by Greenfield, the rough-cut Scot.

They were not friends, these two. There was the difference in their ages – Dickinson turned forty-two at the end of 1822, while Greenfield was only twenty-seven or twenty-eight.[42] But chiefly, Dickinson's friends were Americans, while Greenfield ran with the Scots. Dickinson never ordered an engine from John Bennet; Greenfield never bought one from John Ward. Greenfield's friends were men such as carpenter William Spier, builder Robert Drummond, and masons William Lauder and Thomas McKay. Men in their twenties and early thirties,[43] they were not the old-guard Scots, grown rich in the fur trade, who now ruled the roost in Montreal. Greenfield and his friends were newcomers, tradesmen, and above all, strivers; "desirous of improving their respective Estates," as the legal jargon of the time had it, Greenfield, Lauder, Spier, and contractor Peter Rutherford once sought to pool their skills and resources in a kind of early consortium.[44] Almost every step of Greenfield's career betrays his ambition to get ahead.

He seems to have been among the considerable number of Scots who emigrated to Canada in the years immediately after the War of 1812. Some decorative touches in his home – five prints of Jamaican scenes, four conch shells, and other items – might suggest that he had come a roundabout way via the West Indies. Then again, they may have been meaningless knick-knacks, shells and prints being popular ornaments in North American homes of the day.[45] In the early 1820s Greenfield held the exclusive right to all the plumbing work and repairs for the Montreal Water Works, the city's aqueduct system, then a private concern.[46] Working with lead pipes, he branched out and became a lead merchant as well, a natural progression. But investing in steamers was another matter.

Every one of the early steamers was an experiment. Engineers sought to pack more power into ever-lighter, more compact and fuel-efficient engines; shipbuilders and others played with hull shapes and sizes and the size and placement of water wheels to find the design best suited to the waters on which a boat was to run. This trial-and-error factor helps to account for the monopolistic tendencies of the steamboat owners: after spending large sums for a boat that could turn out to be slow, unwieldy, and costly to operate, they worried that a rival might launch a vessel which would outclass theirs and, by drawing away business, prevent them from recouping their investment, let alone making a profit. Of course, the experimental nature of the boats also deterred all but the most determined challengers, for they too had no guarantee that their boat would do the job.[47] For a man in Greenfield's position, taking up where Thomas Turner and his partners had failed took pluck and resourcefulness. He seems to have been well endowed in both departments.

He showed his brash side when he broke into the steamer business on the busy Montreal-Quebec route. He dabbled in this enterprise from 1822 as the owner of one of the sixty-four shares in the *Laprairie*.[48] But it was with his own steamer, the *Lady of the Lake*, that he entered the Quebec trade in earnest in 1826, single-handedly taking on the big fish – the Molsons, who had dominated the steamer business on this part of the river since 1809, operating now under the name St Lawrence Steamboat Company;[49] and the Montreal Steam Tow Boat Company, owners of the mighty *Hercules*, the first purpose-built steam tug in Canada, constructed in 1823 by Alexander Young, equipped with a 100-horsepower engine made by John Ward, and commanded by George Brush, who had also superintended her construction.[50] When Greenfield entered the picture, the towboat company was owned by more than sixty stockholders representing a who's who – Molsons excepted – of Montreal's business community. It soon came under the control of John Torrance and his nephew, David.[51] In 1829 the company acquired a second boat, the *Richelieu*, also built by Young and fitted with a 45-horsepower Ward engine.[52] Whatever competition existed between them, the Molsons and Torrances – the monopolists, as their detractors came to call them – closed ranks whenever an outsider threatened to encroach on their trade. They would drive the interloper out of business by undercutting his prices, lease his boat, pay him to keep it idle, or press him to sell it outright.

Greenfield went after passenger traffic, freight, and government contracts with a fair degree of success.[53] Matters came to a head in 1829 when the Molsons detached one of their boats, the *Waterloo*, to meet the *Lady of the Lake* head on and drive her from the field. The *Waterloo* was ordered to match the *Lady's* fares and freight rates, no matter how low. The regular rate for steerage passengers was ten shillings; by 8 August the two boats were charging six pence.[54] That year, Greenfield also tangled with John Torrance, who was a co-contractor with him for the transport of military stores and men. He accused Torrance of cutting him out of the contract by steering customers away from the *Lady of the Lake* to the Molson boats. Torrance denied the charge, but not before the commissary general's department had suspended all payments to him when Greenfield threatened legal action.[55]

Surprisingly, Greenfield did not meet his Waterloo in this showdown with his competitors. On 27 October he signed a formal truce with the Molson and Torrance companies, the three parties agreeing to a common fare and freight-rate schedule for the remainder of the year and for the 1830 season.[56] They signed another such price-fixing agreement on 16 April 1831 for the navigation season that year.[57] Finally, on 3 May 1832, with a powerful new boat, the 75-horsepower *Canadian Eagle*, due to be launched within weeks – a far cry from the low-budget *Perseverance*, she was 140 feet long, 24½ feet beam, with a depth of hold of 7 feet 10 inches, and valued at £6,500 – Greenfield sold the Molsons and the Torrances each a one-eighth share in his steamboat business for £1,000 apiece.[58] The transaction provided a welcome infusion of funds while leaving him in control of his two boats. If nothing else, the episode shows him to have been a tenacious scrapper when it came to business.

Greenfield could be just as brash in his private life. In 1825, for example, he fathered a child out of wedlock. Ann Greenfield was born on 13 August. Her mother, Mary McCrimmon, was an illiterate farm girl from Glenelg in Inverness-shire. As an unwed mother with few resources, she would have suffered great hardship had Greenfield not resolved – after taking his time about it – to do the honourable thing: on 21 January 1826, five months after Ann was born, he married her mother. That same day they had the girl christened.[59] Respectable society may have frowned on Greenfield's behaviour, but a generation earlier, had not John Molson, founder of the famous brewery, originator of steam navigation in Canada, and pillar of Montreal society, waited eight years after the birth of the last of his three sons before marrying their mother?

How different a character was Dickinson, a founder of the American Presbyterian Church in Montreal and a stalwart member of the Bible society. Where Greenfield kept a cellar stocked to bursting with beer, wine, and cider,[60] Dickinson was a temperance crusader. Where Greenfield did not disdain the rough-and-tumble of politics – he was involved in a punch-up at the polls with supporters of Patriote candidate Louis-Joseph Papineau in the West Ward of Montreal in 1827[61] – Dickinson steered clear of political activity. Outside his work, the affairs of his church, moral improvement, and charities seem to have been his sole public concerns – at least, the only ones in which he took an active part.

Though they lived by different codes, Greenfield and Dickinson could and did do business, beginning with the link formed between Dickinson's stage line and Greenfield's *Perseverance* in 1822. Dickinson also held an interest in the new 20-horsepower steamer *Dalhousie*, which, as we have seen, went into regular service between Prescott and Kingston that year. In 1823 he introduced steamer service on Lake St Francis with the 16-horsepower *Cornwall*, plying four times a week each way between Cornwall and Côteau. At the same time, he increased the frequency of his stage service to Upper Canada to four round trips a week from three.[62] The *Perseverance*, meanwhile, inaugurated steamer service to Beauharnois, calling at the south-shore village on Tuesdays and Fridays on her way up and down Lake St Louis.[63]

Greenfield and his partners advertised that the *Perseverance* "having formed a line with the steamboat *Cornwall*, on Lake St Francis, Goods will be forwarded from Montreal to Cornwall and intermediate places, with safety and dispatch."[64] And Dickinson, who acted as a freight and passenger agent for the *Perseverance*, boasted that the connection of his stage line "with the Steam Boats between Lachine and Cascades, Coteau du Lac and Cornwall, and Prescott and Kingston, (which are fitted up in a good and comfortable style for the accommodation of Passengers,) renders it both for comfort and despatch, superior to any other mode of travelling in this Country."[65]

If any steamboat projector deserved a prize for perseverance in 1823, however, it was not Greenfield or Dickinson but Thomas Mears. At the relatively advanced age of forty-eight, he finally had a steamer plying on the Ottawa River.

He had pinned his hopes on the *Ottawa* in 1819–20 but she had failed. When Guy Warwick and Company tried its hand at building the engine for the Montreal-Terrebonne steamer *Dalhousie* in 1820, Mears had looked on with interest, as had Philemon Wright and his sons at Hull. They had concluded from the boat's performance that "the engine made by the Warwicks will not answer the purpose … it will not do."[66] Yet for the lumbermen and settlers on the Ottawa, as well as for Mears's and Wright's common business interests, "we must have a regular line for next year and so arranged that their will be no Jumble," Mears wrote to Philemon Wright Jr on 8 November, as the *Ottawa* neared the end of her first and last navigation season.[67]

The following spring, with the *Ottawa* about to be put up for sale, Mears thought that her engine might be a worthwhile investment. He prodded the Wrights: "I wish you would make up your minds on that subject before you come down that you may let me know how to manage as it will no doubt be sold before a long time." At the same time, he forwarded a letter from Samuel Twelves Hudson, engineer of the Montreal Water Works, about the state of Joseph Lough's engine and the prospects for transferring it to a new boat.[68] "Friend tho^ms Mears," the Quaker Hudson wrote at the end of April, in prose stripped of all punctuation,

I now take the liburtey of adressing the[e] with a few lines with respect to the Engine As I have had Sum Convershan with Scott Burt this day as not having opertunity Before as he did not return from Surill [Sorel] until the 28 I had sum words with Wm Brackenrage respecting the same and it is their openions that the Engine may be made to work well when put in proper Order wish may be done with one hunderd and fifty to two hundered pounds I believe and if thou should purchas the whole pleas to take care of the frameing & take particular mishur of the kelsons & bed that the Engine Stands upon as there is no drawings to go by I should like to see the Engin Before it is taken Down that a proper drawing may Be made to your advantages as it Respects time and meterials

Along with everyone else on the Ottawa, Mears was eager to find out whether the *Perseverance* would make it up from Lachine to Point Fortune.[69] After all, transport arrangements between Hawkesbury and Hull hinged on the connections available below, between Point Fortune and Montreal. The *Perseverance* proving no more able than the *Ottawa* to ensure regular service to Point Fortune, Mears turned his back on the lower reaches of the river in 1822 and determined to launch a steamer above the Long Sault. That summer he and the Quebec timber-trading firm of Sheppard and Campbell acquired the engine of the *Ottawa*, and on 30 November he wrote to P. Wright and Sons from Hawkesbury:

I have just time to drop you a line Respecting the Entended Steam Boat Messrs Campbell & Sheppard as also my Self are desirous that you should take a share Mr [William] Grant the builder with 4 men has just arrived and shall commence the building the boat Soon, Should you take a Share or not I Shall feell much obliged to you for your oppinion as to Shape what water She Should draw and any thing that may Strike your mind.[70]

The Wrights had still not come on board on 18 January 1823 when Mears and Sheppard and Campbell hired Scott Burt to make the necessary repairs to the engine and install it in their boat.[71] By the end of March, however, P. Wright and Sons had bought in, and Mears prevailed upon

the Wrights to send down one of their employees, James F. Taylor, to help
out, Burt having expressed the need for an assistant. "We are getting on
well with the Boat," Mears reported on 5 April; "am very happy that Mr
Taylor came down I hope that we will be able to Raise the Steam by the
Middle of May."[72]

Taylor himself kept the Wrights informed of progress. "The Steam boat
will be afloat next week if the water continues to rise as it has done but
she will not be ready this some time yet for Sailing," he wrote on
17 April.[73] Nine days later William Grant exulted, "we have the boat A
Float and She Only Draws Nineteen inches Water with her Engine That
is including four & A half inches keel."[74] At last, on the evening of Saturday, 17 May, Taylor indicated that the boat, now christened, was about
ready to be taken for a spin, though no one was yet prepared to crow.

I take the liberty to address a few lines to you by this mail informing you that
should the weather Permit we intend to start for Hull with the Steam Boat on
Thursday next or Sunday following. She will not be entirely finished then but
Mr Grant & Mr Mears think (as the engine had a bad name before) it is best to
try her before they advertise so that Passengers from a distance may not be
disappointed. She is named the *Union* of the Grand or Ottawa River. You may
expect a number of gentlemen up with her as all within reach of here are intending
to go to Hull first trip.[75]

In a postscript, the assiduous Taylor provided a clue as to why Mears may
have been so "very happy" to see him assist Burt, the engineer:

P.S. our Engineer all most Kicked the bucket Last night, he went to bed Pretty
full in the evening, (in fact every evening Since I have been here) was taken with
a cramp in the Stomach, about twelve O'Clock at night, when Mr Grant and
myself were called upon, he was in terrible distress however we got him relieved
some, but it keeps us back his being sick at this time – he is a little better now
5 OClock PM.[76]

The *Union*, about 125 feet long by $30\frac{1}{2}$ feet in breadth and with her engine
developing 28 horsepower, passed muster. By 17 June her owners were
confident enough to advertise her regular sailings – leaving Grenville and
Hawkesbury for the upward journey of eight to twelve hours every
Sunday and Thursday morning and sailing back from Hull and Richmond
Landing every Monday and Friday.[77] Emery Cushing, the young Montreal
tavern-keeper who operated the Montreal-Grenville mail-stage line with
fellow tavern-keeper John Russell of St Andrew's,[78] immediately saw the
need to synchronize stage and boat services. On 20 June he wrote to
Philemon Wright:

I Commenced Running My Stage twice a weak and I shud like to have the Boat
Run to meat it if the Boat wood leave Granville Wednesday and Sunday and leave
Hull tuesday & Satterday in the morning it wood Meat the Stage at Granville
waiting for it as I under stand that it Arrives thare About two A Clock in the
After Noon At present it Arrives A Day before the Stage and lands on Mr Mears
Side [at Hawkesbury] and I loose All the Passingers Down Mr Mears has gone to
Quebec I told him of this and he Says that he is willing for his boat to Run to
Meat the Stage and I wish get your Sentiments About it.[79]

In the end, the *Union* did run to Grenville, but Cushing had to adjust his
stage schedule slightly to suit the steamer's sailings that summer. Instead
of leaving Montreal on Monday and Friday as they had been doing, the
stages left on Tuesday and Friday so as to reach Grenville the evening
before the boat's 6 a.m. departures on Thursday and Sunday.[80]

"By this accommodation," the owners of the *Union* boasted of their
boat, "the Village of Richmond, and the Townships of Nepean, Goulbourn,
March, Tarbolton, Fitzroy, Beckwith, Huntley, Ramsey, Lanark, Dalhousie, Sherbrook, and the Lands lying Northerly of the Town of Perth, is
nearer the City of Montreal by from 20 to 70 miles of land road, than
by the River St Lawrence."[81] One who could appreciate the improvement
was Thomas A. Turner's brother-in-law, Alexander James Christie. After
working in Montreal for two and a half years as editor of the *Herald*,
Christie had settled with his family on a farm in March Township in 1821.
But in March 1824 he had returned to newspaper work in Montreal, as
editor of Turner's *Gazette*, leaving his family and farm in the charge of
his son.[82] He was in a position to compare travel on the Ottawa before
and after the appearance of the *Union*. A report on the "Improvements
on the Ottawa River" in the *Gazette* of 6 October 1824 was probably
from his hand. It read in part:

We observed a very striking change for the better ... during a late excursion up
the Ottawa river ... But a very few years past – [a] journey thither was an
undertaking ... full of difficulty and subjected the traveller to unavoidable delays,
and inconvenience at almost every point. These seem now changed by the exertions of a few spirited individuals, the means of conveyance, and the
accommodations are such as to render it a tour of pleasure. An excellent stage
from Montreal takes the traveller to St Andrews, a distance of 45 miles – (and
even this part of the rout, we understand is to be soon improved, by a steam boat
which is intended to ply from Lachine to Point Fortune,) ... From this another
excellent stage carries him to Granville, on the north side of the river, or to
Hawksbury on the south, which ever rout he pleases – and where he can have an
opportunity of diversifying his view of some of the richest scenery. Here he joins
a steam boat, built last year by a few public spirited men, with far more regard

to the adoption of a plan beneficial to the public, than to the expectation of present profit to themselves ... With a very complete engine constructed on the safest principles – she is laid out and finished with every regard to accommodations for passengers. Under Captain Grant's management, all who have had opportunity of witnessing it, have expressed themselves satisfied – She performs the distance she has to run from Hawksbury to the Chaudier Falls at Wrightstown [Hull] 70 miles with ease in one day: affording the traveller by this route a happy exchange, from being obliged to perform this journey as formerly in a small canoe, or open boat, liable [to] detention from contrary winds – exposed to the changes of weather – *eaten* by muesquitoes at certain seasons – and having nothing to *eat* but salt pork, perhaps uncooked.

Christie returned to March Township in 1825 and later moved to Bytown, where he launched the *Bytown Gazette*. As for Mears's boat, she continued running for as long as he did. Under Captain William Grant until 1827, then under Mears's former clerk, Eden Johnson, and finally under N. Morehouse, the *Union* ran on the Ottawa until 1830. When the Rideau Canal was almost completed at the end of 1831, she ran there, between Bytown and Merrickville. In 1832, with the canal officially opened, she spent her last full season sailing between Bytown and Kingston under Morehouse.[83] Mears died at Hawkesbury on 16 September that year, at the age of fifty-seven.[84]

On Lake St Louis, meanwhile, the arrangement between the owners of the *Perseverance* and Dickinson continued through 1824. In that time the steamer met with no further damaging accidents like the fire of 1821, though at least two people died as a result of being crushed by her machinery in what were typical mishaps of the time. On 18 November 1822 one man was killed when, standing next to the engine, he "carelessly threw back one of his arms so that it came in contact with the fly wheel, which instantly drew his whole body between the wheel and casement, and crushed him in such a shocking manner that he survived the accident but six hours."[85] The second fatality, on 20 November 1823, points up a dangerous feature in the early steamers in which the walking beam projected through an opening in the deck. A passenger "fell from the deck among the machinery, by which his right leg was torn from his body, and cast a considerable distance; the other parts of his frame were Mangled in a dreadful manner; he died almost immediately. A Coroners Jury brought in a verdict of 'accidental death.'"[86]

Carpenter James Malcolm was hired to make alterations to the *Perseverance* in 1824. The nature of these changes is not known. A newspaper report of 16 April 1825 said simply that she had undergone a "thorough repair."[87] Malcolm's work may have made the boat safer for passengers and crew. Perhaps his alterations also helped to reduce her fuel requirements:

instead of contracting for 600 cords of wood a year, as had been the practice in her first three years, her owners called for only 400 cords from 1824 on.[88] James Ross and Thomas Kerr undertook to supply the wood for that year.[89] Of greater interest are the two men who acted as securities for them – Robert Drummond, a thirty-two-year-old master builder, and stonemason Thomas McKay, age thirty-one. Both had immigrated from Scotland in 1817; given their friendly relations with Greenfield, it is possible that he may have known them in Scotland and come out with them or around the same time. Drummond, who had emigrated as a bachelor, had not only stood witness at Greenfield's wedding but had also advised Greenfield's bride in the drafting of her marriage contract.[90] As for McKay and his wife, Anne Crichton, Greenfield had been a sponsor at the christening of their daughter, Ann, in January 1824. Two years earlier, after McKay had set to work as a contractor on the Lachine Canal, Greenfield and William McMaster had ferried stone for him from a Caughnawaga quarry.[91] Drummond and McKay were to make their names and fortunes as contractors on the Rideau Canal. But first, Drummond was to play a key role in the fate of the *Perseverance*.

All the arrangements on Lake St Louis were shuffled in the spring of 1825 when two new steamers appeared on the scene – the *St Lawrence*, built by McMaster at Lachine for Dickinson's line and equipped with a 32-horsepower Ward engine,[92] and the *St Andrews*, with a 20-horsepower Bennet and Briggs engine, built at Lachine for the St Andrews Steam Boat Company and intended for the Ottawa River trade. The days of a lone puffing boat on the lake were done; from now on, there would never be less than two, and frequently there were more. The stockholders of the *St Andrews* included Bennet and Briggs, Robert Drummond, Thomas Mears, Guy Warwick and Company, and Emery Cushing.[93] Also associated with the boat in 1825 was John Macpherson of Montreal, a Scottish immigrant who had embarked on the forwarding trade in 1822 and who, once he had teamed up with American-born Samuel Crane, would parlay his business into one of the largest inland transportation concerns in Canada. Macpherson acted as freight agent for the *St Andrews* in her first year, the Lachine storehouse of John Macpherson and Company serving as depot for the steamer.[94]

The *Perseverance* began the new season on 19 April, sailing from Lachine to the Cascades as she had done for the last four years. But the *St Lawrence*, launched on 4 May, supplanted her on Dickinson's line. With her more powerful engine, the new boat, commanded by William McMaster, could easily outdo the *Perseverance* in towing the forwarders' boats. One day in June she towed six at a time against a strong head wind.[95] The days of the *Perseverance* were numbered. But now, in an ironic twist, the troublesome rapids at the mouth of the Ottawa came to her rescue.

The *St Andrews*, 80 feet long on deck and 26 feet beam, took her first run at the St Anne Rapids in mid-June. She left Lachine on Sunday, 12 June, under the command of forty-eight-year-old Captain David Nelson, formerly a saddler and harness-maker in Montreal. He was assisted by pilot Charles L. Lighthall, a seasoned captain of Durham boats on the Ottawa, where he had worked for John Macdonell, and by engineer William Black, age twenty-three. Her crew busied themselves taking observations and soundings and placing buoys, as the men of the *Perseverance* had done four years earlier. This operation lasted until Tuesday morning. Then up she went, scaling the rapids in about twenty-five minutes, using a cable and anchor as the *Perseverance* had done. She made Point Fortune in the early afternoon. The next day she ran down from St Andrew's to Lachine in four and a half hours.[96] "One important point which was hitherto doubtful, has been ascertained, namely that there is a sufficient depth of water at the St Ann's rapids to allow Steam Boats to pass," the *Montreal Gazette* observed. "It has also been found that by means of an anchor and cable a boat can be warped up these rapids with little more than half an hour's detention." The *Perseverance* had done the same in 1821, but the writer either ignored the fact or had forgotten it.[97]

If the first trip made by the *St Andrews* proved once more that a steamer could conquer the St Anne Rapids, it also confirmed the difficulty of the feat. While her owners had planned for her to make three round trips a week, they settled for two, promising to launch daily service (except Sunday) as soon as circumstances would allow.[98] Before that happened, the *St Andrews* recorded her first casualty: William Black, her young engineer, fell overboard and drowned at Point Fortune on 22 June.[99] Within a few weeks, the owners of the new *St Andrews* and the old *Perseverance* agreed to work their boats in tandem to serve the Ottawa: the *St Andrews* would run on Lake St Louis between Lachine and the Vaudreuil Rapids, while the *Perseverance* would sail on the Ottawa above the rapids. This way, neither boat would have to struggle up the short but troublesome stretch of swift water. Transferring passengers and freight by land from one boat to the other was a relatively simple matter since they stopped within two hundred feet of each other.[100]

Regular daily service on the lower Ottawa was at last a reality. The *Perseverance* stopped anywhere and everywhere along her route. A customer on shore had only to wave a white cloth and she would pull in. As with Dickinson's operation on the St Lawrence, links were established between land and water transport. Carriages and wagons carried passengers and freight between Montreal and the steamer at Lachine. At Point Fortune, Tait and Davis, a partnership of Rigaud merchant James Tait, a former clerk for the North West Company, and Theodore Davis of Chatham, a New Hampshire-born surveyor, land agent, trader, and co-owner of the

St Andrews, operated carriages and carts to Hawkesbury, linking the boat on the lower waters with Mears's *Union* for travel up to Hull.[101]

Occasionally, on a Sunday the *St Andrews* risked the rapids to take excursionists up to the Lake of Two Mountains.[102] She needed the practice, as it turned out, for in 1826 she would be on her own again on the Lachine–Point Fortune run. The *Perseverance* would be engaged in other business – for Robert Drummond.

Two days after his marriage in January 1826, Greenfield, intending to travel to Europe, entrusted his affairs to Drummond and John Porteous, Montreal agent for the St Maurice Iron Works. He gave them instructions

to take possession of a certain Steam Boat or Vessel now about fitting up as a Steam Boat and which one Horace Dickinson is bound & obligated to deliver at Montreal by Contract; to cause the same to be completed and for that purpose, if necessary, to sell and dispose of any part, portion or share of the said boat and her machinery & apparatus, but not to exceed a sum of fifteen hundred pounds, the remainder, he [Greenfield] ... being desirous of retaining.[103]

The boat in question was the *Lady of the Lake.*[104] Perhaps in naming her after the well-known verse romance of Sir Walter Scott, the Scottish plumber meant to pay a tribute to his Scottish bride. Certainly, like the *Ottawa* before her, her name also alluded to the body of water on which she was built and meant to sail, in this case, Lake St Francis.

Built by Luke Sheay at Rivière Beaudette on the Upper Canada border, the *Lady* was intended to run in opposition to Dickinson's *Cornwall.*[105] Greenfield, challenged by Dickinson on Lake St Louis in 1825, seems to have hoped to fight back by setting up his own line to Upper Canada along the St Lawrence. To succeed, however, he needed more than boats – besides establishing his own steamboat landings on Lake St Francis, with the necessary facilities and staff, he would have to launch a rival stage service to carry his passengers from one landing to another. Here Dickinson unquestionably held the upper hand.

Of the discussions that passed between them, we know nothing but the results. Somehow, Dickinson managed to persuade Greenfield to forget about competing with him on Lake St Francis and to take his boat down to Montreal to embark on a contest with the steamers running to Quebec. Greenfield, a sporting man – in 1829 he would contribute a $50 prize to the Montreal races, to be called the Lady of the Lake Purse[106] – was prepared to gamble. But it was Dickinson who was to take the first big risk. As the price for a continued steamboat monopoly on Lake St Francis, besides paying Greenfield £100 in cash, he agreed to take charge of running the still engineless *Lady,* drawing $2\frac{1}{2}$ feet of water, down the rapids through Lake St Louis and on through the Lachine Rapids to

Montreal, at the opening of navigation in 1826. Canoes, rafts, batteaux, and Durham boats regularly ran the rapids – but a steamer? It had never been done; it had never even been tried. The penalty for failure was steep: Dickinson was to pay Greenfield £1,000 if the boat was damaged or destroyed.[107]

Drummond must have trusted in Dickinson's success, for by 11 March he was offering for sale "a few shares" in the new boat, as Greenfield had authorized him to do.[108] His confidence was not misplaced. On 10 May, Dickinson had the *Lady of the Lake* brought down the rapids "by means of oars, and taking advantage of the unusual height of the river," delivering her safe and sound at Montreal, where she was to be fitted with her engines and machinery.[109]

Besides acting for Greenfield in this matter, Drummond leased the *Perseverance* from him and his associates for the season. He did not operate her as a public conveyance; rather, it seems that he used her to transport workmen and materials, for he was engaged through the summer in building a lock at Vaudreuil to bypass the rapids.[110]

On the Ottawa stage and steamboat line, the *St Andrews*, under Captain Nelson, went back to sailing twice a week from Lachine to Point Fortune, starting on 15 May. Even that was not accomplished without difficulty, it seems, for early in the season, forwarder John Macdonell was touting his Durham boats as "a remedy for the disappointments caused by the non-performance of the Steam Boat St Andrews Packet."[111] Performance was not the only problem faced by the *St Andrews*. On 6 August her engineer, Lawrence Bennet, drowned when he fell off a plank as he was disembarking. He was the second engineer she had lost by drowning in little more than a year.[112] By the time that winter arrived and the *St Andrews* was laid up, however, she had weathered these blows and triumphed: Drummond had built his lock at Vaudreuil.

Contemporary accounts of this feat are confusing; later versions muddy the waters even more by stating that the lock was built in 1815–16 or in the early 1830s.[113] The *Canadian Courant* reported the milestone this way: "By the united exertions of the proprietors of this Boat, a Canal has been cut 500 feet long, 30 feet breadth at the gates, and 5 feet deep, by means of which the dangerous rapids of Vaudreuil and St Andrews are avoided, and the Boat will be enabled to proceed between Point Fortune and Lachine, in perfect safety, and with as much ease as if on the smooth surface of a lake."[114] On the face of it, the reference to St Andrew's, a village located miles upriver from the Vaudreuil Rapids, is nonsense. It must be a misprint for St Anne. John MacTaggart, clerk of works on the Rideau Canal during the first three years of its construction, gave another account, which is annoyingly vague as to the location of Drummond's lock. He remarked that between the Lachine Canal, opened along its full

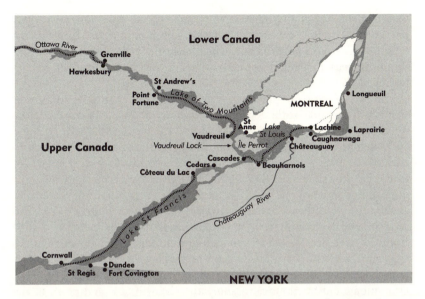

Above: broken lines show the steamboat routes west of Montreal in the mid-1820s before the Vaudreuil lock opened. *Below:* a detail from an 1836 map shows the location of the lock (Justin Stahlman; NA/National Map Collection 19358 1/3).

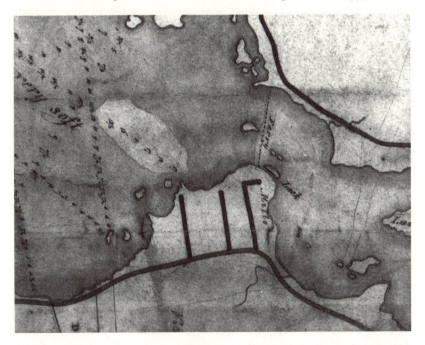

length at the end of 1825, and the Grenville Canal, then under construction on the Ottawa, "a steam-boat lock has been built by Mr Drummond, of dry stone, on a new principle, which answers well; and as it gives him the command of this part of the navigation with his steam-boat, it is to be hoped he will be fully rewarded for his enterprise."[115]

The agreement (see appendix A) that Drummond and Theodore Davis signed with the de Lotbinière family, owners of the seigneury of Vaudreuil, on 24 November 1825 adds some valuable details.[116] Drummond and Davis were authorized to build a canal and lock, "suitable and sufficient to facilitate the navigation of the Ottawa River," across the point of land near the seigneurial flour mill. The lock was to be 30 feet wide and deep enough to allow the passage "at all times, even when the waters are at their lowest, of boats or vessels drawing four feet of water or cribs and rafts of eighty feet in length" – dimensions well tailored to the St Andrews with her 80-foot length and 26-foot breadth. The owners of the seigneury were to be allowed free passage for any wood or craft – steamboats excepted – needed for their mill or manor house. Otherwise, Drummond and Davis were to enjoy the exclusive use and profit of the canal for eleven years from the time of its completion. At the end of eleven years, it was to revert to the owners of the seigneury. It is clear from subsequent events that the privilege acquired by Drummond and Davis was considered to belong to the owners of the St Andrews as a whole and that it was extended beyond eleven years.[117]

As MacTaggart noted, the lock was designed to give the owners of the St Andrews a stranglehold on the steam navigation of the lower Ottawa. This monopoly was to provoke much controversy, particularly after 1830, when the Ottawa Steamboat Company, controlled by Montreal capitalists, took over all the stages and steamboats on the Ottawa.[118] But the first casualty of Drummond's handiwork at Vaudreuil was the Perseverance.

He was supposed to return the boat to the owners at Lachine at the end of the season. On her way down, however, she ran upon the rocks in the Vaudreuil Rapids – "whether by design of the crew, carelessness or misfortune," Greenfield and Fellow were not sure, but they had their suspicions.[119] There she remained, locked in ice through the winter. In February 1827 Drummond promised to salvage her and deliver her at Lachine on the opening of navigation, "free from any damage or harm whatever and in as good, safe and perfect order & Condition" as when he had taken possession of her.[120] By mid-June he still had not done so, and Greenfield and Fellow notified him that they held him responsible for all damages and lost revenue.[121]

Still nothing was done, and the Perseverance sat in the rapids through 1827 and one more winter. Drummond, meanwhile, had moved on to become one of the main contractors on the building of the Rideau Canal.

On 4 June 1828, through his brother-in-law, William Spier,[122] he agreed with Greenfield and Fellow to submit their dispute over the *Perseverance* to arbitration. She was past salvaging now, they said, "part of her engine having been subsequently taken and [the boat] is now lying in different directions along the Shores and exhibits a total wreck." Drummond undertook to pay the owners whatever the steamer was worth at the time he rented her.[123] On 30 July 1828 the arbitrators ruled that, in addition to whatever sum he owed for the rental of the boat, he was to pay her owners £600 in damages, plus interest of 6 per cent from 1 May 1827.[124] Drummond was taken aback. He thought £600 "a sum far higher than I ever expected for such an old boat, but as it is now fixed, so I suppose I must abide by it," he wrote from Kingston. But the arbitrators had overstepped their powers in making reference to rent, he argued; there had been no mention of rent in the arbitration agreement.[125] The matter was not laid to rest until 8 March 1831, when Drummond, Greenfield, and Fellow met in Montreal to ratify the arbitration award and declare their accounts closed.[126]

Other accounts remained open, however. As late as June 1836, the *Perseverance's* owners were still trying to recover a debt of £83 7s. from Philip VanKoughnet of Cornwall.[127] But time and the cholera epidemic of 1832 had taken a heavy toll among them. William Brackenridge, the oldest of the group, had died in 1830 at the age of sixty-five.[128] McMaster, Fellow, and Greenfield had succumbed to the cholera, and their executors or the guardians of their children were left to press their claims.[129] John Bennet had survived the epidemic, but his latest business partnership, with engineer John Henderson, had failed in 1835. Bennet had teamed up with Henderson right after the dissolution of his partnership with Briggs on 29 July 1826. Bennet and Henderson had set up first in George Platt's old nail factory on Wellington Street in the St Ann suburb and then in the St Mary Foundry, which they bought from Thomas Turner. There, in 1831, they had built the engines for the Quebec and Halifax Steam Boat Company's *Royal William*, which two years later had become the first Canadian steamship to cross the Atlantic.[130]

At the time of his death in June 1832, Greenfield had been all in a lather because Bennet had failed him. Sheay and Merritt had delivered the hull of his *Canadian Eagle* in early May as agreed. Counting on a banner year, with this boat and the *Lady of the Lake* scuttling between Montreal and Quebec, a confident Greenfield had taken on the Molsons and the Torrances as "dormant stockholders" on 3 May, selling each group a one-eighth share in his two boats. But Bennet and Henderson, who had pledged to have the boat's 75-horsepower engine installed by 25 June, had been "tardy and dilatory," he complained two weeks before his death. So long as the *Canadian Eagle* remained engineless, the joiners, carpenters,

MR. JOHN BENNET.
Who made the engines for the ' Royal William.'

Engineer John Bennet and the St Mary Foundry, which
he operated with partner John Henderson from 1829 to
1835 (from the *Daily Witness*, 20 March 1897).

and painters could not begin their finishing work. There was no way that
the boat could be ready by 25 June. Bennet and Henderson had left him
high and dry "during the most profitable part of the navigation season,"
he moaned.[131]

It was the height of the cholera season, too; Greenfield died on 28 June.
His widow and William Spier, acting as tutors to his four children,
protested to Bennet and Henderson in August – the engine still was not
ready. Only in October did the *Canadian Eagle* finally leave the foot of
the St Mary's Current, where her engine had been fitted, to receive her
finishing touches in the port of Montreal.[132]

Two years later, in November 1834, Spier sold the crippled *Lady of the
Lake* to a group headed by William Patton of Quebec for £1,000. Her
boiler had exploded on 7 September as she was about to leave Quebec,
killing six people on the spot.[133] The following January, Spier sold the
three-quarters interest still held by Greenfield's estate in the *Canadian
Eagle* to the Molson and Torrance companies for £3,050.[134] Most of the
proceeds from these sales went to pay off Greenfield's debts. In the case

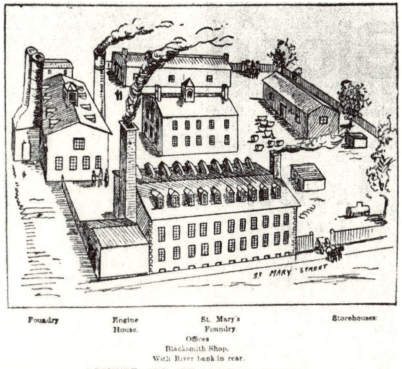

Foundry   Engine   St. Mary's   Storehouses
                 House.   Foundry.
                                 Offices
                            Blacksmith Shop.
                         With River bank in rear.

BENNET AND HENDERSON'S FOUNDRY.

of the *Canadian Eagle,* it was September 1840 before Spier received the final payment for the boat.[135]

Meanwhile, Mary McCrimmon and her children lived in straitened circumstances. She remarried in March 1835, but this union does not seem to have improved her fortunes. In December that year she complained to Spier that she still had not received the £100 to which she was entitled under the terms of her marriage contract with Greenfield. And in the previous twelve months, Spier had given her a grand total of £5 for the support of her children, who, as a result, "are now suffering and enduring great hardships and privations." Pressed, Spier replied, "There are no surplus funds in my hands to pay these demands."[136]

CHAPTER THREE

Horace Dickinson and the "Yankee Swarm"

The cholera of 1832, carried from the British Isles to the St Lawrence aboard jam-packed immigrant ships, raced up the St Lawrence slaying thousands in its path from 8 June, when the first case appeared at Quebec, until the epidemic petered out in the fall.[1] It was a quick killer. Benjamin Thatcher, for example, an innkeeper and stage owner, left Montreal for the United States on Saturday, 16 June, thinking to outrun the scourge. He made it to St John's, all of twenty miles away, where he died the next day.[2]

Horace Dickinson had not counted on the cholera, but he had been banking on the immigration boom. The number of immigrants arriving at Quebec had swelled from 15,945 in 1829 to 28,000 in 1830 and 50,254 in 1831, most of them bound for Upper Canada. Anticipating another great influx in 1832 – 51,746 were to land at Quebec, an estimated 35,000 of them going on to settle in the upper province[3] – and preparing as well to meet the challenge posed by the opening of the Rideau Canal in May, Dickinson had thoroughly overhauled his steamer fleet. He had commissioned new boats and discarded or improved his old ones. To lure immigrants to his Upper Canada Line, he offered them reduced fares.[4] Wednesday, 20 June, found him at his office as usual. Cholera or no, it was, as James Greenfield said, "the most profitable part of the navigation season." Some time that day, Dickinson opened a new ledger – then went home to die within hours, a victim of *Vibrio cholerae*.[5]

At his death, this pillar of Montreal's American Presbyterian Church was said to have "endeared himself by a long residence in this city, to a numerous circle of relatives and acquaintances by whom his memory will long be cherished, as a good neighbour, an honest man, and a pious Christian."[6] That might sound like an off-the-shelf tribute, yet it rings true in his case. He was a straight arrow and pious – too straight and pious, perhaps, the kind of man it is hard to picture cracking a smile. Still, anyone stealing a glance through the window of his drawing-room and catching sight of the two mahogany card tables and the pair of "fancy" card racks might have thought that here was a man who had some fun in him.[7] As for his "long residence" in Montreal, he had spent a mere fourteen of his fifty-one years there: only a newcomer or a young person could call that "long."

Horace Dickinson was born on 17 November 1870 in Hatfield, Massachusetts, on the west bank of the Connecticut River, next to Northampton, the county town of Hampshire County. His Puritan ancestors had been among the founders of Hatfield, and of Hadley across the river, in the mid-seventeenth century.[8] Horace was the fourth of ten children born to Mollie Little and Lemuel Dickinson, a Hatfield landowner and farmer then serving as a militia officer in the Revolutionary War. Barnabas, their fifth child and Horace's future partner in the transport business, was born on 5 May 1783, as the war drew to a close. Land deeds of the early 1800s identified Lemuel Dickinson as General Dickinson, and so he was known for the rest of his life.[9]

For a town founded by rigid Puritans, Hatfield clung to a custom that was far from puritanical. Drunkenness was not countenanced, but every occasion – it might be a birth or simply getting up in the morning, a funeral or just the preacher dropping by – was an occasion to drink. The locals showed a fondness for "flip," a mulled cocktail of cider or beer with a shot of "kill-devil" – their name for the demon rum – eggs, and sugar, seasoned with a dash of nutmeg. Throw in some cream for a special treat, and "flip" became "flannel." For the young boys, there was Egg Pop Day, the first Monday in April, when they were packed off to play for the day with a ration of six eggs, one cup of sugar, and a half pint of rum, to be mixed into a sort of eggnog. The temperance views of the adult Horace Dickinson may have sprung from this boyhood brew.[10]

On 27 December 1804 the sober Horace, eldest of the four Dickinson boys, married Mary Ann Taylor of Westfield, Massachusetts, the daughter of tavern-keeper Colonel James Taylor and his wife, Mary Ann Moseley.[11] Then in 1806 the Dickinsons joined the wave of New Englanders streaming to the frontier lands of northern and western New York.[12] By that time, three of the six girls in the family had died and the others had married Hatfield men. Lemuel, his wife, and their sons – George, age eleven, Lemuel, thirteen, Barnabas, twenty-two, and the married Horace, twenty-five – left their ancestral home for Lowville, New York.[13] This town in newly established Lewis County had been settled in 1798 by families from Mary Ann Dickinson's hometown of Westfield.[14]

Most of the family were to put down roots in the Black River country, if not in Lowville, then in neighbouring Denmark and nearby Champion. Lemuel Dickinson Sr, for instance, was a trustee of the First Ecclesiastical Society in Denmark and a founding trustee of the Lowville Academy. A

traveller passing through in 1816 noted that "General Dickenson" kept a
tavern in Denmark.[15] His wife, Molly, was to die in Champion, Jefferson
County, in 1830, and he in Denmark in 1835. Barnabas, for his part, seems
to have moved from Lowville to Denmark in 1810, and on 24 January
1811 he married a Connecticut-born Denmark girl, seventeen-year-old
Lydia Davenport.[16]

Horace Dickinson and his wife, however, did not remain long in the
area. Their first child, James Taylor, was born in Lowville on 27 October
1806, but the following year they moved to Russell in St Lawrence
County, in the northwestern foothills of the Adirondacks. Russell was a
new town erected that year. The first settlers had arrived in 1806. The
Dickinsons lived almost nine years in the village of Russell, southeast of
Ogdensburg, where their two other children were born – Mary Ann
Moseley, named after her maternal grandmother, on 7 November 1808,
and Dimmis White, named after one of Horace Dickinson's late sisters,
on 28 January 1811.[17]

Shortly before the War of 1812, work began on the Russell Turnpike,
projected to run between Malone and Carthage and cross the Grass River
in their village. Though it was not completed along its full length, the
road, located safely inland from the exposed St Lawrence River shore, was
an important east-west thoroughfare in northern New York State during
the war. That was one factor which led state authorities to choose Russell
as the site for the county arsenal. During the two and a half years of
hostilities, Horace Dickinson served as corporal of the guard at the arsenal.
In February 1813 the enemy sacked Ogdensburg, across the St Lawrence
from the new Canadian village of Prescott and the British Fort Wellington,
but backwoods Russell escaped untouched.[18]

The war left hard feelings on both sides. But the northern states had
generally opposed it, and for practical Americans living in northern New
York and Vermont, hard feelings towards Canada were a luxury. In those
days, when the waterways served as highways and before canals were
built to redirect trade from the border areas to the Hudson River and
New York City, the St Lawrence was their lifeline as much as it was
Canada's. The trade of settlers in those border regions, like Upper Canada's, flowed through Montreal. "Peace having been made between the
United States and England, a great trade had commenced with Canada,"
wrote Jedediah Dorwin, a Vermonter who made his first trip to Montreal
in 1815. Indeed, "the Vermontese pour in plenty on us," the *Montreal
Herald* observed.[19] For entrepreneurs such as Dorwin, not over-concerned
about whether they lived under president or king, post-war Canada
presented all kinds of opportunities. After a few trading expeditions back
and forth across the border, he settled in Canada in 1816. For a Joseph
Lough, American by choice, or a John Ward, American by birth and

conviction, it seemed a good place to open a foundry. Horace and Barnabas Dickinson started a stage line.

From 1 January 1816 they advertised in Kingston and Montreal newspapers a line of winter stages running twice a week between the two cities. Readers were also informed that "another line will leave Ogdensburgh for Utica, every Wednesday and Friday for the convenience of travellers into that part of the country." Somewhat at odds with this, their advertisements in an Ogdensburg newspaper announced the start of weekly stage service to Denmark, but no run as far south as Utica. All these advertisements were signed Barnabas Dickinson or Barnabas Dickinson and Company. This year, while Barnabas himself remained a resident of Denmark – though he spent a couple of months in Montreal that summer – Horace would move to Prescott, to manage the Canadian line.[20]

Founded in 1810, Prescott, in Grenville County, was a hamlet of a dozen houses and fewer than a hundred inhabitants. On the outbreak of the War of 1812, the British built Fort Wellington just east of the village. Like Lachine, Prescott's importance lay not in its size but in its location. Situated at the head of navigation for the Durham boats and batteaux that came up the St Lawrence from Montreal, and at the foot of navigation for the sloops on Lake Ontario, it became an important hub of the forwarding trade, jealously watched by Brockville, a dozen miles to the west. Precisely at the time that the Dickinsons launched their stage line, a post office was established at Fort Wellington, serving Prescott as well as the garrison. Alpheus Jones, then in his early twenties, a member of a prominent Loyalist and Tory family, was named postmaster. Years later he would marry a daughter of Barnabas Dickinson.[21]

The wounds of war were raw and anti-American feeling still ran high in some quarters, particularly among the residents of Upper Canada whose property had been attacked and destroyed in the war. The British authorities sought to discourage American immigration and settlement in the Canadas.[22] Yet, far from blocking the Dickinsons' bid to establish a land transportation and communications link on the strategic route between Montreal and Upper Canada, they helped to finance this American venture by granting the brothers the contract to carry the mails.

Two years before the war the mail service had progressed to the point where a courier travelled between Montreal and Kingston once every two weeks, sometimes on foot. In March 1814 Montrealers William Innis, a former mail courier between Montreal and Vermont, and Thomas Rennie were hired to carry the mails once a week for one year. Together they were paid a total of £250.[23] Then in 1815 Deputy Postmaster General George Heriot, stationed at Quebec but answering to the postmaster general in London, was pressed by officials in Canada to increase the frequency of mail service between Montreal and Kingston to twice a week.

He called for tenders, only to find that no one would provide the service for less than £3,276 a year, or twice the revenue he expected it to generate.[24] The best he could manage was a reorganization of the weekly courier service. As of 9 October 1815, the contract was split and the cost tripled: Innis was hired for one year at £450 to carry the mail once a week between Kingston and Cornwall, while Alexis Pratte of Montreal was paid £300 to handle the shorter Cornwall-Montreal leg. There was to be no more walking – they were required to carry the mail "on horse back or in a light vehicle" and to keep three horses stationed at convenient distances along their respective routes.[25] Perhaps the idea of capitalizing on extra space in their cariole or cutter that winter – and the knowledge that the Dickinsons were after their jobs – led Innis and Pratte to launch a rudimentary passenger service. For surely they, together, must have been the anonymous "Kingston courier" behind the advertisement in the *Canadian Courant* of 2 December:

THE KINGSTON COURIER, Gives notice that he will take two passengers every week, from this place to Cornwall or Kingston, on reasonable terms. He will leave town every Monday evening at six o'clock, and arrive at Cornwall on Wednesdays at six o'clock in the morning and at Kingston by four o'clock afternoon on Thursdays. Persons wishing a passage must be at Mr Gosselin's, New Market place, or leave directions where to be called for.

That is where things stood when the Dickinsons launched their stage line, tailored to Heriot's requirements. They offered twice-a-week service, and as they could count on revenues from the carriage of passengers and parcels, they could afford to carry the mails for a lower price than someone hired exclusively as a courier. On 25 March 1816 Heriot awarded the brothers – both still officially residents of the United States – a two-year contract at £900 a year. The stages were to leave Montreal and Kingston every Monday and Thursday and to reach their destination no later than the Wednesday and Saturday. The brothers were to station "a sufficient number of horses and carriages" along the route. They had to post a bond of £1,000. Horace Dickinson travelled to Montreal to sign the contract for himself and his brother. Former fur trader Daniel Sutherland, the postmaster at Montreal, signed for the Post Office. The service began in the last week of March, though the official starting date was 5 April.[26] The Dickinsons offered Heriot a bargain, and in return, whatever the seasonal fluctuations in passenger and freight traffic, they received what amounted to a subsidy of £900 a year from the Post Office.

Virtually nothing is known of the occupations of Horace and Barnabas Dickinson before this. One might surmise that both must have worked in the cartage or coaching business in Massachusetts. A stage line from

Boston to Albany, New York, via Northampton had been established in 1793, the year that Horace Dickinson turned thirteen and around the time he might be supposed to have started his working life. The following year another line had been opened from Springfield, Massachusetts, near the Connecticut border, up the Connecticut River through Northampton and Hatfield to Dartmouth College in New Hampshire. Westfield, too, where Horace Dickinson found his wife, lay just to the west of Springfield on a stage route from Boston to Albany.[27] The first explicit indication that either of the brothers engaged in such work, however, comes in a sketchy nineteenth-century account of the beginnings of mail service along the Black River of New York:

The first route through the valley was established January 19, 1804. Daniel Gould is said to have been the first carrier. He was succeeded by Reuben Chase soon after, who began in 1804, and performed one trip each week from Utica to Brownville. Mr Barnabas Dickenson of Denmark, was the next mail carrier, and by him a two-horse carriage was first placed upon the route for the accommodation of travellers.[28]

Clearly, by 1816 both brothers knew enough about the transportation business to risk investing heavily in a venture outside their own country; enough, too, to induce the British postal service to hire them, "aliens" that they were, and for two years, when previous mail carriers had been hired for only one year at a time.

The published reminiscences of Jedediah Dorwin, somewhat doctored by an editorial hand, afford a glimpse of the Canadian postal service around the time that the Dickinsons arrived on the scene:

The mail system of that time was a part of the English Postal Service, and the Province had no voice in the matter. The Montreal Post Office was a room about twelve feet square in St Sulpice St., near St Paul. There were no letter-boxes; it was all "general delivery" in its crudest form. The few letters lay scattered about on a table, and had all to be looked over at each application at the door. Very few letters came or went; the mail to Upper Canada was weekly, and the seven days' collection could be contained in one small mail-bag.[29]

The general idea is clear, but the details are telescoped. The post office here spoken of was established in St Sulpice Street (then called St Joseph Street) only in May 1820. It remained there, a cubbyhole tucked away in an auctioneer's yard, until the late summer of 1824.[30] In speaking of a weekly mail service to Upper Canada, however, Dorwin is referring to the days before 1816. He also states that before 1820 "the mails for Upper Canada were carried to Lachine in a cart, or when the roads were bad, on horseback." This account does not seem to jibe with the terms under which the Dickinsons contracted for the job, nor with the fact that from 1816 they operated a *stage* line. But the quality of the rolling stock in these early years did leave much to be desired, and the word "stage" did not mean "stagecoach" – carts, wagons, and all kinds of wheeled vehicles were used. An English traveller spoke of the stage from Cornwall to Prescott in 1816 as "one of the roughest conveyances on either side of the Atlantic."[31] Indeed, the main riverfront road stopped several miles short on both sides of the border between Lower and Upper Canada, which would have made travel by any wheeled vehicle an ordeal. The residents of Charlottenburgh Township, east of Cornwall, complained of this gap in January 1818 in replying to Robert Gourlay's famous questionnaire:

Not having the front main road completed through the first township in the province, called Lancaster, is a great bar against the improvement of this township: the road is already so as to allow the mail stage to run within three miles of the province line: there are also five miles of the province of Lower Canada without a road to join this main road, which makes eight miles in all to complete the land conveyance between the two provinces on this route.[32]

Even where there were roads, there were times in late fall and early spring when mud and the state of the ice on the rivers – too soft or broken for carriages or sleighs, but too thick for ferries to run – made travel by cart or carriage impossible. Stage service was then suspended and the couriers carried the mail on horseback, switching to canoes or other small craft to cross the larger expanses of water. The quality of the vehicles improved quickly enough, but not the condition of the roads. By the mid-1830s the average speed of the coach on the Kingston-Montreal route was four and a half miles per hour, and Deputy Postmaster General Thomas Allen Stayner observed that "the time occupied on this route varies considerably, the roads becoming exceedingly bad in wet weather." On one April day in 1837 it took the stage nineteen hours to cover the forty-odd miles from Côteau to Montreal.[33]

Between Montreal and Kingston lay two hundred miles of bush, bad roads, and few bridges, with here and there a settlement. Launching a stage line was not a simple matter of hitching horses to a wagon and setting off down the road. The Dickinsons had to reconnoitre the route, locate posts every nine or ten miles where horses would be changed, purchase proper horses and equipment – sleighs for the winter; wagons or carriages for the spring, summer, and fall – hire drivers, find booking agents, and round up the capital needed to pay for all that. They must have been at it for a good part of 1815, perhaps drawn by Heriot's call that summer for tenders for a twice-weekly service between Montreal and Kingston. They launched their service in winter, when travellers were few but travelling easier: ice bridged the streams, and snow paved over the rutted muck of the tracks that passed for roads.

To establish their line, the Dickinsons relied on help from both sides of the border. When they signed their first mail contract, Dr Noah Dickinson of Cornwall (he does not appear to have been a close relative but perhaps a distant cousin) acted as one of their two guarantors. He was just the kind of sponsor they needed – a man with roots in the United States, where he had been born, but solidly established in Canada. In the War of 1812 he had served as surgeon of the Glengarry militia. He claimed to have been "approved of as Surgeon by the late Major General Sir Isaac Brock," the British commander killed at the Battle of Queenston Heights in October 1812. He was also intimately connected with the Loyalist establishment by virtue of his marriage to Margaret VanKoughnet. She came from one of Cornwall's premier Loyalist families. Her father had fought in the Royal Regiment of New York in the American Revolution. Her brother, Philip, a future speaker of the assembly of Upper Canada and later an executive councillor, was elected to the legislature for the first time in 1816.[34]

The other guarantor of the mail contract was Vermont-born Thomas Peck, himself a stage operator and Post Office contractor. In the spring of 1814 he had formed a partnership with Isaiah Bangs to operate a livery stable in Montreal, their agreement stipulating that "the Contract made by the said T. Peck and the Deputy Post Master for Conveying the Mail from Montreal to Quebec shall be a joint Concern." In January 1816 Peck and Bangs had launched a stage line to Burlington, Vermont, with several associates south of the St Lawrence and in the United States. At this time, Bangs also served as captain of the Montreal-Quebec steamer *Car of Commerce*. In addition, he and Peck were engaged in the Ottawa River timber trade with Theodore Davis.[35]

Peck and Noah Dickinson were already residents of Canada, but other Americans seem to have moved there specifically to help establish the Dickinson line. Such were Hiram Norton and Asahel Whipple.

The lifelong connection between Norton and the Dickinsons appears to have been formed in Lewis County. Born in Skaneateles, Onondaga County, New York, on 26 February 1799, Norton was a penniless orphan of fourteen when he turned up in Lewis County, where he had relatives in Denmark, home of Barnabas Dickinson. After helping the Dickinsons launch their Canadian stage line, he returned to Lewis County to study at the Lowville Academy in 1818–19; he then moved back to Canada, to Prescott, where he soon operated his own stage services in conjunction with Horace Dickinson, perhaps even as Dickinson's partner. He would later branch out into a wealth of other ventures. From 1831 he would serve as one of the two "popular" members for Grenville County in the Upper Canada legislature, and from 1833 as a commissioner for the building of the St Lawrence canals. "This public spirited gentleman has laid out more money, on buildings and public works in this town, than any other individual," a Prescott newspaper would say of him in the 1830s.[36]

Asahel Whipple, for his part, was saluted near the end of his life as one who had played a key role in establishing the first stage service between Montreal and Prescott. Born on 20 January 1790 in Glocester, Rhode Island, he had spent his childhood near Cooperstown in Otsego County, New York, before moving with his family to the Oswegatchie River town of DeKalb in St Lawrence County when he was about thirteen years old. Both the Cooperstown area and DeKalb were settled by land speculator William Cooper, father of the novelist James Fenimore Cooper. Indeed, Whipple's father, Esek, was one of the band of thirty-four original settlers of DeKalb, led north from Otsego County by William Cooper in May 1803. Asahel Whipple was married at DeKalb in 1811 to Clarissa Church, and the first of their three children – all girls – was born there on 11 August 1812.

The township of DeKalb lay next to Russell, the road between the village of Russell and Ogdensburg passing through it. Circumstantial evidence suggests that the connection between Whipple and Horace Dickinson, nine years his senior, originated when they both lived in St Lawrence County. In Canada, Whipple settled on Lake St Francis, at what is now Les Côteaux (Côteau Landing). The cluster of houses, stables, blacksmiths' shops, and storehouses – one contemporary document called it *"le village de Whipple"* – which he built served as a depot for the Dickinson stage line. He was to command the first steamer on Lake St Francis, the 16-horsepower *Cornwall*, and its successor, the 67-horsepower *Neptune*, before becoming the manager of the line.[37]

The terms of the Dickinsons' first mail contract, including the price of £900 a year, remained unchanged when Horace Dickinson, no longer associated with his younger brother, took care to renew it for five years on 4 October 1817, six months before it was due to expire. Montreal postmaster Daniel Sutherland had succeeded George Heriot as deputy postmaster general by then.[38] If, on paper, Dickinson's contract obligations remained the same as in 1816, he did make one significant change on the ground. Beginning in 1818, when the *Charlotte* inaugurated steamboat service between Prescott and Kingston, he ran his stages only as far west as Prescott during the summer; passengers and mail went on to Kingston by steamer. In winter the stages continued to run all the way to Kingston for another few years.[39]

In the fall of 1818 Dickinson arranged to take over one of the oldest mail routes in the country. He signed a five-year contract with the Post

Office to carry the mails between Montreal and Quebec five times a week. That contract, worth £1,560 a year, was to run from 6 April 1819.[40] The prospect of this new venture undoubtedly was a factor in his decision to leave Prescott in 1818 for Montreal, the big city with its population of 18,000. On 1 May that year he and his family moved into a two-storey house, leased from apothecary Abner Rice, at the corner of Queen and Gabriel (now Ottawa) streets, in the St Ann's suburb.[41] A block north, across the narrow St Pierre River, which ran at the top of Queen Street, stood the Collège de Montréal. The college, fronting on College Street, the extension of St Paul Street west of McGill Street, was a boys' school run by the Sulpician priests. Its students – not just Roman Catholics – came from as far afield as Europe, the Caribbean, and the United States, as well as from just around the corner.[42] In 1818 a James Dickinson, said to be from Cornwall, enrolled. He was probably Horace Dickinson's son, James Taylor Dickinson, who turned twelve in October.[43]

In Montreal, Dickinson kept the stage books for his Upper Canada and Quebec lines at the tavern operated by fellow American expatriates Elisha Lyman and his brother-in-law, Samuel Hedge, "at the sign of General Brock." From an establishment at the corner of narrow St Paul and St Nicolas streets in the heart of the city, they had moved to the Brock Tavern on 1 May 1816, a few months after Dickinson launched his stage line. The tavern stood at the corner of McGill and College streets. McGill Street, site of the hay market, was a broad, new thoroughfare, offering plenty of room for a stage to turn.[44]

It was only natural that Dickinson should fall in with Lyman and Hedge. Both were Massachusetts men like him. In fact, Lyman, ten years his senior, hailed from Northampton; Dickinson probably knew the family from his days in Hatfield.[45] Lyman had moved to Montreal from the border town of Derby, Vermont, in 1815, a year after the death of his first wife. Most people knew him as Deacon Lyman, a title he bore from his role in the founding of the Derby Congregational Church in 1807. Three of his brothers had preceded him to Montreal by several years; one had since died and the other two had returned to the United States.[46]

Hedge, a native of Warwick, Massachusetts, who had married Lyman's younger sister, Lydia, in 1806, had lived in Northampton before moving up the Connecticut River to Windsor, Vermont, and then on to Montreal in 1810. They had remained in Montreal through the war. This proved handy for Lyman. As an American just arrived in town, he could not readily obtain a tavern licence. Hedge, however, already had one: like many Americans who had chosen to stay in Canada through the war, he had pledged allegiance to the king rather than leave the country, as Americans were required to do by Governor Sir George Prevost's proclamation of 9 July 1812. At this early stage, then, Hedge held the licence, it seems, but turned his attention to blacksmithing while Lyman ran the Brock Tavern.[47]

Besides offering food and drink and serving as stage-line rest stops and terminals, inns and taverns often provided a community's only public meeting halls. The Brock Tavern served as one of the gathering places for the American colony in Montreal.[48] These expatriates, hankering for a taste of home in a town much given to whisky, brandy, and beer, might have called for a mug of flip at Lyman's inn and drawn more than a puzzled stare.[49] The irony of an American keeping a tavern named after the late British hero of the War of 1812 was not lost on one wry Montrealer, who commented:

A certain Canadian was so much charmed with our late General Brock that he employed a sculptor to make a wooden statue of the hero of Niagara. It was not finished when this loyal Canadian died; however, his heirs paid the artizan for his labour, and fixed the figure of the General as large as life and in full uniform on a building of theirs, in one of the most frequented streets of this city. The building is at this time leased to an American who keeps public house, and now entertains travellers, and sells his spirituous liquors, at the sign of General Brock. When it is known what an antipathy the General had to Americans, we may with truth say, there never was such an incongruity exhibited to the eyes of the public, nor ever such a method adopted to shew respect to the memory of departed worth.[50]

Montreal, based on a map published in 1839 by William Greig (redrawn by Justin Stahlman).

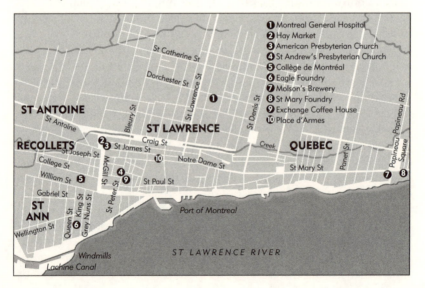

Lyman acted as one of Dickinson's sureties for the Montreal–Quebec mail contract in 1818. His eldest son, William, a druggist, partner with his cousin, William Hedge, in a drugs-and-spices business, was to act in the same capacity in 1824 when Dickinson renewed the Montreal-Kingston contract for five years and signed a one-year agreement to carry the mails between Montreal and Three Rivers.[51]

The Brock Tavern stood at 1 McGill Street. Next door in the same building, at 2 McGill Street, was Cushing's Tavern, operated by Job Cushing, another Massachusetts man and a brother-in-law of Dickinson's landlord, Abner Rice. Job Cushing had moved from Shrewsbury, Massachusetts, to Lower Canada in 1798, first to the Eastern Townships, then to Three Rivers, and on to Montreal in 1814. In 1819 his tavern became the departure point for the St Andrew's and Grenville stage, operated by Thomas Peck, who had his office at 3 McGill Street.[52]

Cushing's son, Emery, was to become, to some extent, Horace Dickinson's counterpart on the Ottawa River.[53] At least a year before his father's death on 2 January 1821, he began running the tavern. Then in April 1821 he took over Peck's share in a six-year Post Office contract which Peck and Philemon Wright had secured in 1819 to inaugurate the mail-stage service between Montreal and Hull. Cushing began by operating the stage line between Montreal and St Andrew's, via Saint-Laurent, Saint-Martin (now part of Laval), Saint-Eustache, and Saint-Benoît; he then branched out into steamboats in 1825 as a co-owner of the *St Andrews*. From that time until his death, he was the manager of the Ottawa stage and steamboat line. He was also involved in winter stage lines to Albany, as was Dickinson, though Cushing associated with partners in Plattsburgh and along the west, or New York, side of Lake Champlain, while Dickinson generally worked with lines running through Burlington, Vermont, down the east side of the lake. From late 1825, after his marriage to Mary Ann Bostwick of Compton in the Eastern Townships – and his move to a new, three-storey stone building at 7 McGill Street – Cushing also operated a stage line from Montreal to the Townships village of Stanstead, on the border across from Derby, Vermont. He and Dickinson seem to have always remained on good terms; when Cushing contracted at the end of 1829 to carry the mails between Montreal and Stanstead, for example, Dickinson signed as his security.[54]

Besides the Hedges, Lymans, and Cushings, Dickinson's early contacts among the Americans of Montreal included John Ward, who set up shop on Queen Street, where Dickinson lived, in the fall of 1819, and the Bigelow brothers, Abijah and Jacob. The Bigelows were natives of Waltham, Massachusetts, and cousins of the future Upper Canadian reform leader Marshall Spring Bidwell.[55] Ward moved to Montreal a year after Dickinson, but the Bigelows had lived there since 1815 at the latest.[56]

Abijah, the younger of the two, operated as a commission merchant until at least 1826.[57] Jacob preferred salaried employment. He is said to have worked as a store clerk in Boston before moving to Montreal. On the founding of the Bank of Canada in 1818, he was hired as discount clerk. He became second teller in the spring of 1819, then first teller the following year.[58] Their baby brother, Increase Sumner Bigelow, born in 1805, was also to spend some years in Montreal.[59]

"There has been, and in time of peace will continue to be, a great influx of Americans, chiefly from the New England States, who are winding themselves into all the most active and ingenious employments," a traveller from Philadelphia noted on a visit to Montreal in 1817.[60] This was an influx of a different character from that of the Loyalist refugees in the 1780s. Most Americans who moved to Canada in the early nineteenth century were not making a political statement, renouncing the republic for the British crown, or fleeing persecution. They were part of the Yankee swarm that left the crowded New England hive after the American Revolution to make a new beginning in Vermont, New York, and points beyond. There was something atavistic in this movement of population, a kind of early, muffled expression of "manifest destiny," but without the sting which that notion would come to convey by mid-century. It is most aptly summed up, not in the sabre-rattling cry of "Fifty-four forty or fight!" of President James Polk's day, but in the entomological comparison of Judge Nathan Ford, one of the founders of Ogdensburg: "It is equally necessary that Yankees swarm as it is for bees."[61]

Many established themselves in Canada, largely undeveloped compared with their native states. In Lower Canada, thousands sought cheap land – or at least a promising speculation – in the Eastern Townships.[62] Others, such as Philemon Wright, found their opportunity up the Ottawa River. Still others favoured Montreal "as a place offering flattering prospects for the employment of active industry."[63] Whether Yankees such as the Bigelows, Cushings, Hedges, and Lymans, New Yorkers such as Alexander Young, or New Jerseyites such as John Ward, they displayed an abundance of initiative and industry.

Travelers record that almost without exception innkeepers in the river towns and along the post roads were Americans. The "American tavern" was an institution welcomed by every wandering European writer. The most prosperous and enterprising storekeepers, as, for instance, in the city of Montreal, were foreigners from New England. The country miller was usually an immigrant from the south; in fact, almost all the mechanics who could perform the duties of a new settlement were of Yankee origin.[64]

Americans in Lower Canada formed as much of an ethnic group as the Scots, English, or Irish. Those last three groups, however, especially the

Scots, the English, and the Irish Protestants, but even many Irish Catholics, acted as if they owned the place. It was an extension of home. No matter how strong the different cultural identities they gloried in or how vastly outnumbered they were by French Canadians, they felt, as British subjects, a kind of collective proprietary interest in a British colony, never hesitating to voice their demands and grievances. The Americans, on the other hand – certainly those of the Montreal commercial and professional classes – stepped gingerly when it came to politics. It was as though they were marked men, which, in a way, they were. In the eyes of stout John Bulls, they were tainted by birth with a double-barrelled variant of original sin called democracy and republicanism, and were not to be counted loyal subjects of His Majesty. When Governor General Lord Dalhousie travelled up the Ottawa River in the summer of 1820, for example, the John Bullish Irish Protestant timber dealer George Hamilton of Hawkesbury is said to have tried his best to dissuade him from stopping at Hull and calling on Philemon Wright. Thomas Mears informed Wright that Hamilton had waylaid the official party at Grenville and "used all his powerfull arguments both with the Govr and others with him to prevent his calling, Saying that you were a pack of disaffect yankes."[65]

The true-blue *Montreal Herald* had stated the anti-American case in its very first issue, on 19 October 1811, in speaking of this "different class of men whose numbers are becoming so great that we cannot pass them without notice." The paper declared them "aliens, citizens, or denizens of a foreign country." Even those who, as a condition of taking up crown lands, had sworn allegiance to the king, remained foreigners: "their oath only qualified them to hold lands, but gave them no right to vote at our elections or serve on our grand and petty Juries." A quarter-century later, an American-born farmer in Stanstead was moved to complain: "The inhabitants of American origin in Lower Canada, have been, heretofore, treated by the Executive Government of the Colony as unfit for offices of honor & trust – even in those parts where they were the principal inhabitants and also, unworthy of their confidence – except in a few instances of great political pliancy."[66]

Trusting in the British crown to protect their rights and institutions, French Canadians until the 1830s were even stouter than loyal Britons in their anti-Americanism. John Bull and Jonathan were cousins, after all, in matters of culture, religion, and language; not so Jean-Baptiste. It might be said that French Canadians resented the British as high capitalists and the Americans as low. The British merchants seemed bent on developing Lower Canada, not for its own sake, but as a cog in the imperial machine and a channel for the trade they controlled, which flowed from Britain to the Great Lakes and beyond. Americans, on the other hand, were often seen as just money-grubbing. In 1807, six years before the United States tried to take Canada by force, a writer in the Quebec newspaper *Le Canadien* opined:

If Canada should be so unfortunate as to fall eventually under American domination, we would soon feel the avidity and grasping spirit of the Americans; born in the bosom of commerce and ever hungering after all kinds of pleasures, an American will do anything to achieve his ends. The ties of blood, so strong in the hearts of men, are non-existent in him. He will leave father, mother, brother, sister, even his wife, as readily as a French Canadian might leave a stranger. The latter would never wish to quit the family home, whereas the former enjoys long journeys and generally moves away from his parents ... An American's prime object is always to buy and sell.[67]

Twelve years later, a correspondent of the same newspaper represented the peaceful post-war invasion of Yankee immigrants as the chief threat to French Canada: "This latter group is increasing at an astonishing rate, and if nothing is done to halt its progress, it will soon swallow all the others."[68]

If officialdom, the *Herald*, and *Le Canadien* cold-shouldered them, American expatriates had a somewhat more sympathetic organ in the *Canadian Courant*, launched in 1807 by Nahum Mower, a native of Worcester, Massachusetts, who had moved to Montreal after a spell as a newspaper publisher in Windsor, Vermont.[69] The *Courant* was a perfectly respectable paper, yet the very incorporation of the word "Canadian" in its name aroused suspicion in the minds of arch-Britons who thought that only someone whose Canadianness was doubtful would feel the need to proclaim it.

In this brittle colonial context, the French Canadians, English, Irish, and Scots – even the Germans and the French – all founded national societies in the mid-1830s, affirming their cultural separateness. Another two decades would pass before American Montrealers felt comfortable enough, and sufficiently free of aspersions on their loyalty, to launch their own. Their New England Society of Montreal was not formally established until 6 March 1854.[70]

In the early decades of the nineteenth century then, American Montrealers lived the immigrant experience – outsiders banding together socially and in business, and maintaining close ties with families and friends back home. Business-minded and rigidly Calvinistic as they may have been, they were not half so bloodless as sometimes portrayed. Footloose when it came to trade and commerce, the men showed their attachment to their homeland in matters of the heart, seeking out American brides across the border or among their fellow expatriates. Jacob Bigelow did so in 1820, marrying Eliza Southgate of Leicester, Massachusetts.[71] Four years later Abijah Bigelow married Susan Maria Phelps of

Windsor, Vermont, a minor for whom Horace Dickinson acted as tutor in the drafting of her marriage contract.[72] Captain George Brush returned to his native Vergennes to marry Eliza Maria Seymour on 12 January 1826.[73] Samuel Ward, John Ward's brother, found the first of his three wives in Montreal's American community in the person of Abigail Hedge, daughter of Samuel Hedge and Lydia Lyman. They were married on 9 September 1830. She died on 4 October of the following year, at the age of twenty-one. In April 1834 Ward went farther afield, marrying his second wife, Mary Jane Bunce, in her hometown of Hartford, Connecticut.[74]

Vermonter Jedediah Dorwin was another who married true to form. His account of how this came about is revealing. After settling in Montreal in March 1816, he worked briefly as a clerk for James McDouall and Company, a firm of commission merchants with which Abijah Bigelow was associated.[75] In May, Dorwin opened a grocery east of the city in what is now the Hochelaga district of Montreal. In the fall he moved closer to town, to the Papineau Road, opposite Molson's brewery and near Joseph Lough's foundry:

I soon formed the acquaintance of Mr Loughs family and Boarded with them. both he and his wife were pleasant pleasant people she being an American Lady. with all their manners and way of living it seemed like home in their family more than any other place I had found in Canada So that time passed more pleasantly than the previous Summer. besides there was an actraction, by the way of a young Lady friend of Mrs Lough from Town who used to visit her once in a while. her name was Miss Isabella Williamson a native of Albany who resided in Montreal with her Brother in Law a Mr Austin Warner, a merchant. An attatchment grew up between us so on the Seventh day of April 1817 we were married by the Rev. Mr Robert Eastern [Easton] of the Presbyterian Church in St Peter Street.[76]

For Dorwin, Montreal became home, though his trading activities would take him from Newfoundland to Chicago.[77]

Shipbuilder Alexander Young, already married when he turned up in Canada, shuttled back and forth across the border in the 1820s and early 1830s. His wife remained in Westport, New York, on the property she had inherited from her father, and Young kept returning there amidst his frequent wanderings. For a while in the 1830s, he operated a shipyard on Lake Ontario at Oswego, New York. In his sixties he apparently accompanied Sir George Simpson, governor of the Hudson's Bay Company, on an overland trip to the Pacific and then spent several years in California and Louisiana, before returning to Westport.[78]

Some Americans in Montreal found it difficult to fit in, partly because of prejudice – real or imagined – against them and partly because of a general expectation that sooner or later the tensions that kept flaring up

John Dod Ward; from an engraving in the Ward Family
Collection at the Butler Library, Columbia University.

between Britain and the United States were bound to lead to another war.
In some cases, it was also because they were only too clearly birds of passage. John Ward, for example, complained of prejudice, claiming that he
was denied contracts for the simple reason that "I am not a Scotchman, a
circumstance of no small importance with some of the wise ones here." He
sought to place American engineers aboard steamers on the St Lawrence
and the Great Lakes "that I may have the general direction of and do the
repairs to the engine … which an 'American' could never be permitted to
do if it was managed by one from 'over the seas.'."[79] Yet while he resented
being treated as an outsider, Ward refused to consider himself anything
but. "I think Jersey my home," he told his father in May 1822. A year
later he elaborated on that thought, giving it as his opinion as well as that
of his brothers, Samuel and Lebbeus, that "of all the places we have ever
been New Jersey is 'rather the best' to live in and the place we all wish to
return to after we have supplied John Bull with all the steam engines that
he wants and the reason we stay here now is because steam engines are
wanted here more than in Jersey and there are fewer to make them."[80]

For Ward, Lower Canada was an opportunity, but not quite a country to call home. His ignorance of the French language did not help. One condition of Jacob Bigelow's appointment as second teller at the Bank of Canada in 1819 was that he know French.[81] He seems to have been one of the few American Montrealers who did. Ward certainly did not. On a trip to Europe in 1828–29, he was somewhat discomfited to discover that France was, of all things, French. After crossing from England to Calais, he found himself "really in a foreign country – the servants spoke french – the house and furniture were french – the dinner french – the mail coach french – every thing FRENCH," he wrote in his diary. The language, like tobacco smoke, made him run for cover, as he did in Brussels when he "dined at the table d'hote – without being able to understand one word spoken during the dinner and concluded I would not do so again but would dine alone hereafter."[82]

Of an altogether different stamp was the hardware merchant Jacob De Witt, a founding director of the Bank of Canada who helped further the careers of both Jacob and Abijah Bigelow. In 1818, for example, he and his brother Jabez Dean De Witt, a hatter, helped Jacob Bigelow post the £1,000 bond required of him when he was first hired by the bank.[83] Born in Windham, Connecticut, in 1785, De Witt had moved to Montreal with his family at the turn of the century.[84] He had learned French and mixed with French Canadians while remaining attached to his American roots. In 1816 he married an American girl, Sophronia Frary, a native of Conway, Massachusetts, whose family had settled in the Eastern Townships near the Vermont border.[85] They would name some of their sons after contemporary American notables – Clinton, after New York governor De Witt Clinton, the driving force behind the building of the Erie Canal; Henry Clay, after the famous Kentucky congressman, secretary of state, and Whig leader; and Caleb Strong, who bore a name that was that of a Massachusetts governor (from Northampton) as well as of his grandson, minister of the American Presbyterian Church in Montreal from 1839 to 1847.[86]

Though he had sworn allegiance to the British crown,[87] De Witt flaunted his American roots in a way that few other American-born Montrealers dared to do. And while most American merchants of Montreal maintained a discreet public silence on the burning political issues pitting the Anglo-Scottish elite against the followers of Louis-Joseph Papineau, he was notable for his support of the Patriote leader. In 1830 he was elected to the Legislative Assembly for the county of Beauharnois, a seat he would hold until the rebellions. In the ensuing decade, as many aggrieved French Canadians lost faith in Britain and came to view American-style democratic institutions as the answer to their prayers, he was one of the few English-speaking members to side with Papineau and his Patriote party. In 1834 he endorsed the compendious statement of Patriote grievances, the 92 Resolutions. The following year he and Louis-Michel Viger and ten other men formed Viger, De Witt and Company to launch the Banque du Peuple, or People's Bank. (A previous attempt by De Witt and sixteen associates, including Abijah Bigelow and Hiram Norton, to launch a Banque du Peuple in 1833 had come to naught.) Papineau's portrait adorned the bank's $5 bills, while on the $2 bills appeared the face of Daniel O'Connell, "the Liberator," Ireland's hero and Britain's bane, then leading a campaign for the repeal of the legislative union of Ireland and Britain. There was no mistaking where De Witt's political sympathies lay. In 1835 he was the founding vice-president of the Montreal headquarters branch of the Patriotic Union, an extra-parliamentary extension of the Patriote party. He stopped short, however, of following the Patriotes into armed rebellion in 1837–38.[88]

Jacob Bigelow's close association with De Witt argues a kinship in their social and political outlook. One hint of such a rapport came in the fall of 1832 when Bigelow was touted as a candidate for the editorship of the "radical" *Vindicator*. Launched in 1828 by Irish firebrand Dr Daniel Tracey, the newspaper tore into the Anglo-Scottish establishment at every opportunity, championing small-scale local enterprise against Montreal capitalists, and the Patriote cause against the entrenched commercial and political elite. De Witt became one of the owners of the paper in 1829, along with bookseller Édouard-Raymond Fabre, whose back shop was the closest thing to a Patriote party office. Publication of the *Vindicator* was suspended at Tracey's death in July 1832. Mention of Bigelow's name in connection with its revival that fall probably sprang from De Witt's involvement and the view of some that the paper should broaden its appeal beyond its largely Irish Catholic readership in Montreal to American settlers in the Eastern Townships. Bigelow did not lack qualifications. At forty-two, after two decades or more in Montreal, he was well acquainted with the public affairs of the province and its people. He was liberal, earnest, stubbornly idealistic; he would give proof of those qualities after his return to the United States, where in the 1840s he would stand as an anti-slavery candidate for Congress at a time when abolitionists could count on few votes and much abuse. But he was no fire-breather – and he did not get the editorship. A temporary editor was in charge when the *Vindicator* reappeared on 2 November, and the following spring the position went to the pugnacious Dr Edmund Bailey O'Callaghan, a French-educated Irishman who was to become a Patriote member of the legislature and a perfervid Papineau lieutenant (which must have complicated relations between his wife, Charlotte Crampe, and her older sister, Elizabeth, who had married into the stout Anglo-Irish Colclough family).[89]

Bigelow, De Witt, and Fabre were also associated with other Montreal and La Prairie men in the ownership of the *Patriote Canadien*, a steamer of 196 tons burden built in 1832 by Sheay and Merritt and equipped with a 60-horsepower engine made by Bennet and Henderson. This was an effort to bring out the capitalist in the habitants around La Prairie and it worked: "Shares were offered at 30 shillings so that the country people could afford them, which did indeed lead almost all of them to buy one or several shares and therefore gave them a more direct interest in encouraging the venture and seeing it succeed." The steamer ran at first as a ferry between Montreal and La Prairie, and from 1834 she challenged the Molson-Torrance boats in the Quebec trade before being bought off by those interests and mothballed.[90]

De Witt also played an important role in Abijah Bigelow's career. Through his intercession, Bigelow became, in December 1821, the first foreign agent of an American insurance company. More of an entrepreneur than his older brother – at one time he sold drafts on New York banks, at another, American lottery tickets – Abijah Bigelow was appointed Montreal agent of the Aetna Insurance Company of Hartford, Connecticut, founded two years earlier. He was notified of his appointment in a letter of 22 December from the company secretary. From this letter it appears that the company hired Bigelow sight unseen, solely on the strength of De Witt's recommendation, and that only the difficulties of conveying documents from Hartford to Montreal had prevented the earlier appointment of De Witt himself to the post. Whatever the shortcomings of the mail service, the letter, which advised Bigelow to waste no time in advertising his services, seems to have reached him within a week: by 1 January 1822 he was advertising in the *Canadian Courant* that the Aetna company "has established an Office in this place, and will be ready in a few days, to insure against loss or damage by fire." The office, at 71 St Paul Street, opened for business at the end of the month. Bigelow was authorized to cover risks of up to $10,000 and paid a commission of 5 per cent on each policy he sold.[91] He busied himself thereafter with this and related activities, encouraging the work of fire societies, the forerunners of modern fire departments, and at one time acting as a sales agent for Cooper's Patent Rotative Fire Engines, made in Hartford. In April 1822 he joined fifty-three other merchants to found the Montreal Committee of Trade, later to become the Board of Trade.[92]

CHAPTER FOUR

New Beginnings

At the time when the *Ottawa* began plying on Lake St Louis and John Ward's first Canadian-made engine propelled the *Montreal* across the St Lawrence to La Prairie, Horace Dickinson had yet to make the jump from land to water transport. But like his brother, who had introduced a two-horse carriage and passenger service on his New York mail run, he too innovated. In the published digest of his reminiscences, Jedediah Dorwin says:

> The vehicles then in use were ordinary carts and trucks, and, for driving, the calèche, a clumsy one horse carriage with two wheels and a spring seat. In 1817, there were but two coaches in the city ... the mails for Upper Canada were carried to Lachine in a cart, or when the roads were bad, on horseback. But Horace Dickinson, an American, was the carrier, and Yankee enterprise must come to the surface, so one fine morning in June, 1820, he drove out of the city along the Upper Lachine Road amid crowds of envious lookers-on, with two horses hitched to a large four-wheeled three-seated farmer's wagon, painted red, the first vehicle of the kind seen in the neighborhood. In a few years, however, they became quite common, but Dickinson again forged ahead by coming out with a four-horse coach.[1]

(Later still came six-horse coaches, which by 1833 were said to be "as common as three eggs for a penny" around Montreal, and by 1834, eight-horse vehicles.)[2]

Dickinson grasped the need for timely innovation to ward off competition. He could be daring, but he was not foolhardy. Unlike other stage operators who doubled as innkeepers, or the bankers, professional men, merchants, tradesmen, and landowners who invested in steamboats as a sideline, he had no other source of income than his transport business. In nursing it along, he sought to minimize the risks. Thus, when he and his brother had launched their stage line between Montreal and Kingston, they had taken care to secure the mail contract; and for long-term security, Dickinson had hastened to renew the original two-year contract for another five years. His first mail contract on the Montreal-Quebec route was also for five years.[3] In association with mail contractor John Easinhart in St John's and other stage operators in Vermont and New York, he also ran a winter stage line from Montreal to Albany in the winter of 1820, but he seems to have begun pulling out of this venture the very next year. His role thereafter appears to have consisted in little more than allowing the Albany line to keep its stage books at his office.[4]

This measured approach may help to explain why, when steamboats were all the rage, Dickinson moved slowly into that line of business. Land transportation he knew well, but as far as is known, he had no experience with water craft and inland navigation. He would not gamble, as the owners of the *Ottawa* had done. Besides, had he even the legal right? The navigation laws, though erratically enforced, stated that an American could not run a vessel between Canadian ports.[5] Nor did Dickinson even form a connection between his stages and the *Ottawa* to speed passengers across Lake St Louis, as he had done with the *Charlotte* in 1818 on the river between Prescott and Kingston. The stages continued to plod overland between Lachine and the Cascades, using ferries to cross the mouth of the Ottawa River.

The *Perseverance* replaced the *Ottawa* on Lake St Louis in 1821 and still Dickinson held back.He may not have had the resources to invest in steamboats then, or his attention may have been diverted by changes on the home front. In May that year he and his family had moved from Queen Street to a three-storey stone house on McGill Street. The property had a good-sized yard and stable. In the adjoining house, at 23 McGill, stood Cyrus Brewster Martin's Union Hotel, "at the sign of the Golden Hands," where Dickinson now kept his stage books. From May 1824 until he left for other quarters in 1826, he would lease both houses, with their common backyard, and sublet number 23. Martin, meanwhile, left for Upper Canada to run the Williamsburgh Stage House, located between Cornwall and Prescott.[6] Dickinson and his family had hardly settled into their new home when his wife died at Côteau on 17 July. She was thirty-nine. Her body was carried back to Montreal for burial.[7] Dickinson was left a single parent with three children ranging in age from ten years to not quite fifteen.

His bereavement and new responsibilities at home may have put him off his stride, but business could not wait. The success of the *Perseverance* in her first year spelled trouble for his Upper Canada Line. He would have noticed a drop in local traffic from Lachine to the Cascades. Perhaps, too, some of his passengers tweaked his ear with reports of the comfort and speed of the steamer compared with the slow bone-shaking they experienced in his stages. The simple fact was that his stages constituted no more than a portage line, a land link between the boat terminals of Montreal in the east and Prescott in the west. He had begun in 1816 with stages running between Montreal and Kingston. Two years later, when the *Charlotte* made her appearance, he had bowed before the superior convenience of steamboat travel and withdrawn his stages from the route between Prescott and Kingston in the summertime. Now the *Perseverance* threatened to force him into a similar surrender between Lachine and the Cascades. And what if a steamer should appear on that other navigable stretch of the route, Lake St Francis? He would be left with no line at all, nothing but disjointed taxi routes from Montreal to Lachine, Cascades to Côteau, and the fifty-mile run between Cornwall and Prescott. Even there, boat owners would soon realize that they had everything to gain from launching their own stage services. To preserve his stage line, therefore, Dickinson had little choice but to take to the water.

There is some slight evidence that he had already faced up to this imperative by the spring of 1821. That May, when François Denaut, *dit* Jérémie, of La Prairie approached John C. Langdon of Troy, New York, to build the machinery for a horse boat, Langdon replied that he could begin working on it "as soon as completed a Boat now Engaged by the said John C. Langdon for Mr Horrace Dickenson of Montreal."[8] This Dickinson boat is a mystery. It was undoubtedly meant for use somewhere along his Upper Canada stage line. Did he ever take delivery of it? Might it have been the horse boat that plied on Lake St Francis before steamers made their appearance there? Such a theory would make sense. It would also be just like Dickinson, in making the transition from land to water transport, to ease into it in this way – with a boat driven by horses, which he knew well, rather than by the unfamiliar power of steam, and on waters where he challenged no entrenched interests and faced no rivals. But that is speculation.[9] No evidence has yet been found to show that Dickinson held a stake in the Lake St Francis horse boat. If indeed he did not, then he reached an accommodation with her owner by 1822, for in that year, as we have seen, she formed a link in the passenger line between Montreal and Upper Canada, as the *Perseverance* did on Lake St Louis.

Alliances of this sort, however, could only be stop-gap measures for Dickinson. They ensured that a transport line operated between Montreal and Upper Canada, but it was no longer his line. Control was necessarily split and revenues had to be shared. To draw revenue from the stretches where boats had supplanted his stages, he had to acquire a share in the boats. If he wanted free rein to manage the whole line, he would have to run his own boats.

Dickinson regained a financial stake in summer travel between Prescott and Kingston in 1822 as a shareholder in the new steamer *Dalhousie*. The boat began by running twice a week, stopping at Brockville and Gananoque on the way. On Lake St Francis he and Asahel Whipple made plans to introduce the *Cornwall*. It may have been in an effort to meet the requirements of the navigation laws that Whipple swore an oath of allegiance to the Crown in the summer of 1822.[10] Beginning the following year, the *Cornwall* made four trips a week each way between Côteau and Cornwall, charging cabin passengers 11s. 3d. and deck passengers 6s. 3d. for the trip up, and 7s. 6d. and 3s. 9d. for the trip down. This dual rate was a common feature on the St Lawrence in the early days of steam traffic, reflecting the fact that a trip upriver, against the current took longer and consumed more fuel than sailing with the current. The *Cornwall* left Côteau on Mondays, Thursday, Fridays, and Saturdays on the arrival of the stage from Montreal and sailed from Cornwall on Mondays, Tuesdays, Fridays, and Saturdays as soon as the stage from Prescott arrived. She stopped at Lancaster and other intermediate points.[11]

As his business grew, Dickinson drew on the Bigelows for help. From 1824, for example, Abijah Bigelow acted as guarantor for every mail contract that Dickinson signed.[12] It is possible that Dickinson's links with the Bigelow family went back, if not to Massachusetts, then to New York.[13] Whatever their origins, the relations between him and the Bigelow brothers were sealed on 17 May 1823, when, at the age of forty-two, Dickinson married their sister, Mercy Amelia, age twenty-eight.[14] The wedding took place not in Barre, Massachusetts, where she lived, nor in Montreal, but in Plattsburgh, New York, a choice seemingly dictated by Dickinson's wish to have the ceremony performed by the Reverend Samuel Whelpley of the American Presbyterian Society. Whelpley had only recently returned to his charge in Plattsburgh after helping Dickinson and others to establish a new church in Montreal.[15] Outside his family and his business, this American Presbyterian Church had now become Dickinson's chief preoccupation.

The insistence of Scottish members of the Presbyterian Church in St Peter Street, generally known as St Andrew's Presbyterian Church, that none but a Scot was fit to be their pastor had led Dickinson and others – among them the Bigelows, the Wards, Jacob De Witt, and Deacon Lyman – to bolt. Samuel Hedge remarked that "although he had no objection to going to heaven, he utterly failed to see the necessity of going there by way of Scotland."[16] On 24 December 1822 the seceders met at the newly refurbished City Tavern, at St Paul and St Peter streets, and founded the American Presbyterian Society of Montreal, of which Dickinson was to be the first treasurer.[17] With De Witt in the chair and Jacob Bigelow as secretary, they resolved to establish their own church, "denominating themselves Presbyterians although not regularly of the established Church of Scotland, nor in connection with same." In many respects, it was a Congregational church.[18] The founders later adopted a set of rules, the preamble of which stated their aims and reflected their earnestness:

Whereas we the undersigned inhabitants of the City and vicinity of Montreal, attached to the good and wholesome laws of our King and Country, … and having no union or connection binding on us to any other religious association, we do believe it to be an incumbent duty on us at this time to exercise and improve our religious privileges, by uniting together, to form and build up a church and congregation in this place according to the pure principles of the gospel … at the same time setting those laudable examples to the rising generation, of relief to the poor and destitute, the discountenance of vice, wherever it appears and the encouragement of virtue, together with charity to all mankind.[19]

There was much there to sting leaders and members of other denominations. Some asked how these men could pretend to belong to no congregation when most had been members of St Andrew's. In claiming to found their church on the "pure principles of the gospel," did they mean to imply that other churches rested on foundations less pure? And some British-born subjects carped about professions of loyalty to king and country pouring from the mouths of Americans whose very deeds here amounted to a repudiation of the king's established churches of England and Scotland.[20]

Without a building or minister of its own, the society cast about for suitable sites and candidates, entrusting the search to a "prudential committee," whose members included Dickinson, Jacob De Witt, Jacob Bigelow, and Samuel Hedge.[21] In seeking a minister, they set their sights high – and left us an insight into their perception of Montreal. Witness Jacob Bigelow's letter sketching their requirements:

It is essential that he should be a man of unblemished character, a scholar of high attainments, his style chaste, and his talents brilliant. He should be a popular preacher with that dignity of deportment which results from sound principles and true piety. As Montreal is a place of considerable refinement it would be particularly desirable that he should possess that urbanity in his manner which would be less desirable in a different place. I am ordered to be explicit in saying that he should be a man of eminent piety and first class talents.[22]

Whelpley helped get the church off the ground, officiating at the first public worship on 23 February 1823. But he was needed in Plattsburgh. Still without its own pastor after more than a year, the society applied for enrolment in the presbytery of New York in May 1824, seeking a candidate there.[23] What to make of this taunting report, larded with puns and sexual innuendo, in the *Scribbler* of 13 May?

The American Presbyterian Church at the northeast corner of McGill and St James streets (NA/C-65419).

Lady Susan Big-below has entered upon her pilgrimage to the South, (some say to South America,) for the purpose of looking out, and importing a clergyman for a new fangled society in Mount Royal, of recent begetting. Report adds that she is clothed with full powers, as the great plenipotentiary, from the sisterhood, to grant to the person she may select, (if he comes directly, and performs to satisfaction,) the privilege of navigating up and down thro' all the navigable channels, large and small, appertaining to the said society.[24]

In this hit at the American Presbyterian Society, "Big-below" is an obvious play on the name Bigelow, suggesting pregnancy or broad hips. A reference to Susan Bigelow, Abijah's wife? But they were married only that 13 May, the magazine's cover date. Besides, she was just nineteen; it seems improbable that the "new fangled society" would have entrusted to one so young the task of seeking out a pastor. Whether it was through "Susan Big-below" or some other agency, Joseph Stibbs Christmas, freshly graduated from the Theological Seminary in Princeton, New Jersey, was invited to preach that spring. He had just turned twenty-one. On 1 August he was ordained and installed as pastor, a position he was to hold until the summer of 1828.[25]

On 4 October a committee that included Dickinson, Jacob De Witt, John Ward, and Daniel Ward Eager purchased a lot at the northeast corner of St James and McGill streets on which to build their church. Builder Moses

Marshall[26] drew up his plans, and in December, masons were invited to submit their tenders at Dickinson's Upper Canada Stage Office. On 13 June 1825 a procession made its way to the building site from the Masonic Hall for the laying of the cornerstone. Members of the congregation, Masons, and members of the bar in their robes were escorted by the grenadier company of the 70th Regiment and the Royal Montreal Volunteer Cavalry. No anti-Americanism there. A scroll deposited in the stone on the occasion identified, among others, the elders of the church and the members of the building and prudential committees. Horace Dickinson, an elder since 31 March 1824, was the only person listed in all three groups.[27] Work proceeded slowly and the congregation, which had been meeting in rented premises, finally occupied the building in April 1827.[28]

William Lyon Mackenzie, the Upper Canadian newspaper publisher and future rebel leader, attended a service at the church in April 1831 and noted: "The congregation is numerous and the people generally well-dressed, forming evidently an important and influential part of the citizens of Montreal. Yet the minister, because he was born in the United States, is forbidden to marry, even the members of his own congregation."[29] In reality, the prohibition affected all churches other than the Roman Catholic, Anglican, and Scottish Presbyterian, not just those with American pastors. No marriages or funerals were performed at the American Presbyterian Church until, in its case, this disability was removed by legislation in 1832.[30] The restriction helps to explain why Dickinson's two daughters were married at other Montreal churches, despite their attachment to their own. On 8 September 1829 Dimmis, the younger of the two, married Lebbeus Baldwin Ward at the Scotch Presbyterian Church in St Gabriel Street. Mary Ann married the Reverend George William Perkins, Christmas's successor as pastor of the American Presbyterian Church, on 7 September 1831 at St Andrew's Presbyterian Church.[31] As regards baptism, however, the laws of men were no match for what Christmas – and Perkins after him – considered a higher law that bound them to "baptize all nations." Baptisms were performed and registered at the church from the first. All five children born of Dickinson's second marriage between 1824 and 1830 were christened there.[32]

In Dickinson's life, then, family, church, and business affairs were closely interwoven. It was a family compact, so to speak, and particularly evident in his business. The Wards built the engines for at least six of the eight steamers which he owned at one time or another. He, for his part, besides giving them his custom, assisted the Wards in other ways, for instance, by helping John Ward to nail down the £4,500 contract to build the engine of the steam tug *Hercules* in 1823.[33] As for the Bigelows, it appears that Abijah sold him fire insurance policies on his scattered assets,[34] besides acting as his security in the mail contracts, while Jacob added a new dimension to the business from 1825: in July that year he began selling insurance against the hazards of inland navigation as agent of the Howard Insurance Company of New York.[35] This was just two months after Dickinson's *St Lawrence* went into operation on Lake St Louis and six months before he undertook to run the hull of James Greenfield's *Lady of the Lake* down the treacherous rapids from Lake St Francis to the port of Montreal. In view of the risk, he had to insure the boat for £1,000, the sum he agreed to pay Greenfield should the boat be damaged or sunk.[36] As far as Dickinson was concerned, Jacob's insurance venture certainly was timely. Abijah followed Jacob's lead in August 1829. While still selling fire insurance for Aetna, he became the agent of the Protection Insurance Company of Hartford, dealing exclusively in inland-navigation insurance.[37] It would be 1830 before Montreal merchants, together with forwarding interests at Prescott and Brockville, dismayed to see profits that could easily be theirs slipping away to capitalists in the United States, took action and formed the Canada Inland Assurance Company.[38]

Increase Sumner Bigelow, who surfaced in Montreal in the late 1820s, used Dickinson's Upper Canada Stage Office for retail ventures of his own. In the fall of 1830 he was peddling Genessee valley apples there. He may also have been associated with his brother Abijah in a clothing store that operated in the building in 1829–30.[39]

No matter what differences may have existed in their personalities, Dickinsons, Wards, and Bigelows were generally of one mind on essentials, from life everlasting to life on the shop floor. The hope of the former hinged on regular work habits in the latter, and that meant – no egg pop. At a time when workmen routinely took grog on the job, strong drink was strictly off limits for Dickinson's boat crews. As vice-president of the Montreal Society for the Promotion of Temperance, founded by the Reverend Joseph Stibbs Christmas in 1828, Dickinson had renounced distilled spirits, pledging with his fellows "that we will entirely abstain from their use, except as a medicine; that we will banish them from our families, that we will not give them to persons employed by us, and that we will use our influence in discouraging their use among our friends."[40]

After Dickinson's death, Abijah and Increase Sumner Bigelow maintained the policy. Referring to one of the steamers they inherited from Dickinson, a writer noted in the fall of 1832 that the crew were distinguished "for their civility and sobriety; as all, from the Captain to the cook, wholly abstain from the use of spirituous or fermented liquors."[41] The implication was that such was not the rule on other boats, and indeed, freshwater sailors could be as foul-mouthed and fond of drink as old salts were reputed to be, and a ration of drink was commonly part of their pay.[42] The Wards were also commended for running a dry shop. While many employers fell behind in their orders because of drunkenness on the job, the *Canadian Courant* noted in July 1830, the Eagle Foundry had just completed on schedule the two engines that would make John Torrance's 150-horsepower towboat *British America* the most powerful steamer in Canada (at least until the next year, when it was trumped by the Molsons' *John Bull*, fitted with Ward engines developing 260 horsepower).[43]

Dickinson's religious convictions inspired in him an inflexible sense of moral duty that clashed with the ways of the worldly and occasionally sparked controversy. One small flap occurred in 1824 after he refused to let his stages carry a bundle of publisher Samuel Wilcocke's *Scribbler* to Quebec. To a man of Dickinson's stamp, this magazine, with its barbs, scandal-mongering, and dirty jokes, would have been something hot off the devil's press. (Might he have been personally offended, too, by that squib of May 1823 about Susan "Big-below" and the "new fangled society"?) The outraged Wilcocke struck back, urging a boycott of Dickinson's transport line. "Contemptible as this fellow's conduct is," he wrote, "it yet deserves the broad notice I take of it, that the public may know the man, and avoid encouraging or patronising him." Most "respectable" people, however, would hardly have taken their lead from the *Scribbler*.[44]

Another controversy erupted in late 1830 as a result of Dickinson's determination to keep his stages and steamboats idle on Sundays. He had not always been such a stickler for Sunday observance. In August and September 1819, for example, when he had increased the frequency of his Upper Canada passenger service to three times a week from two, stages left Prescott and Montreal at 9 o'clock Saturday morning and arrived at their destination on Sunday evening. As the speed of travel improved, thanks mainly to steamboats, the contortions in scheduling testified to his efforts to honour the Lord's Day. By the summer of 1829, a stage left Montreal every weekday at 11 a.m.; on Saturdays it left at 4 a.m., the idea being that it should reach its destination before midnight.

The absence of Sunday service provoked no comment until the fall of 1830, when the Post Office decided to increase the frequency of mail service between Montreal and Upper Canada to five days a week from two, as of 6 January 1831.[45] Dickinson's refusal to send off a mail stage on Saturdays or Sundays that winter meant that the five-day service had to be performed Monday to Friday. Deputy Postmaster General Thomas Allen Stayner therefore ordered the Montreal post office to open for business on Sundays, to collect and sort the mail so that it would be ready to be picked up early on Mondays. Dickinson's observance of the Lord's Day resulted in the postal workers being required to defile it. This was too pharisaical for the *Vindicator*, which sneered at Dickinson, at the same time tarring the whole "pious sect" to which he belonged:

Mr Dickerson [*sic*], who has contracted for conveying the Mails to & from U. Canada has in his establishment some coach wheels and coach horses of a most godly and religious turn of thinking. They have, we are given to understand, absolutely refused to do the smallest act of bodily labour, that might be construed by the pious sect, of which they are most worthy members, into anything like disrespect for the Lord's day. In consequence of these praise worthy scruples, the thing of violating the sanctity of the Sabbath is thrown on the Post Master of this city, his assistants and the people of Montreal.[46]

The editorialist considered it intolerable that Dickinson should salve his conscience at others' expense. He offered a simple solution: "If any man scruple to convey the mails, at any time required, another should be looked for, who would not think the service of the public so objectionable."[47] Fortunately for Dickinson, the radical organ was far from having the ear of government. The Saturday stage, which he had run during the summer and dropped every fall as road conditions deteriorated and steamboats retired for the winter, was reintroduced only in June. It left Montreal at the ungodly hour of 2 a.m. so as to reach its destination before Sunday.[48] It was only in May 1833, it seems, a year after Dickinson's death, that Sunday postal work ended in Montreal; a new stage schedule provided for a 10 a.m. mail pickup on Mondays and other weekdays.[49]

Dickinson's Sabbatarianism was probably inspired by the activities of Evangelicals in his native country, who were waging a like battle. Decrying Sunday mail and stage services, they had formed the General Union for Promoting the Observance of the Christian Sabbath in 1828. Among their chief crusaders were brothers Arthur and Lewis Tappan of New York, who were to become leading figures of the abolitionist movement. The philanthropic Tappans were natives of Northampton, Massachusetts, and as it happened, Arthur Tappan had been in business in Montreal before the War of 1812. What is more, he was an admirer of the Reverend Joseph Stibbs Christmas, who, after leaving Montreal, briefly exercised his ministry in New York: Tappan had joined Christmas's Bowery Presbyterian Church, drawn by its young pastor and its support for anti-slavery.[50] The quixotic tactics of the Sabbath union soon gave it a reputation for dottiness and it did not last, but Sabbatarianism long remained a force on both sides of the border.[51]

Dickinson found time to serve on the executive of church-related bodies such as the Auxiliary Bible Society, the Auxiliary Religious Tract Society, the Canada Education and Home Missionary Society, and the Montreal Society for the Promotion of Temperance.[52] For an enterprising businessman, however, he was singularly absent from public affairs. There were no memberships in committees or associations pressing for changes to commercial or government policies. He took no part in various commissions established for the improvement of roads, the harbour, or inland navigation, for which one would have thought him suited. Unlike many men of his station, he never held an appointment as justice of the peace, and even from the published jury lists his name is noticeably absent. He may have avoided some of these commitments from personal inclination – he was not a public man – or because he could not spare the time. It is possible that some doors were closed to him as an "alien," or that he was considered to lack the right property qualification. In an age when the measure of a man's stake in the country rested on his ownership of real property, Dickinson owned none in Lower Canada until near the end of his life.

But his rigid sense of morality did not blind him to commercial realities. The key to his survival lay in adjusting to developments in the field of transport, especially on the Upper Canada route, his chief interest from first to last. There, as in a game of chess, every one of his moves constituted a pre-emptive strike or parry designed to preserve the integrity of his line.

In 1825 he jettisoned the connection with the aging *Perseverance* to launch his own steamer, the *St Lawrence*, on Lake St Louis with William McMaster, her builder and master. At about the same time, stage owner Emery Cushing and others with interests in the Ottawa valley launched the *St Andrews*. These developments on the water reflected progress on shore. A correspondent of the *Montreal Herald* noted that September "the sudden elevation of the Village of Beauharnois, the building of thirty five Houses, some of them of stone and two stories, in little more than two years, where not a house stood before … A convenient quay has been built, and 2 Steam-boats touch there almost daily."[53]

The *St Andrews* competed with the *St Lawrence* on Lake St Louis, but the Ottawa River was her goal. Her owners secured their hold on the lower Ottawa by building their lock at Vaudreuil in 1826. That fall, work began on the Rideau Canal under the supervision of Colonel John By of the Royal Engineers. Along with continuing efforts to build locks and canals on the Ottawa – work on the Grenville Canal, skirting the Long Sault, had been going on for seven years – these developments heralded the most serious challenge to Dickinson's line: an alternative steamboat route between Montreal and the Great Lakes. Once completed, the Rideau Canal – with its forty-seven locks, each 134 feet long and 33 feet wide – would carry boats, including small steamers, the 125 miles from the Ottawa, opposite Hull, to Lake Ontario at Kingston.

If the announcement of this massive public works project worried Dickinson, others had reason to cheer. "We congratulate you on the prospect of the commencement and early completion of a navigable canal from Kingston to the Ottawa river," Horatio Gates and Company wrote to Philemon Wright at Hull on 4 June 1826; "will not this be the making of you and your country altogether[!]"[54] There were more immediate benefits to be had. The shock waves of a financial crash in England in 1825 had reached Canada by the spring of 1826. Business sagged and several merchants faced ruin. Orders for new ships were suspended, and on 10 April there were layoffs at the shipyards at the foot of the St Mary's Current:[55] "Most work sites are idle. The company established to have ships built in Canada is laying off almost all of its workers, and the few remaining are paid half the usual wages. The government has even stopped all its work on St Helen's Island, Île aux Noix, Quebec &c. – More than three-quarters of the merchants did not manage to sell enough all winter to cover their costs."[56] The building of the Rideau Canal was therefore a godsend for many labourers, tradesmen, and contractors.

But the project was not just a make-work scheme. Improving the Ottawa-Rideau route was seen as a military necessity, a means of securing a safe back way for the movement of troops and supplies between Montreal and the Great Lakes. As a defensive work, the building of canals there was supervised by the military and paid for by Britain. Any such effort on the upper St Lawrence was out of the question: the works would be too vulnerable to capture or destruction in the event of another war with the United States. Seen as an essentially commercial proposition, canal building on the St Lawrence was left to colonial initiative. With prospects dim for any such improvements, the St Lawrence Association, founded in 1824, had explored a variety of less costly schemes to conquer the rapids. One idea it came up with was to harness the power of the current against itself. Cables fastened at the head of the current would be tied to the paddlewheels of shallow-draft steam towboats. The current would turn the paddlewheels, causing them to wind the cables and thus the boat would be cranked up the rapids. Ingenious in theory, the plan came to nothing.[57] So while the Ottawa-Rideau route was the focus of intensive development in the late 1820s, all the upper St Lawrence could boast of were the old military locks, barely able to accommodate Durham boats, between Lakes St Louis and St Francis and a similar private lock at Moulinette, near Cornwall.[58]

It would be a few years, however, before the Ottawa-Rideau route became a reality. The Rideau Canal itself would not open from end to end until 1832. The Grenville Canal, nearly six miles long and featuring seven masonry locks built of stone supplied by Thomas Mears,[59] was completed three years earlier, but it would be of limited use until two other downriver facilities, the lock at Chute à Blondeau and the two-mile Carillon Canal, were built. Contracts for the first were let only in 1829, and work on the Carillon Canal, with its three locks, would not start until 1830.

Both works would be finished by 1834, but even then the Grenville Canal would prove almost as frustrating as helpful to commercial navigation because of its mismatched locks. Four of them were roughly the same size as those on the Rideau, but the three others had been built on the smaller Lachine Canal scale (108 feet by 20 feet). The undersized locks would not be enlarged until the 1870s, meaning that for years the canal was open to only the smallest of steamers.

In the 1820s all the traffic between Montreal and the Great Lakes went on by the St Lawrence route. Dickinson strengthened his hand there in early 1826 by dissuading James Greenfield from launching his *Lady of the Lake* against the *Cornwall* on Lake St Francis. In the process, he secured Greenfield's pledge that he would "not under any pretence whatever, be concerned in any Steam Boat or Vessel in the Lake St Francis to the prejudice and Injury of the said Dickinson." Should Greenfield ever be tempted to go back on his word and try to take the *Lady* back to Lake St Francis, "it would require a team of sea-serpents to tow it up again," as one report put it.[60] That same year, Dickinson made plans to launch a second steamer of his own on the lake, the *Neptune*. The presence of his two steamers was bound to deter any potential challengers.

With her 67-horsepower Ward engine, the *Neptune* was to be the most powerful of Dickinson's steamers. This fact suggests that he and Asahel Whipple had set her a special task. An American guidebook offers some evidence of what that was. *The Northern Traveller and Northern Tour* (1830 edition) asserted that she was built "to pass the rapids at Côteau du Lac, and to take passengers to the village of the Cedars, nine miles further than heretofore by water." That plan must have been quickly dropped because Côteau remained the eastern terminal for steamers on Lake St Francis for more than a decade. In fact, around the same time that plans were made for the *Neptune*, Whipple secured a two-year lease for a waterfront lot at Côteau for the purpose of building a steamer wharf on it. The lease was to run from 1 May 1827.[61] The *Neptune* joined the Upper Canada Line the following September. She was 113 feet long in the keel, 22 feet wide, and drew $31\frac{1}{2}$ inches. How much Dickinson paid for her is not known, but in 1832 she was estimated to be worth £3,520, more than double the value of most of his other steamers.[62] She was built at Côteau by Alexander Young, who would later construct two more boats there for Dickinson.[63]

It was in 1827, too, that Dickinson obtained permission from William Waters, who then kept the Wellington Inn at the Cedars, to build a wharf and storehouse on a lot at the Cascades.[64] Dickinson had a woodyard there, leased from the government the previous year.[65] In 1827, however, he established his main Lake St Louis fuel depot at Beauharnois, a result of the connection that he formed with the Massons.

Eustache Masson, who had only recently moved to Beauharnois from Sainte-Geneviève on the island of Montreal, was one of those country merchants, then found in every district, who traded two ways. As a general storekeeper, he supplied villagers and farmers with a wide assortment of goods. Since hard cash was a rarity, he took in payment their timber, potash, wheat, and other products, which he resold to Montreal contractors, manufacturers, and businessmen. On 12 October 1827 he contracted to supply Dickinson with 800 cords of firewood. The wood, to be supplied as needed and costing a total of £240 (6s. per cord), was enough to keep the *St Lawrence* going for almost two years. Masson built his own wharf, stockpiling the wood on it. In 1831 he formed the partnership of E. et D. Masson with his son, Marc-Damase Masson. Even after Dickinson's death, the Massons would continue to supply the wood for the Upper Canada Line steamers on Lake St Louis, until disaster struck them and Beauharnois in the rebellion of 1838.[66]

At the upper end of the line, a connection was formed in 1827 at Prescott between Dickinson's stages and Robert and John Hamilton's lake steamer *Queenston*. Saturday's stage from Montreal reached Prescott in time to convey passengers to the steamer, which left at noon on Sunday for the trip up Lake Ontario to Niagara via Brockville, Kingston, and York. Similarly, on the downward journey, the steamer that left Niagara on Thursday connected with Friday's stage at Prescott. By 1829, three steamers – the *Queenston*, then belonging to John Hamilton, his older brother Robert's *Alciope*, and the *Niagara*, owned and commanded by John Mosier – were operating in conjunction with the Montreal stages, each sailing on different days between Prescott and Niagara.[67]

Perhaps because his business was more oriented toward passenger traffic than freight, Dickinson, unlike the owners of the *St Andrews*, took no steps to capitalize on the facilities offered by the Lachine Canal. In 1827 David Nelson, the former captain of the *St Andrews*, operated canal boats to haul freight to and from Montreal and the *St Andrews* at Lachine. Edward Connolly, a Lachine innkeeper and sometime prizefighter, succeeded Nelson as captain of the steamer. He was the one in charge on 6 May when she made the first steamboat crossing from Lachine to Caughnawaga. While it did not lead to the establishment of regular steam ferry service to Caughnawaga, this trial crossing suggests that the owners of the *St Andrews* were eager to test new waters in search of business.[68]

More important and portentous in the long run was the purchase of the steamer *William Annesley* by Ottawa River interests that same year. Her builder, Belfast-born William Annesley, who had plied his trade in the United States, Ireland, and England, had devised a method of building vessels which, he claimed, made them faster, safer, stronger, and more

The village of Lachine on the left and, opposite, the Mohawk village of Caughnawaga, c.1826; from an engraving by W. Walton, after John Greaves; the steamer
off Lachine is probably the *St Andrews* or the *St Lawrence* (NA/C-122928).

capacious than those built in the traditional way. His chief innovation
consisted, as he said,

in making the hull of the ship, boat, or other vessel of three or more layers of
planks, the direction of the grain of the alternate layers proceeding from bow to
stern of the vessel, and the direction of the grain of the intermediate layer or
layers passing from one gunwale around and under the vessel to the other gunwale
without being cut or separated by the keel, the whole of these planks being well
pinned, treenailed, or bolted together, without frame timbers, beams, knees, breast
hooks, or stem; the thickness and number of layers of plank must depend upon
the strength required for the tonnage of the vessel and the service in which she
is intended to be employed; for small boats, where great strength is not required,
I sometimes make use of only two courses of planking, that is to say, one outside
longitudinal layer, and one inner transverse layer.[69]

Over time, Annesley had also come to alter the shape of his boats, forsak-
ing the traditional sharp bow and square stern for a canoe-like shape.

    He was in Montreal in the spring of 1824, probably at the urging of
his son, William Jr, a gilder, carver, and mirror-maker.[70] Annesley Jr had
joined in a partnership in March 1823 to build and operate a passenger
ferry between Montreal and Île à La Pierre, just off the south bank of the

St Lawrence between Longueuil and La Prairie. Tenders were called on 22 January 1824 for the construction of a boat with a 72-foot keel, 80 feet long on deck and 16 feet wide, and a 6-foot depth of hold. On 13 May, Annesley Sr contracted with the company to build a steamboat according to his new system, guaranteeing that she would "exceed in strength and velocity the Steam Boats called the Montreal and Laprairie now navigating on the River St Lawrence." To be sure, the owners stipulated that the finished product would be subject to the approval of John Ward and Jahaziel Sherman. At that time, Sherman was himself experimenting with Annesley's designs.[71]

The *William Annesley* was described as a beautiful little boat, built "upon the exact model of a canoe." She was 57 tons burden, 79 feet in length, and 17 feet 2 inches wide, with an iron-braced deck 28 feet broad and a $5\frac{1}{2}$-foot depth of hold. The hull consisted of five courses of planks, "two fore and aft, of one inch pine each, two transverse of half inch oak each, and one outside of one inch Oak, with Deck in three courses of one inch pine each extending to the guards all round." Launched on 30 July, she was fitted with an engine of 20 horsepower built by John Ward. He, in fact, had subscribed for one £50 share in the boat in 1823 – "in case I build the Engine." He got his contract, worth £950.[72]

The boat underwent her first trial on 10 September 1824. By July 1825, when she was registered at Quebec, the more than thirty original shareholders had dwindled to nine. Ward was not among them, nor was Annesley Sr, who may by then have moved on to Upper Canada, where another steamer built on his system, the *Toronto*, had been launched that April. Within a year, ownership of the *William Annesley* passed to contractor and real-estate developer Stanley Bagg and builder Andrew White. Then by December 1826 the word was out that, after a refit that winter, she was to be taken up the Ottawa to ply between Grenville and Hull.[73]

It might be supposed that White, who was to be one of the contractors on the Rideau Canal,[74] was behind this plan. He did buy out Bagg's half-share in the boat on 22 February 1827, only to turn around and sell the whole concern that same day for £900 to a trio from La Prairie – notary and land agent Edmund Henry and carriers Hypolite Denaut, *dit* Jérémie, and Louis-René Bauzet. Their interests had always lain in local traffic between Montreal and the south shore. At this time, besides the steamers *Laprairie* and *Edmund Henry*, they owned most of the shares in the *Montreal*, of which Denaut's brother, François, was captain. Venturing up the Ottawa would have constituted a major departure and, in fact, they did no such thing. The *William Annesley* sat idle until Thomas Mears bought her on 30 August for £875.[75]

If Mears was the intended purchaser from the start, that would account for the report of 1826 that the *William Annesley* was bound for the

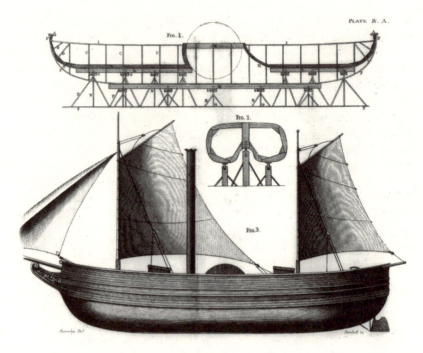

William Annesley's design for a single-wheel steam packet launched in England
in 1822; the *William Annesley/William King*, which Annesley built in Montreal
in 1824, had the same canoe-like shape, but two paddlewheels (reproduced from
Annesley, *A New System of Naval Architecture*, plate iva; courtesy, National
Maritime Museum, Greenwich).

Ottawa. But why had he not bought the boat directly from Bagg and
White? The mystery did not end there. A companion agreement to the
contract of sale bound the vendors, under pain of a £100 penalty, to
pretend that they remained the owners of the boat. They were not to
disclose the sale or any detail of it. The sales contract was drawn up in
English, the secrecy compact in French.[76]

This agreement to deceive stated that "the object of Mr Mears would
be frustrated were it known that such was his views in acquiring the said
boat."[77] But nowhere were Mears's views stated except in a crossed-out
paragraph which the agreement declared to be void: "That the said Mr
Mears does make the acquisition of the said boat only with a view to
prevent the competition which might arise should other persons establish
another steamboat on the Ottawa River where the said Mr Mears already
has one."[78] If Mears's purpose was to deter competition, it is hard to see
how he stood to achieve this by keeping his purchase a secret. His aging

Union, overhauled in 1826, had had the Grenville-Hull route to herself for nearly five years. With work progressing on the Rideau Canal and the new settlement of Bytown rising across from Hull, there was room and business for a second, faster steamer on the Ottawa. It had been public knowledge for almost a year that the *William Annesley* was headed that way; no one would have been surprised to learn that Mears was behind the move.

The affair must be put down to the jockeying for position that went on as powerful Montreal interests, notably John Molson and Sons, prepared to enter the navigation business on the Ottawa. The evidence shows that Mears, already in debt over his head, was in league with – if not acting as a tool of – Montreal merchant Peter McGill, then thirty-eight years of age and vice-president of the Bank of Montreal. It was McGill who signed the sales contract and secrecy agreement, acting in Mears's name; he also guaranteed payment for the boat, in the name of Peter McGill and Company, and he paid for it in full over the next three years.[79]

Five days after the contract of sale was signed, Mears turned up in Montreal to ratify it. On the same occasion he signed a lumber contract with McGill and Horatio Gates which makes clear that he owed the McGill and Gates companies "various large sums of money which he is unable to pay without further support to carry on his business in its various branches."[80] Even more telling is the deed he signed the following day, transferring ownership and control of the *William Annesley* to McGill.[81] The Montreal merchant, it turns out, had signed as guarantor for Mears on 30 August on the express understanding "that the said Steamboat the William Annesley should be transferred to him by an absolute Bill of Sale thereof and that he, the said Peter McGill, should have the Controul thereof so long as the said Thomas Mears shall not have paid the whole sum for which the said Peter McGill thus stands engaged." Any idea that Mears's association with the *William Annesley* was to remain a secret was here exploded since he agreed

to take upon himself to navigate the said Boat, to pay all its expenses & to have the advantage of its earnings, but the whole until due redemption to be made thereof to be under the Controul and Interference of the Said Peter McGill, his heirs and Assigns, whose orders will be executed so far that should he wish the said boat not to ply or to go in another direction, he may do so & his order to be obeyed.

So Mears was to be the ostensible owner, but McGill was to pull the strings. The secrecy agreement thus seems to have been meant to veil McGill's manœuvring more than Mears's.

Stripped of her paddlewheels and machinery, the *William Annesley* was towed through the Lachine Canal and up the Ottawa in the fall of 1827.

RATES OF PASSAGE

FOR THE

OTTAWA
STAGE & STEAMBOATS,

FROM

MONTREAL TO BYTOWN.

CABIN UPWARDS.

	£	s.	d.
From Montreal to Lachine,	0	3	9
Ditto Vaudreuil Locks,	0	10	9
Ditto Lake Two Mountains,	0	12	6
Ditto Carrillon,	0	17	6
Ditto Chatham;	1	0	0
Ditto Grenville;	1	2	6
Ditto Bytown,	1	17	6

CABIN DOWNWARDS.

	£	s.	d.
From Bytown to Grenville;	0	12	6
Ditto Chatham	0	15	0
Ditto Carrillon	0	17	6
Ditto Lake Two Mountains,	1	2	6
Ditto Vaudreuil Locks,	1	3	9
Ditto Lachine,	1	10	0
Ditto Montreal;	1	12	6

DECK UPWARDS.

	£	s.	d.
From Montreal to Lachine,	0	3	9
Ditto Vaudreuil Locks,	0	5	9
Ditto Lake Two Mountains,	0	6	3
Ditto Carrillon,	0	8	9
Ditto Chatham,	0	11	3
Ditto Grenville,	0	12	6
Ditto Bytown,	0	17	6

DECK DOWNWARDS.

	£	s.	d.
From Bytown to Grenville,	0	5	0
Ditto Chatham,	0	7	6
Ditto Carrillon,	0	8	9
Ditto Lake Two Mountains,	0	11	3
Ditto Vaudreuil Locks,	0	11	9
Ditto Lachine,	0	13	9
Ditto Montreal,	0	16	3

STAGE PASSAGE only, from CARRILLON to GRENVILLE, 5s.,
And from GRENVILLE to CARRILLON, 5s.

Passage to Petite Nation from
Montreal 3rd Cabin — £1.10.0
downwards — 1.6.3
deck passengers — 5
downwards — the same as up

Two handbills from about the late 1820s.

TARIFF OF FREIGHT
Between Montreal and Bytown,
PER THE
OTTAWA STEAMBOATS.

				£	s.	d.
From Montreal to Lachine,	- - - per cwt.			0	0	4
Ditto	Vaudreuil Locks,	- -		0	0	10
Ditto	Lake of Two Mountains,	- -		0	1	0
Ditto	Carrillon or Rigaud,	- -		0	1	1
Ditto	Chatham,	- - -		0	1	8½
Ditto	Grenville,	- - -		0	2	1
Ditto	Petite Nation,	- - -				*3.8½*
Ditto	Buckingham,	- - -				*2.10*
Ditto	Bytown,	- - -		0	2	11

ASHES PER BARREL.

			£	s.	d.
From Bytown	to Montreal,	- - -	0	11	3
Petite Nation	to ditto,	- -	0	10	0
Grenville	to ditto,	- -	0	8	9
Chatham	to ditto,	- -	0	6	3
Carrillon	to ditto,	- -	0	3	9
Lake of Two Mountains	to ditto,	- -	0	3	0
Vaudreuil Locks	to ditto,	- -	0	2	6
Lachine	to ditto,	- -	0	1	6

				£	s.	d.
CARRIAGES, &c.	Four Wheel double,	Lachine to Vaudreuil,	- - -	0	7	6
		Ditto to Carrillon,	- - -	0	15	0
		Grenville to Bytown,	- -	0	15	0
	Common Waggon, single, or 2 wheel vehicles	Lachine to Vaudreuil,	- -	0	5	0
		Ditto to Carrillon,	- -	0	10	0
		Grenville to Bytown,	- -	0	10	0

				£	s.	d.
CATTLE, &c.	Oxen each,	Lachine to Vaudreuil,	- - -	0	5	0
		Ditto to Carrillon,	- -	0	10	0
		Grenville to Bytown,	- -	0	10	0
	Cows each,	Lachine to Vaudreuil,	- -	0	3	9
		Ditto to Carrillon,	- -	0	7	6
		Grenville to Bytown,	- -	0	7	6
	Sheep, Hogs & Calves, each,	Lachine to Vaudreuil,	- -	0	2	6
		Ditto to Carrillon,	- -	0	5	0
		Grenville to Bytown,	- -	0	5	0
	Horses, each,	Lachine to Vaudreuil,	- -	0	5	0
		Ditto to Carrillon,	- -	0	10	0
		Grenville to Bytown,	- -	0	10	0

UPWARD OR DOWNWARD.

(Bodleian Library, Oxford, MS.Eng.Lett.c 175, fols. 139r and 140r)

She was renamed the *William King,* after the Royal Staff Corps captain in charge of work on the Grenville Canal, who had been posted back to England that autumn; she would run between Grenville and Bytown in 1828, performing the 56-mile journey in ten hours, where the *Union* often took twice that time. William Grant assumed command of her, while Eden Johnson replaced him as captain of the *Union.*[82]

Beginning in January 1828, on instructions from McGill, Mears pressed the Wrights and Captain Grant, by then the only other shareholders in the *Union,* to come to a final settling of accounts for that boat. For some reason, Grant raised objections and stalled. In June he was warned that his funds to operate the boat would be cut off unless he agreed to arbitration.[83]

Then came news that was to bring a radical change to the navigation on the Ottawa, and ultimately on the St Lawrence as well. "I presume you have heard of the new Boat that is to be built," Mears wrote to Ruggles Wright in August 1828. He was referring to the *Shannon,* a steamer that was to be built at Hawkesbury by Montreal shipwright Richard Fleming, under the supervision of Mears's arch-rival, George Hamilton.[84] She was to be equipped with the two English-made, 28-horsepower engines taken from the Molsons' St Lawrence steamer *Quebec,* launched a decade earlier. The owners were a new joint-stock company, the Ottawa Steamboat Company, dominated by John Molson and Sons, Horatio Gates, and Maine-born hardware wholesaler John Frothingham. "I have a letter from Mr McGill who says that there is no use in trying to keep off the opposition That Molson & Sons find the engine Hamilton Laws Buchanan Alexr Grant &c have taken up the remainder of the Stock and Mr McGill says that our Capt Grant is to command her."[85]

The problem of settling the *Union's* accounts went unresolved, Grant severing his connection with his old partners in 1829, well before Mears and the Wrights finally went to arbitration in April 1831.[86] The new company, meanwhile, was slow in starting up, and the suspense was killing Mears. To make matters worse, the *William King* was badly damaged on 14 October 1829 when she hit a rock and sank; at the same time the *Union* was so decrepit as to be all but washed up.[87]

In January 1830 McGill pulled off a coup that would give him a good bargaining chip in dealing with the new company. He bought the *St Andrews* and the rights to the Vaudreuil lock that went with her.[88] Still, Mears wrote anxiously to Philemon Wright and Sons:

Pray what are we to do with the Union She is quite rotten Between wind and water. I wish you would come down and examine her if she is to be repaired there is not much time to loose. I think she may be repaired to last at all Events one more Season to annoy the opposition We can not Expect to make any money, but we can prevent them I am anxious to see you that we may decide what we will do I hope to see or hear from you soon They are pushing on their new Boat as fast as possible and will no doubt have her done early.[89]

In a postscript, Mears added, "I tried hard to sell out Both Wm King & Union to Molson But they would not Buy they Expect to drive us off of the River into Hudsons Bay." Hearing nothing from the Wrights, he fired off several more letters in the same vein. In mid-March he informed them that McGill had sent word that "he can make no arrangement with Moulson therefore we must Strike or run an opposition."[90]

The *Shannon* was launched on 3 May. Under William Grant's command, she left Hawkesbury on 28 May to begin her regular runs between Grenville and Bytown the next day.[91] She vied for business with the *William King* and the *Union*, but not for long. The heated competition ended within a month, "terminated by the proprietors of the Steamboat Shannon purchasing the Steamboats and Stages on the whole line, from Montreal to Bytown."[92]

The Vaudreuil lock was undoubtedly a key to the bargain. The *Shannon* would have given the new company an edge on the river between Grenville and Bytown, but the lock assured it of virtual control of the whole lower river, an opportunity it hastened to embrace. While the *Shannon* remained on the Grenville-Bytown route, the company ran the *William King* down to Lake St Louis in July, to sail between Lachine and Point Fortune on alternate days to the *St Andrews*.[93]

CHAPTER FIVE

Coming to Grips

Drawn by the potential of the Ottawa-Rideau route, the moneyed men of Montreal left Horace Dickinson in peace on the St Lawrence. He did encounter some competition on Lake St Louis in 1828–29. Strangely enough, two of his American cousins were involved. Though mostly of a small, local nature, the challenges were sufficiently important in his eyes to call for special measures.

Some of the more active residents of Châteauguay and the seigneury of Beauharnois, seeking to improve trade and transportation links with Montreal, had been exploring the possibility of acquiring a boat to provide ferry service between Châteauguay and Lachine. In the summer of 1827 they had approached Silas and Erastus Dickinson, distant younger cousins of Horace and, like him, natives of Hatfield, Massachusetts, who had just begun running a horse ferry, the *Experiment*, between the area of present-day Verdun, on the island of Montreal, and La Tortue (now Saint-Mathieu), near La Prairie.[1] The matter was settled on 22 February 1828 when Silas and Erastus Dickinson formed a joint-stock company with twenty men of Beauharnois and Châteauguay, including Jacob De Witt's younger brother, Charles, a former Montrealer and now a Châteauguay bailiff. When it came to purchasing shares, local support fell short of what the Dickinsons had been led to expect. In the end, they were left holding $72\frac{1}{2}$ of the $87\frac{1}{2}$ shares. But the horse boat had been brought up to Lake St Louis by then, and the *Experiment* went to work as agreed, with Erastus Dickinson in command.[2]

A horse ferry had run between St Anne and Vaudreuil, just above the rapids, from 1823,[3] but the *Experiment* was the first boat of this kind on Lake St Louis. A sidewheeler powered by four horses, she was 68 feet long, 15 feet 9 inches in breadth, but with an extended deck 27 feet wide to carry freight and her machinery, and with a depth of hold of slightly more than 5 feet.[4] While she may not have presented a serious threat to the *St Lawrence*, there was the possibility that her owners might eventually expand their business, perhaps launch a steamboat to challenge Horace Dickinson on other parts of the lake. He would deal with such a challenge.

On 17 February, he had taken over full control of the *St Lawrence*, buying out William McMaster's interest for £940 and a promise to pay off debts owed to Montreal suppliers.[5] Then on 17 April, while ice below the rapids at Point Fortune kept the Ottawa River closed to navigation, he had the *Cornwall* brought down through the rapids from Côteau to Lachine. It marked the first time that a steamer had shot those rapids with her engine, paddlewheels, and all her machinery on board. The *Cornwall* was to run in tandem with the *St Lawrence* between Lachine and the Cascades, leaving Asahel Whipple and the new *Neptune* to handle the traffic on Lake St Francis.[6]

In mid-July, Dickinson strayed from his beaten path and sent the *St Lawrence* up the Ottawa to Point Fortune. The fact that she worked her way up the rapids instead of passing through the Vaudreuil lock suggests that he was defying the monopoly of the *St Andrews*.[7] What Dickinson's motives were it is impossible to say with certainty. He may have meant this intrusion to be a warning to the owners of the *St Andrews*. Nettled by that boat's experimental trip to Caughnawaga the previous year, which he viewed as an incursion on his territory,[8] he was possibly signalling them that he was ready to retaliate on the Ottawa should they take any steps to expand their operations on the St Lawrence. But Dickinson may also have been looking ahead to the completion of the Rideau Canal, still almost four years off, and the opening of the Ottawa-Rideau route. News of the formation of the Ottawa Steamboat Company and its plans to place a powerful steamer on the Ottawa had begun circulating at about the same time that he sent the *St Lawrence* up that river.[9] The new company was positioning itself to outflank his Upper Canada Line once the canal opened. Dickinson may have considered joining battle on the Ottawa-Rideau route itself by placing steamers there as well as on the St Lawrence. In that regard, remarks made the following year about another boat in which he held an interest, the *Dalhousie*, are suggestive. When she became the first steamer to pass under the Cataraqui drawbridge at what was to be the Kingston end of the Rideau Canal, a newspaper remarked; "The *Dalhousie*, we learn, is to be taken as the model of the steam-boats which, at no distant day, are destined to ply on this route."[10] It is even conceivable that Dickinson envisaged the possibility of joining the two routes, sending boats up the Ottawa-Rideau to Kingston and back down by the St Lawrence. Whatever his intentions in 1828, the *St Lawrence*, after making Point Fortune, sailed back to Lachine and did not return to the Ottawa.

Another twist came on 8 August when he leased the *Cornwall* to Gregory Dunning, a Châteauguay farmer, tavern-keeper, and sometime ferryman, and James Perrigo, a merchant of Sainte-Martine, on the Châteauguay River, who had earlier operated a batteau ferry between Lachine and Caughnawaga. The terms of the lease provide an insight into Dickinson's preoccupations. Dunning and Perrigo were required to retain the existing crew; they were to use the boat only as a ferry between Lachine and Châteauguay and not to run her to the Cascades, Beauharnois, or any other part of the St Lawrence where Dickinson operated; and she was not to run on Sundays. The lease was valid for three months at the most. Dunning and Perrigo were to pay 15 shillings for every day the *Cornwall* ran.[11]

By November a group of Châteauguay men that included Perrigo's brother, Robert, had made other arrangements for the following year. For £1,200 they had bought the controlling interest – ten of eleven shares – in the *Montreal*, held by Edmund Henry, Hypolite Denaut, dit Jérémie, and Louis-René Bauzet.[12] The old warhorse had been modified since 1820, when her engine had marked John Ward's first Canadian triumph. A mast and sail had been added to her in 1823, and in the winter of 1826–27 she was said to have been "made much larger."[13] Now she was to compete with the *Experiment* on the ferry run between Lachine and Châteauguay. There was no lease with restrictive clauses forbidding her to sail to other points on the lake or to run on Sundays, as there had been with the *Cornwall*.

No account seems to have survived of when or how the *Montreal* was brought up to Lake St Louis. It must have been in the late fall of 1828. Under Captain Pierre Dupuis of Châteauguay, formerly a smith in Montreal, she went into service on 24 April 1829, when the lake was barely clear of ice. Dickinson's *St Lawrence* did not leave her wintering ground at Beauharnois until five days later; even then, she did not start for the Cascades for another few days because an accumulation of ice, known as *la bride du loup* (the wolf's collar), at the mouth of the Ottawa blocked access to the steamer wharf there.[14]

With the *Cornwall*, *St Lawrence*, *St Andrews*, *Montreal*, and *Experiment*, Lake St Louis was getting altogether too busy. There was business to be done there, certainly, but within limits. Attesting to the growing role of the lakeshore villages, postmasters were appointed in 1829 at Lachine, Châteauguay, and Beauharnois.[15] Curtis Elkins Crossman, the American-born captain of the *St Lawrence*, was chosen to operate the post office at Lachine. At Châteauguay the postmaster was Arthur McDonald, government-appointed inspector of rafts and one of the shareholders in the *Experiment*. Thomas McDonald, a former trader at Montreal who had moved to the village of Beauharnois, was named postmaster there.[16]

Throughout this year, Dickinson pressed on with his campaign to tighten his hold on the lake. His first move came on 22 January when he leased a storehouse and rickety wharf at Lachine from brewer Thomas Dawes. It was a ten-year lease: Dickinson was digging in for the long haul. He was to pay no rent for the first five years, then £15 a year for the second five. In return for this low rent, he was to build "a good and substantial wharf," which would revert to Dawes when the lease expired.[17] That summer he would establish a boat-repair facility on the property, through an arrangement with shipbuilder Jean Desnoyers of Quebec. Dickinson supplied the land and Desnoyers undertook to build an "inclined plain" on which to haul up the boats to be repaired. Desnoyers agreed to repair Dickinson's steamers at the going Montreal shipyard rates, Dickinson reserving the right to claim up to £5 from other steamboat owners who availed themselves of the facilities.[18]

On 27 February he bought Silas Dickinson's $35\frac{1}{4}$ shares in the *Experiment* for £155. Later that year he would pick up Erastus Dickinson's $37\frac{1}{4}$ shares in the boat for the same price.[19] The competition between the *Experiment* and the *Montreal* on the Lachine-Châteauguay run was sharp that summer, and not without incident. On 14 August both boats were entering the mouth of the Châteauguay River, which was crowded with rafts of timber and produce coming out. The space left in the channel was too narrow for the two boats to pass abreast, so they raced to be first in. The more-powerful *Montreal* won the contest, forcing the horse boat to veer off and run up on one of the rafts. No one was injured and the *Experiment* was undamaged, though her passengers were understandably shaken.[20]

Steam technology may have given the *Montreal* the edge over the horse boat between Lachine and Châteauguay, but her operators did not challenge Dickinson elsewhere on the lake. Throughout the summer his *St Lawrence* left Lachine at 1 p.m. every weekday and at 6 a.m. on Saturdays, two hours after the departure times of the Upper Canada stage from Montreal. True to his scruples, he did not operate her on Sundays. That would have left the field clear to the *Montreal*, had her owners chosen to take advantage of the opening. Sunday being Sunday, they did not, beyond running a couple of pleasure excursions around the lake.[21] Besides, it seems that she was too unreliable to win much favour with the locals, "for unless under full way, the boat steered badly and from her boiler being too small, steam would run low. She would get out of the channel, and run aground, which happened often enough to give her a bad name."[22]

Once more, Dickinson did not employ the *Cornwall* on his line this year. At first she remained out of action, undergoing a refit. Then on 27 July he leased her to the St Andrews Steam Boat Company for £150. She went into service on the Ottawa River line two days later, under a

Captain Scott.[23] For the rest of the season, the *St Andrews* continued her scheduled three trips a week from Lachine to Point Fortune, and the *Cornwall* sailed on alternate days, the two boats thus offering a daily service (Sundays excepted) on that route.[24] The leasing of the *Cornwall* was one more coup for Dickinson in staking his claim to Lake St Louis: the lessees had to promise not to run either of their steamers "to the Cascades or Beauharnois and not to injure in any way the said Horace Dickinson in his line from Lachine to Cascades aforesaid."[25]

By the end of the summer, then, he had eliminated one rival, the *Experiment*, by buying up the majority of her shares and disposed of the other, the *St Andrews*, by cutting her out of the Lachine-Beauharnois-Cascades circuit. He also had the repair yard at Lachine, though problems cropped up there soon enough. The facility seems to have been built by 15 September, as agreed, but a month later Dickinson was complaining that Desnoyers had so far been unable to haul the *St Lawrence* up for some badly needed repairs. Worse, he had absconded, leaving no one behind to carry on the work.[26]

New business had also come Dickinson's way. Four days after he leased the *Cornwall*, he secured a contract from the York-based Bank of Upper Canada to transport the regular shipments of cash and bank notes between Forsyth, Richardson and Company, the bank's agents at Montreal, and Alpheus Jones, its representative at Prescott. Dickinson was to be paid £2 for every £1,000 of specie he transported and £3 15s. to cover the expenses of every round trip by the "confidential and suitable person" he was to hire to take charge of the shipments.[27]

Along with the changes on Lake St Louis, improvements were made on Lake St Francis. After Dickinson and Whipple had built their new wharf for the *Neptune* at Côteau in 1827, it had become apparent that facilities at Cornwall were unfit for their new boat. The landing place, they said, was "extremely inconvenient from the narrow channel leading to it & the number of shoals which make it next to impossible to go in or out of the Harbour of Cornwall." They looked for a new landing place and in 1829 built a wharf at the foot of Augustus Street. In December the government of Upper Canada permitted them to occupy two lots adjoining the wharf. On the west side of Augustus Street, they built a warehouse. A half-acre lot on the east side served as a woodyard for the steamer.[28]

For the Dickinson circle in Montreal, the year 1829 was notable for two events, one uniting it, the other presaging its dissolution. First, Lebbeus Ward and Dimmis Dickinson were married, on 8 September.[29] Only a month later John Ward, his wife, and two daughters – they had lost three other girls in six years, the last one only that August – moved to Vergennes. Ward acquired the rights to the Monkton Iron Company property, built a foundry, and prospered. He even ran for public office, something he had never done in Canada: he served as mayor of Vergennes from 1833 to 1836. He then sold his business there and moved to New York.[30]

Ward retained his interest in the Eagle Foundry for three years after his departure from Montreal. He took no hand in the management of John D. Ward and Company but continued to draw his £150 yearly salary. On a visit to Montreal in February 1830, he agreed that his brothers should receive a salary commensurate with their new responsibilities: from £75 a year, their salary jumped to £250, retroactive to 1 October, when John Ward had ceased to be actively involved in the affairs of the company. John D. Ward and Company was finally dissolved on 23 November 1832, when Lebbeus and Samuel Ward bought out their older brother's half-interest for £5,000. The twins then formed a new fifty-fifty partnership, called Ward and Company, to continue running the Eagle Foundry. Each drew a salary of £400 a year.[31]

Fate – and the ten-to-fifteen-year lifespan of hulls and boilers[32] – decreed that the *Montreal*, which had marked John Ward's arrival on the Canadian scene, should give up the ghost soon after his departure. Her demise in the spring of 1830 played into Dickinson's hands, opening a niche for the *Cornwall* on Lake St Louis. The latter boat would not be needed on the Ottawa this year as the new Ottawa Steamboat Company replaced her with the *William King* on the Lachine–Point Fortune run.

Scarred and patched many times in her career, the *Montreal* was said to have been thoroughly overhauled the previous winter.[33] Captain Dupuis, however, may have had his doubts about her. When he hired millwright James Bothwell of Ormstown as engineer on 14 April – for 6s. 6d. a day, plus room and board and a daily allowance of three tots of liquor – he did so not for the navigation season, as such contracts usually stipulated, but "for as long as the steamboat operates during the navigation season of the present year."[34] On 10 May she broke down. The public was told not to worry; she would be back in business in a week. But the *Montreal* does not appear to have run again on Lake St Louis, unless it was to limp downriver to her final resting place. The sale to the Châteauguay men must have been cancelled since the La Prairie trio of Henry, Denaut, and Bauzet were back in possession of their ten shares by 30 June. On that date they complained that the boat was lying at Longueuil in dire need of repairs, but that Guy Warwick and Company, owners of the eleventh share, refused to pay a penny toward the cost of breathing new life into the carcass. And that was the end of the *Montreal*.[35]

With the *Montreal* out of the running, Dickinson, who had by now acquired all but 3 of the $87\frac{1}{2}$ shares in the *Experiment*, was free to make new arrangements in the ferry service between Lachine and Châteauguay. He put the *Experiment* up for sale on 14 July and placed the *Cornwall* on the ferry run with Silas Dickinson in command.[36]

In another development this year, Peter McGill, Horatio Gates, and other Montreal merchants and forwarders formed the Canada Inland Assurance Company to compete with Abijah Bigelow, agent of the Protection Insurance Company, in the business of insuring boats and cargoes on inland waters from Quebec to Detroit. The new concern opened for business in August.[37] It was not long before Bigelow had other woes to contend with. On 15 November his wife, Susan, died. She was only twenty-five and left two young children, ages four and five.[38] For his sister, Mercy Amelia, and her husband, the year ended on a happier note. On 31 December she gave birth to a girl, Ellen Maria. This was the fifth child born to her and Horace Dickinson in a little more than six years. She was also their last. They lived then in the St Mary suburb, in a rented house whose previous tenants had included John Molson Jr, Charles Christopher Johnson, seigneur of Argenteuil, and most recently, a lieutenant of the Royal Staff Corps. The Dickinsons were doing well.[39]

Over the years, Dickinson had made changes to the stage services to Upper Canada as well as in his steamboat arrangements. Operating initially between Montreal and Kingston, he had withdrawn his summer stages from the Prescott-to-Kingston leg, beginning in 1818, and then his winter stages as well. While he held on to contracts to carry the mail between Montreal and Kingston – and all the way to York from 1827 on[40] – he operated his stages only as far west as Prescott, entrusting the business of mail carriage beyond that point to steamers or to other stage owners. From 1823 Hiram Norton ran the stages between Prescott and Kingston. In the winter of 1827 Norton teamed up with Jonathan Ogden to operate a stage line between Kingston and York. Then in 1829 Norton and Vermont native William Weller bought out Ogden's interest. Weller took over full control of the Kingston-York route the following year, Norton continuing to run stages between Prescott and Kingston. Thus in the winter of 1830–31, while Dickinson held the mail contract, he subcontracted the carriage of the mail between Prescott and Kingston to Norton, and between Kingston and York to Weller.[41]

This shortening of the Upper Canada Line was not to everyone's liking, particularly in winter, when there was no choice of travelling on by water. In the mid-1830s a traveller set out his beef in writing, shedding light on the ups and downs of traffic in the early days of Dickinson's stage line and providing a clue as to why he had abandoned the Prescott-Kingston route:

The mail which the Line carries is sent onward [from Prescott] to Kingston by different sorts of conveyances, as suits the convenience of the sub-contractor; but passengers having taken seats at Montreal, not expecting any interruption in the Line, are set down at Prescott, and left to make their way as they best may to Kingston, (a distance of about 70 miles,) where they can again take seats for Toronto and other parts of the Province.

The Exchange Coffee House, whose courtyard served
as the Montreal terminus of the Upper Canada Line
from 1827 to 1839 (from the *Daily Witness*, 7 December 1896/courtesy E.A. Collard).

There was a time when the country was newer, and comparatively poor, when
the population was fewer, and travelling much less than at present, the proprietors
of the Stage Line on this route, who enjoyed the profits of the business during
the summer – when there was most travelling – kept up a comfortable and regular
conveyance during the winter months, though the business was less profitable
during that period, and though, then as now, the portion of the route lying
between Prescott and Kingston was less profitable than any other part.[42]

In Montreal, Dickinson had also relocated his stage office. After five
years on McGill Street, he had moved in May 1826 to temporary quarters
around the corner on College Street, in the same block of buildings as
the Molsons' new Mansion House Hotel, between Longueuil Lane and St
Henri Street, leasing the tin-roofed stone stables behind the hotel.[43] After
only one year there, he moved his office in May 1827 to a new, two-
storey brick building, constructed expressly as a stage office, in the courtyard of Asa Goodenough's Exchange Coffee House.[44] This popular hotel,
located at the northeast corner of St Paul and St Peter streets, was the
former City Tavern, where the American Presbyterian Society had held

its founding meeting in 1822. Goodenough, whom Dickinson may have known in his youth – they came from the same neck of the Massachusetts woods[45] – had leased the premises after the death of the previous occupant and opened his hotel in the winter of 1823–24. It now became a coaching inn. "Judges, lawyers, travellers, all went to the Exchange Coffee House in Exchange Court," George Brush's son later recalled; and Goodenough "kept the establishment in fine style – and good enough it was for the best."[46] He kept the Exchange Coffee House until 1836. The Upper Canada stage office remained in the hotel courtyard until May 1839.[47]

Thomas Fowler, a Scotsman travelling on business in 1831, left a user's-eye view of how the stage-and-steamboat line operated out of Montreal at that time. On Saturday, 11 June, he and a fellow traveller made plans to leave Montreal for the journey upriver:

From Montreal to Prescott is one hundred and forty miles, and the regular fare by the stage is eight dollars; so we engaged a passage for Monday morning ... People going up the country who have heavy luggage, must give it in charge to a forwarder, and they send goods or luggage to any port on Lake Ontario, for about half a dollar per cwt. ... [On Monday morning, 13 June] immediately after four, the coach drove up in front of the building ... The coaches in this country are much larger inside than those of Britain; the back and front seats are sufficiently large to hold three passengers each, with room betwixt for a seat to hold another three; so a full complement in a stage coach here is nine persons. However, there are no outside passengers, neither is there a guard; the tops of the coaches are railed in, and appropriated to convey passengers' luggage, also a place on the back capable of holding two or three trunks; and each passenger is allowed a small trunk or other light luggage. The company here keep coaches in reserve; so when the way bill is made up, there are as many coaches ordered to the office as are required to convey the whole of the passengers. The office of this establishment is in the court of the Exchange Coffee House, St Paul's Street. When the coaches have collected the passengers from the various hotels, they meet here before starting. It appeared by the way bill, that the number of passengers this morning amounted to thirty-four; this required four coaches, and each is drawn by four horses, so when they started from Montreal, within a short distance of each other, in the stillness of a fine summer morning, they presented a lively scene as they drove out the Lachine road.[48]

It was a simple enough matter to supply the requisite number of coaches for the start of a journey. But before the electric telegraph or telephone, how were employees at intermediate points to know how many carriages to prepare to meet the boats? One of them later recorded that "we had no means of knowing how many stages each steamer should

A stagecoach on the road from Montreal to Lachine; from an 1839 watercolour by James Duncan (Bibliothèque de la Ville de Montréal, Album Jacques Viger, plate 258, neg. 214).

require except by the sounding of a bell – one stroke for each stage. We could hear the bell a long distance on the water of course."[49] In a similar manner, a stage driver could warn innkeepers at a distance of the number of guests to prepare for by blowing short blasts on his horn, the number corresponding to the number of his passengers.[50]

While little is known of the stages that Dickinson used in the early days, by about 1830 he had begun to import Concord coaches, manufactured since 1827 by Abbot and Downing of Concord, New Hampshire. At first, he employed them only on the road between Montreal and Lachine. These celebrated flat-topped, round-bottomed vehicles were marvels of their day, well suited to the rugged roads of North America. Light-bodied but with a tough, heavy undercarriage and rugged hickory or ash wheels, they were mainly distinguished by their thoroughbrace suspension. Instead of resting on steel springs, they sat on several thicknesses of leather strapping, or thoroughbraces, running lengthwise under each side of the body and securing it to the undercarriage. Wells Fargo would later

use Concord coaches to criss-cross the American west, and the same
vehicles would make their mark as far away as South America, South
Africa, and Australia.[51]

Besides Fowler, several travellers left a record of their journeys in these
coaches. "They are Yankee made, drawn by four horses, but carry no
outside passengers save one with the coachman," Montrealer Charles
Kadwell noted when he travelled to Upper Canada in 1838.

They are undoubtedly the best adapted to the roads of the country, being very
substantially built, & the springs regulated in such a manner as to obviate as
much as possible the ups and downs of a wretched road, for be it borne in mind,
there are here no turnpikes ... I have only seen but one stage coach in the country,
pretending to anything like the English build; it travelled the Ottawa route, &
was styled L'Hirondelle.[52]

A near-fatal accident aboard the *St Lawrence* in the summer of 1831
shows that not only were stage and steamboat schedules synchronized,
but services were sometimes piggybacked. After leaving the Cascades for
Lachine on 19 July, the boat was caught in a severe thunderstorm. Four
people sought shelter in a mail stage which had been placed on board to
be conveyed to Lachine. As the boat pitched and tossed, the horseless
stage, improperly secured, rolled against the railing and over the side. Two
of those inside, the stage driver and a young boy, managed to jump out
before it fell into the lake. The other two, innkeeper William Waters of
the Cedars and eleven-year-old John Molson, son of John Molson Jr, went
overboard with the coach. The air trapped inside kept it afloat long enough
for Captain Crossman to lower a boat and pull man and boy to safety.[53]

Besides illustrating the degree of integration of stage and steamer travel,
the incident serves as a reminder that it was not always clear sailing for
the boats of the Upper Canada Line, no matter how tame Lakes St Louis
and St Francis might appear compared to the Great Lakes or the open seas.
Nature had tricks up its sleeve here as everywhere. William Lyon Mackenzie experienced more than one of nature's blows this same year when
he journeyed from York to Quebec. He had a close call aboard the Molson
line's *Waterloo* on 18 April when the boat, holed by ice on her first trip
of the season, sank in sixty feet of water near Cap Rouge, just above
Quebec. The crew and all twenty-three passengers survived, scrambling
to shore across the ice floes.[54] Heading home in May, Mackenzie was
aboard the *Neptune* when she nearly came a cropper on Lake St Francis.
A passenger on that trip left a graphic account of the near disaster:

We left Coteau with every prospect of a favourable voyage, but ere we had
proceeded many miles we were caught by one of those squalls, which occasionally

arise in a moment, upon the lakes. Preparations were making in the cabin for dinner, and I was engaged in writing, when my attention was drawn to a confused noise upon deck, while, at the same moment, the vessel gave a heavy lurch, with the sensation of a sudden stop. I was immediately called up by a fellow passenger, and, as I ascended, the engineer rushed past me, pale as death, exclaiming, "We are lost!" I did not at the moment comprehend the full extent of our danger, as the alarm arose, not from the squall alone, but from the machinery having become disordered, the pumps choked, and an explosion immediately expected. All was in confusion upon deck, the captain and mate alone seeming to retain self-possession. A poor Canadian voyageur, who had charge of the helm, fled from his post, calling in despair upon Sainte Marie for aid. Fortunately, a steady fellow, with better nerves and less faith in saints, had been placed beside him, and succeeded in keeping the vessel's head to the wind. At one heavy roll, a general movement took place in the steward's pantry, and nearly a score of bottles, Madeira, brandy, &c. with lots of crockery and crystal, were demolished, with an astounding crash. Bad as this was, too, it was by no means all, for one of those extensive rafts, constructed in winter and moved down in spring to Montreal or Quebec, had gone to pieces just a-head. The logs, now cast loose, were rushing past us in numbers on each side, with a violence which must have inevitably staved the vessel if she had been struck. Neither could we contemplate without dismay eleven poor fellows cast away by the raft. Two or three of them, distinctly observed at a very short distance, seemed to be in the last struggle; and great was our relief by learning (though not until some days afterwards, at Kingston) that they had all, in a most providential manner, by clinging to spars, been carried for several miles, in safety to the American side. For ourselves, by some happy change below, the pumps suddenly cleared, steam resumed its office, and ere we had time to ponder much upon the matter, we were scudding back for Coteau before the gale, which continued to blow for several hours, with unabated violence.[55]

CHAPTER SIX

Swan Song, 1832

In 1831 Horace Dickinson was taking the first steps in a plan to revamp his steamboat service and extend it to a part of the river previously thought out of bounds. But as far as the public was concerned, nothing much changed on the line that year. The horse boat *Experiment* found a buyer in James Wait, who held the ferry rights between Longueuil and the foot of the St Mary's Current, as the shore of the St Mary suburb of Montreal was called. On 6 April, Dickinson sold Wait his 84½ shares in the boat and its equipment – everything but the horses – for £323 10s. 3d., on condition "that the said James Wait shall never interfere with the said horseboat or any other vessel in the ferry between Lachine and Chateauguay or between Lachine and Sault St Louis [Kahnawake], directly nor indirectly, and that he will not sell the said boat to anyone who could interfere with him [Dickinson] in the ferries aforesaid."[1] Otherwise, the *St Lawrence* and the *Cornwall* continued plying as before on Lake St Louis, and the *Neptune* on Lake St Francis.

If his signing a ten-year lease with Thomas Dawes for the wharf and store at Lachine in 1829 had suggested a long-term commitment, Dickinson now went further. For the first time since he had come to Lower Canada, he bought land. On 22 February he acquired from the Bank of Canada a property of about five arpents (one arpent equalled 3,600 square yards, roughly three-quarters of an acre) with a two-storey house, stables, and outbuildings on Lake St Francis, in the seigneury of New Longueuil. This was Asahel Whipple's neighbourhood. Besides the seigneurial dues, Dickinson was to pay the bank £150. Under terms laid down in an 1826 sheriff's sale of the property, he also inherited the obligation to pay retired farmer Jean-Baptiste Prieur, *dit* St-Léger, and his wife the sum of £7 10s. every 1 January for as long as they lived. It was from this same Prieur that Whipple had leased land and obtained the right to build a steamer wharf on it in 1827.[2]

On 31 March, for £300, Dickinson bought another property, this one at Lachine, from William Whitney, a former stage keeper who may have alternated with Curtis Crossman as captain of the *St Lawrence*.[3] The lot, about 127 feet wide and stretching from the river to the king's highway (*chemin du roi*), contained a storehouse and wharf. Before the summer was out, Dickinson became embroiled in a dispute with his neighbour, Joseph Lebœuf, *dit* Laflamme, over the latter's wharf, which jutted out at an angle in front of Dickinson's property. Laflamme's plans to extend his wharf threatened to cut off access for boats and rafts to the property, Dickinson claimed.[4]

These land purchases were part of Dickinson's grand plan. A hint of the changes in store came on 11 June when a new boat built for him by Thomas Mears was launched at Hawkesbury. This was the *Swan*, $93\frac{1}{2}$ feet long, $18\frac{1}{2}$ feet broad, and with a $6\frac{1}{2}$-foot depth of hold. Like the *Ottawa* twelve years earlier, she was brought down to Lachine to be fitted with her engine. But summer passed and then autumn, and the *Swan* lay engineless and unfinished.[5]

It sometimes seems that Dickinson was so focused on his transport business and his church that he had little time for anything else. But in 1831 he and Jacob Bigelow embarked on a quixotic venture unrelated to either of those concerns. They took up the cause of the heirs of François Cazeau, an enterprising Frenchman who had prospered in the Canadian fur trade, then lost all after supporting the rebel side in the American Revolution.[6] Arrested for treason by the British in 1780, his property seized and sold, Cazeau had escaped to the United States, leaving his family behind. Until his death in Paris in 1815 at the age of eighty-one, he pursued his claims against the United States and its wartime ally, France, obsessively. After his death, his children and grandchildren in Canada pursued the matter.[7] In 1818 they were dismayed to learn that an impostor had obtained nearly $43,000 from the Americans in settlement of the claims. What chance did they stand that Congress would pay the same claims a second time, this time to the rightful heirs? But they pressed on. On 14 May 1831 they appointed Jacob Bigelow their agent for a minimum of five years.[8] It was not so much a job as a cause to which he was to devote the rest of his life, or more than twenty years.

Bigelow was no longer first teller of the Bank of Canada. The bank itself, almost dormant and in the hands of liquidators since the mid-1820s, let its charter lapse this year and was absorbed by the Bank of Montreal.[9] The £2,000 bond that Bigelow had posted as a condition of his employment in 1819, renewed in 1823, had been cancelled in April 1824, suggesting that he had left the bank or that it was doing so little business that his bond was no longer needed.[10] As we have seen, in the summer of 1825 he had opened an office as agent of the Howard Insurance

Company of New York. Then in January 1826 he had launched a hat-
manufacturing business with hatter William Eydam, but the partnership
of Eydam and Bigelow had lasted only until June of the following year.[11]

Now, with Dickinson's support, he set out to obtain justice for the heirs
of François Cazeau. Bigelow, Dickinson, and tanner Joshua Hobart agreed
to bear all the expenses of the case. In return, they were to receive half
of any compensation that Bigelow might secure from France or the United
States. In the second half of 1831 Bigelow travelled to Europe; he returned
to Montreal from London aboard the ship *Columbia* in the following
spring.[12] For the American case, he collected supporting statements in
1833 from his friend Jacob De Witt and from Louis-Joseph Papineau,
Horatio Gates, Montreal mayor Jacques Viger, and others. He moved to
Michigan City, Indiana, in 1835 but pressed the case in Washington in
person and through lawyers. At last, in 1844, after years of lobbying and
arguing and after the case had been shuttled between the courts and
government committees, Bigelow was successful. Congress refused to
cover the portion of the claims paid in error to the impostor in 1818, but
offered $27,352.32 as a final settlement.

Whatever fee Bigelow may have earned for his efforts, this was
obviously no get-rich-quick scheme. When he, Dickinson, and Hobart
embarked on the project in 1831, they knew that hope of financial reward
was slight and that "heavy expenses will attend the prosecution of the
said claims." They also knew that it could take years – so many that
Bigelow, then age forty-one, might die before the matter was resolved.
Should that happen, Dickinson and Hobart insisted, they alone, as the
ones paying the bills, were to have the right to name his successor.[13]
How much Hobart contributed, and for how long, is not known. Dickinson, for his part, may have helped to pay for Bigelow's European trip
in 1831–32, but he can have done little more – he died two months after
Bigelow's return.

He was probably drawn into the scheme by Bigelow, whose own
involvement may have gone back to his days at the Bank of Canada: the
bank's assistant bookkeeper, François-Guillaume Reeves (or William
Reeves, as he was known), was a grandson of François Cazeau.[14] Dickinson's commitment to paying for this rainbow chase in 1831 suggests that
he acted from motives more personal than commercial. It also shows that
he had money to spare, even as he was investing heavily in the expansion
of his transport line and bracing for the competition which the opening
of the Rideau Canal would bring.

While changes to the Upper Canada Line seemed to be slow in coming
in 1831, work was progressing apace on the Rideau. The step-like set of
eight locks at the Bytown end of the canal, built by Thomas McKay, were
inaugurated that October. Thomas Mears's worn old *Union*, the pioneer

steamer on the Ottawa River, was accorded the honour of being the first to try the locks.[15] On the evening of Friday, 7 October, before an anxious crowd, "she ascended the eight locks at the entrance of the Canal in as good style as could be expected, albeit she was not built for the service, and never noted for obeying her helm," a witness recorded. "The morning of the eighth beamed bright on the Steamboat at the top of the eight locks. This was a day to be remembered in the annals of our adopted country." The *Union* sailed as far as Merrickville that year.[16]

Merchants on the lower Rideau were eager to take advantage of the new facilities. They could now hope to ship goods in and out by water, via the canal and the Ottawa River, instead of having to pay for costly overland transport to and from the St Lawrence at Brockville. That very October, Smiths Falls merchant William Mittleberger advised his brother, Montreal commission merchant Charles Mittleberger: "I intend to leave in a few days for Montreal, through the Canal by Steam Boat, with a view of making arrangements for the transport of my goods by the Ottawa – and therefore have to request of you not to forward any more by the St Lawrence – If I have my Goods brought by the Ottawas this Fall, the transport from Brockville hence will be a clear saving." But with his very first attempt to have goods shipped up the Ottawa, William Mittleberger was soured on the Ottawa Steamboat Company. A company agent ignored his instructions, resulting in delays in getting his goods to Bytown. Once they reached there, he found that the *Union* had broken down; only by offering to pay a premium was he able to induce Mears, who chanced to be on the spot, to have the steamer haul his goods up the canal as far as Burritt's Rapids. By mid-December, Mittleberger was writing that "the Ottawa Line Co. are determined to be as exorbitant as ever in their forwarding charges; thanks be to God it will not last long, the merchants of Perth & this neighbourhood have very handsomely come forward & proposed to us to undertake to build a Boat, which we will lose no time in doing."[17]

Thus the pattern was set for the decade – the Ottawa-Rideau route would cut into the St Lawrence trade, but the service on the new route would draw endless complaints and spark efforts to launch new steamboat ventures more responsive to local needs and interests. And as Mittleberger's early experience shows, steamboats would be virtually indispensable to Rideau Canal traffic. The waterway had no towpath along which horses – or humans, if necessary – could be employed in pulling barges and other craft, because unlike other canals, the Rideau was not one continuous trench, but a succession of streams, lakes, locks, and flooded swamps. Practically speaking, this meant that all boat movement through the canal would depend on steam towing: whoever operated the steamers would have the run of the canal.[18]

On Lake St Louis, meanwhile, residents of Châteauguay and Beauharnois, still bent on having a steamboat service tailored to their own needs,
were becoming restive again. By the fall of 1831 they were once more in
the market for a boat, this time planning to build their own and to sell
shares at 30 shillings, the same formula resorted to at La Prairie at this
time to finance the building of the *Patriote Canadien*.[19] But Dickinson
headed them off.

His designs became clear in March 1832 as word spread that he was
proceeding with the renovation of his whole fleet. At the beginning of
March he bought the *Dalhousie* outright for the reported price of £1,100
and announced that he was going to run her down from Prescott to Lake
St Francis. She was to operate with the *Neptune* on the Côteau-Cornwall
run, serving such south-shore communities as St Regis and Dundee and
the New York villages of Fort Covington, adjoining Dundee, and Hogansburgh, next to St Regis. The *Neptune* herself, running along the north
shore, was improved, notably by the addition of a ladies' cabin on deck.[20]

On Lake St Louis the *St Lawrence* and the *Cornwall* were discarded.
They may well have been the two steamer hulls that Dickinson scuttled
at Lachine to form a wharf. The 32-horsepower engine of the *St Lawrence*
was being installed in the *Swan*. That explained the delay in equipping
the latter boat the previous year: the *St Lawrence* had been left to finish
the season before being cannibalized.Like the engine of the *St Lawrence*,
the *Cornwall's* 16-horsepower engine was to be recycled, in a boat that
Alexander Young was building for Dickinson at Côteau. She was to be
named *Chateauguay* and to serve as the ferry between Lachine and
Châteauguay (one of her two anchors came from the *St Lawrence*).[21]

Young, in fact, was building two boats at Côteau. The second was to
be called *Henry Brougham*, after Britain's lord chancellor. This tribute
to a member of the British aristocracy may seem out of character for
Dickinson, but there was much in Henry Peter Brougham's career to
appeal to the egalitarian sentiments of a Yankee on British ground. As a
member of the British Parliament for more than two decades, he had
played a prominent role in various liberal causes. After reluctantly agreeing in 1830 to become lord chancellor, which required him to forsake the
House of Commons for the House of Lords, Brougham – now Baron
Brougham and Vaux, or Lord Brougham for short – remained the popular
hero as one of the champions of the monumental struggle for the Reform
Bill of 1832, an effort to bring parliamentary representation into line
with the great social changes stemming from the Industrial Revolution.
(Another of Brougham's achievements would certainly have struck Dickinson, had he lived to hear of it: in 1838–39, he designed the Brougham,
the light, low-slung, closed carriage which bore his name far and wide.)
It is worth noting that Dickinson chose to call his boat by the commoner's

name, the *Henry Brougham*, rather than the *Lord Brougham* or *Chancellor Brougham*.[22]

The *Henry Brougham*, of 198 tons, was to be just under 133 feet long and 18 feet broad midships, with an $8\frac{1}{2}$-foot depth of hold. The Wards were making her 50-horsepower engine. Her job would be to haul freight and tow batteaux. The smaller, less-powerful *Swan*, of 32 horsepower, was reserved for passengers.[23]

There was more to Dickinson's boat-building boom. He had another steamer of quite different design under construction in Upper Canada called the *Iroquois*. She was built at Gananoque and then towed down to Prescott on 8 May to be fitted with her engines. One hundred and thirty feet long, 18 feet beam, and drawing 12 inches of water, she was to sail where no steamer had yet run – up and down the Galop Rapids and Rapid Plat between Prescott and the head of the Long Sault, giving rise to the village of Dickinson's Landing. If she worked out, she would shave almost forty of the fifty miles of bumpy stage travel between Cornwall and Prescott on the Upper Canada Line. It was thought that the special demands placed on her required a different design and different engine from Dickinson's sidewheelers on the lower lakes. She was to be a sternwheeler, a rarity in Canada then – the only other such steamer in operation was the *John By* (see chap. 7). And she was to be driven by two high-pressure, or non-condensing, engines of 25 horsepower. The Wards did not make high-pressure engines. Bennet and Henderson built at least one, in 1833, for a boat that would quickly wind up on Lake St Louis, a second *Montreal*. But Dickinson never dealt with Bennet. So the engines, costing a total of £700, were ordered from Fuller and Copeland of Hartford, Connecticut.[24]

The placing of the sternwheeler *Iroquois* on the turbulent water above Cornwall may have owed something to Barnabas Dickinson. Horace's brother is said to have moved from the United States to Cornwall in 1828. With the expansion of his Upper Canada Line, Horace Dickinson certainly could have used some help. Whether his brother played any part or not,[25] his brothers-in-law did. Abijah and Increase Sumner Bigelow joined Horace Dickinson and Company as partners on 1 April.[26]

On 18 April the *Dalhousie* was run down the rapids from Prescott to Lake St Francis, where, outside the boat channel, the ice lingered. The *Neptune* and the *Swan* were ready to swing into action as soon as the ice broke up on their respective lakes. The *Chateauguay* was ready for service by the end of May. Only the *Brougham* and the *Iroquois* were still in the works when cholera struck in June.[27]

As the death toll mounted steadily in the first couple of weeks, most shopkeepers shut down and those who could fled town for the country. The highest single-day toll in Montreal occurred on 19 June, when 149 people died.[28] Dickinson died the next day. There seems to be no church record of a funeral for him. He may have been among the victims who, in the panicky early days of the epidemic, were buried in haste and without prayers. Cemetery records, however, indicate that a minister was present when he was buried beside his first wife in the Protestant cemetery on the Papineau Road.[29] On 26 August, Barnabas Dickinson died at Cornwall, followed four days later by his four-year-old daughter, Sophia.[30] Jacob Bigelow's son, Joseph Sanford, not quite nine, died on 8 August.[31] Few, if any, families were spared. A traveller recorded on passing through Montreal that "every one seen in the streets showed by his dress that he was mourning the loss of a relative or a friend."[32]

The grim tone was set before the cholera hit. It began with a violent election contest in the West Ward of Montreal, originally pitting *Vindicator*

Gravestones of the Dickinson family circle, Mount Royal Cemetery, Montreal: (foreground, left to right) Abigail Hedge, wife of Samuel Ward; Phebe Caroline and Sarah Ann Dod Ward, children of John Ward; Dimmis White Dickinson, daughter of Horace Dickinson and wife of Lebbeus Ward; behind them stands the headstone of Horace Dickinson and his first wife, Mary Ann Taylor; a stone to the memory of Dickinson's dauther, Sarah Spring, once stood next to Dickinson's (photograph by the author).

Barnabas Dickinson, from a portrait painted c.1832 (St Lawrence Parks Commission, Upper Canada Village).

editor Daniel Tracey, backed by the bulk of French-Canadian and Irish voters as well as a few Americans, against Thomas Phillips and Stanley Bagg, candidates nominated by the Scots, English, and Americans. According to a Patriote sympathizer, the anglophone establishment persuaded Phillips to withdraw in favour of Bagg to avoid splitting the Tory vote: "He [Phillips] was made to retire, because it was thought that as an American, Mr Bagg would rally the great majority, if not all, of the people of like origin which, together with all the Scots and the English & a few weak and perfidious [French] Canadians, could not fail to ensure their victory."[33] The poll was established in the vestibule of the American Presbyterian Church on 28 April, but owing to the brawling, the church's prudential committee refused to let voting go on there. On 2 May the poll was moved east down St James Street to Place d'Armes. There on 21 May, magistrates ordered soldiers to fire into a riotous crowd. Three of Tracey's supporters were killed. The incident sparked an outrage, one more milestone on the path to rebellion.[34]

Public indignation was at fever pitch when the cholera struck. Tracey, the election victor, died on 18 July; Bagg survived. Innkeeper Asa Goodenough's wife, Sophia Preston, succumbed on 27 June. Emery Cushing lost his five-year-old daughter, Cornelia Rachel, on 5 August. Elisha

Lyman's son, Edwin, age twenty-six, died on 20 September. At St John's on 10 July the cholera carried off John Easinhart, Dickinson's former associate, who had held the mail contract between Montreal and Swanton, Vermont. At Quebec, Daniel Sutherland, with whom Dickinson had signed his first mail contract sixteen years earlier, died on 18 August at the age of seventy-six. Joseph Wigfield, engineer of the *Shannon*, died at Grenville on 24 June. At Kingston, James McKenzie, who had commanded the *Frontenac* throughout her ten-year career and then the *Alciope*, before retiring in 1831, died on 27 August.[35]

At Beauharnois, in Damase Masson's household, a rare event was recorded on 30 June: his wife gave birth to triplets. This ray of hope was quickly snuffed out, all three newborns dying within hours. When the village doctor died of cholera on 17 August, Masson's cousin, Luc-Hyacinthe Masson, a twenty-one-year-old medical student, moved to Beauharnois from Montreal to fill in. In the space of twenty-four hours in mid-August, postmaster Thomas McDonald, his mother-in-law, and his young son were wiped out. Damase Masson would succeed McDonald as postmaster that October.[36]

In the midst of this carnage, with many businesses and industries shut up for a time during the summer, completion of the *Iroquois* and the *Brougham* was understandably delayed. Two days after Dickinson's death, his widow, following the practice in cases where a person died intestate, petitioned the Court of King's Bench to appoint tutors to their five minor children. Assisting her in court were the Reverend George W. Perkins and Lebbeus Ward, the children's half-brothers-in-law; their grandfather, Abijah Bigelow Sr; their uncles Jacob, Abijah, and Increase Sumner Bigelow; and forwarder James Henderson, a friend of the family. Mercy Amelia Dickinson was named "tutrix" (or guardian), with Lebbeus Ward as sub-tutor.[37] These two and Perkins, in the name of Dickinson's heirs, immediately instructed Abijah and Increase Bigelow "that you should for the present conduct the business of the late firm of H. Dickinson & Co. under the same name or firm and on the same conditions as heretofore as will appear by articles of Copartnership entered into between the said H. Dickinson and yourselves on the first day of April last." The Bigelows, it turned out, had entered into partnership with Dickinson in the nick of time, their presence ensuring that the business of the Upper Canada Line would continue with the least possible disruption.[38]

Work soon proceeded on the unfinished boats. The *Brougham* tested her engine for the first time on 31 August.[39] It would seem that, from the first, Asahel Whipple's younger brother, Daniel, then age thirty-four, was in command of her.[40] As for the *Iroquois*, originally meant to be ready by early June, a holidaying English army officer recorded in late August:

We saw a steam-vessel which was off the stocks and nearly completed at Prescott, for the purpose of running down the smaller Rapids, and constructed upon a novel principle. The vessel was of great length and extremely narrow in the beam, with six long cylindrical boilers, and the paddles astern, on the supposition that in ascending the stream they will propel the vessel quicker than paddles on the sides, which might retard its progress, by being opposed to the full power of the current. Four rudders were placed equi-distant on the stern, so as to give the steersman more command over the vessel in the violent eddies; and, if the experiment answered in the smaller Rapids, it was intended to attempt the passage of the Long Sault.[41]

The *Iroquois* tried out her engines on the safe waters above Prescott in September. On the 18th of that month, "crowded with all the beauty and fashion of Ogdensburgh and Prescott," she popped up to Brockville. With a ladies' cabin 20 feet long and a gentlemen's of 43 feet, she was "a neat little boat with fine accommodation," said one report. "In the gentlemen's cabin is a table of horse-shoe form which is capable of accommodating seventy-five persons. The ladies' cabin which is on deck, is fitted up in a light and healthy style, with large windows, and comfortable accommodations for the inmates." On 24 September the *Iroquois* made her first run up the rapids from Dickinson's Landing to Prescott, "and although the machinery was new, and the wind ahead, she ascended these rapids with considerable ease, and reached Prescott as soon as the stages by land could have performed the distance."[42]

As the surviving partners in H. Dickinson and Company, Abijah and Increase Sumner Bigelow arranged that one of them, along with sailing master Jeremiah Baldwin, would be on board for the *Iroquois's* every trip that fall.[43] They had ample opportunity to rate her performance. Despite various puffs about the ease with which she breasted the current, it quickly became apparent that she did not measure up. They hired engineer Samuel Hulburt of Prescott to make adjustments to her engines over the winter.[44] At the same time, they petitioned the government of Upper Canada for a remission of the import duties on the engines, pleading the high costs and financial risk to themselves versus the great benefit that the travelling public would reap should Hulburt's alterations make her perform up to expectations. The petition was granted, but the *Iroquois*, which began her first full season on the water the following April under Captain Augustus Barber, continued to experience difficulties.[45] Alfred Domett, a young Englishman who travelled in her in the fall of 1833, could testify to that fact. He left Montreal on Tuesday, 1 October, and found himself at Dickinson's Landing the next day:

At a small village at the Head of the *Long Sault* waited a small steamboat called the Iroquois ... It looks like a long low white wooden house placed in a barge. It draws only 27 inches of water ... It is propelled by a steam engine the piston of which is horizontal and pushes backwards and forwards a beam connected with

The "Iroquois" a steamer w[ith]
the paddle wheel abaft, f[or]
navigating the rapids o[f]
the St Lawrence.

The sternwheeler *Iroquois*; from a drawing by Henry Byam Martin, who travelled
in North America in 1832–33 (NA/C-115050).

the axle of the wheels which are placed at the stern of the boat. It is not of
sufficient power for this undertaking … The boat at times made scarce any
headway at all. The water was not much broken but ran with considerable rapidity.
About the middle of the day we stopped a while in a sort of bay formed by the
curving shore. Ahead of us was a projection of the land beyond which the river
foamed along with a strong and swift motion. We lay crouching under this point
for some time getting up more steam and taking in wood … At length we darted
into the current intending to round the point of land. We were carried by the
stream quite across to the other bank and for a long time had to struggle hard
for every inch of progress we made. We were obliged soon after to throw out a
rope to a team of three horses waiting for us on the bank by whose assistance we
passed the worst part of the river.[46]

Only after extensive work on her engines – including the replacement of
her boilers by Edward Quingly, "the first rate boiler maker in North
America" – in the first seven months of 1834 was the *Iroquois* able to
give a more or less satisfactory account of herself. A test run on 2 August

showed that her speed was twice what it had been the previous season. She returned to service through the rapids on 6 August that year, but in 1835 she was withdrawn from the line. There was talk of her forming part of a new steamer line on the Rideau Canal that year. She was put up for sale in 1836, but her fate is unknown.[47]

It would seem, then, that like the owners of the *Ottawa* years before, Dickinson had miscalculated and launched a steamer unsuited to her purpose. But in a sense the *Iroquois* was the crowning achievement of his career as a St Lawrence steamboat operator. Hints of what he was driving at can be seen as early as 1826 when he ran the hull of James Greenfield's *Lady of the Lake* down the rapids from Lake St Francis to Montreal. More clues came in 1827 when he sought to have the *Neptune* sail beyond Lake St Francis down the Côteau rapids to the Cedars, and in 1828 when he sent the *Cornwall* down the rapids from Lake St Francis to Lake St Louis. The mysterious single trip of the *St Lawrence* up the Vaudreuil Rapids in 1828 may have been part of the same scheme. The *Dalhousie's* run down from Prescott to Cornwall in the spring of 1832, through some of the same swift waters that the *Iroquois* was intended to ply later that year, surely fit the pattern. There was an element of research and development in this punctual shifting of steamers to meet or forestall competition, a continuing investigation into the possibilities of extending steamer navigation beyond those waters deemed navigable. For some, the way to achieve that goal was to build locks and canals. In the absence of such costly improvements, Dickinson was one of those who believed that the boats themselves could conquer some of the rapids. While shallow-draft steamers could indeed shoot all the rapids of the St Lawrence, as his own tests showed and as later developments were to confirm, they could not sail back up the river – except through the Galop Rapids and Rapid Plat, between Dickinson's Landing and Prescott, where the *Iroquois* was the first to run. However imperfectly, she proved that such a trip could be made. The lesson was not lost on other men.[48]

This then was the line that Dickinson built. Besides six steamers, the stage terminals at Montreal and Prescott, and several depots in between, it included twenty stage "establishments," each apparently named after the stage driver on a section of the route, for example, Shoal's Establishment, Nichols' Establishment, Big Nichols' Establishment, Squires' Establishment, and so on.[49] Those east of Cornwall generally consisted of one four-horse coach, four horses, and a harness set; those to the west, of just four horses and a harness set. Other horses and equipment were kept at Montreal, Lachine, Cascades, Côteau, Cornwall, and Williamsburgh and at a depot, identified in the inventory of Dickinson's property as Looker's Establishment, which appears to have been the western extremity of the line, at Prescott.

There were coaches painted in every colour of the rainbow. At Looker's in 1832 were to be found five yellow coaches and one red one, a small vehicle called a coachee, and one red hack, all bearing numbers from 19 to 31. Here, too, were two four-horse wagons painted red, one green two-horse pleasure wagon, one yellow four-horse wagon, two large four-horse sleighs and one black two-horse sleigh, two cutters (one green, one yellow), and a large red lumber sleigh.

Nine extra horses were kept at Williamsburgh, as well as cords of steamboat wood, a covered caravan, and a four-horse covered wagon painted red. At Cornwall there were wagons and horses and cords of steamboat wood. At Côteau there were seven extra horses and a total of twelve wagons, sleighs, coaches, and covered carriages, including one "Pennsylvania wagon" and a "Boston blue coach." There were also two Durham boats belonging to Dickinson, the *Dundee* and the *H. Gates*,[50] a barge, and a batteau. He owned two other batteaux, one large and one small, stationed at the Cascades. Four coaches, numbered 23, 25, 26, and 28, and a wagon called the John Bull were kept at the five establishments between Côteau and the Cascades.

There were three establishments between Lachine and Montreal, where the line's earliest Concord coaches ran. Two four-horse models, one yellow and one blue, and a six-horse model painted chocolate brown were kept at a station identified as Hutchon's Establishment. Three others, all new that year, were parked in Montreal. There were coaches and wagons and sleighs in sheds on College Street, sulkies and mail carts in stables on St Maurice Street. One worn old yellow coach, number 18, was at the blacksmith's for repairs.

The surviving notarial copy of the inventory lists some – not all – of Dickinson's real property but without providing any valuation. It included a lot in Prescott with a two-storey stone house, wooden offices, stables, and sheds, as well as a wharf at Cornwall and some adjoining land. Particularly interesting is a five-acre lot that Dickinson owned at West Williamsburgh, Upper Canada, "on which is erected a large Tavern House Known as the Williamsburgh Hotel, Store, Blacksmiths shop, Stables sheds &c, bought the said lot from Hiram Norton." No indication is given of when Dickinson acquired this property, but one suspects that it was in the mid-1820s, at the time when C.B. Martin, operator of the Union Hotel next door to Dickinson's house on McGill Street, left Montreal for Upper Canada to run the "Williamsburgh Stage House." Presumably, the Will-iamsburgh Hotel and the Williamsburgh Stage House were one and the same. In 1831 it was also referred to as "Campbell's tavern," after William Campbell, formerly a hotel and boarding-house keeper in Montreal, who took over from Martin in 1828, renovating and expanding the establishment. A traveller described this hostelry, midway between Cornwall and

Prescott, as a "snug, comfortable country inn" and "one of the best kept taverns in Canada."[51]

There is no mention at all in the inventory of the Lachine property that Dickinson had bought for £300 the year before from William Whitney "as a convenient place to protect and carry on the said Stage line business." In 1835 Mercy Amelia Dickinson applied to the courts, as guardian of her children, for permission to sell that property, "the said stage line being no longer the property of the said Estate of said late Horace Dickinson, the said lot of ground is now more onerous than profitable to the said minor children." The sale took place on 24 August, the buyer agreeing to respect a lease held on the property by the Canada Steamboat and Mail Coach Company, then the owners of the Upper Canada Line, until the fall of 1836.[52]

Also left out of the inventory is the property that Dickinson had acquired at Côteau in 1831 from the Bank of Canada. In the list of movable goods he owned at Côteau is a misplaced entry, half-erased and marked with an X, for what seems to be "three buildings in Ship Yard." Some indication of what this property might have been is found in a newspaper report of a fire at Côteau in the summer of 1842. According to that report, "the extensive stables and sheds of the stage company at Coteau du Lac were struck by lightning ... and entirely consumed." The contents of the buildings were saved, and the Canada Steamboat and Mail Coach Company suffered no great financial loss because it did not own the buildings: "The buildings belonged to the estate of the late Horace Dickinson, Esquire, and were insured for $600, much under their real value."[53]

Excluding all these lands and buildings – and the new steam ferry *Châteauguay*, for which no valuation is noted – Dickinson left horses, boats, rolling stock, and assorted other movable property, scattered along the St Lawrence, worth £11,767 10. 9d., plus £2,901 7s. 8d. in debts owed to him, for a total of £14,668 18s. 5d. Against that figure must be set £9,461 14s. 8d. in accounts payable and debts due by the estate. Times had certainly changed since the days when Jedediah Dorwin had seen Dickinson leaving Montreal in a red farm wagon, or since William Innis and Alexis Pratte had carried the mails between Montreal and Kingston, each with three horses stationed along his route.

CHAPTER SEVEN

The Rideau Jitters

To some a promise, to others a threat, the Rideau Canal officially opened at the end of May 1832, just before the cholera struck. Colonel John By and a select party, including Robert Drummond, inaugurated the new waterway, sailing from Kingston to Bytown in Drummond's steamer *Rideau* between 24 and 29 May. At Smiths Falls the inhabitants saluted her passage by firing a cannon until it burst. The *Rideau*, which had served as a work boat on the canal since 1829, reached Bytown the same day that the *Union* entered the locks, headed in the opposite direction.[1]

A timely endorsement of the canal came when the chief immigration officer recommended the Ottawa-Rideau route as the best for the throngs of immigrants heading upcountry that summer. (In 1833, however, the Montreal Emigrant Society favoured the St Lawrence route.)[2] But it was not all smooth sailing on the canal. In the early days of the cholera epidemic, magistrates and health authorities at Bytown and Kingston sought to isolate their towns from the disease by halting all shipping and boat traffic.[3] There was also finishing work to be done on the canal, and shallows impeded navigation. It was late July before the *Rideau* carried the canal's first commercial cargo – 200 barrels of flour and 60 barrels of pork – from Kingston to Bytown.[4] In 1833 the canal did not open for steamer navigation until July.[5] And in 1834 the leader of a group of English immigrants who travelled via the Ottawa-Rideau route recorded:

Our passage from Montreal to Kingston, from some trifling accidental occurrences, occupied eight days, and some hours, although usually performed in seven days. At present, the Rideau canal is in its infancy, several parts of it are narrow, many impeded by stumps, and loose floating trees: in some places, there is a sudden turn, with but just room for the steam boat to enter the passage, where, by the removal of about twenty stumps, from the angle, it could be easily widened one half. In one place we passed through a large lake [Cranberry Lake], covered

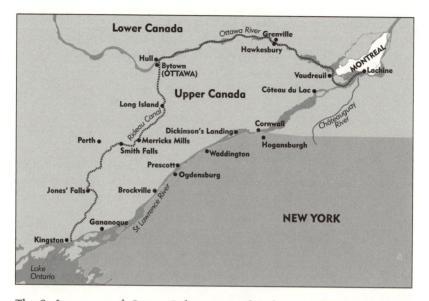

The St Lawrence and Ottawa-Rideau routes, based on an 1827–30 map (NA/ National Map Collection, 11229; redrawn by Justin Stahlman).

with floating islands, formed of the trunks of trees, matted together by coarse grass, and covered with small shrubs, over one of which, our boat, towing along side the steamer, was carried.[6]

The same writer, a Royal Navy surgeon, judged that the steamers on the canal "neither possess the proper form, nor power for the work."[7] Form had certainly been a problem for the *John By*, the first steamer (other than the work boat *Rideau*) built specifically for the canal trade. This sternwheeler, 110 feet long, 33 feet beam, with a 75-horsepower Bennet and Henderson engine, had been built at Kingston in the fall of 1831 for a company of which Drummond was a principal. Placed on the canal, she was immediately withdrawn when found to draw too much water.[8] Drummond had another steamer built, the sidewheeler *Margaret*, which began running on the canal in September 1833 under Captain Morehouse, formerly of the *Union*.[9]

For the region between Montreal and the Great Lakes, the repercussions of the canal project were more far-reaching than the havoc wreaked by cholera. At one end of the waterway were planted some of the seeds of the future city of Ottawa: Bytown and New Edinburgh, the latter pioneered by canal contractor Thomas McKay, who had a gristmill and sawmill in operation there by 1833.[10] At the canal's southwestern extremity, Kingston gained new bustle and a new prominence, personified by

Robert Drummond, who made his home there and showed his faith in the town's prosperity by investing in it: he built a brewery and distillery and became a founding director of the Commercial Bank of the Midland District, and from a contractor on the Rideau, he became the canal's most active user and booster.[11] In early 1832, too, the Montreal-Prescott forwarding firm of John Macpherson and Company rented facilities at Kingston, apparently with the idea of using the Rideau route, when practical, as well as the St Lawrence.[12] Hopes for the canal had spurred the formation of the Ottawa Steamboat Company in the late 1820s; shortly after the canal opened, the company enlarged its Vaudreuil lock to match the dimensions of those on the Rideau – 134 feet long by 33 feet wide – but still kept it closed to all but its own steamers.[13]

On a broader level, the canal can even be seen to have fed the concert of calls from Upper Canada in the fall of 1832 for the annexation of Montreal, which had just been made a port of entry with its own customs establishment. The idea of annexation had gathered steam ever since the failure in the British Parliament in 1822 of an attempt to legislate the union of Upper and Lower Canada. Without a seaport, Upper Canada remained at the mercy of its sister province for its imports. The latter set and levied duties on imports, including those destined for Upper Canada; but the share of duties that should go to Upper Canada was the subject of a running dispute. A decision by Lower Canada to impose a head tax on immigrants in 1832 to help pay for their care exacerbated the problem. Upper Canada was further frustrated by the fact that no matter what steps were taken in its territory – whether it be the Rideau Canal, the Welland Canal connecting Lakes Ontario and Erie since 1829, or canals on the St Lawrence – to improve navigation and the flow of imports and exports, these would meet a dead end in Lower Canada unless that province made corresponding improvements on the St Lawrence above Montreal. Despite occasional encouraging signs, these were not forthcoming.

Under the circumstances, public meetings and newspapers in Upper Canada clamoured for direct access to the sea. Britain should provide this, they said, by giving Montreal and the county of Vaudreuil, the wedge of Lower Canadian land between the Ottawa and St Lawrence rivers, to Upper Canada. That province did not get its seaport, nor had plans for new canals in Lower Canada progressed past the point of studies and surveys when Upper Canada approved a canal-building program for the St Lawrence in 1833. There was renewed agitation for the annexation of Montreal from 1835–36, this time led in the legislature by Drummond's old friend and fellow Rideau contractor Thomas McKay, who had been elected a member for the county of Russell in 1834.[14]

As auspicious as the Rideau development was for Kingston, it caused great agitation downriver, notably at Brockville and Prescott, both dependent on the St Lawrence trade. With a touch of self-delusion, the *Brockville Gazette* dismissed the enthusiasm of Rideau Canal backers in 1832 and suggested that "those who feel an interest in the carrying trade down the St Lawrence may rest contentedly, for it is our impression it will be some time hence before any business of much consequence is done on the Canal."[15] But no one could rest; there was too much at stake. Brockville, the outlet for much of the produce from the Rideau settlements, would soon see that trade begin to flow between Bytown and Kingston. Prescott, a bustling village of about 1,400 by 1833, stood to lose its pivotal role in the forwarding business, estimated to have doubled every three years from 1825. Fourteen steamers and fifty schooners plied between the village and Lake Ontario ports by 1833.[16]

While the Rideau was under construction, a committee had been formed at Brockville in the fall of 1830, chaired by Jonas Jones, to push for legislative action on canal building and other improvements on the St Lawrence.[17] Once the Rideau opened, the need for action became more pressing. A public meeting at Brockville at the end of October 1832 adopted a petition calling for the canalization of the St Lawrence, and it struck a new committee, with Jonas Jones again at the forefront, to collect signatures.[18] The petition, bearing 820 names, was forwarded to the legislature in November and spurred the passage of a law the following 13 February, which provided, at last, for the building of the St Lawrence canals between Prescott and Lake St Francis. They were to be made deep enough for vessels drawing 9 feet of water, and the locks were to be a minimum of 150 feet long (by the time they were built, the required length had been increased to 200 feet) and 55 feet wide.[19] Jonas Jones was named president of the commission appointed to oversee the project; the other commissioners were Hiram Norton, who had launched his political career by defeating Jones in a Grenville County by-election in 1831; steamboat owner John Hamilton, a legislative councillor and brother-in-law of forwarder John Macpherson; Kingston postmaster John Macaulay, former president of a commission on improvements to navigation and future member of the Legislative Council, who was soon to marry John Macpherson's youngest sister; Philip VanKoughnet of Cornwall; George Longley of Maitland, a former reform member of the assembly for Grenville; and Peter Shaver.[20] No sooner had the law passed and the commission met than Jones, Norton, and Longley left for the United States on a canal study tour. Construction of the Cornwall Canal around the Long Sault would begin late in the following year.[21]

Besides sparking this venture, the opening of the Rideau Canal led to a chain reaction of adjustments and realignments among the transport companies on the St Lawrence. The Upper Canada Line, for one, underwent a transformation. In the winter of 1832–33 the major Prescott forwarders Macpherson and Crane (still called John Macpherson and Company at Montreal) and Hooker and Henderson, as well as James McCutchon of Kingston, banded together as Crane, Hooker, McCutchon and Company at Prescott, and Macpherson, Henderson and McCutchon at Montreal, to buy two-thirds of the steamboat interests held by Horace Dickinson's estate. In partnership with Abijah and Increase Sumner Bigelow, operating as A. Bigelow and Company, they would run the forwarding part of the business while A. Bigelow and Company took care of the stage and steamer services.[22]

The new owners were primarily interested in the Upper Canada trade, not in local traffic. One of their first moves was to dispose of the Lachine-Châteauguay ferry boat *Chateauguay*, only a year after she had gone into service. On 10 May, Jacob De Witt bought her for £1,500. He agreed not to run her to the Cascades, in return for which he was guaranteed that the Upper Canada Line would not compete with his ferry service.[23] As a steamboat owner, De Witt showed some of the same concerns as Dickinson: he gave strict orders that the *Chateauguay* was not to run on Sundays, and further, that no alcohol was to be sold on board. He had a captain he could trust in his younger brother, Charles. But De Witt was also intent on encouraging the development of the area which he represented in the assembly. The *Chateauguay* was to be a practical expression of the populist political and economic principles he espoused as a member of the Patriote party. Unlike Dickinson, whose operations had frustrated such efforts, De Witt encouraged local interests to pool their resources and wield a measure of control over the transportation facilities that served their area. Practically speaking, doing so would also spread the financial risk and help solidify his political base. He sold a one-third interest in the boat to thirty-three of his constituents in the county of Beauharnois. He also importuned Horace Dickinson's widow to buy back a one-third share for £500, but in the spring of 1834 she resolutely declined.[24]

Besides disposing of the *Chateauguay*, Dickinson's successors added more horses to their stock of a hundred or so, and acquired more Concord coaches. A. Bigelow and Company negotiated a new contract with the Post Office (no tenders were called) for carrying the mails between Montreal and Kingston six times a week, beginning in April 1833, for £1,195 a year. They gave up the Kingston-York portion, which went to William Weller. Under the new arrangements, the departure time of the stages from Montreal to Upper Canada was rescheduled as of 20 May: they would leave Montreal at 10:30 a.m. instead of at 4 a.m. For travellers who set out on Saturday, there was no longer a mad dash to make Prescott before Sunday. They were taken as far as Cornwall, where they remained until Monday.[25]

Stage lines to Quebec and Albany were left to others, while A. Bigelow and Company joined Ogdensburg businessmen for the season to form the

American Line of Steamboats and Stages between Montreal and Ogdensburg. A. Bigelow and Company owned and operated the service between
Montreal and Hogansburgh, New York, the only part of the line on which
steamboats were used. From Montreal to Côteau the two lines used the
same stages and steamers. They diverged at Côteau, the *Neptune* serving
the Canadian side of Lake St Francis and the *Dalhousie* running to ports
on the New York side. As the *Montreal Gazette* observed, "the distance
travelled by the American line, and by the Upper Canadian line, is exactly
the same, but in the former, the land travelling much exceeds that of the
latter, being in the one case seventy-seven miles, and in the other thirty-
seven." The shorter land travelling on the Canadian side resulted from
the placing of the *Iroquois* on the run between Prescott and Dickinson's
Landing; travellers on the American line covered the fifty-three miles
from Hogansburg to Ogdensburgh by stage.[26]

Alarmed at the juggernaut created by the alliance between Prescott
forwarders and the Upper Canada Line,[27] businessmen in Brockville and
Montreal sprang into action. A group of Montreal merchants issued a
prospectus for a new forwarding concern, the Canada Inland Forwarding
and Insurance Company. Its capital stock of £20,000 was to be split into
800 shares, half of them reserved for Upper Canadian investors. Brockville
merchants met at the office of Moses Maynard Jr on 12 January to endorse
this "counter association" and to propose that, in conjunction with the
forwarding business, a steamboat company, with a capital of £4,000
divided into 160 shares, be formed to offer passenger service. The *Iroquois*
having demonstrated that steamers could run up and down the rapids
between Prescott and Dickinson's Landing, the Brockville group laid plans
to build a bigger, better boat, the *Brockville*, to carry passengers between
Brockville and the head of the Long Sault. Discussions with the Montrealers led to an agreement that a committee of seven Montrealers and five
Brockville men would run the new forwarding company. The articles of
association were signed on 22 January, and the Brockvillites reported on
the arrangements at a meeting of their townsmen six days later. "Several
shares were subscribed on the spot in the Forwarding Association and also
for the proposed Steamboat," the *Brockville Recorder* reported. "We
understand the greater part of the stock of the latter has been taken, that
the other is rapidly subscribing, and that there is the most cheering
prospect of complete success in both undertakings."[28]

With agents W.L. Whiting, erstwhile partner of Samuel Crane, and
Alexander Morris in place at Montreal and Brockville respectively, the
new company opened for business on 23 May, primed to outdo the
forwarders of the Upper Canada Line by offering the "lowest possible
terms" for the carriage of freight.[29] For the passenger trade, it counted
on the *Brockville* to outrun the *Iroquois*. As for the insurance part of the

business, it is worth noting that Moses Maynard Jr, a key figure in the new concern and close friend of its secretary, Montreal commission merchant Charles Mittleberger, was an agent of the Howard Insurance Company of New York, the company for which Jacob Bigelow had once sold inland-navigation policies.[30]

Insurance was a critical factor in St Lawrence transportation. Canadian forwarders and transporters had long disclaimed responsibility for goods lost or damaged in transit, but the courts had ruled against them on this question in 1829–30. They were thus as interested in insurance coverage as the owners of the goods they carried, a factor that probably contributed to the founding of the Canada Inland Assurance Company in Montreal in 1830.[31] What is more, while the dangers of navigation made insurance indispensable on the St Lawrence, the promoters of Ottawa-Rideau traffic held that the comparative safety of their route made it unnecessary there.[32] Offering insurance at reasonable rates was one way for St Lawrence traders to promote trade on their route as they struggled to maintain their ground against the Ottawa-Rideau interests.

The Canada Inland Forwarding and Insurance Company was not alone in grasping this fact. As that company was taking shape, Prescott businessmen secured a charter for the St Lawrence Inland Marine Assurance Company, with an authorized capital of £100,000, split into 8,000 shares of £12 10s. each. Hiram Norton, reform member of the Upper Canada assembly for Grenville, was its first president and Alpheus Jones its secretary-treasurer. Other directors included Samuel Crane, of Macpherson and Crane, and Alfred Hooker, of Hooker and Henderson, the principal forwarding firms operating the Upper Canada Line and together the owners of a clear majority of shares in the St Lawrence Inland Marine Assurance Company.[33]

Considerable friction developed between Prescott and Brockville in the summer of 1833 following the launch of the Canada Inland Forwarding and Insurance Company. Merchants in both towns accused each other of trying to monopolize the transport business on the St Lawrence.[34] By early August the Brockvillites' ambitions had gone beyond running a forwarding company and a single steamer – they were contemplating setting up a whole new line of boats and stages between their town and Montreal. A public meeting was called for 2 September, two days before the scheduled launch of the Brockville, which was to form one link in the chain.[35] Meanwhile, the owners of the Upper Canada Line were said to be planning to build a new steamboat, bigger than the Iroquois, to navigate between Prescott and Cornwall starting in 1834.[36] Not to be outdone, Prescott interests intimated that they planned to build a revolutionary new steamboat that would sail up and down all the rapids between Prescott and Montreal. "Opposition is the life of business," a correspondent wrote teasingly in a Prescott newspaper in breaking the news.[37]

But opposition and one-upmanship between Brockville and Prescott made little sense when their basic goal was the same, that is, preserving and promoting the St Lawrence route in the face of the Ottawa-Rideau alternative. Some conciliatory steps had obviously been taken by the first week of September. Pursuant to notice, a meeting was held at the Brockville courthouse on Monday, 2 September, to lay the groundwork for a new stage-and-steamboat concern with the proposed name of Montreal and Brockville New Steam Boat and Coach Company. A committee consisting mainly of the Brockville and Montreal men behind the Canada Inland Forwarding and Insurance Company and two Cornwall men, Philip VanKoughnet and John Chesley, was appointed to draft the articles of association, organize the sale of stock, and preside over the affairs of the company. At a meeting that Thursday, however, the committee – only six members were present, all from Brockville – delegated Hiram Norton of Prescott to travel to Lower Canada "for the purpose of procuring subscriptions of stock to the Company and carrying into effect the objects of the public meeting held at the Court House on Monday last."[38] Norton, one of the chief backers of the rapids-beating steamer that Prescott merchants planned to build, was well acquainted with the Montreal business community. There was, for one thing, his old connection with the Upper Canada Line. He was also involved at this time with Abijah Bigelow and other Montrealers in the first, abortive effort to launch the Banque du Peuple.[39]

Between the Monday and Thursday meetings of the committee in Brockville, the *Brockville* was launched, on Wednesday, 4 September. Built by Sheay and Merritt of Montreal, she was flat-bottomed, 145 feet long, 22 feet 10 inches beam, and 45 feet wide on deck, with a depth of hold of $7\frac{1}{2}$ feet and a draft of 39 inches. Facilities for passengers included a large drawing-room and bar, a men's cabin, 84 feet long, with twenty-two berths, and a smaller, fourteen-berth women's cabin on deck exhibiting "every luxury that can be found in a lady's boudoir." The boat's stern was decorated with an elaborate carving, representing General Sir Isaac Brock, attended by two female figures. Bigger than the *Iroquois* and a sidewheeler where the latter had her wheel in the stern, she was also more powerful. She was equipped that fall with two horizontal, low-pressure engines of 40 horsepower, built by William Avery of Syracuse, New York.[40] Reports of her trials in January 1834, both in open water and through the rapids between Prescott and Dickinson's Landing, were little short of ecstatic.[41]

But a major change had taken place during the fall in the plans for the new line. Casting aside the anti-monopoly principles of its ally, the Canada Inland Forwarding and Insurance Company, the management committee of the *Brockville* chose to throw in its lot with the owners of the Upper Canada Line. A hint that something was afoot came when the shareholders of the *Brockville* were summoned to meet at Brockville on 7 December to make arrangements for completing the boat and to discuss what was ingenuously termed "other matters of equal importance." At the Saturday night meeting, sparsely attended, the committee presented the five-year agreement it had entered into with the Upper Canada Line partners, that is, the Bigelows, Horace Dickinson's estate, and the forwarders.

This *fait accompli* did not sit well with some of the *Brockville* shareholders present. They complained that they had never been consulted, and besides, had not the original idea been to challenge the Upper Canada Line so as to increase travel and transport facilities and bring fares and freight rates down? Yet it must have been hard to argue realistically against forging links with the Upper Canada Line – no other company operated steamers and stages on the St Lawrence between Dickinson's Landing and Montreal. Barring the immediate creation of a rival passenger line offering comparable facilities, which would require major investments, no other connection was then possible. And if the Upper Canada Line were to proceed with plans to build a new steamer of its own to ply between Prescott and Dickinson's Landing instead of allying itself with the owners of the *Brockville*, the latter boat would be left high and dry. Not surprisingly, opponents of the agreement were outnumbered and the meeting ended by voting its approval of this marriage of convenience.[42]

So the Montreal and Brockville New Steam Boat and Coach Company was stillborn. In its place rose the Canada Steamboat and Mail Coach Company, a joint-stock company with a capital of £25,000 split into 1,000 shares. Abijah Bigelow was appointed manager. As a sop to recalcitrant Brockvillites, their town was to replace Prescott as the western terminal of the line and the fare between Brockville and Montreal was to be the same as that between Prescott and Montreal.[43] As a result of this new state of affairs, when the *Brockville*, under Captain Lonson Hilliard,[44] sailed from Kingston on her first trip to Dickinson's Landing via Ogdensburg on 31 March 1834, it was as a sister boat to the *Iroquois*, rather than as a rival. When the *Iroquois*, then under repair, was at last fit for service in August, she took over the run through the rapids, while the *Brockville* served on Lake Ontario. When the *Iroquois* was finally withdrawn from service in 1835, the *Brockville*, under Captain W.W. Sherman, son of Jahaziel Sherman of Vergennes, Vermont, took over the Prescott–Dickinson's Landing route.[45]

Hilliard was also closely involved in the plans of Hiram Norton, Alpheus Jones, and others to build a shallow-draft steamboat at Prescott that would sail the whole length of the river between Prescott and Montreal.[46] To accomplish this, they proposed to launch a kind of steam catamaran – or "cigar boat," as it was called – based on an experimental design by Henry Burden of Troy, New York,[47] adapted by expatriate American shipwright Nathan Sanford of Prescott.[48] Her two low-pressure,

30-horsepower engines were to be built by the Prescott Foundry and Steam Engine Manufactory, operated by Norton and engineer Samuel Hulburt (Norton, Hulburt and Company) since the fall of 1833. Work began in January 1834. The *Rapid*, as she was called, was launched on 12 June 1834 before a cheering crowd of between 3,000 and 4,000. She appeared to be "as light as a feather, swims like a duck, and draws but 15 inches of water ... a beautiful model, strong as iron and timber could make her, buoyant as a piece of cork, steady as the hills."[49] One who had the opportunity to examine her closely gave this detailed description:

The length of this boat is 179 feet in length by 36 feet 6 inches in breadth, supported by two eliptical cylinders 177 feet in length and 9 feet in diameter, flatter in the bottom than at the top, secured with wrought iron hoops placed 8 feet apart, and planked with $2\frac{1}{2}$ inch plank; the keel is formed of oak ... The two hulls are placed 12 feet 6 inches apart ... The wheel is placed 65 feet from the stern, and the deck extends three feet at each end over the hulls. The after cabin is 55 feet in length by 22 feet in breadth, containing 32 berths, with a removeable partition which separates 3 lengths of berths for ladies. We have been informed by the Architect of this enterprising experiment, that it will require 15,000 pounds weight to sink this boat one inch. Her bearings being 60 feet in length by 18 feet in breadth, she will draw with all on board, wood and water included, 24 inches, and will be propelled by two engines of 30 horsepower connected with one wheel. The shaft of the water wheel is placed about 8 feet above the deck, in order to give a 25 feet wheel, and the engines are upon the deck, for the purpose of fastening them better, this produces an angle of about 10 degrees. The air pumps are within the trunk of the boat, worked by a lever beam through a hole in the trunk. The boilers are built upon the rail-road boiler principle; the outside of a cylindrical form of 5 feet 6 inches diameter, with 28 flues of 7 inches diameter and 13 feet long. A furnace is formed the full size of the outside of the boiler. The whole length of the boiler is 19 feet. They are placed forward of the wheel, side by side, so that one smoke pipe serves for both.

The engines are outside the boilers; and the wheel, boilers and engines, are within the space of 46 feet in length by 20 in breadth.[50]

"Inhabitants of Brockville, will you be outdone by Prescott!" the *Brockville Recorder* expostulated while this wonder was under construction. "Meet them and resolve on action."[51] As it happened, no action was needed: the *Rapid* was a washout. Captain Hilliard may have been among the first to catch on – he bailed out around the time she was launched. When she underwent her trials that summer, it became clear that she drew too much water, and her speed, even in still water, never measured up to her owners' wishes of 18 miles per hour. As a result, they abandoned the idea of running her through the rapids and decided to operate her between Prescott and the head of the Bay of Quinte. On 5 September they published her schedule, which called for two trips a week in each direction. Four days later they summoned the stockholders to meet aboard the boat on 22 September, and on 15 October she was advertised for sale, with the admission that she had been "intended to navigate the Rapids of the St Lawrence, but was found to draw too much water." It was suggested that she was "admirably calculated for the trade between Montreal and Quebec, and could be taken down without any difficulty." There were no takers. At a public sale on 2 June 1835, Norton and Alpheus Jones bought out their fellow shareholders for £1,600, removed her engines, and had them installed in the Toronto-Hamilton steamer *Oakville*, for which they received shares in that boat.[52]

As in the reorganization of 1833, when the forwarders bought into the Upper Canada Line, the creation of the Canada Steamboat and Mail Coach Company brought more changes at the lower end of the line. On Lake St Louis the *Swan*, deemed surplus, was put up for sale at the beginning of April 1834. It would be two years before she found a buyer (in the person of Joseph-Narcisse Pacaud of Nicolet, who would use her on the waters below Montreal). In anticipation of her removal from the line, however, the *Henry Brougham*, used as a towboat in 1833, had been remodelled during the winter and fitted with cabins for passengers. Henceforth she would do double duty.[53]

The sale of the *Chateauguay* and plans to dispose of the *Swan* signalled an end to the exclusionary policy that Dickinson had pursued on Lakes St Louis and St Francis. Barely three months after the *Swan* was offered for sale, another steamer, a new *Montreal*, of about 50 tons burden, 90 feet long, 18 feet beam, and with a 30-horsepower high-pressure engine built by Bennet and Henderson, made her appearance on Lake St Louis. Sheay and Merritt had built her for James Wait for use as a ferry between Montreal and Longueuil in 1833, but on 15 July 1834 he sold a three-quarter interest in her to Emery Cushing, clockmaker Ira Twiss, Silas Dickinson, and the latter's brother-in-law, Charles Sheldon. The sale was conditional on the *Montreal* being run up to Lake St Louis, where the partners proposed to operate her as a ferry between Lachine and Châteauguay. Stripped of her paddlewheels, she was taken up the Lachine Canal to Lake St Louis, where she began service by mid-August. The original purchase agreement fell through, however, and in June 1835 Wait, as "sole owner," sold her outright to Cushing and Twiss for £1,000. That year she sailed regularly between Lachine, Châteauguay, and Beauharnois. In 1836 Cushing and Twiss sold her to Jacob De Witt for £950.[54]

On Lake St Francis, as on Lake St Louis, other steamboats made their appearance. The *Dalhousie* was damaged by fire and sunk in 1834.[55] That year the *Prescott* of Ogdensburg began operating as a ferry between Cornwall and Fort Covington, New York, also touching at St Regis and Hogansburgh. When an accident left the *Neptune* out of commission for about two weeks in the fall, Asahel Whipple hired the ferry to carry the Upper Canada Line's passengers. The following year another ferry, the 6-horsepower *Jack Downing*, named for a popular fictional character created by Maine newspaper publisher Seba Smith, ran twice a day between Cornwall and Hogansburgh under Captain Paul Boynton of Canton, New York.[56]

Nor was that the end of the flurry of activity on the St Lawrence after 1832. Only a few months after the formation of the Canada Steamboat and Mail Coach Company, the Dickinson estate put its shares in the company up for sale in the spring of 1834,[57] at the same time as Horace Dickinson's widow turned down Jacob De Witt's offer of a share in his *Chateauguay*. Then in July, James McCutchon pulled out of the concern to pursue other interests in Kingston.[58] These moves heralded the breakup of the compound partnership formed eighteen months earlier between the forwarders, the Dickinson estate, and A. Bigelow and Company. On 28 August they agreed to fold the concern at the end of the year. Macpherson, Henderson and Company and Crane, Hooker and Company, as the firms were called after McCutchon's withdrawal, liquidated their joint assets at public auctions held at Montreal, Prescott, Kingston, Dundas, and Hamilton between 29 December 1834 and 9 January 1835. Besides fifty open and ten decked barges at Montreal, the schooner *Prescott* at Prescott, and an untold number of Durham boats at various Upper Canadian ports, their holdings included 5,000 of the 8,000 shares in the St Lawrence Inland Marine Assurance Company. As of 31 December 1834, the disentangled companies went their separate ways in the forwarding business under their former names.[59]

The disposition of their joint assets is not known. We cannot say, for instance, how much of an interest each may have retained in the St Lawrence Inland Marine Assurance Company. It is striking, however, that while they put up for auction their controlling interest in that company, as well as some bank stock, they did not offer for public sale any of their shares in the Canada Steamboat and Mail Coach Company. From subsequent developments, it is clear that the Macpherson and Crane partnership and Asahel Whipple remained in control of the Upper Canada Line; James Henderson, the Dickinson family friend, also seems to have retained some stake in the line, either personally or through Hooker and Henderson.[60] A. Bigelow and Company, however, went out of business, and Asahel Whipple succeeded Abijah Bigelow as the Montreal-based manager of the transport line, turning over command of the *Neptune* on Lake St Francis to his son-in-law, William Henry Wilkins. Whipple also seized the opportunity of his move to Montreal to launch a forwarding venture between Montreal and Cornwall with Paul Timothée Masson, former member of the Lower Canada assembly for Vaudreuil and cousin and brother-in-law of Damase Masson, the steamboat line's wood supplier at Beauharnois.[61]

If Mercy Amelia Dickinson's disposal of her late husband's assets indicates that she wished to be clear of the transport business, it seems that Abijah Bigelow, her brother, had thoughts of quitting Canada altogether. This might explain why, after joining in the abortive attempt to launch the Banque du Peuple in 1833 (see chap. 3), he played no part in the renewed, successful attempt in 1835. The widower of forty-one had remarried on 30 January 1834. His second wife, Rebecca Edwards Ogden of Waddington, New York, was the daughter of Gouverneur Ogden, a prominent figure in the Ogdensburg area. The first of their five children was born at Montreal on 18 May 1835, and the rest after they had moved to the United States.[62] In December 1834, at the time of the dissolution of the Upper Canada Line partnership, Bigelow advertised his services as agent of the Aetna Insurance Company, something he had not done for several years. The following August he moved his insurance office into the premises of timber dealer Lumen Vaughan and began handing off the business to the latter's brother, Henry P. Vaughan. By the end of December 1835 Bigelow was out of the business altogether and Henry Vaughan was the Aetna agent.[63] Early in 1836 Bigelow was away in Upper Canada, perhaps disposing of the *Iroquois* and tying up other loose ends of his business affairs.[64] With the political storm clouds gathering in Canada, he and his family then joined the rush to the American west, following his brother, Jacob, and his father to La Porte County, Indiana. Increase Sumner, his unmarried brother and partner, moved to Milwaukee in the Wisconsin Territory.[65]

The scramble of Brockville and Prescott men, in alliance with Montreal interests, to maintain and enhance the viability of the rapids-strewn St Lawrence route after 1832 contrasts with the seemingly calmer pace of progress at Kingston and on the Ottawa-Rideau route generally. Kingston residents, in fact, were rebuked for their lackadaisical response to the changes going on around them. A correspondent who claimed to be a detached traveller, but whose transparent aim was to sting Kingstonians into backing efforts to form a forwarding company to compete with downriver interests, wrote to the *Kingston Chronicle* in September 1833:

On inquiry, I understood that the town is often reprehensible for its imbecile, and consequently inefficient enterprise; that the new and inconsiderable villages of Brockville and Prescott have, through the spirited exertions of a number of their principal inhabitants, established the only forwarding companies now in operation in this delightful and rapidly increasing Province, to the manifest neglect, and in despite of the interests, of this town. Why this is, I am at a loss to comprehend. Kingston is the oldest, and, till recently, the largest and most important town in the colony; its inhabitants are known for their ample means, and many of them for their wealth; and yet I notice that the very necessary and important business [the forwarding company] of which I have been speaking, is like to fall to the ground by the spiritless endeavours proverbial to the good people of Kingston. Why is this so? Let the voice of Kingston reply![66]

One would not be surprised to learn that the writer, who signed "Viator," was one of those involved in efforts to launch the forwarding company, perhaps even Robert Drummond himself. A few days earlier, on 23 September, Drummond had chaired a public meeting at the courthouse to launch the new concern. The meeting voted to establish the Kingston Forwarding Company, with a capital of £15,000, divided into 1,200 shares. A management committee was appointed that included Drummond, then owner of the canal steamers *Margaret* and *Rideau*, as well as of the *John By*, plying on Lake Ontario; John Goldsbury Parker, an American expatriate from New Hampshire, whose *Perseverance* (formerly the *Toronto*) was to run on the canal once his new steamboat, *Kingston*, was ready to replace her on the Bay of Quinte; and foundry owner George Wheatley Yarker, who as a partner in Yarker, Vanalstine and Bennett would launch the steamer *Thomas McKay* on the canal in the spring of 1834.[67] Some £2,000 in stock had already subscribed in the Kingston Forwarding Company when another meeting on 16 October resolved "that the company be now formed," that it be called the Canada Forwarding Company, and, rather vaguely, that the committee "take such steps as the interests of the Company may require," once shares to the value of £6,000 had been subscribed. A new management committee was appointed and authorized to amend the articles of association drafted by its predecessor. Neither Drummond, Parker, nor Yarker sat on the new committee. If not an illustration of dithering, this relaunching certainly betrayed some disunity among Kingston merchants.[68]

As part of the effort to counter the "manifest neglect" of Kingston by the Brockville and Prescott forwarders, John G. Parker planned to run his Bay of Quinte steamer *Kingston* all the way down to Dickinson's Landing, "if practicable," in 1834.[69] Under the command of twenty-seven-year-old Captain Lucius Moody,[70] Parker's steamer, powered by a 45-horsepower Ward engine, made a trial trip to the head of the Long Sault and back on 4–5 April. She did wonderfully, it was said, leaving Dickinson's Landing at 6:30 a.m. on Saturday, 5 April, and reaching Prescott by 1 p.m. This trip proved "that any powerful-engined Steam Boat, not drawing more than five feet of water, can ascend these formidable rapids," the *British Whig* remarked. That boats such as the *Iroquois* and the *Brockville*, "built expressly for the route, should be able to perform the journey we have recorded, is nothing remarkable; the difficulty consists in taking a boat built for deeper waters, and making her do with comparative ease, what the other boats performed with some difficulty." After this exploit, however, the *Kingston* returned to regular duty between Prescott and the Bay of Quinte, under Captain John Ives. She briefly replaced the *Brockville*, out of commission with a broken shaft, on the Prescott–Dickinson's Landing route in early July. Her season came to an abrupt end on 27 November when, holed by ice, she sank at Belleville.[71]

Even more telling of the tensions between Kingston and the downriver interests in 1834 was the to-do over the steamer *St George*, which ran between Prescott and Niagara. She was a top-flight boat, owned by many of the prominent Kingstonians who had built the *John By*.[72] Launched at Kingston on 3 June 1833, she was 142 feet long, 44 feet wide overall, 360 tons burden, schooner-rigged, and with a 90-horsepower low-pressure engine made by Bennet and Henderson. Besides the twenty-four open berths, the men's cabin below deck had two staterooms with two berths in each. The women's cabin consisted of twenty such staterooms. Her commander was an officer of the Royal Navy, Lieutenant James Harper, whose experience included fifteen years of commanding a steam packet on the rough waters between Liverpool and Dublin.[73] On 25 July 1834 the *St George*, pride of Kingston, was boycotted by forwarders at Prescott and Brockville. At Prescott, MacPherson and Crane would not let her take any freight, preferring to ship it aboard the *William IV*, though that steamer was not scheduled to leave port until twenty-four hours after the *St George*. The same thing occurred at Brockville, where forwarders H. and S. Jones detained a batteau full of immigrants for the *William IV* rather than let them sail aboard the *St George*. At the same time, the forwarders were threatening to call on their contacts at the head of Lake Ontario not to ship any goods down by the *St George*. As a result, Captain Harper announced, "the owners of this boat have declined to run her to Prescott and Brockville any more this season."[74]

Several factors may have contributed to this dispute, one of at least three similar controversies in which Captain Harper was embroiled in 1834–35.[75] H. and S. Jones claimed, for example, that the reason they were boycotting the *St George* was that she had often refused to take their freight after they had complained of overcharging. Harper denied any such vindictive behaviour.[76] But the crux of the matter, it seems, was that the *St George* was seen as favouring the Ottawa-Rideau trade over that of the St Lawrence. Because the bulk of imported goods had always had to be picked up at Prescott and, to a lesser extent, at Brockville when the St Lawrence was the only water route to the Great Lakes, it had been the custom for steamers to charge the same price for goods shipped up the lake from those forwarding terminals as from Kingston, even though they were sixty to seventy miles further down. But with goods now coming up the Ottawa-Rideau route to Kingston, the *St George* instituted a policy of charging two pence less per hundredweight for freight shipped upward from Kingston.[77] The implications for Brockville and Prescott – not just for their forwarders – were unsettling, a mark of their declining importance. And woe to them if they chose to respond with tactics such as the boycott of the *St George*, the *Kingston Chronicle* warned, issuing a rather odd threat: "If measures like this affecting the *St George* are persisted in, we are assured that that boat, in connection with the *Commodore Barrie*, will run from Kingston to Toronto five times a week, making a regular line, via the Rideau Canal, from Montreal to Toronto."[78]

Given that Kingston was uniquely placed to benefit from the Rideau Canal, the attempts of its merchants to shore up their trade with Montreal tended to focus on that waterway rather than on the St Lawrence.[79] An important step was taken early in 1834 when Drummond and Emery Cushing, manager of the Ottawa Steamboat Company, met at Bytown to work out a meshing of their transport lines. Spurred no doubt by the redeployment of St Lawrence River forces in the newly formed Canada Steamboat and Mail Coach Company, they sought to streamline their operations by eliminating delays in the transfer of goods and passengers at Bytown, where their lines met. They subsequently advertised a Montreal-Kingston through service for freight and passengers which they called the Rideau and Ottawa Steam Boat Forwarding Company. Cushing was its agent in Montreal, Drummond at Kingston. It was not a full-fledged merger: Drummond and the Ottawa Steamboat Company coordinated their operations but retained the ownership of their respective assets.[80]

It was a busy year for Drummond. In fact, he embarked on two new careers. In May he announced his intention to run as a candidate for the county of Frontenac in the general election to be held that fall. He was nominated in July.[81] In March, following the dissolution of Cormack and Morton (John S. Cormack and James Morton), the partnership that had run his brewery and distillery, he had resolved to operate the business himself. Then on 19 August, perhaps anticipating that political commitments would prevent him from giving due attention to his business affairs, he entered into a brewing, distilling, and forwarding partnership with James McCutchon, who had just pulled out of the Upper Canada Line. The very next day, Drummond was felled by cholera, dying at a moment of particular promise, like Horace Dickinson two years earlier.[82]

Though it claimed fewer victims than the epidemic of 1832, the disease this year sowed its share of death and disruption.[83] Besides Drummond, its victims included Duncan Vanalstine, of Yarker, Vanalstine and Bennett, owners of the *Thomas McKay*; Montrealer Thomas Andrew Turner, who had been a co-owner of the *Ottawa*, that first, ill-fated effort to place a steamboat on the Ottawa River in 1819–20; and mason William McKay, who had recently finished building the Carillon Canal. On the Great Lakes, American steamers stopped calling at Canadian ports for a time. On the Ottawa-Rideau line, James McCutchon stepped into Drummond's shoes, filling in as agent at Kingston. Drummond's canal steamers, *Rideau* and *Margaret*, were put up for sale, as was the *Thomas McKay*.[84]

Drummond's and Cushing's efforts notwithstanding, delays plagued the Ottawa-Rideau service in 1834, largely because of the double use to which the Rideau steamers were put. The five steamers on the canal – the *Rideau*, the *Margaret*, and the *Thomas McKay*, plus John G. Parker's *Toronto* (the *Perseverance* back under her old name) and the *Enterprise*, owned by the Tay Navigation Company of Perth[85] – were used to tow barges as well as to carry passengers. Towing was a tedious process, slowing the steamers between locks but especially in the locks themselves, where vessels proceeded one at a time – first the steamer and then the barges, one after another. "Imagine the pleasure of double or treble Lockage, ascending and descending 47 Locks with three Barges in tow, and a week on the route to Kingston instead of thirty hours," a critic wailed.[86] The *Bathurst Courier* of Perth commented:

We hope, before another season opens we shall have boats expressly for passengers as the system of towing barges has rendered travelling on the Rideau the most perfect humbug imaginable. The last time the *Rideau* came down, she left Kingston at two o'clock on Monday, and did not reach Oliver's until five A.M. on Wednesday, having gone at the rate of a mile an hour. Unless something is done not only to facilitate the passage, but also to add to the comfort and convenience of passengers, and to establish certain hours of arrival and departure at Kingston, Bytown, and all intermediate places, which is quite easily managed, it can never be expected that any one will go that way, who can possibly avoid it; and we think from the business of this year, neglected and ill managed as it has been, it is worth the attention of the Ottawa company, or in short any one of wealth and enterprise sufficient to build a good Boat.[87]

The failure of the boat owners to work together and assign some steamers to towing and others to passenger service thus led the newspaper to invite the Ottawa River monopoly to take an active hand in the Rideau traffic. The 1834 arrangement between Drummond and Cushing had paved the way for just such a step.

In January 1835 the Ottawa Steamboat Company bought Drummond's *Rideau* and *Margaret*, as well as the *Thomas McKay*, and announced: "The Ottawa Steamboat Company having increased their Capital Stock by the purchase of three Steamboats on the Rideau Canal, in order to complete and extend their line to Kingston, will hereafter transact their business under the name of the Ottawa and Rideau Forwarding Company." Besides picking up the three second-hand canal steamers, the company also had a new boat, the *Bytown*, nearly ready for the Rideau trade. Over the winter this steamer, built at Hawkesbury, was fitted with the engine of the *William King*. The latter was retired. Meetings of stockholders in the new company were held at Kingston on 3 February and at Montreal on 16 February. Nearly £4,000 of stock was subscribed by Kingston investors, but the board of directors was made up entirely of Montrealers – John Frothingham, chairman; Emery Cushing, agent (manager); and Peter McGill, John Molson Jr, Thomas Phillips, and John Redpath.[88]

The *Bathurst Courier*, scathing in its denunciation of the previous, rivalrous system, welcomed this concentration of ownership and hoped that "the Ottawa Company will exert themselves to redeem the nearly destroyed character of the Canal."[89] The editorialist went on to explain what, in his estimation, had nearly ruined the Rideau waterway:

Had all its enemies conspired and bought up the influence of every boat and Captain on the Canal last year, with one honourable exception, nothing more could have been done toward its injury and the ruin of the route. We hope the Ottawa Company may buy up every boat on the waters and not subject us to the capricious service of Boats, any individual stock holder in which can turn the boat about at his pleasure, and leave merchandise for months on the way – or to winter in the boat, that would have gone to market, without their interference ... The system of towing barges by regular passage boats will never answer ... Small, low Boats, with extra power expressly for towing, and long light airy boats for passengers, well manned to force through the Locks is what is required.

Besides the changes in the Rideau navigation, the Ottawa and Rideau Forwarding Company had several important changes in store for the Ottawa River. The old *St Andrews*, which had become the first steamer to pass through the completed Ottawa River canals on 24 April 1834, was assigned the task of towing barges through the Carillon and Chute à Blondeau canals, under Captain C.L. Lighthall.[90] The *Shannon*, which had run between Grenville and Bytown for the last five years, latterly under the command of Royal Navy purser Thomas Kains of Grenville,[91] was fitted with two new 40-horsepower Ward engines at New Edinburgh at a cost of £3,400. Besides making and installing her new engines, the Wards were paid £400 to repair and install her old 28-horsepower engines and boilers in the *Nonsuch*, a new boat being built at New Edinburgh under the supervision of George Brush, the veteran master of the Torrance steamboats on the St Lawrence. The *Nonsuch* was to ply between Lachine

The *Shannon* tied up below the locks of the Rideau Canal at Bytown; from W.H. Bartlett's *Canadian Scenery* of 1842 (from the author's collection).

and Carillon, joining the 50-horsepower *Ottawa*, which had been in service on that route since 1833. Once the building of the *Nonsuch* was completed, Brush would become the superintendent of the company at Kingston, superseding McCutchon.[92] On a tour of the Great Lakes in the summer of 1835, he set up agencies for the company at the American ports of Buffalo, Cleveland, Detroit, Oswego, and Rochester, as well as at Cobourg, Hamilton, London, Port Hope, St Thomas, Sandwich, and Toronto.[93]

The *Nonsuch* rivalled the failed *Rapid* of Prescott in the novelty of her design. She was another variant on Henry Burden's "cigar boat." Indeed, Brush had travelled to New York early in 1834 to study Burden's designs.[94] The *Nonsuch* was well named, it seems, for the boat was "of peculiar construction … verily it was a non-such."[95] A writer in the *Kingston Chronicle* described her at length:

Let our readers suppose an impossibility – an oblong square piece of timber 108 feet long, by 31 feet broad, and about 12 feet thick. Groove a channel through the middle of the upper surface of this, 72 feet long, 9 feet wide, and 10 inches deep. Go on *quite through* the block, the remainder of the length, and *turn it over*. Now scoop it out in the roomiest manner possible, to receive a double low pressure engine of 28 horse power each – two Ladies' Cabins, in the prongs of the fork, each having eight berths inclining to midships, and lighted – the starboard one by two, the larboard by three Cabin windows; and four or five side scuttles, with a forecabin the whole breadth, and galleries running to the after Cabins, by each side of the central apartment for the Engine. And let them further conceive this to be a steamer, lightly but closely timbered, and substantially sheathed and planked, with a double rudder adding three feet to its length and then have as good an idea of the 'Nonsuch' as we profess ourselves to give them. We have not quite done yet however, the paddle wheel is placed amidship, where the 10 inch groove ends, and is a little too large being, if we recollect rightly, from 18 to 20 feet diameter, a foot and a half of which is to be removed. The railing is continued quite round the Boat, and going aft from one gangway to the other, supports a number of pillars on which a respectable promenade deck rests. The Gentlemen's Cabin is under this, twenty-four feet by twenty, and to contain sixteen births; but one of the Ladies Cabins will often, in all probability be appropriated to their use.[96]

In June, Brush took the *Nonsuch* through the Rideau to Kingston and down the St Lawrence to Lachine, where she arrived on 1 July. She thus became the first steamer to run all the rapids between Prescott and Lachine. At last, the "long talked of experiment of descending the St Lawrence Rapids in a Steamboat, has been accomplished," a newspaper noted; "it now remains to try those rapids upwards, they only run nine miles per hour, therefore there cannot be much doubt of success, if the Steamboat is properly constructed, but even if it does not at first succeed, it will be an easy matter to do so, with the assistance of iron chains, as proposed by the St Lawrence Association in 1824."[97] But the subsequent history of the *Nonsuch* brought no further triumph. After at most three years of disappointing service on the Ottawa, initially under the command of William Squire of Lachine, a lieutenant in the Royal Navy, she was turned into a boarding house, then run up on the beach at Vaudreuil to serve as a wharf.[98]

By the mid-1830s, then, the Canada Steamboat and Mail Coach Company and the Ottawa and Rideau Forwarding Company enjoyed a virtual monopoly on steamer traffic on their respective routes. The Ottawa and Rideau boasted that its 240-mile route from Montreal to Kingston was much safer than the St Lawrence and therefore cheaper because goods shipped on its line did not need to be insured. The St Lawrence operators claimed that their route, only 190 miles long, was shorter and more direct. Both resorted to dockside touts and tit-for-tat newspaper advertisements to rope in immigrants and other travellers.[99] In April 1836, for instance, the Ottawa and Rideau advertised that, "For Emigrants, this line of communication is particularly advantageous, as they can embark with their luggage on board of decked Barges, which are towed through to Kingston by Steamboats ... without being subjected to the great inconvenience of landing and walking past the Rapids, as is the case by the St Lawrence route."[100]

Macpherson and Crane could not deny that most immigrants on the St Lawrence route, too poor to pay for a coach or steamer and relegated to batteaux or barges, had to trudge around the rapids, carrying their baggage, from one boat landing to another. Some were even enlisted to help work the boats up. With a straight face, the company sought to present this drawback as a plus:

To Emigrants, they would observe that the salubrity of the air on the banks of the St Lawrence, and the opportunities they have of exercising themselves – which is not necessary, however, if disagreeable to them – must prove conducive to their health, and be much more gratifying to their feelings, than to be huddled together on board of a Boat, passing over the still and somewhat stagnant waters of a long, uninteresting, and dreary Canal route.[101]

The Scottish traveller Patrick Shirreff had seen how little conducive to health or gratifying to the feelings travel along the St Lawrence could be for immigrants. Leaving Côteau aboard the *Neptune* one day in mid-August 1833, he noted that the steamer took seven batteaux in tow,

in one of which I counted 110 emigrants, of all ages who were doomed to pass the night on board. Men, women and children were huddled together as close as captives in a slave-trader, exposed to the sun's rays by day, and river damp by night, without protection. It was impossible to look upon such a group of human beings without emotion. The day had been so intensely hot, that the stoutest amongst them looked fatigued, while the females seemed ready to expire with exhaustion ... The navigation up the St Lawrence in batteaux is accomplished by propelling them with poles, and is necessarily tedious. The accommodation is so wretched and irksome, that the emigrants' privations of transport may be said only to commence at Montreal, where they perhaps expected them to end, and when their spirits are ill fitted to bear up against them.[102]

Under the circumstances, it is no wonder that many who had the immigrants' best interests at heart recommended the Ottawa-Rideau route, with its decked barges towed all the way. Still, many people continued to travel the St Lawrence, in some cases, no doubt, for the same reasons that Shirreff did. He had wanted to go by the Ottawa-Rideau, he said, "but the irregularity of the conveyances by this route, and my limited time, induced me to ascend the St Lawrence."[103] In 1836 Macpherson and Crane covered some of their barges to shelter passengers and freight from the elements. And not all immigrants were packed into barges and batteaux; some had the good fortune, if it can be so called, of being packed into steamers. One day in June 1836 the *Neptune* reached Cornwall carrying more than three hundred steerage passengers, besides fifty cabin passengers.[104]

Whatever the company's advantages, fortune frowned on the Ottawa and Rideau in 1836. The run of bad luck might be said to have begun at the end of 1835, with the loss of the *Thomas McKay*. On 21 October the steamer hit a stump in the canal on her way to Kingston and sank in six feet of water. By December the company had decided to build a new boat to replace her; the *Cataraqui* was accordingly constructed at Kingston over the winter and launched the following spring.[105] A late thaw delayed the opening of navigation in 1836. When the ice finally cleared, most of the company's barges were at Lachine and other downriver locations, while most of the freight waited upriver. Then, once the barges had reached Kingston, foul weather prevented them from getting under way for days. The final blow came in mid-June when damage to an overflow dam at Long Island closed the Rideau Canal for almost two months.[106] To fulfill its commitments to its customers, the embarrassed company had no choice but to resort to the much deprecated St Lawrence route. Out of its element and without agents or facilities there,[107] the Ottawa and Rideau, in desperation, found it advisable to absorb the Canada Inland Forwarding and Insurance Company, itself a strong partisan of the St Lawrence route but struggling to stay afloat.[108] The Ottawa and Rideau announced the shotgun wedding with red-faced bluster:

Although a decided preference has justly been given to the Rideau Line, from the superior craft in which goods are forwarded, as well as the certainty with regard to time and diminution of risk attending the transport, yet some objections have been raised to the Canals being closed earlier in the fall than the River St Lawrence, and to obviate these objections the Company intend by this union to keep a full supply of Boats on the St Lawrence, not with a view of doing their business generally by that route, but to accommodate their customers in the Spring and Fall, as well as to meet every possible contingency that might take place on the Canal, and restore to the Company the fullest confidence of the public.[109]

The merger signalled a loss of business and status for Prescott, since the Ottawa and Rideau stated in the same breath: "To facilitate the Transport of Goods destined for the Ports of Lakes *Ontario* and *Erie*, the Company have arranged for their transhipment at both the Ports of Prescott and Kingston, but from its eligibility, intend the latter to be the principal place of transhipment, when the Rideau Canal is reopened." When the canal reopened to traffic in early August, the company resumed

its main operations there but kept a line of twenty freight boats on the
St Lawrence, just in case.[110] While the Ottawa and Rideau championed
Kingston, Macpherson and Crane vaunted the superior merits of Prescott:

> as a place of transhipment, Prescott has advantages over any port at this end of
> *Lake Ontario*. Being at the foot of the unobstructed navigable water, extending
> from that Lake, it is the ultimate destination of all the Steamboats, and the major-
> ity of the Schooners plying thereon … When a cargo can be obtained there, they
> will not, of course, suffer detention at any of the ports above, seeking for freight.
> It is for this reason that Goods are often long kept in Store at these places, obliged
> to wait until a vessel from Prescott calls, which may have room on board for them.
> These advantages are increased, when it is known that freight can be obtained, to
> any of the ports on the Lakes, at as low a rate from Prescott as from Kingston.[111]

More trouble surfaced for the Ottawa and Rideau that fall when disgruntled Bytown-area businessmen, led by the fledgling Ottawa Lumber
Association, announced their intention of launching their own steamboat
line between Bytown and Montreal.[112] They complained of the Ottawa
and Rideau's slow service, high rates, and general insensitivity to their
needs. They faced an old problem, however, in the Vaudreuil lock:

> The Company who own the present line are said to hold the lock at the St Ann's
> rapids [*sic*] as their private property, and will not allow any boat but their own
> to pass that point. It is not necessary to offer any remarks upon the liberality of
> such conduct; but if such an obstacle stands in the way of public improvement
> the sooner it is removed the better. This may be done in various ways. – Let the
> Province purchase the Company's claims and throw open the Lock to all parties
> – or, if this cannot be done, (and there is but little hope of it in the present state
> of Lower Canada) and if no arrangement can be made whereby the new line, to
> be formed, can obtain permission to pass their boats, there is still another expe-
> dient, and for which we believe the state of the place affords every facility, – Lay
> down a warping machine, by which a Steam Boat may be warped up the rapids.[113]

The Ottawa and Rideau ended the year with a loss of more than £7,000
and debts of £8,600.[114] Faced with the threat of opposition on its own
waters after the severe setbacks of the summer of 1836, the company was
open to drastic changes. These were already in the works. Quietly, the
Ottawa and Rideau directors had entered into discussions with Macpherson and Crane. John Macpherson's election to the board of the Bank of
Montreal the previous June had probably facilitated the first probings:
Ottawa and Rideau directors Peter McGill, John Molson Jr, and John
Redpath all sat on the board of the bank, of which McGill was then
president. The rival concerns came to terms by mid-December.[115] No

change was apparent, however, until 28 March 1837, the eve of the Ottawa and Rideau's annual meeting, when it was announced that the company had joined with forwarders Macpherson and Crane, Hooker and Henderson, H. and S. Jones, and Whiting and Chandler (successor to W.L. Whiting and Company)[116] in adopting a common schedule of freight rates. With adjustments, this price-fixing agreement, reminiscent of the modus vivendi reached between James Greenfield, the Molsons, and the Torrances on the Montreal-Quebec steamer route in the late 1820s, was to remain in force through 1840.[117] The next day the committee advised stockholders at their annual meeting that "a change is necessary in the mode of managing the Cos business." The stockholders agreed, giving the committee carte blanche to do what had to be done to restore the company to profitability.[118] Within a few weeks, the Ottawa and Rideau placed the whole of its operations in the hands of Macpherson and Crane, "to secure the efficient management of their business." The announcement was made simultaneously by Ottawa and Rideau chairman John Frothingham and Macpherson and Crane on 18 April.[119]

Apart from the fact that John Macpherson was to direct operations at Montreal and Samuel Crane at Kingston, the terms of their association were not spelled out publicly. Clearly, however, these amounted to more than a fee-for-services management contract, since Macpherson and Crane brought their whole forwarding establishment into the association, besides their knowledge, experience, and administrative abilities. The alliance seems to have been something closer to the pooling of forwarding resources that had taken place between Macpherson and Crane, Hooker and Henderson, and James McCutchon in 1833–34. Yet the term "copartnership," applied to that and other similar mergers, seems never to have been used for their relationship. It remained an "arrangement" or a "business connexion." There was no new company name concocted to designate the union – the names Macpherson and Crane and Ottawa and Rideau Forwarding Company stood, and they became practically interchangeable. From the way that things turned out, Macpherson and Crane may have been assured of a percentage of the profits of their joint operations, without having to shoulder financial responsibility for any losses.

This development came just two days after Emery Cushing, the Ottawa and Rideau's founding manager, died at age forty after an illness of just a few days.[120] Yet it must have been in the works for some time – probably the fruit of that mysterious agreement reached in December. The timing suggests that Cushing had stood in the way of the change and that his sudden death somehow cleared the way for it. Perhaps he himself had opposed it as implying a censure of his management; or some of his fellow directors, conscious of this implication, may have felt qualms about turning over his duties to those who, only yesterday, had been their chief adversaries. Whatever the case, by early May the Ottawa and Rideau's stages from Montreal were departing from Macpherson and Crane's Upper Canada stage office.[121] Macpherson took over at Montreal, while George Brush continued as the Ottawa and Rideau agent at Kingston until the end of the year, when he was succeeded by Alexander Ferguson. A trusted Montreal associate of Macpherson and Crane since at least 1834, Ferguson became a full partner in that firm from 1838.[122]

If the imposition of higher freight rates had stung the Bytowners, this marriage of monopolies did nothing to calm them. "Meetings have been held, and a subscription entered into, with the design of bringing up their goods by Barges rather than pay the freight the company proposes exacting," it was reported in May. Their new enterprise, the Bytown Mutual Forwarding Company, was to concentrate on the carriage of freight and leave the Ottawa and Rideau to handle the passenger trade. The Bytown Mutual bought the small steamer *Tay*, 72 feet long and 20 feet wide, built at Pike's Falls (Port Elmsley) in 1836 in such a way "as to pass all the locks between Montreal and Kingston." Renamed the *Endeavour*, she was placed on the Bytown-Grenville route.[123] At Montreal the company hired freight agent Stephen Finchley away from the Ottawa and Rideau. Unaware of this, several shippers consigned goods to Finchley in the belief that he was still working for the Ottawa and Rideau. Matters were straightened out in June after Macpherson and Crane got wind of what was happening.[124] A one-horse operation, the Bytown Mutual was no match for the combined force of the Ottawa and Rideau/Macpherson and Crane, with their vast resources and 650-odd employees (see appendix D). It would cease operations within two years, and the *Endeavour* would fall into the hands of the Ottawa and Rideau.[125]

That summer, Macpherson and Crane reorganized the towing arrangements on the Ottawa and Rideau line. The route of the canal steamers *Bytown*, *Cataraqui*, and *Rideau* was extended beyond the canal terminal of Bytown, down the Ottawa River as far as Grenville. They were to relieve the *Shannon* of towing duty between Grenville and Bytown, taking charge of the barges at Grenville and towing them all the way to Kingston. In this way, passengers and mail would no longer be delayed at Grenville while the *Shannon* waited for barges coming up from Montreal. At Bytown she would lose no more time and money waiting for Rideau steamers to arrive and pick up the barges she had in tow. This change addressed the Bytowners' standing grievance about delays in the freight traffic up from Montreal as well as passengers' gripes about the tedium of travelling in a steamer used to tow barges. The new scheme was upset when the *Shannon* had to be taken out of service for about a month in August-September and again when the *Bytown* was severely damaged in a gale at Kingston on 19 October. When the *Shannon* went back to towing barges again in 1838, under the press of business after an accident had disabled the *Rideau,* there were renewed complaints of delays.[126]

Sitting pretty on both the St Lawrence and the Ottawa-Rideau routes, Macpherson and Crane at first advised their customers that they would "have it in their power to afford to the public a choice of routes, and will always be particular in attending to instructions which may give a preference to either."[127] But the firm's combined management of steamers and freight boats on the two routes, the spilling over of Rideau steamers into the Ottawa River in 1837, and the breakthroughs made by the *Iroquois,* the *Brockville,* and the *Nonsuch* in running the rapids of the St Lawrence all pointed in one direction – the ultimate joining of the once-competing routes in a single continuous circuit. It would be another three years before steamers accomplished this, but in 1838 the forwarding cartel, including the new firms of William Dickinson and Company and Murray and Sanderson, led the way, shifting their upward traffic to the comparatively safe and sure Ottawa-Rideau route, the barges scooting down the St Lawrence for the return to Montreal. Macpherson and Crane, erstwhile champions of the St Lawrence route, and the Ottawa and Rideau Forwarding Company, sole operators of steamers on the Ottawa-Rideau, took charge of towing the barges of the various firms through the Vaudreuil lock and up to Kingston.[128] In return, the other forwarders seem to have agreed not to invest in steamers that might compete with the Ottawa and Rideau/Macpherson and Crane boats. H. and S. Jones had toyed with the idea of launching a steamer line on the Ottawa-Rideau route in 1838, but did not follow through. None of the forwarders in fact ran steamers there until after the cartel lapsed at the end of 1840, when they rushed into an orgy of boat-building.[129]

The wholesale shift to the Ottawa-Rideau route may have been the result of some muscle-flexing by Macpherson and Crane, but it must be remembered that disruptions caused by the Cornwall Canal works in the last few years may also have contributed to the move. Only one or two small forwarding concerns, such as Whipple and Masson, continued to carry goods up the St Lawrence, and only as far as Cornwall.[130] As he travelled to Upper Canada in the summer of 1838, Charles Kadwell noted: "The greater portion by far of the goods forwarded from Montreal go by this route [Ottawa-Rideau], the Ottawa & Rideau Company established a few years since being a perfect monopoly, rendering the St Lawrence comparatively deserted, & being masters of a lock in a certain situation [Vaudreuil] which governs the whole navigation."[131] When the ninety-one Ottawa and Rideau shares belonging to Emery Cushing's estate were offered for sale in July, they were touted as "a most favourable opportunity for the investment of Capital, from the present flourishing state of the affairs of the Company. The Ottawa and the Rideau Canal being now the route for nearly the whole Freight and Passage to Upper Canada."[132] Indeed, the Ottawa and Rideau's fortunes improved markedly from the moment that Macpherson and Crane took over its operations, and its shares became a sort of blue-chip stock: the company could be counted on to produce an annual return of "ten per cent and a handsome bonus occasionally," a commentator observed in 1841.[133]

The Ottawa-Rideau route from Montreal to Kingston covered more ground, but the travelling time was not significantly longer than on the St Lawrence, where the barges had to be laboriously poled or pulled up the numerous rapids. Lockage fees had to be paid on the Ottawa-Rideau route, but these were relatively light, and the risks being less than those on the St Lawrence, forwarders saved on insurance costs. For the downward journey, however, the St Lawrence was incomparably shorter and faster, the savings in time and absence of fees outweighing the risks.[134]

As a result of these changes, Kingston eclipsed Prescott as a transshipment point, becoming the hub of virtually all the freight traffic on the Great Lakes, the Rideau, and the upper St Lawrence, and of much of the passenger trade. In 1838 Hooker and Henderson, H. and S. Jones, William Dickinson and Company, and Murray and Sanderson all moved their terminals there from Prescott and Brockville.[135] John Macpherson's brother-in-law, John Hamilton of Queenston, whose steamers had run between Prescott and the head of Lake Ontario, made Kingston the eastern terminal of his newly expanded lake line, opening an office there under the superintendence of his agent, William Meneilly. By charter or outright ownership, Hamilton controlled most of the steamers on Lake Ontario in 1838 – *Great Britain, Traveller, St George, Cobourg, Commodore Barrie*, and *Hamilton*.[136] In conjunction with these, the newly reorganized and incorporated Kingston Marine Railway Company, the boat-repair concern founded by John Counter in 1836, launched a daily steamboat line between Kingston and Dickinson's Landing in late June. The company, under president Henry Gildersleeve and with former Montreal shipbuilder Luke Sheay in charge of the shipbuilding and repair works, operated the chartered *Brockville* and the *Kingston* on this route. George Brush, displaced as Kingston agent of the Ottawa and Rideau Forwarding Company, took command of the *Brockville*, while Captain William C. Lawless commanded the *Kingston*. For these two boats, Prescott was just a stop along the route.[137]

The Jones clan of Brockville and Prescott, meanwhile, had teamed up with U.S. interests to run a competing line of passenger steamers on the lake. Their line consisted of the *William IV*, Captain Lonson Hilliard; the new *Sir Robert Peel*, with Captain A.B. Armstrong in command; and the American boats *United States* under Captain James Van Cleve and *Telegraph* under Captain R.F. Child. All but the last boat made Prescott their eastern terminal, connecting there with the 200-ton *Dolphin*, which ran between Prescott and Dickinson's Landing for the Canada Steamboat and Mail Coach Company. These arrangements were upset when the *Peel* was destroyed by rebels in the Thousand Islands at the end of May (see chap. 8).[138] Then in 1839 the *Dolphin*, the *Brockville*, and the *Kingston* all passed under Hamilton's immediate control. To his lake line he added the river services previously operated by the Kingston Marine Railway and the Canada Steamboat and Mail Coach companies, running the *Dolphin* and the *Brockville* between Dickinson's Landing and Kingston.[139]

The five-year agreement under which the Canada Steamboat and Mail Coach Company was set up in 1833 lapsed at the end of 1838, but a new one clearly followed. The company extended its passenger operations to the Ottawa-Rideau in 1839, using the boats and stages of the Ottawa and Rideau Forwarding Company. On the St Lawrence, the company kept up its service from Montreal to Dickinson's Landing, where it connected with Hamilton's lake-and-river line.[140]

CHAPTER EIGHT

A Clearing of the Decks

Cholera epidemics, political tensions, business competition, and the rivalry between St Lawrence and Ottawa-Rideau interests, all capped by the Rebellions of 1837–38, combined to make the 1830s a tumultuous time of attrition. By the end of the decade, such pioneers of inland steam as Horace Dickinson, Emery Cushing, Thomas Mears, James Greenfield, William McMaster, Robert Drummond, and Thomas Turner had all passed away. Even John Molson had died of old age in January 1836, his passing, perhaps more than any other, symbolizing a changing of the guard.

It was not just individuals who vanished. Samuel Crane testified before a parliamentary committee in 1841 that from the opening of the Rideau Canal until the formation of the forwarders' cartel in 1837, competition for the Upper Canada trade had been so stiff that several companies had failed.[1] One early victim was the Canada Inland Assurance Company, the buy-Canadian pioneer in inland-navigation insurance. Launched at Montreal in 1830 under an agreement that was supposed to hold for five years, the company folded on 1 January 1834.[2]

The Prescott-based St Lawrence Inland Marine Assurance Company and the Canada Inland Forwarding and Insurance Company of Brockville and Montreal, both established in 1833, carried on. By spring 1835, however, while the former declared an 8 per cent dividend, Canada Inland Forwarding was reeling, acknowledging that it had yet to show a profit.[3] Racked by internal disputes, it suffered several defections. William Whiting resigned as managing agent at Montreal at the end of 1834 and resumed forwarding on his own – he was later accused of having failed to account for more than £2,000 in company funds. Moses Maynard Jr, another early promoter of the company at Brockville, retired from business.[4] The company, which had given some thought for several months to moving its offices from Brockville to Prescott, finally did so in 1835, hoping to reduce expenses by shortening the distance between its depot and Montreal. At Prescott the company named as its agent Hiram Norton, formerly president of the St Lawrence Inland Marine Assurance Company.[5] By January 1836, Canada Inland Forwarding felt obliged to deny rumours of its imminent demise,[6] only to sell out that June to the Ottawa and Rideau Forwarding Company.

The takeover of Canada Inland Forwarding by Ottawa and Rideau Forwarding made some positions redundant, none more so than those of William Dickinson (no relation to Horace Dickinson) and Edward Hackett, the Canada Inland Forwarding agents at Prescott and Montreal respectively. The Ottawa and Rideau had its own experienced supervisors in George Brush at Kingston, which was soon to draw off Prescott's forwarding trade, and Emery Cushing at Montreal. With support from several Montreal merchants, notably Adam Ferrie, their old boss at Canada Inland Forwarding, Dickinson and Hackett started their own forwarding business in 1837, called William Dickinson and Company in Upper Canada and E. Hackett and Company at Montreal. The following year they joined the other forwarders in shifting their operations to the Ottawa-Rideau route and moving their western terminal from Prescott to Kingston. In 1839 William Dickinson and Company would buy land at Hatters Bay (Portsmouth), opposite the Kingston penitentiary, with plans to make the bay a centre of the timber trade and other industries.[7]

The competition of the mid-1830s could have been even more deadly had railroads, the new steam craze, connected Upper and Lower Canada. Many viewed railroads as the modern alternative to canals, considering them cheaper and easier to build and operate. Various railroad lines were mooted, including at least two from Montreal to Upper Canada and a sixteen-mile one across the seigneury of Beauharnois to link steamers on Lakes St Louis and St Francis, but none was built until the late 1840s.[8] In the case of the latter project, the paralysis of the Lower Canadian legislature from 1836 on frustrated the Beauharnois Railroad Company's repeated efforts to seek a charter, and the enterprise, calculated to halve the travelling time between Lachine and Cornwall, went up in smoke with the Rebellion of 1838.[9] Before the late 1840s, the one railroad that materialized was the Champlain and St Lawrence, a fourteen-mile line between La Prairie and St John's. Opened in July 1836, it connected Montreal with the Lake Champlain steamers.

Quite apart from any larger commercial, political, or social circumstances, the deaths of Horace Dickinson in 1832 and Emery Cushing in 1837 proved crucial to the growth of Macpherson and Crane. It is unlikely that this forwarding firm would have come to dominate steamer traffic on the upper St Lawrence and the Ottawa-Rideau in the 1830s without these and other fortuitous events. This is not to deny the considerable business skills of the partners; on the contrary, it shows that, more than some of their competitors, they had the wits to spot and seize an opportunity and an enviable talent to manage their affairs. The Ottawa and Rideau Forwarding Company certainly recognized this skill in placing its operations in the hands of Macpherson and Crane. It too had capitalized on a couple of timely deaths. If steam transport on the Ottawa-Rideau route was, to all intents and purposes, a monopoly by the time that Macpherson and Crane took it over, it was owing in part to the 1834 deaths of Robert Drummond and Duncan Vanalstine, which had allowed the Ottawa Steamboat Company to gain mastery of the Rideau – and transform itself into the Ottawa and Rideau Forwarding Company – simply by buying up their steamboats. Another accident, the shutdown of the Rideau Canal in 1836, obliged the Ottawa and Rideau to shift its operations to the St Lawrence, where, to fulfill its commitments, it had to swallow the Canada Inland Forwarding and Insurance Company. Rather than use the occasion to establish itself on the St Lawrence, it retreated to familiar waters as soon as the Rideau reopened, shaken and financially weakened, having done little more than tread water and, in absorbing Canada Inland Forwarding, eliminate a rival, albeit a shaky one, of Macpherson and Crane.

More accidents, in the shape of business disputes and miscalculations, led to the disappearance of several important Montreal firms. The Phoenix Foundry closed in the late summer of 1832, after a falling-out between partners Guy and Joseph Warwick.[10] Obadiah Johnson and Acheson Clarke, who opened a foundry in early 1833, closed up shop in November 1834, saddled with what seems a paltry £657 in debts but with only £238 in receivables. In its short existence, Johnson and Clarke had built but two steamboat engines.[11] Around the time that company foundered, the shipbuilding firm of Sheay and Merritt sank under the weight of its debts. Partners Luke Harmon Sheay and Edward Dickson Merritt fled the province, leaving a half-finished ship at their yard. Creditors, judging it to be in their interests that the ship be finished, agreed to suspend all action against the partners if they would return and finish the work. Merritt thereafter continued shipbuilding in Montreal, while Sheay went to work for the Kingston Marine Railway Company.[12]

The engine-building firm of Bennet and Henderson also failed. In trouble from early 1834, the partners blamed their demise on "unexpected losses," their debts amounting to £4,028 by the time they went into liquidation in January 1835. Like Luke Sheay, John Bennet moved to Kingston. Bennet and Henderson engineer John Lowe moved on to Niagara to run the engine foundry of the Niagara Harbour and Dock Company. Another Bennet and Henderson alumnus, George Miller, opened the Perth Foundry at Perth with his father.[13]

The closing of the various Montreal foundries, particularly Bennet and Henderson's, meant that Lebbeus and Samuel Ward, major creditors of both Johnson and Clarke and Sheay and Merritt, were the only engine makers left in Montreal at the start of 1835. But new competition for their Eagle Foundry quickly rose from the ashes of Bennet and Henderson. In the year before his death, John Molson acquired the St Mary Foundry property and leased it to his son, John Jr. In March 1835 the latter formed the St Mary Foundry Company, intending "to establish from the first day of May next an iron & brass Foundery and Steam Engine manufactory" in the premises. He hired former Ward employees Samuel Workman and James Irwin on a five-year management contract. Joined for the purpose in the firm of Irwin and Workman, they agreed to run the business in return for half the profits, while bearing no liability for losses. Workman had occupied a position akin to office manager at the Eagle Foundry; Irwin, who had emigrated to Canada from Ireland in the early 1830s, was an iron founder and engineer whose credits included installing the Ward engines in the Lake Ontario steamer *Constitution* in 1833 and the *Peter Robinson* on Lake Simcoe in 1834.[14] One of their first orders at the St Mary Foundry was a £3,200 contract for a new engine, boilers, and water wheels for the *Adelaide*, the first Canadian steamer on Lake Erie, built in 1831–32 for Robert Hamilton.[15] Irwin and Workman's contract with Molson was cancelled after a fire at the foundry on 1 January 1837. But Molson, who had inherited the property on his father's death, moved quickly to rebuild, and Irwin and Workman agreed to stay on as employees for at least one year from 1 May at an annual salary of £200.[16]

The Eagle Foundry was also hit by fire, as well as by flood and, repeatedly, by thieves in the first half of the decade, but it survived.[17] In fact, the work which the Wards did for the Champlain and St Lawrence Railroad – of which Lebbeus Ward was a director – won plaudits similar to those that had greeted John Ward's steamboat engines in the early 1820s. At the end of 1835, they secured contracts to produce castings for freight cars and various other pieces of equipment for the line. They were also given the job of building the 68-horsepower engine of the *Princess Victoria*, a steamer built by Edward Merritt to run between Montreal and La Prairie in conjunction with the railroad. She was modelled on the *Lexington*, which sailed between New York and Providence, Rhode Island.[18] The following summer the Wards were called to the rescue after the engine of the English-built locomotive was damaged during her trials. They had not quite finished on 21 July, the day of the official opening of the line. As a result, the locomotive pulled only two cars that day, while horses pulled the other ten. By the beginning of August, however, the locomotive was back in working order. At their half-yearly meeting in December, the railroad's shareholders were informed that,

from the time the engine was put in order by the Messrs Ward, and placed in the hands of a competent engineer, it has done, I will venture to say, as good service, in proportion to its power, and has undergone as little repair (about £5) as any engine on this continent, the proof of which is that the engine, from the 3d of August to the 29th November, fifteen weeks, has been in activity one hundred and seven days, and in repair four, during which period it has averaged about five hundred and sixty miles per week, or eight thousand six hundred for the whole period.[19]

In their report to the meeting, railroad chairman Peter McGill and the board of directors also paid tribute to the Wards and to Merritt for their work on the *Princess Victoria*.[20]

After more than a decade in Canada, Lebbeus Ward was solidly established in Montreal. Besides serving on the board of the Champlain and St Lawrence, he had been elected a director of the newly formed City Bank in 1835.[21] He even showed an inclination to speak out on public issues, something that other members of the Dickinson circle had shied away from. In the heated general election of 1834, the last held in Lower Canada before union, he had gone so far as to speak up in favour of Patriote leader Louis-Joseph Papineau.[22] In September 1836 Ward was elected to a broad citizens' committee set up to lay the groundwork for a system of public education in the province, the schools legislation having lapsed as a result of permanent deadlock in the legislature. He was also on the board of the temperance society.[23] He seemed, in short, to have put down roots.

A clear sign of that fact came when he and his twin brother, Samuel, hired a contractor in 1837 to build twin houses, designed by the noted young architect John Ostell. Construction of the semi-detached stone and brick houses on Wellington Street at the corner of King Street, near the foundry, was to begin in May and be finished by October.[24] But for Lebbeus Ward, the pleasure of the anticipated move to the new house was dashed on 24 June when his wife, Dimmis Dickinson, died at the age of twenty-six.[25] A few weeks later he made out his will. Perhaps his wife's death had put him in mind of his own. On the other hand, making out a will was common practice then for middle- and upper-class people about to set out on a long voyage, particularly over the seas. Ward had such a trip in mind: he planned to tour British foundries to study the processes used in the making of heavy iron forgings. On 1 November the childless widower sailed for Liverpool.[26]

An architect's drawing of the facade of the semi-detached houses built for Lebbeus and Samuel Ward in 1837 on Wellington Street in Montreal (ANQM, CN601-134, notary Doucet, no. 24298, 28 March 1837).

He missed the rebellion in Lower Canada that year – from the first skirmish at Saint-Denis in the Richelieu valley on 23 November to the final blow at Saint-Eustache in the county of Two Mountains on 14 December. He also missed the big meeting at the Exchange Coffee House on 28 November, when American Montrealers rallied to take a public stand on the troubles. As disaffected Canadians were being encouraged to count on American support, some eighty-five Americans called the meeting for the purpose of "expressing their conviction that the belief alluded to is unfounded, and declaring a determination to lend their aid in support of the authority of Her Majesty's Government and the maintenance of the laws." The conveners included Ward's brother, Samuel, Asahel Whipple, Curtis Crossman, and John Frothingham.[27] It was an unprecedented gathering. As lawyer Charles Dewey Day told his audience, it was "the first occasion on which a meeting composed exclusively of the inhabitants of this city of American birth and origin, has been convened. From this fact alone, this meeting might be supposed to be a matter of some importance in our eyes."[28] Indeed, this was about its sole significance, besides allaying any lingering fears that the Tories may have had that all the Yankees in town were in league with the rebels.[29] Certainly, it did not alter the course of events.

Martial law, imposed on 5 December in the Montreal district (the whole of southwestern Lower Canada), was lifted the following 27 April. Only four days later a boiler explosion rocked the *Rideau*, commanded by Captain John Morrin,[30] as she prepared to leave Grenville. Two men were killed, and two others severely injured. Excited residents may have been tempted to suspect rebel sabotage: the neighbouring county of Two Mountains had been a hotbed of insurrection. But there was no rebel hand behind the *Rideau's* misfortune. A coroner's inquest found that the steamer's boilers, "old, sagged in the flues, and unprovided with stays," had simply burst under the strain of towing three barges against the spring flood. The *Bytown Gazette* reported that "the public voice ... is loud in blaming the parcimony of the Ottawa and Rideau Forwarding Company as the sole cause of this serious accident." It was the first accident of its kind on the Ottawa River.[31]

One steamer did fall victim to rebel wrath that month, the *Sir Robert Peel*, built by William Parkin[32] at Brockville and launched only a year before, on 19 May 1837. Expecting the Cornwall Canal to open in 1838, her owners planned to operate her between Prescott and Côteau; in the meantime, powered by Ward engines, she plied between Prescott and Toronto.[33] Bill Johnston, so-called commodore of the rebel navy, attacked her in the Thousand Islands on 30 May as she made one of her upward trips. His action was in retaliation for the destruction by loyalist raiders on the previous 29 December of the *Caroline*, an American steamer that had ferried supplies from Fort Schlosser, New York, to rebel troops encamped at Navy Island in the Niagara River. This attack on an American boat in U.S. territory outraged many Americans and led to much sabre-rattling over the next few years. Johnston's men stormed aboard the *Sir Robert Peel* in the dead of night, crying "Revenge for the *Caroline!*"[34]

One passenger aboard the *Sir Robert Peel* who had particular cause to dread that rebel yell was Robert Knight Bullock, formerly of the Lake Ontario steamer *St George* and now captain of the *Neptune*. As he told a traveller that summer, "he had a hand in the taking of the steamer Caroline at Schlosser during the last winter, some time after which he was detained as a spy at Ogdensburgh by the sympathizing crew [rebel supporters] there, who much to their chagrin found out who he was, & what he had been guilty of, a few hours after they had released him, & he had made good his footing on the Canadian shore."[35] Fortunately for Bullock, he was not recognized by Johnston and his men. With the *Peel's* captain and crew and the more than sixty other passengers, he was forced ashore on Wells Island (Wellesley Island), where they were rescued the next day. The boat was burned to the waterline.[36]

That attack occurred just three days after the arrival at Quebec of Lord Durham, sent out from Britain to investigate the causes of unrest and recommend a workable system of government for the Canadas. A group of leading citizens greeted the new governor-in-chief on his first visit to Montreal on 6 July. Lebbeus Ward, back from his European sojourn, was among them. In a formal address, the Montreal worthies offered Durham their co-operation, professing "no other ambition than that of promoting the welfare of all classes of Her Majesty's subjects in these Provinces, and perpetuating the integrity of the Empire."[37] Fine words, but the empire was hardly Ward's priority. Just as incongruous, if not more so, was Damase Masson's greeting of Durham at Beauharnois at the end of July. Masson and his father had been active in Patriote agitation throughout the decade, and they were among the early backers of the Frères Chasseurs, the secret society behind the risings of late 1838. Masson had been relieved of his position as postmaster in January; his father was to flee across the border; his father-in-law, notary André Jobin, elected to the assembly for the county of Montreal in 1835, had just spent two months in jail after several months in hiding; and his cousin, Dr Luc-Hyacinthe Masson, a leading figure among rebels in the county of Two Mountains in 1837, was one of eight prominent rebels whom Durham had banished to Bermuda. Yet when the governor spent a weekend at Beauharnois, Masson read him an address, signed by 430 landholders of the seigneury, praising his treatment of the rebels.[38]

Durham's decision, announced in September, to give up his post was a dispiriting blow not just to those who still looked to him for a liberal solution to the crisis but to moderates of all stripes, wearied of the instability. It added one more cloud to the morose picture that Charles Mittleberger's older brother, Henry, a St Catharines merchant, had painted that summer: "the rebellion and internal disturbances are tearing the province to pieces – this state of suspense is worse than actual war, for it tends to unsettle the minds of people, doubt prevails over confidence, the disloyal are leaving and the state of fear and uncertainty is calculated to unhinge the loyal."[39]

Hiram Norton probably would have qualified as one of the disloyal in the eyes of the Mittlebergers of the day. Indeed, in reporting his departure for the United States, the *Montreal Transcript* linked him by innuendo with runaway rebels and rebel sympathizers.[40] It was an uncomfortable time for men in Norton's position. As an American in Canada, he must have viewed the possibility of war between Britain and the United States, which the rebels were doing their best to provoke, with concern. One of Norton's fellow Prescott residents who thought war likely was Alpheus

Hiram Norton of Prescott, member of the assembly of Upper Canada, 1831–38, left the country in 1838 and moved to Lockport, Illinois (Grenville County Historical Society).

Jones. He actually bet on it, promising to pay a Montreal acquaintance the price of a hat if events proved him wrong.[41]

The border friction certainly affected Joseph Whitney, the American captain of the *Great Britain* (and of the *Queenston* before her), who had fought in the U.S. navy on the lakes in the War of 1812. Around the time of the *Sir Robert Peel* affair, Sir George Arthur, lieutenant-governor of Upper Canada, wrote ominously to the commander-in-chief of the forces: "The Steamer – Great Britain – the largest we have on the lakes belonging to Mr Hamilton is (very improperly) commanded by an American Master." After 1838, Whitney returned across the border and took command of the American steamer *United States*.[42]

But Norton was not only an American; he was a reform politician at a time when anti-reform sentiment raged – and close to home, too. His reform colleague in the representation of Grenville, the hotheaded Loyalist descendant William Wells, fearing arrest, had fled to Ogdensburg in December 1837 and then been stripped of his assembly seat for his alleged involvement in a rebel raid. One of those who supplied evidence against him was the well-placed Alpheus Jones, postmaster, collector of customs, and one of the two Tory candidates whom Norton and Wells had beaten in the last election.[43] Even the no-nonsense Samuel Crane, who had offered himself as the reform candidate for Wells's vacant seat in the spring of 1838 and then backed out, felt the heat. Some thought to incriminate him on the basis of a note found on the body of a rebel killed in the attack on Prescott on 13–16 November. A line in the note read, "Crane has about fifty men in his employ, is friendly." Crane, all business and with nothing of the hothead about him, had no difficulty clearing himself of suspicion. He remained to run successfully in Grenville County in the general election of 1841.[44]

In this climate of fear, suspicion, animosity, and shattered hopes, Norton left his adopted country under a cloud. He was not railroaded out for his political beliefs; nor was he among those reformers who, to make a political point, set up the Mississippi Immigration Society to encourage disgruntled Canadians to move to Iowa.[45] The cloud in his case was of his own making.

His fellow canal commissioners had learned in July 1836 that, through an Ogdensburg front man, he held the contract for supplying hydraulic cement for the Cornwall Canal. They had remonstrated with him then, and he had promised to divest himself of his interest. Soon afterwards, he had produced a document purporting to show that he had transferred the business to a man in Massena, New York. In the summer of 1838, however, word reached the commissioners that Norton still held the contract. He acknowledged the truth of this allegation when the commissioners met at Cornwall on 10–13 July 1838, whereupon his colleagues resolved that "Mr Norton is thereby extremely culpable and blameable for having deceived the Commissioners, and that having so acted, the Commissioners consider it inconsistent for him to retain his situation as one of the Board."[46]

Norton's excuse – that he had tried in vain to dispose of the contract – was unconvincing. Sir George Arthur was undoubtedly apprised of the case when he inspected the canal in August. Commission president John McDonald instructed the secretary to draft a report on the affair for Arthur. It was submitted to the commissioners for their approval at their monthly meeting on 11 September. At their next meeting, on 9 October, a new commissioner took Norton's place.[47] He, meanwhile, left the country. From Lewiston, New York, on 18 October, he dashed off a terse note to the Speaker of the House: "Having removed from the Province of Upper Canada, I beg, most respectfully, to resign my seat as a member of the Commons House of Assembly for the County of Grenville."[48]

So ended Norton's career in Canada. He had entered the country an orphan some two decades earlier to help Barnabas and Horace Dickinson launch their stage line. As he exited, a living reminder of those days went with him: Moss Kent Dickinson, the sixteen-year-old son of the late Barnabas Dickinson and brother-in-law of Alpheus Jones, followed Norton to Illinois to work as his clerk.[49]

Norton may have contemplated moving to Illinois before his undoing. By some accounts, the country had so impressed him, on an earlier visit he had made there with the consulting engineer of the Illinois-Michigan Canal project, that he had made up his mind to move to Lockport, the canal headquarters.[50] There is probably a grain of truth to the story; he may have been preparing his own exit when he introduced a Members' Seat Vacation Bill in the legislature in January 1838.[51] Certainly, the American west exerted an undeniable attraction far and wide. Norton's assembly colleague, William Wells, had himself contemplated moving to Illinois in January 1838 after he had fled across the border.[52] Many unemployed canal workers from Upper Canada were headed that way, lured by the prospect of jobs on the Illinois-Michigan Canal after work on the St Lawrence canals had come to virtual standstill in the spring, the government of Upper Canada having run out of funds.[53] Construction on the Cornwall Canal would not resume until the spring of 1842. It did not take Norton that long to find his niche in Illinois: by summer 1839 he was presiding at Lockport's first Fourth of July celebrations. As a grain merchant at Chicago and Lockport, he rose to prominence, and wielded "great political influence and support," though he sought and won election only once, to the state legislature in 1858. In March 1844 no less a personage than Henry Clay, then in the midst of his campaign to secure the Whig Party presidential nomination, was among the guests when the twice-widowed Norton married an English woman at Mobile, Alabama.[54]

Lebbeus Ward was another who took his leave in the fall of 1838. For him, the Canadian opportunity had passed. The country was in turmoil. In Montreal the family circle was broken. His older brother and the Bigelows had returned to the United States. His father-in-law had died, then his wife, and finally, his two nephews, the last surviving children of Mary Ann Moseley Dickinson and her husband, the Reverend George William Perkins. Within a few months, the Perkinses themselves would move to Connecticut. Ward went to New York, where he established the Hammersley Iron Works, specialists in the forging of heavy wrought-iron pieces.[55] He did not immediately sever his connection with the Eagle Foundry, but an old acquaintance was brought into the business as of 1 January 1839. Under a four-year partnership agreement, George Brush paid £2,540 for a one-third interest in the company, henceforth to be called Ward, Brush and Company. Brush and Samuel Ward would operate the business. As for Lebbeus Ward, off in New York, "his services will be dispensed with but the said Samuel S. Ward & Lebbeus B. Ward will pay the sum of one hundred pounds in lieu thereof."[56]

Lord Durham sailed for England on 1 November. Fighting flared again two days later. Beauharnois, which had remained quiet through the 1837 rising, was this time one of the focal points. Rebels from the surrounding parishes invaded the village on the night of Saturday, 3 November. In the cold, rainy darkness at 6 the next morning, some 150 of them swarmed aboard the *Henry Brougham* as she stopped by to refuel on her way down to Lachine. Captain Daniel Whipple and his crew were taken prisoner, as were some twenty passengers, including old Beauchamp Colclough, in his seventies, and Moses Maynard's old flame, Sarah Ussher, age twenty-one, with her two children, a two-year-old girl and a nursing baby. They would spend the next week in captivity.[57] For part of that time, Alexander Thomson, the *Brougham's* engineer, was held at Damase Masson's house.[58] The boat was disabled and, sometime in the course of the week, sunk at the wharf.[59]

An alarm was raised on Monday, 5 November, when the *Dragon* (later named the *Caledonia*), a small steamer belonging to the Ottawa and Rideau Forwarding Company,[60] appeared headed for the village. Fearing an attack, the rebels took cover behind Masson's woodpiles. The *Dragon*, coming from Lachine, drew close and then veered off west toward the Cascades. On board was Major George Phillpotts of the Royal Engineers, friend and former aide-de-camp to Sir John Colborne, under orders to retake Beauharnois and the *Brougham* and free the prisoners. He was on his way to Lancaster in Upper Canada to gather a force of Glengarry Highlanders and regular troops. Appointed engineer of the St Lawrence canals in 1836, Phillpotts had been pulled from those duties to take charge of the Cornwall Volunteers during the 1837 rebellion. He had returned to his canal work in the spring of 1838, only to see the project put on hold. Durham had then commissioned him to report on the state of inland navigation and on the extent of canal work needed to open up the route between Lake Erie and the Atlantic. Colborne, acting governor since Durham's departure, had called on him in the new emergency. He was to spend the week cruising between Lancaster and Cornwall in the *Neptune*, picking up the volunteers and ferrying them down to Côteau.[61]

By the afternoon of Friday, 9 November, the force was assembled – 889 men from four regiments of Glengarry militia, a small detachment of the Cornwall Volunteer Cavalry, a company of the 71st Light Infantry from Kingston and a detachment of the same regiment from Brockville, and 23 men of the Royal Sappers and Miners. On the Saturday morning, packed aboard the *Neptune* and several barges towed by the steamer, they crossed from Côteau to Hungry Bay, just west of present-day Valleyfield. Lashed by high winds as the troops were disembarking, the *Neptune*, under Captain Bullock, slipped her moorings and drifted in the shallows, scraping bottom. A barge ran aground and was wrecked. Once ashore, the troops began their march to Beauharnois, torching the homes of prominent rebels on the way. A few shots were exchanged as they entered the village that night, and the rebels fled. Loyalists and soldiers exacted their revenge, burning the homes of rebels, real and suspected.[62]

Damase Masson, who – under duress, as he claimed – had acted as interpreter for the insurgents in their dealings with their loyalist captives, had his properties ransacked and destroyed. In what was for him a stroke of bad timing, he had bought out his father's interest in the partnership of E. et D. Masson in April and agreed to pay the first instalment of £200 on 1 November, two days before the rebellion broke out. Now his house and stores lay in ruins. He would supply no more wood to the steamers on Lake St Louis. He moved to Montreal the following year and, like Norton in Illinois, landed on his feet, establishing himself in the wholesale grocery line and prospering in the big-city business world.[63]

Phillpotts reported to Sir John Colborne: "As soon as we had liberated the prisoners, a party was sent to take possession of the steamer *Brougham*, and prevent its being set on fire, in which they succeeded without opposition, though the rebels had scuttled her as soon as they heard of our approach."[64] The steamer was far from a total loss. A member of the Lachine militia who sailed to Beauharnois aboard the *Dragon* on the morning of Sunday, 11 November, later wrote, "The staff officers of the Glengarries and the officers of the 71st were congregated on the deck of the 'Henry Brougham' to meet us, to get what news we had."[65]

The capture of the *Henry Brougham* at Beauharnois on 4 Novembre 1838; from a drawing by Henri Julien illustrating one in a series of articles marking the fiftieth anniversary of the Rebellions of 1837–38 (from the *Montreal Daily Star*, 18 February 1888).

Damase Masson of Beauharnois supplied wood for the Upper Cannada Line steamers on Lake St Louis until the Rebellion of 1838 put an end to his business (reproduced from J. Castel Hopkins, *The Canadian Album*; photograph by Richard Arless Jr).

The *Brougham* lay in four to six feet of water. On the Monday, after surveying the damage, Captain Daniel Whipple went in search of the parts of the boat's machinery which the rebels had removed and hidden. With difficulty, the steamer was refloated and repaired by Friday, 16 November. She sailed for Lachine that day, carrying one of the rebels' homemade cannons – a hollowed log ringed with iron hoops – a rebel flag, and eighty-two prisoners bound for jail in Montreal.[66] Soon afterward, the *Brougham* was laid up for the winter. She would resume her regular route in 1839 under a new name – the *Chieftain*. Macpherson and Crane would later file a claim with the government for £480 in compensation for damage to the *Henry Brougham* (see appendix C). Under the Rebellion Losses Act of 1849, they received £200.[67]

On Lake St Francis the rebellions briefly gave the *Neptune* a companion, the 110-ton steamer *Dolphin*. She had been hired by the government of Upper Canada in 1838 to transport a group of rebel prisoners from Prescott to Cornwall. Doing so meant running down the Long Sault, a feat that the *Dolphin* accomplished on 10 November. Getting her back up the rapids posed a problem. The trip had been undertaken at government risk and expense; it was agreed that if the *Dolphin* could not be brought back up the rapids to Dickinson's Landing, where she was needed, the government would buy her. In the spring of 1839 she was worked up the rapids: it took "four weeks of incessant toil ... with the aid of twenty yoke of oxen, besides horses, capstans and men, added to the working of her engine – the first and probably the last steamer that will ever accomplish the feat." Back in her old waters, the *Dolphin* joined the *Brockville* on the Kingston–Dickinson's Landing route as part of John Hamilton's line of lake and river steamers.[68]

The *Neptune* continued under her old name in 1839, but with a new captain. Forty-year-old James Walker of Sorel, a grandson of Major Edward Jessup, the founder of Prescott, and formerly in command of the Champlain and St Lawrence Railroad steamer *Princess Victoria*, took over from Bullock.[69] A passenger had remarked in 1838 that the eleven-year-old *Neptune* had become, "in nautical language, 'a regular old tub.'"[70] The season of 1839 was to be her last. Work began at Côteau that spring on her intended successor, the *Highlander*, built under the superintendence of Asahel Whipple. Launched on 23 November 1839, the *Highlander* was 180 feet long and 23½ feet beam. She was then fitted with a 100-horsepower Ward engine with an 11-foot stroke, her water wheels of 24 feet diameter making 26 revolutions per minute. She took the *Neptune's* place in 1840, sailing on the run between Côteau and Cornwall with Captain Walker in command.[71] She was said to resemble the Lake Champlain steamer *Burlington*, "that nattiest of natty vessels," launched in 1837, for which the Wards had also built the engine.[72]

Though she would later have her small moment of glory as the first boat through the Cornwall Canal, the *Highlander* was then only one more new steamer. Her contemporary, John Hamilton's *Ontario*, heralded a new era. A big boat, 206 feet outside length, 26 feet beam, and 53 feet broad overall, the *Ontario* was built at Prescott by some eighty men working under the direction of Captain Lonson Hilliard. She was launched on 7 September 1839 and towed up Lake Ontario to Niagara, where she was fitted with two engines of 50 horsepower made by the Niagara Harbour and Dock Company. Hamilton intended her to run up and down the rapids between Prescott and Côteau on Lake St Francis. "The success of this boat is a matter of the greatest consequence to this Province," the *Kingston Chronicle* said at her launch. "If she answers the purpose she is intended for ... the navigation of the St Lawrence, with all its difficulties, will be complete, without the aid of any canal, and the Montreal market will be brought within reach of our farmers."[73]

She proved a fast boat, reaching speeds of close to 20 miles per hour on the smooth waters of Lake Ontario. She also offered superior passenger accommodation – a promenade deck stretching from stem to stern, a large sitting room on the main deck, and below deck, cabins with better-than-average bunks. For men, there were thirty-six berths and four staterooms, each with two berths; the women's cabin offered sixteen berths and four staterooms. But there was a bug in her works. In April 1840, before she was even finished, the shaft of one of her engines broke, causing serious damage to her machinery. Then on 30 June she broke her other shaft while making her way up from Dickinson's Landing to Prescott. She had not yet risked the Long Sault, her pilot and engineer wanting time to get used to her. Until her second crippling accident, Hamilton had had her on the Kingston-Dickinson's Landing run with the chartered *Brockville*. Then, after getting entangled in legal disputes over the boat with Niagara Harbour and Dock, he decided to cut his losses and dispose of the *Ontario*.[74]

William and George Tate of Montreal, partners in the carpentry firm of W. and G. Tate and newcomers to the transport business, were in the market for just such a boat. They needed it to secure the first contract for a mail-steamer line between Montreal and Quebec.

Postal contracts had previously gone to stage-line operators rather than boat owners, largely because of the rigours of the Canadian climate. The icing up of the waterways and harbours in winter meant that steamboats, as a rule, operated only for six or seven months of the year. Rather than hire one set of carriers for the navigation season and another for overland transport during the winter, the Post Office had handed the entire business over to stage owners, who could operate year-round. Of course, mail contractors such as Horace Dickinson and the Canada Steamboat and Mail Coach Company had long sent the mail on by steamboats in summer, on the portions of their routes where it was practical and economical to do so. The Post Office had acknowledged this practice, placing mail boxes on the steamboats and at the same time warning that it would prosecute anyone – passengers, crew members, or other unauthorized persons – caught violating its monopoly by carrying letters for others.[75] But enforcement was impossible and the illicit carriage of mail continued. Witness Charles Kadwell as he set out for Upper Canada in August 1838:

Left Montreal about half past ten A.M. under the auspices of the Upper Canada Mail Coach & Steam Boat Company, per one of their four horse stages numbered 35, having in company three others carrying together between 30 & 40 passengers. I might fairly consider myself a mail-bag on legs, my pockets as well as portmanteau being crammed with letters handed to me by sundry merchants & others (for delivery on the route,) many of whom I knew merely by name, others, not even at all. But such being the habitual custom of infringing on people's good nature, I had to submit. Travellers proceeding (as myself) direct to Toronto or upwards, reach that place three days in advance of the mail, which makes it a desideratum to cheat Her Majesty's Post Office revenue, the mails being carried overland the greater part of the way; a very circuitous route.[76]

For some time, Deputy Postmaster General Thomas Stayner had been convinced of the need to scotch that "desideratum" and speed up the service. In the spring of 1838 he had sought to set up a daily mail-steamer service on Lake Ontario. The Post Office had approached John Hamilton – in Stayner's words, "the principal steamboat proprietor on Lake Ontario, (and the only individual prepared to fulfil such an engagement)." An agreement had been ironed out by 15 June, but Hamilton backed out, concerned that the requisitioning of steamers for government duty in that troubled time would make it impossible for him to guarantee a daily mail run. No satisfactory arrangement was reached until the fall of 1840.[77]

On the Montreal-Quebec route, the Tates had bid to provide a daily mail-steamer service for the 1840 season, in collaboration with the Molson line. They could not do it alone because a daily service required at least two boats and they had only one, the *Lady Colborne*, a fast passenger steamer modelled on the Champlain and St Lawrence Railroad's *Princess Victoria* and launched the year before. But Stayner, apparently dissatisfied, refused to accept their proposal.[78] By August, however, he was prepared to entertain bids for a six-year contract, beginning in the spring of 1841. The successful bidders would have to operate a daily overnight service, except on Sunday, from May through October, taking no more than fourteen hours to deliver the Montreal mail at Quebec and nineteen hours at most for the upward journey. Along the way, the boats were to serve the post offices at Sorel, Port St Francis, and Three Rivers. Every half-hour's delay in completing a run was to cost the contractors a penalty of up to £10; fines for failing to stop at any of the intermediate points ranged from £5 to £20. These were steep penalties, given that the Post Office was not prepared to pay the contractor more than £9 per trip.[79] This time the Tates were determined to secure the business to themselves. To do so, they needed to find a companion for the *Lady Colborne*.

By the time that the official call for tenders came on 10 August – with the deadline for bids only a month away – the Tates were off and running to Prescott to examine Hamilton's steamer. They came to terms with him in an exchange of notes aboard the *Dolphin* as they made their way back to Montreal on 11 August. They offered Hamilton £10,500 for the *Ontario*, "if You will within One Month from this date deliver the said boat over to us in the Port of Montreal in good and sound condition, perfectly water tight withal of the furniture and apurtenences that now belong to her." The *Dolphin* had reached the end of her journey at Dickinson's Landing when Hamilton penned his acceptance of the offer.[80]

He was just as eager to be rid of the *Ontario* as the Tates were to take her. Besides suffering several costly setbacks in court, he had seen another of his boats, the trusty old *Great Britain*, knocked out of commission for a while after being firebombed by a diehard rebel at Oswego, New York, in June[81] – this at a time when his line on Lake Ontario was facing a new challenge from Donald Bethune's expanding fleet.[82] Both men had an eye to the postal contract in the offing for a mail-steamer line between Dickinson's Landing and Toronto – a prize which the rash Bethune would carry off that fall, but which he would have to share with Hamilton.[83] Under the circumstances, Hamilton certainly could do without the financial drain which the idle *Ontario* represented. Though he had one month to deliver her at Montreal, he would need little more than a week.

As a result of her last accident, the *Ontario* had only one engine in working order. Regardless of the steering problems which this one-arm swimming presented, Captain Hilliard, who had spent some time searching for the safest channel through the rapids, ran her down from Prescott, with the help of a Mohawk pilot named Jacques. She became the first fully equipped steamer to shoot all the rapids of the St Lawrence, reaching Montreal at about 6:30 on the morning of 19 August.[84] On that date thirty-one years earlier, Montreal had witnessed the dawn of Canada's steamboat age with the launching of the *Accommodation*. The coincidence went unnoticed.

Ward, Brush and Company was hired to repair the *Ontario*'s broken machinery. But even before they undertook the work, the Tates considered that a demonstration of her powers was in order. On 25 August, with members of the press on board, the *Ontario* made a short hop downriver and back, propelled by her one working, 26-foot sidewheel. She ran downstream at more than 16 miles an hour, then back up St Mary's Current at $9\frac{3}{4}$ miles an hour.[85] The Tates, bidding to provide the mail service for £8 5s. per trip, won their contract.[86] Renamed *Lord Sydenham*, after the new governor general, who was to preside over the union of the Canadas – and who may have played a key role in the Tates' good fortune – the steamer made her first run to Quebec on 10 October.[87]

In the opinion of Sir Richard Bonnycastle of the Royal Engineers, the *Ontario*'s run down the rapids from Prescott to Montreal was an exploit "too hazardous to repeat."[88] Of course, the *Ontario* did not repeat it, nor would any other large steamer do so until the St Lawrence canals were built, allowing these boats to sail back up. But smaller steam vessels could follow in the *Ontario*'s wake and return to Lake Ontario using the Lachine, Ottawa, and Rideau canals, as barges had been doing since 1838.[89] At least two such schemes had been floated before the *Ontario* made her run, and steamers would begin doing just that in 1841, creating a union on the water that paralleled that year's legislative union of Upper and Lower Canada, with its political capital at Kingston and its commercial heart at Montreal.

CHAPTER NINE

Miniature Steamers and Short Circuits

The *Ontario's* successful run down to Montreal overshadowed her equally significant failure: she never ran up and down the Long Sault as she was meant to do. She marked the last serious – and futile – effort to introduce two-way steamboat traffic through a major rapid of the St Lawrence. The fact that John Hamilton made – and abandoned – the effort is indicative of the spirit that prevailed as the gloom of the late 1830s began to lift. After several years of stunted progress and eruptive discontents, there was an impatient determination to break down, or circumvent, long-standing barriers – political, navigational, and others – and to get on with changes which many considered overdue. On the political front, this new spirit would bring the union of the Canadas. Closely tied to that development was the completion of the St Lawrence canals. These two measures would answer Upper Canada's old demand for direct, untrammelled access to the sea.

Even before these courses were settled on – sweetened with a promise of a £1.5 million loan guarantee from Britain – the authorities turned their attention to the Ottawa-Rideau route. In April 1839 the Upper Canadian assembly had lent its weight to the anti-monopoly cause, endorsing a committee report that denounced the hold exercised by the Ottawa and Rideau Forwarding Company and Macpherson and Crane through their ownership of the Vaudreuil lock and of all the steamers on the route. The report claimed that since the opening of the Rideau Canal, transport costs, instead of diminishing, had risen 50 per cent and were much higher than those on the Erie Canal, all as a result of the monopoly. It called on the authorities to buy the Vaudreuil lock or build a public lock at the mouth of the Ottawa; launch a government line of steam tugs or require any private line operating there to tow all boats at a fee to be set by law; and replace all fixed bridges, which impeded the passage of boats through the Lachine and Ottawa canals, with swing bridges.[1] Civil and military authorities would give serious consideration to all three propositions, acting on the first within just a few months.

That summer, at last, it was decided to build a public lock, 190 feet long by 45 feet wide, at St Anne. Not only would it accommodate larger boats than the Vaudreuil lock, but it would also shave twelve miles off a trip up the Ottawa from Lachine, a considerable saving of time and fuel. The newly established Board of Works in Lower Canada called for tenders in October 1839, with construction to begin the following spring.[2] This project signalled the imminent end of the exclusive privilege held since 1826 by the owners of the Vaudreuil lock and, beyond that, of the steamboat monopoly on the Ottawa-Rideau route. "It is high time it should be so," the *Bytown Gazette* commented. "A greater reproach upon a country, was never known, than the fact of allowing a private company, who by no means satisfy the public, to hold the key of the Rideau Canal, a work constructed by the British Government, at the expense of above one million sterling, for so long a period."[3]

The prospect of easy access to the navigation of the Ottawa-Rideau sparked several innovative schemes, none more ambitious than the one drawn up that very October in a round of meetings at the Exchange Coffee House in Montreal. The Montreal and Upper Canadian merchants involved resolved to launch a company, with a capital of £50,000 split into 2,000 shares, that would offer regular steamboat service up by the Ottawa-Rideau route and down by the St Lawrence, and run barges from Montreal as far up as Lake Erie if necessary. They proposed that their Inland Steam Transportation and Forwarding Company should begin operations in 1841 with five iron-hulled steamboats, imported from Britain, fitted with propellers instead of paddlewheels, and employed to tow barges up and down.[4] At the time, there were no iron-hulled boats in Canada and no propeller steamers; no steamer had yet run the "circuit," as the Ottawa–Rideau–St Lawrence triangle would come to be known, and none had ever towed barges down the rapids of the St Lawrence.

As forward-looking at it appeared, there was a whiff of the old about this project. It was an attempt to recreate the failed Canada Inland Forwarding and Insurance Company of 1833–36, on the same anti-monopoly principles but relying on new technology and, of course, on the St Anne lock. Charles Mittleberger, secretary of the earlier venture, was at the heart of the new one, whose prospectus proclaimed:

The intended construction of a Lock at the Rapids of St Ann's, by Government, next summer, will open the communication to Kingston; the key to which is now held by monopolists.

As individual enterprise will be insufficient to establish a firm and wholesome competition in the Trade, the present Company has been projected, and all persons

interested in reducing the enormous charges growing out of the existing monopoly, are now invited to aid in redressing one of the most pernicious grievances in
this Colony.[5]

As it turned out, the Inland Steam Transportation and Forwarding Company never made it past the planning stages.

Engineer William Nunns of Sorel, a veteran of the Torrances' Montreal
Steam Tow Boat Company, came up with a more modest plan. In June
1840, two months before the *Ontario's* path-breaking run, he proposed to
build a steamer to ply between Montreal and Kingston, "propelled by an
engine on an entirely novel construction, and so arranged as to occupy
but a mere trifle of space."[6] His intention, it seems, was to build a boat
small enough to negotiate the 20-foot-wide locks of the Lachine and Grenville canals, using his patented system of retractable paddlewheels and a
compact engine on whose design he had been working since at least 1833.[7]

The same anticipation of Ottawa-Rideau access that spawned these
schemes, coupled with the surge in trade that followed the years of
rebellion, made for important changes in the forwarding trade. Caught
short by a boom in shipments of wheat, flour, and other products from
American and Canadian lake ports in 1840 and an influx of immigrants
– not to mention a major fire at Kingston in April that destroyed some
of their facilities and the breakdown of a lock on the Ottawa that briefly
disrupted operations – the forwarders found themselves under pressure
to expand their carrying and warehousing capacity and to lower their
rates.[8] The boom also contributed to a revival of the forwarding trade on
the St Lawrence, where two new concerns, Ross, Matthie and Company
and Ferguson and McGibbon, sprang up to fill the void created by the
forwarders' wholesale move to the Ottawa in 1838. Under such internal
and external pressures, the Ottawa-Rideau cartel broke up.[9] With the end
of 1840, deregulated competition took the place of what Captain Thomas
Kains of the *Shannon* called "well regulated monopoly."[10] Macpherson
and Crane stopped towing the barges of its competitors and shut the
Vaudreuil lock to all but its own boats. Others scrambled to build their
own steamers and reverted to using the channel through the St Anne
Rapids, pending the completion of the public lock there.[11]

William Matthie of Brockville had been one of the men involved in the
abortive effort to launch the Inland Steam Transportation and Forwarding
Company, acting as secretary at the planning meetings in Montreal in
1839. He had been first clerk and bookkeeper to Moses Maynard and Company when Maynard was involved in setting up the Canada Inland
Forwarding and Insurance Company. On retiring in the spring of 1835,
Maynard had anointed the twenty-three-year-old Matthie his successor
in the general wholesale and retail trade. In the fall of 1840, with the

projected Inland Steam company going nowhere, Matthie set up his own forwarding company, Ross, Matthie and Company, with fellow Brockvillite George Easton, Henry Easton of Kingston, James Ross, in charge at Montreal, and George Augustus Chapman of Morristown, New York, opposite Brockville. They were ready for business on the St Lawrence in 1841.[12]

Like Ross, Matthie and Company, Ferguson and McGibbon was a chip off the old forwarding block. Alexander Ferguson, posted to Kingston on becoming a partner in Macpherson and Crane in 1838, had returned to Montreal by the end of 1839, John Macpherson succeeding him as the firm's resident partner at Kingston. At the beginning of 1841 Ferguson formed a partnership with John McGibbon, former Montreal agent of H. and S. Jones and Company, to carry on the forwarding trade on the St Lawrence.[13] Besides launching a fleet of barges, all bearing three-letter names (*Ant, Bee, Doe*, and so on), they bought the steamer *Dolphin* and ran her down to Côteau on 29 April to serve as a tugboat on Lake St Francis. They also had the small steamer *Aid* built at Prescott that spring for use as a towboat above the Long Sault. The two boats constituted Ferguson and McGibbon's investment – worth 71 shares – in the Union Towing Company. This firm, whose capital stock of £6,000 was split into 240 shares, sought to improve towing on the upper St Lawrence. The *William IV*, salvaged after she had run aground in South Bay the previous fall, was apparently also part of this towing line. Alpheus Jones had bought out his co-owners and converted the once-elegant steamer into a tug for use on the upper St Lawrence, stripping her of "everything on deck that can catch or hold the wind."[14] As the 1841 season began, Ferguson and McGibbon worked aggressively to put Prescott on the forwarding map once more. "Prescott is a busy bustling place," a traveller noted, "despite its great loss of the Forwarding Business, a loss which a new Forwarding firm, Messrs Ferguson and McGibbon, is endeavouring partially to restore."[15]

Confining their trade to the St Lawrence, neither Matthie nor Ferguson made plans to run steamers on the circuit, or even through the rapids below Dickinson's Landing. But others did. William Nunns, for one, had persevered in his plan to run a boat on the circuit. His efforts, however, were to be overshadowed by a new project hatched by the Ottawa-Rideau forwarder Murray and Sanderson.

Donald Murray of Montreal and George Sanderson of Brockville had teamed up in 1838 on Murray's withdrawal from Hooker and Henderson, where he had been a partner for at least three years.[16] At the close of their first year of operation, Murray had demonstrated a social conscience – and a flair for public relations – by organizing a subscription at Montreal for the relief of the families of men killed or wounded in defending Prescott against the cross-border rebel raid in November 1838.[17] Murray and Sanderson again caught the public eye in 1839–40 with a plan to escape the to-and-fro between Montreal and Kingston by running barges between the upper lakes and tidewater. The firm took delivery of the *British Queen* from Brockville shipbuilder William Parkin in October 1839, intending the schooner-rigged barge, with a 130-ton carrying capacity, to sail between the head of Lake Huron and Quebec. "If she succeeds … it will form a new era in our inland navigation, and will be a great saving of that time, labour and waste of property which now unavoidably occurs in the reshipment of goods between the Upper Ports and Montreal and Quebec." The barge did make her first run directly from Kingston to Quebec the following summer, carrying 3,700 bushels of wheat and 300 barrels of flour, without transshipment at Montreal. Even if she did not start from the "upper ports," this trip certainly constituted a breakthrough.[18] On the dissolution of the forwarding cartel at the end of 1840, the partners came up with another attention-getter: they would try to send a propeller-driven steam barge down the St Lawrence to Montreal and then back up by the Ottawa-Rideau route.

Barges similar to those used on British and American canals had been employed on the route since the mid-1830s,[19] but the screw propeller was untried in Canada. In want of information on the subject in the winter of 1840–41, Hamilton Killaly, president of the Board of Works, had had to ask Governor General Lord Sydenham to write to the Admiralty for the results of propeller trials in England. The propeller was only then proving its worth in U.S. trials, thanks to the efforts of Swedish-born engineer John Ericsson, and in Britain, where Ericsson and rival English inventor Francis Pettit Smith had taken out the first two propeller patents within weeks of each other in 1836.[20] Sanderson asked a business acquaintance to check out Ericsson's propeller in New York City in December 1840 and to advise on the prospects for its use on Rideau Canal boats. The report being favourable, Murray and Sanderson wasted no time, placing orders for propeller engines and suitable barges for use in the 1841 season.[21] Two of the engines were to come from the United States, it seems, and one from Nelson Walker, a Montreal jeweller turned engine designer.[22]

Walker's engine, reportedly based on "a mere theoretic sketch" of Ericsson's propeller, was in the works in March, and the barge for which it was meant was sitting in the Lachine Canal by mid-May.[23] But it was a barge built at Brockville by William Parkin and fitted with a high-pressure, 15-horsepower American engine that made the first run. "On the first trial the boat ran from 6 to 7 miles per hour, and so satisfied is Mr Sanderson of its capability and adaptation to the object intended that the Boat was immediately loaded, and he proceeded with it to Montreal."[24] The *Ericsson*, as she was called, 87 feet long and $16\frac{1}{2}$ feet in breadth, carrying 740 bushels of flour and other goods, arrived at Montreal via the

Lachine Canal on 10 June after a sixteen-hour run down the St Lawrence from Brockville. The experiment was deemed a complete success.[25]

A second barge, the *Baron Toronto*, fitted with Walker's propeller, set off unheralded on her first trip to Kingston at the end of June. Within a month, Murray and Sanderson's third propeller barge, the *Propeller*, was also in service. This was not the end of Murray and Sanderson's successes that year. The firm scored another first at the close of the season when the *Baron Toronto* left Kingston on Sunday, 7 November, towing two loaded barges and reached Montreal in three days, having weathered a snow squall on the way. "This shows the practicability of towing from Montreal to Kingston, *via* the Rideau Canal, and downwards, *via the St Lawrence*," the *Gazette* concluded. "The Forwarders who accomplished the trip deserve credit for their enterprise."[26] Without so much as a nod to Nelson Walker, who supplied propeller engines for at least three more small boats, the St Mary Foundry acting as his exclusive agent, Murray and Sanderson thereafter did claim sole credit for introducing propellers on Canadian waters.[27]

Even as the firm was planning its experiment in the spring of 1841, others were hot on the trail. For them, there was no need of propellers – paddlewheelers could negotiate the circuit, providing the boats were small enough to fit the smallest locks on the Lachine and Grenville canals. Only a week after the *Ericsson* had shot the rapids, for instance, William Nunns's 20-horsepower barge *William Henry*, 92 feet long by 16 feet beam, arrived at Montreal from Sorel. She took her first run at the circuit at the end of June, making it back to Montreal on 2 July. With Nunns in command, she completed eight more round trips that year.[28] Captain Lonson Hilliard, for his part, had Thomas Dissett build the 53-ton *Pioneer*, 94 feet long and 14 feet wide, at Prescott that spring. Under Hilliard, she made five trips down to Montreal and back up in her first year.[29] In addition, George S. Weeks, who had moved to Prescott from Clayton, New York, the previous winter and set up a shipyard at the west end of town, built the 51-ton sidewheeler *Grenville* for Hooker and Henderson; she was 94 feet long by 11 feet broad, with a high-pressure engine of 20 horsepower.[30]

Hooker and Henderson, which also had the steamer *Prince Albert* built for the Rideau Canal, joined H. and S. Jones to form the Union Line on the Ottawa and Rideau. The line hired John P. Weir, formerly the Ottawa and Rideau agent at Bytown, to be its agent there. Francis Clemow succeeded him as the Ottawa and Rideau agent. To get around the problem of the rapids at the mouth of the Ottawa, the Jones firm arranged for the contractor of the St Anne lock to warp its boats up, until such time as the lock was completed.[31] H. and S. Jones had a small sidewheeler, the "pollywog" *St David*, built at Brockville by William Parkin. She was equipped with two 15-horsepower high-pressure engines made by inmates of the New York state prison at Auburn. Her fore part was almost the width of the smallest locks, but she was built narrower aft so that her paddlewheels would not protrude beyond the lines of her hull. In late May, shortly before Murray and Sanderson's *Ericsson* made her trial run to Montreal, Captain R.W. Shepherd ran the *St David* down to Lachine. Although she was intended for the circuit, she spent her first few months as a Union Line towboat between Lachine and Carillon.[32] The Jones steamer *Albion*, 102 feet long by 16 feet broad, built by William Parkin at Brockville in 1838–39 and run first on the Bay of Quinte, then on the Kingston-Dickinson's Landing route in 1839–40, moved to the Ottawa River between Grenville and Bytown. In mid-summer the company sent the new sidewheeler *Oldfield*, 104 feet long by 17 feet wide, built at Prescott by George Weeks, down the Rideau and Ottawa canals to serve on the towing run between Lachine and Carillon.[33]

The latter boat was named after Lieutenant Colonel John Oldfield, commander of the Royal Engineers, probably as a mark of gratitude by H. and S. Jones. After the firm appealed to him in early 1841, Oldfield had seen to the removal of the fixed bridges on the Grenville Canal and their replacement by swing bridges. This was a partial fulfillment of one of the recommendations of the Upper Canadian assembly in 1839. There remained the fourteen fixed bridges over the Lachine Canal: they would be taken down in March 1842.[34]

As regards the third recommendation of the assembly – that the government either start a line of steam tugs on the Ottawa-Rideau route or regulate the towing fees charged there – this too was investigated by the military authorities in charge of the canals. A report on the subject of a government towing service was submitted to the commander-in-chief in April 1841. It may be that the single trip up the Ottawa and Rideau canals by the government propeller barge *Union* in August was a kind of practical test. If so, the test was a failure. While Murray and Sanderson's barges covered the distance in about three days, the *Union* took twelve days to travel from Montreal to Kingston, after repeated groundings, breakages, and the jamming of her propeller by submerged stumps and floating logs in the Rideau Canal. For a good part of the trip, she had to be towed by the *William Henry*. The government left steam towing on the route in private hands.[35]

Other than that one trip up by the *Union*, there were no other propeller vessels than Murray and Sanderson's three barges in service in 1841. The *Ericsson* made about fifteen trips on the circuit that year, the *Baron Toronto* about seven, and the *Propeller* twelve. In addition to their propellers, Murray and Sanderson also had placed two new sidewheelers on the Rideau, the *Swan* and the *Vulcan*, the latter built at Brockville by

William Parkin and fitted with two low-pressure engines of 16 horse-power from the St Mary Foundry.[36]

The success of Murray and Sanderson's propeller barges was seen as "likely very soon to lead to a complete change in the forwarding business of the country."[37] Indeed, that summer, Port Stanley forwarding partners J.K. Woodward and Thomas Hutchison made plans to have two propeller schooners built to run between Lake Erie and Montreal. Theirs would be the first Canadian sailing craft fitted with propellers – like the *Vandalia* of Oswego – and the first steam vessels to run from the upper lakes to Montreal.[38]

Murray and Sanderson, for its part, played a role in another break-through in 1841 – the loosening of Macpherson and Crane's grip on the Vaudreuil lock. This was the unexpected outcome of a dispute over an accident that had occurred nearly three years earlier. The mishap itself illustrates the dangers of shipboard drunkenness and shows that boat owners, such as Horace Dickinson in his day, acted out of practical motives, not just moral ones, in prohibiting drinking on the job. The ensuing dispute hints at the chafing which cartel members had felt at their subserviency to Macpherson and Crane, and the outcome helps clear up a misconception about the end of the Vaudreuil lock monopoly.

The chain of events may be said to have begun shortly before the accident itself, with some muscle-flexing by Macpherson and Crane. In September and October 1838 the company successively accused Murray and Sanderson and E. Hackett and Company of breaking the cartel agreements by charging lower forwarding rates than those agreed upon. It stopped towing their barges and threatened legal action. To patch things up and avoid a lawsuit, Murray and Sanderson knuckled under overnight, posting a £300 security for good behaviour. In the case of the complaint against E. Hackett and Company, filed on 26 October, it is not known what steps Hackett and Dickinson took to mollify Macpherson and Crane or to refute the complaint.[39] A prompt settlement was reached, however, because when Macpherson and Crane's steamer *Margaret* left Bytown for Kingston on 31 October, at least one of the six barges it took in tow belonged to E. Hackett and Company. Another belonged to Murray and Sanderson.

According to witnesses, the convoy stopped at a whisky shanty along the canal. The *Margaret's* captain, James Ballentine,[40] his pilot, and most of his crew were soon drunk. As the convoy lurched on through the snowy evening, the steamer's crew disported themselves in their sleeping quarters with three prostitutes. It all made for a rather zigzag course in and out of the channel, as a result of which the barge belonging to Murray and Sanderson ran on some submerged tree stumps near the foot of Long Island. The following morning, deaf to the barge captain's pleas to tow her back out the way she had gone in, the *Margaret's* crew hauled her out sideways, ripping her bottom on the stumps. She sank in fifteen to twenty feet of water. No lives were lost, but all the goods stored below deck went down with her. Ballentine, who was said to be so drunk by then that he was retching over the rail, refused to help raise her and sailed off. Barge and cargo sat submerged for about two weeks before they were salvaged.

Much of this fiasco was set down the following January in affidavits by three barge conductors, two employed by Hooker and Henderson and one by Edward Hackett and Company.[41] Murray and Sanderson solicited these statements in order to press Macpherson and Crane to pay for the damage, but the latter steadfastly disclaimed all responsibility. In January 1840 Murray and Sanderson finally turned to the courts.[42] The case dragged on for a year and a half. While Murray and Sanderson produced witnesses to support its claims, Macpherson and Crane contented itself with cross-examining those witnesses and arguing that the accident had resulted from the carelessness and incompetence of Murray and Sanderson's barge crew.

The two sides settled out of court by 12 July 1841. Under the terms of the settlement, set down in writing on 20 August, Murray and Sanderson agreed to drop all complaints it may have had against Macpherson and Crane "from the beginning of the World to the said twelfth day of July last past." In return, Macpherson and Crane opened the Vaudreuil lock to Murray and Sanderson's barges and propeller boats, and undertook to tow the barges as needed between Lachine and Carillon, all for certain specified fees. The lockage fees were £1 10s. for a second-class barge, £2 for a first-class one, and £2 10s. for every propeller boat. The agreement was valid until the end of 1842, by which time, it was expected, the St Anne lock would be open.[43]

Most writers on the subject credit R.W. Shepherd with single-handedly cracking the monopoly of the Vaudreuil lock.[44] By his own account, Shepherd, as captain of the H. and S. Jones steamer *St David*, had gone searching for a boat channel through the Vaudreuil Rapids in late summer 1841 after work on the government lock had obstructed the channel through the St Anne Rapids.[45] His employer complained to the Board of Works that the lock contractor, whose operations had blocked the channel, was gouging boat owners by charging £2 to tow barges up with a capstan which he had rigged up at the head of the rapids.[46] Finding an alternative route through the Vaudreuil Rapids, of course, would enable the forwarders to escape this imposition while also bypassing the Vaudreuil lock. Shepherd found such a channel, and as the story goes, his demonstration proved so conclusive as to persuade Macpherson and Crane to open its lock to all comers. Although Shepherd's triumphant account, written years afterward, gave rise to this view, he literally claimed no more, as far as the lock was concerned, than to have obliged Macpherson and Crane to open it to the barges of the Union Line for a uniform lockage fee of $8 (or £2 – the same supposedly outlandish price charged for towing by the St Anne lock contractor). Besides, Shepherd said that he found his channel in late August or early September; by then, Murray and Sanderson's boats had been transiting the lock for more than a month.

According to Shepherd, the arrangement between the Union Line and Macpherson and Crane covered more than the Vaudreuil lock: the two firms also agreed to share the towing business, the Union Line to handle the towing between Lachine and Vaudreuil while Macpherson and Crane took care of the business between Vaudreuil and Carillon. If they had come to terms over the lock and the towing, it is rather odd that that very September the Union Line should have begun to tout its fleet of steamers and forty-odd barges as operating "in Opposition to a *long existing* and *Powerful Monopoly.*"[47] Whatever accommodation the two firms may have reached, it did not serve everyone's interests. Nor did Shepherd's new-found channel, for that matter. The following winter the government stepped in, ordering that until the St Anne lock was opened, the contractor there should tow all boats turning up at the St Anne Rapids. To prevent profiteering, the Board of Works was to set the towage fee at a rate just high enough to cover the costs.[48]

Evidently, the end of the Vaudreuil lock monopoly came about, not through the efforts of one man or one company, but from a combination of circumstances that had "softened up" Macpherson and Crane. For the latter, construction of the government lock at St Anne, then well under way, was like the handwriting on the wall.[49] But the government was not the only one doing the writing. On 3 February 1840, at the same time as Murray and Sanderson slapped Macpherson and Crane with the lawsuit over the *Margaret*, the de Lotbinières had notified the Ottawa and Rideau Forwarding Company that its rights to the lock had expired at the end of 1839. They summoned the company to surrender control of the facility, as their agreement provided.[50] Macpherson and Crane and the Ottawa and Rideau seem to have kept this fact to themselves. Had word slipped out that their exclusive tenure was at an end, other forwarders would have bid for access to the contentious lock. The fact that nothing of the sort occurred in 1840, and that Macpherson and Crane still held sway at Vaudreuil in the summer of 1841, suggests that they must have quietly persuaded the de Lotbinière interests to enter into a new arrangement – a lease for a monthly or seasonal fee, perhaps, or for some other financial consideration, and valid at least until the public lock at St Anne opened. Such an arrangement would have served the interests of both parties.[51]

While Macpherson and Crane kept control of the lock, the company suffered a disaster at the upper end of the line before the 1840 forwarding season had begun. A wind-borne spark from the American steamer

Telegraph set fire to the Macpherson and Crane/Ottawa and Rideau Forwarding Company warehouse and offices at Kingston on 18 April. The fire spread to a nearby building where gunpowder was stored. The resulting explosion, besides doing its own damage, helped spread the flames, devastating the centre of town. John Macpherson's own house narrowly escaped destruction. Some 15,000 barrels of flour, whisky, and pork stored in the Ottawa and Rideau warehouse on John Counter's wharf went up in smoke. The company also lost its books, with the record of all accounts receivable; a considerable amount of cash, bills, notes, and other valuable papers; and the Rideau steamer *Cataraqui*, which burned at the wharf. The total loss to the company was estimated at the time at about £20,000.[52] Then the owners of the goods destroyed in the burning of the warehouse filed a series of lawsuits against Macpherson and Crane. Like the suit over the *Margaret*, these legal proceedings would produce unforeseen results down the road.

The Macpherson and Crane/Ottawa and Rideau concern absorbed this blow, which would have levelled many a smaller company, advising customers that business would continue uninterrupted. It was said that "with the gigantic means at the disposal of the Company, however great their loss has been, Messrs M'Pherson & Crane will still lead the forwarding business."[53] The firm set about rebuilding immediately. In recognition of its crucial role in the local economy, the town wharf was placed at its disposal. The company hastened to erect temporary sheds, then a 200-foot-long, two-storey frame warehouse. (The following year it bought three waterfront lots at Portsmouth from William Dickinson and Company on which to build fireproof stone warehouses.)[54] Matters were not helped by the fact that as the season got under way, with an unprecedented volume of lake produce pouring into Kingston, one of the Carillon Canal locks broke down, stopping transport on the Ottawa for most of the month of May. This breakdown, reminiscent of the Rideau Canal mishap that had brought the Ottawa and Rideau to its knees in 1836, created a cargo logjam at Kingston. All available storage facilities were taxed beyond their limit, some goods having to be left exposed to the weather. To dissuade shippers and producers from adding to the stockpile and to protect themselves from damage claims, the cartel forwarders issued a joint warning disclaiming liability for damages to goods stored on their premises.[55] Once the lock was repaired, the forwarders struggled to make up for lost time. For the Ottawa and Rideau, the boom in business was such that, even with the setback of the April fire and the interruption of traffic in May, the company was able to declare a dividend of £3 10s. per share on the year's operations.[56]

With the end of 1840, however, had come the demise of the cartel. In the period of effervescence that followed, some firms had formed new alliances, the Union Towing Company on the St Lawrence and the Union Line on the Ottawa-Rideau. But as king of the hill, Macpherson and Crane at first had stood aloof, spurning the Union Line's offer to pay for the right to use the Vaudreuil lock.[57] Despite that bone of contention, there was a grain of truth in what a Kingston newspaper said in speaking of the Union Line's plans for the 1841 season: "Many persons have insinuated that this Company is started in opposition to the O. & R. Company, and that ruinously low charges will be the consequence; such is not the fact. There is the best understanding between the two establishments, who will not ruin each other to gratify an ungrateful public. A lower priced tariff as compared with that of the last two years, will however, be adopted, the increase in the business justifying the reduction."[58]

The fact is that there was "opposition" between the Union Line and Macpherson and Crane, as indeed there could be rivalry within a company between its steamers as to which was fastest or "which shall be best kept – best found – have the most obliging Captain, and the most civil and respectful crews."[59] But as veterans of the forwarding battles of 1833–36, Macpherson and Crane and the Union Line partners H. and S. Jones and Hooker and Henderson knew well enough that there was a point at which competition became suicidal. Self-interest – what they called "the interests of the trade" – had led them to form a cartel in 1837, just as it had led them to co-operate in other ways from time to time.[60] If there was to be a price war, it would spring from other sources than just the rivalry between Macpherson and Crane and the Union Line.

As early as mid-May, Ferguson and McGibbon's quick, efficient service on the St Lawrence was seen as giving the Ottawa-Rideau forwarders a run for their money.[61] This firm and Ross, Matthie and Company drew some of the trade away from the Ottawa-Rideau. At the same time, the small steamers on the circuit stole a march on the two Ottawa-Rideau companies that had no such boats: Macpherson and Crane and the team of Edward Hackett and William Dickinson. By mid-summer a problem of overcapacity had begun to afflict the forwarders. All these challenges and setbacks, plus the threatened intrusion of firms from as far as Lake Erie in its domain, a lawsuit from Murray and Sanderson that could prove costly if left to proceed to judgment, and R.W. Shepherd's efforts to circumvent the Vaudreuil lock, would have been more than enough to persuade Macpherson and Crane that it was time to yield a little to avoid losing a lot. Reopening the Vaudreuil lock, a doomed asset, may have represented a loss of control, but at least it paid.

If the steamers and barges had been too few to handle the booming trade in 1840, there now were too many. As early as July 1841, John Macpherson and Samuel Crane had told a parliamentary committee that they were laying up excess vessels, and they believed that other forwarders were doing the same.[62] By then, the total number of barges had increased since the beginning of 1840 by perhaps 50 to about 170, and the number of steamers, from about a dozen, had more than doubled. The breakdown by forwarder was roughly as follows:[63]

Company	Steamers	Barges
Macpherson and Crane	12	45
Hooker and Henderson	3	26
H. and S. Jones	3	25
Murray and Sanderson	5	22
Ferguson and McGibbon	2	24
W. Dickinson and Company	0	14
Ross, Matthie and Company	0	14

With some of its barges idled, Macpherson and Crane tried to defuse an old complaint by launching a passenger line – that is, no towing – between Montreal and Bytown that summer. For this purpose, the *Beaver*, a 25-horsepower boat built at Kingston in 1840, fiddle-shaped with recessed paddlewheels amidships, ran between Bytown and Grenville, the towing being left to the ancient *Shannon*.[64] On the run between Lachine and Point Fortune, it seems that the 18-horsepower *Caledonia* (formerly the *Dragon*) was used on the passenger line, while the *Ottawa* handled the towing.[65] The passenger line did not pay enough to cover its expenses, however, and the experiment was abandoned in early August.[66]

While a large company such as Macpherson and Crane could seek to adjust to changing circumstances by redeploying its resources, smaller forwarding firms did not have that flexibility. The partnership of William Dickinson and Edward Hackett, for example, never in a flourishing state, had begun to come unstuck at the same time as the cartel. On 5 December 1840 Hackett had given six months' notice of his intention to dissolve the partnership. In debt and shorn of much of their assets, the partners continued to operate throughout 1841, finally filing for bankruptcy at the end of the year with debts adding up to £5,215 17s. 7d.[67]

Still, more new boats appeared on the scene in 1842 as Matthie's and Ferguson's firms abandoned the St Lawrence to compete on the circuit, the first direct steam navigation links were established with ports beyond Kingston and Montreal, and the older forwarding firms expanded in a bid to keep pace. A couple of independent operators also launched their own small steamers on segments of the route. Thomas Kains, for example, who had served as captain of the *Shannon* until the end of 1840, came out with the *Princess Royal* on the Ottawa.[68] On the Rideau, Lyman Clothier and Company of Kemptville began operating the *Clothier* between Bytown and Kemptville in conjunction with a stage line from

Kemptville to Prescott.[69] Lockmasters' journals for the Rideau Canal show that the number of steamers plying there shot from six in 1840 to no less than thirty.[70]

Macpherson and Crane seems to have undertaken a housecleaning after the 1841 season. Of its six steamers on the Rideau Canal, the *Bytown*, the *Margaret*, and the *Rideau* were retired, and the *Mohawk*, of slightly more recent vintage, was also retired or sold.[71] The *Hunter* remained on the canal, as did the 25-horsepower *Otter*, 103 feet long by 24 feet wide, built at Macpherson and Crane's own yard in Montreal in 1840.[72] The 110-foot *Porcupine*, built at Prescott the same year, with sidewheels $26\frac{1}{2}$ feet in diameter driven by a 45-horsepower engine from the Niagara Harbour and Dock Company, moved to the Ottawa from the St Lawrence. She seems to have supplanted the 80-horsepower *Shannon* as the company's main tug and passenger steamer between Grenville and Bytown.[73] On the Bay of Quinte the firm continued to operate the *Union*, which it had bought at the end of 1840 and lengthened.[74]

The Union Line, which had six steamboats in operation in 1841, put two new paddlewheelers on the circuit. H. and S. Jones contributed the *Pilot*, built at Prescott over the winter and towed down to Montreal to receive a low-pressure "angular" engine made by Ward, Brush and Company. The newly expanded partnership of Hooker and Henderson, invigorated by the addition of young Luther Holton as partner in 1841, added the *Lily*, built over the winter at the Montreal yard of Millar, Edmonstone and Allan and equipped with a 20-horsepower low-pressure engine.[75] On the Ottawa River, H. and S. Jones took up where Macpherson and Crane had left off the previous year, setting up a regular passenger line. The *Oldfield*, refitted as a passenger boat over the winter, ran from Lachine to Carillon, and the *Albion* between Grenville and Bytown.[76]

It must be said that novelist Charles Dickens missed the boat when, after leaving Kingston for Montreal on 10 May 1842, he noted in his travel journal: "we reached Dickenson's Landing, whence travellers proceed for two or three hours by stage-coach: the navigation of the river being rendered so dangerous and difficult in the interval, by rapids, that steamboats do not make the passage."[77] This was true of the larger steamers above Dickinson's Landing and of the Canada Steamboat and Mail Coach Company boats on which he travelled. But small steam vessels had plunged down the rapids in 1841. Perhaps few passengers had dared to risk the ride. The hazards were real: some twenty regular barges were wrecked on the upper St Lawrence that year, sixteen of them in the Cedars Rapids.[78] But steamer passenger service was definitely a reality by May 1842.

From the opening of navigation, Murray and Sanderson charged $6 for cabin fare in its barges between Montreal and Kingston and $3 for steerage. The cabin was on deck, no longer below, an alteration made possible by

A steamer shoots the Lachine Rapids (reproduced from *Eighty Years' Progress*).

the removal of the fixed bridges on the Lachine Canal. On the arrival of the *Ericsson* in Montreal on 19 May, the *Gazette* remarked on "the comfort and convenience enjoyed by the passengers who avail themselves of this mode of conveyance."[79] The next day, Lonson Hilliard's *Pioneer* left Kingston carrying eleven cabin passengers and ran all the rapids, even those at Lachine, reaching Montreal in twenty-six hours. The passengers were all male, which might suggest that the run was considered too risky for the ladies. But one passenger, Thomas Molson of Kingston, a son of the late John Molson, must have been reassured. He was again aboard the *Pioneer* on her next trip down on 10–11 June, and this time he took his daughter along, one of two females on board. Under a master identified as William Cruchit, the boat made twenty-four runs on the circuit that year.[80]

By the *Pioneer's* mid-June trip, shooting the Lachine Rapids – and avoiding the Lachine Canal tolls – had become common practice, enough to elicit a warning from the St Lawrence Inland Marine Assurance Company: "It having been intimated to the Secretary ... that Forwarders, and others, are in the habit of running their Steamboats down the Lachine Rapids, Notice is hereby given, that the Company do not insure any Goods or Vessels down these Rapids."[81] Of course, all of this new passenger business represented increased competition for the Canada Steamboat and Mail Coach Company. From 1 June, Asahel Whipple fought back by cutting the fares charged by the old stage and steamer line.[82]

Murray and Sanderson added two new 75-ton steamers on the circuit in 1842, the 25-horsepower *Dart* and the 32-horsepower *Gem*, both built by the Niagara Harbour and Dock Company. The *Gem*, however, after running throughout June, seems to have been pulled from the service until late September, possibly because of defects in her machinery.[83] The *Propeller* was out of commission for about a month after being rammed and sunk on the Rideau by Hooker and Henderson's *Prince Albert* in June. She was raised and formed part of Murray and Sanderson's thrice-weekly service on the circuit later that summer. She left Montreal every Monday at 6 p.m., the *Dart* at 6 p.m. on Thursdays, and the *Ericsson* on Saturdays at 4 p.m.[84] The *Vulcan*, meanwhile, after starting on the Rideau under Captain Richard Johnston in July 1841, had been removed to the St Lawrence, where she ran at first between Brockville and Dickinson's Landing and then on the Bay of Quinte.[85]

The Lake Erie firm of Woodward and Hutchison made good on its promise to place boats on the circuit. But although it advertised its propeller schooners *St Thomas* and *London* as running between Port Stanley and Montreal, only the *St Thomas* seems to have done so before the company went out of business at summer's end. In offering the *St Thomas* for sale in September, her owners observed, without further detail, that "she has made trips between the Upper Lakes and Montreal." Lest prospective buyers conclude that she was not up to the task, they were advised that "a dissolution of partnership is the alone cause of this vessel being offered to the public for sale." Woodward and Hutchison made a similar pitch in offering the *London* for sale the following spring, but without mentioning any trips to Montreal.[86]

The propeller schooner *Precursor*, 88 feet long and 19 feet broad, launched at Cobourg on 21 May and equipped, like the *St Thomas*, with a 15-horsepower engine from Niagara Harbour and Dock, also ran on the circuit, making six round trips that year.[87] Rideau Canal records show that both the St *Thomas* and the *Precursor* were making their first trips back up to Lake Ontario by mid-July. In September, rather late in the game, the *Montreal Gazette* commented that the arrival of a Lake Ontario boat (which it did not name), variously described as a schooner and a barge, marked "the beginning of a direct trade with Canada West," presumably a reference to ports west of Kingston. The link had already been forged. But regardless of which boat first established the connection, the newspaper had a point: before long, this direct trade "must supersede the present mode of transhipping produce at Kingston, by which expense and loss are necessarily incurred."[88]

The connection was to be extended beyond Canada West in 1843 when Captain William R. Taylor, formerly master of the *St Thomas*, would take the 25-horsepower propeller schooner *Adventure*, built by the Niagara Harbour and Dock Company, all the way from Chicago to Montreal.[89] She was the first British steamer to reach Chicago. In August 1843 the *Adventure* would carry a cargo of flour from Toronto to Quebec to become the first propeller vessel to visit the latter port. And in May 1844 she would make the run down from Toronto to Montreal in a record two and a half days.[90]

Ferguson and McGibbon embarked on an ambitious expansion program in 1842. The company had four steamers built over the winter to ply on the circuit – the propeller barges *Kate* and *Norma*, both equipped with 32-horsepower, high-pressure engines, and the 45-horsepower paddle-wheeler *Quebec*, all built by Montreal shipbuilder Augustin Cantin; and another 32-horsepower propeller barge, *Ann*, built by the Niagara Harbour and Dock Company.[91] Ferguson and McGibbon opened storage facilities at Bytown and rented a large new warehouse at Kingston that could hold 40,000 barrels of flour. On the St Lawrence it moved the *Dolphin*, under Captain Nelson Chamberlain, down from Lake St Francis to Lake St Louis. A new partner, James Morton Millar, joined the firm at Montreal, the company changing its name there to Ferguson, Millar and Company. The partners also teamed up with Quebec merchant David Burnet, the newly elected member of the legislature for Quebec, to form the Quebec and Upper Canada Forwarding Company, offering direct transport of goods between Quebec and Kingston, without costly and time-consuming transshipment at Montreal.[92] This seems to have been an attempt to keep pace with Macpherson and Crane, which had opened an office at Quebec in 1841.[93]

More prudent than Alexander Ferguson and his associates, William Matthie and his partners also expanded beyond the St Lawrence to the triangular route in 1842, but limited their stake in steam to one small paddlewheeler. Ross, Matthie and Company took delivery of the 75-ton *Shamrock* at Kingston in May. Built for £2,250, complete with a 32-horsepower, high-pressure engine, by the Niagara Harbour and Dock Company, the steamer made her first run to Montreal about a month later.[94] But in July she was destroyed in the deadliest Canadian steamboat accident up to that time.[95]

For all the risks that they posed, and the fear and bravado that they had so long inspired, the rapids of the St Lawrence played no part in the calamity. The luckless *Shamrock* left Montreal on the evening of Friday, 8 July. It was only her fourth trip up. She carried no freight but was crammed with passengers – immigrant families from the British Isles. At Lachine the next morning she took three barges in tow, two of them empty and one carrying a few passengers. She set off across Lake St Louis, not quite up to speed because of a leak in her boiler. This was a problem detected on her previous trips but not considered a hazard by her crew or owners. She was about a dozen miles above Lachine, the pressure in her engine at about 70 pounds per square inch – below the maximum 85 pounds allowed by the builders – when the boiler exploded. The force of the blast holed her bow, and the *Shamrock* went down nose first. She drifted about half a mile before settling, stern out of water like a feeding duck, on a shoal or sandbank opposite Nun's Island (Île Saint-Bernard) at the mouth of the Châteauguay River.[96]

Many people died, scalded, drowned, or struck by debris. Over the next few days, bodies were fished out of the river as far down as Boucherville. Ascertaining the death toll was difficult because the passenger money collected, equivalent to ninety-five full fares, was no precise indicator of the number of "souls" transported. As Ross, Matthie explained:

We shipped and received payment for ninety-five adult passengers, a portion of which was composed of children, who were rated as follows – say from three to twelve years of age, half-price; under three years old, free; above twelve years old, full price. These were equal to ninety-five adults on board of passengers. Of those that survive sixty-three adults and three children, leaving, apparently, thirty-two adults to be accounted for, or equal to that, according to the memorandum of their shipment. It is certain, however, that many of those missing are children; and allowing two for every adult, would make the actual number of souls missing about fifty-four.[97]

Initially, in addition to fifty-four passengers, six of the eleven crew members were thought to have died. The casualty estimates varied in the next few days as one or two who had been believed lost turned up alive and some of the injured died of their wounds. Hence the imprecision on the Lachine memorial stone to Mary Thompson's family: the inscription notes that her forty-two-year-old husband and all seven of her children, ages four to fifteen, were among "about 50" immigrants killed aboard the *Shamrock*. In fact, at least sixty-three passengers died, in addition to five of the crew. Of the sixty-seven survivors, only three were children. It is not clear whether the six surviving crew members – among them Captain Thomas Hallinan and first engineer Thomas B. Benedict – were counted in that tabulation.[98]

A coroner's inquest found no fault with captain, crew, or owners, the jury concluding that the calamity was an accident.[99] For many, that was not enough: "the public cannot be convinced even by the verdict of a Coroner's Jury, but that remotely, blame does attach somewhere," a correspondent of the *Montreal Transcript* wrote. "It is evident that steamers do not blow up but in consequence of a faulty construction, originating in some petty economy, by which the proprietors of the vessel are enriched, at the risk of the lives and property of the public."[100] The same theme, with specific allegations, ran through a letter sent to the *Kingston Chronicle* by someone who seemed to possess inside information. The writer alleged that in building the engines of the *Shamrock* and other boats, the Niagara Harbour and Dock Company had cut corners to meet deadlines, and that Ross, Matthie and Company knew this when it accepted delivery of the steamer. Even before these allegations surfaced, the *Transcript* called for a special inquiry, expressing skepticism at the claim that the tiny *Shamrock* had been operating at less than maximum pressure when she was carrying more than a hundred passengers, with all their baggage, and towing three barges against the current.

We cannot help thinking that the power of such steamers as the *Shamrock* is far too small for towing against rapid currents. On canals and lakes they doubtless work admirably but they have not sufficient strength to struggle with the rapid waters of such rivers as the St Lawrence and the Ottawa. And how can it be expected that accidents shall not occur when a single propeller is seen (as was lately the case) dragging twenty one barges, each almost as large as itself, against the current of the Ottawa. The forwarders were obliged, it is true, to reduce the size of these miniature steamers to that of the locks; but there is no reason why several hundred passengers, with their baggage, should be piled upon a small vessel, and that their lives should be endangered by the boat being obliged to tow heavy barges.[101]

The government did not institute a special inquiry, but a grand jury of the Court of Quarter Sessions in Montreal felt duty bound – "as blame must rest somewhere" – to take a close look at the disaster. The panel condemned what it called "the vicious system of high pressure, from which cause the present melancholy accident occurred." It called for a law creating a board of engineers with the power to assess the competence of men such as Benedict, the engineer with four years' experience, whose abilities were deemed inadequate. It also recommended that the legislature appoint an experienced engineer with broad authority, "at each port, to examine, report upon, and certify, the state of efficiency of every steamer previous to her departure, or at periods as may be deemed necessary."[102] A bill would be introduced in 1843 providing, among other things, for the yearly certification of steamers and the phasing out of high-pressure engines on passenger boats, but it never became law.[103]

Ross, Matthie's direct financial loss from the *Shamrock* disaster was comparatively slight. Boat and engine were still under a three-month warranty from the Niagara Harbour and Dock Company.[104] As the boat carried no freight, there was no compensation payable to cargo owners; and because the affair had been ruled an accident, Ross, Matthie was not liable for any loss, injury, or death.[105] But besides the blow to its reputation, the company was deprived of whatever passenger and towing business its one steamer accounted for, and it had to pay others to tow its barges.

Within two weeks of the *Shamrock* disaster, the forwarders regrouped. All the firms operating on the circuit – Ross, Matthie and Company and Ferguson and McGibbon, as well as Macpherson and Crane, Hooker and Henderson, H. and S. Jones, and Murray and Sanderson – subscribed to a new rate schedule.[106] Circumstantial evidence suggests that this new pact constituted a defensive move in the face of a combination of threats which the *Shamrock* incident had brought to a head.

The free-for-all prevailing since the lapse of the 1837–40 cartel had driven down rates to a point where profits, if any, must have been slim. Only a month before the forwarders published their new common rate schedule, Macpherson and Crane had advertised a flat summer rate of 1s. 3d. per hundredweight for all goods carried up from Montreal to Kingston and downward rates of 1s. 3d. per barrel for flour, 1s. 10½ d. per barrel for pork, 3s. 9d. per barrel for ashes, and 5d. per bushel of wheat or other grains. These prices were lower than those which the Canada Inland Forwarding and Insurance Company, "determined upon not being out-rivalled," had charged at the height of the contest between St Lawrence and Ottawa River forwarders in 1835.[107] The new rates set by the cartel in July would be substantially higher. Charges for upward freight were to run from 2s. hundredweight for heavy groceries and hardware to 3s. hundredweight for dry goods and all light and bulky packages. The downward rates for flour, pork, and ashes were 1s. 6d., 2s. 3d., and 3s. 9d. per barrel respectively, and grain was 6d. per bushel.[108]

The struggle for the survival of the fittest among the forwarders might have continued unabated for some time yet had it not been for the announcement on 2 April 1842 of major increases in tolls on the Ottawa River and Rideau canals. The changes were particularly drastic on the Rideau. There, boats had always paid tolls based on the nature and quantity of their cargo and the number of cabin passengers they carried. Now the tolls were to be levied on the vessels themselves, regardless of their load. A steamer passing up or down the length of the canal, for example, was to pay £5 per trip, whether crammed with passengers or empty. Before, it would have paid 4s. per adult cabin passenger (half that for children under twelve). Six other categories of boats and barges were established, based on their tonnage, and a rate was also set for canoes and other small craft. Under the old system, the largest of barges, loaded with a thousand barrels of flour, would have paid a toll of 1½d. per barrel, or

A sketch of a steamer off Pointe-Claire (where the windmill stands, at left) on
Lake St Louis, near where the *Shamrock* blew up in July 1842 (reproduced from
Van Cleve, *Ontario and St Lawrence Steamboat Company's Hand-Book for
Travelers*).

£6 5s. in all. Now, a first-class barge, defined as one measuring 100 to
150 tons, was to pay £31 10s., whether it carried one barrel of flour or a
thousand. On the Ottawa, where the tolls had always been assessed on
the boats, the classification was adjusted to match that on the Rideau and
the rates generally increased. A small steamer passing through all three
Ottawa canals was to pay £2 5s. on the way up and one-third of that, or
15s., on the way down, as opposed to £1 up and 15s. down under the old
schedule. The largest barges, which had paid £4 5s. on the way up and £3
on the way down, were to pay £7 10s. up and £2 10s. down.[109]

Traffic patterns made the increases even steeper than those comparisons
might suggest. Barges were often towed up from Lachine to Kingston
empty or carrying immigrants – as in the case of the *Shamrock's* last
voyage, when she was towing three barges, two empty and one with
passengers – and then loaded with goods and produce to be sent down by
the St Lawrence. Under the old system, a top-class barge used in this way
would have paid £4 5s. to pass up the Ottawa River canals and nothing
on the Rideau. Now the total charge was to rise to £39.

The idea behind the increases was to update the classification of boats,
now that some barges were also steam vessels, and to generate enough

The Macpherson and Crane steamer *Hunter* on Opinicon Lake, part of the Rideau Canal, in 1840; from a watercolour by Thomas Burrowes (AO/C-100017).

revenues from tolls to cover the operating and maintenance costs of the canals. The revenues had always fallen short, partly because most of the barges – and now many of the steamers, too – that travelled up the canals to Kingston returned to Montreal by the St Lawrence. Since the canals were still under imperial control, the funds to pay the deficits came, not out of Canadian pockets, but from the British taxpayer, a situation that was manifestly unfair. The Ordnance Department, which administered the canals, was determined to correct this anomalous situation. But the forwarders, already suffering from their costly rivalry, were utterly unprepared for the new charges. It was not the increases alone that stunned them but also their timing. Though the new toll schedules had been approved by the government on 5 March, they had not been announced until a month later. By then the forwarders had already entered into contracts for the season on the basis of the old tolls. They pleaded their case, arguing that they should have received advance notice of the changes and warning that the new tolls would be counterproductive: instead of raising more revenue, they would lead to an abandonment of the Ottawa-Rideau route, a prospect which many of the towns and settlements along the route viewed with alarm.[110]

The authorities relented. Before the navigation season had even begun, they agreed to suspend the high new tolls "until Her Majesty's pleasure in the premises shall be made known." New schedules adopted on 18 April provided for lesser increases. On the Rideau the old cargo-based toll schedule was reinstated, with slight modifications and the addition of a charge per boat. Steamers were to pay £1 to pass from Bytown to Kingston and half that, or 10s., in the other direction. Barges, Durham boats, and other vessels that carried passengers as well as freight were charged between 3s. and 10s. for the passage up and half as much for the passage down, besides whatever toll they had to pay for the freight. On the Ottawa River the old system of classifying boats in seven categories – small steamer, barge, Durham boat (small barge), packet boat, batteau 32 to 42 feet long, batteau under 32 feet, and skiff, canoe, and similar small craft – was replaced with a new list of nine categories – small steamer, barge of 100 tons or more, barge of 70 to 100 tons, barge of 40 to 70 tons, boat under 40 tons, boat under 40 tons for passengers only, batteau 32 to 42 feet long, batteau under 32 feet, and skiff, canoe, and other. The toll for a steamer passing through the whole line of three canals remained at the old rate of £1 up and 15s. down. The standard rate of £4 5s. up and £3 down for all barges now became the rate charged on third-class barges. The larger barges of 70 to 100 tons and 100 tons or more paid £5 10s. and £6 10s. respectively on the way up and £3 15s. and £4 10s. down. The only boats charged less than formerly were batteaux – £1 5s. up and 15s. down for the larger ones, instead of £1 15s. up and £1 5s. down; and 15s. and 10s. for the smaller ones, compared with £1 5s and 17s. 10d. under the old schedule.[111]

These more modest increases offered the forwarders a respite, but how long would it be before the authorities insisted on charging tolls calculated to cover the canals' operating and maintenance costs? There was another concern for the trade as a whole in the decision to resume construction of the Cornwall Canal in the spring of 1842 and to begin construction later that year of the Beauharnois Canal between Lake St Louis and Lake St Francis. A St Lawrence route, with locks 200 feet long, 55 feet wide, and 9 feet deep, promised more disruption for the forwarders, whose boats were all geared to the Ottawa-Rideau. In the new St Lawrence canals surely lay the death blow to any monopoly on the Ottawa-Rideau, if not to the entire through trade on that route, with its small canals.

It was at the time when these concerns agitated the forwarders that the *Shamrock* blew up. This fiasco affected them all, not just Ross, Matthie and Company, because it raised doubts about the safety of the other steamers on the circuit, and about the integrity of the forwarders themselves. It gave high-pressure engines a bad name and raised new concerns about the common practice of using passenger steamers as towboats. Travellers knew from experience that taking barges in tow made a trip by steamer tediously slow; the *Shamrock* case seemed to demonstrate that the practice was also unsafe. As the *Transcript* observed, there was no reason that the lives of passengers aboard these small steamers should be "endangered by the boat being obliged to tow heavy barges."[112]

For the forwarders, forming a cartel, insofar as it facilitated coordination, was one way of dealing with this problem of public perception and the other pressures they faced. They could try to minimize the use of high-pressure steamers for passenger traffic, or at least arrange that when carrying passengers, these boats would not also tow barges. Collaboration in the management of resources could also help to blunt the impact of higher canal tolls. In cases where boats with no load paid as much as full ones, the different companies might pool shipments to reduce the number of empty or half-empty boats to a minimum. In short, by working hand in hand rather than undercutting each other, the forwarders could hope to offer a more efficient service, make more money, and save more.

But if the cartel was meant to be a lifesaver, it came too late for more than one forwarder. Ferguson and his partners were the first to tumble, in a fall as vertiginous as their rise; they were followed by Ross, Matthie and Company and, more surprisingly, the Ottawa and Rideau Forwarding Company.

A month after the cartel was formed, Ferguson, Millar and Company was reduced to selling the *Dolphin* and the *Aid* and eleven barges, the buyers allowing the company continued use of the boats until they could be resold.[113] In November the *Kate* was holed on the Rideau, and the sudden onset of winter at the end of the month left the *Quebec* and the *Norma*, with several barges in tow, frozen in at Burritt's Rapids. Several other steamers were caught in the same way.[114] This was par for the course for canal navigation – a nuisance but nothing so serious as to lead a young man such as McGibbon, married only one year, to take his own life, as he did in December. The likely cause of his distress soon came to light: in filing for bankruptcy, his partners declared a staggering debt of £31,304 3s. 2d. Their downfall spelled the end of the Quebec and Upper Canada Forwarding Company.[115] A new Quebec Forwarding Company would spring up in its place in 1843, with Ferguson as its agent at Montreal and Millar in charge at Quebec. For £4,600, or about two-thirds of their original cost, the new company bought nine of the barges of the failed Quebec and Upper Canada Forwarding Company and its side-wheeler *Quebec*. It advertised direct links, not just between Quebec and Kingston, but also with Lake Champlain via the newly opened Chambly Canal on the Richelieu River. That year the *Quebec* became the first steamer to sail from Kingston to Quebec and the first to pass through the Chambly Canal.[116]

Ross, Matthie, for its part, was strapped for funds in the fall of 1842 as a result of "the present Commercial difficulties, divers losses in trade, bad debts and other untoward circumstances." Unable to meet the payments on a schooner it had bought for £1,400, it was obliged to return the boat to the seller in October. Still owing "divers large sums of money," it managed to secure protection (a "letter of license") from its creditors in November with a promise to pay its debts in full over an extended period.[117] Matthie's concerns – the Matthie, Easton and Company trading house at Brockville, as well as the Ross, Matthie and Company forwarding business – folded in the course of 1843. By June that year, Matthie had sold the retail part of his business. The rest of his operations were wound up by the end of the year, when his forwarding fleet, offered for sale, consisted of a dozen barges.[118]

The Macpherson and Crane/Ottawa and Rideau Forwarding Company concern gave no indication that it was irrevocably headed for the rocks in the summer of 1842. Having disposed of some of its older steamers, it seemed to be proceeding with the modernization of its fleet. While it had had no steamers making the circuit in 1841, it put four new boats on that run between May and early August. Right after the cartel was formed, it offered twice-daily departures from Montreal for Kingston with the low-pressure, 90-foot paddlewheeler *Charlotte* and the high-pressure propeller barges *Juno*, *Mercury*, and *Meteor*. All three barges were equipped with 25-horsepower Nelson Walker engines. To these circuit boats the company would add a new, low-pressure paddlewheeler, the 92-foot *Bytown*, in 1843.[119]

The fate of the concern seems to have been sealed in November as the season came to a close. One blow fell when the courts turned down Macpherson and Crane's last bid to avoid having to pay for consigned goods destroyed in the Kingston fire of 1840.[120] Another came with the announcement that the objectionable schedule of Rideau Canal tolls that had been suspended in April was to be reinstated. This time the forwarders could not claim that they had been denied fair warning: the new schedule, proclaimed on 5 November and published in the official gazette a week later, was to go into effect as of 1 January 1843.[121] Several towns along the route raised a hue and cry that winter, but failed to shake the resolve of the authorities.[122]

The cartel had no choice but to swallow the pill, but when it published its price schedule for the 1843 season on 15 April, it made a point of highlighting the surcharge attributable to "the greatly augmented Tolls on the Rideau Canal."[123] It also made an effort to rationalize the use of its boats. An indication of this can be seen in the fixed daily passenger service offered by circuit steamers: Macpherson and Crane's *Charlotte* departed from Kingston on Mondays; H. and S. Jones's *Pilot* on Tuesdays; Murray and Sanderson's *Dart* on Wednesdays; Macpherson and Crane's *Bytown* and Hooker and Henderson's *Lily* on Thursdays; the *Pioneer*, part of what appears to have been a reorganized Union Line, on Fridays; and Hooker and Henderson's *Grenville* on Saturdays.[124]

When the Ottawa and Rideau Forwarding Company held its annual meeting in May, the news was not good. For several years the only word from this company, as distinct from Macpherson and Crane, had come in terse notices of its annual meetings or, as had happened for the last time in the spring of 1841, the declaration of a dividend. But in calling on all shareholders to turn out, in person or by proxy, on 13 May, chairman John Frothingham sounded an urgent note, warning that "matters of great importance to the Company will be submitted to the Meeting."[125] There was no hint of what these matters were, and the press carried no account of the meeting. But a few days later Frothingham issued another notice saying that the meeting had resolved to call on stockholders to pay an instalment of £7 10s. per share within a week.[126] The reasons for this urgent demand for funds did not become public knowledge until June, when newspapers carried this brief report:

The Ottawa and Rideau Forwarding Company will be dissolved, and its business closed on the expiration of their agreement with Messrs Macpherson & Crane in December next. The ruinous business of the last two years, and judgments against Macpherson & Crane, amounting to £12,000, for losses at the fire in Kingston, have led to this; and an instalment of £7. 10s. per share is called in to meet demands. The company own large assets, which will probably reimburse the stockholders, if they bring near their value.[127]

This announcement of the fall of the Ottawa and Rideau, a fixture of the Upper Canada trade, seems to have elicited no public comment. At least three factors help to account for this silence. First, critics who had harped on monopoly and inflated forwarding rates may have been at a loss to explain how a company that, in their view, was reaping astronomical profits could suddenly go broke. If anything, the string of failures among the forwarders, not to mention the false starts and quick collapse of challengers promising cut-rate service, suggests that the prices charged were never as outlandish as they were made to appear. If the rates seemed high, then maybe they reflected the high costs of engaging in the forwarding business. The Erie Canal and the port of New York may have been drawing off more and more of the western trade, but perhaps that development had more to do with the advantages which New York presented over Montreal than with the Canadian forwarders' charges.[128] As Captain Henry Twohy, who had commanded the *Rideau* in 1839 and the *Bytown* in 1840, observed years later, "Judging from the Results the Carrying Trade must have been very unsatisfactory as the Forwarders all failed on the River and with a few exceptions Steam Boat proprietors on the Lakes."[129]

A second reason for the lack of any public comment may have been that the disappearance of the Ottawa and Rideau was no hard economic blow to the trade, to the country, or even to Kingston, a city to whose prosperity the firm had greatly contributed in the 1830s. The reason was simple. After thriving under its arrangement with Macpherson and Crane, the Ottawa and Rideau sank under the weight of the business losses and legal liabilities incurred by its partner. Yet the two companies were not so closely tied that the failure of the one should have dragged down the other. When the Ottawa and Rideau was dissolved at the end of 1843, Macpherson and Crane bought up its assets (see appendix E) and carried on business as usual.[130] Thus the Ottawa and Rideau's passing caused scarcely a ripple. At the time, Kingston was gnashing its teeth over a much greater blow: the loss of its status as Canada's capital. In 1844 the seat of government would move to Montreal.

Finally, since it had given Macpherson and Crane the run of the house in 1837, the Ottawa and Rideau had become little more than a name as far as the public was concerned. It was a name that would forever be associated with the early days of the Ottawa-Rideau route – and with complaints of monopoly. But those days were passed, and events that June underscored the fact. On 26 June the public lock at St Anne, the long-awaited answer to the Ottawa and Rideau's Vaudreuil lock, was finally opened. The *Dolphin*, chartered by the lock contractors for the occasion, inaugurated the new lock "to the sound of cannon, and accompanied by the cheers of multitudes on its banks."[131] That same month the Cornwall Canal had been opened to general use, more than six months after its own official inauguration.[132] It was a link in the chain of St Lawrence canals which, by the end of the decade, would eclipse the Ottawa-Rideau as the through route between Montreal and the Great Lakes. The author of *Hochelaga; or, England in the New World* trumpeted the fact:

The most remarkable of the rapids, whose interruption the industry of man is busied to avoid, is called the Cedars. The stream is here pent into several narrow channels among wooded islands, and tumbles fiercely along over its rocky bed. Steamers and other boats constantly venture down this perilous passage, but not unfrequently pay dearly for their temerity. At present they can only return up to the great lakes by the Ottawa river and the Rideau canal, from which they emerge at Kingston, on Lake Ontario; but the works [St Lawrence canals] are going on rapidly, and by them this great round will be saved.[133]

The inauguration of the Cornwall Canal on 25 November 1842 was Asahel Whipple's last hurrah. Like the Ottawa and Rideau Forwarding Company, his day had passed. He retired in 1843; he was fifty-three years old and perhaps not in the best of health. He had begun disengaging himself from business three years earlier, pulling out of his forwarding partnership with Timothée Masson.[134] Perhaps helping to nudge him into retirement were the fires of August 1841 and July 1842 that had successively destroyed the stables of the stage and steamboat line at Dickinson's Landing and Côteau.[135] Times had changed. Whipple had made his mark in the days when steamers were confined to short stretches of the river. "Miniature" steamers were now running circles around his Canada Steamboat and Mail Coach Company. The opening of the Cornwall Canal signalled new challenges; with the Beauharnois Canal then under construction (it was finished in 1845) and work beginning on the enlargement of the Lachine Canal, larger boats would be able to sail back and forth between the Great Lakes and Montreal.

In October 1842 Whipple appeared before a parliamentary committee probing the government's decision to build the Beauharnois Canal. Many people, including his old friends and neighbours at Côteau, objected to the decision, contending that the canal should be built on their side of the river, the north side. In his testimony, Whipple supported their bid, drawing on his years of experience as master of the *Cornwall* and the *Neptune* to point out the difficulties of navigation on the south side of Lake St Francis. But the decision to build the south-side Beauharnois Canal stood.[136]

As work on that project began, the building of the Cornwall Canal was just about completed. Frustrated by ice in his first attempt on 24 November, Captain Erastus H. Stearns succeeded in taking the *Highlander* up through the canal the next day.[137] Whipple was on board to represent the boat's owners. Coming up to the dock at Cornwall, the *Highlander* fired a salute as the militia band struck up "God Save the Queen" and "Rule Britannia," and residents cheered. Some of those cheers were for Whipple. "Indeed," the *Cornwall Observer* remarked, "no person is more worthy of this honour than Capt. Whipple who was instrumental in establishing the *first line* of stages between Montreal and Prescott and to whose unwearied exertions in overcoming many and great difficulties is to be mainly attributed the success of the undertaking, and the efficiency of the present mode of conveyance on this route." The *Highlander* proceeded to Kingston and then left there on 1 December, arriving back at Côteau the next day after stopping for the night at Prescott and making her run down the Long Sault in daylight.[138]

Eveline, the youngest of Whipple's three daughters, was married in the American Presbyterian Church the following February and moved to Burlington, Vermont, where her husband practised law and where her sister, Meribah, lived.[139] That month, Whipple signed his last contract with the Post Office, and in early May he turned over his contract obligations to forwarder James Henderson.[140] Lucius Moody succeeded him as manager of the Canada Steamboat and Mail Coach Company, moving into the Whipple house on McGill Street.[141] Whipple and his wife then followed their daughters to Burlington.

Daniel Whipple retired around the same time as his brother, to be succeeded as captain of the *Chieftain* by Nelson Chamberlain, formerly of the *Dolphin*. Daniel lived out his life on his farm in DeKalb, New York, where he died on 16 February 1855.[142] Asahel's retirement proved much shorter: he died at his home in Burlington on 17 January 1844. An inventory of his Canadian assets showed that he still owned $80\frac{1}{8}$ shares in the Canada Steamboat and Mail Coach Company, each share valued at £25 17s. 9d. Among other effects, he also held three contiguous properties on Lake St Francis, with numerous buildings on them, including six houses, two blacksmith's shops, two carpenter's shops, six stables, a carriage shed, and assorted other sheds. The steamboat wharf stood on one of these properties, its ownership split between Whipple, who held a quarter share, and Horace Dickinson's estate.[143] It is odd to find Dickinson's heirs in possession of this remnant more than a decade after his death, considering that his widow had long ago expressed, in word and deed, a desire to be clear of involvement in his old transport line. The scattering of those heirs to the four winds may have complicated any attempt to dispose of it.

After Whipple's departure, the only members of Dickinson's old circle left in Montreal were his widow, with her four surviving children, and Samuel Ward. He and his twin brother, Lebbeus, had renewed their foundry partnership with George Brush at the end of 1842, stipulating that any of the partners could withdraw on six months' notice.[144] The Ward twins finally did so on 28 November 1845, selling Brush their interests in the Eagle Foundry for £5,306 13s. 4d.[145] Samuel Ward left Montreal the following April. The *Gazette* saw fit to notice his departure in its news columns:

On Tuesday afternoon, one of our most esteemed citizens, S.S. Ward, Esq., left this city for the United States, whither he has gone to reside. Though it rained heavily at the time, numbers of gentlemen accompanied him to the Steamer Prince Albert,[146] to testify their sincere regret at his departure. After having resided in this Province nearly thirty years, Mr Ward has left it in the enjoyment of a most enviable reputation, as a man of business and a member of the Church of Christ; and is followed by the best wishes of a large circle of friends.[147]

Horace Dickinson's widow and her Montreal-born children, all in their late teens or early twenties, seem to have moved to the United States a year or so later.[148]

The children of his brother Barnabas, however, all but one American-born, remained in Canada. After Barnabas's death, his widow and her six surviving children had moved from Cornwall to Prescott. There in 1837 the eldest daughter, twenty-year-old Mary Little Dickinson, had married Alpheus Jones, whose appointment as postmaster dated back to the year before she was born, when the Dickinsons had launched their Canadian stage line and won their first mail contract.[149]

Such reminders of the old days and of old associations were even more marked in the person of Barnabas's youngest son, Moss Kent Dickinson. He had been named after lawyer Moss Kent, who had practised in Coo-perstown and served as state senator for Otsego County in the days of Asahel Whipple's boyhood there, and had then moved to Lewis County, where he had been a trustee of Lowville Academy with Lemuel Dickinson and gone on to serve in neighbouring Jefferson County as a judge, registrar of the Chancery Court, and congressman.[150] In the 1830s Moss Kent Dickinson had himself attended Lowville Academy, Hiram Norton's alma mater, and shortly afterward, at the age of sixteen, had accompanied Norton to Illinois, as we have seen. Returning to Prescott in 1840, he worked as a postal and customs clerk for Alpheus Jones, his brother-in-law, until 1844. He then started in the shipping and forwarding business. His line grew to include some sixteen steamers and sixty barges plying from Oswego, New York, to Quebec and from Ottawa to Whitehall, at the foot of Lake Champlain. A resident of Ottawa through the 1850s and 1860s, he founded the village of Manotick on the Rideau in 1859 and served as mayor of Ottawa from 1864 to 1866. He capped his public career by carrying the county of Russell for Sir John A. Macdonald's Conserva-tive Party in the general election of 1882.[151]

In 1867, two years before he quit the forwarding trade, Moss Kent Dickinson had reorganized his line as a joint-stock company under a familiar name – the Ottawa and Rideau Forwarding Company. In his heyday the *Ottawa Citizen* had dubbed him "King of the Rideau." A thinly fictionalized account of his life was published under that title in the 1970s.[152] It was all rather ironic, considering that to his uncle years before, the Rideau had spelled neither success nor honour, only trouble. More irony lies in the fact that, at least indirectly, Moss Kent Dickinson contributed to the effacing of his uncle's memory. Accounts of his life claim that Dickinson's Landing was founded by, and named after, his father, when it seems much more likely that the village owed its existence and its name to the fact that it was the site chosen as the "landing" for Horace Dickinson's *Iroquois*. But all that is water under the bridge now: Dickinson's Landing vanished in 1958, flooded in the construction of the St Lawrence Seaway.

Appendix A

Lease of privilege, 24 November 1825 (translation):[1]

[The heirs de Lotbinière authorize] Messrs Theodore Davis and Robert Drummond of this city of Montreal, present and accepting, to cut through a point of land in the said Seigniory of Vaudreuille near the mill built at the Lotbinière Rapid, there to open a Canal suitable and sufficient to facilitate the navigation of the Ottawa River, and for no other purpose, of which Canal the said Messrs Theodore Davis and R. Drummond will have the exclusive use … for the time and under the limits and restrictions hereinafter stated and explained, on the condition that the said Canal shall be immediately opened and fitted with the necessary Locks and piers entirely at the costs and expense of the said Messrs Theodore Davis and R. Drummond, beginning to the northeast of the Seigniorial grist mill at a distance of forty feet from the Canal serving the said mill, and to be built in a straight line up to the head of the mill Canal where there shall be left a distance of ten clear feet between the two canals. The canal to be opened will be thirty feet wide inside the Lock and the walls, solidly built and deep enough at all times, even when the waters are at their lowest, for all boats or vessels drawing four feet of water or cribs and rafts of eighty feet in length to pass up and down; the walls will be made of sound oak wood and the lock, where it is underwater, clad in sound hemlock, and above water, in good and sound cedar wood properly squared; and Messrs Theodore Davis and Robert Drummond will have the exclusive use for their benefit of the said Canal for the passage of boats, cribs, rafts or vessels only, and for no other purpose, for the term of eleven years full and complete, reckoned from the day the said canal opens in the ensuing summer for the passage of any boat, crib, raft or vessel as above mentioned, and at the expiration of the said eleven years, the said Messrs Davis and Drummond or their Representatives shall return [the canal] to the heirs Lotbinière or to the proprietor of the Seigniory of Vaudreuille, in good condition and the walls in good order, that the said heirs or proprietor of the said Seigniory of Vaudreuille may use and employ the Canal to such ends and purposes as they may see fit, without having to pay any sum or reimbursement to the said Messrs Davies & Drummond or to their Representatives; with this one reservation that the said [owners] of the said Seigniory of Vaudreuille may use the Canal to pass all the wood or boats, excepting steamboats, needed for the operation, service and use of the existing mill [or any new mills or manufactures] and manor house of the said Seigniory of Vaudreuille free of all charges, without […] in any way obstructing the passage of boats, rafts, cribs or vessels that the said Messrs Davies & Drummond may wish

to pass through; with one further right of the said [owners] of the said Seigniory of
Vaudreuille to open a communication, at their costs and expense, between the said proposed
Canal and the mill Canal, above the Lock ...

From the contract of George Street and John McArthur with Emery Cushing,
16 August 1832:[2]

Specification of Work for the alteration of the Locks at Vaudreuille to alter the present Locks
to the following demensions viz., Thirty three feet wide in the Clear of the Gates and Piers
when completed, and One hundred and thirty four feet in length from the point of the
lower Gate Cill to the point of the Upper Gate Cill, all English measure. The lower Gate
Cill to be placed in the same position and on the same level as the present One[.] The upper
Gate to be extended so far up above the present as to give the length specified, the extra
width to be taken from the south side at the Lower End and from the North Side at the
Upper end. The Cill of the Upper Gates to be on the same level as the present Upper Gates.
The several piers & Chambers to bear the same relative Levels as marked upon the
accompanying Plan[.] in framing the several Piers and other sections great care to be taken
to execute them in a sound workmanlike manner properly braced when necessary to
preserve the best effect. The Gate posts to be bolted to the Other part of the frame work
to resist the weight of the Gates. The whole of the work is intended to be done at the least
possible expence to the proprietors that is to say all useless and superfluous labour omitted
when practicable without effecting the stability of the Work. The greatest height of Water
is supposed will never exceed five feet against the Gates and that only when the Ottawa is
at its greatest height and the St Lawrence being in proportion. The sides of the Chambers
to be framed agreeable to the section, one half of the Cills to extend across the Locks and
sunk down below the bed, the sides to be planked with two inch pine groved and tong[d] at
the Joints and well nailed to be about eleven feet high at the Lowest Gate to the top of the
Cap. The longitudinal rails to be put on in lengths as long as practicable[,] the heading broke
[?] at least equal to the width of two sections[,] the top plate to mortice down upon the
standards and the middle one bolted and bottom one to be well pined [pinned], the whole
to be well backed and filled in with dry stone or Gravel to the top of the planking, no Clay
allowed to be used[;] to put on a pine Casing throughout, about 18 Inches wide and six
Inches in thickness properly pined [pinned] down[;] great care is to be preserved in Sheet
planking in front of the Cills and also in the Wing Piers to prevent as much as possible the
Ingress of the Water. To prepare and properly fix a Pier or Break Water at the Lower End
as marked in the Plan and fill in the same with Stone or Gravel as before mentioned. To
prepare and finish two pair of Lock Gates agreeable to the plan [...] The Contractor is to
Clear out the bottom of the Canal above the Upper Gates to one uniform Level corresponding with the Gate Chamber to extend [words crossed out] and a slope Outwards equal to
about two feet at Base for every one foot in Height, filled with rough stone that will prevent
as much as possible the Canal from being liable to be filled up.

Notification, 3 February 1840:[3]

... We the undersigned public notaries ... at the special Instance and request of Dame Louise
Josephte Chartier de Lotbinière, wife of The Honorable Robert Unwin Harwood of Vaudreuil
... Seignioresse & proprietor in possession of the Fief & Seigniory of Vaudreuil ... did go
to the Office of John Frothingham Esquire of Montreal aforesaid, copartner or Share-holder
in a certain Joint Stock Company at Montreal styled the Ottawa Steam Boat Company &
whereof he the said John Frothingham is an active member being President or Chairman
of the said Company ... Did give Notice unto him, And to the said Ottawa Steam Boat
Company, that the term of time granted unto them by the said Dame Louise Josephte
Chartier De Lotbiniere and her said husband for holding possessing or enjoying certain

rights & privileges in within or about her said Seigniory of Vaudreuil, whereby the said Ottawa Steam Boat Company or certain Individuals on behalf of the said Company did Make & Construct a Certain Lock in or near the Outlet of the Ottawa river between the head of Isle Perrot and the said Seigniory to facilitate the Navigation thereof by their Steamers & other Vessels, expired with the year one thousand eight hundred and thirty nine ... whereby the said lock and all the buildings & improvements made by the said Ottawa Steam Boat Company and now actually being in & within or About the Seigniory aforesaid have fallen to and become and are now the actual property of the said Seignioresse as forming part of the said Seigniory of Vaudreuil, and is and are subject hereafter to her entire Controul to & for her own use & benefit ...; and that she now doth as she will at the opening of the Navigation of the ensuing spring assume the possession & proprietorship thereof and of every part thereof. Whereupon We did also notify the said John Frothingham and the said Ottawa Steam Boat Company and others whom it doth or May concern to quit abandon and give up peaceably & quietly the possession of the said lock and premises and all the rights, privileges & appurtenances to the same attached and heretofore held & enjoyed under all or any Agreements or Agreement, Lease, Sale or *acte* of any description soever made or entered into by and between the said Dame Louise Josephte Chartier De Lotbiniere and Robert Unwin Harwood and the said John Frothingham or others for the account benefit or advantage of the said Ottawa Steam Boat Company or other or others under any other Name style or title.

Appendix B

INVENTORY OF THE SWAN, 1832[1]

This list gives a good idea of the fittings of a small steamer. While inventories exist of other Dickinson boats, this is the only one that provides a room-by-room breakdown.

	£	s	d
The Steamboat "Swan" now running between Lachine and the Cascades, with Engine of thirty two Horse power	1,510.	8.	o
Furniture &c on board			

In Gentleman's Cabin

	£	s	d
One oil cloth Carpet	10.	0.	o
One set Dining Tables (20 ft) cherry	10.	10.	o
One ditto ditto ditto (15 ft) ditto	6.	0.	o
Twelve windsor Chairs	1.	8.	o
Six settees	5.	5.	o
Seven cushions	7.	17.	6
Eight Window Curtains	3.	0.	o
Twenty four soup plates & a lot of sundry plates & dishes	7.	10.	o
Seventy cups & saucers	1.	17.	6
Eight sugar bowls		6.	o
Eight milk pots & six covers		5.	o
Eight slop bowls		2.	o
Sixty egg cups		7.	6
Five Jugs		10.	o
Ten wash basins		12.	6
Three soap boxes		3.	o
Sixty tumblers		15.	o
Fifty four wine glasses		9.	o
Ten salt cellars		5.	o
Two sauce Pots			6
Four pairs Brass candlesticks		10.	o
Four pairs snuffers and trays		8.	o

Item	£	s	d
One pair old candlesticks and snuffers		1.	0
One blue Table cover		5.	0
One small green ditto		2.	6
One Sprinkler		1.	0
Two setts Shoe Brushes		2.	0
Two tin tea Pots		3.	0
Two tin Coffee Pots		4.	0
Four shaving Pots		3.	0
Two Inkstands		2.	6
Two knife Trays		2.	0
Two bread Baskets		2.	0
Two Clothes Brushes		2.	0
Four hair ditto & combs		4.	0
Twenty seven pairs of Nut crackers	1.	0.	0
Sixty five plated tea spoons	5.	8.	4
Fifty four plated Table spoons	9.	0.	0
One plated Soup ladle		10.	0
One dinner bell		2.	0
Three small Table ditto		3.	0
Three sets Castors	4.	10.	0
Two furniture Brushes		2.	0
An oil Pot & can		3.	0
Eight dozen Buck horn large Knives & forks	4.	0.	0
Eight dozen small ditto	3.	0.	0
Six Carvers & forks		10.	0
Four steels		3.	0
One Plate Basket		5.	0
Two small Tubs		5.	0
Two scrubbing Brushes		1.	0
Two dust pans & brushes		4.	0
Two Table Brushes		2.	6
Two corn dusters		1.	0
A corn broom			9
Two Corkscrews		2.	0
One hair floor brush		1.	3
Two chamois		1.	0
Two plate brushes		1.	3
Seven Table clothes	7.	0.	0
Three sponges		1.	3
Thirty one Diaper Napkins	1.	3.	1
Twelve coarse Towels		6.	0
Thirty old ditto (much worn)		7.	6
Twenty four old Napkins (much worn)		9.	0
Two spit boxes		2.	0
Twenty one pillow cases	1.	1.	0
Fifty two sheets	12.	10.	0
Thirty three counterpanes	5.	10.	0
Thirty three Pillows	6.	12.	0
Twenty four pairs slippers	1.	16.	0
Two mattresses	2.	0.	0
Six Blankets	1.	2.	6

In Sailors' Mess Room

Eight Knives & forks		4.	0
Eight tin plates		4.	0
Eight saucers &c		8.	0
One Bread Basket		1.	0
Eight spoons		2.	6
One tea Kettle		2.	0
One Soup Tureen & Ladle		3.	9
One Bench		1.	6

In Cabin Mess Room

Stem and old set castors		2.	6
Twelve small Knives and forks		6.	0
Three large ditto ditto		2.	6
One carver & fork		1.	3
Ten Cups and saucers		2.	6
One sugar bowl		1.	0
One milk Pot			3
Two salt Cellars		1.	0
Three Blue dishes		5.	0
Twelve breakfast Plates		3.	0
Ten cheese plates		2.	0
Ten egg Cups		1.	0
A Vegetable dish & Cover			6
Two Pickle [Gloves?]		1.	0
One sauce Pot			4
Nine plated Tea spoons		2.	0
Six metal ditto		1.	0
Eight large Table spoons		4.	0
A tea Pot		1.	6
One coffee Pot		2.	0
Four table cloths	1.	0.	0

In the Larder

One Butter Box		7.	6
One butter boat			9
A pair steel yards		1.	6
Three Butter plates			6
One Iron meat hook		1.	0

In Ladies Cabin

Two looking glasses	1.	0.	0
One cherry Table	1.	5.	0
Nine old yellow Windsor chairs		18.	0

In cook House

One cooking stove & Tins complete	5.	0.	0
One Collander		1.	6
One Shovel and Tongs		2.	0
One Grid Iron		1.	6
One Wharfle [waffle] Iron		2.	6
One set scewers [skewers]		1.	3
Two ladles		1.	3

Three skimmers	1.	6
Two drudging boxes	1.	3
A choping [*sic*] Knife	1.	0
Four tart Pans	1.	0
A Lamp	1.	0
Four Ponakins [pannikins]	1.	3
A toast Board		3
One steel		6
A rolling pin		3
A dipper	1.	0
One Wood saw	3.	0
An Axe	5.	0
Two buckets	2.	6
Two tubs	5.	0
A scrubbing brush		9
Three Iron sauce Pans	4.	6
One dust Brush		3
One fire Pan	1.	0
A gravy Strainer		6
Five large round tin basins	7.	6
Six Coarse Towels	2.	0
Six pudding dishes	3.	9
A Wood horse	1.	0
A Wood box	5.	0
A flour Pot	1.	3
Three iron spoons		9
One chopper	1.	0
A nutmeg grater		3
A Paste Cutter		9
A flesh Fork		9

In the Bar

Six Kegs with cocks & labels	1.	10.	0
Three large extra cocks		6.	6
Five canisters		10.	0
Two sugar Boxes		7.	6
Four Bar measures		4.	0
Two funnels		1.	3
One dozen and a half pint tumblers		6.	0
Two dozen half pint Tumblers		6.	0
Two dozen & a half Wine Glasses		5.	0
Thirty Pint Decanters	2.	12.	6
Twelve quart ditto	1.	4.	0
Six half pint ditto		7.	6
Five Water Jugs		10.	0
One spice box		7.	6
One sugar bowl		1.	0
A candle box		1.	6
A hammer		1.	6
A pair sugar nippers		2.	0
Two Brass Lamps		5.	0

In Sailors Fore-castle

Eight bed ticks	1.	0.	0
Eight Pillow cases		4.	0
Eighteen blankets		9.	0
Two Lamps		2.	0

In the Pantry

Two tin Kettles		3.	0
Two bottle baskets		3.	0
An ice blanket		2.	6

In store House

A coffee mill		3.	9
A flag [?]	2.	10.	0

On board the "Swan"

One coil (3 in Tor^d) [?] Rope	4.	0.	0
A Remnant (2 in ditto) ditto		15.	0
One Best Bower Chain Cable[2]	–	–	–
Two anchors	7.	15.	6
A chain Hawser[2]	–	–	–
A ship Bell	1.	10.	0
A Glass Lantern		2.	0
A deck ditto (3 lights)		7.	6
Two globe Lanterns		15.	0
Eighteen splint Brooms		3.	0
Three Water Buckets		3.	0
Six Capstan Bars		5.	0
A Jack Screw	1.	0.	0
One marline spike		1.	0
One lead & line		2.	6
Two spars (out Rigers)		2.	6
One brass Gun		3.	0
Two large oil cans		2.	0
One small ditto		1.	0
Four hammer		10.	0
A smith's vice		15.	0
Four Wrenches		15.	0
A sledge Hammer		5.	0
An adze		5.	0
Three augers		5.	0
A Jack Plane		2.	6
Three files			9
An old Jolly boat	2.	10.	0
Three oars		7.	6
A common shovel		2.	0
Two fire Irons		2.	6

[Total   £1,692.   17.   9]

Appendix C

DAMAGE CLAIM FOR THE HENRY BROUGHAM

Lucius Moody gives notice of claim:[1]

Montreal Jany 15th 1846

J.G. Barthe Esq.

    Sir

          I am instructed by the proprietors of the Steam Boat Chieftain that they intend to present a Claim for the damages done that Boat in 1838. She having been Taken possession of by the Rebels at Beauharnois and sunk. I leave this morning to see the Capt who was in Charge at the time & to Collect what information I can in order that the Claim can be brot before the Commissioners not knowing how long they would Sit I was instructed to notify you of their intention.

Yours Respectfully
L Moody
Agent

Rebellion Losses Commission, sitting of 15 May 1851:[2]

1919th Claim was presented by Samuel Crane of the Firm of McPherson Crane & Co. of Montreal representing the late U.C. Steamboat and Mail Coach Company of Montreal No. 1158 under the former Commission and No 1919 in the present under claims £480.00 for damage done to the St Boat Henry Brougham by the Rebels at Beauharnois and being sworn deposed that he is one of the Firm of McPherson Crane & Co. agents of and Co-Owners of the late St Boat and Mail Coach Company, that the present Claim is for the scuttling of the Steam Boat Henry Brougham by the Rebels at the wharf at Beauharnois in November 1838, he has no personal Knowledge of the loss but will prove it by his witnesses.

    Daniel Whipple St Boat Captain being sworn deposed that he was Captain of the Steam Boat Henry Brougham in the Employment of the St Boat and Mail Coach Company in November 1838, that when the Boat was at the wharf in the Village of Beauharnois, a party of armed Rebels ... took possession of the Boat and Scuttled her previous to which they pillaged a few articles, the Boat was five days under Water, and in consequence of being full of water the deck seams burst open and the Boat was otherwise much injured, and the furniture was also greatly injured, they had about 60 or 70 men employed for about five days in raising the boat, they had to pay the men 5/ a day each and upwards and feed them, and he believes the Cost of raising the Boat and afterwards the repairs required to the Boat and Furniture would cost £200 and upwards. the Boat was thus detained from making her usual Trips for twelve days and he believes the Boat was clearing both previous and after the Scuttling the Boat at least $120 per day.

Rebellion Losses Commission, sitting of 20 May 1851:[3]

Alexander Thomson Engineer of the City of Montreal being sworn deposed that he was in the employment of the Claimants in Nov. 1838 as Engineer of the Steamer Henry Brougham and when the boat was at the wharf at Beauharnois she was taken possession of by a party of Rebels and he was taken prisoner by them and was put in the house of Mr Masson. Mr Damase Masson and the family were in the house at the time and did not appear to be under any restraint ... They were very well treated by Mr Masson & his family during their stay with them. Deponent thinks a man named Daigneau stood sentry over them once, and he was the only man he knew. The Rebels scuttled and sank the boat at the wharf. she was under water about 8 or 10 days. he thinks 40 or 50 men were employed in raising the boat. All the furniture was in the water and very much Injured. they had about 60 Burthen on board thinks the damage done to the bedding would be £75 and to the Furniture £100 it cost about £50 in raising the boat. the damage to the Engine £40. the boat had a great deal to do in carrying passengers & towing Vessels – but he cannot say how much she made per day.

They must have had at least £20 of groceries on board – and he believes the Rebels lived on board for two days and must have used any Groceries, liquors and provisions they had on board.

Rebellion Losses Commission, sitting of 31 July 1851:[4]

Michael Murphy Tavern Keeper, Lachine, being sworn deposed that he was employed by the Claimants as a Deck Hand on board the Steamer Henry Brougham in November 1838 and was on board when the boat was taken possession of and sunk by the rebels at the Village of Beauharnois. She was eleven days under water before they could get her up and proceed to Lachine. They had from 60 to 70 men employed in getting her up. He cant say how much they paid the men, thus employed, per day – these men were fed on board – they had great trouble to get men to work, as they were all afraid and they had almost to force men at last – All the beds and bedding were nearly or completely destroyed by being so long under water – The curtains and furniture were also much damaged, but he cant state for what amount – The Boat had a great deal to do in towing, and taking passengers, and he thinks they must have fully lost £30 per day during the time she was sunk. he does not think a dollar a day would be more than they had to pay the men, who were employed in getting the boat up, besides their board which would be worth 2/6 per man p day.

There was some liquor on board, besides provisions but he cannot say that the rebels took any part of them – and he never heard the Captain or Steward afterwards complain of the loss of either the liquor or the provisions. He knows that the rebels took the knives and forks of the mess room – he never heard if they were recovered or not – as he left the boat previous to her being laid up for the winter.

He knows Mr Thompson who was then the Engineer of the Boat and he would credit every thing he has said regarding the Loss. The Steward at that time, is now absent in California. The Crew he believes were all paid during the time the boat was not running the same as if she was – and the crew were also fed during the same time by the Company – neither Captain Daniel Whipple nor the Engineer had any Interest in the Boat.

Appendix D

The present prosperity of the Ottawa and Rideau Forwarding Company, under the prudent management of Messrs McPherson, Crane & Co. begets a deal of envy, and threatens to engender a host of would be rivals. That the latter gentry may have some idea of the immense expense attending the forwarding business, we have procured a hasty account of the 'means and appliances to boot' with which the Company's business is now carried on.

Ten Steamboats, viz – six on the Rideau Canal and four on the Ottawa River, between Lachine and Bytown.

Twenty six large decked barges, average tonnage from 75 to 100 tons.

Twenty four smaller barges and batteaux, from 35 to 60 tons burden.

A Lock at Vaudreuil, that cost £4000 building; the only navigable passage on the Ottawa River.

Four extensive ranges of Ware houses, viz. at Montreal, Kingston, Prescott, and Bytown, beside single warehouses at Lachine, Grenville and Carrillon.

The number of gentlemen employed as Bookkeepers, Clerks, Steamboat Captains & Pursers, amounts to forty five, including about a dozen warehousemen.

The number of men employed as the crews of the steamboats and barges is full six hundred.

Three general offices are located at Montreal, Kingston and Prescott, at each of which places there resides a partner, while agencies are established at Bytown, Toronto, Hamilton, Niagara, Amherstburgh, Coburg and Grenville.

The capital stock of the Company is Fifty Thousand Pounds.

In addition they are now building at Montreal and Prescott, a number of vessels for the ensuing season, including six large barges, to be navigated in summer time on Lakes Ontario and Erie, rigged like schooners.

To the above we may make mention, although we believe them to be the private property of Messrs McPherson, Crane & Co. of a large steam Grist Mill, and Distillery, at Prescott.

We have reason to believe the Ottawa and Rideau Forwarding Company to be the most extensive Establishment of the kind on the continent of America.

Appendix E

The Business Connexion which has subsisted between the "Ottawa and Rideau Forwarding Company," and Macpherson, Crane & Co., since the Fifteenth day of December, 1836, will cease by limitation, on the Fifteenth day of December next; and for the purpose of closing the Business without delay, it is agreed, that the whole Stock in Trade owned by them, and detailed below, shall be sold, at Public Auction, commencing on the Twentieth Day of December next, and to continue till all shall be Sold.

The Stock consists of –

Steamer SHANNON, Propelled by two Engines of 40 Horse Power each, and is in a state of thorough repair.

Steamer OTTAWA, 43 Horse Power, favourably known on the route between Lachine and Carillon.

Steamer PORCUPINE, 45 Horse Power – Is a superior Tow Boat, and has only been running 4 years.

Steamers BEAVER *and* OTTER, 4 and 3 years old, 25 Horse Power each, excellent Passage and good Tow Boats, admitted to be unequalled in their adaptation to the Rideau Canal Trade.

Steamer HUNTER, 25 Horse Power, a comfortable Passage and good Tow Boat.

Steamer CALEDONIA, 18 Horse Power, well known on the route between Lachine and Point Fortune.

Steamers CHARLOTTE *and* BYTOWN, Almost new, and admirably adapted for making the Circuit, ascending to Kingston via the Rideau Canal, and descending by the St Lawrence. They are well and favourably known.

Steamers METEOR, MERCURY, *and* JUNO, Each propelled by a High Pressure Engine of 25 Horse Power, on the Ericson Propeller principle. This is the second season they have been in operation.

Schooners ROSE – THISTLE – SHAMROCK – HENRIETTA – and WM CAYLEY, All constructed after the most approved models, substantially built, and in complete repair; each Vessel is capable of carrying 5000 bushels of Wheat through the Welland Canal.

Barges VICTORIA – ALBERT – WELLINGTON – THISTLE – MARY ANNE – UNION – WESTERN – and CLEVELAND, Staunchly built, and capable of carrying 1300 brls. Flour, each.

Barges QUEEN – ROSE – SHAMROCK – BUCKEYE – EMILY – and OXFORD, Capable of carrying 1100 to 1200 barrels each; in other respects, equal to those named above.

Barges TRAVELLER – HOPE – KINGSTON – TRADER – EMIGRANT – and PERTH, Capable of carrying 900 to 1000 barrels each.

Barges HOCHELAGA – GRENVILLE – ELIZA – ROWENA – NESS – QUAIN – DISSETTE [no. 1] – DISSETTE [no. 2] – WEEKS – ALERT – FAME – and HERO, Nearly new, well suited either for the Ottawa and Rideau route, or the St Lawrence. Capable of carrying 800 barrels each.

Barges DOLPHIN – JANE – CLARA FISHER – IROQUOIS – FRANCES – and ESTHER, Are worthy the attention of persons engaged in the Cord-Wood trade.

All the above craft are rigged and equipped in the best and most complete manner, and will be sold with their Cables, Anchors, and Appurtenances, as they have been running during the past season.

Also a Quantity of Steamboat Wood, at convenient points on the Ottawa River and Rideau Canal. Quantities will be made known at the time of Sale.

Likewise, the Leases for Next Year of the extensive Warehouses on the Corporation Wharf, Kingston; and of the Red Store, and other Premises, including a Marine Railway, situated on the south side of the Lachine Canal here;[2] together with Office Furniture at Kingston, Bytown, and Montreal.

And a Variety of Rigging, Tarpaulings, and Other Articles indispensable about an extensive Forwarding Establishment, and which will be more particularly described in a Catalogue, to be prepared for the day of Sale.

The terms of Sale will be one fourth cash, and the remainder in three equal payments at six, twelve, and eighteen months, with interest on approved indorsed Notes. All Accounts and Obligations due to the concern, to be paid to Macpherson, Crane & Co., and to them all claims against it must be submitted for adjustment.

Applications for further particulars may be made at any of the Offices of Macpherson, Crane & Co., at Kingston, Bytown, or Montreal; or to George Brush, Esq. at the Offices of Messrs Ward, Brush & Co., Montreal.

> J. Frothingham.
> Chairman O. & R. F. Co.
> Macpherson, Crane & Co.

Offers will be received by either of the parties from persons wishing to purchase all, or a portion, of the above Stock by private bargain before the day of Sale.[3]

Abbreviations Used in the Sources

Note: Unless otherwise noted, newspapers and church records cited are from Montreal. Except where there is a possibility of confusion, the names of Montreal newspapers have been shortened to one word, for example, the *Canadian Courant and Montreal Advertiser* becomes the *Courant*. The title *State Trials* is short for *Report of the State Trials before a General Court Martial Held at Montreal in 1838–9*. Notaries are identified by last name only; for full names, see the bibliography.

ANQM	Archives Nationales du Québec, Montreal
AO	Archives of Ontario
APC	American Presbyterian Church
CC	Christ Church
CU	Columbia University, New York, Butler Library, Rare Book and Manuscript Library
DCB	*Dictionary of Canadian Biography*
JAC	*Journals of the Legislative Assembly of the Province of Canada*
JALC	*Journals of the Legislative Assembly of Lower Canada*
JAUC	*Journals of the House of Assembly of Upper Canada*
MMGL	Maritime Museum of the Great Lakes at Kingston
MU	McGill University, Montreal, McClennan Redpath Library, Rare Book Department.
NA	National Archives of Canada
SAP	St Andrew's Presbyterian Church
SGP	Scotch Presbyterian Church in St Gabriel Street
SJM	St James Street Methodist Church
UCQB	*Upper Canada Queen's Bench Reports*
UVM	University of Vermont, Burlington, Bailey-Howe Library, Wilbur Special Collections
ZC	Zion Congregational Church

Notes

PREFACE

1 Dunlop, *Tiger Dunlop's Upper Canada*, 98.
2 *Courant*, 13 October 1819; *Gazette*, 11 September 1834.
3 Bouchette, *British Dominions*, 1:200.
4 Croil, *Steam Navigation*, 319.
5 Morgan, "Steam Navigation on the Ottawa River," 370; Ross, *Ottawa Past and Present*, 48–9.
6 Glazebrook, *History of Transportation in Canada*, 72.
7 Brault, *Ottawa Old and New*, 187.
8 Brault, *Histoire ... de Prescott et de Russell*, 85.
9 Lamirande and Séguin, *A Foregone Fleet*, 3–7.
10 Mills, *Canadian Coastal and Inland Steam Vessels*, 120, and Supplement 2, no. 2925a.
11 Lafrenière, *Le réseau de canalisation de la rivière des Outaouais*, 26–7.
12 Legget, *Ottawa River Canals*, 153.
13 Camu, *Le Saint-Laurent et les Grands Lacs*, 109.
14 The source that Glazebrook cited was a brief item in the *Quebec Gazette* of 25 October 1819. This article, copied from the *Courant* of 23 October 1819, reported that the boat, built at "the head of the Long Sault in the Ottawa River" (i.e., Hawkesbury) and fitted with her engine at Lachine, had just made a trial run on Lake St Louis. It said nothing about the boat operating on the Ottawa.
15 See, for example, Camu, *Le Saint-Laurent et les Grands Lacs*, 110; Glazebrook, *History of Transportation in Canada*, 80–1; Lafrenière, *Le réseau de canalisation de la rivière des Outaouais*, 41.
16 Brault, *Ottawa Old and New*, 187. Of the eight boats Brault named as plying on the Ottawa in 1836, he got one right, the *Shannon*. One, the *Union*, was defunct, and the others were not built before the 1840s.

17 Thomas, *History of ... Argenteuil ... [and] Prescott*, 26–32. This is a printed version of Shepherd's "Memory of Early Steam Boating on the St Lawrence and Ottawa Rivers and Rideau Canals," written in 1894, the manuscript of which is in the R.W. Shepherd Papers at the National Archives (NA, MG 29, A 55/1). One reason for Shepherd's inaccuracy is that he had to rely on the recollections of others for his information on the early days of steamboating. He did not arrive in Canada until 1830, when he was ten years old. Born at Sheringham, Norfolk, England, on 15 December 1819, he began his long career in Ottawa River navigation in 1838 under Captain Redford Robins. In 1847 he and three associates launched the Ottawa Steamers Company, chartered in 1864 as the Ottawa River Navigation Company. R.W. Shepherd was general manager of the company from the late 1850s until 1882, when his son, Robert Ward Shepherd Jr, succeeded him. He died at Como, Quebec, on 29 August 1895 (R.W. Shepherd III, "A Short History of the Ottawa River Navigation Company"; gravestones of Robert W. Shepherd and Henry W. Shepherd, Mount Royal Cemetery, Montreal).

18 ANQM, P345, Fonds Société d'archéologie et de numismatique, D-1/1113, William Mittleberger to Charles Mittleberger, 24 October 1833.

19 Campbell, *History of the Scotch Presbyterian Church St Gabriel Street*, 251–2.

20 *Montreal Daily Star*, 18 February 1888; Mills, *Canadian Coastal and Inland Steam Vessels*, 25; Swainson, *Garden Island*, centrefold list of "Ships built at Garden Island." The *Brougham*, renamed the *Chieftain* in 1839, was long gone by the time the *Star* articles appeared, yet their author mistakenly thought that she was still afloat. The confusion probably arose from the fact that after the *Chieftain* met her end in the 1860s, her owners built a second *Chieftain* in 1874 (and a third in 1903). Julien's drawing may, in fact, be based on the second *Chieftain*.

21 Bonnycastle, *The Canadas in 1841*, 1:61.

22 See, for instance, Ellice, *Diary*, 107, in which the diarist records an encounter with a "Virago of a Stewardess" in the ladies' cabin of a steamer running between Ogdensburg (or Prescott) and Dickinson's Landing in 1838. A Toronto paper, the *Patriot*, in its issue of 1 June that year cited a witness to the rebel attack on the steamer *Sir Robert Peel* in the Thousand Islands the previous night as saying, "The female attendant of the Ladies' Cabin exerted herself most conspicuously in administering to the comfort of the ladies, procuring them clothes, &c. &c."

23 *Courant*, 22 August 1829. A black woman, Margaret Sinclair, was working as a cook aboard the Montreal-Quebec steamer *Quebec* at the time of her death in 1819 (ANQM, CC register, 9 November 1819).

24 Bonnycastle, *The Canadas in 1841*, 1:136.

25 *La Minerve*, 9 May 1836: *"sur nos steam-boats ici, et sur ces même vais-seaux dans les Etats Unis on n'emploie presque que des Canadiens."* The claim is preposterous as regards American steamboats.

26 Besides the *Ottawa*, the only other boat whose full crew is known is the *Union*, for the year 1824. It did not include a single French Canadian. William Grant, its builder, acted as captain; John Cochran was the engineer; William Marshall, John Duck, and John Gray, were hired as seamen (ANQM, notary Griffin, no. 5104, no. 5105, and no. 5106, 20 March 1824).

27 Preston, *For Friends at Home*, 83.

28 Tulchinsky, *River Barons*, 49.

29 In analyzing the chasm that he perceived as existing between French- and English-speakers in 1838, Lord Durham had this to say about the steamboat business between Montreal and Quebec: "Some of the French have lately established steam-boats to compete with the monopoly which a combination of English capitalists had for some time enjoyed on the St Lawrence, and small and somewhat uncomfortable as they were, they were regarded with favour on account of their superiority in the essential qualities of certainty and celerity. But this was not considered sufficient to insure their success; an appeal was constantly made to the national feelings of the French for an exclusive preference of the 'French' line, and I have known a French newspaper announce with satisfaction the fact, that on the previous day the French steamers to Quebec and La Prairie had arrived at Montreal with a great many passengers, and the English with very few. The English, on the other hand, appealed to exactly the same kind of feelings, and used to apply to the French steam-boats the epithets of 'Radical,' 'Rebel' and 'Disloyal.' The introduction of this kind of national preference into this department of business, separated the two races on some of the few occasions on which they had previously been thrown into each other's society" (See Durham, *Report*, 2:40–2).

CHAPTER ONE

1 Required to register as an enemy alien on the outbreak of the War of 1812, Lough identified himself to New York authorities as a twenty-seven-year-old "steamboat maker" from Scotland who had been a resident of the United States for six years (K. Scott, *British Aliens*, 153).

2 *Plattsburgh Republican*, 21 November 1908, "From Rouses Point to New York in 1809," extracts from the diary of Samuel Bridge; Beach, *Lake Champlain*, 79–81; Bellico, *Sails and Steam in the Mountains*, 258, 260, 292; Blow, "Vermont 1"; Philip, *Robert Fulton*, 228–9; O. Ross, *Steamboats of Lake Champlain*, 21–6, 202–3; Z. Thompson, *History of Vermont*,

part 2: 216. The *Vermont* sank when the connecting rod of her engine broke loose and smashed through her bottom.

3 The 240-ton *Ontario*, built at Sackets Harbor, tried her machinery for the first time on 16 April 1817. The 700-ton *Frontenac*, launched at Ernestown (now Bath) on the Bay of Quinte on 7 September 1816 and then taken down to Kingston to be fitted with her 50-hp Boulton and Watt engine, first moved under her own steam on 23 May 1817. She was commanded by James McKenzie, a veteran of the Royal Navy (*Herald*, 10 May 1817; Canniff, *History of the Settlement of Upper Canada*, 602–3; Hough, *History of St Lawrence and Franklin Counties*, 563–4; Lewis, "McKenzie, James"; Lewis, "The *Frontenac:* A Reappraisal"; MMGL, Van Cleve, "Reminiscences," 37, 65).

4 ANQM, notary Griffin, no. 1308, 26 January 1816.

5 Like the better-known Philemon Wright, founder of Hull, Mears was an important figure in the early development of the Ottawa River. Born in Worcester, Massachusetts, on 5 May 1775, he had become a resident of Hawkesbury by June 1804. He is said to have been involved in the building of Canada's first paper mill at St Andrew's (St-André-Est, Quebec) between 1803 and 1805. Although Wright is generally credited with sending the first raft of timber down the Ottawa in 1806, Mears dispatched one down to Montreal in 1805, supplying a boat builder with sawn oak and pine timber. That summer he and partner John Shuter of Montreal acquired from the Algonquin and Nipissing Natives a ninety-nine-year lease to all the islands in the Ottawa River between L'Orignal and the foot of the first rapids south of the Long Sault. At the head of the Long Sault, Mears and his Hawkesbury partner, David Pattee, a fellow American, built a dam and sawmill. He engaged in the timber business for the rest of his life, though he lost his Hawkesbury sawmill and the lease of the islands to George and William Hamilton in 1811–12 after he defaulted on a contract to supply them with timber. This episode seems to have marked the start of a feud between the Hamiltons, supported by British settlers, who went on to establish a flourishing timber business at Hawkesbury, and Mears and Pattee and other members of the American community in the area. Mears, justice of the peace from 1806, was elected to the Upper Canada legislature for Prescott County for two consecutive terms, in 1808 and 1812. During the War of 1812, he served as major of the 1st Regiment of Prescott Militia. Around early 1815 he moved to Montreal with his wife, Polly Harrison, and their children, one of whom, two-year-old Elmira, died there on 14 April.

Documents of 1816 concerning Joseph Lough and Company identified him as a Montrealer, though he cannot have lived there for much more than a year. He moved back to Hawkesbury in 1816: at the end of March that year, on the creation of the Ottawa District, which encompassed the counties of Prescott and Russell, he was appointed sheriff and inspector of shop, still, and tavern licences. He later served as district treasurer (ANQM, notary Chaboillez, no. 8060, 17 October 1807; no. 9673, 21 February 1811; no. 10603, 16 April 1813; notary Doucet, no. 4687, 25 November 1817; notary Gray, no. 1174, 20 June 1804; no. 1380, 26 June 1805; no. 1433, 6 September 1805; no. 1952 and no. 1954, 17 October 1807; no. 2168, 1 October 1808; no. 2660, 23 February 1810; notary Delisle, no. 5101, 25 July 1805; notary Griffin, no. 1029, 24 June 1815; notary Lukin Sr, no. 4262 and no. 4263, 29 March 1809; no. 4370, 26 September 1809; no. 4462, 9 March 1810; SGP register, 15 April 1815; *Boston Evening Transcript*, "Genealogical" column, 19 February 1912, 6 December 1922, and 29 February 1928; *Courant*, 26 September 1832; *Gazette*, 20 November 1822, 18 October 1841; *Herald*, 20 November 1822; Brault, *Histoire ... de Prescott et de Russell*, 36, 50, 130, 210. Brown, *James Brown*, 11–12. Campbell, "A List of the Members of the House of Assembly for Upper Canada," 175–6; S.J. Gillis, *The Timber Trade in the Ottawa Valley*, 66–8, 71–2, 79–80, 91; R.P. Gillis, "Pattee, David"; Gourlay, *Statistical Account*, 283; J.K. Johnson, *Becoming Prominent*, 215. Nourse, *Military Annals of Lancaster, Mass.*, 11, 82, 143–4. Thomas, *History of ... Argenteuil ... [and] Prescott*, 463, 534; *Montreal Almanack* for 1823 and 1825).

6 NA, MG 24, D 12, Dorwin Diaries, 1, part 1: 54–5. Born in New Haven, Vermont, on 25 May 1792, Dorwin moved to Montreal in March 1816 (ibid., 6, 40).

7 Only Brush, born at Vergennes, Vermont, on 6 January 1793, was a Lake Champlain native. Ward, exactly two years younger, was born at Mendham, New Jersey, on 6 January 1795. Young, born at Troy, New York, on 13 February 1789, had settled at Westport, New York, across Lake Champlain from Vergennes, after marrying Jerusha Barber, daughter of the first white settler of the area (CU, Ward Family Collection, "Ward Family Genealogy" file; *Elizabethtown Post*, 2 February 1871; Royce, *Bessboro*, 171; Tulchinsky, "Brush, George," 121; Brush monument in Mount Royal Cemetery, Montreal; Young monument in Westport cemetery).

8 The *Phoenix*, built at Vergennes for the Lake Champlain Steamboat Company, was launched in 1815, shortly after the end of the War of 1812 (*Plattsburgh Republican*, 8 April and 26 August 1815, 11 May and 7 September 1816; Bellico, *Sails and Steam in the Mountains*, 261. Canfield, "Discovery, Navigation and Navigators of Lake Champlain," 688; R. Davison, *The Phoenix Project*, 2–12; Hill, *Lake Champlain*, 197–9; O. Ross, *Steamboats of Lake Champlain*, 31–5).

9 ANQM, notary Griffin, no. 1308, 26 January 1816; notary Huguet-Latour, no. 1197, 8 March 1816, and no. 1204, 15 August 1816.

10 ANQM, SJM register, 9 December 1818; UVM, Guy Catlin Papers, box 1, file 17, 1816–17, documents headed "Vermont Steamboat Co. to Guy

Catlin" and "Advances by G. Catlin for building Champlain." The first
contains the entry under date 28 June 1816: "To Cash paid Lough per
Winans $630.00." The other has a similar entry of the same date: "To
Cash paid Lough $945.00." Catlin was one of the founders of the Lake
Champlain Steamboat Company.

11 ANQM, notary Griffin, no. 1308, 26 January 1816, addendum of 12 July
1816. Mears sold his interest to Wildgoose for £87 10s., plus the refund
of all sums, left unspecified, that he had paid into the concern.

12 *Herald*, 4 January 1817. Doige, *Montreal Directory* (1820 ed.), 109.

13 ANQM, notary Griffin, no. 1916, no. 1917, and no. 1918, 7 July 1817;
Herald, 23 August 1817. Besides the debt to Sherman, Lough owed £2,142
14s. 3d. to the estate of merchant Henry Cox. A native of Sheffield, Yorkshire, Cox married in Montreal in 1816 and then moved to New York,
where he drowned on 7 January 1817 while trying to hop aboard an East
River steamboat (ANQM, SGP register, 10 February 1816. *Herald*, 18 January 1817).

14 Lough was named to the board of the British Methodist Missionary Society for Montreal at its founding meeting on 2 December 1818 (*Herald*,
12 December 1818).

15 On the two types of furnace, see McNally, "Montreal Engine Foundries,"
5–6, 11–12, and Rolando, *200 Years of Soot and Sweat*, 21, 35–7, 41.
Lough's successors at the foundry advertised "a considerable reduction in
the prices of their castings" after they installed a cupola furnace in the
summer of 1820 (*Herald*, 29 July 1820).

16 *Herald*, 23 August 1817.

17 Ibid., 24 January 1818.

18 ANQM, notary Bedouin, no. 1759, 7 February 1823; CU, Diary of John D.
Ward, 1827–30, 2:135, entry of 9 February 1829. *Herald*, 4 January,
19 April, and 4 October 1817, 21 October 1820, 28 March 1821. There
being little mining industry in Upper and Lower Canada then, metal was
at a premium, hence the need for recycling. In January 1817 Lough offered
6d. per pound for old copper and 4d. for brass; that April, Fellow offered
$6\frac{1}{2}$d. for copper and $4\frac{1}{2}$d. for brass.

19 NA, MG 24, D 19, Ward Papers, ff. 1–2, John Ward to Silas Ward, 16 August
1818; UVM, John D. Ward correspondence, John Ward to Silas Ward,
25 May 1816 and 14 April 1817; Borthwick, *History and Biographical
Gazetteer of Montreal*, 334; Canfield, "Discovery, Navigation and Navigators of Lake Champlain," 687–8, 692–3; Tulchinsky, "Brush, George," 121;
MMGL, Van Cleve, "Reminiscences," letter of John Ward's son, Lebbeus
Baldwin Ward, 26 December 1889, tipped in between pages 64 and 65, and
document headed "Copied from original ac[coun]t. in handwriting of John
D. Ward," tipped in between pages 66 and 67. (The letter from Ward's son
says that Daniel Dod built the *Savannah*, which in 1819 became the first

steamship to cross the Atlantic, partly under sail. For Dod's work on that
ship, see Braynard, *S.S. Savannah,* 44–5, 50–1, and 55.) The engine of the
Vermont, removed from the *Champlain* in 1816, was placed a year later in
the *James Caldwell,* the first steamer on Lake George, built by John Winans. Winans was in command of the *Champlain* when the boat, not yet finished, paid a visit to Plattsburgh on 11 July 1816. But Brush was captain
when she began her regular runs between Whitehall and St John's (*Plattsburgh Republican,* 13 July and 7 September 1816).

20 *Herald,* 18 January 1823; *Plattsburgh Republican,* 13 September 1817;
Borthwick, *History and Biographical Gazetteer of Montreal,* 334; Canfield, "Discovery, Navigation and Navigators of Lake Champlain," 692, 707;
Lewis, "The First Generation of Marine Engines," 16; Tulchinsky, "Brush,
George." The *Plattsburgh Republican* published a note from Jahaziel Sherman claiming that the fire was the work of an arsonist and estimating the
loss at close to $40,000.

21 *Herald,* 24 January 1818.

22 NA, MG 24 D 19, Ward Papers, ff. 1–2, John Ward to Silas Ward, 16 August
1818.

23 CU, Ward Family Collection, "Ward Family Genealogy" file. See also H.P.
Smith, *History of Addison County,* 656, 689.

24 J.D. Ward, "An Account of the Steamboat Controversy between Citizens of
New York and Citizens of New Jersey." The *Sea Horse* served as the model
for the *Ontario,* the first American steamer on Lake Ontario (MMGL, Van
Cleve, "Reminiscences," 64). The Fulton-Livingston monopoly was also
responsible for Jahaziel Sherman's move to Lake Champlain. His first
steamboat command, as captain of the Albany Steamboat Company's *Perseverance* on the Hudson River in 1812, had been cut short when Fulton
and Livingston obtained an injunction against the company. A negotiated
settlement gave the Albany interests the exclusive right to steam navigation on Lake Champlain. With businessmen in Burlington and Vergennes,
they founded the Lake Champlain Steamboat Company, and in May of the
following year Sherman moved to Vergennes. With him, he took the
engine of the *Perseverance,* which he placed in the *Phoenix.* This was the
engine that John Ward overhauled and installed in the *Champlain* in 1816;
it was later transferred to the *Congress,* launched in the winter of 1817–18
(Bellico, *Sails and Steam in the Mountains,* 261; Canfield, "Discovery,
Navigation and Navigators of Lake Champlain," 688; R. Davison, *The
Phoenix Project,* 2–12; Dayton, *Steamboat Days,* 36 and 90; Hill, *Lake
Champlain,* 198; O. Ross, *Steamboats of Lake Champlain,* 35).

25 Denison, *The Barley and the Stream,* 77–9. Woods, *The Molson Saga,* 39–
45. For the Molson steamboats, see G.H. Wilson, "The Application of
Steam to St Lawrence Valley Navigation." Wilson traces the Molson
attempts to secure a monopoly on pp. 42–7.

26 ANQM, Cour Supérieure–Montréal, no. 1579, October term 1819, Ward v. Lough; NA, MG 24, D 19, Ward Papers, ff. 3–4, John Ward to Silas Ward, 9 August 1819.

27 Besides the Warwicks, the original owners were, from Montreal, the wholesale produce merchants Horatio Gates and Company (Horatio Gates, Nathaniel Jones, and Charles Bancroft), crockery merchant Zabdiel Thayer, and Hiram Nichols and John Sanford, partners in Nichols and Sanford, auctioneers and brokers (Sanford was a former trading partner of Joseph Warwick); and from La Prairie, merchants Jean-Baptiste Raymond and his son Jean-Moïse. On 3 June 1820, a few days before the boat was registered, they sold carriers Hypolite Denaut, *dit* Jérémie, and Joseph Finsterwaltz, dit Leste, of La Prairie each one eleventh share in the boat (ANQM, notary Doucet, no. 5755, 26 December 1818; no. 7631$\frac{1}{2}$, 3 June 1820; NA, RG 42, E 1, Dept. of Marine, Ship Registers, 183:0170).

28 ANQM, Cour Supérieure-Montréal, October term 1820, no. 541, Francis, Smith & Co. v. Guy Warwick et al., depositions of William McNish Porter, 18 November 1820, and of John Molson, 8 February 1821; notary Desautels, no. 4365 and no. 4366, 2 October 1819; NA, MG 24, D 19, Ward Papers, letters of John Ward to Silas Ward in 1819, notably those of 9 August, ff. 3–4, 16 September, ff. 6–7, 3 October, ff. 9–10, and 4 November, ff. 11–12; *Courant*, 25 August 1819; *Herald*, 11 March and 29 April 1820. The Warwicks had ordered the English engine in June 1819 through the Montreal firm of Froste and Porter, Canadian agent of the Eagle Foundry of Birmingham. The price was £1,050, exclusive of all transport costs and duties.

29 NA, RG 42, E 1, Dept. of Marine, Ship Registers, 183:0170, register of 14 June 1820; *Herald*, 29 April 1820. According to her register, her master was John Melville. In the contract he signed one month later, however, Melville was hired as "mate." Until that spring, he had been mate on the *Car of Commerce*. He later worked as a tailor (ANQM, register of Christ Church, Sorel, 18 April 1819 and 30 April 1820; register of St Pierre Church, Sorel, 30 January 1826; notary Doucet, no. 7778, 20 July 1820).

30 Dorwin, "Montreal in 1816." Dorwin's account is in many ways misleading, particularly in stating that building the *Montreal* was Ward's idea and that her inaugural crossing to La Prairie took place "one fine afternoon in the summer of 1819." Three of her owners – Horatio Gates, Hiram Nichols, and John Sanford – had sought to launch a steam-ferry service between Montreal and La Prairie in 1818. Associated with them were merchant Benjamin Whitney of Kingston, Thomas Porteous, president of the Montreal Water Works, and Deputy Postmaster General Daniel Sutherland of Quebec. Their boat, the *Telegraph*, built by Isaac Johnston, was launched on 25 April that year. She was 84$\frac{1}{2}$ feet long by 28$\frac{1}{4}$ feet broad, with an 8-foot depth of hold, and measured 228 tons. She proved unsuitable and was placed on the Montreal-Quebec run. On 3 June 1822 she was

sold to the Molsons' St Lawrence Steamboat Company. As for the *Montreal,* it is clear from Ward's correspondence, cited above, and from contemporary newspaper accounts that Ward did not begin building her engine until the fall of 1819 and that she did not make her first trip to La Prairie until May 1820 (ANQM, notary Griffin, no. 2081, 5 January 1818; no. 2162, 11 March 1818; no. 4180, 3 June 1822; *Courant,* 25 August 1819, 22 April and 13 May 1820; *Herald,* 2 May 1818, 22, 29 April, and 13 May 1820; G.H. Wilson, "The Application of Steam to St Lawrence Valley Navigation," 58–9).

31 Cordner, *The Vision of the Pilgrim Fathers,* speech by Jacob De Witt, 37–8. See also *Herald,* 10 August 1816. For the construction of the *Car of Commerce* and the installation of her 50-horsepower Boulton and Watt engine, see ANQM, notary Louis Guy, 22 August 1814; and notary Griffin, no. 1107 and no. 1120, 26 August 1815. John Pickard, sent out from England by William Hodgson and Company in 1815 to install and operate the engine, was still engineer of the boat when he died on 16 October 1819. The *Car of Commerce* was wrecked in the St Mary's Current in August 1822 (ANQM, CC register, 18 October 1819; *Courant,* 28 August 1822; *Herald,* 23 October 1819, 28 August 1822, 18 January 1823. See also Lewis, "The *Frontenac:* A Reappraisal," 30).

32 *Courant,* 10 June 1820.

33 CU, Ward Family Collection, "Ward Family Genealogy" file. The child, born on 5 May, was christened Phebe Caroline after Ward's mother, Phebe Dod.

34 Lebbeus Baldwin Ward and Samuel Shipman Ward were born at Chatham, New Jersey, on 7 April 1801. They joined their brother in John D. Ward and Company on 1 May 1825 by oral agreement. The terms of their partnership were not set down in writing until 16 June 1826. John Ward owned half the company and drew a salary of £150 a year; the twins each owned a quarter-interest and were entitled to £75 a year. The agreement was valid for five years (ANQM, notary Doucet, no. 13683, 16 June 1826. CU, Ward Family Collection, "Ward Family Genealogy" file; *National Cyclopaedia of American Biography,* 1:246).

35 The name "Eagle Foundry," often used for John Ward's establishment from 1819, was not adopted until he formed the partnership with his brothers in 1825 and began to make his own castings. Before then, these were made either at the Warwicks' foundry or at the St Maurice Iron Works near Three Rivers. On 28 May 1825 he advertised: "EAGLE FOUNDRY, (St Anns Suburb) – The subscriber informs his friends and the public, that this establishment is now in operation, and that orders for all kinds of castings will be executed with punctuality and despatch, and on resonable [sic] terms." With the opening of the Eagle Foundry, the original plant expanded onto land which John Ward had purchased on 11 September

1824. Adjacent to the property he had bought in 1819, it stretched the width of the block from Queen Street to King Street. While his original boiler shop had stood on Queen Street, the Eagle Foundry fronted on King (ANQM, notary Desautels, no. 4365 and no. 4366, 2 October 1819; notary Doucet, no. 13683, 16 June 1826; no. 20032, 23 November 1832; notary Griffin, no. 5377, 11 September 1824; notary Jobin, no. 3510, 11 September 1824; notary Lindsay, no. 66, 11 September 1824; *Courant*, 28 May 1825, 21 January 1826). Early Ward marine engines for which the castings were made elsewhere include the 40-horsepower one for the *Salaberry* in 1820–21, the 100-horsepower one for the *Hercules* in 1823, and the 45-horsepower one for the *Richelieu* in 1824. See ANQM, notary Bedouin, no. 1061, 14 December 1820, and no. 1759, 7 February 1823; notary Doucet, no. 11376, 17 January 1824, and no. 11504, 3 March 1824; notary Griffin, no. 3430 and no. 3431, 15 December 1820; NA, MG 24 D 19, Ward Papers, ff. 78–83, contract for the *Hercules* engine, 3 February 1823. For a list of engines built for Canadian boats by the foundry to 1854, as well as for an account of its operations, see Lewis, "The Ward brothers, George Brush and Montreal's Eagle Foundry," and Tulchinsky, *River Barons,* 211–16).

36 Born in Aberdeenshire around 1775, Turner had emigrated to Canada by the turn of the century. He worked as a clerk in the trading house of Forsyth, Richardson and Company and then formed Thomas A. Turner and Company, commission merchants, in partnership with Alexander Allison and George Hamilton in 1809. The firm was dissolved in 1812. Turner struck out on his own as an auctioneer and broker. During the War of 1812, he served as second lieutenant in the 5th Battalion of Select Embodied Militia of Lower Canada. By the end of 1815 Turner had teamed up with Allison again and with Allison's brother, John, to form Allison, Turner and Company, commission merchants. John Allison died in 1817, but the company survived another four years. After five years as a bank executive, Turner bought the *Montreal Gazette* in 1822 from publisher James Brown for £1,000. He sold the paper in 1827 to his friend Robert Armour, who had been cashier (general manager) of the Bank of Canada. Turner was twice married, first in 1803 to Ann Bell, who died the following year after giving birth to a daughter, and in 1806 to Marianna McCumming. He died at Montreal on 21 July 1834 at the age of fifty-eight (ANQM, notary Doucet, no. 3535, 21 November 1815; no. 9851, 26 June 1822; notary Gray, no. 3413, 11 April 1812; notary Peltier, no. 2464, 3 September 1832; CC register, 28 May 1803, 8 and 18 March 1804, 12 July 1806; *Courant*, 7 January 1824; *Gazette*, 27 June 1822, 7 June and 27 December 1823, 12 June 1826, 16 April 1832; *Herald*, 25 April and 13 June 1812, 22 February, 24 May, 7 June, 16 August, and 22 November 1817, 6 and 27 June 1818, 11 November 1820, 17 May 1821, 10, 21,

24 January 1824, 14 June 1826; *Minerve*, 21 July 1834; *Vindicator*, 22 July 1834; R. Campbell, *History of the Scotch Presbyterian Church*, 141–2, 240; Denison, *Canada's First Bank*, 1:3, 72–3, 84–6, 100, 104, 122, 124, 143–5, 179, 201; L.H. Irving, *Officers of the British Forces in Canada*, 130–1, 134, 166; Lépine, *Les officiers de milice*, 235, 243; Shortt, *History of Canadian Currency and Banking*, 782–84; *Macmillan Dictionary of Canadian Biography*, 844).

37 *Scribbler* 2, no. 53 (4 July 1822): 7; no. 72 (14 November 1822): 313–14; and no. 61 (29 August 1822): 129. See also Klinck, "Wilcocke, Samuel Hull." It is impossible to say precisely what the writer had in mind when he spoke of Turner's partiality and lack of scruples, but it seems that Turner was not above heavy-handedness. In 1820 he and his brother-in-law, Alexander James Christie, for whom Turner had wangled a job as editor of the *Herald*, appear to have worked hand in hand, in the press and behind the scenes, to discredit Montreal postmaster James Williams with a view to securing Christie's appointment to Williams's place. In another episode, roads inspector Jacques Viger, who was to become Montreal's first mayor in 1833, accused turner of abusing his power as a magistrate to seek revenge after he was fined for failing to maintain the road in front of his property (ANQM, notary Griffin, no. 2976, 26 February 1820; no. 2978, 28 February 1820; MU, CH202.3180, A.J. Christie Correspondence, 1819–21, Deputy Postmaster General Daniel Sutherland to Christie, 13 March 1820; Sutherland to T.A. Turner, 25 April 1820; *Gazette*, 3 and 13 January 1831; *Herald*, 17 and 24 April 1819, 20 May and 13 June 1820; *Minerve*, 21, 23 February, 19 March, and 20 April 1829).

38 ANQM, notary Doucet, no. 5782, 7 January 1819; no. 17254, 12 November 1829; no. 17258, 13 November 1829; no. 17303, 7 December 1829; notary Griffin, no. 1916, no. 1917, and no. 1918, 7 July 1817; no. 2541, 11 March 1819; no. 4086, 26 February 1822; *Herald*, 31 December 1819.

39 ANQM, notary Griffin, no. 2460, 16 January 1819.

40 *Herald*, 24 January 1818. The announcement of their partnership says that Grant and Duff owned about eighty batteaux. The year before, Duff had joined Grant's father, John Grant, in the forwarding partnership of John Grant and Company, operating on the St Lawrence and the Ottawa, but the elder Grant had died on 23 August 1817. At the end of 1818 Duff married Robert Grant's sister, Elizabeth (ANQM, SGP register, 30 December 1818; *Herald*, 3 May and 30 August 1817. See also Stewart, *The Loyalists of Quebec*, 327).

41 Marginal note in ANQM, notary Griffin, no. 2460, 16 January 1819. Wing seems to have set up shop as an innkeeper and forwarder at Lachine in 1818. That year he operated one boat on the Ottawa between Lachine and St Andrew's. He extended his service beyond St Andrew's in 1819, running a boat between Hawkesbury and Richmond Landing (now part of

Ottawa). He drowned at Lachine on 19 August 1819. Two years later his daughter, Henrietta, married forwarder Levi Sexton of Ogdensburg, New York, formerly of Lachine (ANQM, notary Jobin no. 1697, 9 October 1819; no. 1698 and no. 1699, 11 October 1819; and no. 1706, 18 October 1819. *Courant*, 15 May 1819; *Gazette*, 25 August 1819; *Herald*, 31 July 1821; W.H. Reid, *The Presbyterian Church St Andrews and Lachute*, 5).

42 Although none of the contracts of 1819 concerning the *Ottawa* mentions him as a shareholder, Alexander Allison signed up the crew of the boat in 1820, beginning with engineer Adam Hall (ANQM, notary Griffin, no. 2964, 22 February 1820).

43 ANQM, notary Griffin, no. 2471, 23 January 1819.

44 Ibid., no. 2474, 25 January 1819.

45 Molson was not among the original partners in the *Accommodation* venture. Bruce and Jackson had begun building the boat with cabinetmaker John Kay. Kay, however, backed out in March 1809, ceding his rights to Bruce and Jackson for £26 (ANQM, notary Lukin Sr, no. 4258, 22 March 1809). The partnership agreement between Bruce, Jackson, and Molson was signed the following June (ANQM, notary Gray, no. 2395, 5 June 1809). The story of the *Accommodation* has often been told (see the works by Woods, *The Molson Saga*; Denison, *The Barley and the Stream*; and G.H. Wilson, "The Application of Steam to St Lawrence Navigation"). For the *Frontenac*, see Canniff, *History of the Settlement of Upper Canada*, 601–4; Lewis, "The *Frontenac*: A Reappraisal."

46 *Courant*, 20 November 1809; *Quebec Gazette*, 9 November 1809; *Quebec Mercury*, 6 November 1809; G.H. Wilson, "The Application of Steam to St Lawrence Valley Navigation," 14–19, 24; Riddell, "Transportation from Schenectady to Quebec in 1810."

47 ANQM, notary Griffin, no. 2471, 25 January 1819.

48 *Courant* 19 May 1819; *Gazette*, 19 May 1819. Years earlier, Mears and Theodore Davis of Argenteuil had ordered a sloop to be built for them at Hawkesbury (ANQM, notary Lukin Sr, no. 4608, 17 November 1810).

49 ANQM, Cour Supérieure-Montréal, no. 1579, October term 1819, Ward v. Lough; notary Griffin, no. 2794, 5 October 1819; no. 2955, 12 February 1820; no. 2996, 6 March 1820 (regarding Fellow and the *Caledonia*, see also ANQM, Cour Supérieure-Montréal, 1820, no. 646, John Fellow v. Thomas Price; notary Doucet, no. 7027, 24 December 1819; no. 7052, 3 January 1820; no. 7583½, 20 May 1820). It appears that Lough may well have left the country by the end of 1819 (see note 91 below). It is not clear whether he ever paid his debt to Ward, who finally dropped his suit in February 1823. The *Caledonia*, built at a cost of £13,600, was launched from David Munn's Montreal shipyard on 26 August 1817. A brief report on her deficiencies, by engineers Scott Burt and Thomas Price, appeared in the *Herald*, 2 January 1819. Price himself bought one of twenty-five shares

in the boat a month later and became her captain. Turner bought a share
in her for £125 on 23 February 1819, which he disposed of on 24 March
1821 when the boat was sold at auction for £2,710. On 24 April 1822 the
boat was sold for £3,250 to James McDouall of Montreal and John Goudie
and Noah Freer of Quebec, to form part of that trio's contribution to the
establishment three days later of the St Lawrence Steamboat Company –
the "Molson line" – in partnership with John Molson and Sons and others
(ANQM, notary Doucet, no. 5882, 4 February 1819; no. 5943, 23 February
1819; no. 9629, 9 April 1822; no. 9684, 24 April 1822; no. 9934½, 29 July
1822; *Courant*, 26 May 1821; *Gazette*, 7 February 1824; *Herald*, 30 August
1817, 2 January 1819, 23 February and 28 March 1821).

50 *Courant*, 23 October 1819; *Herald*, 23 October 1819. The two boats towed
by the *Ottawa* were either Durham boats or batteaux, which, along with
rafts and canoes, were the common craft on the upper St Lawrence and the
Ottawa River at this time. Both the Durham boat and the batteau were
flat-bottomed, propelled by oars, poles, or sails, depending on the weather
and river conditions, and laboriously poled up rapids or pulled up with
drag ropes. The batteau, in use since the days of New France, was pointed
at both ends, with almost perpendicular sides, and had a carrying capacity
of up to about 4½ tons. The Durham boat, originally designed by Robert
Durham or one of his employees at the Durham Furnace in Bucks County,
Pennsylvania, in the 1730s and introduced to Canada around the time of
the War of 1812, was round-bowed, with a keel and centre board; it had
the light draft of the batteau but better sailing qualities and could carry up
to ten times more freight. The size of these vessels varied, tending to grow
with the requirements of the river trade. Near the end of the War of 1812,
for example, Deputy Commissary General Isaac Winslow Clarke ordered
forty Durham boats for the use of the army, ten of them 50 feet long and
thirty to be 58 feet long. Later boats were up to 90 feet long (ANQM,
notary Griffin, no. 717, 3 December 1814; no. 723, 6 December 1814;
no. 734, 16 December 1814; no. 757, 29 December 1814; no. 890 25 March
1815; Bouchette, *Topographical Description*, 136; Guillet, *Pioneer Travel*,
28–52; Hager, *Mohawk River Boats*; *Eighty Years' Progress*, 133–5).

51 *Courant*, 23 October 1819.

52 The *Herald*, 23 October 1819, was more guarded than the *Courant*, saying, "The Engine is an Eighteen Horse power, was made at the Montreal
Air Furnace, and is we believe the first Steam Engine ever made in Canada." These statements appear to have been wrong on two counts. Not
only had the first Canadian-built marine engine been made in 1809 for the
Accommodation, but in 1815 the firm of Wisely and Moore, "Copper-
Smiths, Plumbers, Gilders, &c. (from London)," which had just set up shop
in Montreal, advertised steam engines for domestic use. Late in the century, the claim was also made that John Ward's engine for the *Montreal*

was the first steam engine made in Canada (*Herald*, 15 July 1815; MMGL, Van Cleve, "Reminiscences," letter of John Ward's son, L.B. Ward, dated 26 December 1829, tipped in between pages 64 and 65; Croil, *Steam Navigation*, 310).

53 Denison, *The Barley and the Stream*, 63–4; Woods, *Molson Saga*, 33–4. Jackson's fate is a mystery. He may have left for England in 1810. That year, when Molson offered him £98 16s. 10d. for his one-third share in the *Accommodation*, he replied "that he would not accept of the offer now made to him, but at the same time wished for a settlement being determined to leave Montreal in a few days in order to go to England to join his wife and family." Loyalist's son Platt, who served as member of the Legislative Assembly for the East Ward of Montreal from 1814 to 1816, died on 9 September 1818. He left a wife, Elizabeth Mittleberger, and seven children. J.H. Dorwin observed that before 1820 and the dominance of the wholesale hardware business in Montreal by Maine-born John Frothingham, "George Platt & Co. were the great hardware men" (ANQM, Cour Supérieure-Montréal, testaments homologués, will of John Platt, no. 53, probated 31 January 1811, and will of George Platt, no. 86, probated 3 November 1818; notary Gray, no. 1074, 12 March 1804; no. 2280, 25 February 1809; and unnumbered *protêt*, 7 May 1810; CC register, 19 December 1805 and 11 September 1818; NA, MG 24, D 12, Dorwin diaries, 1, part 1: 45; Lépine, *Les officiers de milice*, 202; Stewart, *The Loyalists of Quebec*, 305–19, 344, 356).

54 *Herald*, 23 October 1819.

55 AO, MS 821, series A-1–2, John Macdonell Papers, Miles Macdonell to John Macdonell, 5 October 1819.

56 *Courant*, 9 March 1822.

57 ANQM, notary Griffin, no. 2915, 8 January 1820. *Herald*, 6 November 1819.

58 The arbitration bond is in ANQM, notary Griffin, no. 2915, 8 January 1820. The settlement is in a short note appended to Bruce's original contract in the same notary's records, no. 2474, 25 January 1819.

59 ANQM, notary Griffin, no. 2964, 22 February 1820. Hall did not renew his contract at the end of the year. By April 1821 he was working in Vergennes, Vermont. He later went to work for the West Point Foundry at Cold Spring, New York, and in 1833, for the Niagara Harbour and Dock Co. (ANQM, Cour Supérieure-Montréal, October term 1820, no. 541, Francis, Smith & Co. v. Guy Warwick et al., defendants' motion of 9 April 1821 for a rogatory commission to Vergennes to question Adam Hall; Dayton, *Steamboat Days*, 387–8; Lewis, "The First Generation of Marine Engines," 14, 19; Parker, "The Niagara Harbour and Dock Company," 103).

60 ANQM, notary Desautels, no. 4442, 15 December 1819; notary Doucet, no. 7025, 22 December 1819; *Gazette*, 10 November 1819; *Herald*, 22 April 1820; *Spectateur Canadien*, 16 October 1819. From an undated, unsigned

document appended to the deed passed before notary Desautels on
15 December 1819, it seems that Lough and Christophe Duclos Decelles
were to be partners in operating the *Catherine*, Lough building her 28-
horsepower engine for £1,350, and Decelles building the boat for £550. But
the deed itself establishes a partnership between Decelles and merchant
John Pickle Jr to own and operate the boat. It was Pickle who contracted
with the St Mary Foundry for her engine. The *Catherine* ran as a ferry
between Montreal and Longueuil in 1820, then between Montreal and
Sorel. Before her first season was up, her owners complained that Hall had
used defective castings for the engine. Arbiters ruled that the owners had
cause for complaint, though not against Hall. Some of the parts complained of were fine, they said, but "the steam pipe, top of condenser and
man Hole door are defective and were such when delivered from the Saint
Mary Foundery, but not to the Knowledge of Mr Adam Hall." The decision reflected poorly on Allison, Turner's foundry and can not have helped
in their search for new engine contracts. Indeed, they produced no more
engines. Hall's engine was removed from the *Catherine* and put up for sale
in 1821, though it seems that as late as 1825 it had not found a buyer. The
boat itself was offered for sale in 1822 (ANQM, notary Lukin Jr, no. 57,
11 October 1820, and no. 58, 13 October 1820; *Herald*, 28 March and
20 October 1821; 29 June 1822; 8 August 1825).

61 *Herald*, 18 March 1820.
62 Ibid.
63 Barrett, *Richard Barrett's Journal*, 94.
64 ANQM, notary Griffin, no. 3080, April 10, 1820; *Courant*, 29 April 1820;
   Herald, 22 April 1820.
65 ANQM, notary Griffin, no. 3093 and 3095, 19 April 1820; *Herald*, 29 April
   1820.
66 *Courant*, 6 May 1820; *Herald*, 29 April and 6 May 1820.
67 *Courant*, 6 and 20 May 1820.
68 *Herald*, 13 May 1820.
69 Ibid., 15 May 1821. This same year the steamer *Congress* inaugurated
   pleasure excursions on Lake Champlain (see O. Ross, *Steamboats of Lake
   Champlain*, 35–6).
70 ANQM, notary Griffin, no. 2687, 10 June 1819; *Herald*, 14 August 1819.
   See also ANQM, notary Desautels, no. 3807, 27 July 1818, and no. 3810,
   30 July 1818, protests by McArthur against the heirs of John Grant for
   evicting him from the premises he had leased from Grant at Lachine. In
   early 1821 Jones would open another Steam Boat Hotel at the Cascades
   (*Herald*, 21 April 1821; see also advertisement in *Courant*, 6 April 1822,
   and report on his trial for theft in *Herald*, 14 August 1824). Bruce had
   married McArthur's sister, Elizabeth, widow of shoemaker Nicholas
   Fletcher, in 1810 (ANQM, SGP register, 12 November 1810).

71 *Gazette*, 23 October 1826, testimony of H.J. Boulton, solicitor general of Upper Canada, before a committee of the British House of Commons in 1826; *Herald*, 22 May 1819.

72 *Herald*, 6 November 1819, 31 March 1820.

73 Dalhousie, *Dalhousie Journals*, 2:30–1.

74 *Herald*, 29 July 1820.

75 ANQM, notary Griffin, no. 3297, 12 August 1820.

76 *Gazette*, 27 August 1817; Bellico, *Sails and Steam in the Mountains*, 261–2; Canfield, "Discovery, Navigation and Navigators of Lake Champlain," 689–92; R. Davison, *The Phoenix Project*, 12–17; Hill, *Lake Champlain*, 199–200; O. Ross, *Steamboats of Lake Champlain*, 33–5, 203–4. In the mid-1830s a Quebec newspaper claimed that "20 to 30 persons annually drowned while landing or embarking from our steamers" (*Quebec Gazette*, copied in *Vindicator*, 30 October 1834). In 1837 a British newspaper commentary on the subject of steamer accidents recommended half in jest "that an engineer should be hanged every week, and a proprietor every fortnight, till the accidents cease. The executions would not last long" (*Transcript*, 11 November 1837, citing the London *Morning Post*).

77 *Herald*, 28 March 1821. A suggestion was later made that "the engine had a bad name." See chap. 2.

78 NA, MG 24, D 8, Wright Papers, 6:1849–51, Mears to P. Wright & Sons, 27 August 1820. In 1832, when a steamer, also named *Ottawa*, was built for the Ottawa Steamboat Company to sail from Lachine up the Ottawa River, her owners took care to specify in their contract with Montreal shipbuilders Sheay and Merritt that she should not draw more than 2 feet 8 inches. When she turned out to draw 3 feet 10 inches, even without fuel or fittings on board, they complained that this "renders her useless to the said Ottawa Steam Boat Company, as being thus rendered unfit to navigate the waters for which the said vessel was intended." Either this second *Ottawa* was modified or her owners overstated the point, since she went on to sail on the Lachine–Point Fortune run until the 1840s (ANQM, notary Griffin, no. 9904, 1 June 1832; no. 10848, 18 April 1833; no. 10866, 29 April 1833. For her launch, see *Gazette*, 18 and 25 September 1832).

79 This had been a problem with other pioneering steamers: the *Accommodation*, for example, and the *Frontenac* on Lake Ontario. In the latter's first season, merchant John Spread Baldwin, whose York firm held a share in the boat, wrote to a former business partner that she was "really as fine as a vessell as any one would wish to see. She will ruin all the Shipping on the Lake make 3 voyages to their one, but is a very expensive concern & tis thought will not make any thing for her owners She cost £14,500 –'–' H.C. [Halifax currency] burns a great deal of wood & her Capn & Engineer have an immense salary & there are not Travlers & Transport enough

in this country to support such an establishment." When she was sold for £1,550 to stepbrothers Robert and John Hamilton of Queenston in 1825, the *Kingston Chronicle* remarked: "This vessel, though eminently useful and convenient, as respected the accommodation of the public, did not, we understand, remunerate the proprietors. Indeed we believe she was quite a losing concern." Henry D. Twohy, a veteran of Rideau Canal and Lake Ontario steamers, wrote to a correspondent in 1873 that all the boats sailing on Lake Ontario when he arrived in Canada in 1833 had been "ahead of the requirements of the Trade and generally poor investments" (AO, MS 768, Canniff Papers, series A-1, Henry D. Twohy to G.N. Tackabury, 26 December 1873; *Herald*, 22 January 1825; Firth, *The Town of York, 1815–1834*, 39–40).

80 *Herald*, 24 January and 5 May 1821. In spring 1821 Grant advertised that, besides dispatching forwarding boats as needed, he would operate a scheduled packet-boat service between Lachine and Point Fortune twice a week (*Gazette*, 25 April 1821).

81 *Gazette*, 14 March 1821.

82 *Herald*, 12 May 1821, advertisement dated 2 May.

83 *Courant*, 22 May 1821.

84 ANQM, notary Doucet, no. 9178, 9 October 1821; no. 9212, 24 October, 1821; no. 9260, 14 November 1821; no. 9666 and no. 9667, 20 April 1822. *Gazette*, 4 April and 22 August 1821; *Herald*, 18 August and 1 September 1821.

85 *Gazette*, 8 September and 5 December 1821; *Herald*, 6, 13 October and 5 December 1821. For Allison's stoves, see advertisements in *Courant*, 8 September 1821, and in *Herald* 11 June 1825.

86 ANQM, notary Griffin, no. 4031, 4 January 1822; *Courant*, 12 January 1822; *Gazette*, 20 July 1822, 30 August, 4 October, and 8 November 1823, 30 October 1824; *Herald*, 12 December 1821, 11 June and 30 September 1825, 9 September 1826. The foundry that Gray opened at St Catherine burned down on 22 October 1828 (*Courant*, 18 August 1830; *Minerve*, 23 October 1828).

87 *Courant*, 9 March 1822.

88 Ibid., 10 July 1822.

89 ANQM, notary Griffin, no. 4438, 18 January 1823.

90 *Herald*, 11 June 1825. Gray's advertisement, published on 11 June, ran for several months.

91 See ANQM, notary Doucet, no. 7001, 14 December 1819; notary Griffin, no. 4086, 26 February 1822. When an attempt was made in December 1819 to collect on a promissory note which Lough had issued that October, John Halstead, "heretofore his clerk," replied that "Mr Lough hath left the Province." If this statement meant that Lough was not just temporarily

absent but had moved away by the end of 1819, it would explain why Allison, Turner and Company hired "a person of science" to run the foundry
in early 1820. In any case, Lough was referred to as "late of the City of
Montreal" in February 1822 when his debt to Jahaziel Sherman was
assigned to Turner.

92 ANQM, SGP register, 31 December 1825; notary O'Keeffe, no. 287C, 7 February 1826; no. 294E, 14 February 1826; *Courant,* 31 December 1825.

93 Details of the *Louisa's* trip and accident are in ANQM, notary Griffin,
no. 7217, 26 April 1827, and in the *Gazette,* 23 April 1827.

94 James McCutchon was a brother of the rising Scottish-born Montreal merchant Peter McGill (born Peter McCutchon) and a nephew of John McGill,
member of the Legislative Council of Upper Canada. Through his wife,
Minerva Finkle, whom he married at Bath, Upper Canada, on 9 September
1825, McCutchon was also a brother-in-law of Henry Gildersleeve, pioneer builder and master of steamers on Lake Ontario and the Bay of
Quinte, who had married Sarah Finkle the year before. In the early 1820s
McCutchon was associated in business with Lachine forwarder Stephen
Finchley. When Finchley temporarily retired from business in March 1826,
McCutchon bought his stock of Durham boats and batteaux and then
formed a partnership with Finchley's clerk, Curtis Elkins Crossman. That
partnership was dissolved on 19 March 1827, a month before the *Louisa's*
trip (*Courant,* 22 March 1826, 5 January 1828; *Herald,* 7 February 1824,
29 September 1825; *Kingston Chronicle,* 18 April 1823. On Peter McGill's
change of name in 1821, see notice in *Herald,* 17 May 1821; Sweeny,
"McGill, Peter"; Robertson, *Landmarks of Toronto,* 1:223).

95 M.Q. Innis, ed., *Mrs Simcoe's Diary* (Toronto: Macmillan of Canada,
1965), 192, entry for 29 July 1796. The locks she referred to were part of
the "military canals" built between 1779 and 1783 to ease the upward passage of small craft from Lake St Louis to Lake St Francis. Originally six to
seven feet, their width was doubled in 1817. With successive repairs and
overhauls, widenings and deepenings, they proved useful up to the mid-
1840s, serving batteaux and Durham boats up to $12\frac{1}{2}$ feet wide, as well as
canoes and other small craft. A statistical table prepared by the commissary general in 1833 shows that in 1832, 788 batteaux, 451 Durham boats,
and 11 other craft had used the canals, yielding £2,554 10s. in gross revenue. The Cascades locks underwent a major repair in 1833–34, when the
walls were rebuilt and new lock gates installed (*Gazette,* 5 April 1827,
30 March 1833; *Hallowell Free Press,* 5 May 1834; *Kingston Chronicle,*
20 July 1833; Creighton, *Empire of the St Lawrence,* 72; Heisler, *Les
canaux du Canada,* 15–6, 33).

96 *An Excursion through the United States and Canada,* 438.

97 ANQM, notary Griffin, no. 7217, 26 April 1827.

98 *Gazette,* 23 April 1827.

CHAPTER TWO

1 Gourlay, *Statistical Account*, 283.
2 Bouchette, *A Topographical Description*, 135. Furs, which made up 76 per cent of exports in 1770, accounted for only 9.2 per cent by 1810, when timber and produce represented 88.6 per cent (Ouellet, *Histoire économique et sociale*, 37, 175–80).
3 Bouchette, *A Topographical Description*, 135.
4 For an early appraisal of the canal in comparison with the Erie Canal in New York State, see Watson, *Men and Times of the Revolution*, 505–7.
5 *Herald*, 28 March, 5 and 12 May 1821.
6 Ibid., 12 May 1821. The verses were signed "Waverly," after Sir Walter Scott's celebrated hero Waverley. They gave offence, and Waverly did nothing to mollify his critics when he published "A Ticklish Response" in the *Herald* of 22 May.
7 This and two other unnumbered documents pertaining to the *Perseverance* were found out of chronological sequence in ANQM, notary Lukin Jr, between items no. 754 and no. 755, which are both dated 6 December 1824.
8 Ibid. Forbes's note is dated 8 January 1821.
9 ANQM, notary Lukin Jr, no. 73, 31 January 1821.
10 ANQM, notary Lukin Jr, no. 389, 29 August 1822.
11 Besides the *Perseverance*, these boats were the 33-horsepower *Laprairie*, launched in 1822; the 28-horsepower *Lady of the Lake*, launched in 1826; and the 75-horsepower *Canadian Eagle*, launched in 1832. Greenfield's interests in these boats are detailed below.
12 The short-lived Johnson and Clarke engine foundry opened in the spring of 1833 (*Vindicator*, 16 August 1833; see also below, chap. 8).
13 ANQM, notary Griffin, no. 942, 25 April 1815, and no. 1698, 18 January 1817; G.H. Wilson, "The Application of Steam to St Lawrence Valley Navigation," 26; McNally, "Montreal Engine Foundries," 22. A sketch of Bennet's life, published in the *Daily Witness* nearly fifty years after his death, says that he was born in the parish of Culross, near Alloa, Kincardineshire, in 1791. This would mean he was about twenty-one when he landed in Canada and about fifty-eight when he died of cholera in Montreal on 23 July 1849. His burial record, however, gives his age as about sixty-four, and a death notice in the *Gazette* says he was sixty-eight, meaning that he might have been born as early as 1781 and could have been as old as thirty-one when he arrived in Canada. On 25 April 1832 he married Angélique Johnston, daughter of shipbuilder Isaac Johnston. This appears to have been his second marriage: the burial notice for his seven-month-old daughter Catherine on 20 June 1826 says that he was then married to a Catherine Grace. No record of that first marriage nor of

Catherine Grace's death has been found in Montreal (ANQM, SGP register, 20 June 1826, 25 April 1832; SAP register, 24 July 1849; *Gazette*, 24 July 1849; "Witness Jubilee Symposium," 20 March 1897).

14 ANQM, notary Jobin, no. 1769, 26 January 1820. See also no. 1765, 24 January 1820, and no. 1766, 26 January 1820; *Herald*, 26 February 1820.

15 *Herald*, 28 March 1821. The engine is identified as a 10-horsepower in the 1821 contract between the partners, but the model for it is described as a 12-horsepower in an 1835 inventory of Bennet's factory (ANQM, notary Arnoldi, no. 3884, 2 January 1835).

16 ANQM, notary Griffin, no. 3487 and no. 3488, both 26 January 1821. John Fellow may also have worked on a Molson steamer, but in 1822 he was in charge of engine operation (including the hiring of an engineer and fireman) and maintenance for the *Telegraph* when she was sold in June that year to the St Lawrence Steamboat Company. Brackenridge, like John Bennet, was sent out from Britain by Boulton and Watt to install an engine in a Molson steamer, the *Malsham*, launched in 1814. He then went to work for Molson, beginning in October that year. He lived in Quebec at that time, but moved to Montreal early in 1815. At his marriage to a Montreal widow in 1817, he was once more living in Quebec. In 1820 he was back in Montreal: a city directory listed him as an engineer and tavern-keeper (ANQM, notary Doucet, no. 9542, 14 March 1822; notary Griffin, no. 941, 25 April 1815; no. 4102, 14 March 1822; SGP register, 25 October 1817; Doige, *Montreal Directory*, 47; McNally, "Montreal Engine Foundries," 23).

17 ANQM, notary Griffin, no. 6698, 29 July 1826; *Courant*, 26 August 1826.

18 ANQM, notary Lukin Jr, no. 73, 31 January 1821; *Courant*, 30 June and 10 July 1821; *Herald*, 28 March and 12 May 1821. No information has been found on the crew of the *Perseverance* other than that James Dodd, a former steward on the Molson steamer *Malsham*, leased the bar for £10 a month in 1822 (ANQM, notary Doucet, no. 7736, 12 July 1820; notary Griffin, no. 1345, 29 February 1816, and no. 4119, 28 March 1822).

19 In Greenfield's contract with Bennet and Briggs for the 28-horsepower engine of the *Lady of the Lake*, the price was set at "forty pounds Currency of this Province for each & every Horse power." G.H. Wilson quotes the following entry from the diary of Thomas Molson for 14 September 1822: "Mr [John] Ward (an American) told me that he makes Steam Engines for £50 currency for each horse power to 20 horse power, and £47.10 for horse power for any Engine upwards of 20 horse power & likewise puts or erects them up for going at the above prices." In the £950 contract for the building and fitting of the engine of the *William Annesley* in 1824, John Ward undertook to build "A Steam Engine of Twenty Horse power, according to Bolton & Watts' rule for estimating the power of Steam Engines." In 1834 the Ward brothers' Eagle Foundry charged £42 10s. per horsepower for two 40-horsepower engines for the *Shannon*,

an Ottawa River steamer (ANQM, notary Griffin, no. 6173, 6 January 1826; no. 12763, 18 December 1834; notary Lindsay, no. 42, 13 May 1824; G.H. Wilson, "The Application of Steam to St Lawrence Valley Navigation," 127. See also Lewis, "The First Generation of Marine Engines," 9–10, and the same author's "The Ward Brothers, George Brush and Montreal's Eagle Foundry," 30).

20 ANQM, notary Lukin Jr, no. 73, 31 January 1821.

21 ANQM, notary Griffin, no. 2474, 25 January 1819, and no. 2471, 23 January 1819.

22 *Courant*, 30 June 1821; *Herald*, 12 May, 9 and 26 June 1821.

23 *Courant*, 23 June and 10 July 1821; *Gazette*, 11 July 1821; *Herald*, 10 July 1821.

24 *Courant*, 10 July 1821; *Herald*, 10 July 1821.

25 *Herald*, 10 July 1821.

26 *Courant*, 23 June 1821; *Herald*, 8 September 1821. The regular fares between Lachine and Châteauguay were 2s. 6d. for cabin passengers, 1s. 3d. on deck, 5s. for a horse and carriage, and only $7\frac{1}{2}$d. for raftsmen; merchandise was charged at 6d. per hundredweight. Between Lachine and the Cascades the fares were 7s. 6d. in the cabin, 3s. on deck, 7s. 6d. for a horse and carriage, and no cut rate specified for raftsmen; merchandise was shipped at $7\frac{1}{2}$d. per hundredweight. Cabin passengers making a same-day return trip were charged only the one-way fare.

27 *Courant*, 11 August 1821; *Herald*, 11 August 1821.

28 *Herald*, 14 August and 1 September 1821.

29 ANQM, SGP register, 11 January 1822, baptism of Henry McMaster, born 28 December 1821.

30 *Courant*, 15 December 1821.

31 Ibid., 30 June 1821, 24 July 1822. In this first year the link was less than perfect. The stages left Montreal at 11:30 a.m. on Monday and Thursday and at 8 a.m. on Saturday. While the Monday and Thursday stages could conceivably have covered the nine miles from Montreal to Lachine in $1\frac{1}{2}$ hours and arrived in time for the *Perseverance's* 1 p.m. departure for the Cascades, the Saturday stage left Montreal at precisely the same hour at which the steamboat left Lachine (see their respective schedules in *Herald*, 11 May 1822, and *Courant*, 22 June 1822.)

32 It is possible that Dickinson was precluded from forming a link between his stages and the *Ottawa* by Michael Connolly's enterprise in launching the Union Stage Coach to service the steamer. See chap. 1.

33 *Courant*, 24 July 1822. In vaunting "that variety of land and water transport so pleasing to travellers" on the route between Montreal and Upper Canada, the newspaper made a virtue of necessity. The novelty and pleasure soon paled. Carl David Arfwedson, a Swedish traveller who paid a brief visit to Canada in 1834, complained that the constant shifting from

steamer to stage and vice versa on the trip from Prescott down to Montreal made it "one of the most wearisome trips I had in Canada ... It is to
be hoped that the Canadians will remedy this evil, by building stronger
and more suitable steamers, of sufficient power to work against the strong
current. I must also add that they must improve stages and roads, which
are really very indifferent" (Arfwedson, *The United States and Canada*,
2:329–30). Graphic illustrations of the discomforts of travelling in this way
can be found in almost every traveller's account from the 1820s to the
1840s. See, for example, Buckingham, *Canada*, 86.

34 Barrett, *Richard Barret's Journal*, 18–19. On the issue of team boats versus
   steamboats, see Crisman and Cohn, *When Horses Walked on Water*, 27–
   40. Team boats were paddlewheelers powered by horses working a tread-
   mill or turning a capstan or other such machinery. They were suited to
   short ferry service, but rarely used on such a relatively long haul as the
   forty miles from Côteau to Cornwall. The best-known horse boat in the
   Montreal area was the Montreal-Longueuil ferry *Edmond*, built at La Prairie in 1819 for François Denaut, *dit* Jérémie, and powered by ten horses.
   She sailed on through the 1820s, and horse boats continued to be built and
   used as ferries through the century, notwithstanding the view expressed
   when the *Edmond* was built that this kind of horse power had been super-
   seded by steam. In 1833, for example, John Meltimore of Fort Covington,
   New York, built a 1-horse team boat for use as a ferry between Cornwall
   and Massena Point, New York. A horse boat was also launched that year
   between York (Toronto) and what is now Centre Island (ANQM, notary
   Griffin, no. 2691, 16 June 1819; notary Lukin Jr, no. 754 and 755,
   6 December 1824; notary Jobin, no. 3660, 29 March 1825; notary Doucet,
   no. 14907, 3 November 1827; *Brockville Recorder*, 23 August 1833; *Herald*, 24 July 1819, 22 July 1820; *Kingston Chronicle*, 14 September 1833;
   Spectateur Canadien, 14 August 1819, 26 August 1820).

35 *Montreal Gazette*, 13 August 1817; *Herald*, 6, 27 June, and 19 September
   1818; *Kingston Gazette*, 31 March, 21 and 28 April 1818; Canniff, *History
   of the Settlement of Upper Canada*, 604–6; *Eighty Years' Progress*, 141;
   Mills, *Canadian Coastal and Inland Steam Vessels*, 97; Robertson, *Landmarks of Toronto*, 2:846–8.

36 *Courant*, 24 July 1822; *Vindicator*, 11 September 1829. Van Cleve (MMGL,
   "Reminiscences," 39) says that she was built at Kingston by Henry
   Gildersleeve. He gives her tonnage as 150, while Disturnell (*Picturesque
   Tourist*, 150) says she was 350 tons, and Lake Ontario steamboat owner
   John Hamilton put her tonnage at 50 (*Kingston Chronicle*, 22 November
   1843).

37 *Courant*, 14 and 21 April 1819; *Gazette*, 11 April 1819, 11 September
   1822; *Herald*, 5 December 1818, 1 May 1819, 17 August 1822; *Kingston
   Chronicle*, 30 August 1822, 22 November 1843; Disturnell, *Picturesque*

Tourist, 150; Pringle, *Lunenburgh,* 107; Robertson, *Landmarks of Toronto,*
2:849; MMGL, Van Cleve, "Reminiscences," 39.

38 ANQM, notary Doucet, no. 6992, 7 December 1819; no. 7004 and no. 7005,
14 December 1819.

39 ANQM, Cour Supérieure-Montréal, October term, 1820, no. 541, Francis,
Smith & Co. v. Guy Warwick et al.; notary Doucet, no. 7627 and no. 7629,
2 June 1820; no. 7648 and no. 7649, 8 June 1820.

40 For this firm, see notices in *Courant,* 13 May 1820, 5 May 1821, and
Kingston Chronicle, 5 February 1819, 10 August 1821. In 1819 the company operated under the names Levi Sexton and Company at Lachine and
Ogdensburg, New York, Jones and Van Slyck at Prescott, and C.A. Van
Slyck at what is now part of greater Rochester, New York. The four partners in the company then were Prescott postmaster Alpheus Jones and
three Americans – Eri Lusher, one of the owners of the *Ontario,* who had
recently moved from Lachine to Schenectady, New York; Levi Sexton, who
had replaced Lusher as the resident partner at Lachine; and Cornelius
Adrian Van Slyck at Genessee River. Lusher withdrew in the spring of
1820, to be succeeded as partner by American expatriate Samuel Crane. He
became the resident partner at Lachine, the name of the company there
changing to Sexton and Crane.

41 ANQM, Cour Supérieure-Montréal, October term, 1820, no. 541, Francis,
Smith & Co. v. Guy Warwick et al., deposition of John Ward, 14 February
1821; *Gazette,* 31 January 1823; *Kingston Chronicle,* 30 August 1822; Lewis,
"The Ward Brothers, George Brush and Montreal's Eagle Foundry," 32.

42 The only indication of Greenfield's age was found in Protestant Old Burial
Ground Records, book no. 2 (1822–34): 261, 271, kept at the Mount Royal
Cemetery in Montreal. According to those records, he was thirty-eight
when he died in June 1832 and thus was born around 1794. The records
are subject to caution, however: they give Dickinson's age at his death as
forty-five, while his gravestone gives his true age, which was fifty-one.

43 Lauder's age is unknown. Spier was born on 17 June 1801, and thus turned
twenty-one only in 1822. Drummond and McKay were born in 1791 and
1792 respectively (William Spier gravestone, Mount Royal Cemetery.
Bush, "Drummond, Robert"; Bush, "McKay, Thomas").

44 ANQM, notary Griffin, no. 9644, 7 January 1832. The four agreed to form a
three-year partnership, as of 1 January 1832, to practise for their joint
benefit all the trades and business they had previously carried out sepa-
rately. Greenfield transferred the ownership of the two steamers he then
owned to the partnership, whose business was to be "principally confined
to the proprietorship and navigating and sailing of Steam Boats and Vessels on the several Rivers & Streams in the Province of Lower Canada and
in the tendering for and undertaking of Contracts of all or any description
of work than can be by them encompassed within the said Province."

According to an addendum to this deed, Greenfield pulled out of the partnership on 2 May 1832. But an agreement the following month between Lauder and Spier and another contractor to collaborate on work to be done in the port of Montreal names Greenfield and Rutherford as "dormant partners" in Lauder and Spier. After Lauder and Spier was dissolved on 1 January 1835, a public notice indicated that Greenfield's estate and Rutherford had remained partners to the end (ANQM, notary Griffin, no. 9937, 13 June 1832; *Courier*, 21 April 1835).

45 ANQM, notary Griffin, no. 10097, 25 July 1832.

46 *Courant*, 13 December 1823. Greenfield's exclusive arrangement had ended by mid-1828, when another plumber was hired to repair the company's pipes (*Gazette*, 31 July 1828).

47 See Lewis, "The First Generation of Marine Engines," 2–12.

48 ANQM, notary Doucet, no. 13641, 31 March 1826; NA, RG 42, E 1, Dept. of Marine, Ship Registers, 183:0181. The *Laprairie* was built to challenge the *Montreal's* monopoly on the Montreal–La Prairie run. Competition between the two boats was fierce in 1822, when the *Laprairie* began service, but by spring 1823, rivalry gave way to co-operation, and the two boats ran alternately between Montreal and La Prairie and Montreal and Quebec for the Montreal and Laprairie Steamboat Company. In August 1821 Greenfield and two other men had signed as securities for Bennet, Briggs and Burt, who were hired to supervise her construction and to build her 33-horsepower engine. The £1,890 contract stipulated that they were to hire shipwright Jonathan Gorham to build the boat. Gorham had built the steamer *Congress* for the Lake Champlain Steamboat Company in 1817–18 and, with Alexander Young, the *Phoenix II* in 1820 for the same owners (ANQM, notary Bedouin, no. 1301, 29 August 1821; *Courant*, 29 May, 1 June and 27 July 1822, 12 April, 10, 24, 28 May, and 2 July 1823, 25 February 1824; *Gazette*, 5 October and 11 December 1822; *Herald*, 17 July and 1 September 1821, 9 February, 6 March, 8 May, 1, 8, and 19 June 1822, 17 March 1824; Thompson, *History of Vermont*, part 2: 216; Canfield, "Discovery, Navigation and Navigators of Lake Champlain," 707).

49 The St Lawrence Steamboat Company was established on 27 April 1822. John Molson and Sons owned $27\frac{1}{2}$ of the forty-two £1,000 shares in the company (ANQM, notary Griffin, no. 13815 and no. 13816, 29 April 1836; Denison, *The Barley and the Stream*, 92; G.H. Wilson, "The Application of Steam to St Lawrence Valley Navigation," 109).

50 NA, MG 24, D 19, Ward Papers, ff. 78–83, contract for *Hercules* engine, 3 February 1823; *Courant*, 26 November 1823, 26 May 1824; *Gazette*, 14 February and 18 October 1823; Croil, *Steam Navigation*, 310–1. Sailing ships had trouble negotiating the St Lawrence above Quebec against the currents and prevailing winds, and were often stalled for days just below Montreal, unable to overcome the St Mary's Current unaided. The

Hercules was built to tow ships from Quebec into the harbour of Montreal. Launched on 11 October 1823, she had a 100-foot keel, 28-foot beam, and 12-foot depth of hold. Her engine, with a cylinder 55 inches in diameter, cost £4,500. When Brush brought her into the harbour of Montreal with her first transatlantic ship in tow on 23 May 1824, the *Courant* remarked: "The *Hercules* is a beautiful modeled vessel, and was built by Mr Alex. Young of this city, but what mostly excites the astonishment of the curious is, the magnitude, power and simplicity of her engine, which was projected, built, and set up here, by Mr John Dod Ward. It is, probably, the most powerful single engine that was ever applied for the propelling of any vessel in the world; and its performance will no doubt, clearly manifest to the public, that the builder, as a man of science in his profession, is justly entitled to their patronage and support." The earliest evidence of Young's presence in Montreal is a contract he signed there in March 1819 to build a brig. The next winter he was in Vergennes, building the 150-foot-long *Phoenix II*. For at least the next decade, he commuted between Lake Champlain and Montreal, where he kept a shipyard and where he was associated in 1824 with shipbuilder Luke Harmon Sheay. A title deed of Essex County, New York, of 13 February 1826 identified him as a Montrealer, while another of 6 October identified him as a resident of Westport, New York (ANQM, notary Arnoldi, no. 973, 26 July 1831; no. 977, 1 August 1831; notary Doucet, no. 6007, 16 March 1819; notary Griffin, no. 5710, 18 April 1825; no. 7053, 10 February 1827; no. 9552, 31 October 1831; notary Lukin Jr, no. 699, 3 July 1824, and no. 723, 1 October 1824; New York title deeds, Essex County, E:103–4, H:123–4; *Courant*, 16 October 1824; *Elizabethtown Post*, 2 February 1871; *Herald*, 1 June 1825; Canfield, "Discovery, Navigation and Navigators of Lake Champlain," 692, 707; Glenn, *Story of Three Towns*, 339; Royce, *Bessboro*, 171, 223, 607; Thompson, *History of Vermont*, part 2: 216).

51 For a list of stockholders, see ANQM, notary Kimber, no. 264, 15 December 1827; notary Griffin, no. 7714 and no. 7715, 9 May 1828.

52 ANQM, notary Doucet, no. 11376, 17 January 1824; no. 11504, 3 March 1822; notary Griffin, no. 8111, 31 March 1829; *Courant*, 25 August 1824; *Gazette*, 21 August 1824. The *Richelieu* was built at Chambly in 1824 for a group of investors led by Augustus Kuper, brother-in-law of Thomas A. Turner. In his contract with Ward, Kuper stipulated that her engine was to be "similar in form and arrangement to the steam engine on board the Steam tow boat *Hercules*."

53 In September 1826 Greenfield's *Lady of the Lake* was hired by the Montreal Board of Trade for use in surveying Lake St Pierre, a widening of the St Lawrence below Montreal, to determine the practicability of dredging the channel through the lake. In 1828 and 1829 he secured contracts to supply stone to the government's Engineers' Department in Quebec. In

1829 he also won the contract for the transport of military stores and men.
Torrance's company shared this government contract (ANQM, notary Doucet, no. 15651, 13 September 1828; no. 15757, 23 October 1828; no. 15791,
7 November 1828; no. 16392, 17 August 1829; *Gazette*, 18 September
1826, 2 April 1829; *Minerve*, 23 March 1829).

54 *Courant*, 15 August 1829; *Minerve*, 10 and 13 August 1829; *Vindicator*,
13 August 1829. The *Waterloo* was herself a prize which the Molsons had
picked up in the steamboat wars. Originally called *Le Canadien*, complete
with a figurehead of a pipe-smoking habitant, she was built in 1825 by
Jonathan Gorham at La Prairie for Jean-Moïse Raymond. She was
Gorham's last boat – he died on 2 July at age fifty-five, two months after
her launching. Equipped with a 45-horsepower Ward engine, she was 100
feet long on deck, with an 85-foot keel and 25 feet broad, and she had a
7-foot depth of hold. She began running between Montreal and La Prairie
in mid-July 1825. Before the opening of the 1826 navigation season, the
Molsons had persuaded Raymond to sell out. Shortly after the sale, she
was heavily damaged in a fire on 22 April 1826. The Molsons rebuilt her,
adding 12 to 15 feet to her length, and then relaunched her under her new
name on 23 June that year (*Courant*, 30 April, 2, 13, and 20 July 1825, 19,
26 April and 27 June 1826; *Gazette*, 16 July 1825; *Herald*, 4 May and
14 July 1825, 26 April and 15 July 1826).

55 ANQM, notary Griffin, no. 8463 and no. 8464, 12 October 1829; no. 8466,
13 October 1829.

56 Ibid., no. 8483, 27 October 1829. The regular cabin fare from Montreal to
Quebec was set at £1, the return against the current at £1 5s. The steerage
rate both ways was 7s. 6d. Fares were also set for intermediate points, as
were rates for carrying horses, cattle, sheep, and pigs. A concession was
made in Greenfield's case, allowing him to charge 5s. less for cabin fare.
One reason for this may have been that the *Lady of the Lake* was inferior
in carrying capacity and quality. At the time of the cholera epidemic in
1832, a committee established at Montreal to provide shelter for immigrants called on the Board of Health to enforce strict limits on the number
of immigrants which the steamboats could pack in on each run from
Quebec to Montreal. For first-, second-, and third-class boats, the limits
were set respectively at 300, 200, and 100 passengers. The *Lady of the
Lake* was the only boat deemed third class (*Gazette*, 26 June 1832).

57 ANQM, notary Griffin, no. 9347, 16 April 1831. The passenger fares were
the same as in 1829–30, but a more detailed schedule of freight rates was
worked out.

58 ANQM, notary Griffin, no. 9524, 8 October 1831; no. 9634, 31 December
1831; no. 9829, 3 May 1832. Bennet and Henderson agreed to build the
engine for £3,187 10s., Sheay and Merritt to build the boat for £2,000.
Fully equipped, she was valued at £6,500 when Greenfield sold shares in

her to the Molsons and the Torrances. The smaller, older *Lady of the Lake* was then valued at £1,500.

59 ANQM, notary Griffin, no. 6199, 21 January 1826; SGP register, 21 January 1826.

60 A search of his cellar after his death turned up 564 bottles of beer, one 61-gallon cask of beer, 552 bottles of cider, and 96 bottles of claret, plus 174 empties (ANQM, notary Griffin, no. 10097, 25 July 1832).

61 *Minerve*, 26 June 1828, 15 March 1830; *Vindicator*, 12 March 1830.

62 *Courant*, 28 June 1823, advertisement for the *Cornwall*. No steamer plied on Lake St Francis before 1823, although it seems that plans were made to run one there in 1819. On 25 May that year the *Upper Canada Herald* reported that a boat of 80 feet keel and 28 feet beam was under construction at Prescott, intended to run on Lake St Francis. She was to be fitted with a 20-horsepower engine. The *Montreal Herald* of 23 October 1819 said of the *Ottawa*, "We understand she is intended to ply between La Chine and the Cascades, to keep up the communication with the Steam Boat lately built on Lake St Francis." These reports may bear some connection to early plans for the *Dalhousie*.

63 *Courant*, 21 June 1823.

64 Ibid.

65 Ibid., 28 June 1823.

66 NA, MG 24, D 8, Wright Papers, 6:1997–8, Thomas Mears to Philemon Wright Jr, 8 November 1820. Mears was citing the opinion of their mutual friend, Theodore Davis of Chatham. Philemon Wright Sr, born in Woburn, Massachusetts, in 1760, had moved to Canada in 1800 and founded the settlement of Hull. In 1814 his sons Philemon Jr, Tiberius, and Ruggles joined him in the partnership P. Wright and Sons.

67 Ibid.

68 Ibid., 7:2402–7, Mears to Philemon Wright Jr, 30 April 1821.

69 Ibid., 7:2408–9, Mears to Philemon Wright Jr, no date but received by Wright on 11 May 1821.

70 Ibid., 9:3071–2, Mears to Philemon Wright & Sons, 30 November 1822.

71 ANQM, notary Griffin, no. 4438, 18 January 1823. Burt, hired at a total salary of £150 plus room and board, was to start work on 20 January. He must have taken leave soon afterward because on 13 February he was married in Montreal to Catherine McKinnon, a native of Inverness, Scotland (ANQM, SAP register, 13 February 1823).

72 NA, MG 24, D 8, Wright Papers, 10:3208–9, Mears to P. Wright & Sons, 22 March 1823, and 10:3235–7, same to same, 5 April 1823.

73 Ibid., 10:3250–1, James F. Taylor to Tiberius Wright, 17 April 1823. The boat was built on the river shore, her builders counting on the spring flood waters to float her. In the same letter, Taylor reports that Grant says "things are doing pretty well only the water has come a little to quick."

74 Ibid., 10:3260, William Grant to Tiberius Wright, 26 April 1823.

75 Ibid., 10:3278–9, James F. Taylor to Tiberius Wright, 17 May 1823.

76 Ibid. Burt did not "kick the bucket" for another seven years. After serving one year as engineer of the *Union*, he worked at various jobs, including a year with the Halifax Steam Boat Company. On 25 June 1829 his thirty-year-old wife died in Montreal. On 13 September 1830 he himself dropped dead in the street at Niagara. At the time, he was the engineer on the *Alciope*, a steamer plying between Prescott and Niagara and owned by Robert Hamilton of Queenston (ANQM, notary O'Keeffe, no. 632, 14 November 1827; *Courant*, 27 June 1829 and 25 September 1830; Robertson, *Landmarks of Toronto*, 2:855).

77 *Courant*, 18 June 1823; Lamirande and Séguin, *A Foregone Fleet*, 4.

78 ANQM, notary Jobin, no. 2253, 13 April 1821, and no. 2291, 11 May 1821; *Courant*, 26 May 1821.

79 NA, MG 24, D 8, Wright Papers, 10:3309–10, Emery Cushing to Philemon Wright, 20 June 1823.

80 On 20 June, the day Cushing wrote to Wright, Cushing and Russell announced the schedule for their Montreal-Grenville stage line. Published in the *Courant* the next day, the notice advised that the stages "will hereafter run so as to meet the Union Steam Boat on the Ottawa twice a week," leaving Montreal at 8 a.m. Mondays and Fridays, stopping overnight at St Andrew's, and then continuing on to the head of the Long Sault the next day. That meant that Monday travellers arrived at Grenville on Tuesdays and had to wait until Thursday morning for the boat to sail. A new schedule, published in the *Courant* beginning 9 August, provided for departures from Montreal on Tuesdays and Fridays, eliminating that lost Wednesday in Grenville.

81 *Courant*, 21 June 1823. The advertisement named the owners as P. Wright and Sons, Hull; T. Mears, Esq., Hawkesbury; John Campbell, Esq.; and William Shepherd (*sic*), Quebec.

82 ANQM, notary Griffin, no. 2608, 13 April 1819; no. 3529, 20 February 1821; no. 3737, 12 May 1821; no. 3889, 29 August 1821; no. 3969, 3 November 1821; Ballstadt, "Christie, Alexander James"; Bond, "Alexander James Christie, Bytown Pioneer"; Mahaffy, "History of Canadian Publishing," 11–12; Ross, *Ottawa Past and Present*, 39.

83 NA, MG 24, I 9, Hill Collection, 3:689a–e; *Brockville Gazette*, 1 November 1832, copying the *Kingston Chronicle*; *Montreal Gazette*, 24 April 1828, 16 April 1832; Thomas, *History of ... Argenteuil ... [and] Prescott*, 509. The Hill Collection documents show Alexander James Christie acting for Mears's estate in pressing a claim for damage incurred by the *Union* in the Rideau Canal in 1832. The itemized list of damages to the water wheels and engine, totalling £40, was signed by N. Morehouse as master of the steamer. Ross says that the *Union* "finally was abandoned and rotted away

near Edmond's Locks, about six miles south of Smiths Falls" (Ross, *Ottawa Past and Present*, 69).

84 AO, RG 22–155, Court of Probate, will of Thomas Mears, 1 September 1832. *Courant*, 19 and 26 September 1832. Although he died in the waning days of the cholera epidemic of 1832, Mears did not fall victim to the disease, but to "a long and tedious illness."

85 *Herald*, 23 November 1822.

86 *Courant*, 26 November 1823.

87 ANQM, notary Lukin Jr, no. 689, 1 June 1824, and no. 690, 3 June 1824. *Herald*, 16 April 1825. Arbitrators awarded Malcolm £33 16s. 6½d. but did not specify the nature of the materials he furnished or the repairs he made.

88 *Courant*, 15 December 1821, 11 December 1822, 13 December 1823.

89 ANQM, notary Griffin, no. 5036, 27 January 1824.

90 ANQM, SGP register, 21 January 1826; notary Griffin, no. 6199, 21 January 1826.

91 ANQM, notary Griffin, no. 4114, 20 March 1822; SGP register, 13 January 1824; Heisler, *Les canaux du Canada*, 86. After his retirement from steamboating, McMaster did similar work for mason William McKay and carpenter Alexander Crichton, hauling stone from Île Bizard up the Ottawa, where McKay and Crichton were building the Carillon Canal (ANQM, notary Griffin, no. 9270, 10 February 1831, and no. 9353, 25 April 1831).

92 ANQM, notary Doucet, no. 12864, 13 August 1825; notary Jobin, no. 4472, 13 February 1828; *Courant*, 4, 28 May, 15 June 1825; *Herald*, 4 May 1825. The engine of the *St Lawrence*, transferred to the *Swan* in 1832, was described as a 34-horsepower made by the Ward Foundry when the *Swan* was put up for sale in 1834. The 1832 inventory of Dickinson's estate described the engine as 32-horsepower (ANQM, notary Doucet, no. 19686, 2 July 1832; *Gazette*, 29 March 1832, 3 April 1834).

93 *Courant*, 2 April and 22 June 1825; *Gazette*, 14 May 1825. The identity of the owners of the *St Andrews* is perplexing. A notice of December 1830 announced that the debts due to the boat's "Original Proprietors" were to be auctioned on 10 January 1831. The deed of assignment, showing that Robert Drummond had bought up the debts, suggests that the original owners, to the end of 1829, were Drummond, farmer Hugh Brodie of the parish of Lachine, Emery Cushing, Theodore Davis, Montreal lawyer James Charles Grant, Montreal blacksmiths William Kerr and Thomas Biggar (partners in Kerr and Biggar), trader Joseph Lebœuf, *dit* Laflamme, of Lachine, and Guy and Joseph Warwick. David Nelson, the first captain of the *St Andrews*, is not mentioned, yet he owned at least one share, equal to "one fortieth part," which he sold to Emery Cushing in 1827. Montreal merchant Peter McGill also seems to have held an interest in the boat from early 1829, if not sooner. In January that year, purser Andrew Irvine

called on all those with claims against the boat to submit them immediately to Emery Cushing. Then in February, Peter McGill and Company advertised for an engineer and steward for the *St Andrews*. And at the beginning of 1830 McGill, "owner of fourteen Shares thereof as representing Robert Drummond for twelve shares, Thomas Mears for one Share and the Estate of Alexander and Lawrence Glass for one share," bought the remaining eighteen shares in the boat from their fifteen owners, who included David Nelson, Guy Warwick and Company, Kerr and Biggar, Theodore Davis (four shares), Hugh Brodie, and Joseph Lebœuf, *dit* Laflamme, as well as Bennet and Briggs. The fact that Bennet and Briggs, a firm dissolved in 1826, is named as a shareholder in 1830 adds to the puzzle, suggesting that it had acquired an interest in the boat by 1826 at the latest, perhaps in part payment for the engine (ANQM, notary Doucet, no. 17343, 4 January 1830; notary Grant, no. 55A, 7 March 1831; notary Jobin, no. 4379, 7 September 1827; *Courant*, 18 December 1830; *Gazette*, 5 January and 23 February 1829).

94 *Courant*, 25 June, 9, 30 July 1825; JAC, 1841, app. EE, report of the select committee on transport costs, testimony of John Macpherson. Cruikshank, "Macpherson, David Lewis," 682. Macpherson's partners at this time were Arthur Gifford and Alexander McMillan of Prescott. John Macpherson and Company was dissolved at the end of 1825 when Gifford withdrew; it was then immediately reformed under the same name, with Samuel Crane taking Gifford's place. Crane, who was to remain Macpherson's partner for close to thirty years, had begun his Canadian career in the spring of 1820 in partnership with forwarders Alpheus Jones, Levi Sexton, and Cornelius Van Slyck. In late 1821 he had become the partner at Lachine of Prescott forwarder William Lapin Whiting, carrying on business under the name W.L. Whiting and Company at Prescott and as Whiting and Crane at Lachine. On joining John Macpherson and Company in 1825, Crane moved to Prescott, which remained his home for the rest of his life. Macpherson, the son of David Macpherson and Naomi Grant of Inverness, remains largely unknown, unlike his younger brother, David, who would join his firm in 1835 and go on to cap his career as a railway promoter, political organizer, and Conservative senator with a knighthood in 1884. John Macpherson kept out of the public eye and eventually retired to England. In June 1834 he married Matilda Hatt, daughter of Samuel Hatt, seigneur of Chambly and legislative councillor. They had a son, Samuel Hatt Macpherson, on 6 April 1835; Matilda Hatt died two months later (ANQM, CC register, 13 May 1835; register of St Stephen's Anglican Church, Chambly, 5 June 1834 and 1 December 1835; *Courant*, 13 May 1820, 26 January 1822; *Gazette*, 7 June 1834, 28 November 1835; *Herald*, 27 November 1821, 29 March 1826; *Kingston Chronicle*, 10 August 1821; Morris, *Prescott 1810–1967*, 89; Whyte, *Dictionary of Scottish Emigrants*, 2:266; Pietersma, "Crane, Samuel").

95 *Courant*, 4, 28 May, 15 June 1825; *Herald*, 16 April and 4 May 1825. The advertisement for Dickinson's Upper Canada Line in the *Courant* of 28 May is dated 6 May and speaks of the *St Lawrence* as already in service, which would mean that her engines and fittings were on board at her launch.

96 *Courant*, 16 April, 22, 25 June 1825; *Gazette*, 14 May and 18 June 1825. Nelson had worked as a saddler and harness-maker since at least 1802. He seems to have experienced a mid-life crisis in 1820, when he announced that he was quitting the business and seeking a change of occupation. At his death on 23 November 1837 at age sixty, he was a lock-keeper on the Lachine Canal at Lachine (ANQM, notary Gray, no. 777, 12 June 1802; no. 1140, 12 May 1804; notary Bedouin, no. 1957, 20 October 1823; no. 1996, 29 November 1823; register of St Andrew's Presbyterian Church, Lachine, 26 November 1837; *Spectateur Canadien*, 26 February 1820).

97 *Gazette*, 18 June 1825.

98 *Courant*, 2 April, 22, 25 June 1825; *Gazette*, 14 May 1825. Cabin passage from Lachine to Point Fortune cost 10s., deck passage 5s.

99 ANQM, SGP register, 24 June 1825; *Herald*, 25 June and 4 July 1825. James Greenfield was a witness at Black's burial.

100 *Courant*, 9 July 1825, news item and advertisement.

101 Ibid., 2 April, 25 June, 9 July 1825, 13 May, 22 June 1826. See also ANQM, notary Desautels, no. 4897, 26 June 1820; notary Lukin Jr, no. 1189, 5 October 1826. Davis, born in Chesterfield, New Hampshire, in 1777, had moved to the Ottawa Valley in 1799, where he was granted land in the seigneury of Argenteuil by the seigneur, Patrick Murray, for whom he worked as a surveyor. John MacTaggart, clerk of works on the Rideau Canal in the 1820s, said of him: "For local information respecting men and things, there is no equal to my friend Theodore Davis; he knows every *concession line*, can put his hand on all sacred *post marks*, lead you up all wild rivers, show you all mines and minerals, and explain to you the *lumber trade*." Davis served one term as member of the assembly of Lower Canada for Ottawa County from 1830 to 1834. He did not run again in the general election of 1834, but that year was named the first registrar for the county, a position he resigned in 1840. He died suddenly while on a visit to Ruggles Wright at Hull on 15 March 1841 (ANQM, notary Lukin Sr, no. 1478, 11 June 1799; *Gazette*, 30 January, 23, 25 March 1841; *Vindicator*, 27 October 1834; MacTaggart, *Three Years in Canada*, 1:278–9; Thomas, *History of … Argenteuil … [and] Prescott*, 79–80).

102 Such an excursion was advertised in the *Courant*, 9 July 1825, for Sunday, 10 July.

103 ANQM, notary Griffin, no. 6201, 23 January 1826.

104 The square-sterned *Lady of the Lake*, measuring 93 tons, had an 86-foot keel, was 96 feet 9 inches long on deck, 18 feet beam, and 7 feet 9 inches deep. She

had a 28-horsepower Bennet and Briggs engine (ANQM, notary Griffin, no. 6160, 2 January 1826; no. 6173, 6 January 1826; NA, RG 42, E 1, Dept of Marine, Ship Registers, 190: 1 September 1835; *Herald*, 13 May 1826).

105 *Herald*, 13 May 1826.

106 *Gazette*, 7, 28 September 1829.

107 ANQM, notary Griffin, no. 6160, 2 January 1826; *Herald*, 13 May 1826.

108 *Courant*, 15 March 1826. The advertisement is dated 11 March. It appears that no shares were sold in 1826, since Greenfield still held all the stock six years later when he sold a stake in the boat to the Molson and Torrance companies.

109 Ibid., 13 May 1826. *Gazette*, 11 May 1826; *Herald*, 13 May 1826.

110 There does not appear to be any mention of the *Perseverance* in the newspapers during the navigation season this year.

111 *Courant*, 12 May and 3 June 1826.

112 ANQM, SGP register, 9 August 1826; *Courant*, 12 August 1826. Lawrence Bennet appears to have been related to engineer John Bennet, who, along with a David Bennet, signed the burial register.

113 In sketching the efforts made to circumvent the rapids, Ross piles error upon error: "About 1915 [*sic*] a wooden lock was built at Vaudreuil to overcome the Ste Anne Rapids, and Durham boats began to ascend the Ottawa River as far as Point Fortune. In 1816 the St Andrew's Steam Forwarding Company built a wooden lock between Ile Perrot and the mainland of Quebec, but allowed only their own vessels to pass through it. All others had to be 'wound up' the channel by means of a windlass placed on a pier a short distance above the rapids at Vaudreuil, but at a later date Captain R.W. Sheppard [*sic*] found a navigable channel through the rapids and broke up the monopoly" (*Ottawa Past and Present*, 39). Durham boats plied on the Ottawa before the lock was built; no such company as the St Andrew's Steam Forwarding Company existed in 1816; the method Ross describes of pulling boats up by means of a windlass was used, not at Vaudreuil, but at St Anne during the construction of the government lock there in the early 1840s; the owners of the *Perseverance* and the *St Andrews*, among others, had found "navigable" channels through the rapids around Île Perrot long before Captain Shepherd did so in 1841, and the claim that Shepherd broke the monopoly held by the owners of the Vaudreuil lock is an oversimplification (see chap. 9). Glazebrook repeated the error that a St Andrews Steam Forwarding Company built the lock in 1816 (*History of Transportation in Canada*, 80–1). Legget wrote that it was built "as early as 1816" and that "no details can be found of this structure" (*Ottawa River Canals*, 141). Lafrenière dates the building of the lock to 1815–16, and as recently as 1997, in his historical atlas of railways and canals, Andreae makes it 1816 (Lafrenière, *Le réseau de canalisation de*

la rivière des Outaouais, 41; Andreae, *Lines of Country*, 100). In 1863 engineer Thomas Coltrin Keefer wrote that the lock was built in 1832 (*Eighty Years' Progress*, 153). Guillet claimed that navigation "on the Ottawa route was aided by the building of a bateau lock by a private company at Vaudreuil in 1832" (*Pioneer Travel*, 29). The erroneous date of 1816 can be traced to a passage in the report of Canada's commissioner of public works for 1866–67, which says of this lock: "No official record of the date of its construction has been found, but it appears to have been first built in 1816, by the 'St Andrews Steam Forwarding Company'" (*General Report of the Commissioner of Public Works for the Year Ending 30th June, 1867*, 49–50). The confusion over 1832 probably stems from the work done that year to lengthen and enlarge the lock (see ANQM, notary Doucet, no. 19806, 16 August 1832, cited in appendix A).

114 *Courant*, 2 December 1826.

115 MacTaggart, *Three Years in Canada*, 1:237.

116 ANQM, notary Doucet, no. 13143, 24 November 1825.

117 When the *St Andrews* was sold to Peter McGill in 1830, it was expressly stated that along with the boat went the "Canal now or lately in the use of the said Proprietors and particularly the remaining and unexpired term of a lease of priviledge made to Theodore Davis and Robert Drummond by the heirs of the late the Honorable Chartier de Lotbinière by deed passed before the undersigned notaries dated the twenty fourth day of November of the year one thousand Eight hundred and twenty five" (ANQM, notary Doucet, no. 17343, 4 January 1830).

118 On this controversy, see, for example, the letter in the *Vindicator* of 22 November 1833. Commenting on the imminent completion of the Ottawa River canals and the increase in business sure to ensue on the Rideau Canal, the writer observes: "With referrence to this important era in the trade of these Provinces, the public, I apprehend, will learn, with regret, that the 'Ottawa Steamboat Company' have, by purchasing from the Hon. Mr Harwood the exclusive right to the Locks, rented by that gentleman, at Vaudreuil, acquired the entire control of the whole carrying trade on this communication." (Legislative Councillor Robert Unwin Harwood was the husband of Louise de Lotbinière, who had inherited the seigneury of Vaudreuil.) The writer seems to suggest that the Ottawa Steamboat Company had made a new arrangement with the de Lotbinières for the use of the locks. If this is correct, it might explain why the rights granted in 1825 did not lapse eleven years after completion of the lock, as originally stipulated (see chap. 9).

119 ANQM, notary Griffin, no. 7733, 4 June 1828.

120 Ibid., no. 7047, 8 February 1827.

121 Ibid., no. 7293, 18 June 1827.

122 In 1819 Drummond, then twenty-seven or twenty-eight, had married
    Margaret Gentle of Perth, Upper Canada, and in 1822 Spier, just twenty-
    one, had married her sister Catherine (ANQM, SGP register, 23 April 1819
    and 8 November 1822).

123 ANQM, notary Griffin, no. 7733, 4 June 1828.

124 Ibid. The arbitrators were John Henderson and Samuel T. Hudson.

125 Ibid.

126 Ibid.

127 ANQM, notary Arnoldi, no. 4875, 10 June 1836; *Gazette*, 2 June 1836,
    notice by William Spier, dated 19 May. Arnoldi's notarial records also con-
    tain a deed of sale for one half-share in the *Perseverance* by Lot Briggs in
    1836 (no. 4854, 27 May 1836).

128 *Vindicator*, Friday, 30 April 1830.

129 McMaster, whose first wife had died in 1827, was living with his second,
    Jane McMartin, his three children, and his sister when he died on 22 July
    1832, at the age of forty-three. At the time, he was a tavern-keeper at
    Lachine (ANQM, register of St Andrew's Presbyterian Church, Lachine,
    22 July 1832; Cour Supérieure-Montréal, Tutelles et Curatelles, no. 721B,
    7 September 1832; notary Grant, no. 409, 13 September 1832; no. 420,
    1 October 1832). Fellow died eight days later, on 30 July, leaving his
    French-Canadian wife, Josephte Imbault, and a thirteen-year-old daughter,
    Sophia (ANQM, SGP register, 22 December 1816; Cour Supérieure-
    Montréal, Tutelles et Curatelles, no. 576, 7 August 1832; *Courant*,
    4 August 1832). For Greenfield's last days, see below.

130 ANQM, notary Arnoldi, no. 3884, 2 January 1835; no. 4875, 10 June 1836;
    notary Bleakley, no. 127, 24 July 1835; notary Doucet, no. 17303,
    7 December 1829; notary Griffin, no. 9446, 5 July 1831 (re *Royal William*
    engine contract passed before notary L.T. McPherson at Quebec on
    28 August 1830); notary Lukin Jr, no. 2083, 30 November 1830; *Gazette*,
    2 May 1835; *Herald*, 20 September 1826; *Minerve*, 7 October 1830.

131 ANQM, notary Griffin, no. 9524, 8 October 1831; no. 9634, 31 December 1831;
    no. 9829, 3 May 1832; no. 9931, 12 June 1832; *Gazette*, 10 May 1832.

132 ANQM, Cour Supérieure-Montréal, Tutelles et Curatelles, no. 412, 3 July
    1832; notary Griffin, no. 10097, 25 July 1832; no. 10146, 10 August 1832;
    Courant, 30 June and 3 October 1832.

133 ANQM, notary Griffin, no. 12848, 27 January 1835; *Gazette*, 11 and
    13 September 1834; *Vindicator*, 12 and 16 September 1834.

134 ANQM, notary Griffin, no. 12826, 16 January 1835; *Gazette*, 15 January
    1835; *Minerve*, 19 and 22 January 1835.

135 ANQM, notary Griffin, no. 12826, 16 January 1835, and no. 17299, 29 Sep-
    tember 1840.

136 ANQM, notary Doucet, no. 22325, 19 March 1835; notary Blackwood,
    no. 557, 17 December 1835.

CHAPTER THREE

1 Godfrey, *The Cholera Epidemics in Upper Canada,* 14–15, says that the first cases were reported at Montreal on 9 June, Prescott on 16 June, Brockville on 19 June, Kingston on 20 June, Cornwall and York (Toronto) on 21 June, Cobourg on 27 June, and Brantford on 28 June. By early July the epidemic had spread to the Hamilton and London areas, and by August, cases were reported on the Welland Canal. On the Ottawa River the disease had spread to Bytown by 5 July. For the death toll, see Godfrey, 39–40, and Bilson, *A Darkened House,* 48–9, 63, 179–81.

2 *Courant,* 20 June 1832. Thatcher's inn at 87 St Paul Street had served as the Montreal booking office and stage terminal for passengers on the *St Andrews* in 1825. Thatcher was also involved at different times in stage lines to the United States and Quebec (ANQM, notary Desautels, no. 4150, 6 April 1819; *Courant,* 23 January 1819, 9 July 1825, 25 November 1826; *Gazette,* 6 December 1827; *Vindicator,* 13 December 1831).

3 *Minerve,* 16 January 1834; Murray, *A Historical and Descriptive Account of British America,* 3:172–3.

4 *Gazette,* 2 June 1832. The advertisement did not specify what the fares were, but they must have been close to those charged by a group of St Lawrence forwarders who, from early July, established a common rate for immigrants travelling from Montreal to Prescott of 10s. for adults, 5s. for children under twelve, and nothing for "infants in arms." The baggage rate was 4s. per hundredweight. Macpherson and Crane, one of the forwarders involved, had a particular interest in immigrants at this time as an agent at Montreal and Hamilton for the Canada Company, which sought to attract settlers to the Huron Tract and other lands in Upper Canada (*Gazette,* 9 June 1832, 14 August 1832, advertisement dated 7 July).

5 ANQM, notary Doucet, no. 19686, Dickinson inventory, 2 July 1832; notary Griffin, no. 9931, 12 June 1832. The inventory of Dickinson's estate, filed in Doucet's records under the date of 2 July 1832 but closed only on 16 July 1833, runs to 122 unnumbered pages. The reference to the ledger is on the second last page.

6 *Courant,* 23 June 1832.

7 ANQM, notary Doucet, no. 19686, Dickinson inventory, 2 July 1832. These items are listed on the eighth page.

8 Hatfield town clerk's office, Hatfield records; J.T. Dickinson, *Genealogies,* 17; Stott, "The Correct English Origins of Nathaniel Dickinson"; E.V. Smith, *Descendants of Nathaniel Dickinson,* 4–7, 325; Walker, *Historic Hadley,* 1–5, 12, 14, 78–9, 119.

9 See Hatfield Records, Hatfield, Massachusetts; Massachusetts title deeds, Hampshire County, 25:49, 292, and 591; Parish, "The North Country in 1816"; E.V. Smith, *Descendants of Hathaniel Dickinson,* 313.

10 *Hatfield, 1670–1970*, 31; Wells and Wells, *History of Hatfield*, part 2 (reminiscences of Samuel Dwight Partridge): 257.

11 Bates, "Pictures of Westfield," no. 17, 14 July 1869; A.M. Dickinson, *Descendents of Nathaniel Dickinson*, 258; J.T. Dickinson, *Genealogies*, 17; E.V. Smith, *Descendants of Nathaniel Dickinson*, 325.

12 J.T. Dickinson, *Genealogies*, 17; Massachusetts title deeds, Hampshire County, 23:366 and 24:561. See also Darlington, "Peopling the Post-Revolutionary New York Frontier"; Ellis, "Rise of the Empire State"; Fox, *Yankees and Yorkers*, particularly chap. 7, "The Great Migration"; Taylor, *William Cooper's Town*, 4, 89–95. James Taylor Dickinson wrote that his father had moved to New York State "about 1805." If Horace Dickinson and his wife did leave Hatfield that year, it was not before November: on 25 October 1805 he was a witness in one of his father's Hatfield land sales. Lemuel Dickinson himself was still identified as a Hatfield resident on 15 November 1806, when he disposed of the last of his property in the area. It is possible that instead of the family moving in a body, Horace and Barnabas Dickinson set out ahead of their parents and their two younger brothers.

13 E.V. Smith, *Descendants of Nathaniel Dickinson*, 313; Wells and Wells, *History of Hatfield*, part 2 (reminiscences of Samuel Dwight Partridge): 276.

14 Hough, *History of Lewis County*, 6, 8–11, 140; Lockwood, *Westfield and Its Historic Influences*, 2:188–91. Lewis County was established in 1805 and Lowville was made the county seat.

15 Hough, *History of Lewis County*, 91, 163; Parish, "The North Country in 1816."

16 *Cyclopaedia of Canadian Biography*, 238–9; E.V. Smith, *Descendants of Nathaniel Dickinson*, 313, 326. Barnabas Dickinson bought a 100-acre lot in Denmark in May 1810 (New York title deeds, Lewis County, C:27).

17 Durant and Peirce, *History of St Lawrence County*, 427, 430; J.T.; Dickinson, *Genealogies*, 17.

18 Durant and Peirce, *History of St Lawrence County*, 429, 431; Hough, *History of St Lawrence and Franklin Counties*, 468–71, 568.

19 NA, MG 24, D 12, Dorwin Diaries, 1, part 1: 32; *Herald*, 4 March 1815. How much border-dwelling Americans and Canadians depended on each other can be seen from the brisk smuggling and the crafty evasion of U.S. laws against trading with the enemy that went on during the War of 1812. At times, British troops were fed contraband beef. See, for example, Muller, "A 'Traitorous and Diabolical Traffic'"; Edgar, *Ten Years of Upper Canada*, 269, 279, and 281–2; and Dunlop, *Tiger Dunlop's Upper Canada*, 21–2. Referring to the northwestern part of Vermont, Zadock Thompson noted in his *History of Vermont* (part 2: 215): "Previous to the opening of the Champlain and Hudson canal, in 1823, Montreal and Quebec shared

largely in the business of this section, but, since that event, the business with Canada has been comparatively trifling." The canal, linking Lake Champlain to the Hudson River, diverted trade away from Montreal to New York City, just as the Erie Canal, completed in 1825 from Albany to Buffalo, with a feeder later opened to Oswego on Lake Ontario, drew off the trade of the upper Great Lakes.

20 ANQM, notary Desautels, no. 2570, 20 July 1816; *Courant*, 13 January 1816, advertisement dated Montreal, 6 January; *Kingston Gazette*, 13 January 1816, advertisement dated Montreal, 1 January; *St Lawrence Gazette*, 25 December 1817, advertisement dated 27 February 1816. The last advertisement continued to run in this Ogdensburg paper until 6 January 1818. There seems to be no evidence to support the claims made in various historical and genealogical works that Barnabas Dickinson moved to Canada in 1812 and/or secured a contract that year to carry the mail between Montreal and Kingston by boat and stage. See below, note 26.

21 *Gazette*, 15 October 1833, 9 September 1837; Morris, *Prescott*, 17–18, 21, 94–5, 109–12; E.V. Smith, *Descendants of Nathaniel Dickinson*, 342–3. Alpheus Jones, born in 1794, was appointed postmaster on 6 May 1816 and held the job until his death in 1863. From 1819 to 1821 he was a partner in Levi Sexton and Company, forwarders. On 1 January 1823 he formed a forwarding partnership with his cousin, Henry Jones of Brockville; it was dissolved after less than three months, on 25 March 1823, so that Alpheus Jones could accept an appointment as collector of customs at Prescott. The appointment came through on 14 April. His older brothers, Charles and Jonas, were more widely known. Charles, a Brockville miller and businessman, was a member of Upper Canada's House of Assembly from 1821 to 1828, then of the Legislative Council until his death in 1840. Jonas practised law in Brockville, served off and on as a member of the legislature between 1816 and 1828 and again in 1836–37, and was a district court judge and then a judge of the Court of King's Bench from 1837 until his death in 1848. From the mid-1820s the Jones brothers' cousins, Henry and Sidney Jones, operated the Brockville forwarding firm of H. and S. Jones, called H. Jones and Company at Montreal (NA, MG 24, B 98, Alpheus Jones Papers, 1, appointment of Alpheus Jones as customs collector, 14 April 1823; *Courant*, 13 May 1820, 5 May 1821; *Kingston Chronicle*, 5 February 1819, 10 August 1821, 18 April 1823; Chadwick, *Ontarian Families*, 1:167–80. R.L. Fraser, "Jones, Jonas"; McIlwraith, "Jones, Charles"; Richards, "The Joneses of Brockville and the Family Compact"; MacPherson, *Matters of Loyalty*, 18, 45–8; Gourlay, *Statistical Account*, 88).

22 Dunham, *Political Unrest in Upper Canada*, 74. In 1816 Richard Barrett of Jamaica found anti-American sentiment strong as he travelled from Niagara to Montreal. The first Canadian he met after crossing into Upper Canada from New York State "expressed the bitterest animosity against

the Americans, & longed for another trial of strength between the two nations," he recorded. "We afterwards found among all those with whom we conversed a similar animosity against the Yankees as they call them, & it is to be feared that in case of another war, it will rage in all its horrors" (Barrett, *Richard Barrett's Journal*, 39).

23 ANQM, notary Griffin, no. 439, 7 March 1814; Clow, *Report on the Postal System of Upper Canada*, 2; W. Smith, *History of the Post Office*, 99–104, 110. Rennie ceded his job to Joseph Labelle of St Rose on 23 May 1814 (ANQM, notary Griffin, no. 522, 23 May 1814).

24 *Herald*, 12 August 1815; W. Smith, *History of the Post Office*, 104. The call for tenders published in the *Herald* of 12 August allowed that the service "may be performed by the stage waggons running between those places, or with a light carriage drawn by one or two horses, to be changed at certain distances. When the roads are not practicable for carriages, the mails may be forwarded on horseback."

25 ANQM, notary Griffin, no. 1138, 25 September 1815; no. 1146, 2 October 1815.

26 ANQM, notary Griffin, no. 1372 and no. 1373, 25 March 1816. In this postal contract and related bond, the Dickinson brothers were identified as residents of Denmark, New York. But Horace Dickinson was identified as still a resident of Russell on the following 7 June when he sold his 50-acre lot in that village. His oldest child later recalled that in 1816 the family moved from Russell to Prescott. These elements suggest that in setting up the Canadian stage line, Horace Dickinson may have left his family in Russell while using the Denmark home of his brother and partner as his temporary base and business address before relocating to Prescott. Barnabas Dickinson, on the other hand, while he spent the summer of 1816 in Montreal – he leased part of a house there from 14 July to 29 September – remained domiciled in Denmark until the mid-1820s, when he moved to Schenectady and ultimately to Cornwall, Upper Canada, in the late 1820s (ANQM, notary Desautels, no. 2570, 20 July 1816; notary Doucet, no. 5021, 19 March 1818; NA, MG 24, D 8, Wright Papers, Richard Chamberlin to Mr Writh [*sic*], 22 August 1821; New York title deeds, Lewis County, I:119; St Lawrence County, 4:349; J.T. Dickinson, *Genealogies*, 17).

27 Bates, "Pictures of Westfield," no. 8, 5 May 1869; Holmes, "Levi Pease," 255.

28 Hough, *History of Lewis County*, 258. Hough says that the post office in Denmark was established in January 1804; other sources say 1810, which was around the time that Barnabas Dickinson moved there from Lowville (Hough, *History of Lewis County*, 90; Kay and Smith, *New York Postal History*, 163).

29 Dorwin, "Montreal in 1816."

30 From May 1820 the post office occupied a building at 11 St Joseph Street (later renamed St Sulpice). Its previous home had been at St Jean Baptiste

and Notre Dame streets, and before that at the foot of St Vincent Street. In 1821 the *Gazette* published a facetious letter from a writer styling himself Blunder O'Leary on the difficulties he had had in finding the St Joseph Street post office. "Oh Lord," he wrote, "is it possible that in this place, the largest city in the Canadas, you have your Post Office in a back house in an auctioneers yard? Why, Sir, ours in Dublin is a magnificent building placed in one of the grandest streets I ever saw, and is a beautiful specimen of modern architecture." In August 1824 the post office moved from that "inconvenient and unhealthy situation" to a house at 19 St James Street, at the corner of St Laurent (ANQM, notary Bedouin, no. 201, 11 February 1817; *Gazette*, 18 July 1821, 6 October 1824; *Herald*, 9 November 1816, 10 May 1817, 20 May 1820, 1 September 1824).

31 Francis Hall, *Travels in Canada, and the United States*, in 1816 and 1817 (London, 1818), cited in A.B. Smith, *Kingson! Oh Kingston!*, 235. On the types of vehicle used, see Lambert, *Les anciennes diligences du Québec*, 18–25; Talman, "Travel in Ontario before the Coming of the Railway," 96.

32 Gourlay, *Statistical Account*, 279. On the Lower Canadian side, it seems that the road was not built until 1830 (see *Minerve*, 24 June 1830; *Vindicator*, 6 July 1830).

33 *JAUC*, 1836, app. report no. 52, first report of the committee on finance: Post Office department, 1:54; *Vindicator*, 18 April 1837.

34 AO, F 286, Samuel Peters Collection, file 6, indenture of 24 July 1810; RG 22, Court of Probate, Stormont, Dundas and Glengarry, estate file 841. NA, RG 1, L 3, Upper Canada Land Petitions, 156, part 1, D13, no. $17\frac{1}{2}$, 22 January 1821; 156, part 2, D14, no. 73, 31 December 1824; 514a, bundle 10V (1811–16), 21 January 1811; *Cornwall Observer*, 9 January 1837; *Gazette*, 9 November 1826; *Kingston Chronicle*, 11 March 1840; *Vindicator*, 13 February 1831; Canniff, *Medical Profession in Upper Canada*, 338; Harkness, *Stormont, Dundas and Glengarry*, 446–7; Hough, *History of Lewis County*, 291; Pringle, *Lunenburgh*, 85–6; W.D. Reid, *Loyalists in Ontario*, 326. Noah Dickinson does not appear in genealogical accounts of the descendants of Nathaniel Dickinson. Canniff identifies him as "one of the band of U.E. Loyalists," but his name is not on the Loyalist list. Harkness says he was born in Vermont in 1776 and moved to Canada around 1806. But at his death on 28 February 1840, the *Kingston Chronicle* said that he was sixty-two and had lived in Cornwall for more than forty years. Hough notes that a Dr Noah Dickinson registered as a member of the Lewis County Medical Society on 11 September 1807. Harkness says that it was in 1807 that Noah Dickinson married Margaret VanKoughnet, but Reid gives the date as 1811. Margaret VanKoughnet died on 7 October 1826. Noah Dickinson was founding secretary of the Medical Society of the Eastern District in 1831 and later its president. John Moseley, another doctor in the Cornwall area, may also have helped the Dickinsons make

the jump across the St Lawrence from New York. It is possible that he was related to Horace Dickinson's wife: he had a daughter called Mary Ann Moseley, which was the maiden name of Horace Dickinson's mother-in-law and the surname of his oldest daughter (*Gazette*, 26 March 1829; Carter, *Story of Dundas*, 432; Harkness, *Stormont, Dundas and Glengarry*, 445–6; Pringle, *Lunenburgh*, 317).

35 ANQM, notary Desautels, no. 937, 18 April 1814; no. 1260, 16 November 1814; no. 1267, 18 November 1814; no. 1288, 6 December 1814; no. 1292, 9 December 1814; unnumbered hiring contracts found between items no. 1497 and 1500, March–April 1815; no. 2522, 22 June 1816; notary Griffin, no. 681, 4 November 1814; no. 1373, 25 March 1816; notary Lukin Sr, no. 4850, 1 February 1812; notary Thibodeau, no. 3864, 29 January 1815; *Courant*, 13 January 1816; McDougall, "The American Element in the Early Presbyterian Church in Montreal," 121–2. In 1822 Thomas Peck married Catherine Finchley, sister of Lachine forwarder Stephen Finchley. His brother, Ebenezer Peck, was returned as the first member of the Legislative Assembly for Stanstead County in 1829. Thomas Peck died in Montreal on 2 April 1833 (ANQM, SGP register, 26 February 1822; *Vindicator*, 9 April 1833; Bibaud, *Histoire du Canada sous la domination anglaise*, 394).

36 Grenville County Historical Society, Hiram Norton file, Norton's speech at celebrations marking the fiftieth anniversary of Lowville Academy, 21 and 22 July 1858; *Kingston Chronicle*, 6 July 1833, copying the *Prescott Gazette; Statutes of Upper Canada*, 3 William IV, ch. 18, An act granting His Majesty a sum of money to be raised by debenture, for the improvement of the navigation of the River Saint Lawrence; Leavitt, *History of Leeds and Grenville*, 64, 148; Pringle, *Lunenburgh*, 155–6. Norton probably went to Lewis County to live with Almon M. Norton, a tavern-keeper and merchant in Denmark, after whom he seems to have named one of his sons, Charles Almon Norton, born in 1835. The first of his sons, born in 1827, he named Lemuel Dickinson Norton. The first explicit, published reference to his business ties with Horace Dickinson comes in a newspaper advertisement dated 27 June 1823 for the Upper Canada Line: "Stage Books kept at the Stage Office, McGill Street, Montreal, and at H. Norton's in Prescott." Another advertisement, published two years later in a Montreal newspaper, was signed "H. Dickinson & Co., Prescott" – rather than Montreal – suggesting that someone at Prescott, probably Norton, was a partner in the company (*Courant*, 28 June 1823; 28 May 1825; Hough, *History of Lewis County*, 90; Livingston, *Rev. Robert Blakey's Baptisms*).

37 ANQM, notary Charlebois, 12 May 1842; New York title deeds, Otsego County, 7:336–7; St Lawrence County, 2:220; *Cornwall Observer*, 28 November 1842; Brainard, *Wilkins Family*, 80–1; Church, *Descendants*

of Richard Church, 135–6; Hough, *History of St Lawrence and Franklin
Counties*, 288–9. Taylor, *William Cooper's Town*, 321–9 and 389–92, gives
a detailed view of Cooper's land dealings in and around Cooperstown and
at DeKalb. Brainard gives Asahel Whipple's birth place and date, based on
information written in a Whipple family Bible; no record of his birth has
been found in Rhode Island vital records. The title deeds cited above show
that Esek Whipple first bought land from Cooper in Otsego County on
23 May 1792, when Asahel was only two, and in DeKalb on 17 June 1803.
Someone in the Whipple family of DeKalb seems to have worked in the
cartage business on the eve of the War of 1812, since a militia officer
advised the adjutant in charge of the Ogdensburg barracks on 25 May
1812: "You will receive by Whipple, four bbls. of pork, four axes, and one
frying pan, which belong to the troops, together with one bbl. of whiskey,
for their use." Esek Whipple, a veteran of the Revolutionary War who died
in 1833, served six months under arms at Ogdensburg in the War of 1812.
The earliest record found of Asahel Whipple's presence in Canada is a
land deed of 1819 (ANQM, notary Dubois, no. 2271, 18 November 1819;
St Lawrence Republican, 24 December 1833; Hough, *History of St
Lawrence and Franklin Counties*, 618–19).

38 ANQM, notary Griffin, no. 1981, 4 October 1817. Sutherland, a former
partner in the North West Company and a brother-in-law of Theodore
Davis (both had married daughters of Captain Daniel Robertson, a major
landowner in the township of Chatham on the Lower Canadian side of the
Ottawa River) succeeded Heriot as deputy postmaster general in April
1816. He was in turn succeeded by his son-in-law, Thomas Allen Stayner,
in 1827 (*Courant*, 25 August 1832; *Herald*, 31 May 1817; Armour, "Robertson, Daniel"; Martineau, "Stayner, Thomas Allen"; Momryk, "Sutherland, Daniel"; W. Smith, *History of the Post Office*, 114, 153).

39 *Courant*, 30 January, 18 August, and 16 October 1819, 27 May and
29 December 1820; *Kingston Gazette*, 19 May 1818; *Upper Canada Herald*,
9 March 1819. The stage advertisements in the *Courant* do not mention boat
connections, but do show the seasonal alternation of Prescott and Kingston as
the western terminus of Dickinson's stage line. The article in the *Upper
Canada Herald* mentions the steamboat connection, but mistakenly dates the
start of Kingston-Montreal stage service from the winter of 1817–18.

40 ANQM, notary Griffin, no. 2381, 17 October 1818; no. 2528, 4 March 1819.

41 ANQM, notary Jobin, no. 1103, 8 April 1818.

42 See Maurault, *Le Collège de Montréal*.

43 Ibid., 220. Dr Noah Dickinson of Cornwall also had a son called James, but
he was born only in 1819. The records cited by Maurault show that James
Dickinson entered the college in 1818 and left in 1819. James Taylor Dickinson later studied at Yale, where he graduated in 1826. He spent most of
his career as a minister in Connecticut, except from 1836 to 1844, when he

worked as a missionary in Singapore. He died in Middlefield, Connecticut, on 21 July 1884 (Canniff, *The Medical Profession in Upper Canada*, 338; J.T. Dickinson, *Genealogies*, 17; Harkness, *Stormont, Dundas and Glengarry*, 446; E.V. Smith, *Descendants of Nathaniel Dickinson*, 325).

44 ANQM, notary Bedouin, no. 94, 25 March 1816, and no. 103, 25 April 1816; NA, MG 24, D 12, Dorwin Diaries, 1, part 1: 37, 55; *Courant*, 6 January 1816. The demolition, between 1801 and 1817, of the decrepit old walls constricting Montreal led to the development of McGill Street as a major north-south thoroughfare marking the boundary between the city and its western suburbs. At Kingston in these early days, passengers for the Dickinson stages booked seats at Robert Walker's Hotel, then at "the Tavern formerly known by the Sign of the Britannia Inn," and in 1819 at Moore's Coffee House (*Courant*, 6 January 1816, 30 January 1819; *Kingston Gazette*, 11 January 1817; *Les rues de Montréal*, 328).

45 On 8 August 1805 Lemuel Dickinson sold 21 acres of the family homestead at Hatfield plus other land to a Joseph Lyman and Samuel Hinckley. Horace Dickinson witnessed the sale (Massachusetts title deeds, Hampshire County, 23:205).

46 ANQM, notary Chaboillez, no. 7716, 18 December 1806; notary Gray, no. 1706, 8 December 1806; no. 2682, 12 March 1810; no. 3482 and no. 3483, 12 July 1812; Hemenway, *Vermont Historical Gazetteer*, 3:179; Lyman, *Genealogy of the Lyman Family*, 22, 24, 30–1, 50. Elisha Lyman's first wife, Hannah Stiles, niece of the president of Yale University, died at Derby, Vermont, on 25 February 1814. Well before the establishment of the first Canadian bank, Lyman's brother, Lewis, had acted as an agent for a group of U.S. banks in helping to finance Canada's first paper mill at St Andrew's on the Ottawa River in 1806. Lewis and another brother, Micah Jones Lyman, were both involved in the wholesale and retail drug business in Montreal. They were also partners in Lewis Lyman and Company, a trading company dissolved in July 1812, just after the outbreak of war.

47 ANQM, notary Bedouin, no. 103, 26 April 1816; no. 819, 10 February 1820; no. 2794, 7 February 1827; notary Desautels, no. 1058, 28 June 1814; no. 1063, 29 June 1814; no. 1118, 28 July 1814; no. 1206, 5 October 1814; no. 1433, 21 February 1815; no. 2138, 2 February 1816; no. 2324, 2 August 1816; no. 3340, 9 October 1817; notary Griffin, no. 1320, 2 February 1816; NA, MG 24, D 12, Dorwin Diaries, 1, part 1: 37; *Courant*, 30 January 1819, 21 May 1825, 21 October 1826; *Plattsburgh Republican*, 6 January 1816; "Proclamations of the Governor of Lower Canada," 158; Doige, *Montreal Directory* (1820 ed.), 83; Lyman, *Genealogy of the Lyman Family*, 30–1, 60–1. Lyman kept the tavern until the end of 1826. He then moved back to Massachusetts and later to the border town of Champlain, New York, where he died on 21 February 1844. Hedge died in Montreal on 6 January 1830 (*Gazette*, 4 March 1844; *Vindicator*, 12 January 1830).

48 See NA, MG 24, D 12, Dorwin Diaries, 1, part 1: 37, 55; Dorwin, "Montreal in 1816."

49 Flip was not unknown in Canada. See, for example, Ross, *Lancaster*, 21.

50 *Gazette*, 18 November 1816.

51 ANQM, notary Griffin, no. 2381, 17 October 1818; no. 5244 and no. 5245, both 23 June 1824.

52 ANQM, notary Doucet, no. 5998, 15 March 1819; Cleveland, *Sketch of the Early Settlement of Shipton*, 11–12, 14, 19, 21, 28, 31, 33, 35, 43, 63; Elmer Cushing, *An Appeal*, 28–30; Désilets, "Cushing, Lemuel"; Doige, *Montreal Directory* (1820 ed.), 19–20, 99, 115. Job Cushing's move to Montreal in 1814 seems to have been intended as a temporary stopover for he leased two farms in the seigneury of Argenteuil from Thomas Peck that year. The leases may have fallen through. By the fall of 1815 Cushing was operating an inn in Montreal. He rented the tavern property on McGill Street from the spring of 1816 (ANQM, notary Bedouin, no. 113, 17 May 1816; notary Delisle, no. 7109, 21 October 1815; notary Lukin Sr, no. 5270, 10 March 1814, and no. 5287, 2 May 1814).

53 Emery Cushing, fourth child of Job Cushing and Sarah Rice, was born in Shrewsbury, Massachusetts, on 21 November 1796 (J.E. Cushing, *Genealogy of the Cushing Family*, 168–9, 294–5; A.H. Ward, *History of the Town of Shrewsbury*, 254).

54 ANQM, notary Bedouin, no. 818, 10 February 1820; notary Doucet, no. 6350, 17 June 1819; no. 19961 and no. 19962, 19 October 1832; notary Griffin, no. 5068 and no. 5069, 18 February 1824; no. 5579, 18 February 1825; no. 8332, 17 July 1829; no. 8545, 11 December 1829; notary Jobin, no. 2253, 13 April 1821, and no. 2291, 11 May 1821; Cour Supérieure-Montréal, Tutelles et Curatelles, no. 181, 6 April 1822; *Courant*, 26 May 1821, 23 March, 30 April, and 31 December 1825, 18 November and 9 December 1826; *Gazette*, 30 June 1819.

55 Jacob Bigelow was born on 26 August 1790, Abijah on 16 August 1792. Their maternal grandfather, Converse Spring, and Bidwell's maternal grandmother, Sarah Spring, were brother and sister. Jacob and Abijah Bigelow's older brother, Marshall Spring Bigelow, and Bidwell, who was born in Stockbridge, Massachusetts, on 16 February 1799, were both named after their common great-uncle, Marshall Spring, a prominent physician and political figure in Massachusetts. An 1869 letter to Bidwell from Horace Dickinson's son, James Taylor Dickinson, shows that he and his two sisters, both dead by then, were also related to Bidwell through their mother, Mary Ann Taylor. The letter is among the Bidwell Family Papers preserved at Yale University. The fact that James Dickinson discovered this kinship in 1869, long after his father's death, strongly suggests that there was no contact between the Dickinsons and Bidwell while they all lived in Canada (Yale University Library, Bidwell Family Papers, MSS. group 79,

series III, box 6, folder 245, James T. Dickinson to Marshall S. Bidwell, 25 February 1869; *In Memoriam M.S. Bidwell*, proceedings of a meeting of the New York bar honouring Bidwell after his death [n.p., n.d.]; Bigelow, *Bigelow Family Genealogy*, 1:129–30, 262–3; Craig, "Bidwell, Marshall Spring"; Mary-Jo Kline and Joanne Wood Ryan, eds., *Political Correspondence and Public Papers of Aaron Burr* [Princeton, NJ: Princeton University Press, 1983], 2:608; Patterson, "Bidwell, Barnabas").

56 Jacob Bigelow is said to have moved to Montreal around 1810. The earliest documentary evidence of Abijah Bigelow's presence dates from the summer of 1815 (ANQM, notary Desautels, no. 1825, 18 August 1815; SAP register, 24 December 1815; *Herald*, 23 December 1815; Bigelow, *Bigelow Family Genealogy*, 1:262).

57 From at least 1817, Abijah Bigelow was a partner with James McDouall, Daniel Ward Eager, and John Churchill Bush in James McDouall and Company, commission merchants. Jedediah Dorwin's first job in Montreal, in 1816, was as a clerk in their warehouse. James McDouall and Company was dissolved in 1819. Bigelow seems to have continued in business with McDouall for a couple of years, then with Eager. McDouall became a partner of the Molsons in the St Lawrence Steamboat Company in 1822, in which he held five shares. An advertisement for a sheriff's sale in 1830 showed that Bigelow and Eager still jointly owned a commercial property at Lachine at that time (ANQM, notary Bedouin, no. 1171, 7 April 1821; no. 2354, 25 April 1825; and no. 2398, 9 July 1825; notary Doucet, no. 4605, 11 October 1817; no. 4696 and no. 4697, 29 November 1817; no. 5908, 12 February 1819; no. 6584 and no. 6585, 11 September 1819; notary Griffin, no. 13815 and no. 13816, 29 April 1836; NA, MG 24, D 12, Dorwin Diaries, 1, part 1: 40, 45; *Courant*, 3 June 1820; *Herald*, 31 July 1819; *Vindicator*, 20 July 1830).

58 ANQM, notary Doucet, no. 5685, 25 November 1818; no. 6194, 1 May 1819; *Herald*, 13 April 1819, 12 August 1820; Bigelow, *Bigelow Family Genealogy*, 1:262.

59 Bigelow, *Bigelow Family Genealogy*, 1:264. Increase Sumner Bigelow has been confused with his older brother, Jacob, because newspapers abbreviated the names Increase Sumner to J.S. instead of I.S., just as they gave the initials of Deputy Commissary General Randolph Isham Routh as R.J. The substitution in print of the capital "J" for "I" sometimes led to quaint mistakes (the *Transcript* of 8 October 1836, for example, reported: "The Americans speak of adding two new States to the Union, to be called Jowa and Wisconsin"). The fact is, Jacob Bigelow had no middle name or initial.

60 Sansom, *Travels in Lower Canada*, 72.

61 Fox, *Yankees and Yorkers*, 193. For American immigration to Lower and Upper Canada, see chapters 4–5 of Hansen and Brebner, *The Mingling of the Canadian and American Peoples*.

62 The exact numbers are unknown. A writer in 1808 said he had heard that about 15,000 Americans had settled in the Townships. A modern view holds that, "Between 1791 and 1812 the English-speaking population of Lower Canada increased from 10,000 to 30,000 and nearly all of this increase can be attributed to the arrival of the Americans" (Gray, *Letters from Canada*, 349. Rudin, *The Forgotten Quebecers*, 57).

63 E. Cushing, *An Appeal*, 7.

64 Hansen and Brebner, *The Mingling of the Canadian and American Peoples*, 1:77.

65 NA, MG 24, D 8, Wright Papers, 6:1849–51, Thomas Mears to P. Wright & Sons, 27 August 1820.

66 *Vindicator*, 30 October 1835. See also E. Cushing, *An Appeal*, 73–80.

67 *Le Canadien*, 28 November 1807, cited in Ouellet, *Histoire économique et sociale*, 207–8: "Si malheureusement le Canada passoit, dans la suite des tems, sous la domination américaine, on ne tarderoit pas à sentir l'avidité et l'esprit d'accaparement des Américains; né dans le sein du commerce et avide de toutes especes de jouissances, l'Américain est prêt à tout entreprendre pour parvenir à son but. Les liens du sang, qui parlent si fortement dans le cœur de tous les hommes sont parfaitement nuls chez lui. Il peut laisser père, mère, frère, sœur, une épouse même tout aussi aisément qu'un Canadien peut le faire un Etranger. Celui-ci ne voudroit jamais abandonner la maison paternelle, celui-là, au contraire, aime les longs voyages et s'éloigne généralement de ses parens ... Le grand objet pour un Américain est toujours d'acheter et de revendre." According to Ouellet, French Canadians at the time of the War of 1812 saw the Americans not only as military invaders but as purveyors of values rejected by French Canada – commercial and industrial capitalism, republicanism, democracy, and so on. Creighton cites the above passage from *Le Canadien* and other similar material in discussing the clash between merchants and French Canadians (Creighton, *Empire of the St Lawrence*, 125–7, 153–62; Ouellet, *Histoire économique et sociale*, 229–32. See also Greenwood, *Legacies of Fear*, 191–2, 196–202).

68 *Gazette*, 20 January 1819, reproducing an item from *Le Canadien*: "Cette dernière classe augmente étonnemment, et si le pays n'adopte pas bien vite des mesures pour en arrêter les progrès, bientôt cette classe engloutira toutes les autres." The author, who signs himself "Un fidèle sujet," divides the population of Lower Canada into four main groups – native peoples; people of French descent; the English, Scots, Irish, and Germans; and recent American immigrants, supported by their Loyalist forerunners.

69 *Courant*, 10 March 1830, obituary notice. Mower published the *Courant* until 1 May 1829, ten months before his death, when he sold it for £1,000. In a brief farewell message to his subscribers, he remarked that "although not born a British subject, he feels an honest conviction of having

redeemed the pledge he made in the first number, that he 'should make it his duty to become a good subject, and endeavor to persuade others to continue so.'" The newspaper ceased publication in 1834 (ANQM, notary Bedouin, no. 3580, 2 June 1829; *Courant*, 6 June 1829, cited in R. Campbell, *History of the Scotch Presbyterian Church*, 259–60).

70 *Constitution and Bylaws of the New England Society in Montreal* (Montreal, 1854). On the other societies, see *Courant*, 26 June 1830; *Courier*, 28 March, 2 April, and 7 August 1835; *Gazette de Québec*, 18 August 1840; *Minerve*, 2 April and 3 August 1835; Senior, *Redcoats & Patriotes*, 105.

71 *Herald*, 18 November 1820; Bigelow, *Bigelow Family Genealogy*, 1:262. The wedding was on 31 October 1820.

72 ANQM, notary Griffin, no. 5181, 10 May 1824; Bigelow, *Bigelow Family Genealogy*, 1:262–3. The wedding was held on 13 May 1824.

73 *Courant*, 12 January 1826.

74 ANQM, SAP register, 9 September 1830, marriage of Samuel Ward and Abigail Hedge; 6 October 1831, burial of Abigail Hedge; notary Doucet, no. 20446, 24 April 1833; CU, Ward Family Collection, "Ward Family Genealogy" file; *Courant*, 11 September 1830; *Gazette*, 10 April 1834. Lyman, *Genealogy of the Lyman Family*, 60, errs in saying that none of Lydia Lyman's children ever married.

75 NA, MG 24, D 12, Dorwin Diaries, 1, part 1: 1, 40, 45. For Abijah Bigelow's connection with this firm, see note 57 above.

76 ANQM, notary Desautels, no. 3037, 7 April 1817; SAP register, 7 April 1817; NA, MG 24, D 12, Dorwin Diaries, 1, part 1: 54–6. Joseph Lough signed the marriage register as a witness. Austin Warner was a merchant tailor.

77 Dorwin died in Montreal on 12 November 1883 at the age of ninety-one (Tulchinsky, "Dorwin, Jedediah Hubbell").

78 New York title deeds, Essex County, E:103–4, H:123–4, J:231–2, R:489–90, T:447–50, X:45–50, X:89–90, EE: 148–9, WW:286–8; *Elizabethtown Post*, 31 October 1856 and 2 February 1871; Royce, *Bessboro*, 167–72, 223, 405–6, 444; Young monument in Westport cemetery. Young's wife, Jerusha Barber, born 22 September 1789, died at Westport on 6 September 1856. Young died at his daughter's home in Paola, Kansas, on 6 January 1871. His obituary in the *Elizabethtown Post* said, "He kept a careful diary of his trip with Sir George [Simpson]."

79 NA, MG 24, D 19, Ward Papers, ff. 32–4, John Ward to Silas Ward, 30 October 1821; ff. 24–6, same to same, 24 January 1821; ff. 42–4, same to same, 29 May 1823. On a similar clannishness practised by Scots and English, see Rudin, *The Forgotten Quebecers*, 82. Lebbeus Ward picked up his brother's refrain about pro-Scottish prejudice. When the government ordered an engine from the rival firm of Bennet and Henderson in 1829, he observed that the authorities had never inquired whether the Eagle

Foundry could supply it – "the reason probably is we are not Scotchmen." An order placed with a Scottish firm for a steam dredge in 1831 did nothing to allay his sense of grievance (see chap. 8, note 22). But the Wards must have been mollified at last when the Royal Navy awarded the Eagle Foundry a £4,950 contract in 1839 to build two 40-horsepower engines for a steamer intended for the Great Lakes (ANQM, notary Hunter, no. 1176, 15 August 1839; NA, MG 24, D 19, Ward Papers, ff. 52–5, Lebbeus Ward to John Ward, 5 February 1829).

80 NA, MG 24, D 19, Ward Papers, ff. 39–40, John Ward to Silas Ward, 20 May 1822, and ff. 42–4, same to same, 29 May 1823.

81 In seeking a receiving, or second, teller in April 1819, the Bank of Canada stated, "Security will be required and a knowledge of the French language is requisite." This was the position to which Jacob Bigelow was named and for which he posted a £2,000 bond on 1 May (ANQM, notary Doucet, no. 6194, 1 May 1819; *Herald*, 13 April 1819).

82 CU, John D. Ward diaries, 1827–1830, 3:101 and 4:16.

83 ANQM, notary Doucet, no. 5685, 25 November 1818. The De Witts acted in the same capacity in 1819 when Bigelow had to post a £2,000 bond on changing jobs at the bank, and again in 1823 when the £2,000 bond was renewed (ibid., no. 6194, 1 May 1819; no. 10858, 5 July 1823).

84 Richard, "Jacob De Witt," 537–8, dates the arrival of the De Witt family in Canada at 1802 when De Witt was "barely 17 years old." *La Minerve*, 13 March 1834, reports Jacob De Witt as stating that he had been a resident of Canada for thirty-three years. On the face of it, this statement would suggest that the family had arrived in 1801 when De Witt was fifteen.

85 Richard, "Jacob De Witt," 539; Robert, "De Witt, Jacob." The wedding took place at the Anglican church in Dunham. Richard says that Sophronia Frary and her parents were natives (*originaires*) of Hudson, New York. Her baptism record and the inscription on the De Witt family monument in Montreal's Mount Royal Cemetery indicate that she was born in Conway, Massachusetts, on 28 May 1797 (Erskine and American Church, Montreal, APC baptism register, 4 February 1825).

86 ANQM, APC register, 18 October 1835, 1 April 1838, and 6 September 1840.

87 In a legislature debate in 1834, De Witt rebutted a Tory accusation that he had refused to take the oath of allegiance to the Crown at the time of the War of 1812, insisting that he had done so "and that he had done his duty, to the best of his ability, as a British subject, in the 33 years he has lived in Canada" (*Minerve*, 13 March 1834).

88 Richard's "Jacob De Witt" provides an interesting overview of De Witt's career. For the Beauharnois election in 1830, see *Courant*, 16 October 1830; *Minerve*, 23 September, 4, 14, 25 October 1830; *Vindicator*, 12 and 15 October 1830. The *Vindicator* of 16 August 1831 carries a report on a

dinner given to De Witt and his fellow member for Beauharnois by their
electors. For the Banque du Peuple, see Greenfield, "La Banque du Peuple";
the partners in the abortive effort of 1833 are identified on pp. 1 and 97.
The bank's bills are described in *Minerve*, 6 July 1835, and *Vindicator*,
21 August 1835. For the Patriotic Union, formed on 2 May 1835, see
Minerve, 29 May 1835; *Vindicator*, 3 July 1835. In the 1840s, De Witt
would align himself with the moderate reformers under Louis–Hippolyte
La Fontaine. He supported the short–lived movement for annexation of
Canada to the United States in 1849. He was also instrumental in launching the New England Society of Montreal in 1854, five years before his
death on 23 March 1859.

89 ANQM, notary Doucet, no. 19979, 26 October 1832; *Courant*, 3 October
1832; *Minerve*, 16 May and 29 July 1833; *Vindicator*, 2 November 1832,
7 and 14 May 1833, 7 October 1834; Bibelow, *Bibelow Family Genealogy*,
1:262; Packard, *History of LaPorte County*, 207–9, 223–9, 235, 237; Siebert, *The Underground Railroad*, 117; Verney, *O'Callaghan*, 48–9, 56–61.
O'Callaghan married Charlotte Crampe at Sherbrooke on 22 March 1830.
Her sister, Elizabeth, had married Guy Carleton Colclough more than a
decade earlier. The Colcloughs were a martial family settled in the Drum-
mondville aera. The head of the clan, Beauchamp Colclough, known as
Major Colclough, was a former brigade major of the Irish militia of
County Carlow. He was among the passengers of the steamer *Henry
Brougham* held captive by rebels at Beauharnois in 1838 (see chap. 8). His
wife, Catherine, was the niece of eighteenth-century Canadian governor
Guy Carleton, Lord Dorchester. Their youngest daughter, Harriet Rebecca,
and her husband, lawyer Samuel Ussher, settled at Cobourg, Upper Canada, where he served as a captain in the 1st Battalion of Incorporated Militia in the Rebellions of 1837–38. Guy Colclough, agent of the British
American Land Company at Port St Francis in the 1830s, was mortally
wounded in an engagement with rebels in the fall of 1837 at Fort Erie,
Upper Canada, where he was serving as captain of the 103rd Regiment.
O'Callaghan's wife died in childbirth at Montreal on 17 July 1835 (ANQM,
register of Christ Church, Sorel, 3 August 1818, 27 November 1829,
20 and 24 November 1837, 10 March and 2 November 1840; ND register,
19 July 1835; *Courant*, 1 September 1830; *Gazette*, 21 November 1837,
12 November 1840; *Minerve*, 20 July 1835; *Transcript*, 23 November and
5 December 1837; *Vindicator*, 21 July 1835, 23 September, 15 November,
and 6 December 1836).

90 ANQM, 06, M-P26/1/11:24–5, Romuald Trudeau, "Mes tablettes," August
1832: "On a mis les actions à 30s. afin qu'elles fussent à la portée des
gens de la campagne, ce qui en effet les a engagés presque tous à prendre
une ou plusieurs parts, & leur a fait par conséquent contracter un intérêt
plus étroit au succès et à l'encouragement de cet établissement." The

contract for the building of the *Patriote Canadien*, signed before notary
P.E. Leclere on 16 December 1831, has not survived, but it is mentioned in
drafts of a protest by Sheay and Merritt against the boat's owners. A statement of accounts of the Canadian Patriot Steam Boat Company (also called
the Ferry Boat Company) published in 1835 shows that Sheay and Merritt were paid £1,595 18s. 10d. for the hull, which was described as 112 feet
(her register says 114 feet) long, 25 feet broad, with a depth of hold of
8 feet. Benett and Henderson were paid £2,550 for her engine and two
boilers (ANQM, notary Griffin, no. 13651, 11 February 1836, and no.
16955, 9 April 1840; notary Hunter, no. 268, 9 February 1837; no. 293,
10 March 1837; nos. 919 and 922, 5 October 1838; no. 1150, 2 July 1839;
notary Leclere, no. 85, 9 September 1831; no. 106, 2 April 1832; no. 107,
3 April 1832; NA, RG 42, E 1, Dept. of Marine, Ship Registers v. 175: no. 3
for 1832; *Courier*, 21 April 1835; *Gazette*, 26 March 1832, 5, 28 February,
and 5 May 1835; *Minerve*, 22 May, 16 and 30 June 1834, 6, 20 April,
7 and 11 May 1835, 1 June 1837; *Vindicator*, 24 June and 1 July 1834,
6 February, 3 and 10 April 1835, 17 February 1837).

91 *Courant*, 27 December 1820, 2 and 30 January 1822, 29 March 1825;
Gazette, 30 January 1822; Gall and Jordan, *One Hundred Years of Fire
Insurance*, 32, 59–60, 160–1. There is a copy of an Aetna policy sold by
Bigelow in MU, MS 234, Lyman Family Papers, folder marked "William
Lyman & Co., Insurance and financial papers 1835–56." Bigelow's appoint-
ment seems to have predated by only a couple of months that of an agent
at Kingston for the Franklin Fire Insurance Company of New York (see
Kingston Chronicle, 31 May 1822).

92 NA, MG 28, III 44, v. 1, Montreal Board of Trade, Register and Correspondence of the Committee of Trade, 11 April 1822; *Courant*, 17 April 1822,
25 and 28 November 1829, 25 September 1830; *Gazette*, 26 November
1829; *Minerve*, 15 October 1827.

CHAPTER FOUR

1 Dorwin, "Montreal in 1816."

2 *Gazette*, 31 October 1834; *Vindicator*, 30 August 1833.

3 While his Upper Canada mail service continued to grow, Dickinson cur-
tailed his involvement in mail carriage to Quebec after his first £1,560-a-
year contract expired in 1824. That year he entered into a one-year contract that began 6 April, covered only half the route – between Montreal
and Three Rivers – and paid £638 1s. 8d. No contract has been found for
1825–26, but in 1826 Dickinson again contracted to carry the mails
between Montreal and Three Rivers, this time for three years, from 5 April
1826 to 5 April 1829, at the rate of £671 13s. 4d. per year. That was the
last contract he held on the route, though he probably continued as a

subcontractor because the inventory of his effects at his death in 1832 lists a few items "employed in mail contract towards Quebec." He continued to operate a winter passenger service between Montreal and Quebec until 1830–31. The previous winter some enterprising French-Canadian residents of Quebec, Berthier, and Montreal had set up a competing line of stages. In response, Dickinson, who had charged £3 (12d. per league of three miles) for the full distance in 1819–20 and then reduced his rate to £2 10s. (10d. per league) by 1823–24, slashed his price to £1 10s. (6d. per league), half the fare charged a decade earlier. After the winter of 1830–31, he seems to have abandoned the field (ANQM, notary Bedouin, no. 3475, 16 March 1829; notary Doucet, no. 19686, 2 July 1832; notary Griffin, no. 2381, 17 October 1818; no. 5245, 23 June 1824; no. 6547, 7 June 1826; *Courant*, 25 December 1819, 30 December 1820, 29 November 1823, 14 February, and 15 December 1824, 10 December 1825, 27 December 1826, 5 January 1828, 16 December 1829, 27 January, 8 February, and 15 December 1830; *Gazette*, 17 December 1827, 29 December 1828; *Minerve*, 10 January 1828; *Vindicator*, 8 January and 26 January 1830, 13 December 1831; Lambert, *Les anciennes diligences du Québec*, 40–1, 63–4).

4 *Courant*, 30 December 1820, 1 and 18 December 1821, 30 November 1822, 17 January, 20 November, 8 and 18 December 1824, 12 January 1825, 18, 25 November and 9 December 1826, 16 December 1829, 18 December 1830; *Gazette*, 6 and 17 December 1827, 29 December 1828, 8, 15, 16, and 19 January 1829; Lambert, *Les anciennes diligences du Québec*, 54–6. One of Easinhart's mail contracts is found in ANQM, notary Griffin, no. 7780, 7 July 1828.

5 There was some confusion as to the rules governing vessels used for inland navigation. The British navigation act of 1786 required boats to be British owned but exempted them from having to be registered with the customs service. A supplement to the *Herald* of 20 May 1820, however, carried this notice: "The Honble Commissioners of H.M. Customs have decided that Steam Boats, and other Vessels, solely employed in navigating the River Saint Lawrence, are not considered to fall within the exemption contained in the 6th Section of the Act 26th Geo. 3d, Cap. 60, and are required to be registered as well as owned by British Subjects." The *Herald* of 27 May 1820 commented that this interpretation had caused great astonishment. It was to remain a dead letter, however, for boats confined to Lakes St Louis and St Francis and the Ottawa River since no port of registry was accessible to them. Besides, registration was not strictly enforced until after mid-century, though the requirement seems to have been a factor in the seizure and brief detention of the *Hercules* at Quebec in 1825 (*Courant* and *Gazette*, 26 October and 31 December 1825; Bush, *Commercial Navigation on the Rideau Canal*, 23, 56–7; Marcil, *The Charley-Man*, 364–6). The *Kingston Chronicle* of 18 July 1823 published a notice by Christopher A.

Hagerman, collector of customs at Kingston, and a letter signed "Navigator" that cast an interesting light on the enforcement of the laws in Upper Canada. Hagerman's notice, dated 7 July 1823, stated that foreign boats "can no longer be engaged in the Carrying Trade of this Province, instructions having been received from his Majesty's Government to enforce the Navigation Laws, which particularly prohibit their being so employed." The notice stated further that the master and three-fourths of the crew of all vessels carrying goods from one British port to another had to be British subjects. The letter from "Navigator" said in part: "The Collector at this port has invariably ... informed the parties interested, that the employment of foreign bottoms in the home trade, was contrary to the provisions of British Statutes, but he at the same time stated, that *he* should not interrupt a practice which had been so long permitted, without positive instructions to that effect from the Government; these instructions it appears have been some time issued to all the Collectors of the Province, and if I am correctly informed, have been given in consequence of a clause contained in the Canada trade act, passed by the Imperial Parliament after its last session, which recognizes the British Navigation laws as being in full force here, and imposing on the Colonial Government the necessity of strictly enforcing them."

6 ANQM, notary Doucet, no. 5998, 15 March 1819; no. 7239, 20 February 1820; notary Huguet-Latour, no. 1851, 30 March 1824; notary Jobin, no. 2198, 2 March 1821; no. 3348, 9 March 1824; *Courant*, 5 May 1821, 6 May 1829; *Herald*, 13 April 1820.

7 ANQM, SAP register, 19 July 1821; *Courant*, 21 July 1821. The fact that she had borne three children in just over four years (October 1806–January 1811) and then none in the last ten years of her life may hint at a health problem stemming from that last birth. When Dickinson remarried, he proceeded to father five more children in seven years.

8 ANQM, notary Bedouin, no. 1208, 9 May 1821. John C. Langdon was the son and business partner of Barnabas Langdon of Troy, who patented a turntable design for horse-ferry machinery on 5 June 1819. That same year, Barnabas Langdon and a partner had built a boat fitted with this horizontal treadwheel, for use as a ferry across the Hudson River. More than a decade later, a Troy, New York, newspaper referred to Barnabas Langdon as "the inventor of the Horse Ferry Boat, which has come into very general use" (*St Lawrence Republican*, 11 February 1834, copying the *Troy Budget*; Beach, *Lake Champlain*, 81–4; Crisman and Cohn, *The Burlington Bay Horse Ferry Wreck*, 19–26; Crisman and Cohn, *When Horses Walked on Water*, 61–87).

9 Another possibility is that Dickinson had ordered the machinery, not for himself, but for a group of four Montrealers who had formed a partnership to build a horse ferry, the *Non-such*, to run between Montreal and

Longueuil. One of the partners was his friend, baker and flour inspector
Nahum Hall, a native of Keene, New Hampshire; another was Seth
Pomeroy, then operator of the City Tavern (ANQM, Cour Supérieure-
Montréal, 1822, no. 471, Guy Warwick et al. v. Seth Pomeroy et al.; notary
Lukin Jr, no. 112, 5 April 1821).

10 Whipple took the oath on 2 July 1822 before Cornwall postmaster and
magistrate Guy Carleton Wood (see NA, RG 1, L 3, Upper Canada Land
Petitions, 556, no. 43).

11 *Courant*, 28 June 1823, advertisement for *Cornwall*.

12 ANQM, notary Griffin, no. 5244, 23 June 1824, two-year contract Montreal-Kingston; no. 5245, 23 June 1824, one-year contract Montreal-Three
Rivers; no. 6546, 7 June 1826, five-year contract Montreal-Kingston;
no. 6547, 7 June 1826, three-year contract Montreal-Three Rivers;
no. 7109, 5 March 1827, four-year contract Kingston-York.

13 On his own account and through James McDouall and Company, Abijah
Bigelow had business connections in St Lawrence County, New York,
where Dickinson had lived. In the fall of 1816 Bigelow lent $1,000 on
mortgage to a resident of Hopkinton, the town from which Russell was
carved. In 1821 he acted in a land transaction as the attorney for Russell
Atwater, founder of Russell and the man who had sold Dickinson a village
lot there in 1814 (ANQM, notary Doucet, no. 4953, 20 February 1818;
no. 8728$\frac{1}{2}$, 17 May 1821; no. 9290, 1 December 1821; New York title
deeds, St Lawrence County, 4:166, 349, and 6:295; *St Lawrence Gazette*,
21 April 1818; Durant and Peirce, *History of St Lawrence County*, 426).

14 *Courant*, 17 May 1823. Bigelow, *Bigelow Family* Genealogy, 1:129–30.

15 NA, MG 24, D 12, Dorwin diaries, 1, part 1: 104; *Gazette*, 4 April 1823;
Lighthall, *Short History of the American Presbyterian Church of Montreal*, 3, 6.

16 Knowles, "American Presbyterian Church of Montreal," 18; McDougall,
"The American Element in the Early Presbyterian Church in Montreal,"
158–60.

17 *Courant*, 11 December 1822; Bosworth, *Hochelaga Depicta*, 113; Lighthall,
Short History of the American Presbyterian Church of Montreal, 3–6, 38.

18 *Statutes of Lower Canada*, 1 William IV, c. 56, An Act to afford relief to a
certain Religious Congregation at Montreal, denominated Presbyterians;
Knowles, "American Presbyterian Church of Montreal," 19, 42; Lighthall,
Short History of the American Presbyterian Church of Montreal, 4.

19 *Herald*, 5 February 1823. Lighthall, *Short History of the American Presbyterian Church of Montreal*, 4–6.

20 See *Herald*, 5 February 1833, "Strictures upon the Manifesto of the New
'American Association.'"

21 Lighthall, *Short History of the American Presbyterian Church of Montreal*, 4.

22 Ibid.

23 NA, MG 24, D 12, Dorwin Diaries, 1, part 1: 104. Knowles, "American Presbyterian Church of Montreal," 21, 32–3; Lighthall, *Short History of the
American Presbyterian Church of Montreal*, 6–7.

24 *Scribbler* 5, no. 121 (13 May 1824): 124.

25 *Gazette*, 28 July and 4 August 1824; Lighthall, *Short History of the American Presbyterian Church of Montreal*, 7–9; Lord, *Memoir of the Rev.
Joseph Stibbs Christmas*, 9, 47, 54. Christmas was born on 10 April 1803
in Georgetown, Beaver County, Pennsylvania. Asthmatic, of a delicate constitution, he retired from his Montreal charge on grounds of ill health in
1828 and moved to New York. Named minister of the Bowery Presbyterian Church in October 1829, he died five months later, on 14 March 1830.
La Minerve published a fanciful death notice asserting that he was really a
French-Canadian Catholic apostate by the name of Noël (See *Minerve*,
25 March 1830, and rebuttal in *Courant*, 31 March 1830).

26 In 1834 Marshall's son, Aaron Foster Marshall, married Dickinson's niece
by marriage, Frances Maria Bigelow, of Leicester, Massachusetts, daughter
of Marshall Spring Bigelow. The marriage contract was drawn up in Montreal, with Dickinson's widow, Mercy Amelia Bigelow, acting as attorney
for her niece (ANQM, notary Doucet, no. 21518, 7 April 1834).

27 ANQM, notary Griffin, no. 5399, 4 October 1824; no. 5506, 7 January 1825;
Courant, 31 December 1824; *Gazette*, 18 June 1825; *Herald*, 1 and 15 June
1825.

28 Knowles, "American Presbyterian Church of Montreal," 76.

29 Cited in Campbell, *History of the Scotch Presbyterian Church*, 752–3, and
in Lighthall, *Short History of the American Presbyterian Church of Montreal*, 10. Mackenzie himself had been married at Montreal's St Andrew's
Presbyterian Church in 1822, a few months before Dickinson and others
seceded to form the American Presbyterian Church (ANQM, SAP register,
1 July 1822).

30 *Statutes of Lower Canada*, 1 William IV, c. 56, An Act to afford relief to a
certain Religious Congregation at Montreal, denominated Presbyterians;
Lord, *Memoir of the Rev. Joseph Stibbs Christmas*, 144–6.

31 ANQM, SGP register, 8 September 1829; SAP register, 7 September 1831.
Courant, 9 September 1829; *Vindicator*, 13 September 1831; Lighthall,
Short History of the American Presbyterian Church of Montreal, 11.
Perkins was installed as minister on 30 May 1830. Dickinson's son, James,
married twice, in 1832 and 1845, both times in the United States
(J.T. Dickinson, *Genealogies*, 17).

32 For Christmas's explanation of this point, see Lord, *Memoir of the Rev.
Joseph Stibbs Christmas*, 145–6. Dickinson's children by his second mar-
riage were Horace, born 27 January 1824, baptised 8 August 1825; Edward
Sumner, born 20 September 1825, baptised 20 July 1826; Sarah Spring,

born 29 July 1827, baptised 18 November 1827; Charles Perkins, born 8 March 1829, baptised 20 June 1830; Ellen (Ellen Maria), born 31 December 1830, baptised 28 June 1831. The records of these baptisms were found in the original APC registers, January 1825–August 1828 and June 1830–July 1832, consulted at the Erskine and American Church, Montreal. They were not among the microfilmed APC records at the ANQM.

33 NA, MG 24, D 19, Ward Papers, ff. 78–83, contract for the *Hercules* engine, 3 February 1823. The contract bound Ward to repay all advances should experts rule the finished engine unsatisfactory. Dickinson acted as one of Ward's main guarantors. Others included Jacob De Witt, Nahum Mower, and Horatio Gates.

34 At his death, Dickinson owed £338 5s. 2d. to the Aetna Insurance Company (ANQM, notary Doucet, no. 19686, 2 July 1832, seventh page from the end).

35 *Courant*, 16 July 1825; *Herald*, 16 July 1825.

36 ANQM, notary Griffin, no. 6160, 2 January 1826.

37 *Courant*, 12 August 1829, 18 May 1830. In the latter advertisement, Bigelow seems to suggest that he covered risks on the St Lawrence only. He was associated at this time with lawyer Marcus Burritt of Prescott, who handled applications for insurance at that end of the line. In 1834 Burritt would marry Anne Eliza Sexton, widow of Levi Sexton, at the Prescott home of Samuel Crane (*Brockville Recorder*, 4 July 1834).

38 *Courant*, 24, 31 March and 14 August 1830. The joint-stock company, with a capital of £12,500 divided into 1,000 shares, was established at Montreal on 24 March 1830 at a meeting called by merchants Thomas B. Anderson, Horatio Gates, Peter McGill, and George Moffatt. Gates and Moffatt were named trustees along with Henry Jones, partner in the Brockville forwarding company H. and S. Jones (called H. Jones and Company at Montreal). Forwarder John Macpherson of John Macpherson and Company was appointed secretary, as well as agent of the company at Montreal. Jones's cousin, Alpheus Jones, the postmaster and collector of customs at Prescott, was named agent there. The company went into operation in August, prepared to cover risks up to £1,250 on the waters between Quebec and Detroit. The agreement setting up the company was valid for five years.

39 *Courant*, 27 November 1830. *Gazette*, 17 August 1829, 26 August 1830.

40 *Courant*, 23 June 1830; Bosworth, *Hochelaga Depicta*, 188–90. Jacob De Witt was president of the society, Dickinson vice-president.

41 *Gazette*, 30 October 1832.

42 In 1822, for example, the pilot of the *Montreal* had been heard to shout a very uncivil "Hard a–port, you bugger!" before a near collision with the *Laprairie*. The *Montreal's* fireman, blacksmith Nathaniel Walker, was guaranteed three glasses of rum daily – "but no tea or Coffee" – in addition to

his monthly wage of £3 15s. (ANQM, notary Bedouin, no. 1566, 5 March 1822; *Gazette,* 5 October 1822).

43 *Courant,* 31 July 1830.

44 *Scribbler* 4, no. 13 (15 January 1824): 288. Dickinson was not alone in obstructing delivery of Wilcocke's magazine. When *Scribbler* subscriber Philemon Wright complained of difficulties in receiving his magazines at Hull in 1823, Wilcocke told him: "I am informed that Mr [Archibald] Mac-Millan the post master at Grenville takes upon himself to detain them ... Besides I also understand that Mr [Guy] Richards the postmaster at St Andrews has done the same thing." Wilcocke attributed the problem to Deputy Postmaster General Daniel Sutherland's "bad faith & arbitrary conduct" (NA, MG 24, D 8, Wright Papers, 10:3193–4, Wilcocke to P. Wright, 9 March 1823. For an earlier spat between Wilcocke and the Post Office, see the notice by Montreal postmaster James Williams in *Gazette,* 9 November 1822).

45 *Courant,* 6 November 1830.

46 *Vindicator,* 21 December 1830.

47 Ibid., 28 December 1830.

48 Unsigned advertisement in *Courant,* 11 June 1831.

49 *Gazette,* 14 May 1833; *Vindicator,* 28 May 1833.

50 Tappan, *Life of Arthur Tappan,* 13, 44–58, 86–8, 96–102; Wyatt-Brown, *Lewis Tappan,* 53–4. From 1809 to 1812 Arthur Tappan and a partner operated a dry-goods business in Montreal. They returned to the United States on the outbreak of the war. As regards Lewis Tappan, Jacob Bigelow, as "manager" of the Underground Railroad in Washington, DC, worked with him, notably in 1854–55 in the rescue of a fifteen-year-old slave girl who, disguised as a boy, was smuggled from Washington to her uncle in south-western Ontario (Library of Congress, Lewis Tappan Manuscripts, Diary of Lewis Tappan, entries of 19 and 20 July, 30 November and 3 December 1855; letter of Lewis Tappan to Dr Ellwood Harvey, 4 December 1855; Lewis Tappan to J. Bigelow, 3 December and 6 December 1855; Lewis Tappan to Henry Richardson, 27 July 1855; Sarah Tappan to Henry Richardson, 8 December 1855; Siebert, *The Underground Railroad,* 117, 436; Still, *The Underground Railroad,* 177–87, 685–8; Wyatt-Brown, *Lewis Tappan,* 330).

51 In 1841, for example, Sabbatarian pressure dovetailed with efforts by the U.S. postal service to bring its budget under control. Sunday mail service was discontinued on many routes, including that between Albany and the border town of Highgate, Vermont. This development upset Montreal businessmen and prompted a remonstrance from Deputy Postmaster General Thomas A. Stayner because it meant that American mail, as well as overseas mail landed at New York, could no longer be picked up at Highgate

for delivery in Montreal on Monday afternoons. The curtailing of Sunday mail carriage in the U.S. at that time coincided with the introduction of seven-day-a-week mail service in Canada. Prominent Kingstonians protested to the governor about Sunday mail service in 1841–42; in the latter year, Quebecers, including the Anglican bishop and the mayor, vainly petitioned the governor to have the post office in that city closed on Sundays. Sabbatarians did not target only the postal service. In 1834 the assistant minister of St George's Church in Kingston called on steamboat owners to refrain from operating their vessels on Sunday. In 1869, residents of Merrickville called for the Sunday closing of the Rideau Canal (*Gazette*, 20 March, 22 April, 15 June, and 3 July 1841, 26 March 1842; *Hallowell Free Press*, 14 April 1834; *Kingston Chronicle*, 14 July 1841, 16 April 1842; Bush, *Commercial Navigation on the Rideau Canal*, 77–9).

52 *Courant*, 12 and 16 August 1826, 23 June, 4, 8 September 1830, 24 August 1831.

53 *Herald*, 22 September 1825.

54 NA, MG 24, D 8, Wright Papers, 14:5145–7, H. Gates & Co. to P. Wright, 4 June 1826.

55 *Gazette*, 14 April 1826.

56 ANQM, 06,M-P26/1/4, Fonds Romuald Trudeau, "Mes Tablettes," 38–41: "Les chantiers sont presque tous inactifs. La compagnie organisée pour faire bâtir des vaisseaux en Canada renvoye presque tous ses ouvriers, ou si elle s'en réserve quelques uns, ce n'est qu'en leur allouant la moitié des gages ordinaires. Le gouvernement a même arrêté tous ses nombreux travaux dans l'Ile Ste Hélène, l'Ile aux Noix, Québec, &c. – Les trois quarts et demi des marchands n'ont pas vendu à peine dans tout l'hiver pour payer leurs dépenses." The shipbuilding company mentioned by Trudeau was the British North American Ship Building Company, organized by London and Canadian interests. A report on the company's prospectus is found in the *Herald*, 28 May 1825.

57 *Courant*, 3 November 1824, 12 January, 5 February, 4 May 1825; *Herald*, 30 October, 3, 24 November, 1, 11, 15 December 1824, 12 January, 2 February 1825. The prospectus of the association proposed the formation of a joint-stock company "having the exclusive privilege for a certain number of years of navigating the Rapids of the River St Lawrence." The *Courant* was later to claim that the association had been torpedoed "by intrigues in the Capital of Upper Canada" (*Courant*, 4 December 1830).

58 The Moulinette locks were owned and operated by Adam Dixon from 1817 nearly until the time of his death in 1837. Under an agreement of 1 May 1826 with forwarders John Macpherson and Company, McCutchon and Crossman, Donald Duff, and Hooker and Henderson, Dixon agreed to repair his locks, in return for which the forwarders would pay him 2s. 6d. for every batteau and 5s. for every Durham boat they took through. In

1830 he charged 3s. 9d. for "barges" (ANQM, notary Arnoldi, no. 3030, 28 November 1833; notary Griffin, no. 6438, 1 May 1826; *Courant*, 5 May 1821, 10 July 1830; *Gazette*, 20 May 1837; *Herald*, 10 May 1817, 25 April 1818).

59 Legget, *Ottawa River Canals*, 79, 91.

60 ANQM, notary Griffin, no. 6160, 2 January 1826; *Herald*, 13 May 1826.

61 ANQM, notary Charlebois, no. 100, 6 November 1826; notary Doucet, no. 19686, 2 July 1832; *Gazette*, 24 September 1827, 21 April 1828; Dwight, *The Northern Traveller* (1830 ed.), 105. *Neptune* captain Asahel Whipple and George Brush listed the engine as a 67-horsepower in the 1832 inventory of Dickinson's estate. Newspapers referred to it as 70-horsepower, while Dwight's guidebook said 69-horsepower.

62 ANQM, notary Doucet, no. 19686, inventory of Dickinson estate, 2 July 1832; *Gazette*, 24 September 1827. The inventory valued Dickinson's other boats thus: *Dalhousie*, boat and engine, £500; *Swan*, new boat with engine taken from the *St Lawrence*, £1,510; *Henry Brougham* and *Iroquois*, both new but without their engines, £950 and £500 respectively. The *Chateauguay* was noted in the inventory, but without valuation.

63 Young returned to Lake Champlain in the fall of 1827 to oversee repairs and renovations to the steamers *Phoenix II* and *Congress*. At this time, the *Phoenix II* was converted from passenger service to a freight boat (ANQM, notary O'Keeffe, no. 620–6, no. 630, and no. 633, nine related hiring contracts that Young signed between 2 November and 15 November 1827; Bellico, *Sails and Steam in the Mountains*, 263).

64 ANQM, notary Doucet, no. 25023, 27 September 1837. When Waters, named the first postmaster at the Cedars in 1837, offered to let his inn at the Cascades in 1839, it was described as "joining the Steamboat Wharf" (*Gazette*, 13 May 1837; *Transcript*, 26 March 1839).

65 ANQM, notary Mondelet, no. 548, 20 June 1826.

66 ANQM, notary Doucet, no. 22989, 6 October 1835; no. 19686, 2 July 1832; notary Jobin, no. 4407, 12 October 1827; no. 4979, 11 December 1829; no. 5105, 15 July 1833; no. 5332, 18 April 1838; notary Leblanc, no. 2241, 3 August 1832.

67 *Courant*, 8 July 1829; *Gazette*, 31 May 1827. The *Niagara*, built at Brockville as a sailing vessel in 1825, was lengthened and turned into a steamer the following year. The *Alciope*, built at Niagara in 1827–28 for Robert Hamilton, was fitted with the old *Frontenac's* 50-horsepower Boulton and Watt engine, refurbished by the Ward foundry. Besides the *Frontenac's* engine, she had that boat's captain, James McKenzie. In 1831–32 she was remodelled, fitted with two new 60-horsepower, high-pressure engines of American manufacture, and renamed the *United Kingdom*. At the end of 1834 Hamilton, planning to retire, offered her for sale as "the best Sea Boat on Lake Ontario." Her next owner, H.H. Smith of Youngstown, New

York, converted her into a brig and changed her name to *Birmingham* (ANQM, notary Griffin, no. 7531, 9 November 1827; *Brockville Recorder*, 30 August 1832; *Gazette*, 12 April and 6 September 1832, 3 September 1835; *Kingston Chronicle*, 27 December 1835; Lewis, "McKenzie, James," 470; Mills, *Canadian Coastal and Inland Steam Vessels*, 6, 84; Robertson, *Landmarks of Toronto*, 2:852, 854–5; Wightman, "The Adelaide and Early Canadian Steam above Niagara," 17–18).

68 *Gazette*, 3 and 10 May 1827. Connolly's term as captain was brief: he died on 28 August. He was succeeded by Daniel De Hertel of St Andrew's, stepson of Theodore Davis and son-in-law of former *Gazette* owner James Brown (ANQM, register of St Michel church, Lachine, 30 August 1827; *Gazette*, 30 August 1827, 24 July 1828; Armour, "Robertson, Daniel," 716; Thomas, *History of ... Argenteuil ... [and] Prescott*, 80, 108).

69 Annesley, *A New System of Naval Architecture*, 5–16; National Patent Office, London, no. 4240, 8 April 1818, and no. 4549, 5 April 1821, "Specification of William Annesley," 2. The first Annesley steamboat, built at Selby, Yorkshire, was the *Aire*, which ran from July 1821 on the River Humber between Hull and Selby, performing the 55-mile trip in three hours and five minutes.

70 In his *New System of Naval Architecture*, Annesley named his son, Lawson Annesley of Belfast, as agent to handle applications for use of his patent (the premium was 5s. per registered ton). By 1824 Annesley and his son had both moved to Albany, New York. Annesley gave the first sign of his presence in Montreal in the *Gazette* of 8 May 1824. Three days earlier the newspaper had carried a report on the English steamboat *Aire*, "built on Annesly & Lowerby's patent." In its 8 May issue the *Gazette* printed a brief note from Annesley correcting the spelling of his name and stating that he was the sole patent holder. Acknowledging its error, the newspaper noted that in two days Annesley was to start building his first Canadian steamboat "near Hart Logan & Co.'s Ship-Yard." From 20 July, Annesley advertised his patent, offering to give "Estimates, Drawings and instructions to those disposed to adopt the system, and grant Licences to build at Three Shillings per ton register, for Boats and Sea Vessels. During his absence his Son [William Annesley jr] will act for him by Attorney" (*Gazette*, 4 August 1824).

71 ANQM, notary Lindsay, no. 43, 13 May 1824; *Courant*, 22 March 1823, 24 January 1834. Sherman was building the *Mountaineer*, the second steamer on Lake George, New York. Based on Annesley's system, her hull was made of three layers of one-inch oak planks, two fore-and-aft and one transverse. Sherman had a family connection in Montreal at this time. A year earlier, at his request, John Molson had hired his son, Jahaziel B. Sherman, as captain of one of his Montreal-Quebec steamers (ANQM, notary Griffin, no. 5636, 15 March 1825; Bellico, *Sails and Steam in the*

Mountains, 292–3; Van de Water, *Lake Champlain and Lake George,* 286–7; G.H. Wilson, "The Application of Steam to St Lawrence Valley Navigation," 240–1).

72 ANQM, notary Lindsay, no. 42 and no. 43, 13 May 1824; NA, RG 42 E 1, Dept. of Marine, Ship Registers, 184:0078; *Herald,* 14, 28, 31 July 1824.

73 ANQM, notary Bedouin, no. 2466, 10 November 1825; no. 2476, 26 November 1825; no. 2486, 16 December 1825; no. 2488, 22 December 1825; no. 2495, 30 December 1825; notary Doucet, no. 12064, 12 October 1824; no. 13278, 19 January 1826; no. 13491, 2 April 1826; no. 13499, 4 April 1826; no. 13501, 4 April 1826; no. 13704, 22 June 1826; no. 14138, 13 November 1826; notary Lindsay, no. 74, 5 October 1824; no. 75, 6 October 1824; no. 78, 15 November 1824; NA RG 42, E 1, Dept. of Marine, Ship Registers, 184:0078; *Courant,* 11 August 1824, 22 April and 6 December 1826; *Herald,* 11 September 1824, 11 May 1825, 22 April 1826. The *Toronto,* launched at York on 23 April 1825, ran between York and Niagara. Her captain, William Shaw, died on 26 September. In 1826 she was moved to the Prescott–Bay of Quinte route, and in 1834 to the Rideau Canal (*Herald,* 6 October 1825; Lewis, "The Steamer *Toronto* of 1825").

74 White, builder of the cabins on John Molson's first two steamers, the *Accommodation* and the *Swiftsure,* had worked with Bagg as a contractor on the building of the Lachine Canal. On the Rideau he was to work in partnership with Thomas Phillips, another Lachine Canal contractor. For work on the Rideau, Phillips and White were also involved in a consortium with masons Thomas McKay and John Redpath similar to the joint venture of James Greenfield, William Spier, William Lauder, and Peter Rutherford (see chap. 2). White's Rideau associates went on to become prominent businessmen, Phillips and Redpath at Montreal and McKay at what is now Ottawa. White himself died of cholera on 11 July 1832, shortly after the canal opened (*Courant,* 14 July 1832; Heisler, *Les canaux du Canada,* 86; Legget, *Rideau Waterway,* 166–7; Stewart, *Loyalists of Quebec,* 344, 346).

75 ANQM, notary Doucet, no. 14339, no. 14342, and no. 14343, 12 February 1827; no. 14740, 30 August 1827.

76 ANQM, notary Doucet, no. 14740 and no. 14741, 30 August 1827.

77 "l'objet du dit Sieur Mears seroit frustré Sil étoit Connu que tel a été ses vues en faisans l'acquisition du dit Bateau."

78 "Que le dit Sieur Mears fait l'acquisition du dit Bateau que dans la visé d'empêcher la Compétition qui pourroit s'établir par d'autres personnes qui pouroient naviguer un autre bateau à Vapeur sur la Rivière des Outaouais où le dit Sieur Mears en a déjà un."

79 The acknowledgments of McGill's payments totalling £1,045 6d. are annexed to the original deed of sale, ANQM, notary Doucet, no. 14740, 30 August 1827. The connection between Mears and McGill probably dated

from 1809 when McGill (then called Peter McCutchon) and his brother, William McCutchon, both minors, were apprenticed for four years as clerks respectively to Parker, Gerrard, Ogilvy and Company in Montreal and its Quebec branch, John Mure and Company. Mears did business with these firms – in fact, at the time McGill went to work for Parker, Gerrard, Ogilvy, Mears owed the company £700, which he had promised to pay off in timber by 1 August (ANQM, notary Gray, no. 1952, 17 October 1807; no. 2168, 1 October 1808; no. 2397, 6 June 1809; no. 2403, 10 June 1809).

80 ANQM, notary Doucet, no. 14740, 30 August 1827 (with attached ratification by Mears, dated 4 September 1827); no. $14754\frac{1}{2}$, 4 September 1827; no. 15916, 22 January 1829. Gates, born in Barre, Massachusetts, and a resident of Montreal since shortly before the War of 1812, was the leading American businessman in the city. A wholesale merchant and prominent figure in the import-export trade, he was, like Thomas Turner, among the founders of both the Bank of Montreal and the Bank of Canada, serving as president of the former in 1826 and 1832–34 and of the latter in 1826–31. He was named to the Legislative Council in 1833, an appointment that earned him savage attacks from some reformers, who labelled him an "apostate republican." He died of a stroke in April 1834 (*Gazette*, 17 April 1834; *Minerve*, 7 April and 10 April 1834; Robert, "Gates, Horatio"; Shortt, *History of Canadian Currency and Banking*, 776–89).

81 ANQM, notary Doucet, no. $14761\frac{1}{2}$, 5 September 1827.

82 *Gazette*, 3 September and 24 December 1827, 17 April 1828, 4 July 1833; Legget, *Ottawa River Canals*, 76–7, 82–3, 90; Thomas, *History of ... Prescott ... [and] Argenteuil*, 509.

83 NA, MG 24, D 8, Wright Papers, 133:69797–800, Union Steam Boat Co. agreement, 30 April 1827; 17:6149–50, G. King to Tiberius Wright, 8 January 1828; 17:6157–8, Mears to P. Wright & Sons, 12 January 1828; 17:6258–9, Mears to Capt. William Grant, 20 May 1828; 17:6268–73, Mears to P. Wright & Sons, with copy of letter to Grant enclosed, 29 May 1828; 17:6348–9, Mears to Ruggles Wright, 1 July 1828; 17:6391–2, Mears to P. Wright & Sons, 25 July 1828; 17:6415–16, Mears to Ruggles Wright, 15 August 1828; 33:14751–2, P. Wright to Mears, 30 June 1828; 33:14749–50, P. Wright to Grant, 30 June 1828; 19:7085–7, Eden Johnson to P. Wright & Sons, 9 March 1830; 19:7097–8, Mears to Ruggles Wright, 13 March 1830; 34:14946–9, P. Wright to Mears, 16 March 1830; 19:7114–17, Mears to Ruggles Wright, 18 March 1830; 19:7162–3, Eden Johnson to J.L. Morrison, 2 August 1830; Lamirande and Séguin, *A Foregone Fleet*, 4, 6.

84 NA, MG 24, D 8, Wright Papers, 17:6415–16, Mears to Ruggles Wright, 15 August 1828; *Kingston Chronicle*, 15 May 1830. Fleming had built the horse boat *Experiment* for Silas Dickinson in 1826. William Grant would

hire him to build the steamer *Lady Colborne* at Aylmer in 1832 (ANQM, notary Doucet, no. 13564, 27 April 1826; notary Griffin, no. 9907, 4 June 1832. See also below, note 86).

85 NA, MG 24, D 8, Wright Papers, 17:6415–16, Mears to Ruggles Wright, 15 August 1828; *Courant*, 31 October 1829; *Gazette*, 28 July and 13 October 1828, 9 November 1829, 4 July 1833. The Molsons' St Lawrence Steamboat Company, which held sixty-four shares in the new concern, was reported to have received forty of those in payment for the *Quebec's* engines, made by Maudslay and Sons of London. The last captain of the *Quebec*, Thomas Panting Attrill, a purser in the Royal Navy, was himself a resident of St Andrew's in the Ottawa valley (ANQM, notary Arnoldi, no. 4130, 22 April 1835; register of Anglican Church, St Andrew's, 24 February 1825; CC register, 10 August 1828; SGP register, 25 July 1831; McNally, "Montreal Engine Foundries," 24).

86 NA, MG 24, D 8, Wright Papers, 134:69921–8, arbitration bond between P. Wright & Sons and Thomas Mears, 22 April 1831. In 1830 Grant commanded the *Shannon* until sometime early in the summer, when he was sacked – unfairly, according to a Bytown correspondent who penned a long denunciation of the Ottawa River steamboat owners and particularly of the "monopolists" behind the *Shannon*. Grant thereafter worked to extend steam navigation on the Ottawa above Bytown. In 1832 he oversaw the building of the *Lady Colborne* at Aylmer, Lower Canada, for Charles Symmes and other merchants and lumbermen. Launched on 30 October that year, she was fitted with the 30-horsepower engine of the defunct *Montreal*. She was to run under Grant's command between Aylmer and Fitzroy Harbour. At Arnprior in 1836, Grant superintended the building of the *George Buchanan* for Buchanan, Simpson and Company, a firm formed by timber dealer George Buchanan of Arnprior, James Simpson of Smiths Falls, and William Mittleberger of Montreal and Smiths Falls. Launched on 28 October, the *George Buchanan* was 87 feet long on deck by $26\frac{1}{2}$ feet wide, 16 feet 6 inches breadth of beam, with a $6\frac{1}{2}$ foot depth of hold. She plied on the Chats Lake, from the head of the Chats Rapids to the Portage du Fort, carrying freight and towing timber rafts. Grant commanded the *Lady Colborne* in the 1830s, and after an absence of two years in 1840–41, he returned as her captain in 1842 (ANQM, notary Arnoldi, no. 4840, 23 May 1836; notary Griffin, no. 9907, 4 June 1832; *Bytown Gazette*, 30 June, 6 October, and 10 November 1836, 3 June 1841, 25 May 1843; *Courant*, 27 October 1830, 3 November 1832; *Gazette*, 4 July 1833 and 3 May 1842; H.R. Morgan, "Steam Navigation on the Ottawa River," 375–6; R. Reid, *The Upper Ottawa Valley to 1855*, lxxviii, lxxxii).

87 NA, MG 24, D 8, Wright Papers, 18:6906–7, Thomas Brigham to P. Wright, 27 October 1829; 18:6916–17, Mears to Ruggles Wright, 4 November 1829; 19:7097–8, same to same, 13 March 1830; *Courant*, 21 and

31 October 1829; *Gazette,* 13 October 1828, 9 November 1829. The owners apparently hoped to have the *Shannon* running by the spring of 1829, but perhaps owing to problems in selling the stock, work on the boat did not start until the following autumn. The *Gazette* reported in November 1829: "The requisite quantity of stock is now all subscribed by respectable individuals in Quebec and Montreal, and residents in different places on the Ottawa, interested in the trade of that quarter."

88 ANQM, notary Doucet, no. 17343, 4 January 1830. See chap. 2.

89 NA, MG 24, D 8, Wright Papers, 19:7004–6, Mears to P. Wright & Sons, 5 February 1830.

90 Ibid., 19:7097–8, Mears to Ruggles Wright, 13 March 1830.

91 *Gazette,* 27 May 1830; *Kingston Chronicle,* 15 May 1830. The advertisement by John Molson and Sons for the *Shannon* in the *Gazette* of 27 May misidentified her master as J. Grant. Joseph Wigfield, formerly engineer of the *Quebec,* seems to have followed that steamer's engines when they were transferred to the *Shannon.* At his death in 1832, he was working as the engineer of the *Shannon* (ANQM, register of Christ Church, Sorel, 5 December 1825; *Courant,* 4 July 1832).

92 *Courant,* 10 July 1830.

93 Ibid., 4 August and 27 October 1830. In the next few years, the *William King* ran alternately on the Grenville-Bytown and Lachine-Carillon routes (see *Gazette,* 16 and 30 April 1832, 4 and 25 July 1833).

CHAPTER FIVE

1 ANQM, notary Doucet, no. 13564, 27 April 1826; no. 14607, 21 June 1827; no. 14608, 21 June 1827; no. 14659, 11 July 1827. Silas Dickinson, born on 17 September 1794, moved to the Montreal area from Rutland, Vermont, in 1823 and leased the Île aux Hérons at the foot of the Lachine Rapids to farm. Erastus Dickinson, born on 29 April 1798, seems to have joined him around the time that they formed their horse-boat partnership. Both men moved to Châteauguay after forming their association with men of that district. Erastus was identified as a trader at Châteauguay when he married in Montreal on 24 November 1835. Silas, who settled up the Châteauguay River in the area of what is now Mercier, farmed there through the 1830s and on the Île aux Chats, an island in the St Lawrence between present-day Valleyfield and Côteau-du-Lac. He also established a business as a broom-maker. He went bankrupt in 1841 and moved back to the United States in 1842 or 1843 (ANQM, notary Arnoldi, no. 4606 and no. 4607, 10 December 1835; notary Hunter, no. 1446, 13 March 1840; notary Jobin, no. 3060, 5 May 1823; no. 4228, 5 March 1827; notary Leblanc, no. 4720, 17 November 1837; notary Lepailleur, no. 3078, 3 March 1828; notary Sarault, unnumbered deed, 27 October 1838; register

of St Paul's Presbyterian Church, Montreal, 24 November 1835. *JAC*, 1843, app. NN, report of bankruptcy commissioners; *Gazette*, 1 October 1841, 15 December 1842; private correspondence with Alan Dickinson and Diana Rasmussen, descendants of Silas Dickinson).

2 ANQM, notary Arnoldi, no. 163, 22 February 1828.

3 *Courant*, 31 May 1823, 8 July 1826.

4 ANQM, notary Doucet, no. 14659, 11 July 1827.

5 ANQM, notary Jobin, no. 4478, 13 February 1828.

6 *Gazette*, 21 April 1828.

7 Ibid., 24 July 1828.

8 This interpretation can be inferred from the way that Dickinson ran his affairs on Lake St Louis, notably from the terms under which he leased the *Cornwall* this year and in 1829, as outlined later in this chapter.

9 See *Gazette*, 28 July 1828.

10 *Gazette*, 10 September 1829, copying the *Kingston Chronicle*.

11 ANQM, notary Bedouin, no. 3286, 8 August 1828.

12 *Gazette*, 10 November 1828; *Vindicator*, 10 February 1829; Ratio et al., *La navigation à Longueuil*, 47.

13 ANQM, notary Bedouin, no. 1799, 26 March 1823; *Courant*, 6 December 1826.

14 *Gazette*, 30 April 1829; *Minerve*, 2 April 1829; *Vindicator*, 28 April 1829. By one account, the *Montreal* docked at Châteauguay at a wharf built for Michael Connolly, formerly of the *Ottawa*, who now kept an inn at Châteauguay (Sellar, *History of ... Huntingdon*, 259).

15 *Gazette*, 2 April 1829; *Vindicator*, 23 December 1828. The issue of the *Gazette* that announced the imminent opening of post offices at Beauharnois, Châteauguay, and Lachine, as well as at Bytown, also carried a letter from a Châteauguay correspondent who noted that improvements at that village in the past year included "the nomination of a Post Master ... and the accommodation of a large and safe Team boat, to cross the Lake to Lachine." Projects for the coming year included "the preparation of an additional Steam-boat, viz.: – the Montreal, which will run in opposition to the Team-boat, already established."

16 ANQM, notary Arnoldi, no. 163, 22 February 1828; notary Jobin, no. 4940, 12 October 1829; notary Lepailleur, no. 3283, 7 March 1829; SGP register, 1 November 1829; *Courant*, 10 April 1830; *Gazette*, 5 March 1825, 2 April 1829; *Vindicator*, 29 September 1829. Crossman may have had experience in handling the mails before he became captain of the mail boat *St Lawrence*. He had served as clerk for brothers Elijah and Henry Curtis of Montreal, who were involved in the carriage of mail between Montreal and Quebec before Dickinson took it over in 1819 (ANQM, notary Desautels, no. 2379, 20 April 1816; no. 3706, 20 May 1818; no. 4378, 12 October 1819; notary Doucet no. 7730, 11 July 1820).

17 ANQM, notary Jobin, no. 4707, 22 January 1829. Dickinson's successors appear to have held on to this lot after the ten-year term had expired, signing a new three-year lease with Dawes in 1840 (see ANQM, notary Hunter, no. 1690, 31 August 1840).

18 ANQM, notary Bedouin, no. 3670, 3 September 1829; notary Jobin, no. 4904, 21 August 1829.

19 ANQM, notary Jobin, no. 4752, 27 February 1829, and no. 4923, 24 September 1829.

20 *Courant*, 22 August 1829.

21 Ibid., 27 May 1829; *Minerve*, 2 and 30 July 1829. Two Sunday excursions of the *Montreal* were advertised that summer, one for 5 July and one for 2 August.

22 Sellar, *History of … Huntingdon*, 258–9.

23 ANQM, notary Jobin, no. 4896, 27 July 1829; *Courant*, 29 July and 30 September 1829. Borthwick suggests that William Parkyn, an English-born engineer, commanded the *Cornwall* on the Lachine–Point Fortune run. The two newspaper reports cited above, however, give the captain's name as Scott. Parkyn may have served aboard her in some other capacity, such as engineer (Borthwick, *History and Biographical Gazetteer of Montreal*, 176).

24 *Courant*, 25, 29 July 1829.

25 ANQM, notary Jobin, no. 4896, 27 July 1829.

26 ANQM, notary Jobin, no. 4943, 16 October 1829.

27 ANQM, notary Doucet, no. 16353, 31 July 1829.

28 NA, RG 1, L 3, Upper Canada Land Petitions, 556, no. 43, 15 October 1829.

29 ANQM, SGP register, 8 September 1829; *Courant*, 9 September 1829; *Gazette*, 10 September 1829; *Vindicator*, 11 September 1829.

30 CU, Ward Family Collection, "Ward Family Genealogy" file; Diary of John D. Ward, 1:6, 8–10; 4:114; 5:18, 29, 44–51; NA, MG 24, D 19, Ward Papers, ff. 24–6, John Ward to Silas Ward, 24 January 1821; ff. 28–30, same to same, 29 March 1821; 39–40, same to same, 20 May 1822; f. 46, same to same, 5 January 1824; f. 63, Lebbeus Ward to John Ward, 23 July 1829; *Courant*, 7 January 1824, 16 August 1826; H.P. Smith, *History of Addison County*, 677, 692. A stone in the Mount Royal Cemetery in Montreal, moved there from the vanished Protestant cemetery on Papineau Road, commemorates two of the Ward children, Phebe Caroline (5 May 1820–13 August 1826) and Sarah Ann Dod (5 July 1828–7 August 1829). The inscription does not mention the Wards' second child – the first to die – Maria Ann Elizabeth (9 February 1822–3 January 1824), who probably had her own marker, now lost. The Wards had five more children after leaving Canada. From 1837 to 1841 John Ward was a partner in the Novelty Iron Works in New York. He later ran a foundry in Jersey City, New Jersey, and served as a director and (from 1865 through 1867) as vice-president of

the Morris Canal and Banking Company, whose canal ran across northern New Jersey, linking the Delaware River with the Hudson River at Jersey City. He died at his home in Jersey City on 19 May 1873 at age seventy-nine. Laura Roburds, his wife, died there on 28 February 1877 at age eighty (CU, Ward Family Collection, Lackawanna & Western Railroad Co. pass issued to John D. Ward as vice-president of the "Morris Canal & Barge Co.," valid to 31 December 1866. *New York Times,* 20 May 1873, 1 and 2 March 1877; Dayton, *Steamboat Days,* 382; Kalata, *A Hundred Years,* 405, 409, 476, 486, 487, 494–5, 497, 654; Lewis, "The Ward Brothers, George Brush and Montreal's Eagle Foundry," 31).

31 ANQM, notary Doucet, no. 13683, 16 June 1826 and addendum of 17 February 1830; no. 20032, 23 November 1832; no. 20068, 11 December 1832; *Gazette,* 6 December 1832. John Ward maintained business connections with the foundry and with other Montreal businesses into the 1840s (see Tulchinsky, *River Barons,* 215).

32 See Lewis, "The First Generation of Marine Engines," 9. This was the *Montreal's* tenth year in operation.

33 *Courant,* 15 May 1830. For previous accidents and repairs to the *Montreal,* see *Courant,* 7 and 10 June 1820, 27 July 1822, 23 September and 14 November 1824, 6 December 1826; *Gazette,* 12 April 1827; *Herald,* 26 August 1820, 17 November 1824; *Minerve,* 12 and 19 April 1827, 21 July 1828.

34 ANQM, notary Cardinal, no. 122, 14 April 1830.

35 ANQM, notary Griffin, no. 8846, 30 June 1830; *Courant,* 15 May 1830. Over the winter of 1832–33, the engine of the *Montreal* would be placed in the *Lady Colborne* at Aylmer on the Ottawa River (see chap. 4, note 86).

36 *Courant,* 14 July 1830.

37 Ibid., 24 and 31 March, 7 April, and 14 August 1830. It seems that Jacob Bigelow was no longer in the insurance business.

38 ANQM, SAP register, 28 April 1825; *Courant,* 13 April 1825, 19 August 1826, 17 November 1830; *Vindicator,* 16 November 1830; Bigelow, *Bigelow Family Genealogy,* 1:263. The children were Martha Amelia, born 6 April 1825, and Edward, born 15 August 1826. The *Bigelow Family Genealogy* gives the wrong birth and death dates for Bigelow's wife, saying she was born on 27 February 1800 and died on 15 November 1829. Had she been born in 1800, she would have been of the age of majority at her marriage in 1824, which she clearly was not (See ANQM, notary Griffin, no. 5181, 10 May 1824).

39 ANQM, notary Arnoldi, no. 401, 18 March 1829; *Gazette,* 3 July 1824.

40 ANQM, notary Griffin, no. 6546, 7 June 1826; no. 7109, 5 March 1827.

41 *Courant,* 5 January 1828; *Kingston Chronicle,* 25 December 1830; Muntz, "Weller, William," 825. See also the notice of 2 January 1830 by Norton

and Weller, reproduced in Haight, *Country Life in Canada Fifty Years Ago,*
132. Norton also held the contract for carrying the mail between Brockville and Perth from January 1830 (*Gazette,* 10 September 1829).

42 *Courier,* 29 December 1835.

43 *Courant,* 24 May 1826, 2 May 1829, 24 April 1830. The original Mansion
House on St Paul Street, from which Michael Connolly had run his stage
to Lachine in 1820 to meet the *Ottawa,* had burned down in 1821.

44 ANQM, notary Bedouin, no. 3038, 26 October 1827. The lease was retroactive to 1 May 1827.

45 ANQM, notary Daveluy, no. 967, 15 December 1824; *Courant,* 5 May 1824.
When he bought a tavern in Westfield, Massachusetts, in 1811, Goode-
nough was identified as coming from Granby, Massachusetts, just east of
South Hadley (Massachusetts title deeds, Hampshire County, 53:407–8).

46 "Witness Jubilee Symposium," 7 December 1895; *Courant,* 24 January
1824.

47 *Gazette,* 27 April 1839.

48 Fowler, *Journal of a Tour through British North America,* 124–5, 129–30.

49 "Witness Jubilee Symposium," 23 May 1896, reminiscences of Alexander
Milloy.

50 Lambert, *Les anciennes diligences du Québec,* 30.

51 *Gazette,* 11 April 1833, 22 July 1834; Austin, *The Lights of Cobb and Co.,*
42–7; Scheiber, *Abbot-Downing and the Concord Coach,* 5–13.

52 MU, MS 255/1, Charles Kadwell Papers, "Notes, &c. during a Trip from
Montreal to Upper Canada and back, From the 3rd to the 18th August
1838," under date of 4 August. L'Hirondelle, also known by its English
name, the *Swallow,* was imported from England in 1832. One writer placed
its cost at $2,000, but Emery Cushing, acting for the Ottawa Steamboat
Company, picked it up at auction in Montreal for less than one-quarter of
that sum – £92 10s., or $370 – on 5 October that year (*Gazette,* 6 October
1832; J.E. Cushing, *Genealogy of the Cushing Family,* 294–5; Lambert, *Les
anciennes diligences du Québec,* 26).

53 *Courant,* 23 July 1831. The standard procedure was for stages to stop at
the wharf, not to drive right on to the boats, but it seems that piggyback-
ing was common enough on the route that it startled no one. Thirteen
years after the misadventure aboard the *St Lawrence,* a traveller recorded:
"A clumsy stage-coach carried me to Lachine, nine miles from Montreal:
there it was put on board a steamer, borne through Lake St Louis, and
released again at the cascades, to carry us on sixteen miles further to
Coteau du Lac" (Warburton, *Hochelaga,* 1:211–2; see also Lambert, *Les
anciennes diligences du Québec,* 69).

54 MU, MS 475, St Lawrence Steamboat Co., v. 54; *Gazette,* 16, 21, 23 April,
and 21 May 1831. The newspaper of 21 May carried Mackenzie's own
account of the sinking of the *Waterloo,* together with the text of a letter of

thanks from the passengers to Captain Andrew Perry and his crew. Other passengers included Moses Marshall, builder of the American Presbyterian Church, and William Lyman.

55 Fergusson, *Practical Notes*, 82–4.

CHAPTER SIX

1 ANQM, notary Peltier, no. 2012, 6 April 1831.

2 ANQM, notary Charlebois, no. 100 and no. 101, 6 November 1827, and unnumbered deeds signed before the same notary on 4 November and 26 December 1831; notary Crawford, no. 219, 22 February 1831; sheriff Ermatinger, no. 771, 5 January 1826.

3 ANQM, notary Peltier, no. 2008, 31 March 1831. In this notary's copy of the deed of sale, the mention of Whitney as "Captain of the Steam boat St Lawrence" has been crossed out. Three days earlier, however, he was identified as captain of the boat in another deed signed before the same notary. Crossman, as we have seen, was master that July when the stage rolled off the deck of the boat into Lake St Louis. Two years earlier, in September 1829, the baptism record of one of Whitney's children identified him as "Captain of the Steam Boat *St Lawrence*, Lachine," but the will that Crossman's wife made out that October and the baptism record of one of his children in November identified Crossman as her captain. At some time in the 1830s, Whitney operated the Steam Boat Hotel at Lachine (ANQM, notary Jobin, no. 4940, 12 October 1829; notary Peltier, no. 2004, 28 March 1831; SGP register, 13 July 1820, 20 September 1829, and 1 November 1829; *Courant*, 23 July 1831; *Transcript*, 16 May 1839).

4 ANQM, notary Peltier, no. 2143, 2 September 1831.

5 NA, RG 42, E 1, Dept. of Marine, Ship Registers, 175: no. 3 for 1837; *Courant*, 18 June 1831. A copy of the *Swan's* register in ANQM, notary Doucet, no. 25406, 25 May 1838, says she was 147 tons, but the official register cited above gives 80 tons, which seems more probable.

6 Unless otherwise specified, the details of Cazeau's case are taken from Rocheleau-Rouleau, "Une incroyable et véridique histoire," and Gervais, "Cazeau, François."

7 See, for instance, ANQM, notary Doucet, no. 3536 and no. 3537, 21 November 1815; no. 3538, 27 November 1815; no. 3539, 28 November 1815; no. 3542, 9 December 1815; no. 3543, 10 December 1815.

8 ANQM, notary Arnoldi, no. 908, 14 May 1831. See also ANQM, notary Gibb, no. 685, 12 December 1836.

9 Breckenridge, *The Canadian Banking System*, 29, 31, 34; Shortt, *History of Canadian Currency and Banking*, 782–4.

10 ANQM, notary Doucet, no. 6194, 1 May 1819; no. 10858, 5 July 1823. The cancellation of Bigelow's bond is annexed to the latter deed. In June 1830,

as "Teller of the late Bank of Canada," he testified at a forgery trial in Plattsburgh (*Courant*, 3 July 1830).

11 ANQM, Doucet, no. 13280, 19 January 1826; no. 13656, 9 June 1826; no. 14574, 6 June 1827; *Courant*, 18 February 1826, 5 January 1828.

12 *Gazette*, 7 May 1832. Bigelow, *Bigelow Family Genealogy*, 1:262.

13 ANQM, notary Arnoldi, no. 908, 14 May 1831.

14 ANQM, notary Doucet, no. 6179, 28 August 1819.

15 For McKay's work, see Legget, *Rideau Waterway*, 192–5. Though the *Union* was the first boat through the Bytown locks, she was not the first steamer on the canal. That honour went to Robert Drummond's *Rideau*, which had been used as a canal work boat from 1829 (*Courant*, 24 June 1829; *Kingston Chronicle*, 11 July 1829).

16 *Kingston Chronicle*, 21 December 1831; *Vindicator*, 14 October 1831.

17 ANQM, P345, Fonds Société d'archéologie et de numismatique, D1/1113, William Mittleberger to Charles Mittleberger, 27 October, 17, 26 November, 10, and 17 December 1831.

18 See *JAUC*, 1839, 2, part 2: 839–42, report of the select committee on Rideau Canal tolls.

19 *Vindicator*, 28 October 1831.

20 *Gazette*, 8 and 19 March 1832.

21 Ibid., 19 March 1832; *Courant*, 5 September 1832. The inventory of Dickinson's assets at Lachine, begun on 20 July 1832 by George Brush and Augustus Barber, mentions the hulls of two old steamers intended to form a wharf. Continued on 22 July by Barber and Daniel Whipple, the inventory lists an anchor from the *St Lawrence* among the items aboard the *Chateauguay* (ANQM, notary Doucet, no. 19686, 2 July 1832).

22 An early error by a deferential press has resulted in a minor mistake about the proper name of this boat. Before the launch, the *Gazette* ventured that she was "to be called, we believe, the *Chancellor Brougham*." The *Courant* used that name in reporting the trial of the boat's engine in late August. The inventory of Dickinson's estate that summer, however, makes clear that even before her engine was installed, she was called the *Henry Brougham*, the name used in all contemporary accounts except in those early newspaper ones (*Courant*, 5 September 1832; *Gazette*, 16 April 1832; ANQM, notary Doucet, no. 19686, 2 July 1832; for the Brougham carriage, see McCausland, *The English Carriage*, 99–103).

23 NA, RG 42, E 1, Dept. of Marine, Ship Registers, 1416:237–40; *Gazette*, 29 March and 5 September 1832, 11 April 1833. Her register at Kingston in 1849, under the name *Chieftain*, described her as having a figurehead bust.

24 *Brockville Recorder*, 23 February and 17 May 1832; *Courant*, 29 September and 3 October 1832; *Gazette*, 29 March 1832; Lewis, "Iroquois," 17; MMGL, Van Cleve, "Reminiscences," 44. In high-pressure engines, steam

entered the cylinder alternately from top and bottom, driving the piston up and down against the pressure of the waste steam, which was thus forced out through a pipe into the atmosphere in noisy puffs. In low-pressure engines, steam did not act against steam but against a vacuum. An air pump drew off the waste steam from the cylinder, creating the vacuum. The spent steam then passed through a condenser, the water running into a tank to be pumped back into the boiler. The high-pressure engine was noisier but more compact than the low-pressure one, with its air pump and condenser, and generally easier to maintain.

25 *Cyclopaedia of Canadian Biography*, 238–9. This article makes the rather doubtful claim that Barnabas Dickinson was the founder of Dickinson's Landing.

26 ANQM, notary Doucet, no. 19674, 27 June 1832. While this document makes reference to the partnership, no copy of a partnership deed has been found. See below, note 38.

27 *Gazette*, 16 April, 31 May, and 2 June 1832.

28 Bilson, *A Darkened House*, 24.

29 Mount Royal Cemetery, Protestant Old Burial Ground Records, Record of Lots, 49, book no. 2 (1822–34): 261. The records show that the Reverend Edward Black, then of the Scotch Presbyterian Church in St Gabriel Street, was present at the burial, probably as duty minister for that day. They also show that Dickinson had acquired lot 131 in the now-vanished Papineau Road cemetery when his first wife, Mary Ann Taylor, died in 1821. Besides her and Dickinson, the only family member buried in the plot was Sarah Spring Dickinson, a daughter of Dickinson's second marriage, who died of scarlet fever on 4 March 1839 at age eleven (ANQM, ZC register, 5 March 1839. *Gazette*, 7 March 1839).

30 *Courant*, 1 and 5 September 1832.

31 ANQM, APC register, 8 August 1832.

32 Coke, *A Subaltern's Furlough*, 330–1.

33 ANQM, 06,M-P26/1, Fonds Romuald Trudeau, "Mes Tablettes," 10:48: "On fit retirer celui-ci [Phillips], parce que l'on supposait que Mr Bagg comme Américains auroit pour lui la grande majorité si non toute la population de même origine, qui jointe à tous les Ecossais et Anglais & quelques Canadiens lâches et perfides, ne pouvait manquer de leur assurer la victoire."

34 ANQM, 06,M-P21/1, Fonds Romuald Trudeau, "Mes tablettes," 10:46–64; Knowles, "The American Presbyterian Church of Montreal," 231–2.

35 ANQM, ND register, 18 July 1832; SAP register, 28 June 1832; *Courant*, 4, 14 July and 25 August 1832; *Minerve*, 19 July 1832; J.E. Cushing, *Genealogy of the Cushing Family*, 294; Lewis, "McKenzie, James" 469–70; Lyman, *Genealogy of the Lyman Family in Canada*, 30, 37.

36 ANQM, St Clément (Beauharnois) register, 30 June 1832; *Courant*, 4 July and 18 August 1832. *Gazette*, 6 October 1832; Désilets, "Masson, Luc-

Hyacinthe," 499; A. Walker, *Bureaux et maîtres de poste du sud-ouest du Québec*, 3. Gravestone inscriptions in the cemetery of St Edward's Presbyterian Church in Beauharnois indicate that Dr Charles Fleming, age thirty-three, a native of Glasgow, died of cholera on 17 August 1832, and that Thomas McDonald, age twenty-eight, died on 11 August.

37 ANQM, Cour Supérieure-Montréal, Tutelles et Curatelles, no. 385, 22 June 1832. James Henderson had begun a forwarding business in 1824, with agents Averell and Hooker at Prescott, Henry Jones at Brockville, and John Strange at Kingston. By 1826 he had formed a lasting partnership with Alfred Hooker of Prescott. The firm was called Hooker and Henderson in Upper Canada and Henderson and Hooker at Montreal (See ANQM, notary Griffin, no. 6438, 1 May 1826; *Courant*, 31 March 1824).

38 ANQM, notary Doucet, no. 19674, 27 June 1832. Abijah and Increase Bigelow, as the "surviving partners" in Horace Dickinson and Company, and Mercy Amelia Dickinson and Lebbeus Ward, as guardians of the Dickinson children, subsequently published a notice that read: "The business of the Upper Canada Line of Stages and Steamboats heretofore conducted by H. Dickinson & Co. will be and is hereby renewed and continued, by and with the advice and consent of all the parties interested, under the same name and firm" (*Gazette*, 17 July 1832).

39 *Courant*, 5 September 1832.

40 Daniel Whipple, was born in Otsego County, New York, on 13 February 1798. He took part in drawing up the inventory of Dickinson's estate in 1832. That he was in the area, that he is known to have been the *Brougham's* captain a few years later, and that there seems to be no record of anyone else having commanded her in the meantime all lead us to suppose that he was in charge of this steamer from 1832 (ANQM, notary Doucet, no. 19686, 2 July 1832; NA, RG 19, E 5b, Lower Canada Rebellion Losses Claims, 3798:1889, 3799:2172. Brainard, *Wilkins Family*, 82).

41 Coke, *A Subaltern's Furlough*, 327.

42 *Brockville Gazette*, 20 September 1832; *Brockville Recorder*, 17 May 1832; *Courant*, 29 September 1832.

43 *Montreal Gazette*, 30 October 1832, copied from *Grenville Gazette*.

44 *Gazette*, 13 July 1833.

45 NA, RG 1, E 3, Upper Canada State Submissions, 21:8–10, petition of H. Dickinson and Company; *Gazette*, 11 April and 18 June 1833.

46 Domett, *The Canadian Journal of Alfred Domett*, 20. Domett, a friend of the poet Robert Browning, later served briefly as prime minister of New Zealand.

47 *Brockville Recorder*, 15 August 1834; *Gazette*, 17, 22 July and 7 August 1834, 9 July 1835; Lewis, "*Iroquois*," 18.

48 Dickinson received some posthumous credit for his achievement, but one newspaper suggested that the idea for the *Iroquois* came from Hiram

Norton of Prescott. The *Gazette*, on 24 September 1832, saluted the *Iroquois* in these terms: "The public are indebted for this valuable improvement in inland communication, by which rapids, heretofore considered impracticable by steam boats, have been ascended, to the enterprise of the late Horace Dickinson, Esquire, who carried the arrangement almost to completion, before he fell a victim to the pestilence." The same newspaper, on 30 October 1832, copied an item from the *Grenville Gazette* that said: "Steam navigation, through this route, we are informed, was first projected by the late H. Dickenson, Esquire, who did not live to see his magnificent scheme accomplished, but which has since been brought into successful operation by the surviving partners in the firm." But the *Brockville Recorder* of 27 September 1832 commented: "We understand the credit for the suggestion and preliminary movements for the erection, of this boat, is ascribed to H. Norton, Esq. M.P. whose former enterprises for public accommodation are extensively known."

49 These and other details of Dickinson's assets are taken from the inventory of his estate: ANQM, notary Doucet, no. 19686, 2 July 1832.

50 These may have been two boats that forwarders Hooker and Henderson had bought in 1826 from Ainsworth and Lee of Cape Vincent, New York. The *H. Gates* was in Dickinson's possession by 1829 (ANQM, notary Bedouin, no. 2602, 20 May 1826; notary Jobin, no. 4863, 8 June 1829).

51 *Courant*, 5 May 1821, 6 May 1829; *Herald*, 13 April 1820; *Minerve*, 10 May 1827; Fergusson, *Practical Notes* 86, 90; Fowler, *Journal of a Tour through British North America*, 137.

52 ANQM, notary Jobin, no. 5230, 24 August 1835; notary Peltier, no. 2008, 31 March 1831.

53 ANQM, notary Crawford, no. 219, 22 February 1831; *Cornwall Observer*, 18 July 1842.

CHAPTER SEVEN

1 *Brockville Gazette*, 31 May and 7 June 1832; *Courant*, 6 June 1832; *Kingston Chronicle*, 26 May and 9 June 1832. The *Rideau*, 80 feet long, 15 feet beam, with a 6-foot depth of hold, was launched near Kingston on 6 June 1829 with her 12-horsepower engine on board. She served, among other things, to pump out coffer dams during the building of the canal, hence her nickname "Pumper." A story persists that *Pumper* was her original name and that it was changed to *Rideau* for the opening of the canal, but at her launch in 1829 she was identified as the *Rideau*. Some confusion exists about her status from the summer of 1832 on. Mills says that a new steamer called *Rideau*, 80 feet long and 27 feet in breadth, was built at Merrickville that year and that the first *Rideau* was retired in 1833. A report in the *Kingston Chronicle* of 25 August 1832 seems to support that

claim: "Mr Drummond's new boat the Rideau, arrived here yesterday in order to receive her Engine. She is a beautiful model, measuring eighty feet in length, and twenty-seven in breadth; has excellent accomodation for fourteen gentlemen and eight ladies. She is about to make her trips upon the Canal in about a month hence." But Mills also says that less than a year later, this second *Rideau* was rebuilt and made 15 feet longer. Indeed, in June 1833 the *Gazette* reported that Drummond's *Rideau* was "now lengthening and undergoing repairs at Kingston." It seems rather improbable that a steamer should undergo such major modification after only a few months of operation, or that Drummond, whose new steamer *Margaret* was about to be launched and who had just invested heavily in the lemon *John By* (see note 8 below), would have undertaken such an expensive proposition. It would seem more likely that the original *Rideau*, having served her purpose as a work boat, was converted into a freight and passenger boat in 1832 and then lengthened in 1833. In his history of Merrickville, Larry Turner makes no mention of any such steamer being built there (*Courant*, 24 June 1829; *Gazette*, 30 August 1832, copying *Kingston Chronicle* of 25 August, 18 June 1833; Brault, *Ottawa Old and New*, 52; Bush, *Commercial Navigation on the Rideau Canal*, 7, 92; Legget, *Rideau Waterway*, 56; Mills, *Canadian Coastal and Inland Steam Vessels*, 96, and Supplement 2, no. 2444a; A.H.D. Ross, *Ottawa Past and Present*, 68–9).

2 *Gazette*, 6 September 1832, 3 January 1833.
3 Bilson, *A Darkened House*, 12–13, 26; Bond, "Alexander James Christie, Bytown Pioneer," 30.
4 *Hallowell Free Press*, 24 July 1832.
5 *Brockville Recorder*, 28 June 1833; *Gazette*, 25 July 1833.
6 Brydone, *Narrative of a Voyage with a Party of Emigrants*, 51.
7 Ibid.
8 *Brockville Gazette*, 13 September 1832; *Brockville Recorder*, 13 September 1832, 7 June 1833; *Courier*, 12 April 1836; *Kingston Chronicle*, 24 December 1831, 21 January, 28 April, and 26 May 1832, 29 June and 27 July 1833; *Montreal Gazette*, 16 April 1832, 7 May 1833, 19 August 1834, 9 June 1835; *Vindicator*, 28 December 1830; Bush, *Commercial Navigation on the Rideau Canal*, 95; Lewis, "*John By*"; Mills, *Canadian Coastal and Inland Steam Vessels*, 63; A.H.D. Ross, *Ottawa Past and Present*, 68. The *John By* was described in 1832 as "propelled by a low-pressure engine of 75 horse power; – boilers on the bows; wheels on the stern; 33 feet beam; $9\frac{1}{2}$ feet hold; her cabins are neatly fitted up; that for the gentlemen, which is below, contains 30 bearths; and the ladies', directly above, 19 bearths; a promenade deck of 112 feet." Drawing too much water for the Rideau, she ran between Prescott and the Carrying Place, at the head of the Bay of Quinte, in 1832. Her master, Henry Lelievre of Perth, son of

a French naval officer who had switched to the British side during the French Revolution, was chosen by a vote of the shareholders on 19 May that year. In the spring of 1833 Drummond bought out his fellow shareholders, replaced her 75-horsepower engine with two 30-horsepower engines made by Sheldon, Dutcher and Company of York, and ran her between York and Hamilton, under Captain William Kerr. She was wrecked that year off Port Credit. Her engines were salvaged and placed in the *Oakville*, launched at Oakville in 1834 (see below, note 52). The *John By's* original owners, who had formed a company in December 1830 specifically "to navigate the Rideau Canal by steam," had miscalculated. This mistake was surprising, given that they were scarcely novices. Besides Drummond, the committee named to oversee the building of the boat consisted of James McKenzie, the Royal Navy veteran who had served as captain of the *Frontenac* and now commanded the *Alciope*, Henry Gildersleeve, the Connecticut native who had worked on the construction of the *Frontenac* and then built and commanded the *Charlotte* and *Sir James Kempt*, Donald Bethune, John Kirby, David John Smith, and John Strange.

9 *Kingston Chronicle*, 13 July, 7 and 21 September 1833.

10 Ibid., 29 June 1833; Walker and Walker, *Carleton Saga*, 323–30. From April 1833 McKay offered lots for sale in New Edinburgh, saying that he had "just got in operation a superior Grist Mill with seven Run of Stones, and a Saw Mill, with two Run of Saws, which render the situation more desirable for location."

11 *Bathurst Courier*, 29 August 1834; *Brockville Recorder*, 6 June 1834; *Gazette*, 16 April 1832; *Kingston Chronicle*, 17 March and 7 April 1832, 8 March, 23 August, and 15 November 1834; *Statutes of Upper Canada*, 2 William iv, ch. 11, An Act to incorporate certain Persons under the style and title of the President, Directors and Company, of the Commercial Bank of the Midland District (18 January 1832).

12 *Kingston Chronicle*, 21 January 1832.

13 ANQM, notary Doucet, no. 19806, 16 August 1832.

14 The case for annexation was widely covered in the press. See, for example, *Bathurst Courier*, 20 February 1835; *Brockville Gazette*, 13 December 1832; *Brockville Recorder*, 6 and 20 December 1832; *Bytown Gazette*, 15 December 1836; *Courant*, 3 November 1832; *Kingston Chronicle*, 25 February and 7 March 1835; *Montreal Gazette*, 2 and 9 October 1832, 10 December 1836, 7 and 10 April 1838; *Morning Courier*, 7 March 1835, 23 January 1836; *Minerve*, 15, 18, 22 February and 5 December 1836, 30 January 1837; *Vindicator*, 18 November, 2 and 23 December 1836. See also ANQM, 06, M-P26/1/11, Fonds Romuald Trudeau, 36–7 and 41–2; Arthur, *The Arthur Papers*, 1:184–7; Bertrand, *Histoire de Montréal*, 2:95–6; Creighton, *Empire of the St Lawrence*, 224, 283–5, 301; Dunham, *Political*

Unrest in Upper Canada, 71–2, 119. Claude G. Charron, *La partition du Québec* (Montreal: VLB Editeur, 1996), traces today's political agitation over the partitioning of an independent Quebec back to this annexation movement and beyond, to the Constitution Act of 1791.

15 *Brockville Gazette*, 31 May 1832. Two years later the *Grenville Gazette* voiced a similar opinion in raining on Kingston's parade: "The Kingstonians, good folks, are full of glee since the opening of the Rideau Canal. It is astonishing with what rapidity they magnify mole hills into mountains. The *Chronicle* ... has a longwinded sophisticated dissertation on the ideal profits which the government must derive from the revenue arising from this important channel of intercommunication; but it is all in prospect, and we are sure it will always continue to be so" (*Brockville Recorder*, 30 May 1834, copied from *Grenville Gazette*).

16 *Gazette*, 15 October 1833; R. Reid, *The Upper Ottawa Valley to 1855*, lxxiv, lxxv; Turner, *Perth*, 45.

17 *Courant*, 24 November 1830; I. MacPherson, *Matters of Loyalty*, 38–41. On the committee with Jones were Andrew Norton Buell, George Crawford, George Longley of Maitland, John McDonald of Gananoque, Alexander McMillan, Alexander Morris, and William L. Whiting.

18 *Brockville Recorder*, 25 October and 1 November 1832. The members of this committee were, besides Jones, John Bogert, Andrew N. Buell, Samuel Crane, George Crawford, Paul Glasford, Elnathan Hubbell, Alfred Hooker, Alpheus Jones, Daniel Jones, George Longley, George Malloch, John McDonald, Alexander McMillan, William McQueen, Justus S. Merwin, Alexander Morris, and William L. Whiting.

19 *Brockville Recorder*, 22 November 1832. *Statutes of Upper Canada*, 3 William IV, ch. 18, An act granting His Majesty a sum of money to be raised by debenture, for the improvement of the navigation of the River Saint Lawrence (and later amendments: 4 William IV, ch. 40; 7 William IV, ch. 45; 1 Victoria, ch. 57); I. MacPherson, *Matters of Loyalty*, 42–3.

20 ANQM, CC register, 23 October 1833; *Brockville Recorder*, 21 February 1833; *Courant*, 22 September 1821; *Gazette*, 22 October 1833; *Kingston Chronicle*, 26 October 1833; *Vindicator*, 20 December 1831; *Statutes of Upper Canada*, 3 William IV, ch. 18; Baskerville, "Hamilton, John"; Chadwick, *Ontarian Families*, 1:148–9; Fraser, "Jones, Jonas"; Fraser, "Macaulay, John"; Otto, "Longley, George." Macaulay, the only commissioner not named in the law, was appointed when one nominee declined to serve. Hamilton had married Macpherson's sister, Frances Pasia, in the 1820s. He acted as a witness at Macaulay's wedding to Helen Macpherson in Montreal in October 1833.

21 *Gazette*, 7 March 1833; Fraser, "Jones, Jonas," 459.

22 *Gazette*, 7 January and 11 April 1833. Asahel Whipple may have been a partner in A. Bigelow and Company; see note 60 below.

23 ANQM, notary Doucet, no. 20491, 10 May 1833; *Gazette*, 4 April 1833; *Vindicator*, 17 and 21 May 1833.

24 ANQM, notary Cardinal, unnumbered deeds of 3 July 1833 and 9 July 1833; notary Doucet, no. 21498, 28 March 1834. Charles De Witt is identified as the captain in various wood contracts for the steamer in the fall of 1833. He later bought up several of the shares which his brother had sold to residents of the area. During the Rebellions of 1837–38 or immediately afterward, John McEachern of Ormstown succeeded him as captain. Jacob De Witt seems to have been the sole owner of the steamer by January 1842, when he hired engineer William Kerr of Montreal to build and install two new furnaces and two new boilers. A boiler explosion aboard the boat the previous 20 November had killed her French-Canadian fireman (ANQM, notary Cardinal, unnumbered deeds of 25 October, 28 October, and 11 November 1833, 29 September and 15 October 1834, 27 October and 16 December 1836, 7 March 1837; notary Doucet, no. $27570\frac{1}{2}$, 22 January 1842; notary Martin, no. 828, 3 April 1837; *Bytown Gazette*, 9 December 1841; *Montreal Gazette*, 28 March 1839).

25 *Gazette*, 11 April, 14, 16 May, and 18 June 1833; *Vindicator*, 28 May 1833; *JAUC*, 1836, app., first report of the committee on finance: Post Office department, 22, 25–8, 53.

26 *Gazette*, 11 April, 30 May, and 18 June 1833. The Ogdensburg partners were S.H. Clark, W. Cleveland, and C.R. Pierce. On the operation of this American line, see *Gazette*, 11, 18, and 20 July 1833, and Shirreff, *A Tour through North America*, 142–4.

27 The merger prompted McMillan, McDonell and Company (Alexander McMillan and Archibald McDonell) to issue this notice on 12 January 1833: "It having been reported and circulated through Upper Canada, that *all* the Forwarding houses in *Prescott* had united with H. Dickinson & Co. in their line of *stages* and *steam-boats*, we beg leave to state that we *are* an exception" (*Brockville Recorder*, 17 January 1833).

28 *Brockville Recorder*, 17, 31 January and 7 February 1833; *Gazette*, 23 February, 21, 25 May 1833; *Statutes of the Province of Canada*, 7 Victoria, ch. 54, An act to authorize the president of the committee of the Canada Inland Forwarding & Insurance Co. [Adam Ferrie] to sue for the recovery of debts owed to the company. Among the leading figures in the company were Montrealers Adam Ferrie and Charles Mittleberger and, at Brockville, Paul Glasford, Robert Harvey, Jonas Jones, Moses Maynard Jr, Alexander Morris, Henry Sherwood, and forwarder William L. Whiting. Ferrie, who had moved to Canada in 1829 at the age of fifty-two, after a long business career in Scotland (see his *Autobiography* and Tulchinsky, "Ferrie, Adam"), was to be the chairman of the company, and Mittleberger, the twenty-seven-year-old son of a Montreal tailor, its secretary. The management committee of the *Brockville* consisted of Harvey, Jones, Maynard,

Brockville auctioneer Fordyce L. Lothrop, and George Crawford of Cornwall.

29 *Gazette*, 23 February and 25 May 1833.

30 Maynard advertised as agent of the Howard Insurance Company from December 1831. His relations with Mittleberger went beyond business, as a letter he wrote in the fall of 1833 shows. Mittleberger had just informed Maynard that the latter's marriage proposal to "Miss P——" had been refused. The lady is thought to have been Mittleberger's sixteen-year-old cousin, Sarah Platt, youngest surviving daughter of George Platt. "It is to you Mittleberger I have made confession of love for the only woman I ever have loved – for God's sake guard it truly," a crushed Maynard wrote, concluding wistfully, "Will you sometimes take the trouble to let me Know that She is as happy as it is my wish She should be." Sarah Platt went on to marry lawyer John Ussher Jr of Chippawa, formerly of Montreal, in September 1835. In 1838 she was on board the *Henry Brougham* when the steamer was captured by rebels at Beauharnois (see chap. 8). She and her husband later moved to Peterborough (ANQM, P345, Fonds Société d'archéologie et de numismatique, D-1/1120, Moses Maynard Jr to Charles Mittleberger, 8 November 1833; CC, register 10 September 1835; SAP register, 12 February 1817; notary Arnoldi, no. 1657, 3 May 1833; notary Doucet, no. 22924, 9 September 1835; notary Gibb, no. 6882, 5 August 1843; *Brockville Recorder*, 25 April 1834).

31 *Courant*, 26 September 1829, 11 December 1830. On 22 March 1828 forwarders John Macpherson and Company, James McCutchon, Hooker and Henderson, and H. and S. Jones had issued a joint notice disclaiming liability "as Forwarders or Common Carriers on the river St Lawrence, for the hazard and dangers of the navigation hence to Montreal." The notice ran in the *Gazette* through most of 1828 and 1829. On the formation of the Canada Inland Assurance Company in 1830, Henry Jones, of H. Jones and Company, the Montreal arm of H. and S. Jones of Brockville, became a trustee of the insurance company, and John Macpherson its secretary (*Courant*, 14 August 1830; *Gazette*, 10 April 1828).

32 See, for instance, the Ottawa and Rideau advertisements in the *Kingston Chronicle*, 12 April 1834, and the *Gazette*, 19 April 1834. Partisans of the St Lawrence route disputed the claim that insurance could be dispensed with on the Rideau, arguing that a breakdown anywhere along the canal could hold up traffic there for weeks (*Brockville Recorder*, 30 May 1834).

33 *Statutes of Upper Canada*, 3 William IV, ch. 20, An Act to Incorporate certain persons under the name and title of the Saint Lawrence Inland Marine Assurance Company; *Gazette*, 18, 20 April 1833; *Kingston Chronicle*, 29 June 1833. The first board of directors, elected on 10 June, consisted of Samuel Crane, Robert Harvey, Alfred Hooker, Alpheus Jones, Jonas Jones, Sidney Jones, George Longley, Alexander McMillan, Justus S. Merwin,

Alexander Morris, and Hiram Norton. On 13 June, Norton was named president, Morris vice-president, Alpheus Jones secretary-treasurer, and Longley and Merwin trustees. In Montreal, subscription books were kept at the office of Mathias Link, of forwarders McMillan, Link and Company (called McMillan, McDonell and Company at Prescott). Norton remained on the board for two years, serving as vice-president the second year. Jonas Jones succeeded him as president in 1834. Alpheus Jones remained secretary-treasurer into the 1840s. Jonas Jones's brothers-in-law, David B. Ogden Ford and Chilion Ford, were the company's agents at Brockville and Montreal respectively. David Ford was also a member of the board of directors from 1834. The copartnership of forwarders Macpherson and Crane and Hooker and Henderson held 5,000 of the 8,000 shares in the company, according to a listing of their joint assets in December 1834 (*Gazette*, 18 December 1834, 9 and 19 May 1835; *Kingston Chronicle*, 7 June 1834, 16 May 1835).

34 *Brockville Recorder*, 28 June and 5 July 1833. It was not just the river trade that was a concern, but traffic up and down Lake Ontario as well. Seeing that Prescott forwarders were forming ties with the owners of lake schooners in 1834, St Catharines merchant Henry Mittleberger suggested to his brother, Charles, of the Canada Inland Forwarding and Insurance Company, that the company's agent at Brockville should "favour those schooners which deliver their cargoes at Brockville in preference to those who go to Prescott and touch there [Brockville] on their return – perhaps he does, but I have an object in mentioning the thing – *viz*. would it not be well to form a line of Schooners on the lake in connexion with the Inland Forw^g & In. Co. at fair fixed rates by which the Co. would be enabled to make their charges for the whole route up & down, those vessels would have constant employment and the consigner of produce would find an unbroken responsibility until his property had reached its destination" (ANQM, P345, Fonds Société d'achéologie et de numismatique, D1/1126, Henry Mittleberger to Charles Mittleberger, 28 May 1834).

35 *Brockville Recorder*, 16 August 1833; *Gazette*, 17 August 1833; *Kingston Chronicle*, 10 and 17 August 1833.

36 *Gazette*, 6 August 1833.

37 *Brockville Recorder*, 23 August 1833, copied from *Grenville Gazette*; *Montreal Gazette*, 24 August 1833.

38 *Brockville Recorder*, 6 September 1833; *Kingston Chronicle*, 7 September 1833; *Minerve*, 12 September 1833. Jonas Jones was to accompany Norton. The committee appointed to draft the articles of association consisted of Andrew N. Buell, John Chesley, George Crawford, Ephraim Dunham, Adam Ferrie, Daniel Jones, Jonas Jones, George Longley, Fordyce L. Lothrop, Colin McDonald, Moses Maynard Jr, Charles Mittleberger, James Morris, Henry Sherwood, Joseph Shuter, and Philip VanKoughnet. Paul

Glasford, who chaired the meeting on 2 September, must also have been a member, for he again chaired the meeting of 5 September that sent Norton to Lower Canada.

39 Greenfield, "La Banque du Peuple," 1, 97.

40 *Brockville Recorder*, 10 January 1834; *Gazette*, 10, 12 September and 24 October 1833, 23 January 1834; *Kingston Chronicle*, 17 August 1833, 28 June 1834; *St Lawrence Republican*, 10 September 1833. Avery, foreman at E. Lynds and Son of Syracuse, also built the engines for the American steamers *Black Hawk*, *United States*, and *William Avery*. For the *Black Hawk*, later renamed *Dolphin*, see below, note 138. The *United States*, 145 feet long, 26 feet beam, with two 60-horsepower engines, and launched in 1831, was considered the top American steamer on Lake Ontario, the counterpart of John Hamilton's *Great Britain*, the "monarch of the lakes," built at Kingston in 1830, with her two 90-horsepower engines made by Bennet and Henderson. The *William Avery*, launched in 1833, ran between Ogdensburg and Niagara in 1834, at first under Captain W.W. Sherman, and was dismantled in 1835 (*Courier*, 27 August 1835; *Gazette*, 12 April and 6 September 1832, 26 March 1833; *Kingston Chronicle*, 10 August and 5 October 1833; Cattermole, *Emigration*, 54–6; Hough, *History of St Lawrence and Franklin Counties*, 564–5; MMGL, Van Cleve, "Reminiscences," 71, 77).

41 *Brockville Recorder*, 10 January 1834; *Kingston Chronicle*, 4, 18 January and 28 June 1834.

42 *Brockville Recorder*, 6 and 13 December 1833.

43 Ibid., 13 December 1833; *Gazette*, 22 July 1834.

44 Hilliard had previously served as purser aboard the *Great Britain*, and from 1835 he was to command the lake steamer *William IV*. His wife, Maria Ann See, whom he had married in 1833, was the daughter of David See, then agent at Sorel for the Molson and Torrance steamboat lines (ANQM, register of Christ Church, Sorel, 14 November 1833 and 21 August 1838; ZC register, 7 December 1846; *Courier*, 8 June 1835; *Gazette*, 22 July 1834; *Kingston Chronicle*, 11 April 1835; *Vindicator*, 22 November 1833).

45 *Courier*, 18 April 1835; *Gazette*, 18 March, 3 June, 8, 17, 22 July, 4 and 14 August 1834, 21 April and 30 May 1835; *St Lawrence Republican*, 1 April 1834. For the first month of the 1834 season, W.W. Sherman had commanded the *William Avery*, he then switched to the *Oswego*. Both were American steamers plying between Ogdensburg and the head of Lake Ontario. By late 1835 the *Brockville* was reported to be under the command of a Captain Brown (*Brockville Recorder*, 9 May 1834; *Kingston Chronicle*, 27 September 1834, 21 November 1835; *St Lawrence Republican*, 29 April, 6, 27 May, and 29 July 1834; Hough, *History of St Lawrence and Franklin Counties*, 565; MMGL, Van Cleve, "Reminiscences," 77).

46 *Kingston Chronicle,* 25 January 1834. The project was formally organized at a public meeting held at Prescott on 14 January 1834 under the chairmanship of Alexander McMillan, with William Benjamin Wells acting as secretary. The meeting appointed a managing and building committee consisting of Hilliard, McMillan, Alpheus Jones, Hiram Norton, and Joseph Whitney, captain of the *Great Britain,* all of Prescott; Henry Gildersleeve of Kingston; and John McDonald of Gananoque. It was estimated that the boat could be built for £5,000. The stock was split into 800 shares of £6 5s. each.

47 The Scottish-born Burden, superintendent of the Troy Iron and Nail Factory, built his 300-foot steamer, *Helen,* in 1833–34. Equipped with a 75-horsepower engine, she made her first trip from New York to Troy in $12\frac{1}{2}$ hours in July 1834. Plagued by bugs in her propulsion system and several accidents, she soon proved a disappointment. Had they awaited the outcome of Burden's experiment before following in his footsteps, the builders of the *Rapid* might have spared themselves much grief. But theirs was not the only "cigar boat" built to ply on Canadian waters. The *Northumberland,* built on the Burden principle, began running on Rice Lake in 1835 and was said to ascend the rapids near Peterborough with ease. In 1837 the 6-horsepower *Henry Burden,* described by one passenger as "a funny little steamer like a raft upon tubes – no bottom & one wheel," began running as a ferry on Lake St Francis between Fort Covington, New York, and Cornwall under her builder, Captain Paul Boynton of Canton, New York. In 1839 she was taken around by the Ottawa River and Rideau Canal to Kingston and then down to Ogdensburg, where she ran as a ferry to Prescott. The English traveller James Silk Buckingham saw her there in the summer of 1840 and was impressed: "Two long hollow tubes, of about a foot in diameter, and painted at each end, are placed parallel to each other on the water, at a distance of from ten to twelve feet apart. On these tubes a platform is laid across, surrounded by a railing; and in the centre of the whole is a water-wheel or paddle, between the tubes, worked by a small engine. The tubes having much less hold of the water than a boat's hull would have, the whole fabric is propelled with great speed by small power, because of the little resistance or friction; I should conceive it highly advantageous to introduce this principle more extensively in steam-rafts on rivers, as combining economy, speed, and capacity for burden, in a greater degree than almost any other form of construction." By 1837 Burden had set aside his "cigar boat" ideas and come up with a design for a boat with a single hull, sharp at bow and stern. The novelty this time was that his steamer, the *Diamond,* was "entirely flat at the bottom, having upright sides formed with light timber fastened together crosswise." Burden eventually took over the Troy Iron and Nail Factory, which became one of New York State's largest iron foundries (NA, RG 43, Dept. of

Railways and Canals, c 1, v. 1878, Nicholson's Rapids lockmaster's journal, entry of 20 July 1839; v. 1972, Jones' Falls lockmaster's journal, entry of 22 July 1839; *Albany Argus*, 13 September 1833, 10 July and 2 August 1834, 30 April 1838; *Courier*, 27 May 1835; *Cornwall Observer*, 5 October 1837; *Gazette*, 20 July 1837; *Hallowell Free Press*, 14 July and 25 August 1834; *Kingston Chronicle*, 15 and 22 February 1834; *Minerve*, 19 September 1833, 19 June and 14 July 1834; *Transcript*, 9 November 1837; *Vindicator*, 24 January, 15, 22 July, and 22 August 1834; Buckingham, *Canada*, 85; Crisman and Cohn, *The Burlington Bay Horse Ferry Wreck*, 32, 50; Crisman and Cohn, *When Horses Walked on Water*, 94–5, 107–8; Ellice, *Diary*, 68; Hough, *History of St Lawrence and Franklin Counties*, 565).

48 *Kingston Chronicle*, 2 August 1834; *Patents of* Canada, no. 146, 23 May 1834, "A new and useful improvement in the principle of building steam vessels"; MMGL, Van Cleve, "Reminiscences," 46. Sanford was not the only one to work at "improving" Burden's model. At the beginning of 1834, Barnabas Langdon of West Troy, New York, came up with a twin-hulled design supposedly more buoyant than Burden's. Montreal auctioneer and sometime forwarder Norman Bethune, brother of Lake Ontario steamboat owner Donald Bethune, secured two patents for his own improvements that year. Believing that Burden's boat would capsize should one of its two hulls spring a leak, he came up with a design for a boat "of an elliptical form, combining the shape of a body of a fish called the Flounder, and the throat and chest of a common frog, which may be constructed either of wood or of iron." He sought to launch a joint-stock company to build two such boats for the Montreal-Quebec trade, but nothing seems to have come of the proposal (*Gazette*, 18 February 1834; *Hallowell Free Press*, 5 May 1834; *Kingston Chronicle*, 15 February and 7 June 1834; *Minerve*, 7 April 1834; *St Lawrence Republican*, 11 February 1834; *Vindicator*, 24 January and 8 April 1834; *Patents of Canada*, no. 34, 4 February 1834, "Improvement in the construction of steam vessels and other water craft," and no. 38, 14 August 1834, "A new and useful model for building and constructing steam vessels and other descriptions of water craft").

49 *Brockville Recorder*, 11 October 1833; *Gazette*, 17 June 1834; *Hallowell Free Press*, 30 June 1834; *Kingston Chronicle*, 25 January, 8 February, and 17 May 1834; *Minerve*, 19 June 1834; Lewis, "The First Generation of Marine Engines," 18–19.

50 The description, taken from the *Montreal Herald*, was published in the *Hallowell Free Press*, 28 July 1834, and in the *Kingston Chronicle*, 2 August 1834.

51 *Brockville Recorder*, 17 January 1834.

52 Ibid., 15 August 1834; *Gazette*, 12, 19, and 28 August 1834, 6, 9 June, 29 September, and 5 December 1835; *Kingston Chronicle*, 6, 13 September and 18 October 1834; *Vindicator*, 1 August 1834; MMGL, Van Cleve,

"Reminiscences," 46. The *Rapid's* engines replaced the two Sheldon and Dutcher engines, salvaged from the *John By*, which had been installed in the *Oakville* in 1834 (see above, note 8). The *Oakville* was renamed *Hamilton* in 1836 and then *Union* after she was sold by Douglas Prentiss of Kingston to the Ottawa and Rideau Forwarding Company in 1840. As the *Union*, she ran on the Bay of Quinte (*Courier*, 12 April 1836; *Gazette*, 5 December 1840, 2 July 1841).

53 *Gazette*, 3 April and 22 July 1834, 31 May 1836; *Minerve*, 1, 9, and 30 June 1836; *Vindicator*, 27, 31 May and 28 June 1836. Pacaud bought the *Swan* in May 1836 for $5,000.

54 ANQM, notary Blackwood, no. 393, 13 June 1835; notary Cadieux, no. 203, 15 July 1834; notary Doucet, no. 23703, 23 July 1836; notary Griffin, no. 12445, 14 August 1834; *Gazette*, 19 July 1834; *Minerve*, 27 May, 22, 25 July, and 12 December 1833, 5 June, 17, 31 July 1834; *Vindicator*, 18 June, 23 July 1833, 20 May, 6 June, 1, 18 July 1834. The hitch in the 1834 sale probably stemmed from questions about Wait's title to the boat. In March 1833 he had agreed to sell a half-interest in the *Montreal* to merchant Logan Fuller. It seems that sale fell through (see ANQM, notary Arnoldi, no. 1584, 7 March 1833).

55 *Gazette*, 15 July 1834. No details of this accident have been found other than those contained in this item, which reported that arrangements were being made to raise the boat. The following summer, when there was talk of a new Rideau Canal forwarding company to be formed at Kingston, newspapers reported: "Among the boats named as likely to be engaged are the *St Andrews*, *Dalhousie*, *Iroquois* and *Enterprise*." That appears to have been the last heard of the *Dalhousie*, as well as of the *St Andrews* and the *Iroquois* (*Gazette*, 9 July 1835, copying the *Bathurst Courier*).

56 *Gazette*, 4 and 18 November 1834, 19 May 1835. In 1830 Boynton had built the small steamer *Paul Pry* at Heuvelton, New York, up the Oswegatchie River from Ogdensburg. She was used for a time as a ferry between Ogdensburg and Prescott. Boynton built the *Jack Downing* at Carthage, Jefferson County, New York, in 1834. She was hauled overland to Sackets Harbor, where she was launched. According to Hough, she was meant to serve as a ferry between Ogdensburg and Prescott, "but used for this purpose a short time at Waddington, and afterwards run from Fort Covington to Cornwall." In 1837 she was replaced as a ferry by Boynton's new steamer, *Henry Burden*, and her engine was transferred into that boat. Besides designing, building, and operating steamboats, the multi-talented Boynton also apparently "made clocks, watches, a Piano after his own fashion, & pistols ... without locks" (Ellice, *Diary*, 68; Hough, *History of St Lawrence and Franklin Counties*, 564–5; MMGL, Van Cleve, "Reminiscences," 71, 77).

57 *Gazette*, 15 May 1834.

58 Ibid., 17 July 1834.

59 Ibid., 9 and 18 December 1834, 15 January 1835.

60 The bank stock offered for sale consisted of forty shares in Kingston's Commercial Bank of the Midland District and ten shares in Montreal's City Bank. It is impossible to say exactly when Whipple had acquired a share in the line. Certainly, he was more than a simple employee in Dickinson's day. It also seems likely that he was one of the partners in A. Bigelow and Company, formed in 1833. The earliest explicit reference to him as one of the "proprietors of the line of stages and steamboats between Montreal and Prescott" is found in an 1833 wood contract for the steamboats on Lake St Louis (ANQM, notary Jobin, no. 5105, 15 July 1833). He is publicly identified as one of the owners of the line in a newspaper article in the summer of 1834. In January 1835 he was among the principals who signed the notice of the dissolution of the partnership of A. Bigelow and Company with the forwarders. A hint of James Henderson's involvement in the line after 1834 comes from the fact that in February 1843 he and Whipple jointly signed the contract to carry the mails in summer between Montreal and Dickinson's Landing and in winter between Montreal and Prescott (see ANQM, notary Griffin, no. 19673, 8 May 1843; Gazette, 22 July 1834, 15 January 1835).

61 ANQM, notary Arnoldi, no. 4853, 24 May 1836; register of the Catholic church of St Geneviève, 9 November 1818; Cornwall Observer, 30 October 1835; Courier, 1 and 6 October 1835; Gazette, 28 April, 30 May, and 11 July 1835; Vindicator, 2 and 13 December 1831, 20 January 1832; Brainard, "The Wilkins Family," 44, 49–50. Wilkins, a native of Portsmouth, New Hampshire, married the eldest of Whipple's three daughters, twenty-year-old Meribah, at Côteau on 18 December 1832. P.T. Masson was elected to the legislature in a by-election in December 1831. He did not run in the general election of 1834.

62 Gazette, 4 February 1834, 19 May 1835; Bigelow, Bigelow Family Genealogy, 1:263. Rebecca Edwards Ogden was the fourth daughter of Gouverneur Ogden of Waddington, New York. Later that year her older sister, Mary Seton Ogden, married George William Usborne of the timber-trading firm of Atkinson, Usborne and Company of Quebec (Gazette, 12 September 1835).

63 Gazette, 5 March 1835, advertisement dated 22 December 1834; Herald, 17 November 1835, advertisement dated 3 August 1835, 29 January 1836, advertisement dated 22 December 1835. Henry P. Vaughan was replaced as Aetna agent within six months. He seems to have only recently moved to Montreal from New York on the dissolution of the trading partnership of H.P. Vaughan and Company of New York, L. Vaughan and Company of Montreal, and R.A. Goodenough and Company of Toronto. R.A. Goodenough was Rollin Austin Goodenough, son of Montreal hotel keeper Asa

Goodenough of the Exchange Coffee House, the Upper Canada Line terminus. Asa Goodenough's daughter, Caroline, was the wife of Lumen Vaughan of L. Vaughan and Company (ANQM, CC register, 25 December 1827; notary Easton, no. 3566, 24 February 1849; *Herald*, 29 January 1836; *Minerve*, 9 May 1836; *Vindicator*, 10 May 1836).

64 ANQM, notary Griffin, no. 13706 and no. 13707, 3 March 1836.

65 *Gazette*, 6 January 1838; Bigelow, *Bigelow Family Genealogy*, 1:129–30, 262–4; Packard, *History of La Porte County*, 140–2, 211, 237, 434. Abijah Bigelow moved to La Porte, the county seat. Like his brother Jacob, he too became involved in politics in Indiana. In December 1839 he was one of four delegates from Clinton Township to the Whig Party convention. He ran unsuccessfully as the Abolitionist candidate for county auditor in 1843 and as one of three Whig candidates for county commissioner the following year. He subsequently moved to Cincinnati, Ohio. Regarding the movement of population to the American west in 1836, the *Gazette* reported at the end of May that the steamer *United States* had recently sailed up Lake Ontario from Ogdensburg with "800 passengers, nearly all emigrants from the northern States to the 'far West.' The *Oswego* has also carried large numbers, bound in the same direction, to Lewiston [New York]." In June, reports from Hamilton and Detroit spoke of an unprecedented "tide of emigration flowing into and through Michigan," amounting to an estimated one thousand people a day. Many of these were Americans, but Lower Canadians were also reported on the move: "An immense tide of emigration towards Illinois and Michigan has commenced lately throughout the parishes on the banks of the Richelieu ... It is limited to [French-] Canadian farmers, who are selling off their property, and are bent upon establishing themselves in 'the far west.' Three hundred have left St John's this season with this intention, principally young men, and almost every steamboat that leaves carries off from twenty to thirty" (*Courier*, 24 May 1836; *Gazette*, 31 May 1836; *Vindicator*, 3 and 7 June 1836).

66 *Kingston Chronicle*, 28 September 1833. A similar sales pitch, playing on the pride of Kingstonians, was used in the summer of 1835 to promote bank stock, and in the fall of 1835 to solicit support for the establishment of the Kingston Marine Railway Company, a ship-repair facility. (ibid., 1 July and 28 November 1835).

67 *Gazette*, 18 June 1833; *Kingston Chronicle*, 27 July, 31 August, 21 and 28 September 1833, 5 April 1834; Guillet, *Lives and Times of the Patriots*, 118; Lewis, "The First Generation of Marine Engines," 19; Robertson, *Landmarks of Toronto*, 2:842, 858. Yarker's father, Robert Yarker, had been first teller at the Bank of Canada in Montreal when Jacob Bigelow began there. As for Parker, he became the first prominent Upper Canadian rebel suspect to be arrested in 1837. One of fifteen rebels who took part in a

daring jailbreak from Fort Henry in August 1838, he was soon recaptured. Ordered transported to Australia without trial, he and several other prisoners were in transit in England when they were freed by a British court in 1839. Parker spent the rest of his life in the United States (ANQM, notary Desautels, no. 4781, 13 March 1820; *Bathurst Courier*, 10 August 1838; *Gazette*, 3 and 10 September 1839; *Kingston Chronicle*, 15 April 1835, 4 September and 30 November 1839; *Herald*, 12 August 1820; *Transcript*, 23 and 26 February 1839; Arthur, *Arthur Papers*, part 1: 130–1, and part 4: 266; Guillet, *Lives and Times of the Patriots*, 117–18, 201–7).

68 *Brockville Recorder*, 27 September and 11 October 1833; *Gazette*, 17 October 1833; *Kingston Chronicle*, 19 October 1833.

69 *Kingston Chronicle*, 5 April 1834. Launched in the spring of 1833, the *Kingston* had been found "unfit for navigation" at her trial on 20 July that year. Over the next month, she had had to undergo a major overhaul, including the addition of false sides, consisting of $1\frac{1}{4}$-inch boards, to steady her. Finally, on 30 August she left Kingston on her first trip up the Bay of Quinte. In June 1834 she was said to be "the best running boat on the river" after she had run from Brockville to Prescott in fifty-three minutes. She was 110 feet in length, 16 feet beam, and 32 feet wide on deck, and had sleeping accommodation for forty – twenty-eight berths in the men's cabin below deck, twelve in the women's on deck (*Gazette*, 26 March and 18 June 1833; *Hallowell Free Press*, 30 June 1834; *Kingston Chronicle*, 27 July and 31 August 1833, 29 November 1834).

70 Her regular captain in 1834 was John Ives. Moody had commanded her in 1833 after serving as captain of Parker's other steamer, *Perseverance*, the renovated old *Toronto*, built in 1825. He went on to work as purser on the *Great Britain* under Captain Joseph Whitney and then commanded the *St George* from 1837 or 1838. In 1843, he would succeed Asahel Whipple as manager of the Canada Steamboat and Mail Coach Company in Montreal, holding that position until 1849. The following year he owned and commanded his own steamer, the 138-ton *British Empire*. In 1852 he was master of the *Jenny Lind*, which ran between Ogdensburg and Montreal for the Ontario and St Lawrence Steamboat Company. There are several tantalizing hints of some link between him and Horace Dickinson and the Bigelows, so much so that one cannot help but wonder whether Moody might have got his start working for the Upper Canada Line. To begin with, his parents hailed from Amherst, Massachusetts, the same area as Horace Dickinson; in fact, his mother, Sally, was a Dickinson. Moody himself was born at Canton, St Lawrence County, New York, on 24 July 1806, a year or so before Horace Dickinson settled in that county. On 29 January 1834, the day before Abijah Bigelow's wedding at Waddington, Moody married Julia Ann Guest at nearby Ogdensburg. At the time, he lived in Prescott. He and his wife named one of their sons, born in 1837, Horace

Dickinson Moody, though it is not clear whether this was after the founder of the Upper Canada Line or some closer family connection of the same name. Finally, Moody's brother-in-law, Silas Wright, a close friend and ally of President Martin Van Buren and future governor of New York, was chairman of the Senate finance committee during Van Buren's presidency (1837–41) – years when Jacob Bigelow was seeking financial compensation from the American government for the heirs of François Cazeau (ANQM, APC register, 4 September 1860. NA, RG 42, E 1, Dept. of Marine, Ship Registers, 175: no. 14 for 1850; *British Whig,* 7 April 1838; *Gazette,* 18 June 1833, 20 February 1834; *Kingston Chronicle,* 5 April and 29 November 1834, 14 February 1835; *St Lawrence Republican,* 4 February 1834; *Vindicator,* 18 April 1834; "Witness Jubilee Symposium," 23 May 1896, reminiscences of Alexander Milloy; Hough, *History of St Lawrence and Franklin Counties,* 567; E.V. Smith, *Descendants of Nathaniel Dickinson,* 433; MMGL, Van Cleve, "Reminiscences," 47; Van Cleve, *Ontario and St Lawrence Steamboat Company's Hand-Book for Travelers,* 4, 6; information on the Moody family from the St Lawrence County Historical Association, Canton, New York).

71 *Gazette,* 8 July 1834; *Kingston Chronicle,* 29 November 1834, 14 February 1835; *Vindicator,* 18 April 1834. The *Kingston* was raised and repaired, and sailed the following year between Prescott and the head of the Bay of Quinte under Captain N. Calder, formerly purser aboard the Lake Ontario steamer *Britannia* (*Kingston Chronicle,* 18 April 1835).

72 *Gazette,* 18 June 1833. Among the owners of the *St George* identified in a report on a meeting of shareholders held on 28 November 1834 were John Kirby, Thomas Kirkpatrick, Anthony Manahan, Hilary Dupuy, John Counter, Walter McCuniffe, William Wilson, Lieutenant Colonel J.R. Wright, commander of the Royal Engineers at Kingston, John Strange, and David John Smith. Smith bought the *St George* from his fellow owners for £7,250 on 2 March 1835 (*Courier,* 7 March 1835; *Gazette,* 24 January and 13 June 1835; *Kingston Chronicle,* 29 November 1834, 4 March 1835).

73 *Brockville Recorder,* 7 June 1833; *Gazette,* 26 March and 18 June 1833; *Kingston Chronicle,* 6, 27 July and 10 August 1833, 5 and 12 April 1834; Robertson, *Landmarks of Toronto,* 2:859.

74 *Brockville Recorder,* 22 August 1834; *Kingston Chronicle,* 26 July 1825. The *William IV,* built at Gananoque by Jesse Wood of New York and about the same size as the *St George,* was launched in the fall of 1831 and fitted with a 100-horsepower Ward engine. Sidney Jones was one of her principal stockholders, with Henry Gildersleeve, Alpheus Jones, John McDonald, Alexander McMillan, and Lieutenant Colonel J.R. Wright of the Royal Engineers. She was commanded at this time by Charles Paynter, formerly captain of the *Hercules* towboat between Montreal and Quebec. She grounded and sank in the fall of 1840; raised with difficulty, she was

bought by Alpheus Jones, who ran her as a tugboat between Dickinson's Landing and Kingston (*Brockville Recorder*, 2 and 9 June 1831; *Gazette*, 12 April 1832, 18 June 1833, 3, 14, 21, 24 November and 26 December 1840, 20 May 1841; *Kingston Chronicle*, 10 March 1832; I. Scott, *Yesterday's News*, 74).

75 In November 1834 the merchants of Port Hope voted to boycott the *St George*, alleging that Harper was biased against them. This spat was resolved the following spring. In the summer of 1835 the crew of the *St George* corralled passengers who had just arrived at Kingston by the Rideau to keep them from going aboard the *Great Britain* (*Courier*, 10 July 1835; *Kingston Chronicle*, 29 November, 20 and 27 December 1834, 14 January and 8 April 1835).

76 *Brockville Recorder*, 1 and 22 August 1834.

77 *Kingston Chronicle*, 26 July 1834.

78 Ibid. Built at Kingston in 1833–34 by Henry Gildersleeve for the Bay of Quinte service, the *Commodore Barrie* was launched on 9 May 1834. She was 133 feet long, 35 feet broad overall, with 8 feet 9 inches depth of hold, and powered by two 35-horsepower Ward engines. Her captain was Redford S. Robins, who was to command the *Bytown* on the Rideau Canal in 1835–36 and the *Ottawa* between Lachine and Carillon from 1837. The *Commodore Barrie* was lost off Presqu'ile on 30 April 1842 after colliding with a schooner (*Gazette*, 28 April 1835, 7 May 1842; *Kingston Chronicle*, 28 September 1833, 5 April and 10 May 1834, 27 September 1835; Robertson, *Landmarks of Toronto*, 2:877; Thomas, *History of ... Argenteuil ... [and] Prescott*, 27–8).

79 The *Kingston Chronicle* laid down the patriotic line: "Apart from the general usefulness of the Canal, the town of Kingston is likely to be benefited by it in an especial manner; it therefore becomes our inhabitants to promote its interests as far as they are able; and accordingly, our duty to set forth its advantages" (*Brockville Recorder*, 23 May 1834, reproducing an article from the *Kingston Chronicle*).

80 *Kingston Chronicle*, 12 April and 24 May 1834.

81 Ibid., 17, 31 May, 7 June, 12 and 26 July 1834.

82 Ibid., 8 March and 23 August 1834. It seems that Drummond was indebted to McCutchon's brother, Peter McGill. After Drummond's brewery-distillery burned down on 27 September 1835, McGill notified the Alliance Fire Insurance Company to withhold payments to Drummond's estate on the grounds that Drummond owed his firm "large sums of money" (ANQM, notary Arnoldi, no. 4486, 7 October 1835; *Courier*, 3 October 1835).

83 Bilson, *A Darkened House*, 70–84; Godfrey, *The Cholera Epidemics in Upper Canada*, 40–9. Bilson says that at least 1,500 people died at Quebec and 882 at Montreal. Reports from Kingston spoke of anywhere from

95 to 265: "Sir John Colborne himself believed that a more accurate death toll was 150. Yet the number of cases and deaths in a town with a resident population of about 4,800 was enough to cause considerable fear." Godfrey says that by mid-August 9 deaths had been reported at Brockville and 7 at Cornwall, and by 1 September, 59 at Prescott.

84 ANQM, CC register, 21 July 1834; *Gazette*, 14 August 1834; *Kingston Chronicle*, 27 September, 8 and 15 November 1834; *Minerve*, 21 July 1834; *Vindicator*, 22 July and 5 August 1834; Wise, "Tory Factionalism," 219–20.

85 The Tay Navigation Company, organized on 26 April 1831, built the Tay Canal, consisting essentially of four small locks on the River Tay linking Perth to the Rideau Canal. Well before the locks were completed in 1834, the company decided to build a steamer, the *Enterprise*, to ply between Perth, Bytown, and Kingston. Shares were offered for sale at £10 apiece in the summer of 1832. The *Enterprise*, 83 feet by 19 feet, was launched at Perth on 3 April 1833 and then fitted with two 10-horsepower engines at Kingston. She began operating in the fall of 1833, under a Captain Elliott, formerly of the Royal Navy; later her master was a William Richards. Her cabins below deck offered twelve berths for men and six for women. But the Tay proved too shallow for her, and her difficulties there made her the butt of jokes. She was broken up in 1836 (*Bathurst Courier*, 31 July 1835; *Brockville Recorder*, 30 August 1832, 11 April and 28 June 1833; *Gazette*, 3 October 1833; Legget, *Rideau Waterway*, 141; Mills, *Canadian Coastal and Inland Steam Vessels*, 39, and Supplement 2, no. 902; Turner, *Perth*, 46–7).

86 *Bathurst Courier*, 23 January 1835; *Kingston Chronicle*, 17 May 1834.

87 *Bathurst Courier*, 17 October 1834.

88 Ibid., 23 January 1835; *British Whig*, 30 March 1835; *Gazette*, 24 January, 5, 7, 21 February, and 28 April 1835; *Kingston Chronicle*, 31 January, 4 February, 11 March, and 4 April 1835; *Courier*, 18 April 1835. Major stockholders at Kingston included Joseph Bruce, John S. Cartwright, John Counter, Henry Gildersleeve, Thomas Kirkpatrick, and George W. Yarker. John Redpath, age thirty-nine, married Robert Drummond's nineteen-year-old niece, Jane Drummond, at Kingston that September (*Kingston Chronicle*, 12 September 1835. *Minerve*, 17 September 1835).

89 *Bathurst Courier*, 23 January 1835.

90 *Hallowell Free Press*, 5 May 1834; Lafrenière, *Le réseau de canalisation de la rivière des Outaouais*, 34.

91 Born near Chatham, England, Thomas Kains is said to have joined the Royal Navy at fourteen and moved to Canada in 1818. He settled at Grenville, buying a sawmill from Thomas Mears. Three years later he married Mary MacMillan, daughter of Grenville postmaster Archibald MacMillan. He became captain of the *Shannon* in the early 1830s and remained so until the end of 1840, when he devoted himself to developing a spa at the

Georgian Springs, a property he owned near the popular Caledonia Springs resort, inland from L'Orignal. In 1842 he came out with his own steamer, *Princess Royal,* which ran between Grenville and Bytown. Thomas says that he was called back to naval duty in England on the outbreak of the Crimean War in 1853 and died in Montreal four years later (ANQM, register of Anglican Church, St Andrew's, 17 December 1821; *Bathurst Courier,* 23 January 1835; *Bytown Gazette,* 11 June 1840, 4 May 1843; *Montreal Gazette,* 4 July 1833; *Hallowell Free Press,* 5 May 1834; *Kingston Chronicle,* 24 May 1834; *Transcript,* 3 September 1841; Disturnell, *The Picturesque Tourist,* 242. Thomas, *History of ... Argenteuil ... [and] Prescott,* 368, 374, 644).

92 ANQM, notary Griffin, no. 12763, 18 December 1834; *Bathurst Courier,* 23 January 1835; *British Whig,* 2 April 1835; *Gazette,* 5 February 1835; *Morning Courier,* 18 April 1835. Brush had successively commanded the Montreal-Quebec steamers *Hercules, St George, British America,* and *Canada* for John Torrance's towboat company. In his move to the Ottawa and Rideau Forwarding Company, he was followed by another *Canada* hand, purser William A. Bowen, who was given command of the canal steamer *Rideau* in 1835 and then of the *Bytown* in 1836. As for McCutchon, after leaving the Ottawa and Rideau, he was involved in 1836 in plans to revive his brother Peter McGill's Marmora Iron Works in Upper Canada. By 1840 he was a resident of Toronto, where he lived in the house of his late uncle, John McGill, until 1870 (*Bathurst Courier,* 13 May 1836; *Morning Courier,* 9 February 1836; *Gazette,* 28 April 1835, 16 May 1840; Lundell, *The Estates of Old Toronto,* 51; Robertson, *Landmarks of Toronto,* 1:223).

93 Bush, *Commercial Navigation on the Rideau Canal,* 104.

94 *Vindicator,* 24 January 1834.

95 "Witness Jubilee Symposium," 5 June 1897, reminiscences of William Dickson.

96 *Kingston Chronicle,* 1 July 1835.

97 *Courier,* 3 and 10 July 1835. A scheme similar to the one advanced by the St Lawrence Association was proposed in an 1835 pamphlet by its former secretary, James George of Quebec (*Courier,* 27 May 1835).

98 Thomas, *History of ... Argenteuil ... [and] Prescott,* 28. Thomas reproduces Robert Ward Shepherd's "Memory of Early Steam Boating on the St Lawrence and Ottawa Rivers and Rideau Canals," the manuscript of which is in the R.W. Shepherd Papers, MG 29, A 55/1, at the National Archives. Shepherd says that the *Nonsuch* was "commanded by Capt. James Greaves, afterward chief of Rural Police at Vaudreuil." In 1835, however, her commander was William Squire. Shepherd does not say exactly how long she ran, but in noting the first trip of a new Rideau steamer, the *Hunter,* under Captain Morehouse in September 1838, the *Bathurst*

Courier reported that the new boat had a 28-horsepower engine formerly belonging to the *Shannon*. This would have been one of the *Shannon's* two old 28-horsepower engines that had gone into the *Nonsuch*. It would seem, then, that the *Nonsuch* was out of service by the summer of 1838 (ANQM, register of St Andrew's Presbyterian Church, Lachine, 20 December 1835; *Bathurst Courier*, 7 September 1838; *Gazette*, 28 April 1835; *Kingston Chronicle*, 1 July 1835).

99 *British Whig*, 22 September 1835; *Gazette*, 22 and 24 May 1834; *Vindicator*, 2 July 1833; Bush, *Commercial Navigation on the Rideau Canal*, 104.

100 *Gazette*, 21 April 1836.

101 Ibid., 23 April 1836.

102 Shirreff, *A Tour through North America*, 143.

103 Ibid., 142.

104 *Gazette*, 3 May and 21 June 1836; *Minerve*, 5 May 1836.

105 *Courier*, 6 May 1836; *Gazette*, 22 December 1835; *Kingston Chronicle*, 24 October 1835.

106 MU, MS338, Ottawa & Rideau Forwarding Co., report of the committee of management for the year ending March 1837, 29 March 1837 (most of this document is reproduced in R. Reid, *The Upper Ottawa Valley to 1855*, 190–3); *Gazette*, 14, 21 June, 7, 16 July, and 6 August 1836; Bush, *Commercial Navigation on the Rideau Canal*, 69; Legget, *Rideau Waterway*, 165–6.

107 The Ottawa and Rideau did have some barges which, since 1835, had been fitted with masts and sails to enable them to run down the St Lawrence if necessary. Few actually did so, it seems, though the company did advertise at the opening of navigation in 1836 that for the downward traffic, its barges would travel by the Rideau or the St Lawrence "as circumstances require" (*Gazette*, 21 April 1836; *Kingston Chronicle*, 22 July 1835).

108 ANQM, notary Arnoldi, no. 4100, 7 April 1835; MU, MS338, Ottawa & Rideau Forwarding Co., report of the committee of management for the year ending March 1837, 29 March 1837; *Courier*, 12 January and 14 March 1835; *Gazette*, 24 May and 20 September 1834, 6 January, 11, 25 April, 24 and 29 September 1835, 21 June 1836. According to the Ottawa and Rideau management committee report, the offer of a merger came from the Canada Inland Forwarding and Insurance Company and "entailed great extra expense on the [Ottawa and Rideau] Co. without yielding a proportionable profit besides having taken in their stock at a high valuation. The only thing that can be said in its favour was the necessity to which the agents were reduced to do something to prevent the total loss of their business & enable them to fulfil existing Contracts and thereby prevent a great loss."

109 *Gazette*, 28 June 1836.

110 Ibid., 13 September 1836

111 Ibid., 23 April 1836.
112 *Bytown Gazette,* 17 and 24 November 1836; *Transcript,* 31 December 1836.
    The Ottawa Lumber Association was formed on 1 March 1836, with
    George Buchanan as chairman and Alexander James Christie as secretary
    (Lower, *Great Britain's Woodyard,* 164–5; R. Reid, *The Upper Ottawa
    Valley to 1855,* 127–9).
113 *Bytown Gazette,* 17 November 1836.
114 MU, MS338, Ottawa & Rideau Forwarding Co., report of the committee of
    management for the year ending March 1837. The committee for 1836–37
    consisted of chairman John Frothingham, Peter McGill, Emery Cushing,
    John Redpath, John Molson Jr, and John Fisher (*Gazette,* 2 April 1836).
    The only change in 1837–38 was that Thomas Phillips replaced Fisher.
115 The first indication of an 1836 pact comes in a notice in the *Gazette* of
    28 October 1843 in which the two companies refer to a "Business Connex-
    ion which has subsisted between the 'Ottawa and Rideau Forwarding Com-
    pany,' and Macpherson, Crane & Co. since the Fifteenth day of December,
    1836." Macpherson remained on the board of directors of the Bank of
    Montreal until 1839. From 1840, after he moved to Kingston, he served as
    a director of the Commercial Bank of the Midland District (*Gazette,* 7 June
    1836, 11 June 1841, 15 June 1842; *Kingston Chronicle,* 12 July 1843;
    Upper Canada Herald, 7 July 1840; Denison, *Canada's First Bank,* 2:421).
116 In 1837 William L. Whiting and Company became Whiting and Chandler
    at Montreal and S.B. Whiting and Company at Brockville. William Whit-
    ing's partnership with S.B. Whiting and Thomas Chandler was dissolved on
    12 March 1838. Around that time, he appears to have moved to Chicago
    (*Gazette,* 28 March 1837, 15 March 1838, 3 October 1839; *Patriot,* 4 May
    1838).
117 *Bathurst Courier,* 21 April 1837; *Gazette,* 28 March 1837, 17 May 1841;
    JAC, 1841, app. EE, report of the select committee on transport costs, testi-
    mony of Francis Henderson, of Hooker and Henderson.
118 MU, MS338, Ottawa & Rideau Forwarding Co., minutes of annual general
    meeting 29 March 1837, and report of the committee of management for
    the year ending March 1837.
119 *Gazette,* 25 April 1837, notice dated 18 April.
120 ANQM, APC register, 19 April 1837; notary Hunter, no. 341, 24 April 1837,
    and no. 351, 8 May 1837; *Gazette,* 18 April 1837; *Vindicator,* 18 April
    1837. The nature of Cushing's ailment was not specified in the newspaper
    obituaries, but smallpox had been raging in Montreal since the end of 1836
    and cases of scarlet fever also abounded that spring, both diseases result-
    ing in many deaths (*Minerve,* 9 January 1837; *Transcript,* 16 February,
    9 and 11 March 1837).
121 *Gazette,* 6 May 1837. Cushing's widow, Mary Ann Bostwick, took over
    responsibility for her late husband's Montreal-Bytown postal contract,

hiring men to carry the mails on the route (see ANQM, notary Hunter, no. 345, 3 May 1837; no. 469, 2 October 1837; no. 490, 24 October 1837; and no. 929, 16 October 1838.

122 ANQM, notary Arnoldi, no. 3476, 24 May 1834, and no. 4835, 21 May 1836; notary Hunter, no. 328, 8 April 1837; *Gazette*, 14 April 1838, 27 April 1841. On Ferguson's becoming a partner, the name of the firm remained Macpherson and Crane at Kingston, but at Montreal, John Macpherson and Company became Macpherson, Crane and Company.

123 *Bytown Gazette*, 11, 17, 24 May, 14 June 1837; *Montreal Gazette*, 10 June and 1 July 1837; *Morning Courier*, 17 August 1836; *Transcript*, 17 June 1837. The *Bathurst Courier* reported in May 1837 that the Bytown Mutual Forwarding Company had also bought the steamer *Kingston* for use on the Rideau Canal. That report appears to have been in error, as was one in the *Montreal Gazette* in March that the *Kingston* was to be taken through the Welland Canal to ply on Lake Erie. While it seems that some shares in the *Kingston* were sold that spring (six shares had also been offered at a Kingston auction in July 1835), reports later that year placed her on the run between Prescott and the Bay of Quinte (*Bathurst Courier*, 7 April and 19 May 1837; *Gazette*, 4 March, 1 and 22 April 1837; *Kingston Chronicle*, 22 July 1835).

124 *Gazette*, 3 June and 1 July 1837. Finchley was something of a rogue. In the early 1820s he had been convicted of assault and battery and fined for speeding – riding his horse "faster than at a moderate trot" through the streets of Montreal – and for some reason, from lieutenant in the militia, he was busted back to the ranks. When he advertised in 1823 that he had formed forwarding connections with the *Frontenac* and other Lake Ontario boats, a lake forwarder took out an advertisement to deny that any such arrangements had been made. At the time, James McCutchon acted as Finchley's agent at Kingston and Curtis E. Crossman was his clerk at Lachine. Finchley announced his retirement from forwarding in 1826 and sold his business to McCutchon and Crossman. But he was back in business by 1829; besides doing some of his own forwarding that year, he signed a contract to supply batteaux to St Lawrence forwarders John Macpherson and Company, Hooker and Henderson, and James McCutchon, and S. Finchley and Sons advertised as agent for the Ottawa Steamboat Company. He seems to have continued as a contractor and agent for other forwarders from then on. One of his sons, Charles, a minor, went to work as a clerk and accountant for John Macpherson and Company in 1832. Stephen Finchley worked for the Ottawa Steamboat Company in 1834 and then switched to the rival Canada Inland Forwarding and Insurance Company in 1835, only to be sacked that April. He was promptly rehired by the Ottawa company's successor, the Ottawa and Rideau Forwarding Company, with whom he remained through 1835–36; he then signed up with

the new Bytown Mutual Forwarding Company (ANQM, notary Arnoldi,
no. 1037, 3 January 1832; no. 1170, 7 April 1832; notary Gibb, no. 1540,
14 September 1837; notary Griffin, no. 4164, 18 May 1822; no. 8023,
22 January 1829; *Courant*, 10 April 1824, 22 March 1826, 27 May and
26 September 1829; *Gazette*, 2 November 1822, 7 January 1824, 25 April
and 2 May 1835, 21 May 1836; *Montreal Herald*, 21 December 1822,
18 January 1823; *Kingston Chronicle*, 18 April 1823; *Upper Canada
Herald*, 6 May 1823).

125 NA, MG 24, D 8, Wright Papers, 134:70178–9, resolution of the Bytown
    Mutual Forwarding Co., 6 May 1839; *Bytown Gazette*, 17 and 24 January
    1838, 28 August 1839. That last issue of the *Bytown Gazette* reprinted an
    article from the *British Whig* that said: "This year the [Ottawa and
    Rideau] Company took the 'Endeavour' off the Grenville Canal, and
    brought her to Kingston where her engine has been completely over-
    hauled and new boilers constructed." The editor of the *Bytown Gazette*
    commented that the *Endeavour* would be worse than useless because she
    could not pack an engine powerful enough to tow barges and did not have
    sufficient accommodation to be a passenger boat. But it is scarcely credible
    that the Ottawa and Rideau would have gone to the expense of repairing
    the boat had she truly been a lost cause. She was towed up to Kingston by
    the Ottawa and Rideau steamer *Hunter* in May 1839 and was out of circu-
    lation until late August, when she made a few appearances on the Rideau
    Canal and then vanished – at precisely the time when a steamer called the
    Mohawk appeared there out of the blue. It seems likely that the *Mohawk*
    was a reincarnation of the *Tay/Endeavour*, the change of name perhaps
    meant to erase memories of her previous deficiencies. Little is known of
    the *Mohawk* except that she formed part of the Ottawa and Rideau
    steamer fleet through 1841 (NA, RG 43, Dept. of Railways and Canals, C1,
    v. 1878, Nicholson's Rapids lockmaster's journal, entries of 7 May, 23, 27,
    29 August, and 5 September 1839; v. 1972, Jones' Falls lockmaster's jour-
    nal, entries of 9 May, 20, 24, and 26 August; *Bytown Gazette*, 29 April
    1841; Mills, *Canadian Coastal and Inland Steam Vessels*, Supplement 2,
    no. 1899a).

126 *Bytown Gazette*, 23 August and 27 September 1837, 16 May 1838; *Mon-
    treal Gazette*, 9 September 1837; Bush, *Commercial Navigation on the
    Rideau Canal*, 106. For complaints about delays and irregular service, see
    Bytown Gazette, 20, 27 October and 17 November 1836, 17 May 1837,
    13 June 1838.

127 *Gazette*, 25 April 1837.

128 ANQM, notary Hunter, no. 905, 19 September 1838, and no. 937, 27 Octo-
    ber 1838; *Bytown Gazette*, 9 May 1838; *Kingston Chronicle*, 26 May 1838;
    Montreal Gazette, 20 April 1839; *Transcript*, 8 May 1838. No copy has
    survived of the cartel agreements which Macpherson and Crane made with

the other forwarders in 1838, but the notarized documents cited above contain excerpts. These make it clear that in return for abiding by a common rate schedule, the forwarders were promised towing for their boats "between Lachine and Kingston *via* the Ottawa River & Rideau Canal" by Macpherson and Crane. Article 19 of the agreement with Edward Hackett and Company, dated 17 April 1838, established a £2,000 penalty for any violation of the terms. A copy of the "articles of agreement between Murray & Sanderson and Macpherson, Crane & Co. – dated 24th April 1838" was presented in evidence in a lawsuit in 1840, but it is no longer in the court file (ANQM, Cour Supérieure-Montréal, no. 589, Donald Murray et al. v. John Macpherson et al., February term, 1840).

129 For H. and S. Jones's ambitions, see the *Bytown Gazette*, 25 April 1838.

130 *Cornwall Observer*, 9 May 1839. Along with Whipple and Masson, another small forwarding firm active on the St Lawrence around this time was Anderson and Garfield of Cornwall. In addition, Murray and Sanderson may have played a minor role in forwarding up the St Lawrence: at its founding in 1838 the firm advertised that, besides operating on the Ottawa-Rideau route, it was prepared to ship goods "to places below Prescott via the River St Lawrence" (*Gazette*, 21 November 1840; *Patriot*, 4 May 1838).

131 MU, MS255/1, Charles Kadwell Papers, "Notes, &c during a Trip from Montreal to Upper Canada and back, From the 3rd to the 18th August 1838." The passage is found under date of 4 August.

132 *Transcript*, 17 July and 14 August 1838. The going price for Cushing's shares is not known. In April 1835, shortly after the Ottawa and Rideau Forwarding Company came into being, its stock was said to total £22,500, split into 426 shares. Each share, then, would have had a nominal value of roughly £52 16s., but seven months later, 9 shares changed hands at a reported price of £24 each. In 1839 the total stock was said to be £50,000 (*Courier*, 16 April and 26 November 1835; *Transcript*, 10 October 1839).

133 *Gazette*, 11 July 1839, 19 May and 23 June 1841; *Transcript*, 1 August 1840; R. Reid, *The Upper Ottawa Valley to 1855*, 195–6. The company declared a dividend at the end of its 1838–39 financial year, the value of which is unknown. Its profits for 1839–40 were estimated at about 40 per cent, and at the end of the 1840–41 season, it paid another dividend, this time of £3 10s. per share.

134 *Gazette*, 13 September 1836; *Transcript*, 8 May 1838. For the Rideau Canal tolls, see Tulloch, *The Rideau Canal*, 156–7. For tolls on the Ottawa canals, see *Courier*, 5 April 1836; *Gazette*, 23 April 1839.

135 *Bytown Gazette*, 9 May 1838.

136 *British Whig*, 7 April 1838; *Bytown Gazette*, 25 April 1838; Lewis, "Until Further Notice", 23–4.

137 *Statutes of Upper Canada*, 1 Victoria, ch. 30, An Act to Incorporate sundry persons, under the name of the Kingston Marine Railway Company; *British Whig*, 7 April, 16 June, 13 July 1838; *Gazette*, 30 June 1838; *Kingston Chronicle*, 22 April 1843; *Transcript*, 16 November 1837; Angus, "Counter, John," 162; Lewis, "Until Further Notice," 27–8.

138 MU, MS255/1, Charles Kadwell Papers, "Notes, &c during a Trip from Montreal to Upper Canada and back, From the 3rd to the 18th August 1838," entry under date of 4 August; *British Whig*, 7 April and 13 July 1838; Lewis, "Until Further Notice," 24, 27–8, 32–3. The Joneses later unsuccessfully sued John Hamilton for breach of contract, claiming that he had reneged on an agreement whereby their two steamers, *William IV* and *Sir Robert Peel*, and his six were to share in a government contract that Hamilton had obtained to transport troops and munitions that year and for which he was paid £8,000 on 1 January 1839 (UCQB, 3:170–2, Jones v. Hamilton). The *Dolphin* was formerly the American boat *Black Hawk*, built at French Creek (Clayton), New York, by George S. Weeks in 1833 and equipped with an engine made by William Avery. She was 125 feet long and 30 feet broad over all. She had sailed between French Creek, Ogdensburg, and Kingston until 1835, when she had begun running from Ogdensburg to Dickinson's landing. A report in 1836 said that she had been sold to "Canadian interests," refitted, and renamed the *Dolphin*, and that she had begun running between Prescott and Dickinson's Landing. Two years later, however, she was said to be still "a Yankee boat ... chartered by the Messrs. Jones, of Brockville" (*British Whig*, 13 July 1838; *Courier*, 26 April 1836; *Gazette*, 26 March and 18 June 1833, 13 and 20 June 1835; Hough, *History of Franklin and St Lawrence Counties*, 564; MMGL, Van Cleve, "Reminiscences," 77).

139 *Gazette*, 9, 20 April, 8 and 15 June 1839.

140 Ibid., 20 April 1839. What the terms of the new agreement were, or what changes may have taken place in its ownership, is not known. The Canada Steamboat and Mail Coach Company did not own any of the boats on the Ottawa-Rideau. That it had access to Ottawa and Rideau Forwarding Company vessels on that route in 1839 probably stemmed from Macpherson and Crane's connection with both companies.

CHAPTER EIGHT

1 JAC, 1841, app. EE, report of the select committee on transport costs, testimony of Samuel Crane.

2 *Gazette*, 30 November 1833.

3 Ibid., 26 March and 11 April 1835.

4 ANQM, notary Arnoldi, no. 4100, 7 April 1835; notary Gibb, no. 4329, 2 April 1841. *Gazette*, 3 January, 25 April, 2 May, 24 and 29 September

1835, 10 March 1841; *Bathurst Courier*, 10 April 1835; *Statutes of the Province of Canada*, 7 Victoria, ch. 59, An Act to authorize the president of the committee of the Canada Inland Forwarding and Insurance Company to sue for the recovery of debts owed to the company; UCQB, 8:192–202, Ferrie v. Jones. Besides Whiting and Maynard, the Montreal firm of J. and J. Scott and Company also pulled out, and in April 1835 Stephen Finchley was sacked as the company's freight agent shortly after being hired. At a directors' meeting that month, secretary Charles Mittleberger accused company accountant Samuel Tubby of cooking the books. Tubby sued for slander, but a jury ruled against him. His and Whiting's alleged "defalcations" and other debts owed to the company remained an issue into the 1850s.

5 *Courier*, 14 March 1835; *Gazette*, 11 April 1835. Venting his anger at the Brockville Board of Police for barring steamers from entering or leaving port on Sundays, an irate correspondent had written to the *Brockville Recorder* in the fall of 1834: "If anything can induce the Canadian Inland Forwarding & Insurance Company to change their Head Quarters, this arrangement should … The good people of Prescott may congratulate themselves on this act of our Police, as doubtless all the Merchants of the upper Country and Steam Boat proprietors will find it prudent to ship direct to head Quarters for a little fore-sight may easily predict that all forwarding will from such circumstance concentrate there" (*Brockville Recorder*, 3 and 10 October 1834; Leavitt, *History of Leeds and Grenville*, 190).

6 *Courier*, 12 January 1836. The notice by company chairman Adam Ferrie is dated 31 December 1835.

7 ANQM, notary Doucet, no. 24359, 17 April 1837; notary Griffin, no. 14986, 6 April 1837; notary Hunter, no. 689, 11 December 1837; no. 725, 21 February 1838; no. 756, 26 March 1838; no. 1078, 22 April 1839; *Courier*, 12 January 1836; *Gazette*, 28 June 1836, 22 April 1837; *Kingston Chronicle*, 21 August 1839; Ferrie, *Autobiography*, 25; McKendry, *Historic Portsmouth Village*, 1–2, 40, 47. In April 1837 Ferrie and several other Montreal merchants entered into a three-year pact to forward all their goods through Hackett and Dickinson and to advance them a total of up to £2,000, in return for preferential freight rates and other advantages. Besides Ferrie, the merchants were John Smith, William Bradbury, William Ritchie and Company, and Playfair, McLean and Company. When Hackett and Dickinson joined the Ottawa-Rideau forwarding cartel in April 1838, they were allowed to continue charging preferential rates to these clients (see ANQM, notary Hunter, no. 937, 27 October 1838). The three-year pact between Hackett and Dickinson and the Montreal merchants was cancelled on 10 January 1839.

8 *Courant*, 24 November 1830; *Gazette*, 11 June 1825, 21 April 1828, 19 October 1833, 14 August 1834, 13 June, 7 and 28 July 1840; *Minerve*,

24 October 1833; *Transcript,* 16 June 1840; Mika and Mika, *Canada's First Railway,* 11–14; Tulchinsky, *River Barons,* 169–86.

9 Mackey, "The Railroad that Never Was." The railway was to follow the line of a projected canal for which surveys had been made in 1833–35 (*Gazette,* 27 August 1836, 10 August 1842; *Kingston Chronicle,* 14 February 1835).

10 ANQM, notary Arnoldi, no. 3090, 14 December 1833; notary Doucet, no. 19919, 2 October 1832; no. 19998, 6 November 1832; no. 20362, 25 March 1833; *Gazette,* 22 September 1832, 29 September 1835; *Minerve,* 9 January 1834; *Vindicator,* 10 December 1833. Guy Warwick died on 21 November 1833, at age forty-seven. Joseph Warwick survived until 13 July 1837, when he died at age fifty-five (ANQM, CC register, 25 November 1833; *Transcript,* 15 July 1837).

11 ANQM, notary Doucet, no. 22067, 12 November 1834; *Vindicator,* 21 June 1833. Johnson and Clarke built the engines for the 92-foot *Union Canadienne,* which began running as a ferry between Montreal and Longueuil in August 1833 and was destroyed by fire at Chambly on 9 July 1836, and for the Three Rivers ferry *Trois Rivières* (ANQM, notary Doucet no. 21220, 7 January 1834; NA, RG 42 E 1, Dept. of Marine, Ship Registers, 175: no. 6 for 1834; *Gazette,* 12 July 1836, 2 January 1837; *Minerve,* 14 March, 10, 17 June, 15, 26 August, 3 and 28 October 1833, 15 May, 17 July, and 15 September 1834; *Vindicator,* 10 May, 18 June, 16, 27 August, and 4 October 1833, 25 February, 25 March, 8 April, 1, 18 July, 16 September, and 7 November 1834; Ratio et al., *La navigation à Longueuil,* 52–6).

12 ANQM, notary Arnoldi, no. 2056, 7 November 1833; no. 3529, 6 June 1834; no. 3845 and no. 3846, 12 December 1833; no. 3879, 29 December 1834; no. 3882, 30 December 1834; no. 3902, 9 January 1835; no. 3919, 20 January 1835; no. 3927, 22 January 1835; no. 3928, 23 January 1835; notary Griffin, no. 15900, 13 March 1838; *Gazette,* 18 December 1834, 5 February and 13 June 1835. For details on some vessels built by Sheay and Merritt and by Merritt alone after 1834, see Bosworth, *Hochelaga Depicta,* 177–9. Merritt was born at Bedford, New York, on 7 September 1802. Sheay, probably also American-born, died at Kingston on 12 October 1842, at age forty-four (ANQM, CC register, 30 September 1834; *Gazette,* 17 October 1842).

13 ANQM, notary Arnoldi, no. 3345, 5 April 1834; no. 3884, 2 January 1835; notary Bleakley, no. 127, 24 July 1835; *Bathurst Courier,* 31 July 1835, 25 June 1838; *Gazette,* 2 May 1835; Parker, "The Niagara Harbour and Dock Company," 103. Bennet returned to Montreal in 1844 (Mackay, *Montreal Directory for 1845–1846,* 24; "Witness Jubilee Symposium," 20 March 1897).

14 ANQM, notary Griffin, no. 12965, 24 March 1835; *Gazette,* 18 June 1833, 24 May and 21 June 1834, 24 March 1835; *Minerve,* 26 March 1835,

22 February 1836; James Irwin gravestone, Mount Royal Cemetery, Montreal. It seems that Workman's successor at the Eagle Foundry was Curtis E. Crossman, who is known to have been in charge of the office in the 1840s (he died in 1847). Crossman's last known steamer command, after the *St Lawrence* and the *Swan* on Lake St Louis, was the *Ottawa* for the Ottawa and Rideau Forwarding Company in 1835 and possibly 1836. In the latter year he ceased to be postmaster at Lachine (ANQM, notary Easton, unnumbered deed of 16 April 1844, "Notification & Protest at the request of William Watson & al to & v. George Brush Esqre, Deputy Returning Officer"; no. 1134, 20 September 1845; ZC register, 20 December 1847; *Gazette*, 10 April 1835; A. Walker, *L'Île de Montréal – L'Île Jésus*, 4).

15 ANQM, notary Griffin, no. 13245, 11 August 1835; *Gazette*, 18 June 1833; Wightman, "The Adelaide and Early Canadian Steam above Niagara." The *Adelaide* had originally been fitted with the Boulton and Watt engine that had successively powered the *Frontenac* and the *Alciope*. In 1835 her owners were Robert Hamilton's younger brother, James Hamilton of St Thomas, and James Cummings of Chippawa. The contract stipulated that the new engine was to have a cylinder of 48 inches diameter with a 7-foot stroke. The two boilers were to be "somewhat similarly made to the boilers on Board the Steam Vessel 'Black Hawk' [renamed *Dolphin* in 1836]." The foundry was to supply six workers to assemble and install the machinery at Chippawa so that the boat would be ready for action by 1 May 1836. One foundry employee who probably went to Chippawa for this purpose was engineer William Parkyn (see below, note 32).

16 ANQM, notary Gibb, no. 846, 13 February 1837, and no. 874, 21 February 1837; notary Griffin, no. 14720 and no. 14721, 27 January 1837; no. 14935, 23 March 1837; *Gazette*, 3 January 1837; *Minerve*, 2, 5 January and 24 July 1837; *Vindicator*, 3 and 7 January 1837.

17 *Gazette*, 1 April, 24 May, 6 and 13 September 1834, 25 July, 15 September, and 3 October 1835; *Minerve*, 31 March 1834; *Vindicator*, 25 January 1833, 1 April and 23 May 1834. A fire in one of the foundry buildings on 24 July 1835 resulted in a delay of more than a month in the reconditioning of a second-hand engine for the steamer *Trois Rivières* (for this contract, see ANQM, notary Doucet, no. 2241, 12 February 1835).

18 ANQM, notary Arnoldi, no. 4595, 28 November 1835; NA, RG 42, E 1, Dept. of Marine, Ship Registers, 175: no. 3 for 1836; *Courier*, 17 December 1835, 29 March 1836; *Gazette*, 24 February and 17 December 1835, 19 April, 5, 14 May, 19 and 28 July 1836; *Minerve*, 16 May 1836; *Vindicator*, 13 May 1836. Of the *Princess Victoria*, 170 feet long, 20 feet beam, and 10 feet depth of hold, a Montreal newspaper said: "The model of this boat differs materially from those hitherto built on the St Lawrence." "Extra length of keel has been found to have the same effect in reducing the draught of water, as breadth of beam and flatness of bottom, with this great

advantage, that a long narrow boat, like that of the Railroad Company's, drawing an equal quantity of water with a short flat bottomed boat, will run much faster" (*Courier*, 10 June 1835, 19 April 1836; Dayton, *Steamboat Days*, 183).

19 *Minerve*, 25 July 1836; *Vindicator*, 22, 26 July and 20 December 1836; Mika and Mika, *Canada's First Railway*, 29–39.

20 *Vindicator*, 20 December 1836.

21 *Gazette*, 2 June 1835. Ward was not re-elected at the annual meeting in June 1836, but his brother, Samuel Ward, succeeded him and remained a director until the mid-1840s. In 1841 he held thirty shares in the bank. Other long-serving directors included John Frothingham, chairman of the Ottawa and Rideau Forwarding Company, and James Henderson of Hooker and Henderson, who were elected president and vice-president respectively of the bank in 1843 (*Courier*, 7 June 1836; *Gazette*, 3 June 1837, 5 June 1838, 8 June 1841, 8 June 1842, 13 June 1843; *JAC*, 1841, app. C, extract from the books of the City Bank).

22 *Vindicator*, 31 October 1834. Ward's words of appreciation had come after he heard Papineau speak at the opening of the poll in the West Ward of Montreal on 28 October. He considered that the Eagle Foundry had been cheated in 1830–31 when the Montreal Harbour Commissioners, after consulting the Wards, had awarded the contract for the engine of a steam dredge to the Glasgow firm of Claude Girwood and Company. Delays and ballooning costs turned the contract into a running political "scandal," in the eyes of the Patriote-dominated House of Assembly. In his speech of 28 October 1834, touching on many issues, Papineau denounced the harbour commissioners for ordering the dredge from Scotland, "instead of getting it made in Montreal as they could easily have done ... at the Messrs Wards' Foundry," thereby depriving local workers and businesses of their due. Ward let the Patriote newspaper *Vindicator* know that, in his opinion, "every word uttered by Mr Papineau was correct, and that he might have said a great deal more." Given the temper of the times, this comment was tantamount to an endorsement of the Patriote party and would have been perceived as such by most people. The Patriotes went on to sweep the province (*Courier*, 5 March 1835; *Minerve*, 30 October 1834, 21 December 1835; *Vindicator*, 29 October 1834; see also G.H. Wilson, "The Application of Steam to St Lawrence Valley Navigation," 166–70).

23 *Vindicator*, 9 September 1836, 21 February 1837.

24 ANQM, notary Doucet, no. 24298, 28 March 1837. The total price for the two houses was £636 17s. 6d.

25 ANQM, APC register, 26 June 1837; *Transcript*, 29 June 1837. No more is known about the cause of her death than about Emery Cushing's two months earlier (see chap. 7, note 120).

26 ANQM, notary Doucet, no. 24845, 13 July 1837; *Gazette*, 7 November 1837; *New York Times*, 16 June 1885. Ward sailed from New York aboard the ship *England*. In the records of notary Doucet, the title page of his will misidentifies it as that of his brother, Samuel Ward, and bears the erroneous date 13 July 1835. A reference to the one-page will itself makes clear that it is Lebbeus's of 13 July 1837. This will revoked an earlier one made by Lebbeus which, along with one by his wife, is found in the records of the same notary (ANQM, notary Doucet, no. 19285 and no. 19286, 14 January 1832). Samuel Ward made out two wills before Doucet, one in the cholera summer of 1834, shortly after his second marriage – his intended made out a will at the same time – and the other in 1839 on the eve of a trip to Britain (ANQM, notary Doucet, no. 21845 and no. 21846, 16 July 1834; no. 26264, 10 September 1839).

27 *Gazette*, 25 November 1837; *Transcript*, 28 November 1837.

28 *Gazette*, 30 November 1837; *Transcript*, 30 November 1837.

29 The participation of some American residents in the political agitation of the 1830s and the border friction sparked by the Rebellions of 1837–38 did nothing to endear Americans generally to the Tory-hearted. See editorial in *Gazette*, 3 September 1841.

30 Morrin (sometimes written Moran), described by a steamer passenger in 1841 as "one of the most civil Captains on the line" of the Ottawa and Rideau, commanded the *Rideau* in 1838, the *Hunter* in 1839–40, and the *Otter* in 1841 (NA, RG 43, Dept. of Railways and Canals, C1, v. 1950, 1972; *Bytown Gazette*, 30 September 1841; *Montreal Gazette*, 14 April 1838).

31 *Bytown Gazette*, 16 May 1838. Fears were rife that the rebels would try to sabotage the Rideau Canal. Rumours of rebel sabotage also flew in June when an acciental fire destroyed the Molson steamer *Varennes* at Saint-Ours on the Richelieu River (*Transcript*, 21 June 1838; Tulloch, *The Rideau Canal*, 8–9).

32 Boat builder William Parkin must not be confused with engineer William Parkyn, builder of the first Canadian-made iron-hulled steamer in 1843 (see chap. 9, note 146). Parkin worked as a shipwright in Montreal in the early 1830s; he was married there in 1831 and then moved to Brockville, where in the 1840s he served on the Board of Police, forerunner of the town council; in 1850 he was elected to the first town council, serving as deputy reeve. Parkyn, born in St Austell, Cornwall, in 1807, settled in Montreal in 1823 and continued to reside there until his death in 1876. He was married at Montreal, first in 1833 to Margaret Holmes and, after her death in 1847, to Catharine A. Henwood. He had gone to work for John Molson Jr's St Mary Foundry in 1835. He and two other foundry employees, returning from an assignment in Upper Canada – probably connected with the installation of a new engine in the *Adelaide* at Chippawa in the

winter of 1835–36 (see note 15 above) – narrowly escaped drowning after their stage plunged into the icy St Lawrence at Côteau du Lac on 20 January 1836. In 1840 Parkyn formed a partnership with Molson to operate the foundry. From 1845 through 1849 he leased the foundry, operating it under his own name (ANQM, notary Doucet, no. 11164, 10 October 1823; notary Gibb, no. 5954, 2 December 1842; CC register, 18 September 1831; SAP register, 22 June 1833; Gravestones of William Parkyn and Margaret Holmes in Mount Royal Cemetery, Montreal; *Cornwall Observer*, 22 January and 16 May 1836; *Gazette*, 23 January and 14 May 1836; *Minerve*, 25 January and 16 May 1836; *Vindicator*, 26 January 1836; Borthwick, *History and Biographical Gazetteer of Montreal*, 176; Dubuc and Tremblay, "Molson, John," 632; Leavitt, *History of Leeds and Grenville*, 190–1; Mackay, *Montreal Directory 1845–6*, 244; Tulchinsky, *River Barons*, 208, 217).

33 *Brockville Recorder*, 27 April 1837; *British Whig*, 21 July 1838; *Gazette*, 18 April and 23 May 1837, 25 June 1838. The *Sir Robert Peel*, 153 feet long and 20 feet beam, was fitted with two Ward engines, with cylinders 39 inches in diameter and 10 feet stroke. According to one of her owners, David B. Ogden Ford, she had cost about $45,000. Ford and Joseph Jones of Brockville and William Bacon of Ogdensburg each owned one-quarter of the boat. The other fourth was then held jointly by Ford, Henry Jones, and George Sherwood, all of Brockville, as trustees for the creditors of Horace Billings and Company. Robert Harvey, one of three partners in the latter company, was a founding director of the Canada Inland Forwarding and Insurance Company and the St Lawrence Inland Marine Assurance Company, and also a director of the company that had built the *Brockville*. Shortly after the *Peel* incident, he wrote to Alpheus Jones of the need to obtain an affidavit from first mate Roderick McSween, who had been injured in the attack on the boat (NA, MG 24, B 98, Alpheus Jones Papers, 1, Robert Harvey to Alpheus Jones, 9 June 1838).

34 *Bathurst Courier*, 8 June 1838; *Gazette*, 28 February 1839; *Transcript*, 5 and 7 June 1838; Guillet, *Lives and Times of the Patriots*, 156–62. Van Cleve says that the *Caroline* was built at New York in the 1820s, sold for use in North Carolina, returned to New York, and then sent up to Lake Ontario via the Erie Canal. A Buffalo newspaper, however, reporting her arrival in that port in 1834, said that she had been built in South Carolina and run up to the Great Lakes via the St Lawrence (*Hallowell Free Press*, 14 July 1834, quoting the *Buffalo Journal*; MMGL, Van Cleve, "Reminiscences," 78.) The *Caroline* case long gnawed at men such as Johnston. It was partly in retaliation for her destruction that Benjamin Lett firebombed John Hamilton's steamer *Great Britain* at Oswego, New York, on 6 June 1840. The boat was slightly damaged in the incident, but no one was injured. Arrested nearby, Lett was convicted of arson on 22 June and

sentenced to the maximum prison term of seven years, but he escaped on the way to the state prison at Auburn. The following month he and Johnston issued a proclamation from "on board the Flag Ship Revenge," warning Americans to steer clear of British steamers for their own safety and to avoid "patronizing a party who hate Democracy, and who have exulted and triumphed in THE BURNING OF THE CAROLINE AND MURDER OF AMERICAN CITIZENS!" (*Gazette*, 13 June, 4, 9, and 11 July 1840; *Transcript*, 13 and 18 June 1840).

35 MU, MS255/1, Charles Kadwell Papers, "Notes, &c during a Trip from Montreal to Upper Canada and back, From the 3rd to the 18th August 1838" entry under date of 4 August.

36 *Bathurst Courier*, 8 June 1838; *Toronto Patriot*, 1 June 1838; Robertson, *Landmarks of Toronto*, 2:870.

37 *Transcript*, 7 and 10 July 1838.

38 *Courant*, 16 and 30 October 1830. *Gazette*, 30 July 1838; *Minerve*, 4 and 14 October 1830, 27 March, 3 April, 19 May and 16 October 1834, 19 and 26 November 1835, 10 August 1837; *Vindicator*, 12 and 15 October 1830, 25 March and 4 April 1834, 11, 20, and 25 November 1835; Désilets, "Masson, Luc-Hyacinthe"; Désilets, "Masson, Marc-Damase"; Fauteux, *Patriotes de 1837–1838*, 318–9; Greenwood, "Jobin, André"; Senior, *Redcoats & Patriotes*, 156; A. Walker, *Le comté de Beauharnois*, document 1–1.

39 ANQM, P345, Fonds Société d'archéologie et de numismatique, D1/1128, Henry Mittleberger to Charles Mittleberger, 23 July 1838. Born at Montreal on 20 January 1802, Henry Mittleberger had been apprenticed at the age of sixteen to Queenston merchant William Smith. In the 1820s he worked as a clerk for St Catharines merchant William Hamilton Merritt, projector of the Welland Canal. He was associated with Merritt in this and other ventures for many years (ANQM, CC register, 1 February 1802; notary Doucet, no. 5017, 18 March 1818; Merritt, *Biography of the Hon. W.H. Merritt*, 52, 68, 81, 88, 131).

40 *Transcript*, 21 March 1839.

41 NA, MG 24, B 98, Alpheus Jones Papers, 1, James Holmes to Alpheus Jones, 16 May 1838.

42 *Gazette*, 27 April 1839, 23 October and 9 November 1841; Arthur, *The Arthur Papers*, 1:124, 129. Whitney died of typhus fever at his home in Lewiston, New York, on 12 October 1841.

43 NA, MG 24, B 98, Alpheus Jones Papers, 1, Major George Phillpotts to Alpheus Jones, 6 February 1833; *Gazette*, 31 May 1838, 7 March 1839; *Minerve*, 11 July 1836; *Transcript*, 7 and 19 June 1838; *Vindicator*, 21 June and 1 July 1836; J.K. Johnson, "Wells, William Benjamin"; Spragge, "Read, John Landon."

44 *Bytown Gazette*, 18 April 1838; *Montreal Gazette*, 22 March, 10 April, and 6 December 1838, 2 and 16 March 1841; *Upper Canada Herald*, 7 July

1840. For Crane's character, see the article taken from the *Journal of Education for Upper Canada* (February 1859) in Morris, *Prescott*, 89–91. Crane, the only reform candidate in the by-election of 2 April 1838, withdrew after failing to get the poll moved from Merrickville to a more central location.

45 For the scope of the exodus, its causes, and the work of the Mississippi Immigration Society, see Longley, "Emigration and the Crisis of 1837 in Upper Canada."

46 *Appendix to JAUC*, 1839, 2, part 1, report of the commissioners on the improvement of St Lawrence navigation, 75, 77–8.

47 Ibid.; *Kingston Chronicle*, 25 August 1838. One commissioner present at the July meeting, Peter Shaver, voted against the resolution to expel Norton.

48 *JAUC*, 1839, 5. The note was read into the record on 27 February 1839, opening day of the session. Norton must have left Canada sometime in the first two weeks of October: his five-month-old son, John Lyman Norton, was baptised at Augusta, just outside Prescott, on 30 September (Livingston, *Rev. Robt. Blakey's Baptisms*).

49 *Cyclopaedia of Canadian Biography*, "Moss Kent Dickinson," 238–9; E.V. Smith, *Descendants of Nathaniel Dickinson*, 343. Dickinson was born in Denmark, New York, on 1 June 1822.

50 *Biographical Encyclopaedia of Illinois*, 411; Woodruff et al., *History of Will County*, 306.

51 *JAUC*, 1837–38, 23, 79, 109, 115, 123, 124.

52 *Gazette*, 31 May 1838. "I should think Illinois offers the most advantages," Wells had written to his father on 27 January 1838 as he weighed his options.

53 Longley, "Emigration and the Crisis of 1837 in Upper Canada," 33; Heisler, *Les canaux du Canada*, 69, 72. See also the report of the commissioners on the improvement of St Lawrence navigation in *Appendix to JAUC*, 1839, 2, part 1: 43–84. The *Bytown Gazette* of 3 October 1838 announced the death at Dresden, Illinois, of William Harvey, age twenty-six, formerly of Brockville "and for some years Contractor for a large portion of the St Lawrence Canal. Mr Harvey had recently entered into contract for very extensive works on the Illinois Canal, to which place he had but just removed with his family." The *Transcript* of 22 January 1839 reported the death "a short time since" of a man of the same name, whom it identified as a former clerk of Hooker and Henderson at Prescott, residing at Waterford, Indiana.

54 *Brockville Recorder*, 28 March 1844; *Gazette*, 7 March 1839; *Transcript*, 21 March 1839; *Biographical Encyclopaedia of Illinois*, 411–12; Leavitt, *History of Leeds and Grenville*, 148; Lee, "A Diary of the Illinois-Michigan Canal Investigation, 1843–1844," 62; Stevens, *Past and Present of Will*

County, 93; Woodruff et al., *History of Will County,* 305–6, 341, 363, 434–6. Norton had married his first wife, Harriet Morey of Augusta, outside Prescott on 19 May 1822. After her death, he married Rhoda Kingsley Warner of Prescott on 22 May 1826. She died at Lockport, Illinois, on 30 January 1843. His third wife was Elizabeth Safier, of Manchester, England. Norton himself died at Lockport on 1 April 1875 (Grenville County Historical Society, Hiram Norton file, typewritten account of his funeral copied from the *Joliet Daily Sun,* 5 April 1875; *Gazette,* 28 February 1843; *Herald,* 29 May 1822; Livingston, *Rev. Robt. Blakey's Marriages*).

55 ANQM, APC register, 23 February and 6 March 1838; *New York Times,* 16 June 1885; *Transcript,* 2 and 4 August 1838; *National Cyclopaedia of American Biography,* 1:246; Lewis, "The Ward Brothers, George Brush and Montreal's Eagle Foundry," 31; Lighthall, *Short History of the American Presbyterian Church of Montreal,* 11; E.V. Smith, *Descendants of Nathaniel Dickinson,* 342. All three Perkins children born in Montreal died in infancy, as a stone in Montreal's Mount Royal Cemetery records: Frances Ward, one and a half, on 12 August 1834; James Dickinson, two and a half, on 22 February 1838; and Henry Martyn, six months, on 5 March 1838. Lebbeus Ward, who had no children by his first wife, had at least two by his second, Abby Pratt. Born Abby Dwight Partridge in Hatfield, Massachusetts, she was a cousin of his late wife. They married in 1839. In New York, Ward served on various public bodies, including the Metropolitan Police Board, and was elected as a Whig member of the state legislature in 1851. He moved to Morristown, New Jersey, in 1867 but died in New York at the Madison Avenue home of his son Willard P. Ward on 15 June 1885. Another son, Dr Samuel Baldwin Ward, was an early promoter of the Adirondacks as a health and leisure resort (CU, Ward Family Collection, "Ward Family Genealogy" file; *New York Times,* 16 June 1885; *National Cyclopaedia of American Biography,* 1:245–6).

56 ANQM, notary Doucet, no. 25796, 31 December 1838; *Gazette,* 5 January 1839. Brush was on his own for the last few months of 1839 when Samuel Ward was visiting England and Scotland. On his return, Ward wrote, "In our business, we are getting on very well and I find Mr Brush a very good and useful partner" (NA, MG 24, D 19, Ward Papers, Samuel Ward to Silas Ward, 30 December 1839).

57 *Montreal Daily Star,* 18 February 1888, interview of François-Xavier Prieur; *State Trials,* 2:151–2, 531–2; Ellice, *Diary,* 128–37; Prieur, *Notes d'un condamné politique,* 90–2; Rapin, "Récit des troubles de 1838." Colclough and Sarah Ussher may have been travelling together since the two families were connected through the marriage of Colclough's daughter, Harriet Rebecca, to Samuel Ussher of Cobourg (see chap. 3, note 95). While the rebels feared that the *Brougham* might be carrying an armed force, there were only two soldiers on board – Lieutenant Hyde Parker of

the Royal Artillery and Amos Lister, deputy assistant commissary general.
Another passenger, Cornwall shopkeeper Martin Carman, was a lieutenant
in the Cornwall Dragoons, a militia unit formed earlier that year to gather
intelligence and help maintain a dispatch service between Montreal and
Kingston. The other passengers were Dr James Campbell of Brockville;
Romain Robitaille of Sillery Cove, near Quebec City, returning from
Hamilton, Upper Canada, where he had been working for the timber firm
of Calvin, Cook and Company of Garden Island; Thomas McMahon of
Ameliasburgh, Upper Canada, brother of the Reverend Patrick McMahon
of St Patrick's Church in Quebec; Duncan McDonell and John S. McDou-
gall, both from Cornwall; Dr Daniel Ewen McIntyre and merchant
D. McNicol from the Lancaster area; a Mrs McIntyre from Côteau; A.
Farewell; U.C. Poultney; Anna Maria Griffin and her brother, Edward; and
R. Young, H.N. Clarke, and a man identified only as Mr Clement. One
report also mentioned a Mrs Kennedy of Lancaster (ANQM, Événements de
1837–38, no. 2048, 9 November 1838, deposition of Romain Robitaille; SAP
register, 12 February 1817; notary Doucet, no. 22924, 9 September 1835;
NA, MG 24, B 98, Alpheus Jones Papers, 1, Chilion Ford to Alpheus Jones,
5 November 1838. Cornwall Observer, 6 November 1838; Courier, 12 September 1835; Gazette, 8 and 20 November 1838, 12 November 1840; Kingston Chronicle, 7, 21 November, 1 December 1838; Ellice, Diary, 137–42;
Guillet, Lives and Times of the Patriots, 164, 175; Senior, From Royal
Township, 121, 142, 200).

58 State Trials, 1:318–20. Deputy Assistant Commissary General Amos Lister
was held in the same room. The identity of several Brougham crew members is not known. Her pilot was probably Owen O'Neill, an Irish immigrant who had settled at Lachine in the 1820s. He is known to have been
her pilot in 1837 and is thought to have occupied that position since 1832
or 1833. Michael Murphy, another Lachine Irishman, was one of her deck
hands (for O'Neill, see ANQM, register of St Michel Church, Lachine,
10 June 1833; 6 June 1837; for Murphy, see appendix C).

59 State Trials, 1:318–20, 2:151–2; Ellice, Diary, 134; Rapin, "Récit des troubles de 1838." The boat was scuttled sometime after the night of Monday,
5 November, when passengers and crew held on board were rousted from
their beds and ordered off. Coincidentally, the Brougham's former consort,
Swan, was also seized on the morning of 4 November, downriver at Port
St Francis – not by rebels, but by soldiers, after she was involved in a plan
to attack Sorel (David, Les Patriotes de 1837–1838, 119–20; Filteau, Histoire des Patriotes, 405–6).

60 The Dragon seems to pop up out of nowhere at the time of the 1838 rising
and then vanish. The Caledonia was a small, 18-horsepower steamer
known to have been owned and operated by the Ottawa and Rideau Forwarding Company/Macpherson and Crane after the rebellions. That they

were one and the same boat can be deduced from two statements. A few weeks after the 1838 uprising, Deputy Commissary General C.J. Forbes of Carillon, commanding the volunteers in his neighbourhood, appealed for help in locating his luggage, "which was put on board the Barge in the Port of Montreal, on the 6th inst., that conveyed the Arms and Ammunition to Carillon, and is supposed to have been transhipped into the *Ottawa* Steamer *Dragon,* at the time the said barge was stranded at the Isle D'Orval, between La Chine and St Annes; and in which case may probably have been sent on to Bytown or Kingston, on the following trip up the *Ottawa* made by the *Dragon.*" Twelve years later, seeking compensation for damage done to the *Caledonia* in the rebellion, Macpherson and Crane explained that in the fall of 1838, "Ex Depty Commissary General Forbes took possession of the steamer without Claimants consent at Lachine for the purpose of transporting Troops and Baggage from Lachine to Carillon, and ... she was driven ashore on the Isle Dorval, where she remained twelve hours." Despite the glaring discrepancy in these two statements – was it a barge or the steamer that ran aground? – they clearly refer to the same incident. But there was no steamer called *Caledonia* in the area in 1838. One can only conclude that the boat Macpherson and Crane referred to in 1850 as the *Caledonia* was known in 1838 as the *Dragon.* To suggest that the *Dragon* could have been operated by anyone else but Macpherson and Crane in 1838 is to forget that the firm ran the only steamers between Lachine and Point Fortune or Carillon at that time (NA, RG 19, E 5b, Rebellion Losses Claims, 3797:1262–3; Fraser, *Canadian Pen and Ink Sketches,* 94; Guillet, *Lives and Times of the Patriots,* 202; Mills, *Canadian Coastal and Inland Steam Vessels,* Supplement 1, no. 809a; Phillpotts, "Report of 17 November 1838"; *Gazette,* 4 December 1838, 28 October 1843; *Transcript,* 1 July and 14 August 1841).

61 *L'Ami du Peuple,* 25 June 1836; *Gazette,* 17 April 1838; *State Trials,* 2:147–9; Heisler, *Les canaux du Canada,* 40–1, 47, 87; Mann, *A Particular Duty,* 123–4; Phillpotts, "Report of 17 November 1838"; Senior, *From Royal Township,* 134; Senior, *Redcoats & Patriotes,* 28, 71–2; Tucker, *Canadian Commercial Revolution,* 28–31.

62 JAC, 1842, app. z, report of the select committee on the Beauharnois Canal, testimony of Hubert Sauvé, dit La Plante; Grey, *Crisis in the Canadas,* 150–1, 161–2; Mann, *A Particular Duty,* 124–6; Phillpotts, "Report of 17 November 1838"; Prieur, *Notes d'un condamné politique,* 99–101.

63 ANQM, notary Jobin, no. 5332, 11 April 1838; NA, RG 19, E 5b, Rebellion Losses Claims, 3783: no. 515 and no. 516; *State Trials,* 1:318–20, 321–3; Ellice, *Diary,* 139, 148. In 1843 Masson petitioned the legislature for £1,670 16s. 4d. in compensation for the damages he had suffered. Eight years later he was awarded £865 9s. 10d. under the Rebellion Losses Act of 1849. His father's estate received £637 17s. 17d. In Montreal, Masson set

up as a wholesale and retail grocer. He was one of the founding directors of the Montreal City and District Savings Bank in 1846, and fifteen years later he was one of the founders of the Merchants' Bank. He also served on the boards of the Richelieu and Ontario Navigation Company and of several insurance companies. He was elected a Montreal city councillor in 1855 and served for several years as chairman of the city finance committee. He was reckoned a stout Conservative in politics. At his death on 23 April 1878 at age seventy-three, the press said nothing of his political activities at Beauharnois but that he had taken "an active part" in the troubles of 1837–38 (*Gazette*, 23 April 1878; *Herald*, 23 April 1878; JAC, 1843, 5 October; JAC, 1852–53, app. vv, "Rapports des pertes de la Rebellion de 1837 et 1838," claims no. 515 and no. 516, reports of 9 June and 14 July 1851; Hopkins, *The Canadian Album*, 5:117; Désilets, "Masson, Marc-Damase"; Smyth, *The First Hundred Years*, 14, 164).

64 Phillpotts, "Report of 17 November 1838."

65 Fraser, *Canadian Pen and Ink Sketches*, 102–3.

66 ANQM, Événements de 1837–38, no. 2067, deposition of Pierre Peltier, 30 November 1838; Grey, *Crisis in the Canadas*, 150; Phillpotts, "Report of 17 November 1838"; Rapin, "Récit des troubles de 1838."

67 JAC, 1852–53, app. vv, "Rapports des pertes de la Rebellion de 1837 et 1838," claim no. 1919; Grey, *Crisis in the Canadas*, 208–9. The *Chieftain* remained on the lake until 1848, when, with the St Lawrence canals completed, she was sold to Calvin, Cook and Company at Garden Island, off Kingston, for use as a tug. She was registered at Kingston in 1849. In a builder's certificate attached to her registration, Alexander Young stated that he had built the steamer at Côteau in 1832 for Calvin and Cook, "who were the first purchasers thereof." The Calvin, Cook partnership did not even exist in 1832 (NA, RG 42, E 1, Dept. of Marine, Ship Registers, 1416:237–40; Calvin, *Saga of the St Lawrence*, 16–17, 123–33; Boyd, *The Story of Garden Island*, 3; Swainson, "Calvin, Dileno Dexter"; Swainson, *Garden Island*, [5]).

68 *Gazette*, 9, 27 April and 15 June 1839; Croil, *Steam Navigation*, 326; Guillet, *Lives and Times of the Patriots*, 201.

69 *Cornwall Observer*, 9 May 1839. Before becoming master of the *Princess Victoria* in 1837, Walker had been captain of the Torrances' Montreal–La Prairie ferry *Britannia*. He was born at Sorel on 3 December 1798, the son of Irish military surgeon James Walker and Abigail Jessup. Up to the end of 1830, the baptismal records of the children of Walker and his wife, Susanne Hus-Le Moine, whom he married in 1822, identify him as a farmer at Sorel. In 1832 the baptismal record of his sixth child gives his occupation as *navigateur*. His older brother, Hamilton Walker (1782–1830), who had settled at Prescott, was named a judge of the Bathurst and Johnstown District courts in 1823 and served as the assembly member for

Grenville County from 1824 to 1828 (ANQM, register of Christ Church, Sorel, 20 January 1799, 24 January 1812, 11 May 1822, 3 October 1831; register of St Pierre Church, Sorel, 29 December 1822, 12 October 1824, 31 December 1826, 7 January 1829, 30 December 1830, 30 November 1832; NA, RG 42, E 1, Dept. of Marine, Ship Registers, 175: no. 5 for 1834 and no. 3 for 1836; *Brockville Recorder*, 21 September 1830; *Minerve*, 9 May 1836; *Vindicator*, 6 May 1836; J.K. Johnson, *Becoming Prominent*, 232–3; White, *Pages from the History of Sorel*, 41, 43, 47–9).

70 MU, MS255/1, Charles Kadwell Papers, "Notes, &c during a Trip from Montreal to Upper Canada and back, From the 3rd to the 18th August 1838" entry under date of 3 August.

71 *Gazette*, 30 April and 30 November 1839; *Kingston Chronicle*, 27 May 1840. Walker remained in command of the *Highlander* until his sudden death at Côteau on 24 June 1841. He was succeeded by Erastus H. Stearns, previously agent of the Canada Steamboat and Mail Coach Company at Dickinson's Landing (ANQM, register of Christ Church, Sorel, 28 June 1841; *Gazette*, 25 June and 16 July 1841; *Kingston Chronicle*, 10 November 1838; *Transcript*, 3 July 1841).

72 The quoted phrase is taken from the *Gazette*, 5 July 1843. The 405-ton *Burlington*, built for the Champlain Transportation Company and launched at Shelburne Point, near Burlington, on 22 June 1837, was 190 feet long, 25 feet beam, and 9 feet depth of hold and fitted with two 100-horsepower engines. She was commanded by Captain Richard W. Sherman, son of Jahaziel Sherman. Charles Dickens, who sailed in her from St John's to Whitehall in 1842 at the close of a visit to Canada, spoke of her in rapturous terms as an incomparable "floating palace" (*Gazette*, 17 and 21 October 1837; *Vindicator*, 4 July 1837; Canfield, "Discovery, Navigation and Navigators of Lake Champlain," 707; Dickens, *American Notes*, 194).

73 NA, RG 42, E 1, Dept. of Marine, Ship Registers, 175: no. 1 for 1841; *Gazette*, 7 March, 21 May, 31 August, and 19 September 1839, 13 October 1840; *Kingston Chronicle*, 7, 11, and 14 September 1839; Parker, "The Niagara Harbour and Dock Company," 104, 106. According to her register (in Montreal under her new name, *Lord Sydenham*), she measured 325 tons, $196\frac{1}{2}$ feet in length, $24\frac{1}{2}$ feet beam, and $9\frac{1}{2}$ feet depth of hold, and was square sterned, with one deck, a cornucopia head, no masts, and no galleries.

74 *Gazette*, 16 April, 16 May, 14, 18 July, 17, 26 August, and 13 October 1840; *Transcript*, 28 May and 9 July 1840; *Upper Canada Herald*, 28 April, 12 May, and 23 June 1840; Lewis, "Until Further Notice," 32; UCQB, old series, 2nd ed., 6:381–405, Hamilton v. The Niagara Harbor and Dock Co.

75 See the Post Office notices in the *Gazette*, 17 April 1828, and the *Herald*, 12 May 1821 and 17 June 1826. In the 1890s Alexander Milloy, who began working for the Canada Steamboat and Mail Coach Company in 1840,

cited the following vignette in recalling how and why people high and low
had connived at evading the Post Office monopoly: "Among the incidents
of the mail coach times, when the service was neither so good nor so cheap
as to-day were the visits we used to have from old Mr Adam P. Ferrie, so
well known then and afterwards. He would come up with his usual whis-
per, 'I was too late to get anything into the mail, do ye ken onybody gawn
up the day?' Of course we always found some one for him." Ferrie was
then a member of the Legislative Council of the united Canadas ("Witness Jubilee Symposium," 23 May 1896). See also letter signed "D.T." in
Gazette, 16 May 1844.

76 MU, MS255/1, Charles Kadwell Papers, "Notes, &c during a Trip from
Montreal to Upper Canada and back, From the 3rd to the 18th August
1838," entry under date of 3 August.

77 *Kingston Chronicle*, 1 August 1838; *Quebec Gazette*, 8 and 13 May 1839;
Lewis, "Until Further Notice," 23–7. For an instance of government requisitioning of one of Hamilton's boats, see Spragge, "The Steamship *Traveller* and the Rebellion of 1837." For other steamers used for naval service
that year, see K.R. Macpherson, "List of Vessels Employed on British Naval
Service on the Great Lakes, 1755–1875," 178–9.

78 ANQM, notary Griffin, no. 16448, 21 January 1839; NA, RG 42, E 1, Dept. of
Marine, Ship Registers, 175: no. 1 for 1840; *Gazette*, 21 May 1839, 27 June
1840; *Transcript*, 21 May 1839, 11 June 1840. The *Lady Colborne* was built
by Edward Merritt, and her engine by the St Mary Foundry.

79 ANQM, notary Pelton, no. 1102, 8 October 1840; *Quebec Gazette*,
12 August 1840.

80 ANQM, notary Griffin, no. 17242, 24 August 1840; *Le Canadien*, 17 August
1840; *Gazette de Québec*, 13 and 17 August 1840; *Quebec Gazette*, 12, 14,
and 17 August 1840; *Transcript*, 15 August 1840.

81 Lewis, "Until Further Notice," 32–3. For the bombing, see note 34 above.
The following winter, Hamilton sold the *Great Britain's* two 80-horse-
power engines for £4,000 to the Tates for their towboat *North America*,
launched in July 1841, and he sold the hull to the Royal Navy, which used
it as a storage hulk (ANQM, notary Griffin, no. 17575, 23 February 1841,
and no. 17707, 7 April 1841; NA, RG 42, E 1, Dept. of Marine, Ship Registers, 175: no. 18 for 1842; *Gazette*, 30 March 1841; *Kingston Chronicle*,
3 March 1841; *Transcript*, 31 July 1841; JAC, 1841, app. EE, report of the
select committee on transport costs, letter of Sidney Jones to W.H. Merritt, 12 August 1841; Mills, *Canadian Coastal and Inland Steam Vessels*,
Supplement 2, no. 1187).

82 *Gazette*, 27 April and 14 December 1839, 14 April, 4, 14 July and
17 December 1840, 21 August 1841; Baskerville, "Donald Bethune's Steamboat Business," 141. Hamilton's lake line consisted of the chartered *William IV*, *Cobourg*, *Commodore Barrie*, and, on the Bay of Quinte, *Henry*

Gildersleeve, built by the Kingston Marine Railway Company in 1839, to which he added the *Niagara*, built over the winter of 1839–40 by Niagara Harbour and Dock. In 1840 Bethune owned and operated the *Britannia*, which he had chartered to the government during the rebellions, and the *Burlington*; he also acquired the *Gore*, built by Niagara Harbour and Dock in 1838–39, and he placed an order with the same company for another steamer, the *Princess Royal*, which would be launched in August 1841.

83 *Gazette*, 15 and 17 December 1840, 13, 23, 30 January, 22, 24 April, 2 June, and 21 August 1841, 25 January, 2 April, 7 July, and 2 August 1842; Baskerville, "Bethune, Donald"; Baskerville, "Donald Bethune's Steamboat Business," 142; Baskerville, "Hamilton, John"; Lewis, "Until Further Notice," 38–42; Robertson, *Landmarks of Toronto*, 2:875. Under the Post Office contract, awarded on 5 December, the route had to be covered in thirty-six hours. Five steamers were needed. For the first year, the lake portion of the service was performed by Hamilton's *Niagara*; the *St George*, owned by David John Smith, uncle of Bethune's wife; and the *City of Toronto*, a new boat built by the Niagara Harbour and Dock Company for Andrew Heron and Captain Thomas Dick and launched on the last day of 1840. The *Brockville* and the *Henry Gildersleeve*, chartered by Hamilton, carried the mail between Kingston and Dickinson's Landing. For 1842 it was agreed that Bethune would operate on the lake and Hamilton on the river. Bethune's new *Princess Royal* replaced the *St George*. Hamilton sold off at least a part interest in the *Niagara* (renamed *Sovereign* in 1843) to John Elmsley and again employed the *Brockville* and the *Henry Gildersleeve* while having a new riverboat, the *Canada*, built at Prescott.

84 *Gazette de Québec*, 20 August 1840; *Kingston Chronicle*, 22 August 1840; *Montreal Gazette*, 20 October 1843; *Quebec Gazette*, 17, 21, and 26 August 1840; *Transcript*, 20 August 1840; *Upper Canada Herald*, 18 August 1840; JAC, 1842, app. z, report of the select committee on the Beauharnois Canal, testimony of the pilot Jacques. Croil gave the date of this milestone as 19 October 1840; in his published lecture to the science students of McGill University, Weir made it 19 August 1841. Hilliard may have gained useful information for the *Ontario's* run down the rapids from the experience of the *Raftsman* in the spring. With steering oars at bow and stern, the hull of that 100-foot steamer, built by Calvin and Cook at Garden Island, had been run down to Montreal, where she received her boiler. She had then gone on to Lévis, opposite Quebec, to receive her engine. Beginning in July, she was used to tow timber rafts between Montreal and Quebec (*Quebec Mercury*, 7 July 1840; Calvin, *Saga of the St Lawrence*, 117; Croil, *Steam Navigation*, 326; Weir, *Beginnings of the St Lawrence Route*, 17).

85 *Le Canadien*, 21 and 24 August 1840; *Gazette de Québec*, 27 and 29 August 1840; *Quebec Gazette*, 17 August, 21, and 28 August 1840; *Transcript*, 27 August 1840.

86 ANQM, notary Pelton, no. 1102, 8 October 1840.

87 *Montreal Gazette*, 13 October 1840; *Quebec Gazette*, 15 October 1840; *Quebec Mercury*, 13 and 15 October 1840. Of Sydenham's role, John Robert Godley, alluding to the low fares and rapid service between Montreal and Quebec in 1842, wrote in his *Letters from America* (1:73–4): "All this cheapness and rapidity of communication is Lord Sydenham's doing: when he came out [1839], one company had the monopoly of the St Lawrence steam navigation, charged any price they pleased, and spent sometimes from twenty-four to thirty-six hours *en route*. Lord Sydenham proposed to them a reduction of time and charge, and upon their refusal offered the mail and the government patronage to another company to induce an opposition: the consequence is the unexampled benefit to the public which I have stated."

88 Bonnycastle, *The Canadas in 1841*, 1:93.

89 A writer reported from Prescott in the spring of 1841: "There are here two other steam boats, of a small size, nearly finished. These vessels have less than twenty feet beam, and are intended to make the entire tour of the River and Canal, going down the Rapids to Lachine, and ascending the Ottawa, via the Grenville Canal, to Bytown, and so on the [to?] Kingston and Prescott again, via the Rideau Canal. Of the success of this scheme I cannot speak, but I think it extremely doubtful" (*Gazette*, 20 May 1841).

CHAPTER NINE

1 *JAUC*, 1839, 2, part 2: 839–42, report of the select committee on Rideau Canal tolls. Two years earlier, in response to a petition from Kingston merchants denouncing the Ottawa and Rideau monopoly, the assembly had adopted an address to the king calling for the building of a lock at St Anne. The 1839 committee report was dismissed by a commentator in the *Quebec Gazette* as a "course of sophistries" of W.H. Merritt, father of the Welland Canal, backed by a House of Assembly whose members, "almost all merchants or traders, are willing to take advantage of the rise both in produce and merchandize, but utterly oppose the slightest advance in the tariff of freight." Merritt, then member of the assembly for Haldimand, was a long-time advocate of St Lawrence canals. He was a dogged critic of the Ottawa-Rideau monopoly, pressing his attack in 1840 in a series of letters he wrote for the press under the pseudonym of "An Upper Canadian" and, after the legislative union of 1841, as chairman of a parliamentary committee on transport costs (*Montreal Gazette*, 8 July 1837, 2, 12, 23, 26 May, 23, 25, 27, 30 June 1840, 17 September 1841; *Quebec Gazette*, 17 May 1839; *JAC*, 1841, app. EE, report of the select committee on transport costs; Merritt, *Biography of the Hon. W.H. Merritt*, 214–15).

2 *Bytown Gazette*, 25 April 1838, 7 August 1839; *Montreal Gazette*, 8 July 1837, 1 May 1838, 7 May, 13 August, 12 October 1839, 2 June 1840; *Transcript*, 21 July 1842, 29 June 1843; Heisler, *Les canaux du Canada*, 95; Lafrenière, *Le réseau de canalisation de la rivière des Outaouais*, 40–2; Legget, *Ottawa River Canals*, 141–3; Arthur, *Arthur Papers*, 3:179.

3 *Bytown Gazette*, 7 August 1839. Like Merritt and the Upper Canada committee of 1839, the Toronto Board of Trade complained in 1840 that the St Anne lock would have little effect on freight rates so long as one private company ran the steamers on the Ottawa-Rideau (*Montreal Gazette*, 7 July 1840).

4 *Bathurst Courier*, 29 November 1839, cited in R. Reid, *The Upper Ottawa Valley to 1855*, 195; *Bytown Gazette*, 26 September, 24 October, and 14 November 1839; *Montreal Gazette*, 5 November 1839.

5 *Gazette*, 5 November 1839. Besides Mittleberger, the members of the provisional board were Montreal businessmen Joseph Shuter (chairman), Thomas B. Anderson, James Scott, Theodore Hart, and Judah Benjamin; and from Upper Canada, William Stewart of Bytown, William Bell of Perth, William Matthie of Brockville, John McEwan of Gananoque, John H. Greer of Kingston, Charles Bockus of Picton, Benjamin Davy of Belleville, and Chester Culver of Niagara.

6 *Gazette*, 11 September 1834; *Transcript*, 13 June 1840. Nunns told an inquest into the fatal boiler explosion aboard the *Lady of the Lake* in September 1834: "I am a professed engineer, and have been in the employ of the Tow Boat Company for ten years." He was then working as engineer on the Torrance steamer *St George*.

7 *Gazette*, 14 January and 6 February 1834; *Patents of Canada*, no. 50, 4 December 1839, "Certain new and useful improvements in the construction of steam engines"; no. 52, 20 June 1840, "New method of constructing steamboats and other vessels propelled by paddle-wheels."

8 *Gazette*, 19 May, 2 and 4 June 1840, 6 April 1841; *Transcript*, 2, 4, and 6 June 1840; see also Creighton, *Empire of the St Lawrence*, 341, 343–4. On criticism of the forwarders' treatment of immigrants, see also *Bytown Gazette*, 4, 11, 18, and 25 June 1840.

9 *Gazette*, 6 April and 17 May 1841; JAC, 1841, app. EE, report of the select committee on transport costs, testimony of Francis Henderson of Hooker and Henderson.

10 Kains used the phrase in 1838 in replying to a fastidious passenger who capped a list of complaints about service aboard the *Shannon* ("several of the party had table spoons given them to stir their tea with!") with the words: "So much for monopoly" (*Bytown Gazette*, 13 and 20 June 1838).

11 The *British Whig* of Kingston reported in the spring of 1841 on the forwarding plans for that year: "The Ottawa and Rideau Company (Messrs

M'Pherson & Crane), relieved from the intolerable burden of towing the entire of the Upper Country Imports from Lachine to Kingston, will devote the whole of their Steamboats and Barges to the conveyance of goods consigned to their especial custody, as usual, via the Rideau Canal." The *Montreal Gazette* commented ironically: "The 'intolerable burden,' of which one may have been relieved, will fall on the shoulders of others. Whether the bearing of it will be as profitable to them, we cannot say" (*Gazette*, 6 April 1841).

12 *Bathurst Courier*, 10 April 1835; *Brockville Recorder*, 15 November 1855; *Gazette*, 5 November 1839, 3 September 1840, 6, 22, and 24 April 1841; *Kingston Chronicle*, 2 January 1841. Matthie, born in Alloa, Scotland, in 1811, and George Easton were partners in Matthie, Easton and Company, a Brockville importer-wholesaler-retailer of dry goods, groceries, crockery, and glassware. James Ross and Henry Easton joined with Matthie, Easton and Company to launch the forwarding venture. Matthie and Ross may have been connected by marriage: Matthie had married a Hannah Ross of Brockville on 30 October 1838. Matthie, Easton and Company operated under that name until 1843, but the name of Matthie's forwarding partnership changed frequently, usually reflecting the addition or withdrawal of a partner. At first, it was called Ross, Matthie and Company at Montreal, and Easton, Ross and Company at Brockville and Kingston. On Henry Easton's retirement in April 1842, Ross, Matthie and Company became the name of the company at Brockville and Kingston, while the Montreal concern, joined by merchant William Atkinson, adopted the name Atkinson, Matthie and Company. After Atkinson withdrew in November 1842, Matthie, Easton and Company and James Ross continued their association under the names Ross, Matthie and Company at Montreal and Easton, Ross and Company upriver. None of the company names included the name Chapman, though George Chapman was also a forwarding partner of Matthie's in 1841–43 (ANQM, notary Gibb, no. 5792, 22 October 1842; no. 5865, 9 November 1842; no. 6630, 17 May 1843; *Gazette*, 15 October 1840, 19 April and 24 November 1842; *Kingston Chronicle*, 14 November 1838).

13 ANQM, notary Gibb, no. 171, 13 April 1836, and no. 3369, 7 December 1839; notary Hunter, no. 328, 8 April 1837; *Gazette*, 27 April and 26 May 1841; *Kingston Chronicle*, 21 December 1839. The company was called McGibbon and Ferguson at Prescott and Kingston. Ferguson was succeeded as the Montreal partner in Macpherson and Crane by David L. Macpherson, John Macpherson's younger brother, who had joined the firm as a clerk in 1835 at the age of sixteen. McGibbon's successor as the Jones agent at Montreal was David Ford Jones, eldest son of Jonas Jones. He became a full partner in H. and S. Jones in 1843, but the company retained the names H. and S. Jones at Kingston, Brockville, and Bytown and

H. Jones and Company at Montreal (*Courier*, 12 May 1843; *Gazette*, 17 May 1841; Cruikshank, "Macpherson, David Lewis").

14 ANQM, notary Gibb, no. 5605, 26 August 1842; NA, MG 24, B 98, Alpheus Jones Papers, 1, Alexander Ferguson to Alpheus Jones, 27 February 1841; *Gazette*, 3, 14, 21, 24 November and 26 December 1840, 3, 22 April, 1, 17, 20 May and 2 July 1841, 5 May 1842, 11 April 1843; Mills, *Canadian Coastal and Inland Steam Vessels*, 5, and Supplement 2, no. 57. Alpheus Jones's brother, Jonas, as well as their cousins, Henry and Sidney Jones, McGibbon's former employers, may have had a stake in the new towing company.

15 *Gazette*, 20 May 1841.

16 *Gazette*, 4 June 1835, 19 April 1838; *Toronto Patriot*, 4 May 1838. The firm was called Sanderson and Murray at Brockville and Kingston. Murray, who had worked as Adam Ferrie's clerk in Scotland, had been sent across the Atlantic in 1827 to help run the latter's Canadian business concerns (Ferrie, *Autobiography*, 17).

17 NA, MG 24, B 98, Alpheus Jones Papers, 1, Donald Murray to Alpheus Jones, 8 December 1838; same to same, 12 December 1838; account book no. 1, entry under date 24 January 1839. The *Transcript*, on 5 February 1839, reported: "The Families of the brave Volunteers and Militia who were killed and wounded in the action of the 13th and 16th of November last at Prescott, acknowledged with the deepest feelings of gratitude the receipt of £94 by the hands of Donald Murray Esq. contributed by the humane in Montreal for their immediate relief."

18 *Kingston Chronicle*, 9 October 1839, 22 August 1840.

19 *Gazette*, 23 April and 3 May 1836, 20 March, 20 May, and 15 June 1841; *Minerve*, 22 August 1833, 5 May 1836; *Vindicator*, 10 May 1836; Bush, *Commercial Navigation on the Rideau Canal*, 17–19.

20 Bush, *Commercial Navigation on the Rideau Canal*, 12–13; Croil, *Steam Navigation*, 67–70, 252; Dayton, *Steamboat Days*, 310–11, 361; Greenhill and Giffard, *Steam, Politics & Patronage*, 132–62; Merritt, *Biography of the Hon. W.H. Merritt*, 226–7, letter of Hamilton H. Killaly to W. Hamilton Merritt, 9 February 1841.

21 *Gazette*, 20 March and 20 May 1841; *Kingston Chronicle*, 24 March 1841; W.C. Church, *Life of John Ericsson*, 1:107–10; Palmer, "The *Vandalia* and Her Line Mates: Trend Setters"; MMGL, Van Cleve, "Reminiscences," 83–7. On Murray and Sanderson and the introduction of propellers in Canada, see Neilson, "The First Propellers at Kingston." Some newspapers reported that Murray and Sanderson ordered four propeller engines; if so, they may have later scaled back that order because they put only three propeller boats into operation. Sanderson's request for information also resulted in the introduction of the propeller on the American side of Lake Ontario at the end of 1841. His New York acquaintance, knowing little about steam

machinery, invited Lake Ontario steamboat captain James Van Cleve, then on a visit to the city, to help him out. Van Cleve was so impressed with the propeller's potential that he acquired a share in the patent rights for Ericsson's propeller on the Great Lakes. As part of the deal, he had to have a propeller boat plying on the lakes within a year. The 91-foot, sloop-rigged propeller steamer *Vandalia*, built for him and his partners at Oswego, made her first trip in November 1841.

22 Nelson Walker, sometime jeweller, silversmith, and watchmaker, must not be confused with James Nelson Walker, a machinist, "jobbing smith," and manufacturer of printing presses, also active in Montreal at this time. It was the jeweller, not the machinist, who was the engine designer. Born in Montreal on 21 March 1799, the son of an English hairdresser who had immigrated to Canada only four or five years earlier, Nelson Walker was married and established in his trade by the end of 1824. He lost a seven-year-old son, Edmund Farrar Walker, in the cholera epidemic of 1832. (Another son, Frederick Kenneth, born in June 1834, died when he was barely one year old.) In 1833 Walker was president of the company that owned the *Patriote Canadien*. A statement of the steamer's accounts in 1835 showed that he supplied a clock for her. He sold out his forty-three shares in the steamer at 10s. a share in 1836. He was named paymaster of the Montreal Volunteer Rifle Corps by Sir John Colborne in November 1838. Around that time, his social standing rose: deeds of January and October 1839 described him as a former silversmith and trader or merchant, "now Gentleman," though as late as March 1840 he was elsewhere described as a "trader." Letters patent were granted to "Nelson Walker, gentleman," for his propeller designs in 1841–42 (see notes 23 and 27 below). A Kingston newspaper referred to him in January 1842 as a "civil engineer," but Montreal directories listed no Walker among the city's engineers. They gave no occupation for him, identifying him simply as a resident of Craig Street (ANQM, notary Arnoldi, no. 1597 and 1598, both 15 March 1833; notary Doucet, no. 11521, 10 March 1824; no. 12218, 6 December 1824; no. 23726, 5 August 1836; notary Gibb, no. 4891, 24 November 1841; notary Hunter, no. 992, 21 January 1839; no. 1222, 1 October 1839; no. 1334 and no. 1335, 16 December 1839; no. 1441, 10 March 1840; no. 1452, 7 March 1840; no. 1634, 22 July 1840; no. 1761, 15 October 1840; notary Pelton, no. 520, 30 November 1838; no. 597, 5 February 1839; CC register, 14 April 1799, 1 August 1832; 4 July and 18 July 1835; *Courier*, 21 April 1835; *Gazette*, 12 October 1795, 24 April 1841; *Kingston Chronicle*, 19 January 1842; *Transcript*, 6 July 1841; Mackay, *Montreal Directory*, 1842–43 to 1847).

23 *Gazette*, 20 March and 15 May 1841. While Walker was reported to have worked from a sketch of Ericsson's propeller, the patent he secured was for an engine based on Francis P. Smith's design. See *Patents of Canada*,

no. 54, 24 March 1841, "Improvements upon 'Smith's Patent Archimedian Screw.'"

24 *Bytown Gazette*, 1 July 1841.

25 NA, RG 42, E 1, Dept. of Marine, Ship Registers, 175: no. 2 for 1846; *British Colonist*, 23 June 1841; *Gazette*, 12 and 14 June 1841.

26 NA, MG 31, A 10, Andrew Merrilees Collection, 30: file 3, and 31: file 4; RG 42, E 1, Dept. of Marine, Ship Registers, 175: no. 1 for 1846; RG 43, Dept. of Railways and Canals, C 1, v. 1878, 1917, 1950, 1957, and 1972; *Bytown Gazette*, 2 December 1841; *Montreal Gazette*, 2 July, 13 November 1841; *Transcript*, 5 August 1841; Mills, *Canadian Coastal and Inland Steam Vessels*, Supplement 2, no. 238a. The *Baron Toronto* disappeared from the circuit after the 1841 season. A brief item in the *Transcript* of 7 November 1843 mentioned an unpowered barge of this name, loaded with 1,000 barrels of flour, being towed down from Kingston to Montreal by the *Ericsson*.

27 *Gazette*, 20 February 1844; *Kingston Chronicle*, 19 January 1842. Walker improved his propeller by the fall of 1841, devising a "guard propeller," using iron hoops to brace the propeller tips and protect them from flotsam (*Gazette*, 13 November 1841; *Patents of Canada*, no. 55, 18 January 1842, "An improved method of constructing the propellers by him [Walker] discovered and invented, and for which he obtained a patent, dated 24th March, 1841").

28 NA, RG 43, Dept. of Railways and Canals, C 1, v. 1950 and 1972 (besides giving the names of boats, these lockmasters' journals, respectively for The Narrows and Jones' Falls, also name the masters); *Gazette*, 19 June 1841; *Transcript*, 6 July 1841; Mills, *Canadian Coastal and Inland Steam Vessels*, 126, and Supplement 2, no. 3095. The *William Henry* had room for twelve cabin passengers, besides cargo. Mills identifies her as a propeller boat, but contemporary records do not.

29 NA, RG 43, Dept. of Railways and Canals, C1, v. 1972; *Gazette*, 20 May and 3 August 1841; Bush, *Commercial Navigation on the Rideau Canal*, 215–16; Mills, *Canadian Coastal and Inland Vessels*, 92, and Supplement 2, no. 2229.

30 NA, RG 42, E 1, Dept. of Marine, Ship Registers, 175: no. 1 for 1848; *Gazette*, 17 December 1840, 20 May and 2 July 1841; Mills, *Canadian Coastal and Inland Steam Vessels*, 51.

31 NA, RG 8, British Military and Naval Records, C series, 59:349–50; *Bytown Gazette*, 26 September 1839, 16 January 1840, 21, 28 January, 17 June and 30 September 1841; *Montreal Gazette*, 6 February, 6 April, 19 May, and 2 July 1841; Bush, *Commercial Navigation on the Rideau Canal*, 215; Mills, *Canadian Coastal and Inland Steam Vessels*, 94, and Supplement 2, no. 2270. The *Montreal Gazette* of 2 July 1841 mentioned that a Hooker and Henderson steamer called *Victoria*, "nearly finished," is

to ply on the Rideau Canal, but there is no record of any boat of that name on the canal in 1841 or 1842. Perhaps referring to the same boat, other issues of the same paper spoke of a "good-sized steamboat" building for Hooker and Henderson that was to ply as a towboat on the Rideau, powered by the engines of the *Burlington*, a steamer built at Oakville in 1836 and bought by Hooker and Henderson in early 1841, but destroyed by fire at Toronto that spring. Possibly the putative *Victoria* turned out to be the *Oak*, a steamer that made its appearance on the canal in May 1842 under Captain Charles Wells (see NA, RG 43, Dept. of Railways and Canals, C1, v. 1950 and 1972; *Montreal Gazette*, 22 April, 19, 20 May, and 2 July 1841).

32 *Gazette*, 22 April, 19, 20, and 27 May 1841. The *Gazette* reported that the engine was made at the prison, but perhaps it was constructed at the nearby Commercial Iron Works of C.C. Dennis and partners, which employed prison labour (see Palmer, "The *Vandalia* and Her Line Mates: Trend Setters," 16). In his reminiscences of early steamboating, Shepherd recalled taking the *St David* down from Brockville to Lachine in July 1841. It was actually 26–27 May. She made her first trip up the Rideau in September (see NA, RG 43, Dept. of Railways and Canals, C1, v. 1972; Thomas, *History of ... Argenteuil ... [and] Prescott*, 28).

33 NA, RG 42, E 1, Dept. of Marine, Ship Registers, 175: no 5 and no. 24, 1849; *Gazette*, 17 December 1840, 19 May and 2 July 1841; *Kingston Chronicle*, 17 August and 4 December 1839; *Upper Canada Herald*, 17 March and 26 May 1840; Mills, *Canadian Coastal and Inland Steam Vessels*, 6, 87, and Supplement 2, no. 80, no. 2091; Robertson, *Landmarks of Toronto*, 2:872; Thomas, *History of ... Argenteuil ... [and] Prescott*, 29–31.

34 NA, RG 8, British Military and Naval Records, C series, 59:335–6, H. & S. Jones to Lt. Col. J. Oldfield, 1 February 1841; *Gazette*, 8 February, 24 March, 16 April, 3 and 5 May 1842; *JAC*, 1841, app. EE, report of the select committee on transport costs, letter of Sidney Jones to W.H. Merritt, 12 August 1841. The Joneses had apparently first thought of calling their boat *Dragon* (see *Gazette*, 19 May 1841).

35 NA, RG 8, British Military and Naval Records, C series, 59:378–84, copy of the log of the *Union* and related correspondence. A notebook containing this log, but with no indication as to the boat's name, is in MU, MS228, Rideau Canal, Log of a steamer from Montreal to Kingston, 13–25 August 1841. Most of this log has been published in Bush, *Commercial Navigation on the Rideau Canal*, 98–100. Hardly anything is known of the *Union*. She was still in government service in 1847 (see NA, RG 8, British Military and Naval Records, C series, 61:144).

36 NA, MG 31, A 10, Andrew Merrilees Collection, v. 30 and 31; RG 43, Dept. of Railways and Canals, C1, v. 1878, 1950, 1957, 1972; *Gazette*, 22 April, 19, 20 May, and 2 July 1841; *Kingston Chronicle*, 9 December 1843;

Transcript, 14 August 1841; Mills, *Canadian Coastal and Inland Steam Vessels*, 114, 122, and Supplement 2, no. 2812 and no. 2997. Slight discrepancies in the lockmasters' records make it difficult to state the number of trips categorically. In addition, the *Ericsson* and the *Baron Toronto* each made two trips down the Rideau, but it is not known whether they continued down the Ottawa. The *Propeller* is recorded only as going up the Rideau, meaning that she came down the St Lawrence each time. Unlike the other two barges, which sometimes towed as many as three barges, she did not do any towing. The *Gazette* of 31 July 1841 reported four propeller barges on the circuit, but this appears to have been a mistake (see note 63 below). Mills, however, identifies the *Swan* as a propeller boat, though he says she was built at Brockville only in 1844.

37 *Montreal Gazette*, 2 August 1841; see also *British Colonist*, 23 June 1841; *Bytown Gazette*, 1 July 1841; *Montreal Gazette*, 14 September 1841.

38 *British Colonist*, 28 July 1841; *Gazette*, 19 August 1841. For the *Vandalia*, see *Kingston Chronicle*, 4 December 1841; Palmer, "The *Vandalia* and Her Line Mates: Trend Setters"; MMGL, Van Cleve, "Reminiscences," 83–7.

39 ANQM, notary Hunter, no. 905, 19 September 1838; no. 906, 20 September 1838; no. 937, 26 October 1838. Murray's former boss, Adam Ferrie, agreed to be jointly liable with Murray and Sanderson for the £300 penalty they were to pay for any future violation of the cartel arrangements. By an agreement of 17 April 1838 with Macpherson and Crane, E. Hackett and Company was liable to a penalty of £2,000 for any deviation from the cartel arrangement.

40 In 1833–34 Ballentine (also written Ballantine or Ballantyne) had commanded the American steamer *Caroline* when she ran between Ogdensburg and Kingston. He was master of Macpherson and Crane's *Margaret* through 1838–39, the *Rideau* in 1840, and the *Porcupine* in 1841. He was no longer on the Rideau in 1842 (NA, RG 43, Dept. of Railways and Canals, C1, v. 1972; *Gazette*, 18 June 1833, 22 July 1834; *Kingston Chronicle*, 26 April and 3 May 1834).

41 ANQM, notary Gibb, no. 2694, 7 January 1839; no. 2695, 8 January 1839; and no. 2699, 11 January 1839. It is possible that Ballentine was not drunk but ailing. On 10 November the lockmaster at Jones' Falls noted that John Moran (Morrin) was in command of the *Margaret*, replacing Ballentine, who was "sick" (NA, RG 43, Dept. of Railways and Canals, C1, v. 1972, entry of 10 November 1838).

42 ANQM, Cour Supérieure-Montréal, no. 589, Donald Murray et al. v. John Macpherson et al., February term, 1840.

43 ANQM, notary Gibb, no. 4680, 20 August 1841.

44 See, for instance, Camu, *Le Saint-Laurent et les Grands Lacs*, 111; Croil, *Steam Navigation*, 318–19; Heisler, *Les canaux du Canada*, 46; Lafrenière, *Le réseau de canalisation de la rivière des Outaouais*, 41; Legget, *Ottawa*

River Canals, 156–7; Morgan, "Steam Navigation on the Ottawa River," 373; A.H.D. Ross, *Ottawa Past and Present,* 44–5.

45 Shepherd's account, part of his "Memory of Early Steam Boating on the St Lawrence and Ottawa Rivers and Rideau Canals" (NA, MG 29, A 55/1, R.W. Shepherd Papers), has been published in Reid, *The Upper Ottawa Valley to 1855,* 198–200, and Thomas, *History of ... Argenteuil ... [and] Prescott,* 28–9. Lafrenière mistakenly locates Shepherd's channel in the St Anne Rapids (*Le réseau de canalisation de la rivière des Outaouais,* 41).

46 JAC, 1841, app. EE, report of the select committee on transport costs, letter of Sidney Jones to Hamilton H. Killaly, 14 July 1841.

47 *Bytown Gazette,* 30 September 1841.

48 *Gazette,* 8 February 1842.

49 At the beginning of 1841, Samuel Crane had written that he expected the lock to be opened by the end of the year. In March, tenders had been called for the lock gates (*Bytown Gazette,* 21 January 1841; *Montreal Gazette,* 23 March 1841).

50 ANQM, notary Griffin, no. 16865, 3 February 1840.

51 One might be tempted to see some quid pro quo in the loan of £700 made to Louise de Lotbinière, seigneur of Vaudreuil, and her husband by Peter McGill in 1842 (ANQM, notary Griffin, no. 18685, 23 September 1842).

52 *Gazette,* 21, 23, 30 April, 23 and 30 May 1840, 26 October 1841, 22 March, 7 May, 4 June, and 1 December 1842. One of Macpherson and Crane's lawyers in its lengthy court battles resulting from the fire was a young John A. Macdonald. The future prime minister was then one of Macpherson's fellow directors of the Commercial Bank of the Midland District.

53 Ibid., 28 April 1840; *Upper Canada Herald,* 21 April 1840.

54 *Gazette,* 28 April and 19 May 1840, 24 April and 8 June 1841, 3 May 1842.

55 *Upper Canada Herald,* 5 May, 2 and 23 June 1840; Legget, *Ottawa River Canals,* 162.

56 *Gazette,* 19 May 1841.

57 JAC, 1841, app. EE, report of the select committee on transport costs, letter of Sidney Jones to Hamilton H. Killaly, 14 July 1841.

58 *British Whig,* reproduced in the *Gazette,* 6 April 1841.

59 *Bytown Gazette,* 7 October 1841.

60 In 1828, for example, John Macpherson and Company, James McCutchon, Hooker and Henderson, and H. and S. Jones had issued a joint notice disclaiming liability for damages caused by the hazards of navigation. To cope with the influx of immigrants during the cholera crisis of 1832, John Macpherson and Company, McMillan, Link and Company, W.L. Whiting, Hooker and Henderson, H. Jones and Company, and Norman Bethune had set a common fare schedule and between them had dispatched two barges

daily from Montreal to Prescott. On several occasions in the 1830s, groups of forwarders had together contracted with rivermen to haul their batteaux, Durham boats, and barges up the rapids of the St Lawrence (*Gazette*, 10 April 1828, 14 August 1832; for boat-hauling and other similar arrangements, see ANQM, notary Arnoldi, no. 1170, 7 April 1832; no. 1507, 29 December 1832; no. 1629, 1 April 1833; no. 3030, 28 November 1833; no. 3060, 4 December 1833; no. 3079, 10 December 1833; notary Griffin, no. 8023, 22 January 1829; notary Hunter, no. 328, 8 April 1837).

61 *Gazette*, 18 May 1841.

62 JAC, 1841, app. EE, report of the select committee on transport costs, testimony of John Macpherson and Samuel Crane, 7 July 1841.

63 *Transcript*, 4 June 1840; JAC, 1841, app. EE, report of the select committee on transport costs, testimony of John Macpherson, Charles Mittleberger, and George Sanderson. The figures do not include Alpheus Jones's St Lawrence towboat *William IV*. Nor do they include the *Pioneer* and the *William Henry*, which operated independently, at least until 1843. They were advertised with two other steamers that year under the heading of "Union Line Forwarding," the *Pioneer*, still commanded by Hilliard, being sometimes referred to as forwarder "J.A. Glassford's boat" (see *Kingston Chronicle*, 15 July 1843; *Transcript*, 5 and 12 September 1843). The total of five steamers assigned to Murray and Sanderson is based on the fact that the firm had three propeller barges – *Baron Toronto*, *Ericsson*, and *Propeller* – in operation by the fall of 1841, besides the Rideau steamers *Swan* and *Vulcan*. In the evidence given to the parliamentary committee, only Murray and Sanderson was identified as running propeller vessels. It had three such boats, according to Charles Mittleberger; two, according to Samuel Crane. The committee's report does not record what, if anything, Sanderson had to say on this point.

64 *Gazette*, 27 June 1840, 2 July 1841; *Transcript*, 14 August 1841; Mills, *Canadian Coastal and Inland Steam Vessels*, 13, and Supplement 2, no. 258. Macpherson and Crane had contemplated setting up a passenger line since at least the previous winter (see letter of Samuel Crane in *Bytown Gazette*, 27 December 1840; Crane speaks of a plan to put a new 80-horsepower steamer on the Ottawa in 1841, but no such boat appeared).

65 It is not clear exactly what the arrangements on the lower end of the line were. In mid-June the *Caledonia* was advertised as about to start running three times a week as a passenger boat from Lachine to Point Fortune. At that time, she was meant to cater mainly to the spa clientele of Caledonia Springs (see *Transcript*, 1 July and 14 August 1841).

66 *Transcript*, 14 August 1841.

67 ANQM, notary Gibb, no. 6576, 6 May 1843; no. 6589 and no. 6589 (no. 2), 8 May 1843; no. 7366, 2 April 1844; no. 7377 and no. 7378, 6 April 1844; notary Hunter, no. 1111, 15 May 1839; no. 1125, 1 June 1839; no. 1508,

24 April 1840; no. 1553, 15 May 1840; no. 1589, 12 June 1840; no. 1602, 24 June 1840; no. 1643, 29 July 1840; no. 1644, 30 July 1840; no. 1732 and no. 1733, 26 September 1840; no. 1845, 7 December 1840; no. 1860, 15 December 1840; no. 1880 and no. 1881, 16 January 1841; no. 1883, 18 January 1841; no. 1890 and no. 1891, 21 January 1841; no. 1893, no. 1894, and no. 1895, 22 January 1841; *Gazette*, 5 February 1842; *JAC*, 1843, app. NN, report of bankruptcy commissioners; Ferrie, *Autobiography*, 25; McKendry, *Historic Portsmouth Village*, 1–2, 40, 47. In 1841 the partners must have operated on sufferance since by January that year they had sold or mortgaged their four schooners and fourteen barges, £281 11s. 3d. worth of shares in the Bay of Quinte steamers *Henry Gildersleeve* and *Sir James Kempt*, £250 of stock in the Kingston Marine Railway Company, a property in Montreal, and other assets.

68 *Bytown Gazette*, 6 May 1841 and 4 May 1843.

69 *Brockville Recorder*, 21 September 1843; *Bytown Gazette*, 2 February and 4 May 1843; *Kingston Chronicle*, 21 May 1842. Lyman Clothier's father, Lyman Clothier Sr, an American, had been the first settler on the site of what became Kemptville, where he had built a flour mill in 1814 (*Transcript*, 21 March 1839; Leavitt, *History of Leeds and Grenville*, 55, 77, 136).

70 See NA, MG 31, A 10, Andrew Merrilees Collection, v. 30 and 31; RG 43, Dept. of Railways and Canals, C1, v. 1878, 1950, 1957, and 1972.

71 The *Mohawk* is believed to have begun her career as the steamer *Tay*, built in 1836, bought and operated by the Bytown Mutual Forwarding Company in 1837–38 under the name *Endeavour*, and then acquired by the Ottawa and Rideau Forwarding Company, fixed up, and rechristened *Mohawk* (see chap. 7, notes 123 and 125). She was not listed among the assets of the Ottawa and Rideau fleet in 1843 (see appendix E).

72 NA, RG 42, E 1, Dept. of Marine, Ship Registers, 175: no. 32 of 1850; *Bytown Gazette*, 30 September 1841; *Montreal Gazette*, 2 July 1841, 3 May 1842, 28 October 1843; Mills, *Canadian Coastal and Inland Steam Vessels*, Supplement 2, no. 2154.

73 *Bytown Gazette*, 3 August 1843; *Montreal Gazette*, 25 and 30 June 1840, 2 July 1841, 28 April 1842; Mills, *Canadian Coastal and Inland Steam Vessels*, Supplement 2, no. 2248.

74 *Gazette*, 5 December 1840. See also chap. 7, note 52.

75 *Brockville Recorder*, 10 August 1843; *Gazette*, 7, 21 April, 21 June, and 5 July 1842; Bush, *Commercial Navigation on the Rideau Canal*, 197; Klassen, "Holton, Luther Hamilton"; Mills, *Canadian Coastal and Inland Steam Vessels*, 70, 92, Supplement 1, no. 1664, and Supplement 2, no. 1664 and no. 2222. Holton, a future finance minister, went to work as a clerk for Hooker and Henderson in 1836 and became a junior partner on 1 April 1841. He was then twenty-four. Francis Henderson, who had spoken for

the company before the parliamentary committee on transport costs in the summer of 1841, appears to have been a partner by 1838. By early 1843 the company seems to have changed its name – at least at Montreal, where it had been known as Henderson and Hooker – to Henderson, Hooker and Company. The partners were identified then as James Henderson and Holton at Montreal, Alfred Hooker at Prescott, and Francis Henderson at Kingston (see ANQM, notary Gibb, no. 4587, 5 November 1841; no. 6265, 10 February 1843; no. 6413, 14 March 1843; JAC, 1841, app. EE, report of the select committee on transport costs, testimony of Francis Henderson; *Patriot*, 4 May 1838; Tulchinsky, *River Barons*, 42–3).

76 *Gazette*, 28 April 1842. Thomas, *History of ... Argenteuil ... [and] Prescott*, 30.

77 Dickens, *American Notes*, 189.

78 *Gazette*, 10 November 1841. See also notice regarding losses by the St Lawrence Inland Assurance Company in *Gazette*, 11 November 1841.

79 Ibid., 2, 5, and 20 May 1842.

80 NA, RG 43, Dept. of Railways and Canals, C1, v. 1972; *Gazette*, 14 July 1842.

81 *Gazette*, 13 July 1842; the notice is dated 12 June. See also J.R. Godley, *Letters from America*, 1:237–9.

82 *Gazette*, 1 June 1842. The advertisement offers reduced fares without specifying what they are.

83 NA, RG 43, Dept. of Railways and Canals, C1, v. 1950, 1972; *Gazette*, 11, 17 June and 14 July 1842; *Kingston Chronicle*, 3 August 1842; Parker, "The Niagara Harbour and Dock Company," 109. The *Gem* was advertised as leaving Montreal for Kingston on 11 June 1842, but she was absent from Murray and Sanderson advertisements for the rest of that year (see, for example, *Kingston Chronicle*, 2 July 1842). At the start of her 1843 season, she was billed as a "splendid new steamer" (*Gazette*, 13 June 1843). The boiler of the *Dart* exploded in the spring of 1844, killing two people (*Brockville Recorder*, 23 May 1844).

84 NA, RG 43, Dept. of Railways and Canals, C1, v. 1972; *Courier*, 26 August 1842; *Gazette*, 28 June and 5 July 1842; *Kingston Chronicle*, 17 August 1842.

85 NA, RG 43, Dept. of Railways and Canals, C1, v. 1972; *Gazette*, 2 April 1842; *Kingston Chronicle*, 30 March and 27 July 1842. Roderick McSween, first mate on the *Sir Robert Peel* when she was burned by rebels in 1838, was captain of the *Vulcan* in 1842 when she ran to Dickinson's Landing. L.R. Weller took over in July when she switched to the Bay of Quinte service.

86 NA, RG 43, Dept. of Railways and Canals, C1, v. 1972; *Gazette*, 2 and 19 August 1841, 24, 26 March, 2 April, 4 May, and 27 September 1842; *Kingston Chronicle*, 16 April 1842; *Kingston Herald*, 6 June 1843; Mills,

Canadian Coastal and Inland Steam Vessels, 71, 107, and Supplement 2, no. 1680 and no. 2616; Parker, "The Niagara Harbour and Dock Company," 106; Wightman, "The Evolving Upper Canadian Steam Packet Service, 1816–1850," 19. The *St Thomas,* 95 feet long by 20 feet beam, was launched on 15 April 1842 at the Kingston Marine Railway Company yard and fitted with a 15-horsepower engine made by the Niagara Harbour and Dock Company. The *London,* also built by the Kingston Marine Railway Company and launched on 6 June 1842, ran in 1844 between Montreal and Cobourg under Captain A.J. Baker (*Gazette,* 24 May 1844).

87 NA, RG 43, Dept. of Railways and Canals, C1, v. 1972; *Gazette,* 5 and 29 July 1842; *Kingston Chronicle,* 28 May 1842; Mills, *Canadian Coastal and Inland Steam Vessels,* 94, and Supplement 2, no. 2257; Parker, "The Niagara Harbour and Dock Company," 106. Mills says that she was "designed for screw but given experimental 'sweeping paddles'" (for this invention of engineer Nicol Hugh Baird, see *Gazette,* 27 July and 19 August 1841; *Patents of Canada,* nos. 77 and 176, issued on 30 May 1845 and 12 January 1842). In her first year, however, she was a propeller boat. One other steamer, the sidewheeler *Lord Stanley,* belonging to Stanley Bagg and Matthew Campbell and used to tow timber rafts and haul freight between Lachine and Carillon in 1842, was of a size suited to the circuit, but she did not run to Kingston. Built by Edward Merritt in 1842, she was 89 feet long and 18 feet beam, and fitted with a 30-horsepower Ward, Brush and Company engine, with a 27-inch cylinder and 8-feet stroke. She may have run as far as Bytown in 1843 (ANQM, notary Gibb, no. 6242, 4 February 1843; no. 6585, no. 6587, and no. 6588, 8 May 1843; no. 7369, 3 April 1844; no. 7389, 11 April 1844; no. 7418, 4 May 1844; notary Easton, no. 18, 29 November 1843; notary Hunter, no. 1868, 30 December 1840; *Courier,* 12 May 1843; *Gazette,* 20 January, 7 and 21 March 1844; *Transcript,* 29 August 1843; Mills, *Canadian Costal and Inland Steam Vessels,* 71, and Supplement 2, no. 1692).

88 NA, RG 43, Dept. of Railways and Canals, C1, v. 1972; *Gazette,* 13 September 1842.

89 *Bytown Gazette,* 3 August 1843; *Montreal Gazette,* 30 June, 6 and 7 July 1843; *Transcript,* 3 June 1843; Mills, *Canadian Coastal and Inland Steam Vessels,* 4, and Supplements 1 and 2, no. 49; Parker, "The Niagara Harbour and Dock Company," 109.

90 *Gazette,* 17 May 1844; *Transcript,* 31 August 1843; Wightman, "The Evolving Upper Canadian Steam Packet Service, 1816–1850," 19. In 1844 the *Adventure,* still under Captain Taylor, and the propeller steamer *Beagle* ran between Montreal and Toronto for the Toronto St Lawrence Steam Navigation Company. Charles Mittleberger was the firm's agent at Montreal until June, when, unable to get along with some company employees, he resigned (ANQM, notary Easton, 28 June 1844; *Gazette,* 17 May and 20 May 1844).

91 *Courier*, 12 May 1843; *Gazette*, 7 April, 2, 5, 18 May, 2 June 1842; Mills, *Canadian Coastal and Inland Steam Vessels*, 8, 64, 97, and Supplement 2, no. 153, no. 1522, no. 2022a, and no. 2808.

92 *Gazette*, 26 March, 7, 16 April, 11 July, and 17 December 1842; *Kingston Chronicle*, 30 April 1842; Poulin, "Burnet, David."

93 ANQM, notary Pelton, no. 1403, 17 August 1842; *Gazette*, 23 April 1842.

94 *Gazette*, 18 June and 11 July 1842; *Kingston Chronicle*, 14 May, 16 July 1842; Parker, "The Niagara Harbour and Dock Company," 109.

95 The worst steamer accident in Canada up to that time was the fire that destroyed the Molson steamer *John Bull* on 10 June 1839, killing some forty people (*Gazette*, 11 June 1839. *Transcript*, 11 and 13 June 1839).

96 *Gazette*, 11, 13, and 22 July 1842.

97 Ibid., 11 July 1842.

98 Ibid., 11, 13, 14, 21, 22, 23 July 1842; Memorial stone for Thomas Cousins of Yorkshire and his seven children, graveyard of St Stephen's Anglican Church, Lachine. Cousins's wife, Mary Thompson, died at Kingston in 1876 and was buried beside this marker. The *Shamrock's* crew consisted of the captain, two engineers, two pilots, two firemen, and four sailors.

99 *Courier*, 11 and 12 July 1842; *Gazette*, 13 July 1842; *Kingston Chronicle*, 16 July 1842.

100 *Transcript*, 21 July 1842.

101 Ibid., 19 July 1842. For allegations about the *Gem*, see *Kingston Chronicle*, 3 August 1842.

102 *Gazette*, 28 July 1842.

103 *Bytown Gazette*, 9 November 1843; *Montreal Gazette*, 25 October 1843; JAC, 1843, 37, 69. Introduced on 12 October 1843, the bill, which would have established a presumption of misconduct in all fatal steamer accidents, received a second reading on 24 October and was referred to a committee, where it died. The *Montreal Gazette* of 25 October reported that this bill had "excited the alarm and disgust of the commercial community." No one could object to certification, but prohibiting high-pressure engines was preposterous, the newspaper said. "Every body who knows any thing of mechanics, knows that high pressure engines may be made as safe as low pressure ones, and from their greater economy and compactness; the majority of those boats passing over the Rapids, or through our Locks and Canals, will be furnished with engines on the high pressure principle. The forbidding such boats to carry passengers will be oppressive and vexatious in the extreme." See also Godley, *Letters from America*, 1:95–7.

104 *Gazette*, 13 July 1842, testimony of James Ross at the coroner's inquest.

105 *Transcript*, 9 August 1842. In commenting on a suggestion made in a Toronto paper that those injured in the explosion and the heirs of the passengers who were killed should sue the boat's owners, the *Transcript* observed

that under the civil law of Canada East, as opposed to the common law of Canada West, common carriers were not liable for losses resulting from an accident.

106 *Gazette*, 23 July 1842.

107 Ibid., 11 April 1835, 14 June 1842. The rates advertised by the Canada Inland Forwarding and Insurance Company in 1835, exclusive of insurance, were 2s. 6d. per hundredweight for all goods shipped up to Prescott, Brockville, or Kingston; and downwards, 2s., 3s. and 5s. respectively per barrel of flour, pork, and ashes, and $7\frac{1}{2}$d. per bushel of wheat.

108 Ibid., 23 July 1842.

109 *Canada Gazette*, 2 April 1842, no. 27: 258–9; *Montreal Gazette*, 29 March and 2 April 1842. For the old schedule of tolls, see Tulloch, *The Rideau Canal*, 156–7.

110 *Bytown Gazette*, 24 November 1842; *Montreal Gazette*, 9, 19, 21, and 26 April 1842; Tulloch, *The Rideau Canal*, 153.

111 *Canada Gazette Extraordinary*, 20 April 1842; *Montreal Gazette*, 23 April 1839; Tulloch, *The Rideau Canal*, 153, 157–9. In appendix C of her study, Tulloch lists the different schedules of tolls charged on the Rideau from 1832 to 1903, but misses the one proclaimed on 5 March 1842, which provoked the outcry. She claims that the schedule proclaimed on the following 18 April came into force only in 1843, when, in fact, it went into effect immediately. For the 1843 tolls, see below, note 121.

112 *Transcript*, 19 July 1842. The forwarders's concern at the impact of the *Shamrock* explosion on their operations can be seen in two advertisements published by Murray and Sanderson and H. and S. Jones shortly after the incident. In advertising the *Dart* and the *Ericsson*, Murray and Sanderson said: "These Boats have Locomotive Boilers, with Copper Flues, which have been upwards of 12 months in use, and are considered by the first Engineers the surest Boilers in use. They run the Rapids always in day light." H. and S. Jones gave a similar reassurance about the *St David:* "It is now 15 months since she commenced running. The Boilers have been well tested and the utmost care will be observed for the safety and comfort of the Passengers" (*Kingston Chronicle*, 27 and 30 July 1842).

113 ANQM, notary Gibb, no. 5605, 26 August 1842.

114 *Bytown Gazette*, 1 December 1842.

115 ANQM, notary Gibb, no. 7581, 7 September 1844; no. 7583, 9 September 1844; *Gazette*, 18 December 1841, 24 December 1842, 20 April and 2 May 1843, 3 and 15 February 1844; JAC, 1843, app. NN, report of bankruptcy commissioners. McGibbon had married Margaret Shaw at Kingston on 4 December 1841. Advertisements for the disposal of the bankrupt firm's assets in the spring of 1843 provide an idea of the size of its operation. Advertised for sale at an auction scheduled for 11 April were eleven fully rigged barges, as well the steamers *Dolphin* and *Aid* – all the vessels that

Ferguson, Millar and Company had sold in August 1842, though they had retained the use of them to the end. Seemingly unaware of that earlier transaction, creditors of the firm objected to their sale in 1843 as a dilapidation of the bankrupt estate before "assignees" (trustees) had been appointed. A further auction was advertised for 31 May of fifteen other barges belonging to the company, its propeller boats *Ann, Kate,* and *Norma,* and the twenty-five shares it held in the Ottawa and Rideau Forwarding Company. The capacity of the barges ranged from 625 to 700 barrels of flour. From 24 May, Ferguson, Millar's three-storey stone warehouse in Montreal was offered for sale by the Bank of Montreal. Another auction advertised from 8 June offered an assortment of chains, cables, sails, oars, poles, and other fittings, as well as a crane (ANQM, notary Griffin, no. 19586, 11 April 1843; *Gazette,* 11 April, 5, 19 May, 8, 9, and 10 June 1843).

116 *Bytown Gazette,* 20 April and 6 July 1843; *Montreal Gazette,* 20, 29 April, 2 May, and 13 June 1843; *Quebec Mercury,* 20 June 1843.

117 ANQM, notary Gibb, no. 5792, 22 October 1842, and no. 5865, 9 November 1842. Creditors included Ferguson, Millar and Company, Hooker and Henderson, Macpherson and Crane, and Murray and Sanderson.

118 ANQM, notary Gibb, no. 6630, 17 May 1843; *Brockville Recorder,* 17 August 1843, 1, 8 February, 9 May, 27 June 1844; *Gazette,* 25 January 1844. Matthie formed a new trading company at Brockville in April 1844, in partnership with the Montreal firm of Scott, Tyre and Company (James Scott and James Tyre). His new firm was called William Matthie and Company, but Matthie held only a one-third interest. Matthie's partnership with Scott, Tyre, formed for three years, was renewed for another two in 1847. At his death in Brockville in November 1855 at the age of forty-four, he was a partner in the firm of Matthie, Robertson and Company (ANQM, notary Gibb, no. 7380, 6 April 1844; *Brockville Recorder,* 15 November 1855; Mackay, *Montreal Directory,* 1845–46, 244).

119 NA, RG 42, E 1, Dept. of Marine, Ship Registers, 175: no. 21, 22, and 33 for 1850; *Gazette,* 7 April, 26 May, and 11 August 1842, 10 June 1843; Bush, *Commercial Navigation on the Rideau Canal,* 171, 193, 204; Mills, *Canadian Coastal and Inland Steam Vessels,* 18, 24, 64, 78, Supplement 1, no. 382, no. 1864, Supplement 2, no. 382, no. 528, no. 1509, no. 1853, no. 1864. The ship registers state that the *Charlotte,* the *Bytown,* and the *Juno* were all built by Macpherson and Crane at Montreal.

120 *Gazette,* 1 December 1842; *Kingston Chronicle,* 21 May, 4 June 1842, 30 April 1845; UCQB, Old Series, 2nd ed., 6:360–81, Ham v. McPherson [*sic*] et al. After two trials in the case of *Ham v. Macpherson et al.,* each of which ended with a ruling upholding the plaintiff's claim for £806 13s. 4d., Macpherson and Crane sought a third trial, but a panel of judges in the Court of Queen's Bench turned the firm down. On the same occasion, the

court upheld two other verdicts against the company, one for £2,787 16s. and the other for £1,596. Macpherson and Crane did eventually win one case stemming from the fire, but it did not involve damaged goods, and the company had to fight all the way to the Judicial Committee of the Privy Council to carry its point. This was a suit brought by John Counter, who claimed that, as Macpherson and Crane had agreed to lease certain buildings before they were destroyed in the fire, the company should be held responsible for rebuilding and repairing them, even though no lease had been signed and Counter was building one and repairing the others when the fire occurred (UCQB, Old Series, 2nd ed., 1:374–84, Counter v. Macpherson and others).

121 *Canada Gazette,* 12 November 1842, no. 59: 484–5. There was one concession: for journeys up the Rideau from Bytown, empty boats or those carrying only immigrants, salt, or coal would be charged half the regular toll. But a new charge was added: if a steamer carried the least bit of freight, besides passengers, as many did, it would be assessed the same fee as a third-class barge, meaning that instead of paying the steamer toll of £5, it would pay £18 18s. Tolls on the Ottawa canals remained as they had been through 1842.

122 *Bytown Gazette,* 24 November 1842, 12 January, 2, 16, and 23 February 1843; *Montreal Gazette,* 20 and 22 April 1843; *Transcript,* 22 April 1843. In its issue of 16 February 1843, the *Bytown Gazette* suggested that the way to raise canal revenues was not to charge higher tolls, but to increase trade on the Rideau – by making Bytown the capital of Canada!

123 *Gazette,* 2 and 15 May 1843. The cartel members were the same as in 1842, minus the failed house of Ferguson and McGibbon, but with the addition of James M. Millar, acting for the Quebec Forwarding Company. From 17 June, the cartel advertised a reduction in rates, omitting all reference to the increased canal tolls (Ibid., 17 June 1843).

124 *Transcript,* 15 June 1843. The report in the *Transcript* also suggested that freight hauling may have been the subject of a concerted effort at rationalization, with circuit steamers carrying cargo previously shipped by barge. Another sign of coordination was that Macpherson and Crane's *Porcupine* took the place of H. and S. Jones's *Albion* as a passenger boat between Grenville and Bytown, connecting with the Jones steamer *Oldfield* on the lower part of the river. The *Albion* moved to the Bay of Quinte (*Gazette,* 6 July 1843; *Kingston Chronicle,* 24 June 1843).

125 *Gazette,* 27 April 1843.

126 Ibid., 18 May 1843. As soon as the notice appeared in the papers, the liquidators of Ferguson and McGibbon's estate, which held twenty-five shares of Ottawa and Rideau stock, put the shares up for sale (Ibid., 19 May 1843).

127 *Kingston Herald,* 6 June 1843; this paragraph was reproduced in the *Montreal Gazette,* 12 June 1843.

128 On New York as a rival of Montreal, see Tucker, *Canadian Commercial Revolution*, 33–45. Taking a potshot at the cartel in 1843, the *St Catharines Journal* reported that "the Buffalo forwarders have taken contracts for conveying flour from thence to Albany, at the exceedingly low rate of 56 cents per barrel; and to N.Y. for 60 to 65 cents – while our *public spirited forwarders*, below, have all combined and *raised* the price of transportation, between Montreal and Kingston, from 1s. 3d. to 1s. 6d. (at which it was carried last year,) to 2s. 3d. per barrel of flour down; and 3s. 3d. to 4s. 6d. per cwt. on merchandize, up." The writer omitted to mention that the principal reason for these higher prices was the huge increase in canal tolls (*Bytown Gazette*, 1 June 1843, copying the *St Catharines Journal*).

129 AO, MS 768, Canniff Papers, series A-1, Henry D. Twohy to G.N. Tackabury, 26 December 1873; NA, RG 43, Dept. of Railways and Canals, C1, v. 1950 and 1972; *Gazette*, 11 July 1839, 2 June 1840.

130 *Gazette*, 4, 28 October, 12, 23 December 1843; *Kingston Chronicle*, 27 December 1843; *Transcript*, 4 January 1844.

131 *Gazette*, 29 June 1843; *Transcript*, 27 and 29 June 1843.

132 *Cornwall Observer*, 28 November 1842; *Gazette*, 2, 15, and 23 May 1843; JAC, 1843, app. Q, report of the Board of Works for 1843.

133 Warburton, *Hochelaga*, 1:212–13.

134 ANQM, notary Hunter, no. 1520 and no. 1521, 30 April 1840; *Cornwall Observer*, 28 May 1840. From the dissolution of Whipple and Masson on 22 April 1840, the business was continued under the name Masson, Finchley and Farlinger, with Thomas S. Finchley, formerly manager of Whipple and Masson, and Thomas Farlinger of Dundee joining Masson as partners.

135 *Cornwall Observer*, 18 July 1842; *Gazette*, 10 August 1841. The fire at Dickinson's Landing on 6 August 1841 killed fourteen horses and destroyed several carriages. The loss was estimated at £2,000. The fire of 12 July 1842 at Côteau razed the sheds and buildings owned by Horace Dickinson's estate (see chap. 6) and destroyed a quantity of hay and oats, but the rest of the contents, including twenty-two horses, were saved.

136 JAC, 1842, app. Z, report of the select committee on the Beauharnois Canal; see also *Gazette*, 23, 24, 25 June, 7, 16 July, and 10 August 1842.

137 *Gazette*, 24 November, 1 and 3 December 1842.

138 *Cornwall Observer*, 28 November 1842; *Kingston Chronicle*, 14 December 1842; Glazebrook, *History of Transportation in Canada*, 85; Merritt, *Biography of the Hon. W.H. Merritt*, 258. In 1843 the *Highlander*, under Captain Erastus Stearns, would form a mail and passenger line between Côteau and Kingston with the *Henry Gildersleeve*, under Captain William Bowen, and John Hamilton's new *Canada*, under Captain William Lawless (*Gazette*, 2 May 1843; *Kingston Chronicle*, 12 July 1843).

139 ANQM, APC register, 18 November 1840, 16 February 1843; Brainard, "Wilkins Family," 50, 81–2; *Gazette*, 19 November 1840, 23 February

1843. Eveline Whipple's husband was Burlington lawyer Benjamin Jewett Fenney. Whipple's eldest daughter, Meribah, and her husband, one-time *Neptune* captain William Henry Wilkins, had moved to Burlington around 1836. The latter was a partner in the forwarding firm Smith and Wilkins there. In 1840 the second daughter, Abigail Church Whipple, had married Burlington merchant William Andrew Selden at the American Presbyterian Church in Montreal. They were still living in Montreal in 1844, but later moved to Burlington (see ANQM, notary Gibb, no. 7294, 13 February 1844, and no. 7514, 8 July 1844; New York Surrogate Court records, St Lawrence County, 2 February 1855, case no. 1529).

140 ANQM, notary Griffin, no. 19673, 8 May 1843. Henderson had co-signed the mail contract with Whipple.

141 ANQM, APC register, 9 December 1843 (Moody is identified as "Agent of the Upper Canada Steam Boat and Mail Coach Company" in the baptismal record of his son, Lucius Dickinson Moody); Mackay, *Montreal Directory*, 1842–43, 1843–44, and 1844–45; "Witness Jubilee Symposium," 23 May 1896, reminiscences of Alexander Milloy. Born on 6 January 1822 in Kintyre, Argyllshire, Milloy was an orphan when he moved to Canada with his grandmother in 1830. He went to work for the Canada Steamboat and Mail Coach Company in 1840, boarding with Asahel Whipple. "Captain Whipple was my old manager in the company, and his was a good Christian family, whose influence kept me from wandering," he recalled in old age. "I had been attending the Rev. Dr Mathieson's Scotch Presbyterian Church on St Peter street, but my residence with Capt. Whipple's family attracted me to the American Presbyterian Church, with which I have been connected ever since. I was brought to Sunday-school by Capt. Whipple's daughters, and attended it regularly." After the Whipples left, Milloy lived with the Moodys; he succeeded Lucius Moody as chief agent of the Canada Steamboat and Mail Coach Company in 1849. In the 1860s he was a key figure in the organization and administration of the Canadian Navigation Company, a joint-stock company formed to take over the assets of a bankrupt John Hamilton in 1861. The company merged with the Richelieu Company in 1875 to become the Richelieu and Ontario Navigation Company, the core firm in the creation of Canada Steamship Lines in 1913. When he retired in 1888, Milloy was traffic manager of the Richelieu and Ontario (see Lewis, "The Canadian Navigation Company"; Collard, *Passage to the Sea*, 13–68).

142 ANQM, register of St Stephen's Anglican Church, Lachine, 2 May 1844, and *Gazette*, 31 May 1844 (advertisement by Lucius Moody for the stages and steamboats between Montreal and Kingston) both identify Chamberlain as master of the *Chieftain*; Brainard, "Wilkins Family," 82. According to a petition for letters of administration filed with the Surrogate Court of

St Lawrence County, New York, on 2 February 1855 (case no. 1529), Daniel Whipple left no widow or children.

143 ANQM, notary Charlebois, inventory of the common property of Clarissa Church and Asahel Whipple, 8–9 February 1844; notary Gibb, no. 7294, 13 February 1844, and no. 7514, 8 July 1844; Vermont Probate Court records, Chittenden County, 1854, no. 1190, estate of Asahel Whipple; *Gazette*, 25 January 1844; *St Lawrence Republican*, 20 February 1844. For Whipple's properties on Lake St Francis, see also three unnumbered title deeds (*titre nouvel*) in his name in ANQM, notary Charlebois, 12 January 1843.

144 ANQM, notary Doucet, no. 28001, 31 December 1842.

145 ANQM, notary Easton, no. 1277, 28 November 1845. Lebbeus Ward signed the necessary papers in New York before lawyer Marshall Spring Bidwell. Brush formed a partnership with merchant Sidney Seymour, possibly a brother-in-law, in 1849, and the firm operated for a time under the name of Brush and Seymour. In 1852 Brush's eldest son, George Seymour Brush, joined him in the business. Brush Sr died in Montreal on 21 March 1883. His son carried on the business until his own death on 23 February 1906 (ANQM, notary Gibb, no. 11636 and no. 11637, 5 March 1849; Tulchinsky, "Brush, George"; Brush monument, Mount Royal Cemetery, Montreal).

146 The *Prince Albert* was the first Canadian-built iron-hulled boat. William Parkyn built her hull and engine at the St Mary Foundry in 1843 for William Dobie Lindsay, commissioner of the Champlain and St Lawrence Railroad. Launched on 9 July 1843, she provided the same Montreal–La Prairie service for the railroad as the *Princess Victoria* had performed since 1836. An iron-hulled navy steamer for Lake Ontario had been shipped in pieces from England the previous year. By the time the *Prince Albert* was launched, a line of iron-hulled propeller steamers was operating between St John's and New York (NA, RG 42, E 1, Dept. of Marine, Ship Registers, 175: no. 1 for 1844; ANQM, notary Gibb, no. 5954, 2 December 1842, and no. 6147, 13 January 1843; *Gazette*, 18 January 1844; *Quebec Mercury*, 3 June 1843; *Transcript*, 13 August 1842, 11 July 1843).

147 *Gazette*, 27 April 1846; Lighthall, *Short History of the American Presbyterian Church of Montreal*, 36. Samuel Ward died on 18 December 1879 in Hartford, Connecticut, where he had been president of the Hartford Gas Company (CU, Ward Family Collection, "Ward Family Genealogy" file; *Hartford Courant*, 19 December 1879).

148 J.T. Dickinson, *Genealogies*, 17; Mackay, *Montreal Directory*, 1842–43 to 1848; E.V. Smith, *Descendants of Nathaniel Dickinson*, 342. City directories show that until about 1845 the widow M.A. Dickinson lived on "Wellington, near King street." The same location was given for Samuel Ward's house: they probably lived next door to each other in the semi-detached

houses which Samuel and Lebbeus Ward had built in 1837. Mercy Amelia Dickinson then moved to 15 Cheneville Street. Her name is absent from directories after 1847.

149 *Gazette*, 9 September 1837; Chadwick, *Ontarian Families*, 178; E.V. Smith, *Descendants of Nathaniel Dickinson*, 342–3. Mary Little Dickinson and Jones were married on 23 August 1837. She was Jones's second wife. His first, Frances Jones, a cousin, had died in 1836.

150 *Plattsburgh Republican*, 2 June 1838; Hough, *History of Lewis County*, 1, 163; Hurd, *History of Clinton and Franklin Counties*, 135, 178, 197; Taylor, *William Cooper's Town*, 231, 235–41, 244, 247, 249–50, 253–5, 272–4, 275, 284–5, 289, 305–12, 316, 347–8. Kent, whose better-known older brother, James, was a judge of New York's Supreme Court and then state chancellor, died at Plattsburgh, New York, on 30 May 1838 at age seventy-two.

151 *Gazette*, 20 July 1897; *Ottawa Evening Journal*, 19 July and 20 July 1897; *Cyclopaedia of Canadian Biography*, 238–9; Turner, "Dickinson, Moss Kent." For some time in the 1840s, Dickinson was in partnership with John Jones of Montreal and Francis Clemow, the former Bytown agent of the Ottawa and Rideau Forwarding Company and later a Conservative senator. The partnership, operating under the names Dickinson, Jones and Company at Kingston, F. Clemow and Company at Bytown, and Clemow, Jones and Company at Montreal, was dissolved in 1849. In September that year, Dickinson leased the steamer *Mohawk*, with an option to buy her, and formed a forwarding partnership to operate her with Montreal engineer James Turnbull. On his own account, he also leased the *Grenville*, with the backing of Samuel Crane (ANQM, notary Easton, no. 3585, 9 March 1849; notary Isaacson, no. 1143, 4 September 1849; no. 1144, 5 September 1849; *Bytown Gazette*, 17 June 1841; Morris, *Prescott, 1810–1967*, 88–9).

152 Carroll, *King of the Rideau*. See also Bush, *Commercial Navigation on the Rideau Canal*, 122–4; Turner, "Dickinson, Moss Kent." Moss Kent Dickinson died at his Manotick home on 19 July 1897.

APPENDIX A

1 ANQM, notary Doucet, no. 13143, 24 November 1825.

2 ANQM, notary Doucet, no. 19806, 16 August 1832. While the contract refers to an accompanying plan, no plan is attached to the surviving copy of this document.

3 ANQM, notary Griffin, no. 16865, 3 February 1840.

APPENDIX B

1 Taken from the inventory of Horace Dickinson's estate, ANQM, notary Doucet, no. 19686, 2 July 1832.

2 No value is given for these items, which are also marked with an X in the margin.

APPENDIX C

1 NA, RG 19, E 5b, Lower Canada Rebellion Losses Claims, 3775: no. 23. The claim was filed before the second commission of inquiry into rebellion losses, established on 24 November 1845 by Governor General Sir Charles Metcalfe. It was listed as claim no. 1158, "Damage sustained by the Captain of the Steamer Henry Brougham, £480" (see *First Report of the Commissioners Appointed to Enquire into the Losses Occasioned by the Troubles during the Years 1837 and 1838*, 28).
2 NA, RG 19, E 5b, Lower Canada Rebellion Losses Claims, 3798:1889. This commission, the third and last to inquire into rebellion losses, was established under the Rebellion Losses Act of 1849 (12 Victoria, ch. 58).
3 Ibid., 3798:1925–6.
4 Ibid., 3799:2172.

APPENDIX D

1 *Transcript*, 10 October 1839, copied from the *British Whig*. The mention of "partners" residing at Montreal, Kingston, and Prescott properly refers to Macpherson, Crane and Company, not to the Ottawa and Rideau, a joint-stock company that had no partners as such and whose affairs were administered by a management committee.

APPENDIX E

1 *Gazette*, 28 October 1843.
2 This marine railway may bear some connection with the "short piece of railroad" built on the banks of the Lachine Canal in the 1820s by John Macpherson and Company (see *Courant*, 16 January 1830).
3 The auction scheduled for 20 December was put off until January. The notice of postponement in the *Gazette*, 12 December 1843, again listed the company's assets, but grouped by their location.

Bibliography

MANUSCRIPT SOURCES

Canada

ARCHIVES NATIONALES DU QUÉBEC À MONTRÉAL
Cour Supérieure, District de Montréal
Documents relatifs aux événements de 1837–38
06,M-CL 601–2/8 and 2/9, Licitations, adjudications, ventes par le shériff Frederick William Ermatinger, 1824–26
06,M-P26/1, Fonds Romuald Trudeau, "Mes tablettes"
P345, Fonds Société d'archéologie et de numismatique (papers belonging to the Château Ramezay, Montreal, but kept at the provincial archives)
Notaries: George Dorland Arnoldi; Thomas Bedouin; John Gerbrand Beek; James Blackwood; William Bleakley; Jean-Marie-Pantaléon Cadieux; Joseph-Narcisse Cardinal; Joseph-Amable Charlebois; William Nicholas Crawford; Paul-Édouard Daveluy; Jean-Guillaume Delisle; Louis Demers; Joseph Desautels; Nicolas-Benjamin Doucet; Antoine-Alexis Dubois; William Easton; Isaac Jones Gibb; James Patrick Grant; Jonathan Abraham Gray; Henry Griffin; Étienne Guy; Louis Huguet-Latour; William Stewart Hunter; Charles Huot; John Helder Isaacson; André Jobin; Antoine-Télesphore Kimber; Pierre Lamothe; Ovide Leblanc; Pierre Edouard Leclère (Leclerc); François-Georges Le Pallieur (Lepailleur); John Beek Lindsay; Peter Lukin Jr; Peter Lukin Sr; Louis-Séraphin Martin; Jean-Marie Mondelet; Richard O'Keeffe; Joseph Papineau; Jean-Baptiste-Généreux Peltier; Thomas J. Pelton; Pierre Ritchot; Louis Sarault; Louis Thibodeau
Church registers: Anglican Church, St Andrew's; American Presbyterian Church, Montreal; Christ Church, Montreal; Christ Church, Sorel; Notre Dame, Montreal; Scotch Presbyterian Church, St Gabriel St, Montreal; St Andrew's Presbyterian, Lachine; St Andrew's Presbyterian, Montreal; St Clément, Beauharnois; Ste Geneviève Catholic Church, Ste Geneviève; St James Street

Methodist, Montreal; St Joseph de Soulanges, Les Cèdres; St Michel, Lachine; St Pierre, Sorel; St Paul's Presbyterian, Montreal; St Stephen's Anglican, Lachine; Zion Congregational, Montreal

ARCHIVES OF ONTARIO, TORONTO
F 286, Samuel Peters Collection
MS 768, Canniff Papers
MS 821, John Macdonell Papers
RG 22, Court of Probate records

GRENVILLE COUNTY HISTORICAL SOCIETY, PRESCOTT
Hiram Norton File

MCGILL UNIVERSITY, MONTREAL
CH 202.3180, Alexander J. Christie correspondence, 1819–21
MS 228, Rideau Canal
MS 234, Lyman Family Papers
MS 255/1, Charles Kadwell Papers, "Notes, c. during a Trip from Montreal to Upper Canada and back, From the 3rd to the 18th August 1838"
MS 338, Ottawa and Rideau Forwarding Company
MS 475, St Lawrence Steamboat Company logbooks

MARITIME MUSEUM OF THE GREAT LAKES, KINGSTON
James Van Cleve, "Reminiscences of the Early Period of Sailing Vessels and Steam Boats on Lake Ontario, with a History of the Introduction of the Propeller on the Lakes and other Historical Incidents, 1877" (microfilm copy)

MOUNT ROYAL CEMETERY, MONTREAL
Protestant Old Burial Ground Records

NATIONAL ARCHIVES OF CANADA, OTTAWA
MG 24, B 98, Alpheus Jones Papers
MG 24, D 8, Wright Papers
MG 24, D 12, Dorwin Diaries and Journals
MG 24, D 19, Ward Papers
MG 24, I 9, Hill Collection
MG 28, III 44
   Vol. 1, Montreal Board of Trade, Register and Correspondence of the Committee of Trade April 1822–May 1828
MG 29, A 55/1, R.W. Shepherd Papers
MG 31, A 10, Andrew Merrilees Collection
RG 1, E 3, Executive Council, Upper Canada: Submissions to the Executive Council on State Matters
RG 1, L 3, Upper Canada Land Petitions

RG 4, B 19, Lists of Jurors, 1811–35 (Montreal)
RG 8, C, British Military and Naval Records
RG 19, E 5b, Department of Finance, Lower Canada Rebellion Losses Claims, 1837–55
RG 42, E 1, Department of Marine, Ship Registers
RG 43, Department of Railways and Canals, C1 (Rideau Canal)

United Kingdom

NATIONAL PATENT OFFICE, LONDON
William Annesley's patents no. 4240, 8 April 1818, for England and Wales, and
no. 4549, 5 April 1822, for the British colonies

United States

COLUMBIA UNIVERSITY, NEW YORK, BUTLER LIBRARY
John Dod Ward diaries, 1827–30
Ward Family Collection

HATFIELD TOWN CLERK'S OFFICE, HATFIELD, MASS.
Hatfield records of births, marriages and deaths 1668–1838, compiled by Eric
Sawicki

MASSACHUSETTS TITLE DEEDS
Franklin County Registry of Deeds, Greenfield
Hampden County Registry of Deeds, Springfield
Hampshire County Registry of Deeds, Northampton

NEW YORK STATE HISTORICAL SOCIETY, COOPERSTOWN
William Cooper Papers (copies), Documents relating to the Whipple family (orig-
inals at Hartwick College, Oneonta, N.Y.)

NEW YORK SURROGATE COURT RECORDS
Lewis County, Otsego County
St Lawrence County

NEW YORK TITLE DEEDS
Essex County clerk's office, Elizabethtown
Lewis County clerk's office, Lowville
Otsego County clerk's office, Cooperstown
St Lawrence County clerk's office, Canton

UNIVERSITY OF VERMONT, BURLINGTON, BAILEY-HOWE LIBRARY
Guy Catlin Papers
John D. Ward correspondence, 1816–17, 1833

VERMONT PROBATE COURT RECORDS
Chittenden County, Burlington.

YALE UNIVERSITY, NEW HAVEN, CONN.
Bidwell Family Papers

NEWSPAPERS AND PERIODICALS

Bathurst Courier, Perth
Brockville Gazette
Brockville Recorder
Bytown Gazette
Canadian Courant, Montreal
Cornwall Observer
Hallowell Free Press
Kingston Chronicle (later the *Chronicle & Gazette*)
Kingston Gazette
La Minerve, Montreal
Montreal Gazette
Montreal Herald
Montreal Transcript
Morning Courier, Montreal
St Lawrence Gazette, Ogdensburg, NY
St Lawrence Republican, Ogdensburg, NY
Scribbler
Le Spectateur Canadien, Montreal
Upper Canada Herald, Kingston
Vindicator, Montreal

Note: Information was also culled from isolated issues of other newspapers, such as the *British Whig* of Kingston, the *Quebec Gazette* and the *Quebec Mercury*, the *New York Times*, the *Boston Evening Transcript*, the *Plattsburgh Republican*, the *Elizabethtown Post* in Elizabethtown, NY, the *Montreal Daily Star* and *Daily Witness*, and the Toronto *British Colonist* and *Patriot*.

GOVERNMENT PUBLICATIONS

Canada Gazette
Journals of the House of Assembly of Upper Canada
Journals of the Legislative Assembly of Lower Canada
Journals of the Legislative Assembly of the Province of Canada
Statutes of Lower Canada
Statutes of Upper Canada

Statutes of the Province of Canada
Upper Canada Queen's Bench Reports

OTHER PUBLISHED SOURCES

Andreae, Christopher. *Lines of Country: An Atlas of Railway and Waterway History in Canada*. Erin, Ont.: Boston Mills Press, 1997.

Andreas, A.T. *History of Chicago from the Earliest Period to the Present Time*. Chicago: A.T. Andreas Co., 1886.

Angus, Margaret S. "Counter, John." DCB 9:162–3.

Annesley, William. *A New System of Naval Architecture*. London: G. & W. Nicol, 1822.

Arfwedson, C.D. *The United States and Canada in 1832, 1833, and 1834*. 2 vols. London: Richard Bentley, 1834.

Armour, David A. "Robertson, Daniel." DCB 5:714–6.

Armstrong, Frederick H. "Richardson, Hugh." DCB 9:657–8.

– "Torrance, David." DCB 10:683–5.

– "Torrance, John." DCB 9:792–5.

Arthur, Sir George. *The Arthur Papers*. Charles R. Sanderson, ed. 3 vols. Toronto: Toronto Public Libraries and University of Toronto Press, 1943–59.

Audet, F.-J. *Les députés de Montréal (ville et comté), 1792–1867*. Montreal: Éditions des Dix, 1943.

Austin, K.A. *The Lights of Cobb & Co*. Adelaide, Australia: Rigby Limited, 1967.

Ballstadt, Carl. "Christie, Alexander James." DCB 7:182–4.

Barrett, Richard. *Richard Barrett's Journal New York and Canada 1816*. Thomas Brott and Philip Kelley, eds. Winfield, Kans.: Wedgestone Press, 1983.

Baskerville, Peter. "Bethune, Donald." DCB 9:48–50.

– "Donald Bethune's Steamboat Business: A Study of Upper Canadian Commercial and Financial Practice." *Ontario History* 67, no. 3 (September 1975): 135–49.

– "Hamilton, John." DCB 11:377–9.

Bates, W.G. "Pictures of Westfield As It Was." A series of 41 articles in the *Western Hampden Times* (Westfield, Mass.), 17 March 1869–3 August 1870 (typed copy at the Westfield Athenaeum).

Beach, Allen P. *Lake Champlain as Centuries Pass*. Basin Harbor, Vt: Basin Harbor Club and Lake Champlain Maritime Museum, 1994.

Bellico, Russell P. *Sails and Steam in the Mountains: A Maritime and Military History of Lake George and Lake Champlain*. Fleischmanns, NY: Purple Mountain Press, 1992.

Bertrand, Camille. *Histoire de Montréal*. 2 vols. Montreal and Paris: Beauchemin/Plon, 1935–42.

Bibaud, Michel. *Histoire du Canada sous la domination anglaise*. Montreal: Lovell & Gibson, 1844; repr. New York: Johnson Reprint Corp., 1968.

Bigelow, P., ed. *The Bigelow Family Genealogy*. 2 vols. Flint, Mich.: The Bigelow Society, 1986.

The Biographical Encyclopedia of Illinois of the Nineteenth Century. Philadelphia: Galaxy Publishing Co., 1875.

Bilson, Geoffrey. *A Darkened House: Cholera in Nineteenth-Century Canada*. Toronto: University of Toronto Press, 1980.

Blow, D.J. "*Vermont I*: Lake Champlain's First Steamboat." *Vermont History* 34, no. 2 (April 1966): 115–22.

Bock, Margaret B. *Descendants of Nathaniel Dickinson: Corrections and Additions to the Publication of 1978 Compiled by Dr Elinor V. Smith*. N.p.: Eastman Publishing, 1987.

Bond, C.C.J. "Alexander James Christie, Bytown Pioneer: His Life and Times 1787–1843." *Ontario History* 56 (1964): 16–36.

Bonnycastle, R.H. *The Canadas in 1841*. 2 vols. London: Henry Colburn, 1841.

Borthwick, J.D. *History and Biographical Gazetteer of Montreal to the Year 1892*. Montreal: John Lovell & Son, 1892.

Bosworth, Newton. *Hochelaga Depicta; or, The History and Present State of the Island and City of Montreal*. Montreal: William Greig, 1839.

Bouchette, Joseph. *The British Dominions in North America, or, a Topographical and Statistical Description of the Provinces of Lower and Upper Canada, New Brunswick, Nova Scotia, the Islands of Newfoundland, Prince Edward, and Cape Breton, including Considerations on Land-granting and Emigration, to which are annexed Statistical Tables and Tables of Distances, &c. 2 vols*. London: Henry Colburn and Richard Bentley, 1831.

– *A Topographical Description of the Province of Lower Canada, with Remarks upon Upper Canada, and on the Relative Connexion of both Provinces with the United States of America*. London: W. Faden, 1815; repr. St-Lambert, Que.: Canada East Reprints, 1973.

Boyd, Marion Calvin. *The Story of Garden Island*. Kingston, 1983.

Brainard, E.P.H. "The Wilkins Family of Amherst, New Hampshire. Compiled for Mr Frederic Henry Wilkins of New York City, August 1909." Copy of typescript in the Fletcher Free Library, Burlington, Vt.

Brault, Lucien. *Histoire des comtés unis de Prescott et de Russell*. Ottawa: Le Droit, 1965.

– *Ottawa Old and New*. Ottawa: Ottawa Historical Information Institute, 1946.

Braynard, F.O. *S.S. Savannah, the Elegant Steam Ship*. Athens, Ga: University of Georgia Press, 1963; repr. Mineola, NY: Dover Publications, 1988.

Breckenridge, R.M. *The Canadian Banking System, 1817–1890*. Toronto, 1894.

Brown, A.O. *James Brown, a Biography and Family History*. Privately printed, 1967.

Browne, George W. *The St Lawrence River*. New York: G. Putnam's Sons, 1905; repr. New York: Weathervane Books, n.d.

Brydone, James M. *Narrative of a Voyage with a Party of Emigrants, Sent out from Sussex, in 1834, by the Petworth Emigration Committee, to Montreal,*

Thence up the River Ottawa and through the Rideau Canal, to Toronto, Upper Canada. Petworth, England: Printed by John Phillips, 1834.

Buckingham, J.S. *Canada, Nova Scotia, New Brunswick and the other British Provinces in North America, with a Plan of National Colonization.* London: Fisher, Son & Co., 1843.

Bush, Edward F. *Commercial Navigation on the Rideau Canal, 1832–1961.* History and Archaeology 54. Ottawa: Parks Canada, 1981.

– "Drummond, Robert." DCB 6:220–1.

– "McKay, Thomas." DCB 8:551–4.

Calvin, D.D. *A Saga of the St Lawrence: Timber and Shipping through Three Generations.* Toronto: Ryerson Press, 1945.

Campbell, Robert. *A History of the Scotch Presbyterian Church, St Gabriel Street, Montreal.* Montreal: W. Drysdale & Co., 1887.

Campbell, W.W. "A List of the Members of the House of Assembly for Upper Canada from 1792 to the Union in 1841." *Transactions of the Royal Society of Canada,* 3rd ser., 4 (1911), section 2: 169–90.

Camu, Pierre. *Le Saint-Laurent et les Grands Lacs au temps de la voile, 1608–1850.* Montreal: Hurtubise HMH, 1996.

Canfield, T.H. "Discovery, Navigation and Navigators of Lake Champlain." *The Vermont Historical Gazetteer* 1 (1867): 656–707.

Canniff, W. *History of the Settlement of Upper Canada (Ontario), with Special Reference to the Bay of Quinte.* Toronto: Dudley & Burns, Printers, 1869.

– *The Medical Profession in Upper Canada, 1783–1850.* Toronto: William Briggs, 1894.

Carroll, Catherine L. *King of the Rideau.* Manotick, Ont.: Rideau Valley Conservation Authority, 1974.

Carter, J.S. *The Story of Dundas, Being a History of the County of Dundas from 1784 to 1904.* Toronto: St Lawrence News Publishing House, 1905.

Cattermole, W. *Emigration: The Advantages of Emigration to Canada.* 1831; repr. Toronto: Coles Publishing Co., n.d.

Chadwick, E.M. *Ontarian Families.* 1894; repr. Lambertville, NJ: Hunterdon House, 1970.

Church, J.A. *Descendants of Richard Church of Plymouth, Mass.* Rutland, Vt: The Tuttle Co., 1913.

Church, W.C. *The Life of John Ericsson.* 2 vols. New York: Charles Scribner's Sons, 1890.

Cleveland, Edward. *A Sketch of the Early Settlement of Shipton, Canada East.* Richmond, CE, 1858; repr. Sherbrooke, Que.: Page-Sangster Printing Co., 1964.

Clow, Helen M. *Report on the Postal System of Upper Canada to 1867.* Internal research report for Upper Canada Village, Morrisburg, Ont.

Coke, E.T. *A Subaltern's Furlough: Descriptive of Scenes in Various Parts of the United States, Upper and Lower Canada, New Brunswick, and Nova Scotia, during the Summer and Autumn of 1832.* London: Saunders and Otley, 1833.

Collard, E.A. *Chalk to Computers: The Story of the Montreal Stock Exchange.* Montreal, 1974.

– *Passage to the Sea: The Story of Canada Steamship Lines.* Toronto: Doubleday Canada, 1991.

Cordner, John. *The Vision of the Pilgrim Fathers: An Oration, Spoken before the New England Society of Montreal, in the American Presbyterian Church, on 22nd December 1856, by Rev. John Cordner ... (with the Proceedings at the dinner).* Montreal: Henry Rose, 1857.

Craig, G.M. "Bidwell, Marshall Spring." DCB 10:60–4.

Creighton, Donald G. *The Empire of the St. Lawrence.* Toronto: Macmillan, 1956.

Crisman, K.J., and A.B. Cohn. *The Burlington Bay Horse Ferry Wreck and the Era of Horse-Powered Watercraft.* Study submitted to the Vermont Division for Historic Preservation, May 1993.

– *When Horses Walked on Water: Horse-Powered Ferries in Nineteenth-Century America.* Washington: Smithsonian Institution Press, 1998.

Croil, James. *Dundas; or, A Sketch of Canadian History, and More Particularly of the County of Dundas.* Montreal: B. Dawson & Son, 1861.

– "History of Canadian Steam Navigation." In *Canada: An Encyclopaedia of the Country,* 3:298–312. Toronto: Linscott Publishing Co. [1896–1900].

– *Steam Navigation and Its Relation to the Commerce of Canada and the United States.* Toronto: William Briggs, 1898; repr. Toronto: Coles Publishing Co., 1973.

Cruickshank, Ken. "Macpherson, David Lewis." DCB 12:682–9.

Cushing, Elmer. *An Appeal, Addressed to a Candid Public; and to the Feelings of Those Whose Upright Sentiments and Discerning Minds, Enable Them to "Weigh it in the Balance of the Sanctuary."* Stanstead, Que.: Printed for the author by S.H. Dickerson, 1826.

Cushing, J.E. *The Genealogy of the Cushing Family.* Montreal: Perrault Printing Co., 1905.

A Cyclopaedia of Canadian Biography: Being Briefly Men of the Time. G.M. Rose, ed. Toronto: Rose Publishing Co., 1886. (Cover title: *Representative Canadians*).

Dalhousie, Lord. *The Dalhousie Journals.* Marjory Whitelaw, ed. 3 vols. Ottawa: Oberon Press, 1978–82.

Darlington, J.W. "Peopling the Post-Revolutionary New York Frontier." *New York History* 74, no. 4 (October 1993): 340–81.

David, L.-O. *Les Patriotes de 1837–1838.* 1884; repr. Montreal: Jacques Frenette Éditeur, 1981.

Davison, G.M. *The Fashionable Tour in 1825: An Excursion to the Springs, Niagara, Quebec and Boston. Saratoga Springs,* NY: G.M. Davison, 1825. (Eight editions were published between 1825 and 1840, the later ones bearing the title, *The Traveller's Guide through the Middle and Northern States and the Provinces of Canada.*)

Davison, R., ed. *The Phoenix Project: A Report from the Champlain Maritime Society with Funds from the Vermont Division for Historic Preservation.* 1981.

Dayton, F.E. *Steamboat Days*. New York: Frederick A. Stokes Co., 1925.

Denison, Merrill. *The Barley and the Stream: The Molson Story*. Toronto: McClelland and Stewart, 1955.

– *Canada's First Bank: A History of the Bank of Montreal*. 2 vols. Toronto: McClelland and Stewart, 1966–67.

Desilets, Andrée. "Cushing, Lemuel." DCB 10:211–12.

– "Masson, Luc–Hyacinthe." DCB 10:499–500.

– "Masson, Marc–Damase." DCB 10:500–1.

Dever, Alan. "Raymond, Jean–Baptiste." DCB 6:634–6.

– "Raymond, Jean–Moïse." DCB 7:739–40.

Dickens, Charles. *American Notes*. 1842; repr. New York: St Martin's Press, 1985.

Dickinson, A.M. *Descendents of Nathaniel Dickinson*. Compiled by Addie M. Dickinson and the Dickinson Association. 1955.

Dickinson, James T. *Genealogies of the Lymans of Middlefield, of the Dickinsons of Montreal, and of the Partridges of Hatfield*. Boston: Privately printed, 1865.

Dictionary of Canadian Biography. Vols 5–12. Toronto: University of Toronto Press, 1972–90.

Disturnell, John. *The Picturesque Tourist, Being a Guide through the Northern and Eastern States and Canada*. New York: J. Disturnell, 1844.

Doige, Thomas. *The Montreal Directory &c.: An Alphabetical List of the Merchants, Traders and Housekeepers Residing in Montreal*. Montreal: James Lane. 1st ed., 1819; 2nd ed. 1820.

Domett, Alfred, *The Canadian Journal of Alfred Domett: Being an Extract from a Journal of a Tour in Canada, the United States and Jamaica, 1833–1835*. E.A. Horsman and Lillian Rea Benson, eds. London, Ont.: University of Western Ontario, 1955.

Dorwin, J.H. "Montreal in 1816: Reminiscences of Mr J. Dorwin." *Montreal Daily Star*, 5 February 1881.

Dubuc, Alfred, "Molson, John." DCB 7:616–21.

– "Montréal et les débuts de la navigation à vapeur sur le Saint–Laurent." *Revue d'Histoire économique et sociale* 45 (1967): 105–18.

– and Robert Tremblay. "Molson, John, [Jr]." DCB 8:630–4.

Dunham, Aileen. *Political Unrest in Upper Canada, 1815–1836*. London: Longman, Green and Co., 1927; repr. Toronto: McClelland and Stewart, 1963.

Dunlop, William. *Tiger Dunlop's Upper Canada*. Toronto: McClelland and Stewart, 1967. (Contains "Recollections of the American War 1812–1814," first published serially in 1847, and *Statistical Sketches of Upper Canada for the Use of Emigrants, by a Backwoodsman*, first published in 1832).

Durant, S.W., and H.B. Pierce. *History of St Lawrence County*. New York and Philadelphia: L.H. Everts & Co., 1878; repr. Interlaken, NY: Heart of the Lakes Publishing, 1982.

Durham, Lord. *Report on the Affairs of British North America*. C.P. Lucas, ed. 3 vols. Oxford: Clarendon Press, 1912.

Dwight, Theodore. *The Northern Traveller; containing the Routes to Niagara, Quebec, and the Springs; with Descriptions of the Principal Scenes, and Useful Hints to Strangers.* New York: Wilder & Campbell, 1825. (Other editions consulted were those of 1830, 1831, 1834, and 1841.)

Edgar, Matilda. *Ten Years of Upper Canada in Peace and War, 1805–1815; Being the Ridout Letters.* Toronto: William Briggs, 1890.

"1837–1838." a series of historical articles published in thirty issues of the *Montreal Daily Star,* 28 September 1887–18 February 1888 to mark the fiftieth anniversary of the rebellions.

Eighty Years' Progress of British North America Showing the Development of Its Natural Resources, by the Unbounded Energy and Enterprise of Its Inhabitants... London: S. Low & Marston; Toronto: L. Stebbins, 1863.

Ellice, Jane. *The Diary of Katherine Jane Ellice.* Patricia Godsell, ed. Ottawa: Oberon Press, 1975.

Ellis, David M. "Rise of the Empire State, 1790–1820." *New York History* 56, no. 1 (January 1975): 5–27.

Errington, Jane. "Kirby, John." DCB 7:469–73.

– "Markland, Thomas." DCB 7:583–5.

An Excursion through the United States and Canada during the Years 1822–23. By an English Gentleman. London: Baldwin Gradock & Co., 1824; repr. New York: Negro Universities Press, 1969.

Fauteux, Aegidius. *Patriotes de 1837–1838.* Montreal: Éditions des Dix, 1950.

Fergusson, Adam. *Practical Notes Made during a Tour in Canada and a Portion of the United States in MDCCCXXXI.* Edinburgh and London: W. Blackwood and T. Cadell, 1833.

Ferrie, Adam. *Autobiography Late Hon. Adam Ferrie.* n.p., n.d. (written in 1856).

Filby, P. William, et al., eds. *Passenger and Immigration Lists Index.* 3 vols. with supplements. Detroit: Gale Research Co., 1981–95.

Filteau, G. *Histoire des Patriotes.* 1938; repr. Montreal: Éditions de l'Aurore, 1975.

First Report of the Commissioners Appointed to Enquire into the Losses Occasioned by the Troubles during the Years 1837 and 1838, and into the Damages Arising Therefrom. Montreal, 1846.

Firth, Edith G., ed. *The Town of York, 1815–1834.* Toronto: Champlain Society/ University of Toronto Press, 1966.

Fowler, Thomas. *The Journal of a Tour through British North America to the Falls of Niagara; Containing an account of the Cities, Towns, and Villages along the Route, with a Description of the Country, and the Manners and Customs of the Inhabitants, &c. &c. Written during the Summer of 1831.* Aberdeen: Lewis Smith, 1832.

Fox, Dixon R. *Yankees and Yorkers.* New York: New York University Press, 1940.

Fraser, John. *Canadian Pen and Ink Sketches.* Montreal: Gazette Printing Co., 1890.

Fraser, Robert L. "Jones, Jonas." DCB 7:456–61.

– "Macaulay, John." DCB 8:513–22.

Gall, H.R., and W.G. Jordan. *One Hundred Years of Fire Insurance, Being a History of the Aetna Insurance Company, Hartford Connecticut, 1819–1919*. Hartford: Aetna Insurance Company, 1919.

General Report of the Commissioner of Public Works for the Year Ending 30th June, 1867. Ottawa, 1868.

Gervais, Jean–François. "Cazeau, François." DCB 5:173–4.

Gillis, Robert P. "Hamilton, George." DCB 7:379–83.

– "Pattee, David." DCB 8:688–9.

Gillis, Sandra J. *The Timber Trade in the Ottawa Valley, 1806–54*. Manuscript Report, 153. Ottawa: Parks Canada, National Historic Parks and Sites Branch, 1975.

Glazebrook, G.P. de T. *A History of Transportation in Canada*. Toronto: Ryerson Press, 1938.

Glenn, Morris F. *The Story of Three Towns: Westport, Essex and Willsboro, New York*. n.p., 1977.

Godfrey, Charles M. *The Cholera Epidemics in Upper Canada, 1832–1866*. Toronto: Seccombe House, 1968.

Godley, John Robert. *Letters from America*. 2 vols. London: John Murray, 1844.

Gourlay, Robert. *Statistical Account of Upper Canada*. Toronto: McClelland and Stewart, 1974. (Abridgement by S.R. Mealing of Gourlay's two-volume work of 1822).

Gray, Hugh. *Letters from Canada Written during a Residence There in the Years 1806, 1807, and 1808*. London: Longman, Hurst, Rees & Orme, 1809.

Greenfield, R.S. "La Banque du Peuple, 1835–1871, and Its Failure, 1895." Unpublished MA thesis, McGill University, 1968.

Greenhill, Basil, and Ann Giffard. *Steam, Politics & Patronage: The Transformation of the Royal Navy 1815–54*. London: Conway Maritime Press, 1994.

Greenwood, F. Murray. "Jobin, André." DCB 8:433–5.

– *Legacies of Fear: Law and Politics in Quebec in the Era of the French Revolution*. Toronto: The Osgoode Society/University of Toronto Press, 1993.

Grey, Charles. *Crisis in the Canadas, 1838–1839: The Grey Journals and Letters*. William Ormsby, ed. London: Macmillan & Co., 1965.

Guilbault, Nicole. *Henri Julien et la tradition orale*. Montreal: Éditions du Boréal Express, 1980.

Guillet, E.C. *The Lives and Times of the Patriots*. Toronto: Thomas Nelson and Sons, 1938.

– *Pioneer Inns and Taverns*. 5 vols. in 2. Toronto: Ontario Publishing Co., 1964.

– *Pioneer Travel*. Early Life in Upper Canada Series, 4. Toronto: The Ontario Publishing Co., 1939.

Hager, R.E. *Mohawk River Boats and Navigation Before 1820*. Syracuse, NY: Canal Society of New York State, 1987.

Haight, Canniff. *Country Life in Canada Fifty Years Ago: Personal Recollections and Reminiscences of a Sexagenarian*. Toronto: Hunter, Rose & Co., 1885.

Hall, Basil. *Travels in North America in the Years 1827 and 1828*. 2nd ed. 3 vols. Edinburgh and London: Cadell & Co. and Simpkin & Marshall, 1833.

Hansen, Marcus L., and J.B. Brebner. *The Mingling of the Canadian and American Peoples*. Vol. 1. New Haven, Conn.: Yale University Press, 1940.

Harkness, J.G. *Stormont, Dundas and Glengarry: A History, 1784–1945*. Oshawa, Ont.: Mundy–Goodfellow Printing Co., 1946.

Hatfield, 1670–1970. Northampton, Mass., 1970.

Heisler, John P. *Les canaux du Canada*. Cahiers d'archéologie et d'histoire no. 8. Ottawa: Parcs Canada, Lieux historiques canadiens, 1980. (Published in English as *The Canals of Canada*).

Hemenway, A.M. *The Vermont Historical Gazetteer*. 5 vols. Burlington and Brandon, Vt, and Claremont, NH, 1867–91.

Heywood, Robert. *A Journey to America in 1834*. Cambridge [England]: Privately printed at the University Press, 1919.

Higginson, Maria. *The Village of Hawkesbury, 1808–1888: The Era of "Hamilton Brothers."* Hawkesbury, Ont., 1961.

Hill, R. Nading. *Lake Champlain, Key to Liberty*. Woodstock, Vt: The Countryman Press, 1991.

Holmes, O.W. "Levi Pease, the Father of New England Stage-Coaching." *Journal of Economics and Business History* 3, no. 2 (February 1931): 241–63.

Hopkins, J. Castel. *The Canadian Album: Encyclopedic Canada or, The Progress of a Nation*. Toronto: Bradley Garretson Co., 1896.

Hough, F.B. *A History of Lewis County in the State of New York from the Beginning of Its Settlement to the Present Time*. Albany: Munsell & Rowland, 1860.

– *A History of St Lawrence and Franklin Counties, New York, from the Earliest Period to the Present Time*. Albany: Little & Co., 1853.

Hurd, D.H. *History of Clinton and Franklin Counties, New York*. Philadelphia: J.W. Lewis, 1880; repr. Plattsburgh, NY: Clinton County American Revolution Bicentennial Commission, 1978.

"Internal Communication in Canada." Note C in *Report on Canadian Archives, 1897*, 57–85. Ottawa: Queen's Printer, 1898.

Irving, L.H. *Officers of the British Forces in Canada during the War of 1812–15*. [Welland, Ont.] Canadian Military Institute, Welland Tribune Printing, 1908.

Irving, Washington. *Journals and Notebooks*. Vol. 1 (1803–06). Nathalia Wright, ed. Madison, Wis.: University of Wisconsin Press, 1969.

Johnson, Arthur L. "The Transportation Revolution on Lake Ontario, 1817–1867: Kingston and Ogdensburg." *Ontario History* 67, no. 4 (December 1975): 199–209.

Johnson, J.K. *Becoming Prominent: Regional Leadership in Upper Canada, 1791–1841*. Montreal: McGill-Queen's University Press, 1989.

– "Manahan, Anthony." DCB 7:579–81.

– "Wells, William Benjamin." DCB 11:913–15.

Jones, Louis, ed. *Growing Up in the Cooper Country: Boyhood Recollections of the New York Frontier.* Syracuse, NY: Syracuse University Press, 1965.

Judd, S. *History of Hadley (Including the Early History of Hatfield, South Hadley, Amherst and Granby, Massachusetts).* Springfield, Mass.: H.R. Huntting & Co., 1905; repr. Camden, Maine: Picton Press, 1993.

Kalata, Barbara N. *A Hundred Years, A Hundred Miles: New Jersey's Morris Canal.* Morristown, NJ: Morris County Historical Society, 1983.

Kay, John L., and Chester M. Smith. *New York Postal History: The Post Offices and First Postmasters from 1775 to 1980.* State College, Pa: American Philatelic Society, 1982.

Kingsford, William. *The Canadian Canals: Their History and Cost, with an Inquiry into the Policy Necessary to Advance the Well-being of the Province.* Toronto: Rollo & Adam, 1865.

Klassen, H.C. "Holton, Luther Hamilton." DCB 10:354–8.

Klinck, Karl F. "Wilcocke, Samuel Hull." DCB 6:814–16.

Knowles, David C. "The American Presbyterian Church of Montreal, 1822–1866." Unpublished MA thesis, McGill University, 1957.

Lafrenière, N. *Le réseau de canalisation de la rivière des Outaouais.* Ottawa: Parks Canada, 1984.

Lambert, Pierre. *Les anciennes diligences du Québec: Le transport en voiture publique au XIXe siècle.* Sillery, Que.: Éditions du Septentrion, 1998.

Lamirande, A.E., and G.L. Séguin. *A Foregone Fleet: A Pictorial History of Steam-Driven Paddleboats on the Ottawa River.* Cobalt, Ont.: Highway Book Shop, 1982.

Leavitt, T.W.H. *History of Leeds and Grenville, Ontario, from 1749 to 1879.* Brockville: Recorder Press, 1879; repr. Belleville, Ont.: Mika Silk Screening, 1972.

Lee, G.A., ed. "A Diary of the Illinois-Michigan Canal Investigation, 1843–1844." *Illinois History and Transactions for the Year 1941,* 48 (1943): 38–72.

Legget, Robert. *Ottawa River Canals and the Defence of British North America.* Toronto: University of Toronto Press, 1988.

– *Rideau Waterway.* Toronto: University of Toronto Press, 1955.

Lépine, Luc. *Les officiers de milice du Bas-Canada, 1812–1815.* Montreal: Société généalogique canadienne-française, 1996.

Lewis, Walter. "The Canadian Navigation Company (1861–1875)." *FreshWater* 1, no. 1 (Spring 1986): 4–14.

– "The First Generation of Marine Engines in Central Canadian Steamers, 1809–1837." *Northern Mariner* 7, no. 2 (April 1997): 1–30.

– "The *Frontenac*: A Reappraisal." *FreshWater* 2, no. 1 (Summer 1987): 28–39.

– "Iroquois." *FreshWater* 5, no. 2 (1990): 17–19.

– "*John By*." *Freshwater* 1, no. 1 (Spring 1986): 31–3.

– "McKenzie, James." DCB 6:469–71.

– "The Steamer *Toronto* of 1825." *FreshWater* 1, no. 2 (Autumn 1986): 26–9.

- "Until Further Notice: The Royal Mail Line and the Steamboat Trade of Lake Ontario and the Upper St Lawrence River, 1838–1875." Unpublished MA thesis, Queen's University, Kingston, 1983.
- "The Ward Brothers, George Brush and Montreal's Eagle Foundry." *FreshWater* 4 (1989): 29–33.
Lighthall, G.R. *A Short History of the American Presbyterian Church of Montreal, 1823–1923.* Montreal: The Herald Press, 1923.
Livingston, Edwin A., compiler. *Rev. Robt. Blakey's Baptisms (1821–41), Parish of Augusta, Anglican.* n.p., n.d.
- *Rev. Robt. Blakey's Marriages (1821–27), Parish of Augusta, Anglican.* n.p., n.d.
Lockwood, J.H. *Westfield and Its Historic Influences, 1669–1919.* 2 vols. Springfield, Mass.: Privately printed, 1922.
Longley, R.S. "Emigration and the Crisis of 1837 in Upper Canada." *Canadian Historical Review* 17 (1936): 29–40.
Lord, E. *Memoir of the Rev. Joseph Stibbs Christmas.* Montreal: John Lovell, 1868.
Lower, A.R.M. *Great Britain's Woodyard: British America and the Timber Trade, 1763–1867.* Montreal: McGill-Queen's University Press, 1973.
Lundell, Liz. *The Estates of Old Toronto.* Erin, Ont.: Boston Mills Press, 1997.
Lyman, Arthur. *Genealogy of the Lyman Family in Canada.* Montreal: The Beaver Hall Press, 1943.
McCausland, Hugh. *The English Carriage.* London: The Batchworth Press, 1948.
McDougall, Elizabeth A. "The American Element in the Early Presbyterian Church in Montreal (1786–1824)." Unpublished MA thesis, McGill University, 1965.
McIlwraith, Thomas F. "Jones, Charles." DCB 7:452–4.
Mackay, R.W.S. *The Montreal Directory for 1842–3.* Montreal: Lovell & Gibson & Robert W.S. Mackay, 1842. (Also directories for 1843–44, 1844–45, 1845–46, 1847, and 1848).
McKendry, Jennifer. *Historic Portsmouth Village, Kingston.* Kingston: The author, 1996.
McKenzie, Ruth. "Gildersleeve, Henry." DCB 8:325–7.
- *Leeds and Grenville: Their First Two Hundred Years.* Toronto: McClelland and Stewart, 1967.
Mackey, Frank. "The Railroad that Never Was." *Châteauguay Valley Historical Society Journal* 25 (1992): 21–4.
The Macmillan Dictionary of Canadian Biography. W. Stewart Wallace, ed. 4th ed., rev., enl., and updated; W.A. McKay, ed. Toronto: Macmillan of Canada, 1978.
McNally, Larry S. "Montreal Engine Foundries and Their Contribution to Central Canadian Technical Development, 1820–1870." Unpublished MA thesis, Carleton University, Ottawa, 1991.
MacPherson, Ian. *Matters of Loyalty: The Buells of Brockville, 1830–1850.* Belleville, Ont.: Mika Publishing Co., 1981.

Macpherson, K.R. "List of Vessels Employed on British Naval Service on the Great Lakes, 1775–1875." *Ontario History* 55 (1963): 173–9.

MacTaggart, John. *Three Years in Canada: An Account of the Actual State of the Country in 1826–7–8.* 2 vols. London: Henry Colburn, 1829.

Magill, M.L. "Kirkpatrick, Thomas." DCB 9:431–2.

Mahaffy, R.U. "History of Canadian Publishing." *The National Publishing Directory*, 1–49. Toronto: Prestige Books of Canada, 1964.

Mann, Michael. *A Particular Duty: The Canadian Rebellions, 1837–1839.* Wilton, England: Michael Russell, 1986.

Manning, Helen Taft. *The Revolt of French Canada, 1800–1835.* Toronto: Macmillan Company of Canada, 1962.

Marcil, Eileen R. *The Charley-Man: A History of Wooden Shipbuilding at Quebec, 1763–1893.* Kingston: Quarry Press, 1995.

Martineau, André. "Stayner, Thomas Allen." DCB 9:742–3.

Maurault, O. *Le Collège de Montréal, 1767–1967.* 2nd ed. Montreal: Antonio Dansereau, 1967.

Mays, Herbert J. "McDonell, John." DCB 7:552–4.

Merritt, J.P. *Biography of the Hon. W.H. Merritt, M.P.* St Catharines, Ont.: E.S. Leavenworth, 1875.

Mika, Nick, and Helma Mika. *Canada's First Railway – The Champlain and St Lawrence.* Belleville, Ont.: Mika Publishing Co. 1985.

Miller, Carman. "Gray, John." DCB 6:296–7.

Mills, John. *Canadian Coastal and Inland Steam Vessels 1809–1930.* Providence, RI: The Steamship Historical Society of America, 1979. Supplements 1 and 2, 1981 and 1983. (Mills's list is now online at http://www.marmus.ca).

Momryk, Myron. "Sutherland, Daniel." DCB 6:743–6.

The Montreal Almanack. Montreal: Nahum Mower, 1823; Whiting and Mower, 1825.

Morgan, Eleanor W. *Up the Front: A Story of Morrisburg.* Toronto: Ryerson Press, 1964.

Morgan, H.R. "Steam Navigation on the Ottawa River." *Ontario Historical Society Papers and Records* 23 (1926): 370–83.

Morris, J.A. *Prescott, 1810–1967.* Prescott, Ont.: The Prescott Journal, 1967.

Muller, H. Nicholas. "A 'Traitorous and Diabolical Traffic': The Commerce of the Champlain-Richelieu Corridor during the War of 1812." *Vermont History* 44 (spring 1976): 78–96.

Muntz, Madelein. "Weller, William." DCB 9:825–6.

Murray, Hugh. *A Historical and Descriptive Account of British America.* 3 vols. Edinburgh: Oliver & Boyd, 1839.

The National Cyclopaedia of American Biography. New York: James T. White & Co., 1892.

Neilson, Rick. "The First Propellers at Kingston." *FreshWater* 2, no. 2 (autumn 1987): 4–8.

Nelles, H.V. "Loyalism and Local Power: The District of Niagara 1792–1837." *Ontario History* 58 (1966): 99–114.

Noël, Françoise. "Henry, Edmé (Edmund)." DCB 7:394–6.

Notman, W., and F. Taylor. *Portraits of British Americans*. Montreal: William Notman, 1867.

Nourse, H.A. *The Military Annals of Lancaster, Massachusetts, 1740–1865*. Lancaster, 1889.

O'Dette, L.A. *Glimpses, Glances, Sideswipes of Dickinson Landing*. Ottawa: T&H Printers, 1982.

Otto, Stephen. "Longley, George." DCB 7:510–11.

Ouellet, Fernand. *Histoire économique et sociale du Québec, 1760–1850*. 2 vols. Montreal: Fides, 1971.

– and Benoit Thériault. "Wright, Philemon." DCB 7:926–9.

Packard, Jasper. *History of LaPorte County, Indiana*. LaPorte: S.E. Taylor & Co., 1876.

Palmer, R.F. "The *Vandalia* and Her Line Mates: Trend Setters." *FreshWater* 3 (1988): 14–20.

Parish, George. "The North Country in 1816." Document published in five successive issues of the *Watertown Daily Times* (Watertown, NY), 29 December 1936–4 January 1937.

Parizeau, G. *L'assurance contre l'incendie au Canada*. Montreal: Éditions Albert Lévesque, 1935.

Parker, Bruce A. "The Niagara Harbour and Dock Company." *Ontario History* 72, no. 2 (June 1980): 93–121.

Passfield, R.W. *Building the Rideau Canal: A Pictorial History*. Don Mills, Ont.: Fitzhenry & Whiteside/Parks Canada and the Canadian Government Publishing Centre, 1982.

Patents of Canada, from 1824 to 1849. Toronto: Lovell & Gibson, 1860.

Patterson, G.H. "Bidwell, Barnabas." DCB 6:54–9.

Philip, Cynthia Owen. *Robert Fulton, a Biography*. New York: F. Watts, 1985.

Phillpotts, G. "Report of 17 November 1838 by Maj. George Phillpotts to Sir John Colborne." *Montreal Gazette*, 20 November 1838.

Pietersma, Harry. "Crane, Samuel." DCB 8:181–3.

Poulin, Pierre. "Burnet, David." DCB 8:115–16.

Preston, R.A. ed. *For Friends at Home: A Scottish Emigrant's Letters from Canada, California and the Cariboo, 1844–1864*. Montreal: McGill-Queen's University Press, 1974.

Price, Karen. "Le métier de soldat à Côteau-du-Lac (Québec) 1780 à 1856." *History and Archeology* 15 (1979): 3–38. Ottawa: Parks Canada.

Prieur, F.-X. *Notes d'un condamné politique de 1838*. 1864; repr. Montreal: Éditions du jour, 1974.

Pringle, J.F. *Lunenburgh or the Old Eastern District*. Cornwall, Ont.: The Standard Printing House, 1890; repr. Belleville, Ont.: Mika Publishing Co., 1980.

"Proclamations of the Governor of Lower Canada 1792–1815." *Report of the Public Archives for the Year 1921*, appendix B. Ottawa: King's Printer, 1922.

Rapin, Charles. "Récit des troubles de 1838 dans le comté de Beauharnois." *Le Progrès* (Valleyfield, Que.), 13 August–15 October 1897.

Ratio, P.-J., C. Côté, and A. Rubi. *La navigation à Longueuil*. Longueuil: Société d'histoire de Longueuil, 1996.

Reid, Richard, ed. *The Upper Ottawa Valley to 1855: A Collection of Documents*. Toronto: The Champlain Society, 1990.

Reid, W. Harold. *The Presbyterian Church St Andrews and Lachute, Quebec, 1818–1932*. n.p., 1979.

Reid, William D. *The Loyalists in Ontario: The Sons and Daughters of The American Loyalists of Upper Canada*. Lambertville, NJ: Hunterdon House, 1973.

Répertoire d'architecture traditionnelle sur le territoire de la Communauté urbaine de Montréal: Architecture commerciale II – Les Hôtels, les immeubles de bureaux, and *Architecture commerciale III – Les Magasins, les cinémas*. Montreal: Communauté urbaine de Montréal, 1983, 1985.

Report of the State Trials before a General Court Martial Held at Montreal in 1838–9: Exhibiting a Complete History of the Late Rebellion in Lower Canada. 2 vols. Montreal: Armour & Ramsay, 1839.

Richard, Louis. "Jacob De Witt (1785–1859)." *Revue d'histoire de l'Amérique française*, no. 3 (1949–50): 537–55.

Richards, Elva M. "The Joneses of Brockville and the Family Compact." *Ontario History* 60, no. 4 (December 1968): 169–84.

Riddell, W.R. "Transportation from Schenectady to Quebec in 1810." Offprint from *Canadian National Railways Magazine*, December 1927.

Robert, Jean-Claude. *Atlas historique de Montréal*. Montreal: Art Global/Libre Expression, 1994.

– "De Witt, Jacob." *DCB* 8:219–20.

– "Gates, Horatio." *DCB* 6:277–80.

Robertson, J. Ross. *Landmarks of Toronto*. 6 vols. Toronto: J. Ross Robertson, 1894–1914.

Rocheleau–Rouleau, C. "Une incroyable et véridique histoire: l'affaire Cazeau, 1776–1893." *Bulletin de la Société historique franco–américaine*, 1946–47, 3–31.

Rolando, V.R. *200 Years of Soot and Sweat: The History and Archeology of Vermont's Iron, Charcoal, and Lime Industries*. Burlington, Vt: Vermont Archeological Society, 1992.

Ross, A.H.D. *Ottawa Past and Present*. Ottawa: Thorburn & Abbott, 1927.

Ross, Ewan. *Lancaster Township and Village*. Ste-Anne-de-Bellevue, Que.: Imprimerie coopérative Harpell, 1982.

Ross, Ogden. *The Steamboats of Lake Champlain 1809 to 1930*. 1930; repr. Quechee, Vt: Vermont Heritage Press, 1997.

Royce, Caroline Halstead. *Bessboro: A History of Westport*, Essex Co., N.Y. n.p., 1902.

Rudin, Ronald. *Banking en français: The French Banks of Quebec, 1835–1925*. Toronto: University of Toronto Press, 1985.

– *The Forgotten Quebecers: A History of English-Speaking Quebec, 1759–1980*. Quebec: Institut québécois de recherche sur la culture, 1985.

Les rues de Montréal: Répertoire historique. Montreal: Éditions du Méridien, 1995.

Sansom, Joseph. *Travels in Lower Canada*. London: Printed for Sir Richard Phillips and Co., 1820.

Scheiber, H.N. *Abbot–Downing and the Concord Coach*. Concord, NH: New Hampshire Historical Society, 1989. Offprint from *Historical New Hampshire* 20, autumn 1965.

Scott, Ina G. *Yesterday's News, Today's History*. Gananoque, Ont.: 1000 Islands Publishers, 1982.

Scott, Kenneth. *British Aliens in the United States during the War of 1812*. Baltimore: Genealogical Publishing Co., 1979.

Sellar, Robert. *The History of the County of Huntingdon and of the Seigniories of Châteauguay and Beauharnois*. 1888; repr. Huntingdon, Que.: The Huntingdon Gleaner, 1975.

Senior, Elinor K. *From Royal Township to Industrial City: Cornwall, 1784–1984*. Belleville, Ont.: Mika Publishing Co., 1983.

– *Redcoats & Patriotes: The Rebellions in Lower Canada, 1837–38*. Canadian War Museum Historical Publication, no. 20. Stittsville, Ont.: Canada's Wings, 1985.

Shepard, C.J. "McDonald, John." *DCB* 8:533–5.

Shepherd, R.W. "A Short History of the Ottawa River Navigation Company." *Steamboat Bill* 4, no. 23 (August 1947): 25–7; no. 24 (December 1947): 55–6.

Shirreff, P. *A Tour through North America together with a Comprehensive View of the Canadas and United States as Adapted for Agricultural Emigration*. Edinburgh: Oliver & Boyd, 1835.

Shortt, A. *History of Canadian Currency and Banking, 1600–1880*. Toronto: Canadian Bankers' Association, 1986. (Compilation of forty-eight articles originally published in the *Journal of the Canadian Bankers' Association*, October 1896–October 1906, and January 1921–October 1925).

Shortt, Edward. *The Memorable Duel at Perth*. Perth: The Perth Museum, 1970.

– ed. *Perth Remembered*. Perth: The Perth Museum, 1967.

Siebert, Wilbur H. *The Underground Railroad from Slavery to Freedom*. 1898; repr. New York: Russell & Russell, 1967.

Smith, Arthur B., ed. *Kingston! Oh Kingston!* Kingston: Brown & Martin, 1987.

Smith, Elinor V. *Descendants of Nathaniel Dickinson*. N.p. The Dickinson Family Association, 1978.

Smith, H.P. *History of Addison County, Vermont*. Syracuse, NY: D. Mason & Co., 1886.

Smith, William. *The History of the Post Office in British North America.* Cambridge: Cambridge University Press, 1920.

Smyth, T. Taggart. *The First Hundred Years – History of the Montreal City and District Savings Bank, 1846–1946.* Montreal: 1946.

Spafford, H.G. *A Gazetteer of the State of New York.* Albany: Solomon Southwick, 1824; repr. Interlaken, NY: Heart of the Lakes Publishing, 1981.

Spragge, George W. "The Steamship *Traveller* and the Rebellion of 1837." *Ontario History* 52, no. 4 (1960): 251–6.

Spragge, Shirley C. "Read, John Landon." DCB 8:743.

Starr, F.F. *The Miles Morgan Family of Springfield,* Massachusetts, in the Line of Joseph Morgan of Hartford, Connecticut, 1780–1847. Hartford, 1904.

Stevens, W.W. *Past and Present of Will County.* Chicago: The S.J. Clarke Publishing Co., 1907.

Stewart, Victoria M., ed. *The Loyalists of Quebec, 1774–1825.* St-Lambert, Que.: Heritage Branch-Montreal of the United Empire Loyalists' Association, 1989.

Still, William. *The Underground Railroad.* New York: Arno Press and New York Times, 1968.

Stott, Clifford L. "The Correct English Origins of Nathaniel Dickinson and William Gull, Settlers of Wethersfield and Hadley." *New England Historical and Genealogical Register* 152 (April 1998): 159–78.

Swainson, Donald. "Calvin, Dileno Dexter." DCB 11:139–41.

– *Garden Island: A Shipping Empire.* Kingston: Marine Museum of the Great Lakes, 1984.

Sweeny, Robert. "McGill, Peter." DCB 8:540–4.

Talman, James J. "Merritt, William Hamilton." DCB 9:544–8.

– "Travel in Ontario before the Coming of the Railway." *Ontario Historical Society Papers and Records* 29 (1933): 85–102.

Tappan, Lewis. *The Life of Arthur Tappan.* 1871; repr. Westport, Conn.: Negro Universities Press, 1970.

Taylor, Alan. *William Cooper's Town: Power and Persuasion on the Frontier of the Early American Republic.* New York: Alfred A. Knopf, 1995.

Thomas, Cyrus. *History of the Counties of Argenteuil, Quebec, Prescott, Ontario.* Montreal: John Lovell & Son, 1896; repr. Belleville, Ont.: Mika Publishing Co., 1981.

Thompson, Zadock. *History of Vermont, Natural, Civil, and Statistical, in Three Parts, with a new Map of the State and 200 Engravings.* Burlington, Vt: Chauncey Goodrich, 1842.

Tucker, Gilbert N. *The Canadian Commercial Revolution, 1845–1851.* 1936; repr. Toronto: McClelland and Stewart, 1964.

Tulchinsky, Gerald. "Brush, George." DCB 11:120–1.

– "Cantin, Augustin." DCB 12:158–9.

– "Dorwin, Jedediah Hubbell." DCB 11:267–8.

– "Ferrie, Adam." DCB 9:258–60.

- "Redpath, John." DCB 9:654–5.
- *The River Barons: Montreal Businessmen and the Growth of Industry and Transportation, 1837–53.* Toronto: University of Toronto Press, 1977.

Tulloch, Judith. *The Rideau Canal – Defence, Transport and Recreation, 1832–1914.* History and Archeology 50. Ottawa: Parks Canada, 1981.

Turcotte, Gustave. *Le Conseil Législatif de Québec, 1774–1933.* Beauceville, Que.: L'Éclaireur, 1933.

Turner, Larry. "Dickinson, Moss Kent." DCB 12:257–9.
- *Merrickville, Jewel on the Rideau: A History and Guide.* Ottawa: Petherwin Heritage, 1995.
- *Perth: Tradition & Style in Eastern Ontario.* Toronto: Natural Heritage/Natural History, 1992.

Van Cleve, James. *The Ontario and St Lawrence Steamboat Company's Hand-Book for Travelers to Niagara Falls, Montreal and Quebec and through Lake Champlain to Saratoga Springs.* Buffalo, NY: Jewett, Thomas & Co. and Geo. H. Derby and Co., 1852.

Van de Water, F. *Lake Champlain and Lake George.* New York: Bobbs-Merrill Co., 1946.

Verney, Jack. *O'Callaghan: The Making and Unmaking of a Rebel.* Ottawa: Carleton University Press, 1994.

Walker, A.M. *Historical Hadley: A Story of the Making of a Famous Massachusetts Town.* New York: Grafton Press, 1906.

Walker, Anatole. *Les bureaux et maîtres de poste du sud-ouest du Québec.* Montreal: 1982.
- *Le comté de Beauharnois.* Montreal, 1978.
- *Le comté de Châteauguay.* Montreal, 1979.
- *Le comté de Huntingdon.* Montreal, 1979.
- *Le comté de Soulanges.* Montreal, 1977.
- *Le comté de Vaudreuil.* Montreal, 1978.
- *L'Ile de Montréal – L'Île Jésus.* Montreal: Le marché philatélique de Montréal, 1987.

Walker, Harry, and Olive Walker. *Carleton Saga.* Ottawa: Carleton County Council, 1968.

[Warburton, G.D.] *Hochelaga; or, England in the New World.* 2 vols. London: Henry Colburn, 1846.

Ward, Andrew H. *History of the Town of Shrewsbury Massachusetts from Its Settlement in 1717 to 1829.* Boston: Samuel G. Drake, 1847.

Ward, John D. "An Account of the Steamboat Controversy between Citizens of New York and Citizens of New Jersey, from 1811 to 1824, Originating in the Asserted Claim of New York to the Exclusive Jurisdiction over All the Waters between the Two States." *Proceedings of the New Jersey Historical Society 9,* no. 3 (1860–64): 117–34.

Watson, Winslow C., ed. *Men and Times of the Revolution; or, Memoirs of Elkanah Watson, including His Journals of Travels in Europe and America, from the year 1777 to 1842, and His Correspondence with Public Men, and Reminiscences and Incidents of the American Revolution*. 1856; repr. Elizabethtown, NY: Crown Point Press, 1968.

Weir, Arthur. *The Beginnings of the St Lawrence Route: A Lecture Delivered before the Science Students of McGill University*, January 1899. Toronto: Biggar, Samuel & Co., 1899.

Wells, D.W., and R.F. Wells. *A History of Hatfield*, Massachusetts, 1660–1910. Springfield, Mass.: F.C.H. Gibbons, 1910.

White, Walter S. *Pages from the History of Sorel, 1642–1958*. Berthierville, Que.: Imprimerie Bernard, n.d.

Whyte, Donald. *A Dictionary of Scottish Emigrants to Canada before Confederation*. 2 vols. Toronto: Ontario Genealogical Society, 1986–95.

Wightman, W.R. "The Adelaide and Early Canadian Steam above Niagara." *Fresh-Water* 6, no. 2 (1991): 17–22.

– "The Evolving Upper Canadian Steam Packet Service, 1816–1850." *Freshwater* 9, no. 3 (1994): 3–22.

Wilson, G.H. "The Application of Steam to St Lawrence Valley Navigation, 1809–1840." Unpublished MA thesis, McGill University, 1961.

Wilson, L.M. *This Was Montreal in 1814, 1815, 1816 & 1817*. Montreal: Privately printed for the Château de Ramezay, 1960.

Wise, S.F. "Tory Factionalism: Kingston Elections and Upper Canadian Politics, 1820–1836." *Ontario History* 57 (1965): 205–25.

– and Robert Craig Brown. *Canada Views the United States: Nineteenth-Century Political Attitudes*. Toronto: Macmillan of Canada, 1967.

"The Witness Jubilee Symposium." Historical pieces published in Saturday editions of the Montreal *Daily Witness*, 7 December 1895–30 October 1897.

Wood, William. *All Afloat: A Chronicle of Craft and Waterways*. Chronicles of Canada Series, vol. 31. Toronto: Glasgow, Brook & Co., 1920.

Woodruff, G.H., W.H. Perrin, and H.H. Hill. *The History of Will County, Illinois*. Chicago: William LeBaron Jr, 1878.

Woods, Shirley, Jr. *The Molson Saga, 1763–1983*. Toronto: Doubleday Canada, 1983.

Wright, C.A. *The Hatfield Book*. Springfield, Mass.: 1908.

Wyatt-Brown, B. *Lewis Tappan and the Evangelical War against Slavery*. Cleveland, Ohio: Press of Case Western Reserve University, 1969.

Index